BizTalk™ Server Developer's Guide

Peishu Li

Osborne/McGraw-Hill

New York Chicago San Francisco
Lisbon London Madrid Mexico City
Milan New Delhi San Juan
Seoul Singapore Sydney Toronto

McGraw-Hill/Osborne
2600 Tenth Street
Berkeley, California 94710
U.S.A.

To arrange bulk purchase discounts for sales promotions, premiums, or fund-raisers, please contact McGraw-Hill/Osborne at the above address. For information on translations or book distributors outside the U.S.A., please see the International Contact Information page immediately following the index of this book.

BizTalk™ Server Developer's Guide

1234567890 CUS CUS 01987654321

Book p/n 0-07-222226-3 and CD p/n 0-07-222225-5
parts of
ISBN 0-07-213338-4

Publisher Brandon A. Nordin
Vice President & Associate Publisher Scott Rogers
Acquisitions Editor Jim Schachterle
Project Editor Lisa Wolters-Broder
Acquisitions Coordinators Emma Acker, Timothy Madrid
Technical Editor Scott Woodgate
Copy Editor Mike McGee
Proofreader Cheryl Abel
Indexer Jack Lewis
Computer Designers Peter Hancik, Melinda Moore Lytle, Roberta Steele
Illustrators Michael Mueller, Lyssa Wald
Series Design Roberta Steele

This book was composed with Corel VENTURA™ Publisher.

About the Author

As the Technical Development Manager, Peishu Li directs edeagroup development teams in the analysis, development, testing, and deployment of enterprise and e-commerce applications based on Microsoft technologies and platforms, including the .NET framework. Peishu has been awarded Microsoft certifications as both a Microsoft Certified Professional (MCP) and the elite status of Microsoft Certified Solutions Developer (MCSD). He has more than 12 years of industry experience and has expertise in developing distributed enterprise applications and EAI/B2B integration solutions using a variety of tools and technologies, including Microsoft Visual Studio; Web Technologies (IIS/ASP, ASP.NET, XML/XSLT, SOAP, and Web Services); EAI/B2B tools (BizTalk and NEON); Message Oriented Middleware (IBM MQSeries and MSMQ); Component Technologies (COM/DCOM, MTS, and COM+); Relational Database Management Systems (Sybase and SQL Server); Data Access Technologies (OLEDB/ADO, RDO, ODBC, ADO.NET); Modeling Tools (UML/Object Modeling and Data Modeling); and Project Management.

Peishu is the author of *Visual Basic and COM + Programming by Example*, published by Que. He holds an M.S. degree from Sam Houston State University, and a B.S. degree from Wuhan Institute of Chemical Engineering in Wuhan, China. Peishu lives in Plano, Texas, with his wife, Xiaofang, and son, Jeff.

You can reach Peishu at pli@wt.net.

This book is deicated to my father, Xiao-Nong Li

Contents

Acknowledgments

This book took me more than 10 months to write. That's a long time compared to the average six-month period for a typical book of this size. During this process, I've received a great deal of help from a lot of people who deserve my sincere appreciation.

First and foremost, I would like to thank Scott Woodgate, the Microsoft BizTalk Technical Product Manager. Scott's contribution went above and beyond the normal duty of a technical reviewer. Besides assuring the technical accuracy of the content, Scott offered content suggestions, helped structure and lay out chapters, and kept me abreast of up-to-the-minute software information. This book would not have been possible without him. Cheers, Scott!

I also want to thank many people at Osborne/McGraw-Hill, including Jim Schachterle, Tim Madrid, Emma Acker, Lisa Wolters-Broder, and Mike McGee. Writing a book is like aiming at a moving target—so many changes have been taken place with BizTalk technologies since I got started last December. The creative editorial team has helped me make this book of the highest quality possible. I look forward to working with all of you again in the future.

I also want thank Megan Stuhlberg and Jan Shanahan at Microsoft, for providing me with access to the most recent software and other materials.

Finally, I want to thank to my wife, Xiaofang, and my son, Jeff, for their understanding, encouragement, and sacrifices that helped me accomplish writing my second book shortly after my first one.

Introduction

In less than three years, BizTalk has evolved from a buzzword into a solid .NET enterprise server, with hundreds of implementations in production in such companies as Ford, Verizon, Merrill Lynch, and J.C. Penney, and in government agencies in the U.K. and the U.S. Department of Defense.

Microsoft BizTalk Server provides a rich set of services and infrastructures that enable you to build complete, end-to-end EAI and B2Bi solutions. If you've ever used Enterprise Integration Application (EAI) or Business-to-Business integration (B2Bi) products, such as NEON and WebMethods, in the past, you can certainly appreciate what Microsoft BizTalk Server has to offer. As with any enterprise software product and package, it takes time to master BizTalk Server and its related technologies. This book provides practical guidelines and examples for managing all aspects of BizTalk Server, including developing, deploying, and administrating BizTalk solutions.

Who Should Read This Book

This book is for anyone who wants to learn how to implement EAI, B2B solutions using BizTalk Server technologies, including software developers, system architects, system administrators, and IT managers. To get the most out of this book, previous experience in the following Microsoft tools and technologies will be helpful: Visual Basic, VBScript, Active Server Pages (ASP), COM/DCOM/COM+, and MSMQ. If you feel that you need to refresh your skills in these areas, you can read related books such as *Visual Basic and COM+ Programming By Example* (ISBN 0789724588). In addition, the first three appendixes of this book provide extensive coverage of XML, XSLT, and MSXML parsers, in case you are not familiar with these technologies, which are key to effectively working with BizTalk Server.

What's in the Book

This book covers all aspects of developing, deploying, and administering BizTalk Server. You might have noticed that we deliberately avoided using the version number "2000" in the title of this book. That's because we decided to cover both versions of BizTalk Server, 2000 and 2002. We also designed the book in such a way that both BizTalk Server 2000 and 2002 users will benefit from it. Additionally, we have included exclusive chapters that discuss BizTalk Server Accelerators for RosettaNet and HIPAA, for added value.

This book is divided into eight parts:

Part I, *Introducing BizTalk*, contains two chapters that give you an overview of BizTalk. Chapter 1, *BizTalk Initiative,* introduces three components of BizTalk initiatives and discusses the BizTalk Framework. Chapter 2, *Introducing BizTalk Server 2000,* gives a fundamental understanding of the services, tools, and architecture of BizTalk Server 2000. It also helps you install BizTalk Server 2000.

Part II, *BizTalk Server 2000 Messaging Services,* has four chapters on everything you need to know to master BizTalk Server 2000 Messaging Services, including an overview of messaging services (Chapter 3, *Introducing BizTalk Server 2000 Messaging Services*); how to use tools to create BizTalk specifications (Chapter 4, *Working with Specifications*); maps (Chapter 5, *Mapping Specifications*); and working with the messaging services (Chapter 6, *Managing BizTalk Server Messaging Services*).

Part III, *BizTalk Server 2000 Administration,* discusses how to use the administrate BizTalk Server and Server Groups (Chapter 7, *BizTalk Server Administration*) as well as how to track your business documents (Chapter 8, *Tracking Interchanges and Documents*).

Part IV, *BizTalk Server 2000 Orchestration Services,* focuses on another important BizTalk Server service–process orchestration. Two chapters cover the fundamentals of BizTalk Server Orchestration Services, such as how to use BizTalk Orchestration Designer to dynamically manage business processes (Chapter 9, *Orchestrating Business Process*) as well as such advanced topics as managing long-running transactions, debugging, and exception-handling techniques (Chapter 10, *Advanced XLANG Schedules*).

Part V, *Extending BizTalk Server 2000,* demonstrates how to extend the basic services of BizTalk Server 2000 by leverage its extensible architecture. Chapter 11, *Building Custom Components,* teaches how to build custom functoids, preprocessors, and application integration components (AIC) or BizTalk Adapters to extend BizTalk Server messaging services. Chapter 12, *Integrating with Commerce Server,* illustrates how to leverage the built-in support of Microsoft Commerce Server 2000 to integrate with BizTalk Server 2000 for catalog management and order-form integration to provide end-to-end e-commerce solutions.

Part VI, *Building Vertical Market Solutions Using BizTalk Server Accelerators,* covers Microsoft BizTalk Server Accelerators for the high-tech IT industry (Chapter 13, *BizTalk Server Accelerator for RosettaNet*) and the healthcare industry (Chapter 14, *BizTalk Server Accelerator for HIPAA*).

Part VII, *Bizet–BizTalk Server 2002*, provides you with everything you need to work with BizTalk Server 2002, including the new unique features of BizTalk Server 2002 (Chapter 15, *Introducing BizTalk Server 2002*) and the enterprise administration, deployment, and monitoring capabilities provides by Microsoft Application Center 2000 and Microsoft Operations Manager 2000 (Chapter 15, *Managing with Application Center and MOM*).

Appendixes A through C of this book cover XML and related technologies, including the basics (Appendix A, *XML Fundamentals*), XSLT (Appendix B, *XSL Transformation (XSLT)*), and how to use MSXML parsers (Appendix C, *Building XML Applications*). Appendix D, *Creating Windows Script Components,* teaches you how to build COM components in XML scriptlets as one of the technology implementations for BizTalk Server Orchestration Services. All of the appendixes were treated as formal chapters and are meant to provide you with a one-stop solution.

On the CD

To help you to work with the examples presented in the chapters of this book, the companion CD contains all of the book's the source code, organized by chapter.

Additionally, two useful tools are provided:

The XSLT utility (a VBScript file, XSLT.vbs, that can be found in the Tools\XSLT folder on the CD) be executed from the command line to generate XSLT output documents. You can use this utility to work with the examples in Appendix B.

BizTalk Server 2002 ships with an enhanced version of the BizTalk Configuration Assistant (BTConfAssistant) tool, with the capability of exporting/importing receive functions in addition to BizTalk messaging objects. Unfortunately, this functionality is not included in the BizTalk Server 2000 version of BTConfigAssistant. To help those BizTalk Server developers who are using BizTalk Server 2000, a Readme.doc, along with necessary code files, is provided under the Tools\BTConfigAssistant folder, which describes how to modify the source code of the BTConfigAssistant sample of BizTalk Server 2000 to handle receive functions.

PART I

Introducing BizTalk

OBJECTIVE:

- BizTalk, enabling software to speak the language of business! In Part I, we introduce the BizTalk initiative and BizTalk Server 2000.

CHAPTER

1

BizTalk Initiative

IN THIS CHAPTER:

To better understand BizTalk and the motivation behind the BizTalk initiative, it is worth mentioning the challenges system integrators have faced over the decades in their efforts to build Enterprise Application Integration (or EAI) and business-to-business (or B2B) electronic commerce (or e-commerce) solutions.

Typical enterprises use different software applications and platforms to support different areas of their business. Some of these applications may be built in-house, whereas others may be purchased from third party software vendors. For example, in an auto manufacturing company, the accounting department may use a Java application running against an Oracle database on a Sun Solaris UNIX system. The purchasing department may take advantage of a Visual Basic application with an SQL Server database backend running on a Microsoft Windows NT Server. Yet the human resources department may utilize a legacy system built in COBOL and running on a DB/2 database on an IBM AS400 mainframe system. The list goes on and on…. In order to conduct their business more effectively and stay competitive, organizations need to integrate these different applications and systems together as if they were one big application. As mentioned above, however, these applications and platforms are built using different programming tools, which run on different platforms, storing and processing data in different formats. Worse yet, these applications and platforms were never meant to work together—all of which has created many unique challenges to the EAI. Proprietary data storage formats and the application programming interfaces (or API) for accessing and manipulating these data make it extremely difficult for applications to exchange data efficiently and in a controllable manner.

The fast growth of the Internet and the World Wide Web has brought many business opportunities to organizations, allowing them to conduct business over the Web with their trading partners. At the same time, this has also brought organizations many new challenges in addition to issues regarding integration efforts within the organizational boundary. In B2B integration scenarios particularly, organizations also need to tackle such unique concerns as security, privacy, and repudiation.

The first step in addressing these issues is to implement standardized ways of describing common vocabularies used to illustrate and construct the data as well as the content models of the data itself. The *data* we are talking about here is often referred to as a *Business Document*—for example, a purchase order or an invoice. In order to alleviate data exchange between applications, some standards and specifications have been proposed, published, and adopted by standard bodies, organizations, and independent system integrators. These include earlier standards such as Electronic Data Interchange (or EDI) and emerging standards such as eXtensible Markup Language (or XML). Although EDI provided many benefits in helping streamline basic transaction flows between business trading partners, the complexity and high cost of implementation have restricted its use only to those large companies and organizations who can afford using it. On the other hand, XML, powered with its accompanying languages such as XSLT (eXtensible Stylesheet Language Transformation) and XML Schemas, has proved to be a more flexible and efficient language for describing the contents and structure of business documents. As a result, XML has been adopted by the industry at an astonishing speed.

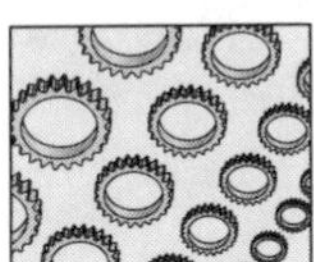

NOTE

Appendixes A to C of this book contain comprehensive coverage of XML and its related technologies, including XML, XSLT, and XML Schema.

Using a standard language such as XML is only the first step in resolving issues involving EAI and B2B integration. The process of building these integration solutions is complicated and challenging. Which is exactly what BizTalk initiative wanted to address.

BizTalk initiative consists of three key components:

- The ***BizTalk.org*** Web site. This is a community started by Microsoft and supported by a wide range of organizations including SAP, CommerceOne, Ariba, and others. It provides a globally available repository and library for organizations and system integrators to publish and share schemas (vocabularies and structure) for constructing BizTalk documents.
- The ***BizTalk Framework*** is a specification for designing and developing XML messaging solutions. Built on top of many open Internet standards and protocols such as XML, SOAP (Simple Object Access Protocol), HTTP, and SMTP, this framework provides guidelines for constructing and passing BizTalk documents between applications and business partners.

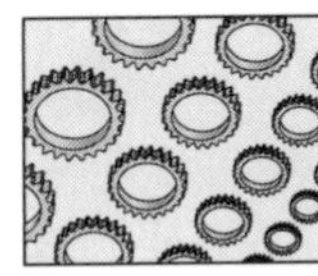

NOTE

For information about the SOAP Protocol, visit MSDN SOAP Developer Resources at: ***http://msdn.microsoft.com/soap/default.asp***

- Microsoft ***BizTalk Server 2000*** is the industry's first comprehensive tool that unites EAI and B2B integration with its unique BizTalk Orchestration technology, allowing organizations to easily build dynamic business processing between applications both within the organization and across business partnerships.

In this chapter, we discuss the BizTalk Framework 2.0, introduce BizTalk.org and BizTalk Server 2000. Chapter 2 will then explore BizTalk Server 2000 in more detail. The rest of the book will cover related technologies, tools, and how to use them to build BizTalk solutions, focusing on the use of BizTalk Server 2000.

The BizTalk Framework

The rapid adoption of XML and XML-related solutions by the EAI and B2B integration industries provided a standard way for specifying the vocabularies and content models of business data. These efforts, however, only solved half of the problems. Organizations and business trading partners still have to face a broad range of interoperability issues. They need a platform- and technology-neutral specification for the design and development of XML-based messaging solutions for communication between organizations and business trading partners. This is exactly where the BizTalk Framework steps in. The BizTalk Framework 2.0 is a specification that provides a general overview of the BizTalk conceptual architecture, centering on two key concepts: *BizTalk Documents* and *BizTalk Messages*. BizTalk Framework provides detailed specifications for constructing BizTalk Documents, BizTalk Messages, and their secure transport over a number of Internet-standard and transfer protocols. It also provides guidelines for reliable delivery of BizTalk Documents, and instructions for handling BizTalk Document attachments. The following sections will introduce the BizTalk architecture, explaining BizTalk Documents, BizTalk Messages, and other terminologies. We will also discuss the structure of a BizTalk document, including its header, body, and attachments. We will look at how to reliably deliver (exchange) a BizTalk document, how to secure BizTalk documents, as well as how to bind different transports in BizTalk documents to ensure authentication, integrity, non-repudiation, and privacy . Finally, we will introduce the BizTalk Framework 2.0 Developer's Toolkit, a technical design framework and programming interface for managing arbitrarily complex BizTalk Framework documents.

The BizTalk Architecture

The implementation model of the BizTalk Framework is composed of three distinct logical components or layers:

- The *BizTalk Framework Compliant Server* (or *BFC Server*) is implemented as a set of services providing the XML messaging functions specified in the BizTalk Framework 2.0. Microsoft BizTalk Server 2000 is an example of a BFC server.

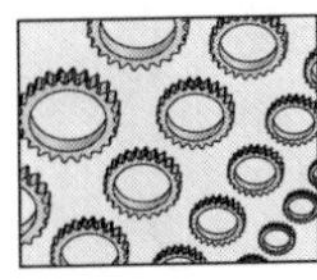

NOTE

BizTalk Framework 2.0 introduced several new features over BizTalk Framework 1.0, including adoption of the SOAP 1.1 specification as the format of BizTalk Messages.

- An ***Application*** that is a line-of-business system which stores and processes the business data and logic. Appropriate adaptors that are responsible for facilitating, emitting, and consuming Business Documents and communicating with a BFC server are also considered part of the application.
- ***Transport***. This is the mechanism by which the actual interchange of BizTalk Messages between BFC servers takes place, ensuring messages are physically carried from the source business entity to the destination business entity. Examples of transports include HTTP, SMTP, and message-oriented middleware (or MOM) such as MSMQ, MQ Series, or JMS (Java Messaging Services). The BizTalk Framework is independent of transport protocols. The choice of a specific transport protocol is completely up to the solution implementer.

Figure 1-1 illustrates a typical example of how the BizTalk Framework may be implemented.

As shown in Figure 1-1, Application A constructs a BizTalk document, packs it into a BizTalk message, and sends it to BFC Server A to be processed. BFC Server A transmits the BizTalk message through appropriate transports and protocols to BFC Server B which may process portions of the document before passing it on to Application B.

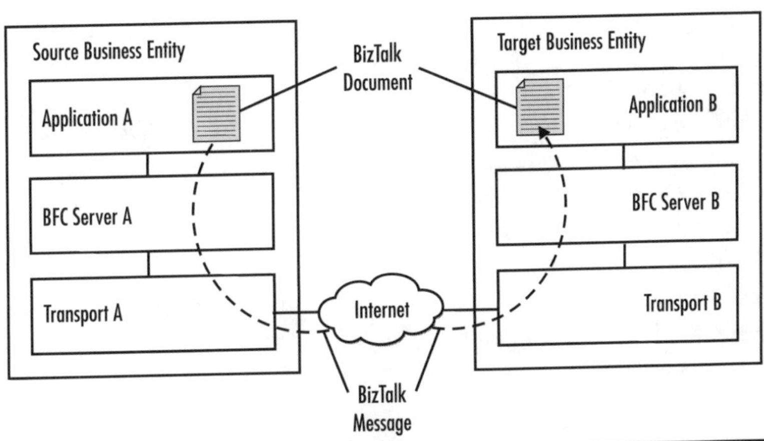

Figure 1-1 *A sample implementation of the logical layering model of the BizTalk Framework*

The *BizTalk document* is a SOAP 1.1 message, also called a SOAP *Envelope*, which is essentially a well-formed XML document. A BizTalk document contains a header section and a body section. The header section includes instructions for document routing, document identification, delivery service requesting, attachment cataloging, document securing, and transport binding. The header section of a BizTalk document uses a special set of XML tags associated with the namespaces defined in the BizTalk Framework. These special tags are called *BizTags* in the BizTalk Framework specification. We will discuss these header instructions in detail later in this chapter. The body section of the BizTalk document contains one or more business documents—well-formed XML documents containing business data. These could be purchase orders, invoices, payments, or any other type of business information.

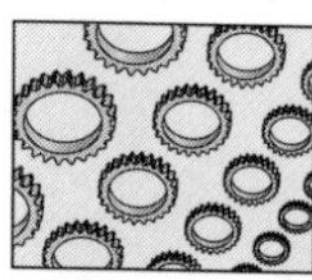

NOTE

XML uses elements as the basic building blocks for describing its data. BizTags are actually XML elements and are case sensitive. (XML elements and namespaces have been explained in greater detail in Appendix A.)

In Figure 1-1, Application A generates a BizTalk document which may contain one or more business documents (possibly with some attachments as well), and transmits these business documents (under the umbrella of the BizTalk document) to Application B by submitting it to BFC Server A. Either the application or the BFC server could be responsible for constructing the BizTalk document, along with the business documents, depending, of course, on the implementation of the BFC server. BFC Server A then processes the document and any attachments and constructs a BizTalk message which is appropriate for the underlying transport protocol. A *BizTalk message* is the unit of wire-level interchange between BFC servers. The BizTalk Framework compliant source or destination of a BizTalk message is also called an *Endpoint* (not shown in Figure 1-1). The BFC server (A in this case) uses information contained in the header section of the BizTalk document (defined by a set of BizTags) to determine the correct transport-specific destination address. The server then hands the BizTalk message to the transport layer which in turn transmits the BizTalk message to BFC Server B through the appropriate transport (Transport B in this case). The BizTalk Framework does not specify which interfaces should be used between the business applications, the BFC servers, and the transport layer. These interfaces are completely implementation-specific.

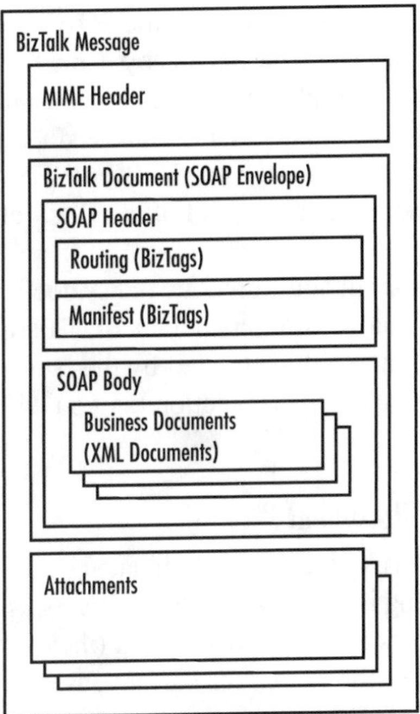

Figure 1-2 *The structure of a BizTalk message*

The Overall Structure of a BizTalk Document

Figure 1-2 depicts the structure of a BizTalk message which contains a BizTalk document (an SOAP envelope). The BizTalk document or SOAP envelope has two sections—the header section contains BFC server processing instructions (routine and content catalog, or *manifest*) described in BizTags, whereas the body section contains one or more business documents. Optionally, a BizTalk message can also have attachments and a Multipart Internet Mail Extensions (MIME) header.

The Body of a BizTalk Document

The body section of a BizTalk document (designated by a SOAP envelope *Body* element) holds a business document (a well-formed XML document that contains business data, such as a purchase order) or multiple business documents—for example, a purchase order document along with an associated shipping document.

In the latter case, the BizTalk Framework uses the SOAP encoding rule to encode data targeted by multiple references. It achieves this by using the XML ID attributes and relative URIs. In the case of multiple business documents, the BizTalk Framework also provides a way to uniquely distinguish business documents from other direct child elements of the Body element. It uses the SOAP-ENC:root attribute with a value of 1 to signal that the immediate child of the Body element is actually a business document.

It is also worth noting that in addition to business documents, the Body element of the BizTalk message can also contain another BizTalk message. In this case, however, the BizTalk message will be treated by the BFC server like any other business document, ignoring its header section (as you will see in the following paragraphs).

The Header of a BizTalk Document

The header section of a BizTalk document (designated by a SOAP envelope *Header* element) provides processing instructions for BFC servers using appropriate BizTags, including mandatory BizTags for describing routing (the *endpoints* BizTag), document identification, and properties (the *properties* BizTag), as well as optional BizTags for delivery services (the *services* BizTag), document cataloging (the *manifest* BizTag), and process management (the *process* BizTag).

Processing BizTalk Documents

In this section, we will take a close look at the processing instructions specified in the header section of BizTalk documents.

Routing

The *endpoints* BizTag under the header section of a BizTalk document contains *from* and *to* BizTags, which in turn contain two *address* BizTags, respectively. These BizTags provide source and destination information specified as names of business entities. The names used to represent business entities are usually business-related abstractions and are not necessarily reflections of physical transport endpoints. For example, "Purchase Orders" and "Purchase Approver" are preferable names for source and destination to "http://POServer/POSubmit.asp", and "http://POServer/POProcess.asp." This abstraction makes it possible to use multiple transports and/or endpoints and replace them over time without changing the names of the business entities defined in the BizTalk document. The exact routing and delivering logic of the BizTalk document is completely up to the BFC server that processes the BizTalk document.

The use of the *from* and *to* BizTags as well as the *address* subtags is mandatory. In addition, the BizTalk Framework also provides a mechanism that forces the BFC server to understand and process the *endpoints* header entries by means of a SOAP-ENV:mustUnderstand attribute with a value of 1.

Document Properties

Under the *properties* BizTag of the BizTalk document header section, there are four mandatory sub-tags: *identity*, *sentAt*, *expiresAt* and *topic*, as summarized in the following table:

BizTag	Description
identity	A URL reference that uniquely identifies the BizTalk document. To guarantee universal uniqueness, you can use the Universally Unique Identifiers (UUIDs) or some cryptographic hash algorithms such as MD5 to encrypt the business document.
sentAt	The timestamp that indicates when the document was sent, or when the properties element was created in relation to the transmission-retry behavior (something discussed later in this chapter). The sentAt BizTag uses a combination of date and time of day values as defined in the ISO 8601 (called *timeInstance* data type in BizTalk Framework).
expiresAt	The expiration timestamps of the BizTalk document. Beyond the point specified by this BizTag, the document should be considered expired and should not be processed or acknowledged by the destination business entity even if it is successfully delivered. In synchronous scenarios, you should leave some room to accommodate the error in time due to the processing of the document. The expireAt BizTag uses the timeInstance data type.
topic	A URL that uniquely identifies the overall purpose of the BizTalk document. The topic BizTag can be used to verify that the content of a BizTalk document is consistent with its intent. The topic can be either specified by the sending application or be inferred by the BFC server by checking the namespace URI of the first business document.

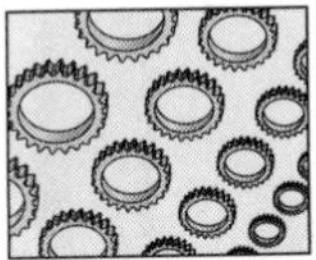

NOTE

The ISO 8601 is an international standard for representing date and times in a standardized way so data will not be misinterpreted when transferred across national boundaries.

As with the routing BizTags, the properties BizTag also uses the SOAP-ENV:mustUnderstand attribute with a value of "1" to mandate the recipient BFC server to understand and process its contents.

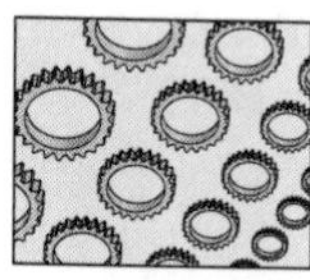

NOTE

Due to the transport-independent nature of the current version of BizTalk Framework and the fact that the latency for messages in a typical BizTalk scenario is usually high, it is recommended to use the absolute expiration time instead of the maximum latency, or TTL (time to live).

Reliably Delivering BizTalk Documents

Delivery instructions of a BizTalk document are specified under the optional *services* BizTag. Under this services tag, there are two more child tags, *deliveryReceiptRequest* and *commitmentReceiptRequest*; both are optional. The deliveryReceiptRequest tag requests a delivery receipt from the destination business entity as a confirmation of a reliable delivery of the BizTalk document. The commitmentReceiptRequest tag asks for a commitment receipt from the receiving end so that the sender will know about the processing commitment of the destination business entity. Appropriate receipts (delivery and/or commitment) will be sent to the address specified under their relative *sendTo* subtags with a timestamp specified by the *sendBy* tag. The addresses are typically the source business entity.

When the services BizTag is present, the same SOAP-ENV:mustUnderstand = "1" attribute is used for the recipient BFC server to understand and process its contents (i.e., to send appropriate receipts upon request).

Both delivery receipt and commitment receipt are standard BizTalk messages, or SOAP envelopes. Even though the body of a delivery receipt is always empty, the empty Body BizTag is still required for the document to be qualified as a BizTalk message. The body of a commitment receipt on the other hand can either be empty or contain one or more business documents.

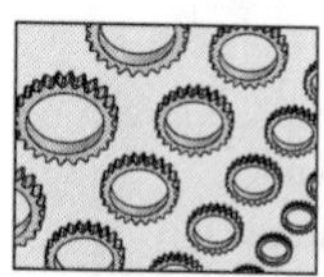

NOTE

Empty tags are also called empty elements in XML terminology and are discussed in Appendix A.

The content of a delivery receipt is specified by the following BizTags under the *deliveryReceive* BizTag of the header section:

BizTag	Description
identity	A URL that uniquely identifies the original BizTalk document sent by the BFC server at the source business entity.
receivedAt	The receiving timestamp for the BizTalk document acknowledged by the delivery receipt.

The commitment receipt uses the *commitmentReceipt* BizTag under the header section with the following subtags:

BizTag	Description
identity	Similar to the identity tag used for the delivery receipt.
decidedAt	The processing decision timestamp for the BizTalk document acknowledged by the commitment receipt.
decision	The actual decision, either positive or negative.
commitmentCode	Specifies a more specific status of the processing decision, analog to a fault code (optional).
commitmentDetail	Detailed description about the process decision (optional).

Both delivery receipt and commitment receipt requires that the recipient BFC server understand its contents by using the same mechanism described earlier.

Certain required behaviors have to be met for the BFC servers at both the source and destination business entities in order to ensure the reliable delivery of the business documents.

The BFC server on the sending side (the source business entity) has to do the following:

- Add a delivery receipt request at the header section of the BizTalk document via the deliveryReceiptRequest BizTag.
- Before submitting the BizTalk document, persist the document in a durable storage, such as a relation database.
- Establish a retry mechanism by specifying two parameters: a retry interval (either fixed or configurable) and a maximum retry count. The sending BFC server should keep retrying (resubmitting the BizTalk document) until a requested delivery receipt is received or the deadline specified by the sendAt BizTag expires or the maximum retry count is exceeded. The content of the BizTalk document being transmitted should not be altered in any way during retries (this includes changing the header). Specifically, even the timestamp specified by the sentAt BizTag should remain the same as it was when the document was first transmitted. The transports used for different retry transmissions do not have to be the same, though.
- At the end of the delivery process of a BizTalk document, if the sending BFC server has not received the expected delivery receipt from the receiving BFC server, then the delivery of the BizTalk document is considered failed. When this occurs, the sending BizTalk server needs to notify the source application appropriately.

The receiving BFC server needs to do a little bit more to ensure a reliable delivery of the BizTalk document:

- Upon receiving the BizTalk document, the receiving BFC server needs to persist the accepted document to a permanent storage.
- For each accepted BizTalk document, including those that are copies or duplicates of previously received documents (recognized by the identity), transmit a receipt back to the source BFC server at the address specified by the sendTo BizTag. The receipt is constructed using the structure described earlier in this section. If the document is received past the time instance specified by the expiresAt BizTag, no receipt will be sent. If the document is received before the time instance specified by the expiresAt BizTag but after that cited in the sendBy BizTag, a delivery receipt still needs to be sent.
- Additionally, the destination BFC server may perform an *idempotent* delivery to appropriate applications to make sure that the BizTalk document is delivered exactly once to its intended recipient application, despite the fact that the document may be received multiple times because of retries at the sending side or errors in transport behavior. Idempotent delivery or *Idempotence* refers to the ability of a BizTalk document to be transmitted and accepted more than once, with the same effect as being transmitted and accepted only once. Idempotence can be achieved by persisting (archiving) all the BizTalk documents (except for those that are expired) accepted to a durable store (such as a relational database). Usually archiving the identity of the BizTalk document is sufficient, provided that the identity is universally unique (for instance, the identity is represented by a UUID).

CAUTION

Though very rare, there is still a possibility that a BizTalk document may actually be successfully delivered, verified, and processed by the destination BFC server, yet for some reason (such as a transport failure) its delivery and/or commitment receipt may get lost. In this case, as a result, the source BFC server may generate a failure report based on the recommended behavior discussed earlier.

As you may have noticed from the previous discussion, there are three different deadlines that may be involved in a BizTalk document. The following table summarizes the distinct semantics of these deadlines:

Deadlines	Associated BizTags	Explanation
Delivery deadline	sentBy subtag of the deliveryReceiptRequest BizTag	This deadline concerns acceptance of the BizTalk document by the destination. The delivery receipt must be received by the source before the delivery deadline.
Commitment deadline	sentBy subtag of the commitmentReceiptRequest BizTag	This deadline concerns examination of content, verification of ability, and willingness to process the BizTalk by the destination. When requested, the commitment receipt must be received by the source before the commitment deadline.
Processing deadline	expiresAt	This deadline is the point in time beyond which the BizTalk document will be considered null and void if unprocessed. After this deadline, the document must not be delivered to the application at the destination end for processing, nor should any receipts (delivery and/or commitment) be sent to the source.

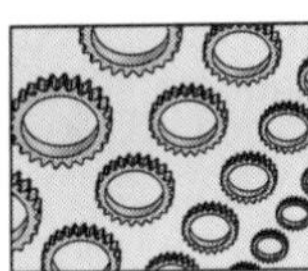

NOTE

The BizTalk Framework does not explicitly specify the required behaviors for the source and destination business entities regarding commitment receipts. Rather, it provides a standard framework which allows such application- and/or implementation-specific semantics to be expressed at the wire level.

Handling Attachments

A BizTalk document can optionally carry attachments with its business documents, as sometimes required by the business process. The attachments are usually in binary forms such as an image file—for example, a photocopy of a signed time card. As illustrated in Figure 1-2, the primary BizTalk document, along with one or more attachments, comprise the compound content of a BizTalk Message.

The BizTalk Framework specifies a standard way to associate a primary BizTalk document with one or more attachments in a multipart Multipurpose Internet Mail Extensions (or MIME) structure for transport. Most Internet transports can handle transporting MIME-encoded content. In case of the HTTP protocol, some special considerations are required (these will be discussed later in the chapter).

The document catalog, specified by the *manifest* BizTag under the header section, includes references (specified by the *reference* BizTags which are usually Universal

Resource Identifiers or URIs) to both the business documents and the attachments. The business documents are specified by the *document* BizTag underneath the reference tag with an *href* attribute (similar to the href attribute for HTML) which points to the URI of the business document. The attachments are specified by the *attachment* BizTag underneath the reference tag, which also uses *href* attributes to reference the URIs of the attachments. Both the business document and the attachments can optionally have some descriptions, specified by the *description* BizTag, under the reference tag.

Managing Processes

The BizTalk Framework uses an optional *process* BizTag under the header section to specify process-management information. If the process tag is present, the SOAP-ENV:mustUnderstand = "1" attribute must be used to mandate the recipient BFC server to understand its contents and successfully process the BizTalk document. The following table summarizes the subBiz Tags under the process BizTag:

BizTag	Description
type	A URI reference that represents the type of business process involved. It is a pattern of interchange between multiple BizTalk documents. For example, the process of purchasing a computer laptop can be specified as "Laptop_Purchase_Process."
instance	A URI reference that uniquely identifies a specific instance of the business process associated with the BizTalk document. A common way is to extend the *type* of a URI with a fragment identifier such as a sequence number. For example, an instance regarding the process of purchasing a laptop could be expressed as "Laptop_Purchase_Process#10001."
Detail	An optional BizTag that allows you to include further information as needed for the process. This tag can contain custom tags (non-BizTags) which provide the flexibility to describe the process in more detail.

Securing BizTalk Documents

When trading partners conduct business over the Internet, security is an important consideration. The data being exchanged must be secured for authentication, integrity, non-repudiation, and privacy. BizTalk handles security at the individual message, document, or attachment level, instead of at the transport level. As a result, single-hop privacy security protocols, such as Secure Socket Layer (or SSL), are not sufficient. The BizTalk Framework supports Secured MIME (or S/MIME) protocol version 3 when securing BizTalk messages, documents, and attachments.

BizTalk offers three types of securing modes:

- Encryption
- Signing (only supports the detached signature, multipart/signed mode)
- Both encryption and signing

The BizTalk Framework allows the header of the BizTalk document to be encrypted separately—and differently—from its body and attachments. This granular securing capability satisfies most B2B security scenarios in which the BizTalk document can be carried in clear for intermediaries and infrastructure components processing without compromising the privacy. The standard SOAP referencing is used to identify the encrypted documents and/or attachments by their *href* attribute.

Binding the Transports

The BizTalk Framework currently supports two transport protocols, Hyper Text Transfer Protocol (or HTTP) and Simple Mail Transport Protocol (or SMTP).

HTTP is a request/response, or synchronous transport protocol. This does not quite fit into the asynchronous messaging architecture of the BizTalk Framework. As a result, an HTTP successful response code (2xx status code) does not have the conventional meaning in the BizTalk messaging context. In other words, the source BFC server should not rely on the standard HTTP response code for ensuring a successful delivery or commitment. Instead, the delivery and/or commitment receipts mechanism described earlier in this chapter should be used as specified by the framework. To work around the limitation posted by the synchronous nature of the HTTP protocol (and the SOAP protocol which currently uses HTTP as the transport protocol), some asynchronous technologies, such as message queuing, can be used in conjunction with the HTTP protocol to provide a more robust solution.

The SMTP protocol, on the other hand, fits pretty well into the BizTalk messaging infrastructure because SMTP is also an asynchronous protocol. As a result, binding SMTP transport is more straightforward. SMTP is completely compatible with MIME and fully supports its semantics.

BizTalk Framework 2.0 Developer's Toolkit

The BizTalk Framework 2.0 Developer's Toolkit (formally BizTalk Jumpstart Kit envelope and Plug-In components) is a programming framework which allows Visual Basic developers to quickly build COM components based on appropriate

BizTalk schemas (XML schema documents). The COM components created by using the toolkit provide an object-oriented abstraction of the underlying BizTalk documents, hiding the complexity of processing an XML document through the Document Object Model (or DOM).

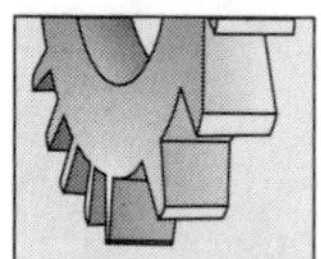

TIP

You can download the toolkit from Microsoft BizTalk Web site at ***http://www.Microsoft.com/downloads/release.asp?ReleaseID=24869*** *as a zipped file, btfdt.zip. Alternatively, if you have installed Microsoft BizTalk Server 2000, you should be able to find the uncompressed files of the toolkit under the following directory:* ***<BizTalk Server Installation>\SDK\Messaging Samples\BTFDevToolKit\.***

The toolkit can be used on both Windows 2000 and NT 4 with SP 4 or above.

Introduction of the Toolkit

The design of the toolkit is based on two logic abstractions, the *envelope* and *plug-in* concepts that map to the SOAP envelope and the business documents contained in the Body section of the BizTalk document as defined in the BizTalk Framework 2.0.

The SOAP envelope is represented by a COM component with a ProgId of BTFEnvelope.Envelope in a form of three ActiveX dll files, BTFEnvelopeXX.dll. Here the XX represents the different version of MSXML DOM parsers to be used, 20 for 2.0, 26 for 2.6, and 30 for 3.0, respectively. You will need to register the appropriate BTFEnvelope object on the target machine before you can use it. To register, run the Regsvr32.exe at the command line prompt. For example:

```
Regsvr32 C:\BTFDTK\BTFEnvelope30.dll
```

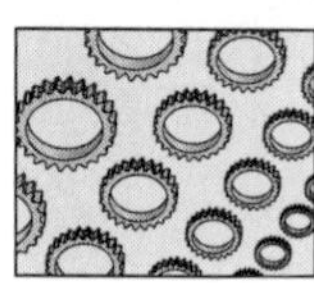

NOTE

You can register only one of the three BTFEnvelopes because they all share the same CLSID. Choose the version that is the same as the MSXML DOM parser version registered on the target machine. The default BizTalk Server 2000 installation comes with MSXML parser 3.0. We will discuss BizTalk Server 2000 installation in Chapter 2. MSXML parsers are discussed in Appendix C.

In addition, the toolkit also provides a plug-in COM interface along with a code generation wizard in the form of a Visual Basic 6.0 Add-in.

The plug-in interface is provided as a type library which only defines the MSPlugIn.PlugIn2 interface but does not contain any implementation. As with the BTFEnvelope, the plug-in type library comes with three forms, msplugin20.tlb, msplugin26.tlb, and msplugin30.tlb, corresponding to the three versions of MSXML

DOM parsers. To register these type libraries, you need to run the accompanying registry file, Plugin2.reg. Before you can use this file, however, you need to open it with a text editor such as NotePad and modify the paths underneath the ..\Win32 key so that they correctly point to the location of the MSPluginXX.TLB file.

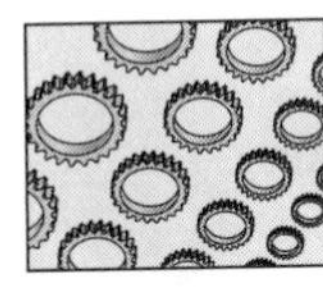

NOTE

The registry file Plugin2.reg that comes with the toolkit is a Windows 2000 registry file. In order to make it work under NT 4, you also need to replace the first line "Windows Registry Editor Version 5.00" with "REGEDIT4".

To set up the Code Generation Wizard (Visual Basic 6.0 Add-in), you need to do the following:

1. Copy the SchemaPlugInGenerator.dll to <Visual Studio Installation>\Common/MSDev98\AddIns\ and register it. Visual Basic IDE will use this dll to launch the Code Generation Wizard and generate the plug-in code.
2. Copy the pigen.ini (the plug-in add-in configuration file) to the same location as the SchemaPlugInGenerator.dll.
3. Copy the class templates, Microsoft Plugin class instance.cls, Microsoft PlugIn collection instance.cls and Microsoft Plugin Main.cls, to <Visual Studio Installation>\VB98/Templates\Classes\.
4. Copy the XML helper module modXMLHelper3.bas to <Visual Studio Installation>\VB98\Template\Code\.

Use the Toolkit

The toolkit comes with two Word documents, EnvelopeAndPlugin.doc and UsingPluginGenerator.doc. The former explains the design and architecture of the toolkit in great detail, including the relationship between the BTFEnvelope and the plug-ins. The latter demonstrates how to use the plug-in generator to create the plug-in COM objects from a sample BizTalk schema, and how to use the generated COM objects in different scenarios. In this section, we will walk through the plug-in code generation process by using a sample purchase order BizTalk schema that can be downloaded from BizTalk.org (we will introduce BizTalk.org in the next section of this chapter): **http://schemas.biztalk.org/BizTalk/zi0124pf.xml**. This sample purchase order BizTalk schema defines the structure of the business document, the purchase order XML document. You can directly view this downloaded BizTalk schema in Internet Explorer 5 or as shown in Figure 1-3.

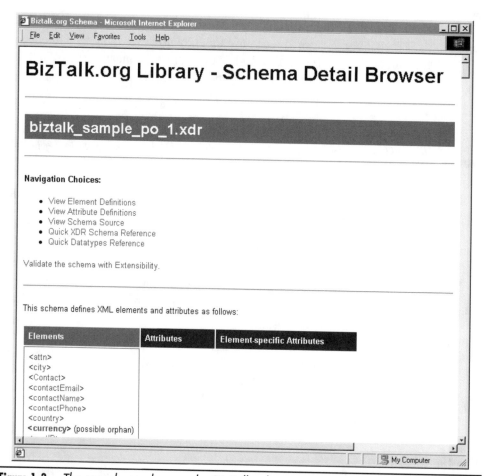

Figure 1-3 *The sample purchase order BizTalk schema in Internet Explorer*

TIP

The schema has a reference to an XSL stylesheet which outputs the XML document to an HTML document, as you see in Figure 1-3. If you are not connected to the Internet, you will need to download the stylesheet (g9boxjl2.xsl) from the BizTalk.org Web site at: ***http://schemas.biztalk.org/BizTalk/g9boxjl2.xsl*** *and save the stylesheet to the same directly as the purchase order BizTalk schema (zi0123pf.xml). You also need to modify the stylesheet reference in the schema so it points to the local version of the stylesheet. To do this, open the schema (zi0123pf.xml) in a text editor and change the second line of text from*

```
<?xml-stylesheet type="text/xsl"
href="http://schemas.biztalk.org/BizTalk/g9boxjl2.xsl"?>
```

to

```
<?xml-stylesheet type="text/xsl" href="g9boxjl2.xsl"?>
```

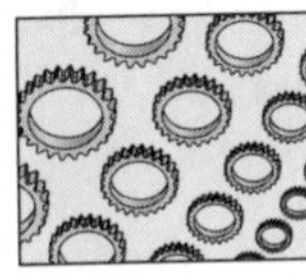

NOTE

Don't worry if you are not comfortable with the XML, XML schema, XSL stylesheet, or XML DOM terminologies used in this section. In Appendix A, B, and C of this book, you will learn about XML and all its related technologies.

Now, let's use this sample purchase order BizTalk schema to demonstrate how to use the plug-in Code Generator Wizard to create COM objects, and how to use the generated COM objects to manipulate the instances of purchase order documents without explicitly using the more complicated XML DOM programming model.

First, you need to start a new ActiveX DLL project from Visual Basic 6.0, name the project POSample, and remove the default class module by right-clicking the class module from the Project Explorer and selecting Remove Class1, as shown in Figure 1-4.

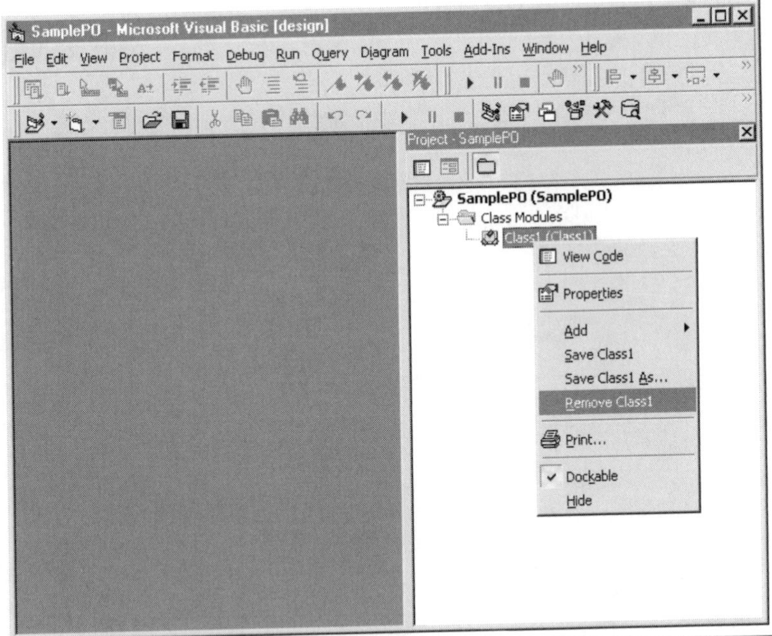

Figure 1-4 *Remove Class1 from the POSample Visual Basic project*

Now you are ready to run the plug-in Code Generator Wizard. If the toolkit has been installed and set up correctly as described in the preceding section, you should be able to access it from the Add-In Manager of the Visual Basic IDE, as shown in Figure 1-5.

After verifying that the plug-in code generator has been appropriately installed, you can start using it for this example: From the Add-Ins menu of Visual Basic IDE, select MS Schema Plug-in Generator. You will see an introductory screen of the MS Plug-in Generator Wizard. Click the Next button to take you to Step 1 of the wizard. Here you can select the XML schemas from which you can generate the corresponding plug-in object. You can load the schema either from a URL or from a local file. In this example, you choose the purchase order schema file you downloaded (zi0123pf.xml). The wizard screen will now look like the one in Figure 1-6. To view the entire schema in the wizard, click anywhere on the schema and press the down-arrow key on your keyboard.

Click Next to see Step 2 of the plug-in generator wizard (Figure 1-7) where you can specify a namespace for the XML document (XML namespaces will be explained in Appendix A). You can either specify the namespace here or keep the default value "YOUR_ORGANIZATION" and manually change it later from the classes generated by the wizard. For now, just keep the default and click Next.

Now you should see Step 3 as shown in Figure 1-8, the last step of the plug-in generator wizard. In this step, you will have a chance to name the classes created by the wizard. By default, the wizard will use the element names (tags) in the schema as the

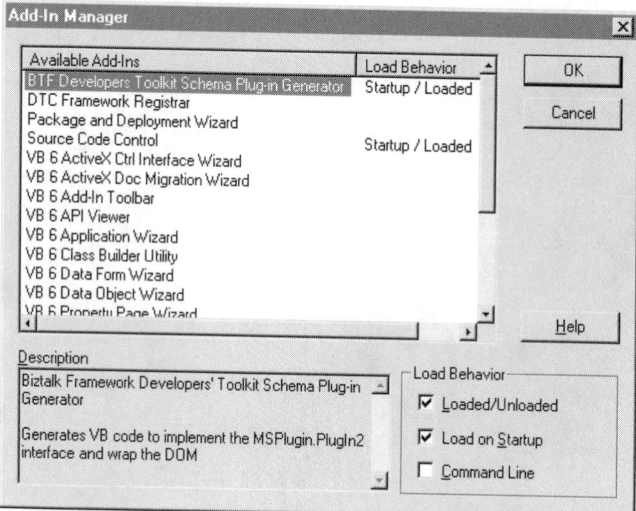

Figure 1-5 *The BTF Developer's Toolkit Schema Plug-in Generator in the Visual Basic Add-In Manager*

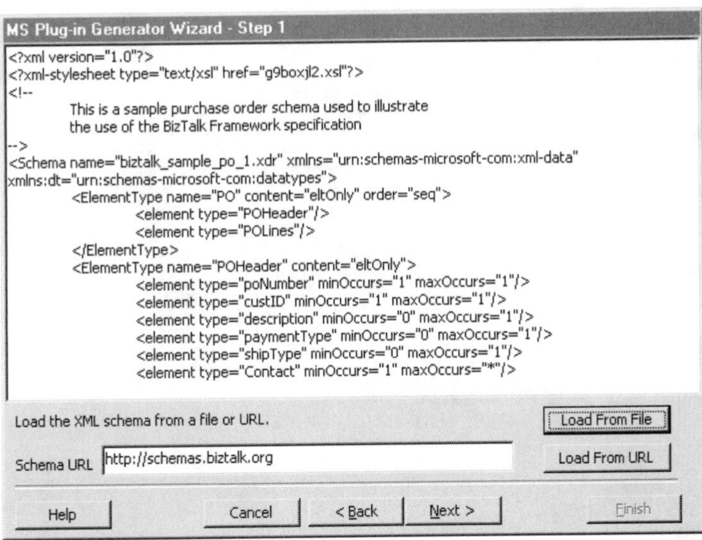

MS Plug-in Generator Wizard - Step 1
<?xml version="1.0"?>
<?xml-stylesheet type="text/xsl" href="g9boxjl2.xsl"?>
<!--
This is a sample purchase order schema used to illustrate
the use of the BizTalk Framework specification
-->
<Schema name="biztalk_sample_po_1.xdr" xmlns="urn:schemas-microsoft-com:xml-data"
xmlns:dt="urn:schemas-microsoft-com:datatypes">
<ElementType name="PO" content="eltOnly" order="seq">
<element type="POHeader"/>
<element type="POLines"/>
</ElementType>
<ElementType name="POHeader" content="eltOnly">
<element type="poNumber" minOccurs="1" maxOccurs="1"/>
<element type="custID" minOccurs="1" maxOccurs="1"/>
<element type="description" minOccurs="0" maxOccurs="1"/>
<element type="paymentType" minOccurs="0" maxOccurs="1"/>
<element type="shipType" minOccurs="0" maxOccurs="1"/>
<element type="Contact" minOccurs="1" maxOccurs="*"/>
Load the XML schema from a file or URL.
Load From File
Schema URL
http://schemas.biztalk.org
Load From URL
Help
Cancel
< Back
Next >
Finish

Figure 1-6 *Step 1, the schema has been loaded into the plug-in generator wizard*

class names. It may replace some special characters that violate Visual Basic naming conventions (such as classes containing an underscore character). In this example, you will use the default names for the classes. You can also specify the specific MSXML

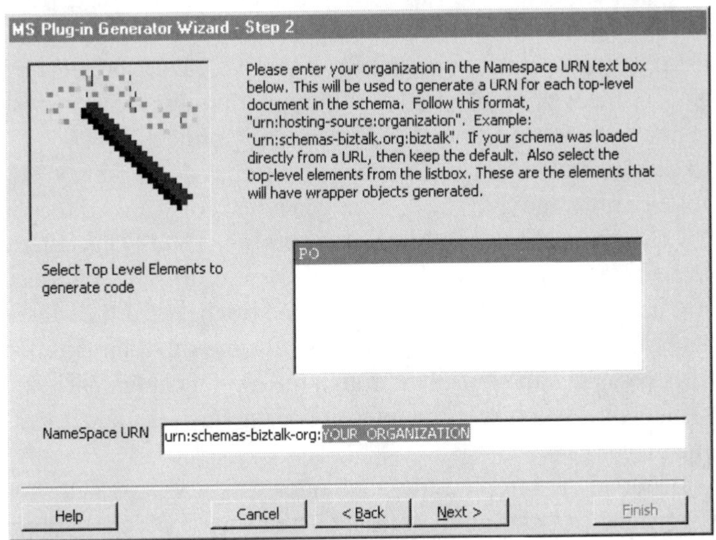

MS Plug-in Generator Wizard - Step 2
Please enter your organization in the Namespace URN text box below. This will be used to generate a URN for each top-level document in the schema. Follow this format, "urn:hosting-source:organization". Example: "urn:schemas-biztalk.org:biztalk". If your schema was loaded directly from a URL, then keep the default. Also select the top-level elements from the listbox. These are the elements that will have wrapper objects generated.
Select Top Level Elements to generate code
PO
NameSpace URN
urn:schemas-biztalk-org:YOUR_ORGANIZATION
Help
Cancel
< Back
Next >
Finish

Figure 1-7 *Step 2, specify a namespace*

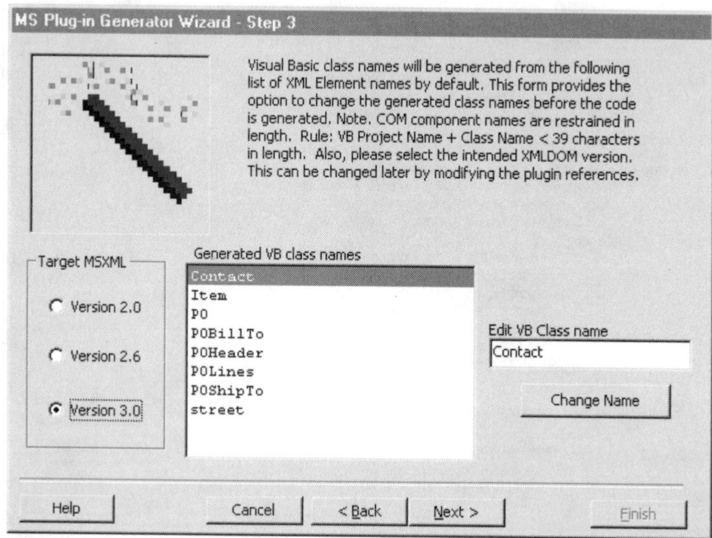

Figure 1-8 *Step 3, rename classes and specify MSXML parser versions*

parser version used on your computer in this step. Let's assume that you have MSXML 3.0 installed, so you will select Version 3.0 as shown in Figure 1-8.

Clicking Next will bring you to the last screen of the plug-in generator wizard. There you can save the current settings as the default for the future. If you click the Finish button, the wizard will start generating the code for you. After a few seconds, you will end up with a completed Visual Basic ActiveX DLL project, with all the classes created by the wizard and ready for compilation. Figure 1-9 illustrates the Project Explorer view of the SamplePO Visual Basic project.

Now, let's see what the plug-in generator wizard has done. As you can see in Figure 1-9, eleven class modules have been generated for you. All the class modules except for PO.cls are marked as **PublicNotCreatable**. The PO.cls corresponds to the top-level element (tag) underneath the Body element of the BizTalk document, the **PO** element. The rest of the class modules created by the wizard correspond to sub-elements of the PO element, or collections of some sub-elements. Therefore, you can only access the sub-elements through the top-level element—in this case, the PO element. As a result, the integrity of the business document has been guaranteed.

You can download the sample code, POSampleClient.vbp, which shows you how to use the wizard-generated plug-in objects to create a PO purchase order document defined by the BizTalk schema from the Web site of this book, located under the

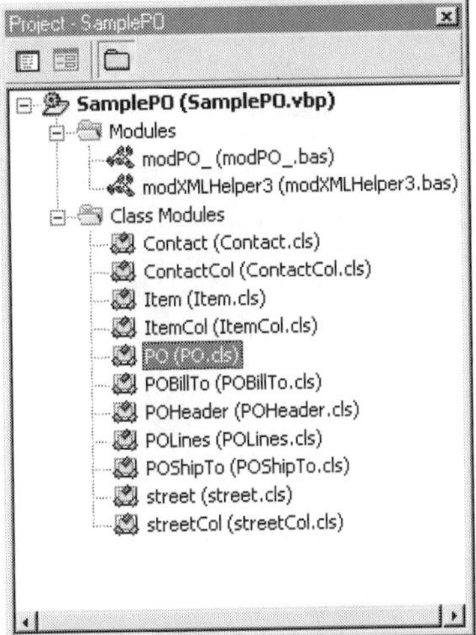

Figure 1-9 *The generated code modules of the POSample Visual Basic project*

Chap01\POSample\Client directory. The following listing illustrates the code that uses the plug-in objects to create an XML purchase order document:

```
Private Sub cmdCreatePO_Click()
  'Assume that you set the following references in the Project:
  'BTF Envelope Object (for example, BTFEnvelope30.dll);
  'Microsoft Plutin2 Type Library (for example: msplugin30.tlb);
  'Microsoft Scripting Runtime (scrrun.dll);
  'SamplePO.dll (the one you just created using the Toolkit).
  Dim oPO As New SamplePO.PO
  Dim oEnv As New BTFEnvelope.Envelope
  Dim oPlugIn As MSPlugin.PlugIn2
  Dim oFSO As New Scripting.FileSystemObject
  Dim oFile As Scripting.TextStream
  Set oPlugIn = oPO

  On Error Goto CreatePO_Err
  oEnv.manifest.addReference oPlugIn.DocumentElementName, _
    oPlugIn.Namespace, "MY_Namespace", oPO

  With oPO.POHeader
    .poNumber = "1234567890"
```

```
        .custID = "10001"
        With .POShipTo
          .attn = "John Smith"
          .Addstreet = "123 Rose Road"
          .city = "Any town"
          .stateProvince = "Any State"
          .postalCode = "AS 12345"
          .country = "USA"
        End With
        With .POBillTo
          .attn = "John Smith"
          .Addstreet = "123 Rose Road"
          .city = "Any town"
          .stateProvince = "Any State"
          .postalCode = "AS 12345"
          .country = "USA"
        End With
        .Contact.Item(1).contactName = "John Smith"
        .shipType = "UPS Next Day Air"
        With oPO.POLines.Item(1)
          .Line = "1"
          .partno = 123
          .qty = 20
          .unitPrice = 1.99
          .totalAmount = .qty * .unitPrice
        End With

    End With
    Set oFile = oFSO.CreateTextFile(App.Path & "\SamplePO.xml", True)
    oFile.WriteLine oEnv.XML
    MsgBox "Sample PO has been created!"

    Set oPO = Nothing
    Set oEnv = Nothing
    Set oPlugIn = Nothing
    Set oFSO = Nothing
    Set oFile = Nothing
    Set oPlugIn = Nothing
    Exit Sub
  CreatePO_Err:
    Msgbox Err.Description
  End Sub
```

Copy the sample project to your local drive and verify that all the preferences are appropriately set. Start the project and click the Create PO button on the form. You will see a message box indicating the PO document has been created (you can find the created PO XML document in the same directory where you installed the sample project on your local computer). Its file name is SamplePO.xml. Figure 1-10 illustrates the generated purchase order in Internet Explorer 5.5 (for brevity, the SOAP envelope tags are not shown in the figure).

In addition to creating a full BizTalk Framework 2.0–compliant document (the SOAP envelope) as you did in the preceding example, you can also use the COM objects generated by the toolkit to build regular, well-formed and valid XML

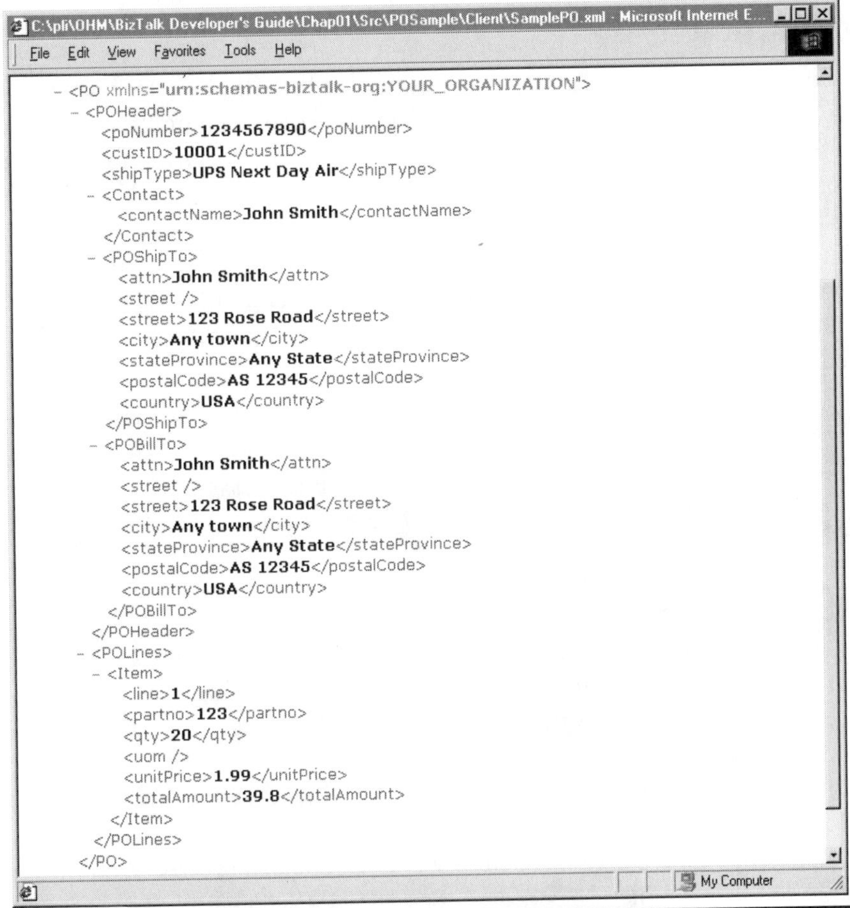

Figure 1-10 *SamplePO.xml in Internet Explorer 5.5*

documents. For other scenarios regarding the toolkit, refer to the documentation, UsingPluginGenerator.doc, that accompanies the toolkit. This document also lists some known issues of the toolkit and appropriate workarounds.

The BizTalk Framework 2.0 Development Toolkit provides a great way to simplify creating BizTalk documents or business documents based on a specific XML schema. This can be extremely helpful, as you will see later in this book, when we discuss using the BizTalk Editor (an XML tool that comes with BizTalk Server 2000) to create, edit, and manage *Specifications* (BizTalk Server-specific XML schemas).

BizTalk.org

The second part of the BizTalk initiative is the BizTalk.org web site, accessible at http://www.biztalk.org/. The original BizTalk.org steering committee consisted of more than a dozen industry leaders in EAI and B2B integration firms, including Microsoft, Ariba, Boeing, CommerceOne, Compaq, Dell, I2, NEON, RosettaNet, SAP, and Siebel Systems. The committee has since served its purpose and is disbanded. The BizTalk.org web site nevertheless carries on their work, providing a rich repository of BizTalk schemas and a growing community devoted to the exchange of best practices in BizTalk and XML. It also contains links to other related resources.

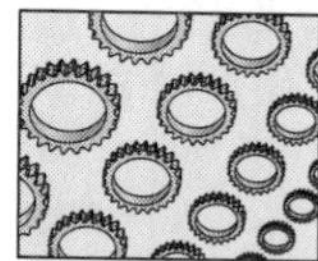

NOTE

There will be some significant changes to BizTalk.org in the coming months. By the time this book is published, the BizTalk.org may look very different than what is described in this section.

A Repository of BizTalk Schemas

As an important part of its makeup, BizTalk.org provides a library of BizTalk schemas contributed by more than 50 organizations, including such industries as Accommodation, Food, Agriculture, Forestry, Fishing, Construction, Education, Finance, Insurance, Health Care, Social Assistance, Information, Management, Manufacturing, Professional Services, Scientific, Real Estate, Rental, Leasing, Retail, and Wholesale Trade, etc.

Membership to the BizTalk.org library is free. You can browse the library for appropriate BizTalk schemas or search for a specific schema by keyword. Figure 1-11 shows 41 BizTalk schemas found using the keywords "purchase order."

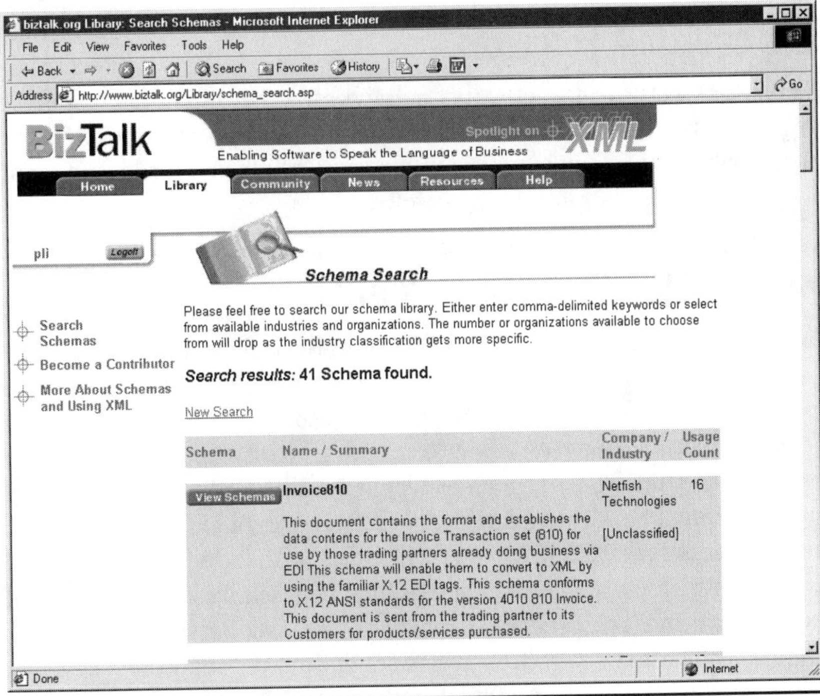

Figure 1-11 *BizTalk schemas in BizTalk.org library*

You can download the BizTalk schema and read related documentation. You can also contribute (register) your own schema to the library so it can be shared around the globe.

A BizTalk Developer Community

Today, the BizTalk.org web site offers many discussion forums on BizTalk, XML, and other related technologies. Current threads of discussion include the ABC's of Schemas, BizTalk Framework Q&A, BizTalk Server Q&A, Community Projects, General, (BizTalk) Jumpstart Kit, Newbies Corner, Riots, Raves and Rants, XML by industry, XML Pub-Casual discussions, XML Schema-experts, and XML Schema–learners. The community provides learning experiences and opportunities for the exchange of ideas and good practices regarding XML, EAI, and B2B integration activities.

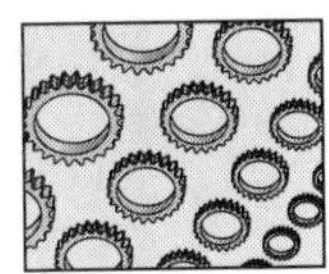

NOTE

By the time you read this, these BizTalk discussion forums will have migrated to MSDN.

A Source of BizTalk Resources

The BizTalk.org web site also contains rich links to other important resources, including BizTalk Framework specifications and white papers, third-party vendors, Microsoft XML Parser download, BizTalk Server 2000 downloads, and more.

Microsoft BizTalk Server 2000

The third part of the BizTalk initiative is Microsoft BizTalk Server 2000. Released on December 12, 2000 by Microsoft, BizTalk Server is the first BFC server to be completely compliant with BizTalk Framework 2.0 specifications. In addition, BizTalk Server 2000 provides a wealth of services, including messaging and orchestration services that greatly facilitate integrations within the organizational boundary (EAI) and between external business trading partners (B2B integration). This book will focus on BizTalk Server 2000. Chapter 2 will give you an introduction to the basics, including BizTalk Server architecture and its important services. Part II through Part IV will have in-depth and comprehensive coverage of BizTalk Server 2000, including its messaging and orchestration services, server administration, application development, the integration of BizTalk Server with other Microsoft .NET servers, as well as ways of extending BizTalk Server services. Part VI contains some case studies that will showcase how to use BizTalk Server 2000 in real world applications.

Chapter in Review

In this chapter, we have introduced you to the BizTalk initiative, including:

- BizTalk Framework 2.0, the backbone of BizTalk initiative
- The BizTalk.org web site, a dedicated BizTalk schema repository and developer community
- BizTalk Server 2000, the first BizTalk Framework 2.0-compliant server that reliably delivers XML-based messaging and orchestration services

CHAPTER

2

Introducing BizTalk Server 2000

IN THIS CHAPTER:

A Brief History of BizTalk Server

BizTalk Server 2000 Services

BizTalk Server 2000 Tools

BizTalk Server 2000 Architecture

Installing BizTalk Server 2000

Chapter in Review

As a BTF 2.0-compliant server, BizTalk Server 2000 fully implemented the messaging services defined in BizTalk Framework 2.0, including data integrity, security, reliable messaging, guaranteed once-only delivery, key document formats, etc. Another unique and exciting feature of BizTalk Server 2000 is its orchestration services which enable you to build dynamic business processes that span applications, platforms, and businesses over the Internet. In addition, BizTalk Server 2000 provides an execution platform that integrates loosely coupled, long-running transactions (up to months in length) either within the organizational boundary (EAI integration) or between business trading partners (B2B integration). In this chapter, we will introduce you to all the important services, tools, and architecture of BizTalk Server 2000. Let's start with an introduction to the history of BizTalk Server.

A Brief History of BizTalk Server

In the third quarter of 1999, Microsoft launched the BizTalk initiative to facilitate the EAI and B2B integration. To let people start implementing XML-based messaging solutions using the BizTalk framework, Microsoft soon released the first version of the BizTalk Jumpstart kit, distributed as part of a free CD-ROM or download titled "Microsoft Windows DNA XML Resource Kit." In February 2000, BizTalk Jumpstart Kit 2.0 (also called version L) was released with a lot of enhancement and improvement. In April 2000 at the Professional Developer Conference (PDC), Microsoft distributed a Technical Preview version of BizTalk Server 2000 to thousands of the conference participants. This was the first time the developers got a chance to see the server form of the BizTalk product. The Beta version of BizTalk Server 2000 was made available in summer of the year 2000, adding orchestration services as well as other important features and tools. By December 2000, Microsoft officially announced the RTM (Release to Manufacturing) of BizTalk Server 2000. To help you get a better idea of the evolution of the BizTalk server product, in the following sections we will briefly introduce the features of these different versions of BizTalk Server releases.

BizTalk Jumpstart Kit

The BizTalk Jumpstart Kit (or BizTalk JSK) was released as a transient tool aimed at helping developers start engineering BizTalk applications—like BizTalk Framework 1.0-compliant XML messaging solutions for EAI and B2B integration—

using Microsoft Visual Studio development tools. Although the Jumpstart Kit has now been replaced by BizTalk Server 2000, it is still worthwhile to take a look at the JSK for several reasons. First, BizTalk JSK demonstrates a great design pattern for building loosely-coupled, XML-based messaging solutions. Second, all the services, components, and tools in BizTalk JSK are available in source code, which is a great learning tool. And finally, BizTalk Server 2000 can only run on Windows 2000 servers, where you can use both BizTalk Jumpstart Kit and BizTalk Server 2000 to build complete BizTalk solutions on both Windows NT and Windows 2000. Figure 2-1 illustrates the architecture of the BizTalk Jumpstart Kit.

As shown in Figure 2-1, BizTalk JSK provides a set of Core Services, Transport Adapters, and Administration Tools. It also supplies a set of development tools and frameworks for developers to build custom (COM) components that glue BizTalk services (the core services) and business logic together. In addition, the JSK also provides a couple of utility (helper) services to streamline the integration process.

Core Services and Transport Adapters

Transport adapters are COM components that wrap appropriate protocol APIs (SMTP, HTTP, MSMQ, etc.) and expose these APIs as a set of methods of appropriate COM objects.

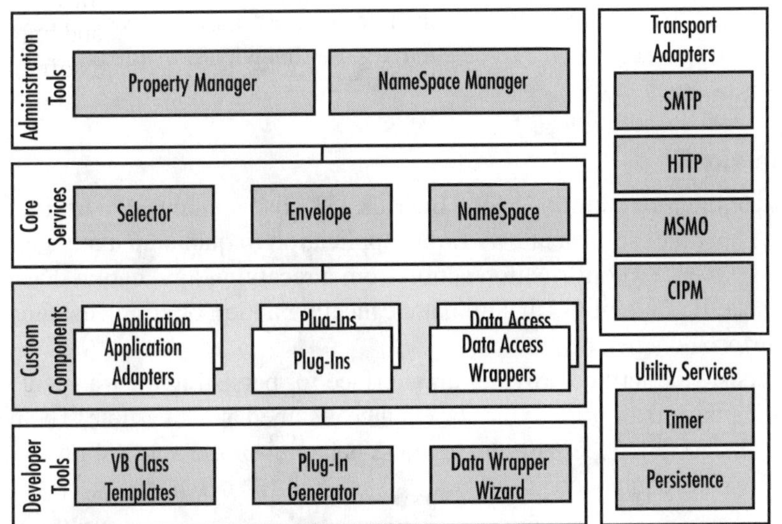

Figure 2-1 *The BizTalk Jumpstart Kit architecture*

The Selector component consists of two COM objects. The Selector.Select object provides a simple interface for transport adapters to submit an incoming message to an MSMQ persistent queue. The Selector.Engine object retrieves the message persisted by the Selector.Select object routes it to an appropriate application adapter for processing based on information provided by the Envelope component and the Namespace component.

Development Infrastructure

BizTalk JSK provides a framework and an infrastructure for developers to build glue COM components that tie different services together.

Application adapters are XML message consumers that process XML messages and perform appropriate business logics. BizTalk JSK provides a Visual Basic class template which defines the IXMLMessage2 adapter interface.

The Plug-In components and the plug-in generator are similar to the ones introduced in Chapter 1 when we discussed the BizTalk Framework 2.0 Developer's Toolkit. As a matter of fact, the BTF 2.0 Developer's toolkit is developed on the basis of BizTalk JSK's plug-in generator.

Optionally, you can also build appropriate Data Access Wrapper components that are responsible for communication between the application adapters and the database layers. BizTalk JSK comes with an MTS Data Wrapper Wizard which automatically creates the Data Access Wrapper component for you. Because the Data Access Wrapper is implemented as a COM DLL, you can only use this wizard inside an ActiveX DLL type of Visual Basic project.

Utility Services

To facilitate the programming tasks, BizTalk JSK also contains two utility helper services. This timer service allows for an application to queue up a message for later processing. In case a confirmation action from a receiving application doesn't occur within a specific time limit, an automatic canceling action or compensating action can be performed when desirable.

The Persistence service provides an interface for persisting the transient state information into a data store so the state can be resumed at a later time. The persistence utility can be used to cope with the stateless behavior of the application adapters that are usually MTS components.

Additional Features

In addition to the core services and the development infrastructure described in the previous sections, BizTalk JSK comes with some administration tools that allow you to define the relationship between a particular message type and a specific application adapter.

The configuration information (meta data) and the state of messages are stored in an SQL Server database, named ADCUMH. MSMQ is used as an asynchronous messaging tool for robust messaging delivery.

All the services, utilities, and tools of BizTalk JSK are shipped as both binary deliverables and source code. They provide a very good design pattern for building loosely-coupled, XML-based messaging solutions. You can use the JSK to build BizTalk applications that run on Windows NT platforms. Because all the JSK services are implemented as COM components, most of them can be reused in non-BizTalk applications as well.

CAUTION

The applications you built using BizTalk Jumpstart Kit are BizTalk Framework 1.0-compliant.

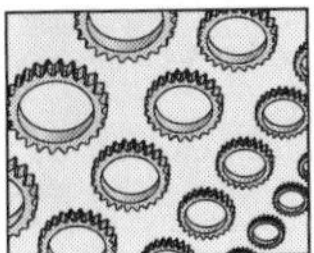

NOTE

BizTalk Framework 1.0 (formally titled "BizTalk Framework v1.0a Independent Document Specification") is available at BizTalk.org from the following URL: ***http://www.biztalk.org/Resources/BTF1_0.doc.***

Vertical Industry SDKs

To facilitate developing BizTalk solutions using the Jumpstart Kit, Microsoft has published several BizTalk Framework SDKs for some vertical industries, including a Banking Framework SDK, a Healthcare Framework SDK and a Securities Framework SDK. Each of these industry-specific BizTalk Framework SDKs is built on top of the BizTalk Jumpstart Kit. Each SDK contains an introductory documentation, an installation guide, a Framework Programmer's Guide, and a Framework SDK Specification.

Framework SDK Specifications are based on specific industry specifications and/or standards. For example, the Banking Framework SDK Specification is based on the Interactive Financial Exchange (IFX) Business Specification, while the Healthcare Framework SDK is based on the Healthcare Information Portability and Accountability Act of 1996 (HTPAA), and the Securities Framework SDK Specification is based on STPML (Straight Through Processing Markup Language) Message Specification.

Each industry-specific Framework SDK also ships with sample applications as well as source code. These Framework SDKs provide a great set of tools when building BizTalk solutions for specific industries. Because they are built on top of BizTalk Jumpstart Kit, all of them are BizTalk Framework 1.0-compliant. To make them BizTalk Framework 2.0-compliant, some modification to the JSK must be done as described in the previous section.

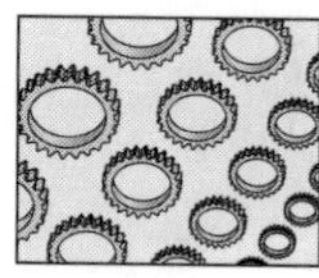

NOTE

BizTalk Jumpstart Kit v2.0 can be downloaded at: ***http://www.Microsoft.com/downloads/release.asp?releaseID=20615.*** *BizTalk Framework SDKs are available at MSDN Online Library, under Other SDK Documentation and then BizTalk Framework SDKs.*

BizTalk Server 2000

On December 12, 2000, Microsoft announced the RTM (Release To Manufacturing) of BizTalk Server 2000. By the time you read this, the evaluation copy of the BizTalk Server 2000 should already be available for download from the Microsoft BizTalk web site at: **http://www.microsoft.com/BizTalk**. In this final version of BizTalk Server 2000, the features of BizTalk Server 2000 can be categorized into the following three areas:

1. Building Dynamic Business Processes:

   BizTalk Server 2000 provides a complete set of visual tools for developers to quickly and easily build dynamic business processes (BizTalk Orchestration Designer), generate XML schemas (BizTalk Editor), transform XML documents (BizTalk Mapper), and build business trading relationships (BizTalk Messaging Manager).

2. Enterprise Application Integration (EAI) and Business-to-Business electronic commerce (B2B eCommerce) support:

   Internally BizTalk Server 2000 uses XML exclusively for document exchange. BizTalk Server 2000 supports multiple transports including HTTP, HTTPS, SMTP, and numerous file formats, including EDI (ANSI X12 and UN EDIFACT), flat file, etc. In addition, the compliance protocol as the underlying BizTalk Framework 2.0 with SOAP 1.1 specification and the open binding adapter architecture add a great extensibility and interoperability to the BizTalk Server 2000.

3. Security, Reliability and Scalability:

   BizTalk Server 2000 uses Windows 2000 security features to ensure secure communications with trading partners over the Internet. BizTalk Server 2000 supports public-key infrastructure, digital signatures, and encryption. It also supports Secure/Multipurpose Internet Mail Extensions (S/MIME) and third-party security products. BizTalk Server 2000 completely supports the reliable document delivery functionality defined in the BizTalk Framework 2.0 such as sending, receiving, and queuing messages with exactly once semantics, synchronously and asynchronously, as well as receipt generating and delivery capability. BizTalk Server 2000 allows you to cluster (BizTalk) servers together to support scalability. In addition, BizTalk Server 2000 provides tracking and monitoring functionality for document exchange.

In the next few sections of this chapter, we will introduce BizTalk Server 2000 services, tools, and architectures, and then conclude the chapter by helping you to install and set up BizTalk Server 2000. Along the way, we'll familiarize you with BizTalk Server 2000's comprehensive tutorial.

BizTalk Server 2000 Services

BizTalk Server 2000 provides a rich set of messaging and orchestration services that developers can leverage to build EAI and B2B integration solutions.

Messaging Services

BizTalk Messaging Services include receive functions, transport services, data parsers and serializers, reliable document delivery, and secure document exchange.

Receive Functions

BizTalk Server 2000 uses *receive functions or scripts* to automatically monitor and pull documents from a disk directory or a queue of Microsoft Messaging Queuing. A BizTalk Server 2000 receive function allows BizTalk server(s) to automatically receive incoming documents from a specific location. Figure 2-2 illustrates the relationship between a sending business application, a receive location, and a generic BizTalk Server receive function.

BizTalk Server 2000 supports two types of receive functions: the File receive function and Message Queuing (MSMQ) receive function. The receive location in Figure 2-2 could be either a file system or a MSMQ queue, depending on the specific type of receive function you created. As you will see in Chapter 6, you can either use the BizTalk Administration management tool (a Microsoft Management Console or MMC snap-in) to declaratively create a receive function or use the Windows Management Instrumentation (WMI) Scripting Type Library with a scripting language, such as VBScript, to programmatically create a receive function.

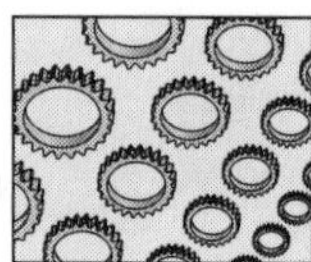

NOTE

You will also learn more about receive functions and WMI in Chapter 6.

In addition to the built-in receive functions, you can also submit documents using Active Server Pages (ASP) scripts via HTTP or HTTPS protocols or using Microsoft Exchange script via SMTP protocol.

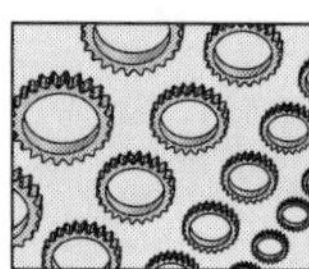

NOTE

The primary difference between the two types of receiving functions are performance. Particularly, the Message Queuing-based receiving function is highly optimized because it's in a known environment, allowing you to cache OLE DB Session objects, and so on. Whereas on the File-based mechanisms, you need to break down and bring up the sessions each time.

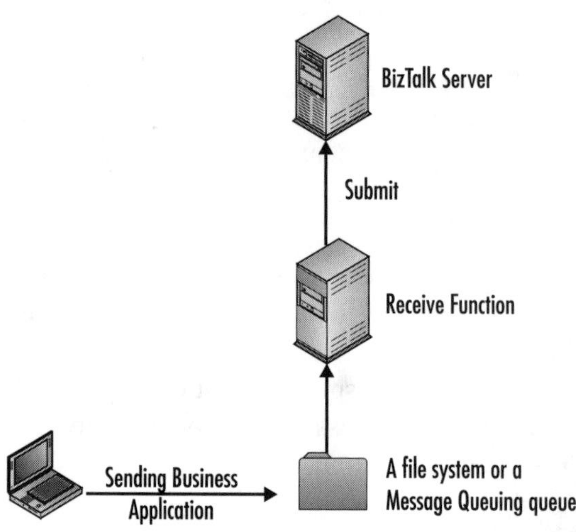

Figure 2-2 *A BizTalk Server 2000 receive function*

Transport Services

BizTalk Server 2000 supports a set of transport services for transmitting documents to their destinations. BizTalk Server 2000 transport services include network protocols such as HTTP, HTTPS, SMPT, File Systems, Message Queuing (MSMQ), and Application Integration Components (AIC). Having these transport services built into the infrastructure of BizTalk Server 2000 greatly simplifies your job as a developer. You don't need to write your own transport code to directly interact with network protocols. Rather, you use the tools provided by BizTalk Server 2000 to declaratively define and bind these protocols to your applications.

A special type of BizTalk transport service is called *Loopback*. Loopback allows the return of current state data to the application from which the state data originated.

Data Parsers and Serializers

A parser is a BizTalk Server 2000 component that translates non-XML files into XML files. Supported data parsers can handle translating a variety of industry document standards, including EDI (ANSI X12 and UN/EDIFACT), XML, of course, as well as flat files (either delimited or positional or a combination thereof). The built-in parsers in BizTalk Server 2000 can handle almost all your parsing needs. In the occasional case where these built-in parsers can't do want you want, you can build and register your own custom parser components for converting non-XML documents into XML (using the IBizTalkParserComponent interface) or convert the document from XML back to its native format (using the IBizTalkSerializerComponent interface).

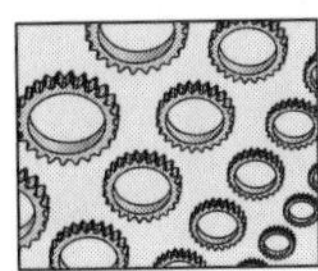

NOTE

The IBizTalkParserComponent and IBizTalkSerializerComponent interfaces will be introduced in Chapter 11.

BizTalk Server 2000 allows you to define a document specification for a specific business document, say a purchase order, and validate instances of purchase orders against the specification. Non-valid documents will be placed into a suspended queue for further analysis.

Reliable Document Delivery

BizTalk Server 2000 Messaging Services provides a set of configurable properties that supports reliable document delivery. The properties you can configure include setting service windows for sending documents, receiving receipts, setting retry counts and retry intervals, and so on. BizTalk Server 2000 also supports all the reliable messaging features of the SOAP envelopes defined in BizTalk Framework 2.0 (recall our discussions in Chapter 1).

In addition, BizTalk Server 2000 includes other robust and reliable features, such as queuing documents to a central location and implementing a rollover mechanism to cope with system failure.

Secure Document Exchange

To support secure document exchanges, BizTalk Server 2000 uses encryption/decryption based on public-key technology. It also supports digital signatures.

Orchestration Services

BizTalk Orchestration is a new technology for creating and orchestrating business processes that span time, as well as various organizations and applications. BizTalk Server 2000 Orchestration Services supports features such as separating definition from implementation, dynamic processes, "any-to-any" integration, concurrency and synchronization, long-running transactions, management, and monitoring.

XLANG Schedules

BizTalk Server 2000 allows you to graphically design (using a Visio drawing) a business process flow and bind this process to appropriate applications (technology components called *implementations*) to create an execution plan. The compiled execution plan is an XML document called *XLANG schedule*. XLANG is an XML-based language that describes the logic sequencing of business processes as well as applications (implementations). XLANG schedules are controlled by the XLANG Scheduler and the XLANG Engine. The XLANG Scheduler is a COM+ application that is loaded when you install BizTalk Server 2000. This COM+ application is used to host running instances of XLANG schedules. The XLANG engine, on the other hand, is a service that runs XLANG schedules. It controls the activation, execution, *dehydration*, and *rehydration* of an XLANG schedule. Dehydration is a process that stores all state information for an XLANG schedule instance in a persistent data store (a SQL Server database) while the XLANG Scheduler waits to receive a message before executing the next action in the business process. In contrast, a rehydration is a process to retrieve all state information of a pending XLANG schedule instance from the persistent data store after a message is received by the XLANG Scheduler. The state information of XLANG Scheduler is stored in the Orchestration Persistence SQL Server database.

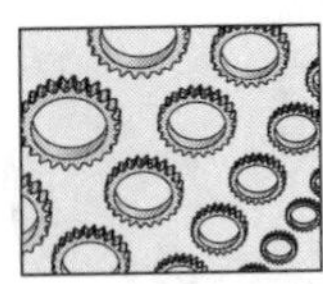

NOTE

BizTalk Server 2000 Messaging Services and Orchestration Services will be discussed in Part II and Part IV, respectively.

Implementations

Technology components that you can bind to business processes in BizTalk Server 2000 Orchestration Services are called *implementations*. BizTalk Server 2000 currently supports four types of implementations: COM components, Windows Script components, Messaging Queuing (MSMQ), and BizTalk Messaging Services. The BizTalk (Server 2000) Message Services itself could be an implementation in an XLANG schedule. As you will learn later in this book, there are several other ways in which you can incorporate BizTalk Server 2000 Messaging Services and Orchestration Services together.

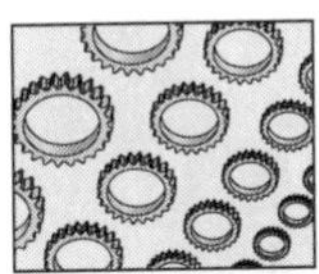

NOTE

Windows script components are covered in Appendix D.

BizTalk Server 2000 Tools

BizTalk Server 2000 offers a complete set of tools that allows you to use and manage its messaging and orchestration services, administrate the servers, monitor and track documents, and construct and transform XML files. In this section, we will briefly introduce important tools available in BizTalk Server 2000.

BizTalk Messaging Manager

Figure 2-3 shows the GUI interface of the BizTalk Messaging Manager (previously named as BizTalk Management Desk in Technical Preview and beta versions of BizTalk Server 2000). The BizTalk Messaging Manager is a web application tailored solely to perform dedicated tasks for managing BizTalk Messaging Services. The screen shown in Figure 2-3 is the custom client application that is a dedicated web browser for accessing and managing BizTalk Messaging Services objects (organizations, messaging ports, envelopes, etc.) The server site functionality of the BizTalk Messaging Manager was built as a bunch of ASP files sitting on the Internet Information Server (IIS) 5 .0 web server. Figure 2-4 illustrates the MessagingManager application in IIS 5.0.

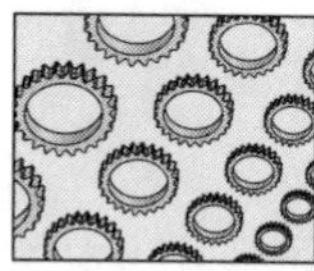

NOTE

You will learn how to use the BizTalk Messaging Manager in Chapter 5.

BizTalk Orchestration Designer

The BizTalk Orchestration Designer (previously introduced in the Beta version of BizTalk Server 2000 as BizTalk Application Designer) is a very neat tool and one of the most exciting features in BizTalk Server 2000, allowing you to draw your flow of business processes and bind them with technology implementations. The BizTalk Orchestration Designer is built as a custom application on top of Microsoft Visio 2000, a great graphic drawing tool with extensive programmatic accessibility.

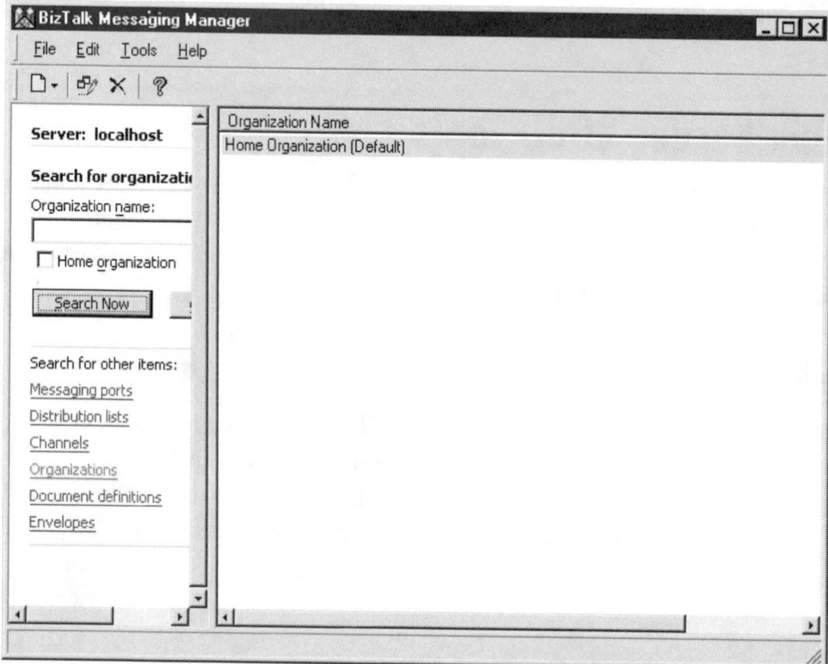

Figure 2-3 *The BizTalk Messaging Manager*

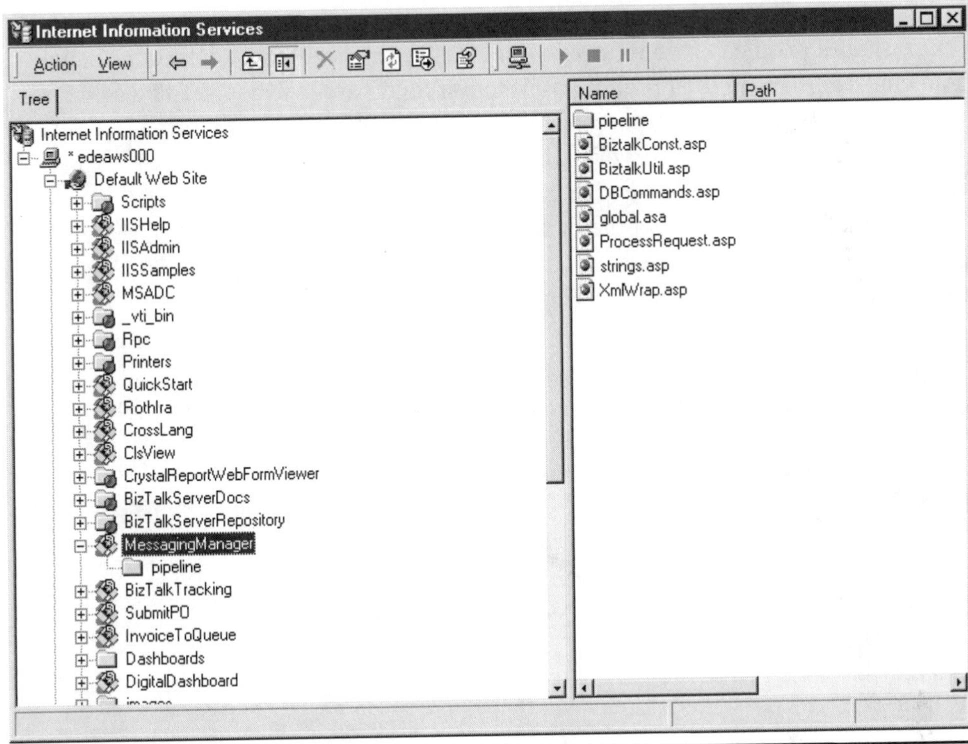

Figure 2-4 *The MessagingManager application in IIS 5.0.*

Figure 2-5 illustrates part of the sample process flow from the BizTalk Server 2000 tutorial. As you can see from this illustration, the drawing areas are separated into two parts, one on the left side and the other on the right. There are also two separate stencils on each side, Flowchart and Implementation, respectively. On the left hand side, you draw the flow of your business processes using the shapes from the Flowchart stencil and then connect the shapes together under the title "Use Flowchart Shapes to Draw a Business Process." Then you select the appropriate technical implementation by dragging a shape from the Implementation stencil on the right hand side and placing it on the right under the title "Use Implementation Shapes to Implement Ports." The BizTalk Orchestration Designer provides binding wizards that help you bind implementations to appropriate actions. The rectangular blocks between the flowchart and the implementations are *port shapes*. They are automatically generated when you place an implementation shape on the drawing area.

You can conditionally direct the process flow by using Decision shapes or While (loop) shapes. You can manage concurrency by using the Fork and/or Join shapes. You can also manage long running transactions and handle exceptions by using the Transaction shape and the Abort shape.

There are two tabs in the BizTalk Orchestration Designer, as shown in Figure 2-5 in the left lower corner. The entire drawing is hosted in the Business Process tab. You use the Data tab to direct the data flow between different ports. The completed orchestration process can then be compiled into an XLANG schedule which can be executed by the BizTalk XLANG Engine.

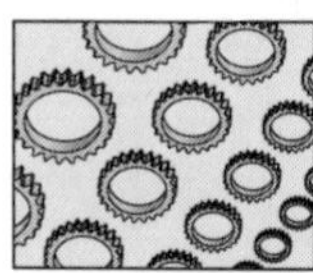

NOTE

You will learn more about how to use the BizTalk Orchestration Designer in Chapter 9.

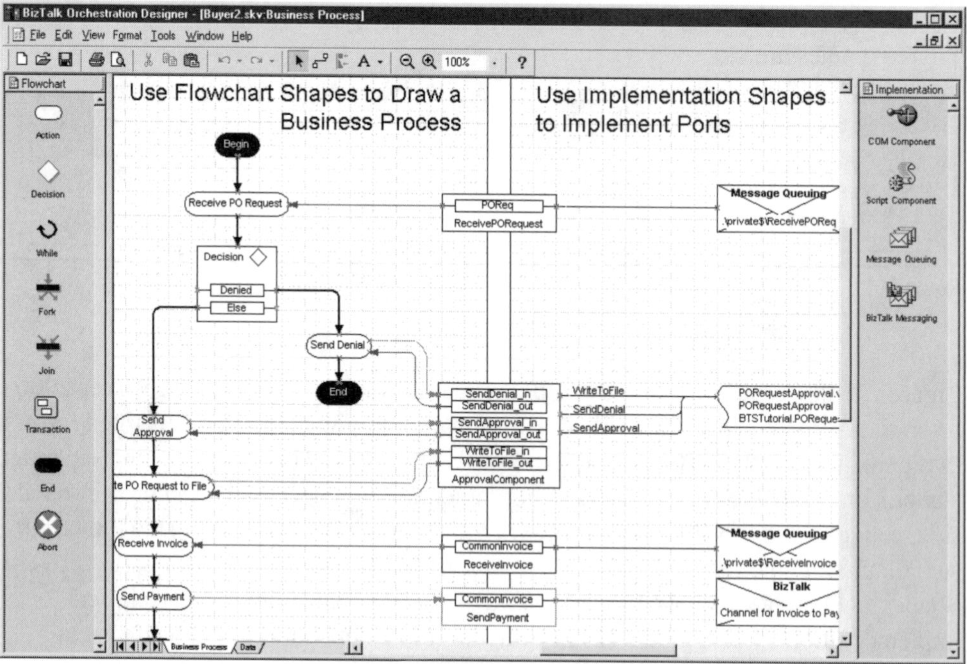

Figure 2-5 *The BizTalk Orchestration Designer*

BizTalk Server Administration

BizTalk Server 2000 provides a Microsoft Management Console (MMC) snap-in, BizTalk Server Administration, as shown in Figure 2-6. Using the BizTalk Server Administration console, you can manage BizTalk Servers and Server Groups, Shared Queues, and receiving functions. BizTalk Server 2000 provides *shared queues* management capabilities for you to manage documents and *interchanges* (an interchange is a group of related documents). Shared queues are logic objects and are mapped to the physical data (the information) of documents and interchanges that are stored in the Shared Queues SQL Server database. So don't confuse the shared queues with the queues in message queuing (MSMQ). The shared queues are very useful for monitoring the progress of documents processed in BizTalk and troubleshooting problems, especially when used together with the BizTalk Document Tracking tool that will be introduced in the next section.

The meta data about BizTalk servers, server Groups, receiving functions and shared queues are stored in the BizTalk Messaging Management SQL Server database. The BizTalk Server Administration tool uses the Windows Management Instrumentation (WMI) provider to access and manage the BizTalk messaging management database.

NOTE

You will learn how to use the BizTalk Server Administration tool to manage and administrate BizTalk servers as well as WMI in Chapter 7.

BizTalk Document Tracking

Like the BizTalk Messaging Manager, the BizTalk Document Tracking is another stand-alone Web application that is used to track documents. Figure 2-7 shows the GUI interface of the BizTalk Document Tracking application. Figure 2-8 shows the various components of the application in IIS 5.0. The BizTalk Document Tracking application is a querying and reporting tool that accesses the BizTalk Tracking SQL Server database. It provides flexible query and search capabilities and also allows you to view the actual documents in their native formats and in XML formats.

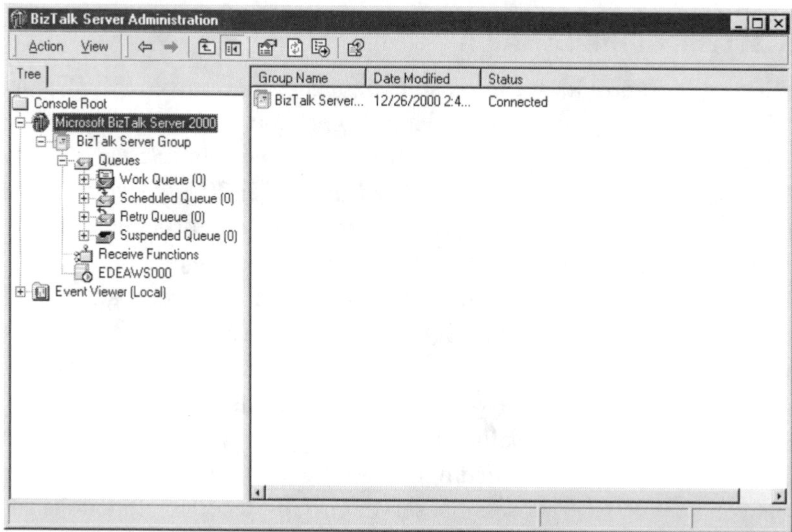

Figure 2-6 *The BizTalk Server Administration*

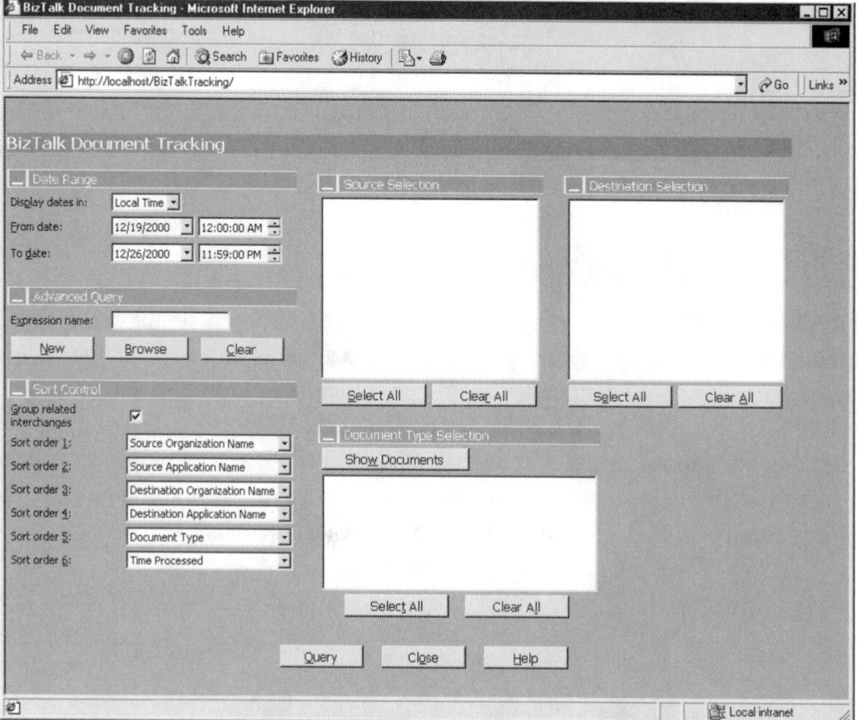

Figure 2-7 *The BizTalk Document Tracking*

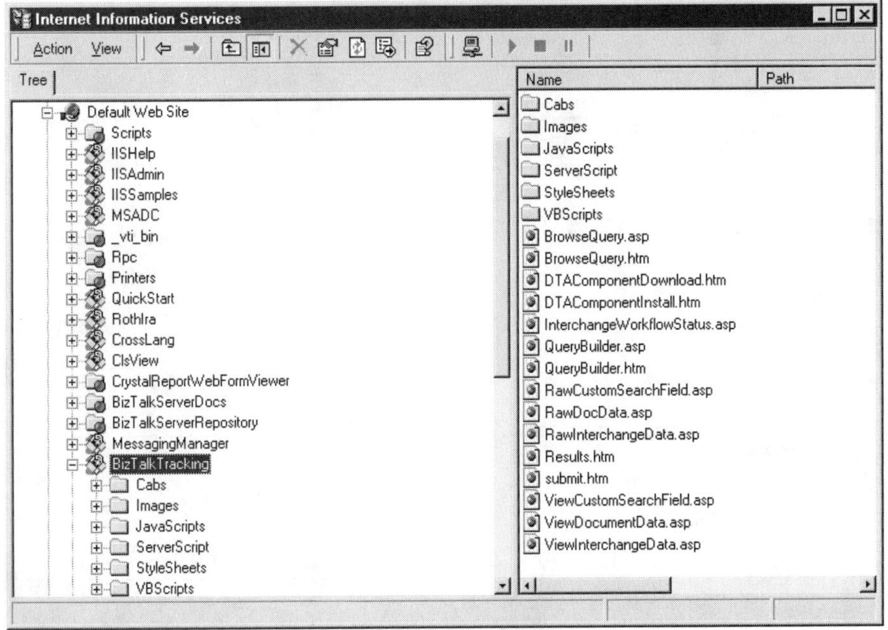

Figure 2-8 *The BizTalkTracking Web application in IIS 5.0*

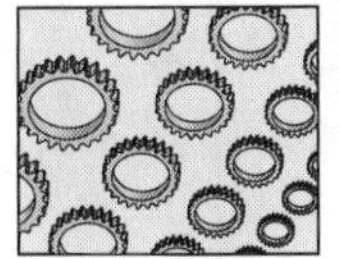

NOTE

The BizTalk Document Tracking Web application will be covered in Chapter 7.

XML Tools

In addition to management and development tools for managing BizTalk servers, services, and documents, BizTalk Server also provides two XML tools which developers can use to graphically create XML schemas and transformations.

You can use the BizTalk Editor (see Figure 2-9) to create BizTalk Server-specific XML schemas called *specifications*. The BizTalk Mapper (see Figure 2-10) allows you to declaratively define a *map* (an XML document with an embedded XSL stylesheet) for transforming two different BizTalk specifications (XML schemas).

The BizTalk Editor allows you to import XML schemas, Document Type Definitions (DTDs), or instances of existing XML documents of a specific type. The BizTalk Mapper supports direct mapping between the fields of two different XML schemas, as well as complicated relationships such as aggregation, calculation, and custom transformations.

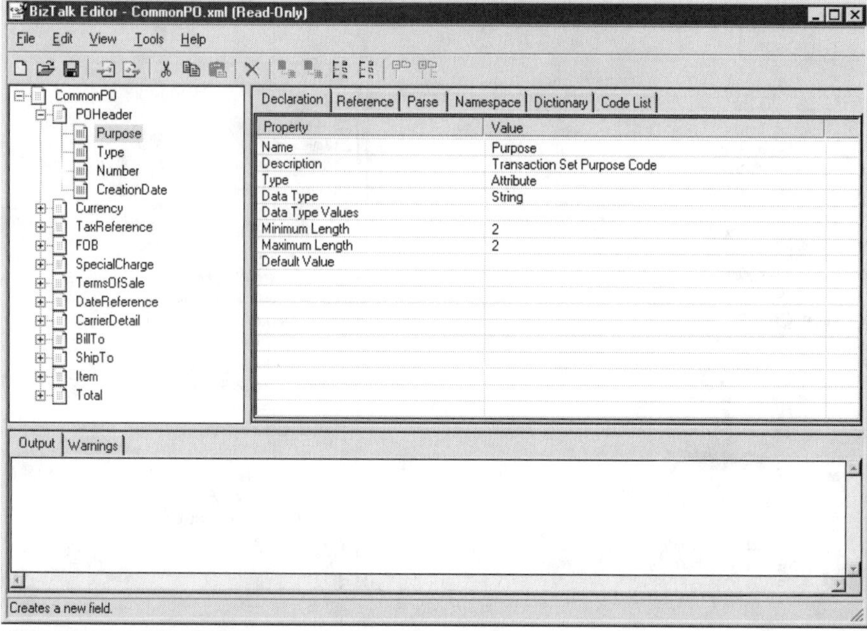

Figure 2-9 *The BizTalk Editor*

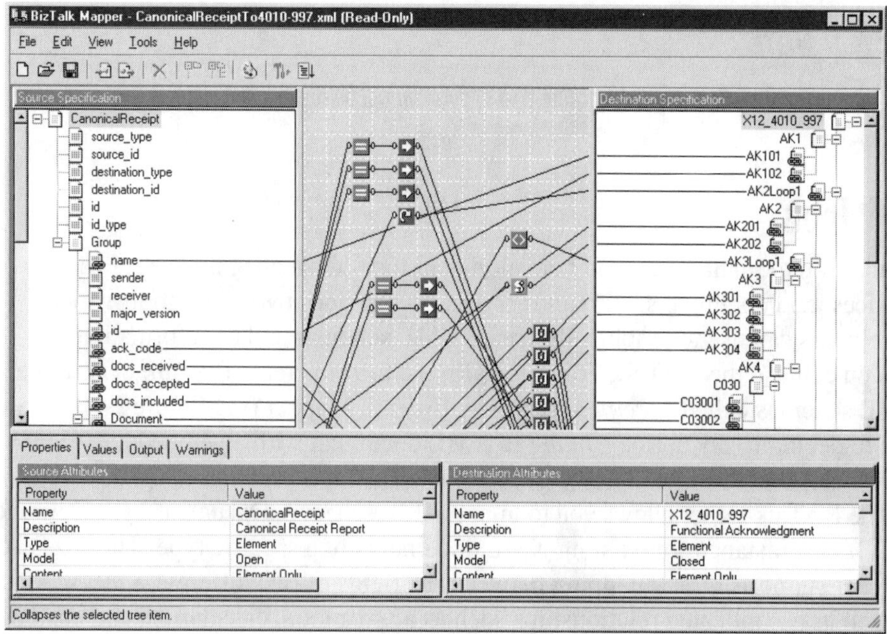

Figure 2-10 *The BizTalk Mapper*

The specifications and maps created using BizTalk Editor and BizTalk Mapper are accessed through a mechanism called *Web Distributed Authoring and Versioning (WebDAV)*. WebDAV is an HTTP 1.1 extension that exposes a hierarchical file storage media such as a file system, over the Web via an HTTP connection. WebDAV supports document authoring and versioning by locking documents to prevent users from accidentally overwriting each other's changes. It also allows users to share and work with server-based documents.

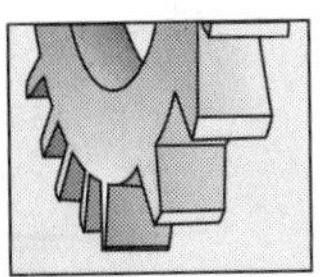

TIP

For more information about WebDAV, read the technical article by Craig Neable and Sean Lyndersay, "Communicating XML Data Over the Web with WebDAV" from MSDN online at: ***http://msdn.microsoft.com/xml/articles/xmlandwebdav.asp****.*

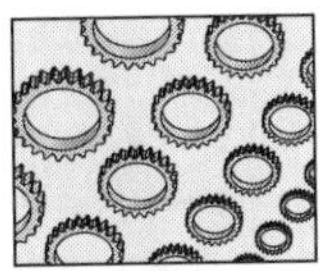

NOTE

You can learn about XML Schemas and DTDs in Appendix A, while BizTalk Editor and BizTalk Mapper will be covered in Chapters 4 and 5, respectively.

BizTalk Server 2000 Architecture

In the previous sections, we reviewed individual pieces of BizTalk Server 2000. Now let's look at the big picture of BizTalk Server 2000, and see how the pieces fit together.

BizTalk Server Architecture Overview

Figure 2-11 illustrates the overview architecture of BizTalk Server 2000.

As shown in Figure 2-11, BizTalk Server 2000 provides powerful integration services (messaging and orchestration), a rich set of administration and management tools (Orchestration Designer, Messaging Manager, Administration Console, and Document Tracking Web application), a robust execution environment (XLANG Scheduler, XLANG Engine, and receive functions), numerous transport protocols (HTTP, HTTPS, SMTP, MSMQ, File, etc.), reliable data stores and a number of data access mechanisms (Windows Management Instrumentation API, and WebDAV). With all these features and components, it's evident BizTalk Server 2000 offers a complete set of tools and services for building robust EAI and B2B integration solutions.

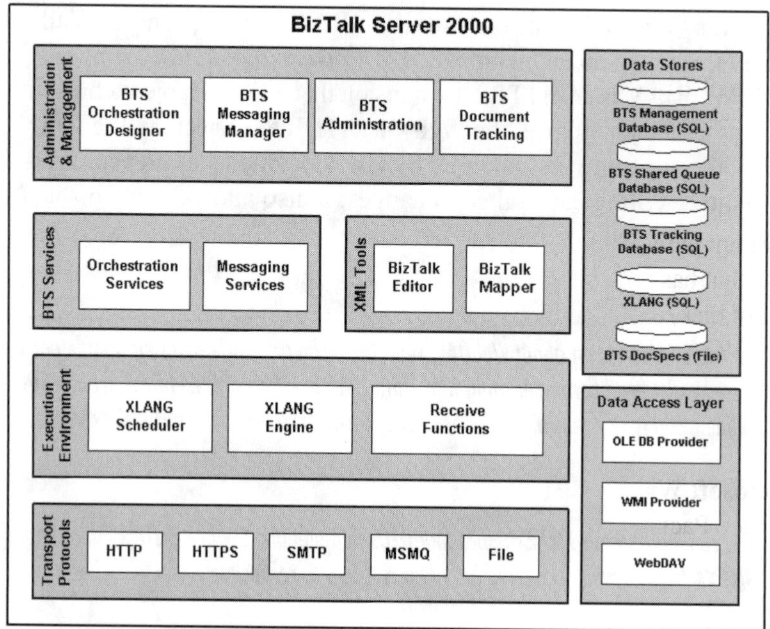

Figure 2-11 *The architecture of BizTalk Server 2000*

BizTalk Server Messaging Objects

In addition to using the BizTalk Server Messaging Manager, BizTalk Server 2000 also provides a BizTalk Messaging Configuration object model so you can programmatically create and configure BizTalk Server messaging objects (organizations, messaging ports, channels, envelopes, document definitions, etc.). This will allow you to automate the process of setting up and configuring the BizTalk Server messaging services and streamline the deployment process.

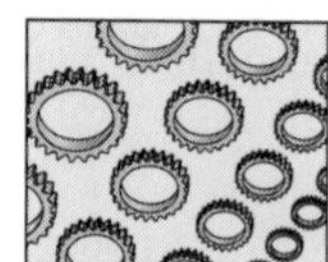

NOTE

We will discuss the BizTalk Messaging Configuration object model in Chapter 6.

Installing BizTalk Server 2000

In this section, we will walk you through the process of installing the BizTalk Server 2000. After you successfully install BizTalk Server 2000, we will also help you set up the BizTalk Server 2000 tutorial so you can start experimenting with BizTalk Server right away.

BizTalk Server 2000 Installation

The process of BizTalk Server 2000 installation is pretty straightforward. It does have a few prerequisites, however.

System Requirements

The minimum hardware requirements necessary to install BizTalk Server 2000 include a machine that has an Intel Pentium 300 processor or the equivalent, 128 MB of RAM, a 6 GB hard disk, a CD-ROM drive, a network adapter card, keyboard, a nice monitor of course (VGA or Super VGA), and lastly a mouse or compatible pointing device.

On the software side, you will need to have the following product packages loaded on the machine before installing BizTalk Server 2000:

- Microsoft Windows 2000 (Professional, Server, or Advanced Server) with Service Pack 1 (MSMQ 2.0 and IIS 5.0 should be configured)

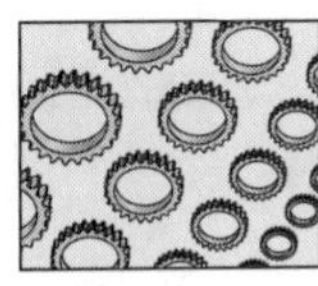

NOTE

MSMQ and IIS are not part of the default Windows 2000 installation, although they are shipped with the Windows 2000 CD. If you have not set up and configured these services yet, you need to do so for the BizTalk services to function. Refer to the Windows 2000 online documentation regarding how to set up MSMQ and IIS 5.0.

- Microsoft Internet Explorer 5.0 or higher
- Microsoft Visio 2000 SR-1A or newer versions
- Microsoft SQL Server 7.0 Service Pack 2 or higher, or SQL Server 2000

Installation

Now that you have a nice machine that meets the minimum hardware requirements with all the required software installed, it's time to install BizTalk Server 2000. Insert the BizTalk Server 2000 CD into the CD-ROM drive. The Welcome screen of the Microsoft BizTalk Server 2000 Setup (see Figure 2-12) should appear after a few seconds.

Click the Next button on the Welcome screen. After the License Agreement, Customer Information, and Destination Folder steps, you will see the Setup Type screen (see Figure 2-13).

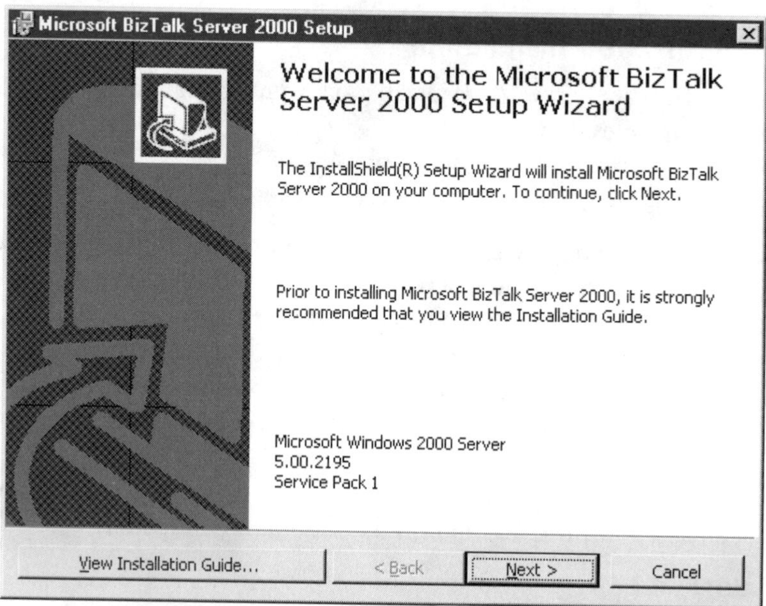

Figure 2-12 *The Welcome screen*

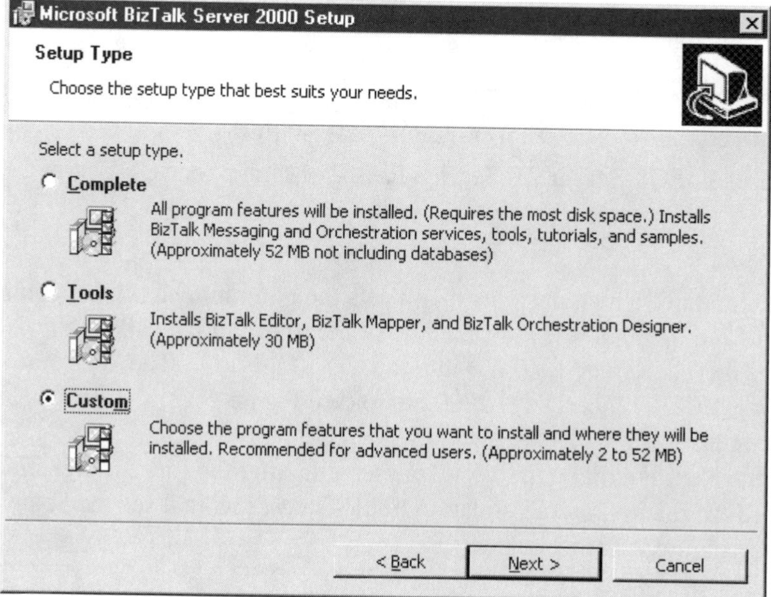

Figure 2-13 *Select a Setup Type*

The options are clearly explained on the Setup Type screen. Let's select Custom to see what the available options are, then we'll click the Next button. The Custom Setup screen (see Figure 2-14) appears.

As shown in Figure 2-14, available options include the Documentation, Messaging, and Orchestration Services, BizTalk Orchestration Designer tool, and the XML Tools (BizTalk Editor and BizTalk Mapper). You also have the option of installing the BizTalk Server Software Development Kit (SDK) and Samples. Let's go ahead and select all of them this time. You can use the Add/Remove Programs applet in the Control Panel to remove the options later if you decide you don't need them anymore.

Next you will see the Configure BizTalk Server Administrative Access screen (see Figure 2-15) where you can specify the name of the BizTalk Server Administrator Group. The default name is BizTalk Server Administrators. Optionally, you can specify a description of the group. Keep the defaults and click the Next button.

On the next screen (see Figure 2-16), you select the logon account for BizTalk Server services. The default is the Local system account which will allow anyone who has access to the system to access BizTalk Server services. You can also

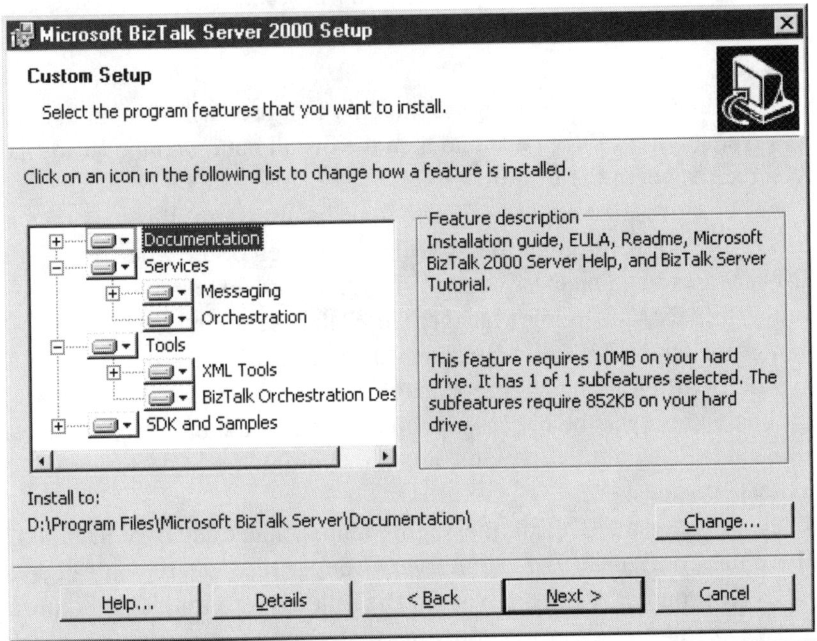

Figure 2-14 *Select the options you want to install*

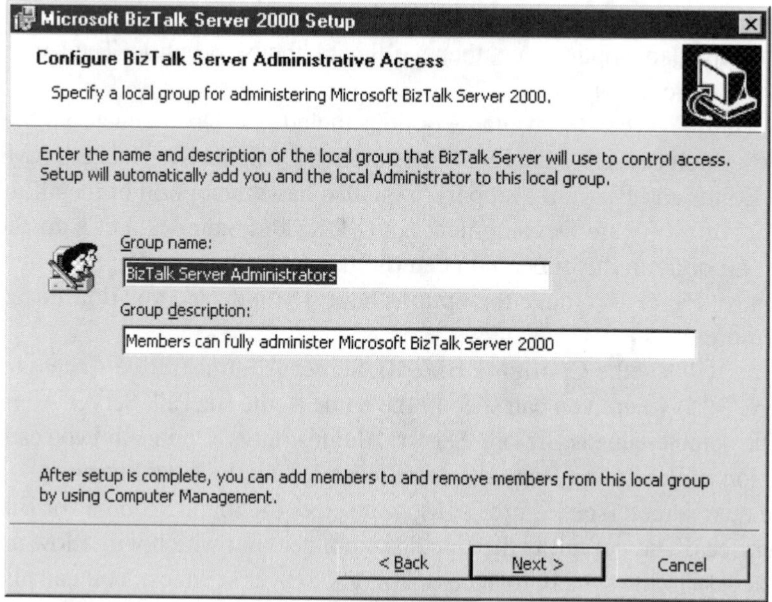

Figure 2-15 *Configure BizTalk Server Administrative Access*

specify a particular network domain user so only that user will be able to access the BizTalk Server services. Click Next and then the Install button on the Ready To Install Program screen to begin the install.

After you've completed copying files to your local system (this may take a couple of minutes), you will be brought to the Welcome screen of the Microsoft BizTalk Server 2000 Messaging Database Setup Wizard. Click Next and you will see the Configure a BizTalk Messaging Management Database screen (see Figure 2-17). The default name for the BizTalk Messaging Management Database is InterchangeBTM. You can specify different messaging management databases for different BizTalk server groups. Should this be the case, you need to give them different names. You also need to provide the username and password to the SQL Server so you can create the database.

Click Next to have the BizTalk messaging management database installed. Soon you will see the Configure a BizTalk Server Group screen where you can create a BizTalk Server group or select an existing BizTalk Server group (see Figure 2-18). For the new BizTalk Server group you will create, you can specify a Group name for it. The default Group name is BizTalk Server Group. This Group name will be shown in the BizTalk Administration MMC snap-in (see Figure 2-6 earlier in this chapter).

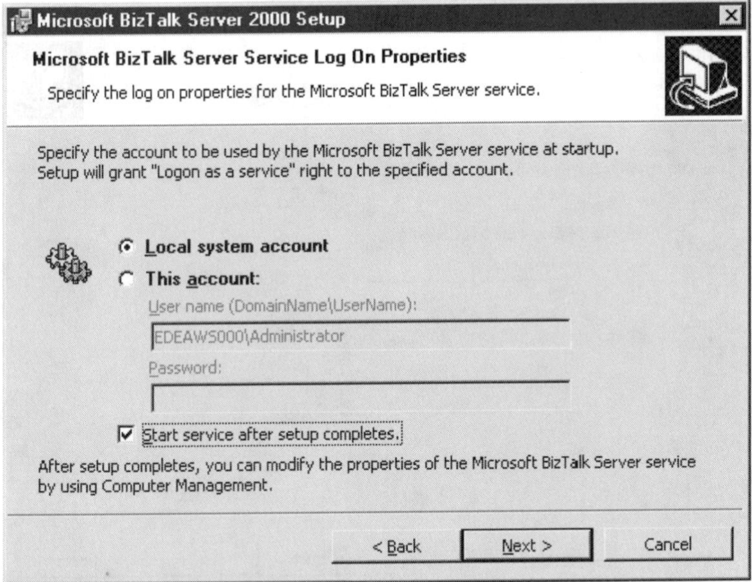

Figure 2-16 *Specify the logon properties for BizTalk Server services*

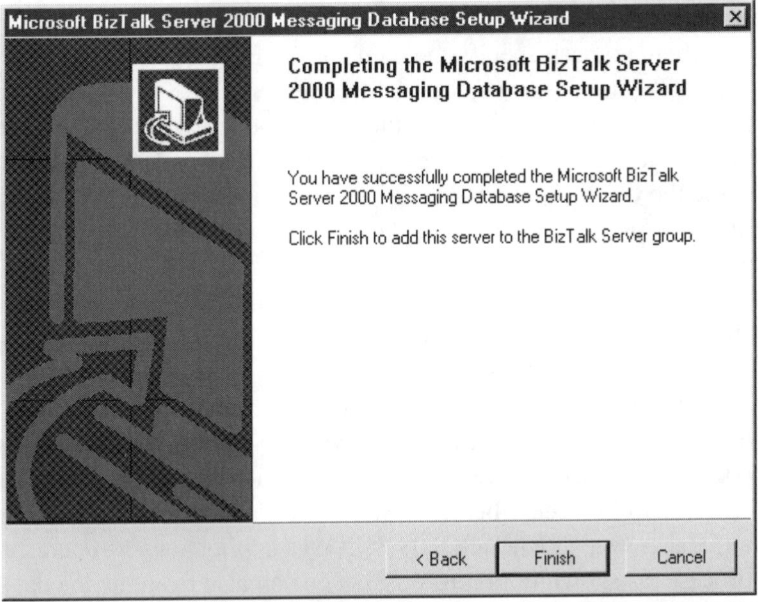

Figure 2-17 *Install the BizTalk Messaging Management Database*

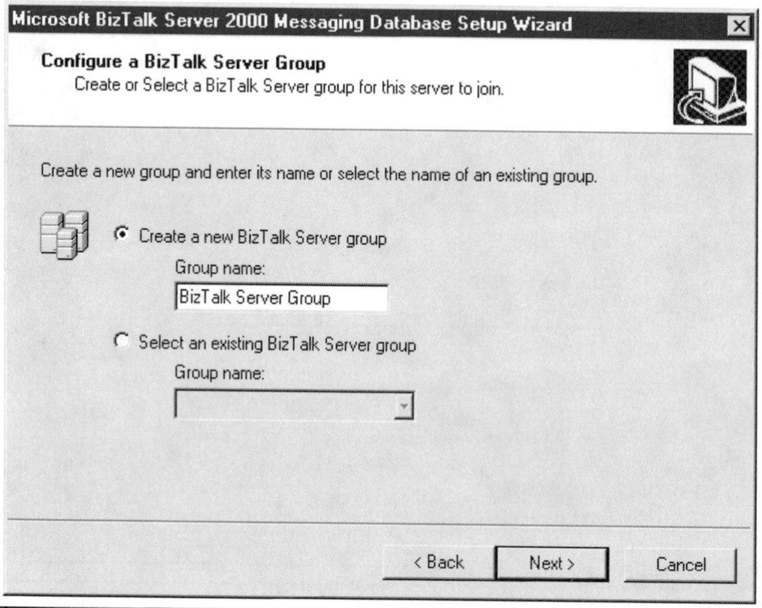

Figure 2-18 *Specify a BizTalk Server group*

Clicking Next will bring you to the Configure a Tracking Database screen (see Figure 2-19) where you can specify the name of the BizTalk Tracking Database and input the user name and password for the SQL Server where you want to install the tracking database. The default name for the tracking database is InterchangeDTA.

Click Next to have the BizTalk Tracking database installed. When it is finished, you should see the Configure a Shared Queue Database screen (see Figure 2-20). The default name for the Shared Queue database is InterchangeSQ.

Click Next to install the Shared Queue database. After a few more clicks on the Next buttons on a few of more screens, you should come to the Configure a default Orchestration Persistence Database screen (Figure 2-21). The default name for the orchestration persistence database is XLANG.

Click the Finish buttons on the Configure Orchestration Persistence Database screen and the Completing the Microsoft BizTalk Server 2000 Setup Wizard screen and voilá, you have completed the BizTalk Server 2000 installation. If you open the Component Services MMC snap-in (accessible from Start | Programs | Administration Tools), you will notice that several BizTalk Server COM+ applications were created during the setup process (as shown in Figure 2-22). You can also examine the databases created during the installation process in the SQL Server Enterprise Manager (as shown in Figure 2-23).

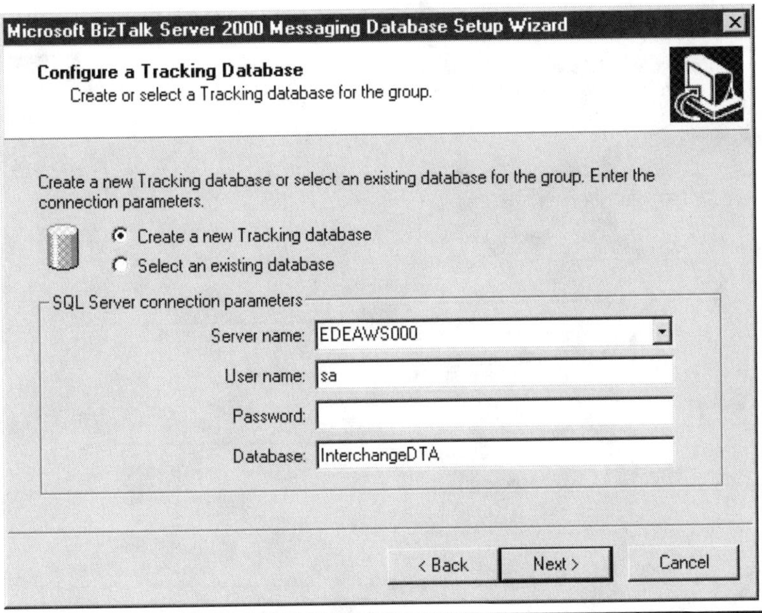

Microsoft BizTalk Server 2000 Messaging Database Setup Wizard

Configure a Tracking Database
Create or select a Tracking database for the group.

Create a new Tracking database or select an existing database for the group. Enter the connection parameters.

- (•) Create a new Tracking database
- ( ) Select an existing database

SQL Server connection parameters

Server name: EDEAWS000
User name: sa
Password:
Database: InterchangeDTA

< Back | Next > | Cancel

Figure 2-19 *Install the BizTalk Tracking database*

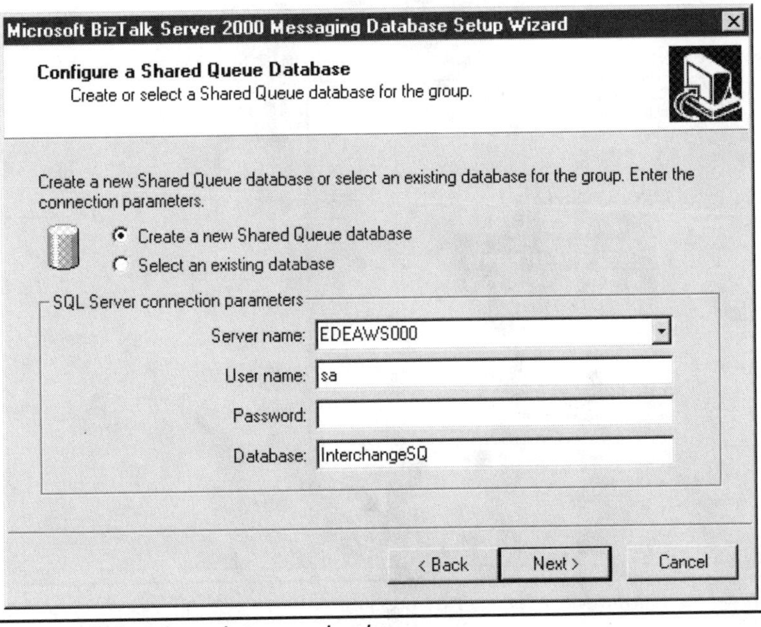

Microsoft BizTalk Server 2000 Messaging Database Setup Wizard

Configure a Shared Queue Database
Create or select a Shared Queue database for the group.

Create a new Shared Queue database or select an existing database for the group. Enter the connection parameters.

- (•) Create a new Shared Queue database
- ( ) Select an existing database

SQL Server connection parameters

Server name: EDEAWS000
User name: sa
Password:
Database: InterchangeSQ

< Back | Next > | Cancel

Figure 2-20 *Install the Shared Queue database*

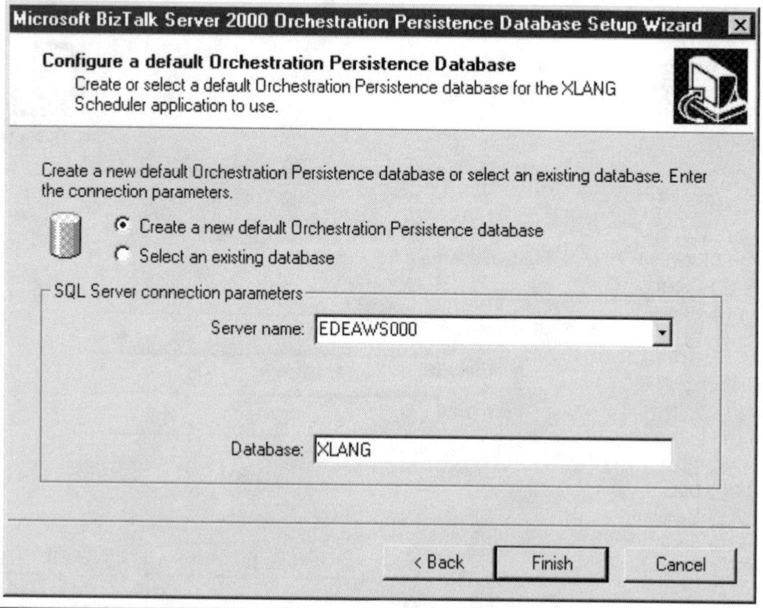

Figure 2-21 *Install the Orchestration Persistence database*

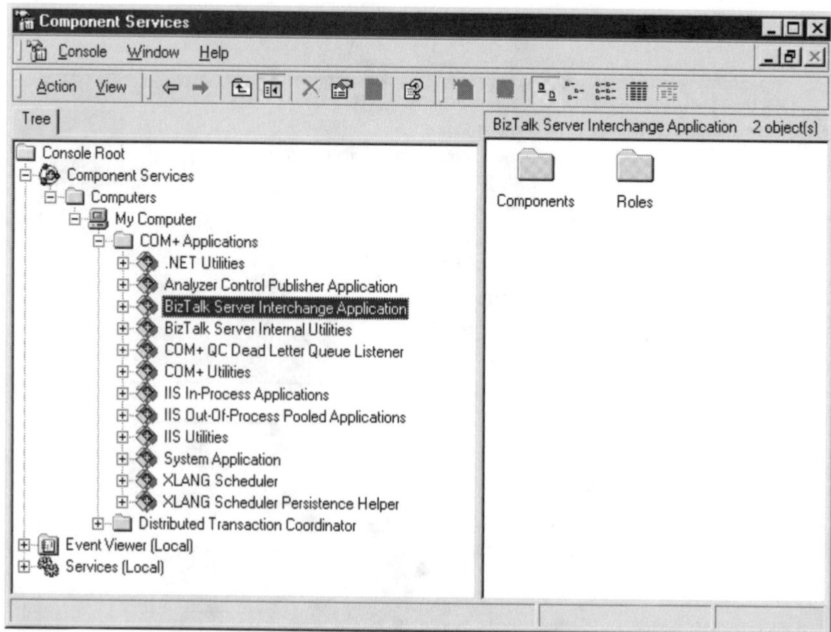

Figure 2-22 *The installation process has created several BizTalk Server COM+ applications*

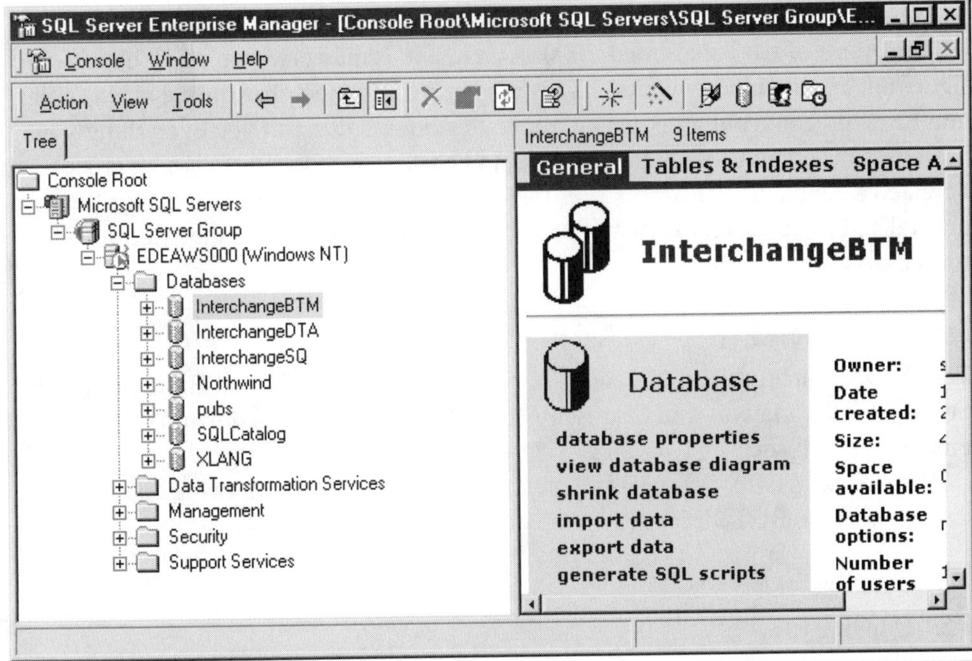

Figure 2-23 *BizTalk Server 2000 databases in SQL Server Enterprise Manager*

Introducing the BizTalk Server 2000 Tutorial

Now it's time to jump into the water! The best place to start is the BizTalk Server 2000 Tutorial that has been revised from the tutorial on the Beta server. In this tutorial, you will have an opportunity to set up and use BizTalk Server 2000 Orchestration Services and Messaging Services to build a B2B automated procurement process between two fictitious business trading partners, ProElectron, Inc. (the buyer organization) and Bits, Bytes, & Chips, Inc. (the seller organization). The tutorial teaches you how to use BizTalk Orchestration Designer, BizTalk Messaging Manager, BizTalk Editor and BizTalk Mapper tools. The revised tutorial now has four modules:

1. Modeling Business Processes
2. Creating Specifications and Maps
3. Configuring BizTalk Messaging Services
4. Completing the XLANG Schedule

This tutorial is a comprehensive example that covers many important services and functions of BizTalk Server 2000. As a result, it may take you a few days to figure out exactly how it works. It may also bring you much frustration when things don't exactly come out as expected. Since this book will teach you everything you need to know about BizTalk Server 2000, to help you speed up the learning process, I created a couple of VB scripts files that can automate the setup process for the tutorial and reduce a lot of frustration for beginners who play with the tutorial for the first time.

Set Up the Tutorial

To help you quickly set up the tutorial, I have provided two Visual Basic Script files, Setup_BTSTutorial.vbs and ConfigureBuyerSeller.vbs, that are downloadable from this book's web site.

The first script file, Setup_BTSTutorial.vbs, performs the following tasks as described in the BizTalk Server online documentation:

1. Creating folders
2. Copying files
3. Creating local Web site folders (setting up virtual Web directories)
4. Creating message queues

The second script file, ConfigureBuyerSeller.vbs, is an enhanced version of the script file, ConfigureBuyer.vbs, that came with the tutorial. The revised file now contains scripts that configure BizTalk Server Messaging Services components for both the buyer organization and seller organization.

Follow these steps to set up the tutorial:

1. Copy the file Setup_BTSTutorial.vbs to the following destination <BizTalk Server Install>\Tutorial\Setup\ and double-click on the Setup_BTSTutorial.vbs file in Windows Explorer. You should see a message box that confirms the BizTalk Server 2000 Tutorial Preliminary setup was completed.
2. Double-click the file Install_POtoInvoice.vbs file in the same folder (<BizTalk Server Install>\Tutorial\Setup\). You should see a message box that confirms the installation (of the POtoInvoice AIC component) has been completed.

3. Copy the ConfigureBuyerSeller.vbs file to <BizTalk Server Install>\Tutorial\Setup\MessagingConfigurationScript folder and double-click on it. You will see a message box after a few seconds that confirms the Tutorial (Buyer/Seller) configuration installation has been completed.
4. Browse to the folder <BizTalk Server Install>\Tutorial\Components\POReqApproval\Solution and right-click the file PORequestApproval.wsc and select Register. You should see a message box that indicates the registration succeeded.

Test the Results

Now we're ready to test the tutorial. Double-click the ExecuteTutorial.exe executable file in the <BizTalk Server Install>Tutorial\Schedule\Solution folder to start the client application of the tutorial. For the Schedule File, click the Browse for Schedule button and select the Buyer2.skx files from the <BizTalk Server Install>Tutorial\Schedule\Solution folder. For the Data File (PO Request), click the Browse for Data File button and select the POReqAccept.xml file from the <BizTalk Server Install >\Tutorial\Schedule\SampleData\ folder. Click the Start XLANG Schedule button and two message boxes should appear. One says Execute Tutorial Successfully Passed Data to XLANG Engine. Another message box confirms that the document has been approved (see Figure 2-24) and displays the content of the POReq XML document. Click OK to dismiss these message boxes.

If everything works fine, you should see a payment XML document in the C:\TutorialFiles\Seller\ folder (This folder was created by the script file Setup_BTSTutorial.vbs), as shown in Figure 2-25.

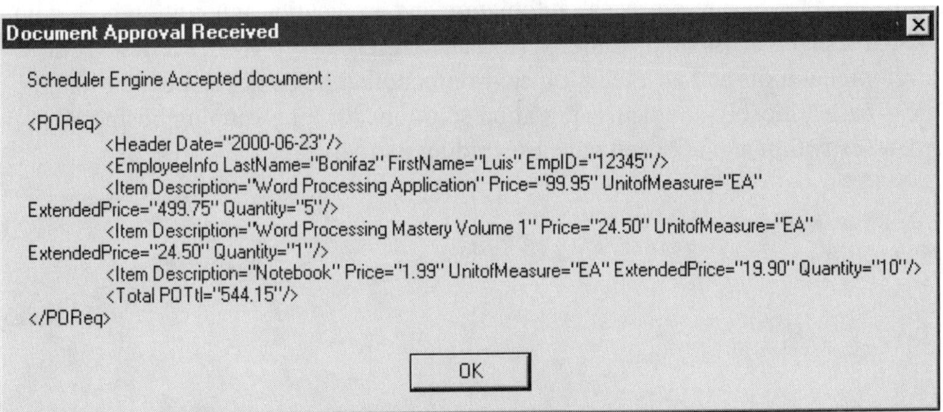

Figure 2-24 *The Document Approval Received message box*

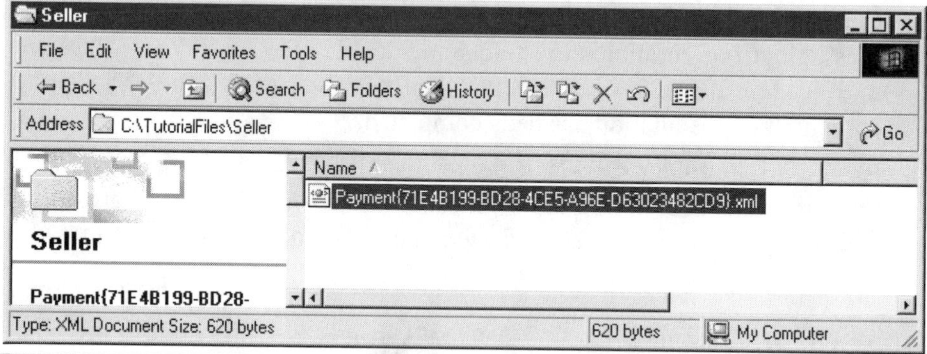

Figure 2-25 *The Payment XML document in the Seller folder*

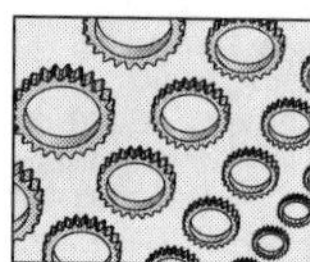

NOTE

If things didn't go smoothly, the BizTalk Server 2000 Tutorial documentation has detailed information about how the tutorial works. Later in this book, you will learn how to use the BizTalk Document Tracking and BizTalk Server Administration tools, as well as the Journaling features of Microsoft Message Queuing to debug and troubleshoot BizTalk messaging and orchestration problems. Later, you can come back to the tutorial and make it work by yourself.

Chapter in Review

BizTalk Server 2000 is a new member in the Microsoft .NET Server Family. It can be used for business-process automation and application-integration both with and between business organizations. BizTalk Server 2000 provides a rich set of development tools and an execution environment that helps developers build XML-based, loosely-coupled, integration solutions for long-running business processes within and between business trading partners.

PART

II

BizTalk Server 2000 Messaging Services

OBJECTIVE:

- Mastering BizTalk Server 2000 Messaging Services

CHAPTER

3

Introducing BizTalk Server 2000 Messaging Services

IN THIS CHAPTER:

To integrate different applications and systems together, either within a business organization or between business trading partners, a mechanism is needed by which one application (the source) can interact with another application or applications (the destinations). One way of doing this is by letting the source application call the destination application via its native Application Programming Interfaces (APIs), as illustrated in Figure 3-1.

This is a tightly coupled integration model which has a number of drawbacks. First, the integration logic is somehow hard-coded into the source application and tied to the exact syntax requirements of the particular version of the API (usually proprietary). Should the target application change (for example, be upgraded to a newer version of the product), the dependency between the source and destination applications will be subject to break. Second, when a new destination application needs to be added to the integration picture, appropriate code has to be added to the source application, probably through new API calls. Third, it is often very difficult, if not impossible, for the source application to interact with the destination application through its native APIs, especially when the two applications are developed in different languages and running on different platforms. Worse yet, if either the source or the destination application (or both) could be legacy applications, that doesn't expose any APIs for other applications to access their data programmatically. Finally, the highly distributed nature of applications and systems involved in the Enterprise Application Integration (EAI) and Business-to-Business Electronic Commerce (B2B e-Commerce) integrations makes the tightly coupled approaches extremely difficult to build and expensive to maintain.

Due to these limitations, most integration implementations today, including both EAI and B2B integrations, take a loosely coupled approach. In a loosely coupled integration environment, instead of directly interacting with the destination application, the source application sends a message to a middleware application which processes the message (i.e., interprets message and performs necessary transformations, aggregations, etc.) and invokes the destination application on the behavior of the source application. Messaging queuing products such as Microsoft Message Queuing services and IBM MQSeries are often used in the middleware application to provide asynchronous processing functionalities and, as such, have earned a name as Messaging Oriented Middleware (MOM). In B2B

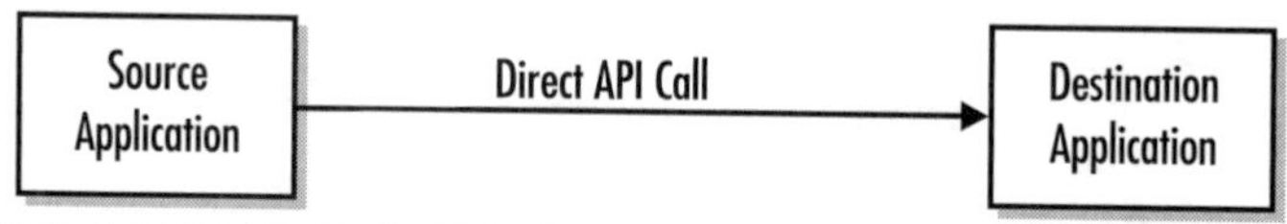

Figure 3-1 *A tightly coupled integration model*

scenarios where integration takes place between two business trading partners, MOM technologies are usually used in conjunction with other transport protocols or private network connections such as the Value Added Networks (VAN) in Electronic Data Interchange (EDI) integrations. Figure 3-2 illustrates a loosely coupled integration environment in which the middleware application provides a messaging solution.

To process a message sent by the source application, the middleware application usually needs to parse the message, validate the message against appropriate specifications, manipulate the message according to appropriate business rules, route the message to the appropriate transports, if necessary, and finally deliver the message to the destination applications.

By abstracting the integration logic into the middleware application, the source application is no longer tied to the destination application. All the source application needs to do is compose a message and send it to the middleware application. The latter takes care of processing the message and interacting with the appropriate destination applications.

Figure 3-2 is an extremely simplified picture of a loosely coupled integration model. A middleware application usually further partitions the API interaction logic into dedicated modules, known as *Application Adapters* or *Protocol Adapters*—there are two types of adapters—transport adapters that deliver to an application, and thicker adapters that both deliver and format/translate (amongst other things). By separating API interaction from the message processing, the middleware application becomes more flexible and can focus on the messaging processing of the integration, such as parsing, validation, routing, and delivery of the messages.

BizTalk Server 2000 Messaging Services fits into the profile of the kind of middleware application just described, and provides a more comprehensive messaging solution for both EAI and B2B integrations.

In this chapter, we will introduce BizTalk Server 2000 Messaging Services and its architecture. We will discuss what BizTalk Messaging (Manager) objects are and explain how the BizTalk Server messaging engine uses them to provide messaging services. We will also discuss how to get messages (documents) to and from BizTalk Server.

Figure 3-2 *A loosely coupled, messaging-oriented integration model*

BizTalk Messaging Services Architecture

The job of BizTalk Server 2000 Messaging Services is to receive a document from a source application or organization, process the document, and deliver it to the destination. During this process, the BizTalk Server messaging engine may perform a set of tasks including parsing the document from its native format to an intermediate XML format, validating the documents against appropriate specifications, changing the document from one format to another, serializing the document from the intermediate XML format to the native format required by the destination application, and finally transporting the document to the destination. Depending on the complexity requirements, the BizTalk Server messaging engine may perform some or all of the tasks mentioned in this paragraph. Figure 3-3 illustrates the architecture of BizTalk Server 2000 Messaging Services.

As shown in Figure 3-3, a source application can send a document to BizTalk Server in a couple of ways. For example, it can use the *IInterchange* COM interface to directly submit a document by calling the Submit or SubmitSync method. But this is tightly coupled and discouraged, and also performs worse than the Message Queuing and File receive functions because there can be no database caching of OLEDB objects and it receives a single document at a time. If the source application is not capable of invoking methods of COM objects (actually, this is ALWAYS preferred, even if it can do COM), it can use one of two types of *receive functions* (File or Message Queuing) to send the document indirectly to BizTalk Server as a loosely coupled intermediate point from any source. After BizTalk Server receives a document from the source application, it will perform a set of tasks (as we mentioned earlier) to process the document through a set of *BizTalk (Server) Messaging (Manager) Objects*. By the end of this process, BizTalk Server will deliver the document to the destination application through an appropriate *transport service*.

In this chapter, we will discuss the concepts of BizTalk Messaging Objects, their relationships and dependencies. Then we will explain how to send a document to the BizTalk Server. Finally, we will discuss how to use the supported transport services in BizTalk Server 2000 to deliver the document to its destination.

Understanding BizTalk Messaging Objects

BizTalk Server Messaging Services processes documents through a set of configurable objects. Because BizTalk Messaging Manager (the topic of Chapter 6 of this book) uses these configurable objects to configure and manage BizTalk messaging services,

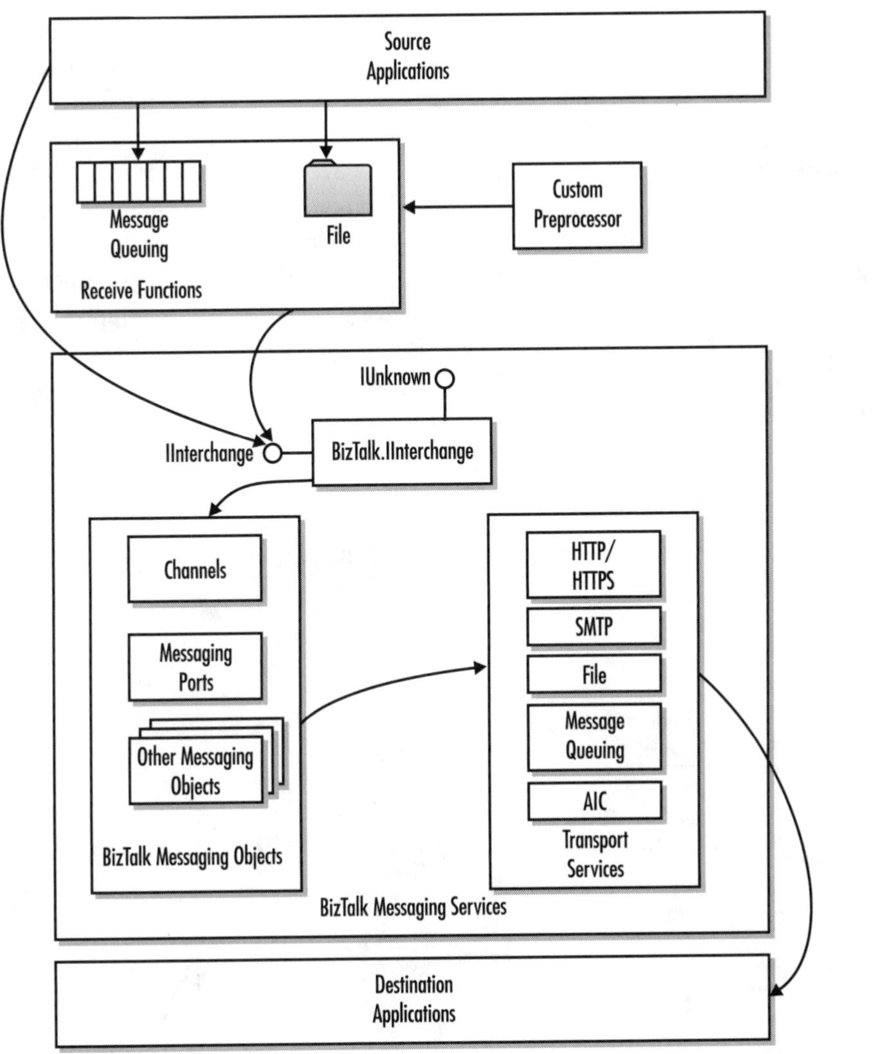

Figure 3-3 *The architecture of BizTalk Server 2000 Messaging Services*

these objects are known as *BizTalk Messaging Manager Objects* in BizTalk Server 2000 documentation. For the purpose of our discussion here, we will refer to them as BizTalk Messaging Objects or simply as Messaging Objects. The metadata of these messaging objects are stored in the BizTalk Messaging Management database.

In Chapter 6, you will learn how to create and manage these messaging objects by using the BizTalk Messaging Manager tool. You will also learn how to programmatically create and configure these messaging objects by using the BizTalk Messaging Configuration Object Model. In order to get the most out of BizTalk Server 2000 Messaging Services, however, you must have a thorough understanding of these messaging objects. You need to know what they are, what they do, when to use them, as well as the various relationships and dependencies that exist between them. This is exactly what we intend to accomplish here.

Figure 3-4 illustrates a typical BizTalk messaging scenario in which most of the BizTalk Messaging Objects (the raised rectangles) are used. Each of these messaging objects tells the BizTalk messaging engine to perform some specific tasks.

Organizations

Organizations are used to define and identify the parties involved in a messaging flow. Essentially, they represent the origination and destination of a message flow.

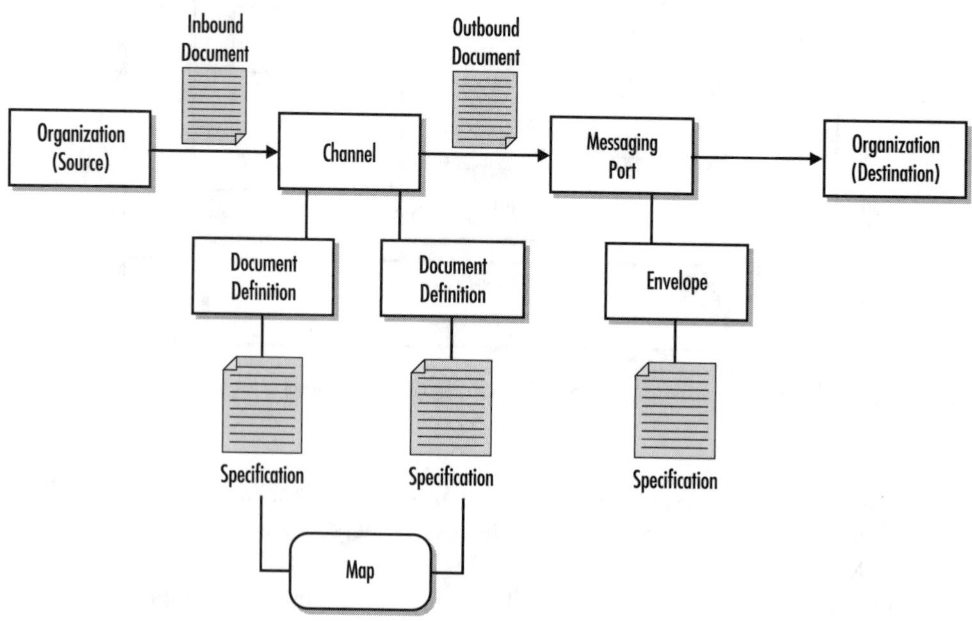

Figure 3-4 *BizTalk Server 2000 messaging objects*

Trading Partner Organizations

Trading partner organizations usually represent business entities, including trading partners of external organizations as well as business units of your own organization. You can designate trading partners to identify and document the source and destination of a messaging flow. You define one organization for each trading partner you work with.

Applications

In addition to organizations, you can also use *applications* to designate both sources and destinations. Each application must belong to an organization, which can have zero, one, or more applications.

Applications enable you to be more specific in identifying the parties involved in a messaging solution. For example, in a supply chain integration project, instead of using a generic organization "Supplier XYZ" to identify one of your trading partners, you can use applications to further identify those systems used in Supplier XYZ's company. You may add two applications, "Order Processing System at XYZ" and "Invoicing System at XYZ" to the organization "Supplier XYZ." Each of these applications handles a different messaging task. One application processes the purchase order document sent from your organization, another sends an invoice document to your organization.

You don't have to map an application messaging object to a physical executable application. Just like an organization messaging object, an application messaging object is simply an identifier. These identifiers are helpful in tracking, and especially in self-routing, as you will see later in this chapter.

Home Organization

BizTalk Server 2000 provides a built-in organization, *Home Organization,* to represent your organization. Home organization has a default name of "Home Organization." You can rename it to a name more representative to your organization, if you so choose. You cannot delete the home organization, however. Neither can you add more home organizations.

Home organization cannot be directly designated as a source or destination in your messaging configuration. You have to create appropriate application objects and add them to the home organization. Then you can use applications instead of home organizations as the source or destination in the messaging configuration. Indeed, you can only add applications to the home organization from the BizTalk Messaging Manager. You can, however, add applications to other organizations in code through the BizTalk Messaging Configuration Object Model.

Using Organizations and Applications

The name of an organization has to be unique within the BizTalk Server scope. The name of an application, meanwhile, must be unique within the organization to which it belongs (i.e., the names of applications within an organization have to be unique). Although BizTalk Server won't prevent you from using same names for applications that belong to different organizations, it is a good practice to use unique names whenever possible.

BizTalk Server 2000 uses *organization identifiers* to uniquely identify an organization. An organization identifier consists of three properties: a *name*, a *qualifier* and a *value*. The Name property can be the organization name or an alias and must be unique. The combination of the qualifier and value must also be unique.

There are two types of organization qualifier: *custom* and *standard*. To create a custom organization identifier, you can assign a unique name, and a unique pair of qualifiers and values. To create a standard organization identifier, you select a name from a list of about 45 predefined names, such as DUNS (Dun & Bradstreet), Federal Maritime Commission, IATA (International Air Transport Association), etc. The qualifier for the standard organization is also predefined and read-only. You still need to set the Value property, though, which must also follow the uniqueness rules as just described.

For any given organization, you can create more than one identifier. In this way, you can use aliases to identify the sample organization in different scenarios. You must also assign one of them as the default identifier. When you create an organization, BizTalk Server will create a default custom identifier for you, using the name of the organization for the Name and Value properties of the identifier. It will then set the Qualifier property to "*OrganizationName*." You cannot delete or modify this organization identifier, but you *can* re-assign another identifier as the default identifier. As we will explain later in this chapter, this is very useful for the routing purposes, including EDI routing and self-routing.

An application has only one property, a Name. The uniqueness constraint for applications is set at the organization level (i.e., the name of applications must be unique within the organization to which they belong). Applications at different organizations may have the same name. As a good practice, however, you should never use the sample name to refer to different applications, even though they may belong to different organizations.

TIP

In a complex integration project, you may have to create a lot of organizations and applications. To make your solution extendable and maintainable, you need to apply a good scheme that can generate distinct yet consistent identifiers for organizations and applications while allowing for future growth in them.

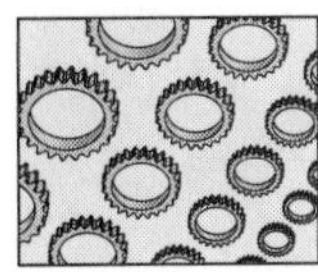

NOTE

Organizations and applications are simply identifiers (see preceding explanation). As a result, organizations and applications alone do not provide enough information for the BizTalk Server messaging engine to figure out the messaging flow. Neither, however, do the documents. As we will explain later in this chapter, you need three things to route a document: the source organization (or application), the destination organization (or application), and the document definition. As shown in Figure 3-4, you need to assign organizations and/or applications either as sources of channels or destinations of messaging ports to guarantee the flow of messaging. Channels and messaging ports will be discussed shortly in the next two sections.

Channels

A *channel* object provides a set of processing instructions to the BizTalk Server messaging engine, including the source of the document, validation and/or transformation rules for inbound and outbound documents, and document tracking options. In addition, a channel enables you to set a *filtering expression*, deal with receipts (for EDI only), control security, and set some advanced properties.

Specifying the Sources

You must specify a source for a channel. The source can be either an organization or an application. In the case of the Home Organization, you can either create an appropriate application first, and then assign it as the source application of a channel. Alternatively, you can create the application on-the-fly by clicking the New button that is next to the Name box for the application in the channel wizard. You can't directly use the Home Organization as the source of a channel. In addition, you can also assign an *XLANG schedule* as the source of a channel.

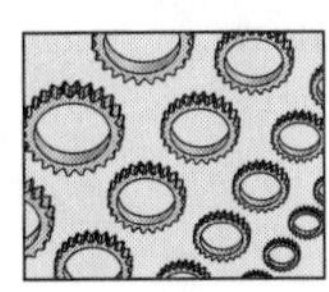

NOTE

XLANG Schedule is an XML application used by the BizTalk Server Orchestration Services. XLANG schedules will be discussed in Chapters 9 and 10.

You can also specify an open source for a channel. A channel with an open source is referred to as an *open channel*. In an open channel, the source of the document can be either specified in the document itself or passed as a parameter when you submit the document directly through the IInterchange interface. If the document is submitted to the BizTalk Server through a receive function which uses an open channel, you must specify the source in the receive function. We will discuss the IInterchange interface and BizTalk Server receive functions later in this chapter.

Validating and Transforming

As shown in Figure 3-4, you must specify *document definitions* for the inbound and outbound documents. An inbound document is the document submitted to the BizTalk Server which then flows into an appropriate channel. An outbound document is the document that has been processed and flows out of a channel. As you will see later in this chapter, a document definition provides a mechanism for validating the document. If the format of the inbound document does not match the format of the outbound document (which is often the case in typical B2B integration scenarios), you must also specify a *map* that transforms the inbound format to the outbound format.

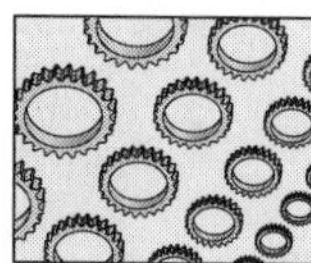

NOTE

We will discuss document definitions a little later in this chapter. BizTalk maps will be covered in Chapter 5.

Tracking Documents

In a channel, you can specify whether to log the inbound and/or outbound document into the BizTalk Server Tracking Database. You can further specify if the native document format or the intermediate XML format should be logged, or both. Take an EDI document for example: specifying the native document format for tracking will result in the document contents being logged in the tracking database in the EDI format.

In addition to document metadata tracking options, you can also specify which fields of the inbound document should be logged into the tracking database. The tracking fields you specified in a channel configuration are within the scope of the channel. If you want some fields in an inbound document to be logged by all the channels, you need to create and configure a document definition and specify the fields to be logged. The fields specified in the document definition are thus referred to as *global tracking fields*.

Filtering

In a channel, you can specify a filtering expression for an inbound document so the BizTalk Server messaging engine can decide whether it should invoke a channel based on the filtering expression. A filtering expression is a valid *XPath expression.* When a document is submitted to the BizTalk Server, the messaging engine compares the value of the field (or fields) against the value specified in the XPath expression to decide if the channel should be invoked.

CAUTION

Be aware that there is a performance implication associated with the filtering, because the BizTalk messaging engine needs to take extra steps to deal with filtering.

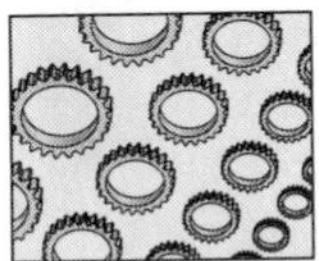

NOTE

For readers who are not familiar with XPath, refer to Appendix B of this book which has complete coverage of XSLT and XPath, with plenty of examples.

Dealing with Receipts

When configuring a channel, you can specify whether the channel expects a receipt from the destination for the document you send. You can also specify if the channel should generate a receipt to the source for the document you received.

BizTalk Server 2000 provides two ways for handling receipts, depending on the format of the document being processed. If the document or the *interchange* (a collection of one or more documents that comprise a single transmission) uses the XML format, you can configure BizTalk Server Messaging Services using *reliable messaging* to process receipts automatically (it doesn't use the channel receipt properties to process receipts). The reliable messaging feature of BizTalk Server 2000 supports BizTalk Framework 2.0 protocol for guaranteed, once-only document delivery (see Chapter 1 for more information about BizTalk Framework reliable delivery). For documents or interchanges that use non-XML formats (such as two flavors of EDI formats supported by the BizTalk Server or custom formats, X12 and EDIFACT), you may have to configure the channel properties to process receipts. In this scenario, you need to use an additional channel dedicated to process the receipt and send it to the source of the document or interchange.

In either case, besides channels, you also need to configure other BizTalk messaging objects such as messaging ports, envelopes, and so on. (We will discuss these and other BizTalk messaging objects shortly in this chapter.) Moreover, you will also need to configure BizTalk Server properties to support receipt processing.

In addition, you can always build your own custom solutions to handle the processing of receipts. This strategy is especially useful in scenarios where the destination of the document does not use BizTalk. The custom solution approach gives you more flexibility but also implies more responsibility since it must be compatible with the receipt processing semantics documented in BizTalk Framework 2.0 specification.

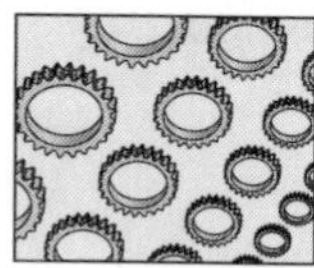

NOTE

In this chapter, we introduced the concepts of handling receipts using the BizTalk messaging services. Receipts processing will be discussed in Chapter 6.

Security and Advanced Properties

You can configure the security properties of a channel to specify if the server should verify the encryption and signature for the inbound document or the signature certificate of the outbound document.

You can also set some advanced channel properties, such as a group control number for EDI documents, retry counts and intervals, and so on. In addition, you can override properties of other messaging objects such as messaging ports, *distribution lists*, and *envelopes* (all three will be discussed later in this chapter).

Document Definitions

As shown in Figure 3-4, when you configure a channel to process a document, you may want to validate the document (either the inbound or outbound document, or both). If the format of the inbound document does not match the outbound document, you may need to specify a map that transforms the format of the inbound document to the format of the outbound document. A *document definition* contains address information about where the *specification* is stored (in a form of URL) so the BizTalk messaging engine will be able to load the underlying specification during the run-time using WebDAV protocol. A specification is a BizTalk Server-specific XML document (an annotated XDR schema) that specifies the structure and constraints of a document and a map using an annotated XSLT document that transforms one specification into another. We will discuss specifications and maps in Chapters 4 and 5, respectively.

If the inbound and outbound documents are the same, you can use the same document definition for both, and no map is needed (actually, if the same document definition is used for both inbound and outbound documents, the map will be disabled). A document definition is a reusable object that can be used in any number of channels.

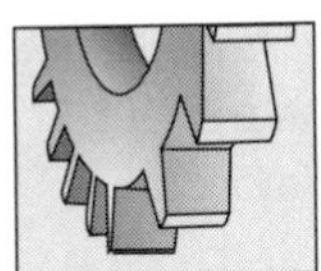

TIP

If you don't want to validate the documents at all—for example, the document is in binary format, or you submit a pass-through document—you can create a document definition without associating it with a specification. When you create a document definition without pointing to a specification, however, you need to be aware of the consequences of doing this. For instance, the document will not be validated, the document will not be loaded by any parser and because of this you cannot transform the inbound and outbound documents if their formats are not the same, and you cannot specify global tracking fields or selection criteria as we will discuss next.

Global Tracking Fields

For an XML document that has an associated specification, you can choose which fields you want to log to the Tracking database. The designated fields will be tracked for all document instances by every channel that uses this document definition for their inbound documents. Because the scope of these tracking fields applies to all channels, they are referred to as global tracking fields.

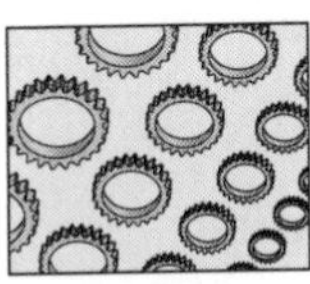

NOTE

Tracking only applies to inbound documents. In the case of outbound documents, the global tracking fields will be ignored by the BizTalk messaging engine.

TIP

Because the tracking data are stored in a SQL Server database—the tracking database—you can utilize these data to create meaningful reports which analyze interesting business trends.

Selection Criteria

When processing EDI (X12 or EDIFACT) documents, it is important to include the document *selection criteria*. Selection criteria constitute a unique set of name-value pairs that BizTalk Server uses to process EDI documents.

For inbound EDI documents, the server relies on selection criteria to uniquely identify and select a document definition because the document definition name is not available within individual EDI documents. For outbound EDI documents, BizTalk Server uses selection criteria to create the functional group header information in the envelope (envelopes will be described later in this chapter).

BizTalk Server extracts document-related data from the functional group header (the GS header of an X12 interchange and the UNG header of an EDIFACT interchange, as summarized in the next two tables).

The following table describes the X12 header elements:

Name	GS Element	Required
functional_identifier	GS01	Yes
application_sender_code	GS02	Yes
application_receiver_code	GS03	Yes
standard_version	GS08	Yes

The following table describes the EDIFACT header elements:

Name	UNG Element	UNH Element	Required
functional_identifier	0038	S009, 0065	Yes
application_sender_code	S006, 0040	Not used	No
application_receiver_code	S007, 0044	Not used	No
standard_version_type	S008, 0052	S009, 0052	Yes
standard_version_value	S008, 0054	S009, 0054	Yes

By matching the values of the data in the group header to the values of the selection criteria specified in a document definition, the server is able to uniquely identify the appropriate document definition.

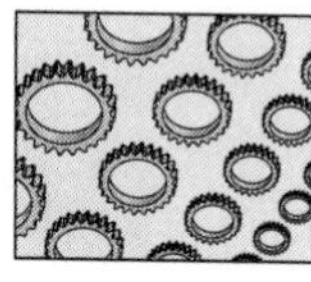

NOTE

You must type the selection criteria names exactly as they appear in the preceding tables. For example, functional_identifier/GS01 and application_sender_code/GS02 are valid selection criteria.

Messaging Ports and Distribution Lists

When a channel finishes processing the inbound document, the outbound document (which could be the same as the inbound document) is sent to a messaging port (refer to Figure 3-4). A messaging port is a BizTalk messaging object that is responsible for providing information to the BizTalk messaging engine to transport documents to a specified destination by using a specified transport service.

Messaging Port Properties

When you create or configure a messaging port, you can specify its destination, transport properties, envelope information, and security properties.

You can configure the destination of a messaging port to an organization, an application, or an XLANG schedule. You can also declare an open destination messaging port. As in the case of an open channel, if the messaging port is configured to use an open destination, then the missing information has to be provided elsewhere (for example, in the document itself or specified in the receive function or passed as a parameter in the Submit calls). The destination information must be provided when the document is submitted, either as the parameter of the call or specified as the destination in the receiving function, depending on which method is used to submit the document. Alternatively, this destination information can be specified inside the document itself. If an open destination is declared in a messaging port, the port can transport documents only to organizations. You can't choose open source and open destination simultaneously, however.

The transport properties of a messaging port include the transport services (protocols) and the specific address where the document is sent. You must specify at least one transport, the *primary transport*. You may also specify an optional *Backup transport* to improve the robustness of your document delivery process. In addition, you can specify a service window that defines a specific time range for transporting the document.

In a messaging port, you can specify if an envelope will be used. For EDI documents, you can further specify the delimiters and an interchange control number. We will discuss envelopes shortly in this chapter.

The security properties you can specify in a messaging port include encoding types, encryption types, and digital signatures.

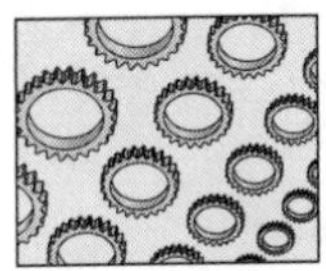

NOTE

For open messaging ports, the encryption security properties are disabled because the destination organizations are unknown.

Distribution Lists

BizTalk Server 2000 also allows you to create a distribution list, which is essentially a group of messaging ports. In this way, you can submit the same document to a number of destinations simultaneously. For example, a supplier can send an updated product catalog to all of its customers.

To use a distribution list, you need to create messaging ports first. Instead of attaching these messaging ports to a channel, you assign them to a distribution list, as illustrated in Figure 3-5.

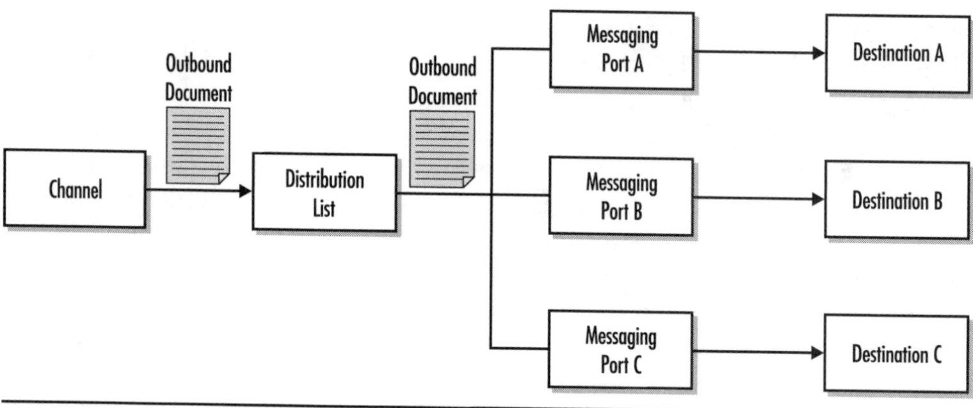

Figure 3-5 *A distribution list*

Envelopes

In BizTalk Server 2000, an envelope is a messaging object that encapsulates electronic business data for transports. An envelope usually contains a header with an optional footer that provides BizTalk Server information to either open inbound interchanges or create outbound interchanges.

BizTalk Server 2000 supports several formats for an envelope, as described in the following table:

Interchange Format	Requires an Envelope?	Comments
CUSTOM XML	Yes	To process inbound interchanges with a custom XML format, you must create an envelope with a custom XML format. You also need a specification for the envelope. When you submit custom XML interchanges, however, BizTalk Server 2000 can locate the appropriate envelope without a name reference. If you use an envelope with a custom XML format, you may choose a specification for the envelope. If you don't pick a specification, however, BizTalk Server will automatically select the BizTalk Framework 2.0–compliant format (which isn't reliable because you are using the format, not the protocol in this instance—hence the reliable envelope).

Interchange Format	Requires an Envelope?	Comments
X12 or EDIFACT	No	For inbound interchanges with EDI X12 or EDIFACT formats, you do not need an envelope. Neither do you need to specify the envelope name in the submit call parameters. If you use an envelope with one of these EDI formats, the specification of the outbound documents must have a matching format.
FLATFILE	Yes	To process inbound interchanges with a flat-file format, you must create an envelope with a flat-file format. You must also specify the envelope name in the submit call parameters.
CUSTOM	Yes	Custom formats are those not supported by BizTalk Server 2000's default parsers and serializers. To process interchanges with a custom format, you need ro create an envelope with a custom format. In addition, you need to create and register custom parsers for inbound interchanges and custom serializers for outbound interchanges. We will discuss custom parsers and serializers in Chapter 11.
RELIABLE	No	Interchanges with the reliable format are compliant with BizTalk Framework 2.0. You do not need to create an envelope with a reliable format for BizTalk Server to process inbound interchanges with a reliable format. Neither do you need to specify the envelope name in the Submit call parameters.

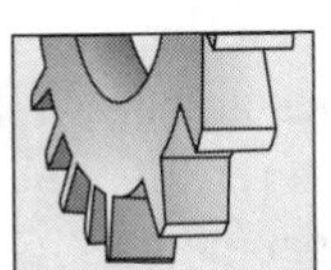

TIP

If you submit an interchange that uses the wrong type of envelope format, the interchange will end up in the Suspended Queue of BizTalk Server and you will receive a message reading "Parser Failure." If you specify a wrong type of envelope format for the outbound interchange, the interchange will also end up in the Suspended Queue, but this time accompanied by a message of "Serializer Failure."

Relationships and Dependencies

By now, we have discussed all the messaging objects for BizTalk Server 2000 Messaging Manager (and the messaging services). In this section, let's take a moment to summarize what we have learned so far and draw a clear high-level picture of a typical BizTalk Server 2000 messaging process.

Organizations and/or applications can be used to identify the source and destination of a document transporting (messaging) flow. A special organization, the Home Organization, is used to identify your company, which hosts all the applications running at your company in the integration.

When BizTalk Server receives a document, it locates the appropriate channel, directing the server how to process the document. In a channel, you can specify the inbound and outbound documents by using document definitions to help validate them. If the inbound and outbound documents do not match each other, you need to create a map to change the format from the inbound document to the outbound document. You can specify an organization, an application, or an XLANG schedule as the source of a channel, or you can declare an open channel whose source information is provided either as the submit call parameters or inside the document itself. At the end of the process, the channel hands the output document to a messaging port.

Whereas a channel specifies the source of the messaging flow, a messaging port determines the destination of the document. A messaging port provides information such as transport protocols and their addresses so the BizTalk messaging engine knows where to send the document.

There are also dependencies between BizTalk messaging objects you should be aware of when you try to create, edit, or delete these messaging objects using the BizTalk Messaging Manager or the Configuration Objects Model API. Figure 3-6 illustrates the dependencies between messaging objects.

In Figure 3-6, an object on the starting side of an arrow is dependent on an object on the ending side of the arrow. For example, Object A → B should read as Object A relies on Object B.

You must create the dependent objects first before you can specify them as dependent objects. For example, you need to first create a specification (not necessarily a messaging object, as will be explained in Chapter 4), then create a document definition that refers to this specification, after which you can create a channel that refers to the document definition. Conversely, you must delete the dependent object first before you delete the independent object. For instance, you must delete a channel before you can delete the document definition or the source organization on which the channel depends. These kinds of dependencies between BizTalk Server messaging objects are similar to the referential integrity relationships between entities in a relational database.

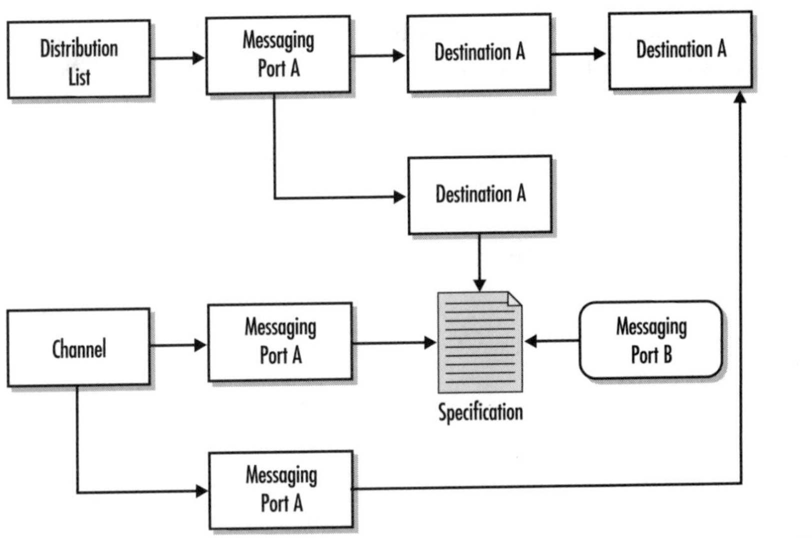

Figure 3-6 *The dependencies between different messaging objects*

Submitting Documents

Having discussed BizTalk Server messaging objects, let's see how to send a document (a message) to BizTalk Server.

Direct Submitting

For an application that can interact with COM objects, you can directly call the *Submit* or *SubmitSync* method of the IInterchange interface to submit a document to BizTalk Server either asynchronously or synchronously. As we mentioned earlier, this is not encouraged, though, due to the performance issue.

Asynchronous Submitting

The Submit method submits a document to BizTalk Server asynchronously. Documents submitted by the Submit method will be placed in a queue (an object that maps to the data stored in the Shared Queue SQL Server database) for processing, and the control returned to the caller immediately. The syntax of the Submit method for Visual Basic or VBScript is as follows:

```
oInterchange.Submit(
        lOpenness, _
        Document, _
        DocName, _
        SourceQualifier, _
        SourceID, _
        DestQualifier, _
        DestID, _
        ChannelName, _
        FilePath, _
        EnvelopeName, _
        PassThrough
)
```

The Submit method can take eleven input parameters, most of which are optional. Some parameters are mutually exclusive with other parameters, however. The following table summarizes the use of input parameters for the Submit method.

Parameter	Data Type	Description
lOpenness	BIZTALK_OPENNESS_TYPE enumeration	This parameter is required. Its value indicates whether a channel or messaging port should be open (as will be explained after this table).
Document	String	A string buffer that stores the content of the document. You must use either the Document parameter or the FilePath parameter (to be explained later), but not both.
DocName	String	The name of the document definition for the inbound document. You cannot use this parameter if the PassThrough parameter (to be explained later) is set to True.
SourceQualifier	String	The qualifier of the source organization. If the PassThrough parameter is set to True, this parameter will be optional. You cannot use this parameter if the ChannelName parameter is specified.

Parameter	Data Type	Description
SourceID	String	The value of the qualifier of the source organization. For example, OrganizationName. If the PassThrough parameter is set to True, this parameter is optional. You cannot use this parameter if the ChannelName parameter is specified.
DestQualifier	String	The qualifier of the destination organization. If the PassThrough parameter is set to True, this parameter will be optional. You cannot use this parameter if the ChannelName parameter is specified.
DestID	String	The value of the qualifier of the destination organization. For example, OrganizationName. If the PassThrough parameter is set to True, this parameter will be optional. You cannot use this parameter if the ChannelName parameter is specified.
ChannelName	String	The name of the channel to be used. Specifying the channel name will provide better performance because it directs the BizTalk Server messaging engine to bypass the channel searching and matching process. Unless the PassThrough parameter is set to True, this parameter will be optional, depending on whether the routing information is provided by other means. Routing will be explained later in this chapter.
FilePath	String	The path of the document to be submitted. This parameter is mutually exclusive with the Document parameter explained earlier.
EnvelopeName	String	An optional parameter specifying the name of the envelope for the inbound interchange.

Parameter	Data Type	Description
PassThrough	Long	A flag parameter indicating how the server should process the document. When set to True, encryption, decoding, or signature verification will all be bypassed. This could be useful in processing binary documents.

The following table lists the BIZTALK_OPENNESS_TYPE enumerations:

Enumeration Constant	Value	Meaning
BIZTALK_OPENNESS_TYPE_NOTOPEN	1	The instance of the object is not open.
BIZTALK_OPENNESS_TYPE_SOURCE	2	The source organization of this instance of the object is open.
BIZTALK_OPENNESS_TYPE_DESTINATION	4	The destination organization of this instance of the object is open.

The following code segment illustrates how to create an instance of the IInterchange object:

```
'In Visual  Basic applications
Dim oInterchange As Object
Set oInterchange = CreateObject("BizTalk.Interchange")

'In .vbs scripting files
Dim oInterchange
Set oInterchange = CreateObject("BizTalk.Interchange")

'In ASP pages
<%
Dim oInterchange
Set oInterchange = Server.CreateObject("BizTalk.Interchange")
%>
```

Synchronous Submitting

To submit a document synchronously to BizTalk Server, you call the SubmitSync method of the IInterchange interface. The SubmitSync method returns an optional response document when provided. The syntax of the SubmitSync method is slightly different from the Submit method and looks like this:

```
oInterchange.SubmitSync( _
      lOpenness, _
      Document, _
      DocName, _
      SourceQualifier, _
      SourceID, _
      DestQualifier, _
      DestID, _
      ChannelName, _
      FilePath, _
      EnvelopeName, _
      PassThrough, _
      SubmissionHandle, _
      ResponseDocument _
)
```

As you can see, most of the parameters of the SubmitSync are the same as the Submit method. It only adds two parameters to the Submit method. Both are output parameters and of variant data types.

The *SubmissionHandle* output parameter returns a unique identifier for the submitted document or interchange. The returned value (the handle) can be used to query the Tracking database for the status of the interchange or document submitted (by calling the *CheckSuspendedQueue* and *GetSuspendedQueueItemDetails* methods of the IInterchange interface if, and only if, tracking of the interchange is enabled). If more than one document is submitted—for example, an interchange is submitted—BizTalk Server will only return a single handle. You can still use this handle to check the status of the interchange and all related child documents, however.

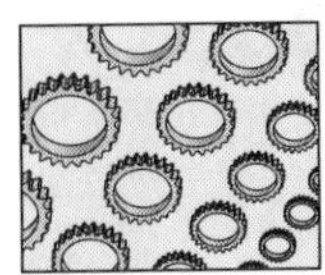

NOTE

Calling the SubmitSync method are usually not a good idea. There are no checkpoints in the Shared Queue database and there is an affinity to single processing machines, thus the scalability decreases. For more information, read the deployment white paper which explains how to create a synchronous façade to asynchronous processes. You can get all the technical white papers from the BizTalk product web site: http://www.Microsoft.com/biztalk/.

The *ResponseDocument* output parameter can capture the response object returned by the BizTalk Server, if available.

The SubmitSync method has several limitations:

1. It only works for a single channel match. If more than one channel matches the parameters, an error will be returned.
2. It only works for single document interchanges. If the interchange being submitted contains multiple documents, an error will be returned.
3. This method does not support distribution lists.

Using Receive Functions

In addition to the IInterchange interface, BizTalk Server 2000 provides *receive functions* that enable you to submit documents to BizTalk Server. This can be very useful for source applications that don't support COM interactions. Even if you do have COM interactions, they are preferred because they are loosely couple systems and are optimized for higher performance.

Receive functions are BizTalk Server Administration objects that can be used to submit documents indirectly to BizTalk Server. Receive functions enable applications to post documents or interchanges to either a file location or a queue of the Message Queuing Services. A BizTalk Server monitors these locations, retrieves the matching documents or interchanges, and submits the document or interchanges to the BizTalk messaging engine to process. Receive functions use an event-based monitoring mechanism instead of polling to detect the arrival of a document or interchange. Note that the "polling location" in the Receive Function wizard is simply a convenient way to specify a file location or queue name. The underlying mechanism used by the BizTalk Server 2000 messaging engine is event-driven. Once a document or interchange arrives in a monitored location defined by a receive function, BizTalk Server will submit it to the messaging engine to process and remove it from the posted location.

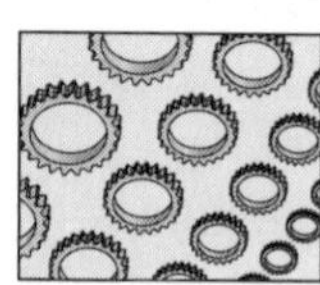

NOTE

Submitting a document from a receive function is always asynchronous. For scenarios in which synchronous submitting is desirable—for example, you want to use the Loopback *transport protocol—you must call the SubmitSync method instead of using the receive functions.*

BizTalk Server 2000 supports two types of receive functions: File receive functions and Message Queuing receive functions. You use the BizTalk Server Administration MMC snap-in to create and configure both types of receive functions.

TIP

Receive functions have some dependencies on messaging objects (such as envelopes, channels, document definitions, and source and destination organizations). In Chapter 6, you will learn how to use BizTalk Messaging Manager to create and configure messaging objects. To help you work with the exercises that discuss creating receive functions, a script file (Config_BTS_Chap03.vbs) has been provided for you. Download the file from this book's web site. Once you've saved it to your hard disk, double-click it in Windows Explorer. This will automatically configure the messaging objects for the remaining examples in this chapter. Alternatively, you can run this file from the DOS prompt by navigating to the directory where you saved it and typing ***cscript Config_BTS_Chap03.vbs****. If you run the file from Windows Explorer, you will see a series of messages confirming that the appropriate messaging objects have been successfully created. If you choose to execute it from the DOS prompt, the messages will go to the console screen instead.*

File Receive Functions

A File receive function monitors a file location and is activated when a file matching the specified type arrives in the specified location.

The following illustrates the process of creating a simple File receive function:

1. Select Start, Microsoft BizTalk Server 2000, and then BizTalk Server Administration. Choose Expand Microsoft BizTalk Server 2000, then BizTalk Server Group (or whatever name you've chosen for it) to display the Receive Functions node.
2. Right-click the Receive Function and select New | File Receive Function as shown in Figure 3-7; the Add a File Receive Function dialog box appears as shown in Figure 3-8.
3. In the Name text box, type **Test_File_Receive_Func**. You can optionally add some comments in the Comment text box.
4. From the drop-down box under Server On Which The Receive Function Will Run, select the server where you want the receive function to run, or keep the default server name that appears.
5. In the File Types To Poll For text box, type ***.xml** to specify you are only interested in receiving XML documents.
6. Bypass the Preprocessor drop-down box (preprocessors will be explained later in this chapter).
7. Bypass the User Name and Password text boxes. A username and password are required only when the receive location is protected.

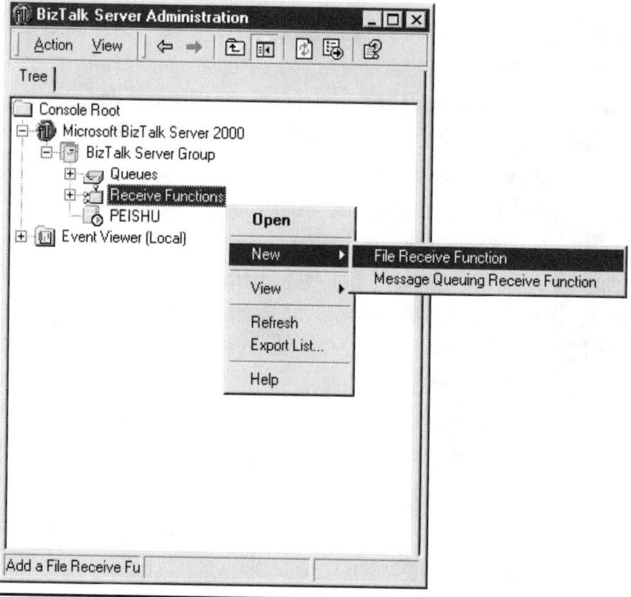

Figure 3-7 *Create a new File Receive Function*

Add a File Receive Function

Name: Test_File_Receive_Func

Comment (optional):

Server on which the receive function will run: PEISHU

File types to poll for: *.xml

Polling location: C:\Temp\In

Preprocessor:

User name:

Password:

Click the Advanced button to customize this receive function for documents that are not self-routing, or to specify openness or pass-through options.

Advanced

OK Cancel Help

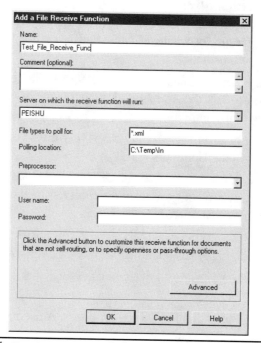

Figure 3-8 *Add a File Receive Function dialog box*

8. Click the Advanced button to bring up the Advanced Receive Function Options dialog box (see Figure 3-9).
9. The Openness drop-down box allows you to specify one of the BIZTALK_OPENNESS_TYPE enumerations discussed earlier in this chapter. Make sure the default option is set to Not Open.
10. The Submit With a Pass-through Flag check box serves the same purpose as the PathThrough parameter in the Submit and SubmitSync method. Leave it unchecked.
11. In the Envelope Name drop-down box, you can specify an envelope for the inbound document or interchange. Leave it as "<None>" (the default) for this exercise.
12. Select "Test_Channel" from the Channel Name drop-down box. This channel was created by the Config_BTS_Chap03.vbs scripts.
13. As soon as you select a channel name in Step 12, the Document Definition Name, Source Selected, and Destination Selected are all disabled. This works the same as the Submit and SubmitSync functions: document definition, source organization, and destination organization are three pieces of information that

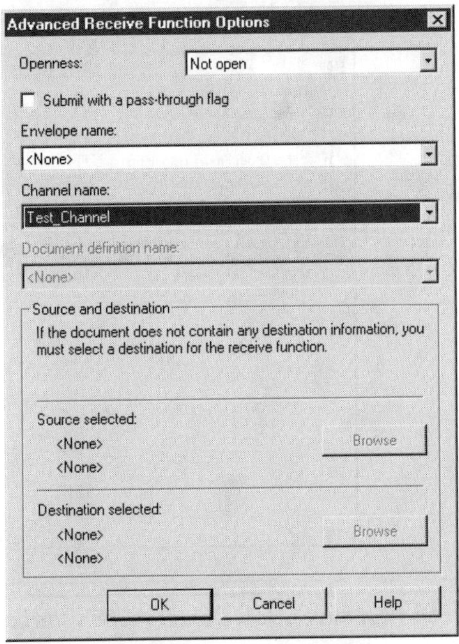

Figure 3-9 *Advanced Receive Function Options dialog box*

help BizTalk Server locate an appropriate channel. If you already selected a channel, the channel searching and matching processes will be bypassed, making these options pointless. If you don't specify a channel, however, you will have to denote some or all of these options, unless they are specified in the document itself.

14. Click OK to return to Add a File Receive Function and then click OK to close it. You should see the File receive function Test_File_Receive_Func appear in BizTalk Server Administration (see Figure 3-10).

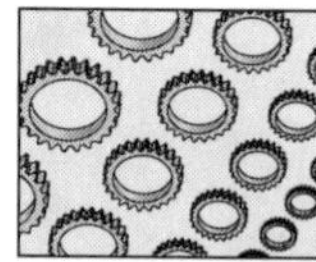

NOTE

When using file receive functions, the location where the document is dropped must be an NTFS share. If you have a non-NTFS share (a UNIX share, for example), you need to copy the document to an NTFS share where the File receive function is configured to.

Message Queuing Receive Functions

A Message Queuing Receive Function monitors a specified queue in Messaging Queuing Services (formerly MSMQ). The process of creating a Messaging Queuing

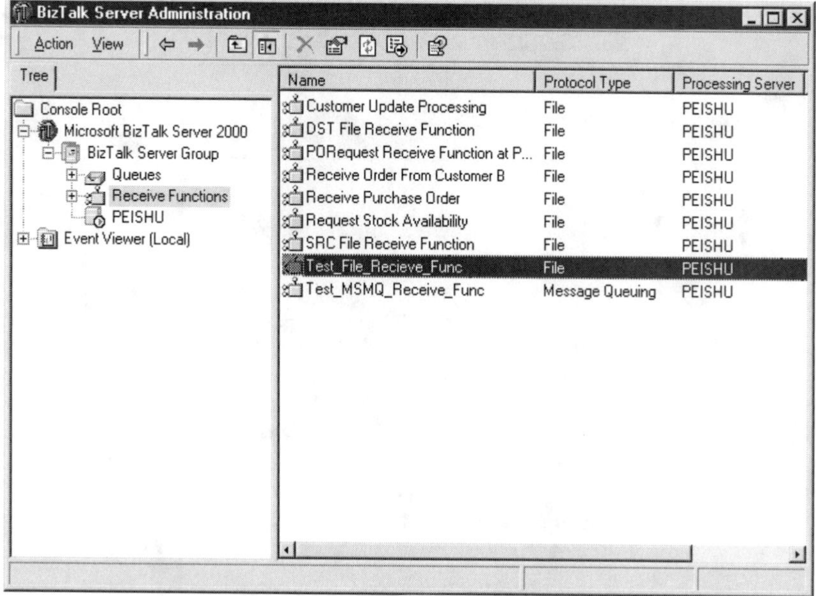

Figure 3-10 *Receive functions in the BizTalk Server Administration MMC snap-in*

receive function is very similar to creating a File receive function, with a couple of exceptions:

1. Unlike in the File receive function, you cannot restrict the type of files received in the queue.
2. Instead of monitoring a file location in a Messaging Queuing receive function, you need to specify a queue name as shown in Figure 3-11.

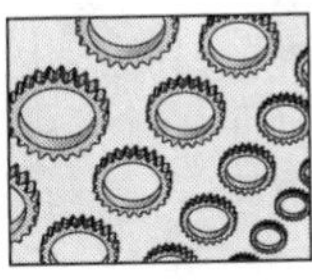

NOTE

The location you specify the receive function to monitor must pre-exist, or else the receive function is disabled. To reenable it, open the receive function and uncheck the disabled box. Similarly, the queue you specified in a Messaging Queuing receive function must also pre-exist. To create a private queue, open the Computer Management MMC snap-in, expand Services and Applications | Message Queuing. Right-click Private Queues and select New | Private Queue. The Queue Name dialog box

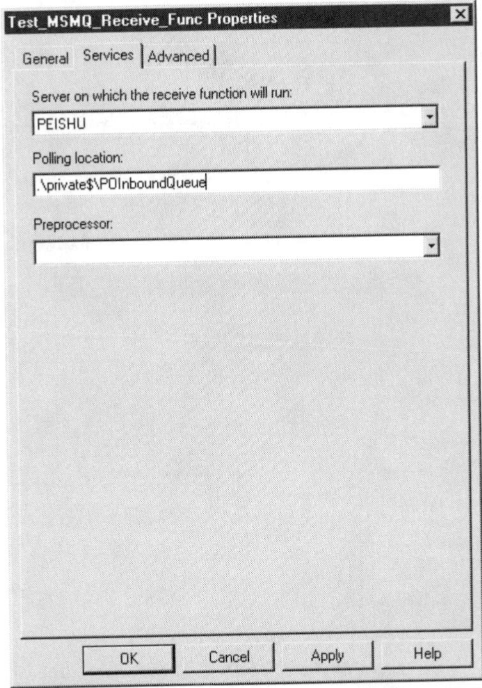

Figure 3-11 *A Messaging Queuing receive function*

appears (see Figure 3-12). Type a name in the private$\ text box. You may also specify a transactional queue by selecting the Transactional check box. (If you do so, all the messages you send to this queue must be transactional.) Click OK. The queue will appear in Computer Management (see Figure 3-13).

CAUTION

If you refresh the view in Computer Management, the queue name will appear as lowercase even though the name is actually mixed case, as in our example. The queue names in Messaging Queuing are case sensitive. This means you should refer to the queue name exactly as it was created, not as it is displayed in Computer Management. For example, if you create a private queue and name it "POInboundQueue", you should refer to the name of the queue in code as ".\private$\ POInboundQueue" not as ".\private$\ poinboundqueue" even though it may appear in the Computer Management MMC snap-in this way.

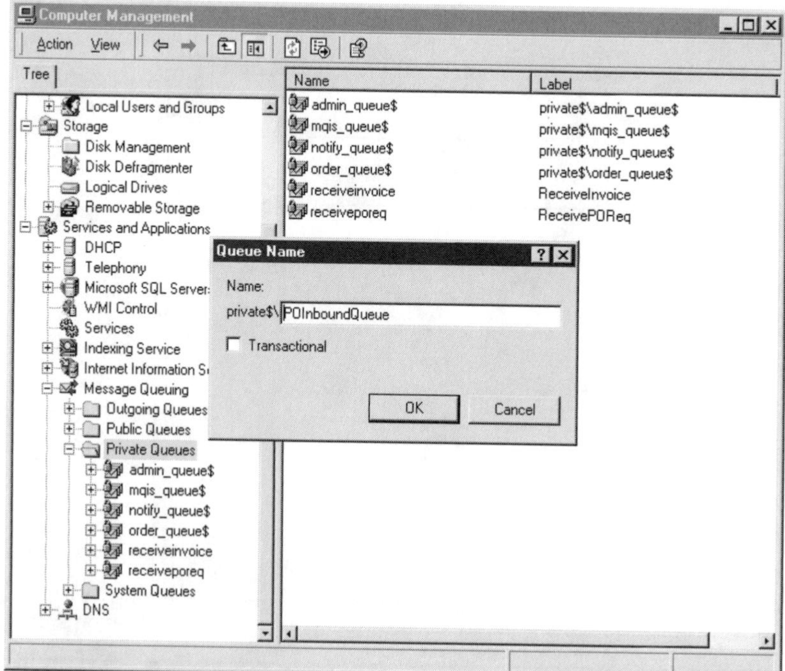

Figure 3-12 *Create a private queue*

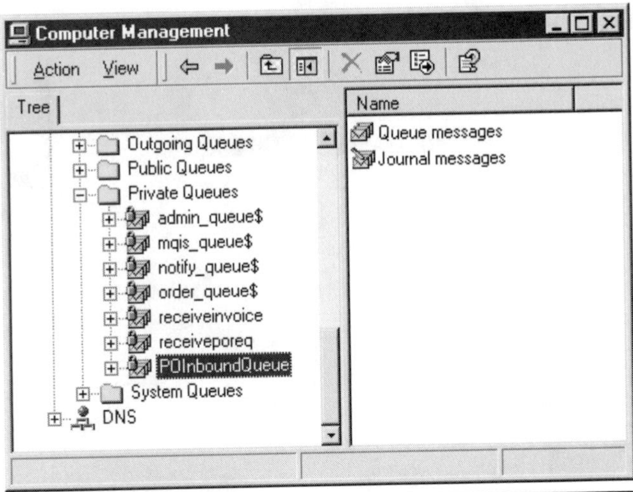

Figure 3-13 *A new private queue appears in Computer Management*

Custom Preprocessors

When BizTalk Server receives a submitted document, it will launch one of its built-in parsers to parse the document. BizTalk Server 2000 ships with four built-in parsers, XML, EDIFACT, EDI X12, and Flat File parser. To view these parsers, open BizTalk Server Administration, right-click the BizTalk Server Group, and select the Parsers tab as shown in Figure 3-14. You can change the order of these parsers by clicking the up and down arrow.

If the format of the inbound document (or interchange) is specified in an envelope, BizTalk Server will invoke the appropriate parser accordingly. If the format information is not available, BizTalk Server will try to parse the document by testing the built-in parsers in the order specified. If all these parsers fail to parse the document, BizTalk Server will place the document in the Suspended Queue and mark it as Parse Failure. If the format of the document falls outside the built-in parsers, you will need to create a custom parser in C/C++ by implementing the IBizTalkParserComponent interface (this will be discussed in Chapter 11).

There are also scenarios in which you may want to preprocess the document or interchange before submitting the document or interchange to BizTalk Server. For example, you may want to unzip a file prior to submitting it. BizTalk Server 2000 provides a Custom Preprocessor framework to deal with these preprocessing scenarios. A registered preprocessor can be selected when you configure a receiving function (see Figures 3-8 and 3-11).

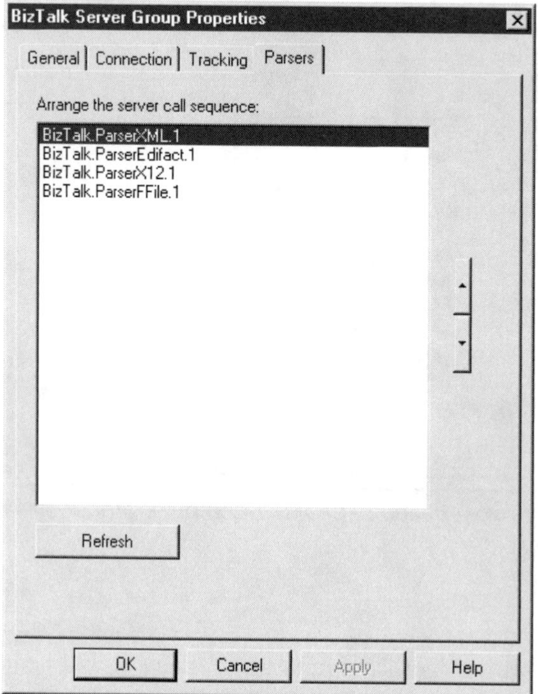

Figure 3-14 *Built-in parsers in BizTalk Server 2000*

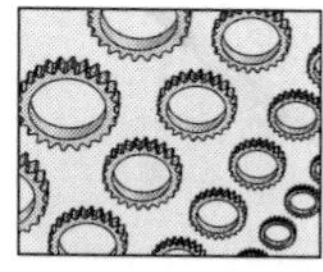

NOTE

You will learn how to create a preprocessor and have it appear in the Preprocessor drop-down list of the receive functions in Chapter 11.

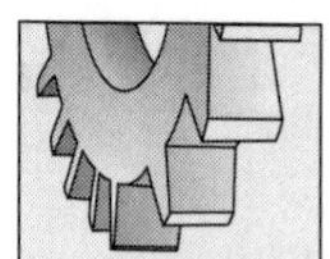

TIP

Whenever possible, use receive functions, especially the Message Queuing receive function instead of calling submit methods. Message Queuing receive functions are optimized for best performance and scalability. However, Messaging Queuing has size limitations on the messages (documents or interchanges)—the maximum size of each message is limited to 4 megabytes (MB) and the total size possible for stored messages in a queue is 2 gigabytes (GB), under Windows 2000 (this part changes only in Windows XP). You should be aware of these limitations as well as other trade-offs when deciding which approach to choose. Use Message Queuing then File Receive then COM in that order.

Document Routing

When BizTalk Server receives a document or interchange, it needs to locate an appropriate channel to process it. This process is referred to as *routing*. To route a document, BizTalk Server needs three pieces of information: the source organization, the destination organization, and the document definition of the inbound document or interchange.

There are many ways to provide routing information to BizTalk Server:

1. Specify the routing information in the input parameters of a Submit or SubmitSync method call. This is referred to as *Call-based routing*.
2. Specify the routing information in the inbound document itself—a process known as *Self-routing*.
3. Specify the routing information in a receive function.
4. Split up the routing information using different combinations of the preceding options.
5. Directly specify the channel name in either the call parameter or a receive channel.

The Number 5 option is the most efficient method (if you know which channel is going to be used beforehand), because it avoids the searching and matching channel process of the server. Under certain circumstances, you can predict which channel to select until you receive the document. In these cases, you have to use one of the other methods to specify routing information. If the same routing information has been specified in several places, the information in the input parameters or receive functions will override those in the document itself.

Transporting Documents

Now that we have discussed BizTalk Server messaging objects, as well as how to get a document or interchange into the BizTalk Server (submitting). How do you get the message (the outbound document or interchange) out of BizTalk Server? When we discussed messaging ports earlier, we mentioned they have some properties which can be specified as transport protocols (called transport services) and may be used as addresses associated with the protocol, if applicable.

Transport Services

BizTalk Server 2000 supports a number of transport services in the box (you can also add other transports such as FTP, and so on), as summarized in the following table:

Transport Service	Description	Address Syntax
HTTP	A transport that uses HyperText Transfer Protocol (HTTP). The document is sent to a valid web site.	http://www.bizpartner.com/poprocessor.asp
HTTPS	A transport that uses Secure HyperText Transfer Protocol (HTTPS). The document is sent to a valid secure web site.	https://www.bizpartner.com/poprocessor.asp
SMTP	A transport that uses the Simple Mail Transfer Protocol (SMTP). The document is sent to an e-mail address.	mailto:btsadmin@bizpartner.com
File	A transport that uses the SendLocalFile component. The document is delivered to a file location.	For file://C:\dir\filename.ext Note: Details regarding file name format follow this table.
Messaging Queuing	A transport that uses Microsoft Messaging Queuing Services. The document is sent to a queue.	DIRECT=OS:.\private$\InvoiceProcessing
Application Integration Component (AIC)	A transport that uses the AIC protocol. AIC is a BizTalk Server 2000 specific infrastructure that extends its messaging services.	{11111111-1111-1111-1111-111111111111} (The GUID of the AIC) Note: AIC is discussed in greater detail in Chapter 11.
Loopback	A transport that returns the outbound document of a channel to a business application, component, or XLANG schedule that submitted the inbound document using a synchronous submit call.	Not Applicable. Note: This transport type is available only for a messaging port that sends documents to an application.

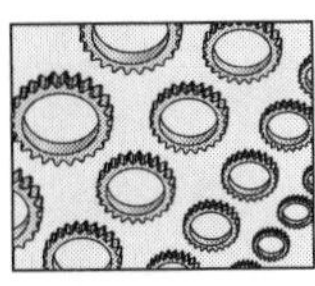

NOTE

When using the File transport service, you can mix predefined symbols with any static characters you specified in the address (in order to specify the file name). For example, if you set Address as "file://C:\Invoices\Invoice_%tracking_id%.xml", the actual file name would become something like "C:\Inovice\Invoice_{12345678-90AB-CDEF-1234-567890ABCDEF}. This is useful because you guarantee a unique file name each time, with no-appending (unlike the other constants that follow). The following table summarizes the symbols provided by BizTalk Server 2000 which can be used in the file name:

Symbol	Description
%tracking_id%	A system-generated GUID to uniquely identify the file.
%document_name%	The name of the document definition for the inbound document processed by BizTalk Server.
%server%	The name of the host server that processed the document.
%uid%	A counter that increases over time, represented in milliseconds, which is reset whenever the server is restarted.
%datetime%	A timestamp in GMT (Greenwich Mean Time) format.

BizTalk Server Messaging Services in Action

We have covered a lot of concepts, terms, and theories in this chapter. Before we finish though, let's look at a very simple example to get an idea of how BizTalk Server Messaging Services works.

Remember, before we started creating out test File receive function (Test_File_Receive_Func), we executed a script file (Config_BTS_Chap03.vbs) to automatically create and configure several BizTalk messaging objects. Now we will use these messaging objects and the File receive function to run a quick test. The following table lists the messaging objects created by the scripts:

Messaging Object	Description
Test_Org_Src	The source organization
Test_Org_Dst	The destination organization
Test_Doc	The document definition
Test_Channel	The channel
Test_Port	The messaging port

Create two folders C:\Temp\In and C:\Temp\Out and create a simple XML document TestData.xml as follows:

```
<TestData>Test Data</TestData>
```

Now, drop the TestData.xml document in the C:\Temp\In folder; it should disappear after a few seconds. Check the C:\Temp\Out folder. You should see a file there that looks something like the one in Figure 3-15.

Here is how it works:

1. The File receive function we created earlier (Test_File_Receive_Func) monitors the C:\Temp\In directory for XML documents. When it detects the arrival of the TestData.xml file, it submits it to the specified channel, Test_Channel.
2. In the Test_Channel, we have specified the Test_Doc as the document definition for both inbound and outbound documents, so no map is needed. In addition, for the sake of simplicity, we did not associate a specification with the document definition.
3. The Test_Channel then directs the document to the messaging port, Test_Port, that has configured a Local File Transport Service with an address specified as "file://C:\Temp\Out\Test%tracking_id%.xml".

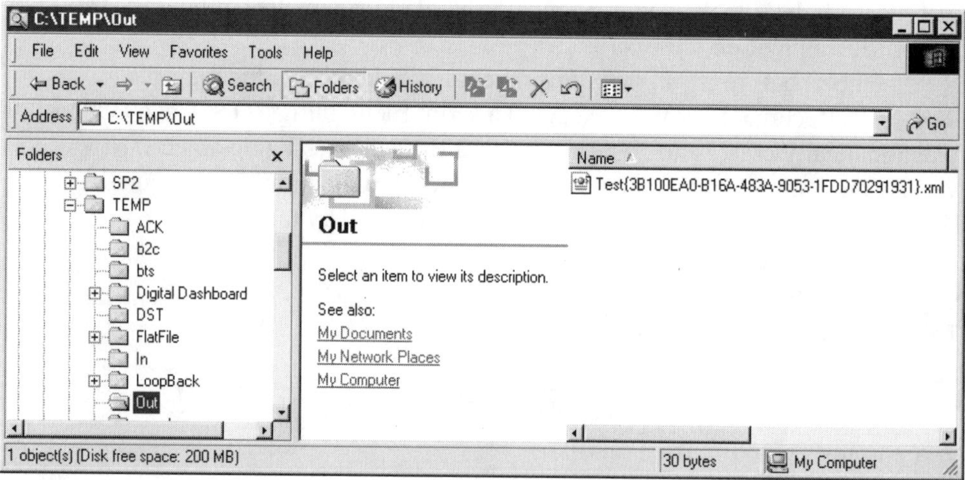

Figure 3-15 *The outbound document is dropped in a local file*

4. At the end of the process, the file ends up in the C:\Temp\Out directory as shown in Figure 3-15.

Whereas this example isn't extremely useful in a real world situation, it does demonstrate how the BizTalk Server 2000 Messaging Services works. Creating messaging solutions using BizTalk Server 2000 for a complex scenario involves a great deal of planning and designing. A thorough understanding of the available messaging objects and where and how to use them, as well as the relationships between them, is fundamental.

Chapter in Review

In this chapter, we introduced BizTalk Server 2000 Messaging Services. We looked at messaging objects, discussed ways of submitting documents to BizTalk Server, and transporting them to their destinations. The information in this chapter will act as a solid foundation for the next three chapters, positioning you to create sound messaging solutions using BizTalk Server 2000.

CHAPTER

4

Working with Specifications

IN THIS CHAPTER:

Introducing Specifications

The BizTalk Editor

Creating Specifications

Chapter in Review

In the last chapter, we introduced BizTalk Server 2000 Messaging Services. One of the most important aspects of BizTalk Messaging Services is how it processes business documents. Processing a document using BizTalk Messaging Services usually involves parsing the inbound document (excepting pass-through scenarios) from its native format into an intermediate XML format used by BizTalk Server (if the inbound document is not already in XML format), transforming the intermediate XML format of the inbound document into another intermediate format for the outbound format if they are different, and serializing the intermediate format of the outbound format to the format required by your business partner, if necessary. The intermediate XML document formats for inbound and outbound documents are known as *specifications* in BizTalk Server 2000 terminology. The information on which BizTalk Server bases these transformations is called a *map*. BizTalk Server 2000 provides two great XML tools, BizTalk Editor and BizTalk Mapper, to enable you to create and translate specifications (see Figure 3-4).

In this chapter, we will discuss BizTalk specifications and teach you how to use BizTalk Editor to work with specifications. Map and BizTalk Mapper are the topics of the next chapter.

Introducing Specifications

Let's start with BizTalk specifications. First, we will explain what a BizTalk specification is, and what it looks like. Then we will introduce the BizTalk Editor's environment, explain its properties and functionalities, and show you a variety of ways in which you can use BizTalk Editor to create specifications. Finally, we will conclude this chapter by creating some specifications in a variety of formats supported by BizTalk Server 2000.

A specification is a BizTalk Server 2000-specific XML document that defines the structure and validation rules of a document processed by BizTalk Server 2000. It is important to understand that BizTalk Server 2000 uses specifications not only for documents using XML formats but also for documents in well-known EDI formats, flat file formats, as well as custom formats (which will be explained later in this chapter). Using a standard format (XML in this case) to define documents, regardless of their native formats, gives BizTalk Server Messaging Services an open and extensible architecture. Document definitions (which were introduced in the last chapter) are actually pointers to corresponding specifications (although there are exceptions in which you can create a document definition without associating it to a specification, as was explained in the last chapter as well). Specifications help the

BizTalk messaging engine to parse inbound documents into XML formats (if they are not already in the XML format) and serialize outbound documents to their native formats. By using specifications, BizTalk Server is able to describe any document format in XML format, regardless of its native format.

Supported Document Formats

The built-in parsers and serializer of BizTalk Server 2000 can deal with a number of formats, including standard formats such as XML and EDI (X12 and EDIFACT), legacy formats such as flat files (delimited, positional, or a combination of both). If the inbound document does not fall into any of these supported formats, BizTalk Server 2000 provides an infrastructure enabling you to implement custom parsers and serializers to read/write from (and to) custom formats.

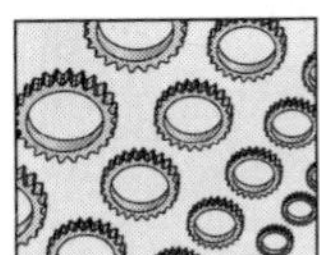

NOTE

We will discuss custom parsers and serializers in Chapter 11.

XML Documents

XML documents are relatively easier to define than other formats within the context of BizTalk specifications. A specification for an XML document is very straightforward because BizTalk-specific elements (those under the BizTalk Server namespace) are empty—for example, the <b:SelectionFields/>, <b:RecordInfo/> and <b:FieldInfo/> elements.

EDI Documents

Prior to the invention of XML, many companies, especially large companies and government agencies, have been using EDI (Electronic Data Exchange) as a standardized format to electronically exchange business documents on line. By using EDI, companies can ensure that documents being exchanged are constructed, interpreted, and processed in a correct and consistent manner. By eliminating paper-based, manual processes, EDI provides more efficient, lower TOC and a more accurate alternative for exchanging business documents between business partners. However, the implementation and maintenance costs associated with EDI solutions are typically so high only large companies can afford to use them to trade with their equally enormous trading partners, and despite the fact that EDI technologies have been around for almost four decades it has not triggered the B2B revolution. In addition to the high implementation and maintenance cost, EDI documents are somewhat cryptic, as you will see in an upcoming example.

XML has overcome the limitations of EDI and has been rapidly adopted in EAI and B2B integration industries. However, most large companies and government agencies today still rely heavily on EDI implementations to support their business document exchange for both EAI and B2B scenarios. Most of these EDI applications are enormous, complicated, and took years to build. The efforts involved in replacing an existing EDI system with an XML system are similar to rewriting a mission-critical enterprise application, if not greater. As a result, a commonly chosen approach is to allow both EDI and XML to coexist peacefully, while gradually replacing expensive EDI systems with XML alternatives.

A single product for EAI and B2B integrations, BizTalk Server 2000 supports two widely recognized EDI formats: X12 and EDIFACT. The X12 standards were developed by the Accredited Standards Committee (ASC) X12 in 1979 and approved by the American National Standards Institute (ANSI). X12 standards are primarily used in North America. The European community developed its own EDI standards, titled Guidelines on Trade Data Interchange (GTDI). In order to create a single international EDI syntax, the United Nations Economic Commission for Europe (UN/ECE) and the Working Party on Facilitation of International Trade Procedures (WP4) consolidated both X12 and GTDI and created the UN/EDIFACT (or simply EDIFACT) standards. In 1987, the International Organization for Standardization (ISO) adopted EDIFACT and made it an international standard. The X12 and EDIFACT standards are functionally equivalent, although the underlying structures are slightly different. For demonstration purposes, we will focus our discussion of EDI primarily on X12 in this book.

The process of developing, reviewing, and publishing an X12 standard typically takes three years. To overcome this lengthy process, the Data Interchange Standards Association (DISA)—the ASC X12 Secretariat—publishes the entire set of X12 standards (called an X12 release) on an annual basis. An X12 release includes the latest ANSI-approved standards, as well as new draft standards approved by the ASC X12 that year. An X12 release is identified by a six digit number code that consists of three parts. The first three digits are assigned by ANSI and represent the version number. The fourth and fifth digits represent the release number, and the last digit represents the subrelease number. For example, the code for X12 Version 4, Release 1 is 004010—referred to as X12 4010. In the box, BizTalk Server 2000 supports X12 2040, 3010, 3060, and 4010 releases, with each release containing about a dozen standards. The parser and serializer support all of X12 and EDIFACT, so you can create any schema that fits into these guidelines or obtain them from a third party. Figure 4-1 illustrates what an X12 4010 document—a purchase order (X12 4010 Standard 850)—looks like.

Header

```
ISA*00**00**01*A01*01*A02*010318*1723*U*00400*000001002*0*P*>~
GS*PO*Northwind*Supplier*20010318*1723*1002*X*4010~
ST*850*0001~
```

Body

```
BEG*00*SA*123456789**19960722~
PER*SA*Laura Callahan~
DTM*118*20010318~
N3*2817 Milton Dr.~
N4*Albuquerque*NM*87110*USA~
PO1**36**21.35~
PID*F****Chef Anton's Gumbo Mix~
PO1**12**30~
PID*F****Uncle Bob's Organic Dried Pears~
PO1**24**38~
PID*F****Rattlesnake Canyon Grocery~
CTT*3*2040.6~
```

Trailer

```
SE*10*0001~
GE*1*1002~
IEA*1*000001002~
```

Figure 4-1 *A sample EDI X12 850 purchase order*

As shown in Figure 4-1, an X12 document consists of three parts: a header, a trailer, and a body. The header signifies the beginning of an EDI X12 document. A header starts with an Instrument Society of America (ISA) declaration, followed by the functional groups indicated by GS and the transaction set header (ST). The trailer marks the end of the EDI X12 document, with SE, GE, and IEA corresponding to ST, GS, and ISA, respectively, indicating the ending of these individual subsections. The header and trailer are collectively referred to as an electronic envelope. The body of an X12 EDI document, meanwhile, contains the core business data. In this purchase order example, the body contains the beginning segment of the purchase order (BEG): the contact name information (PER), date and time information (DTM), shipping address (N3 and N4), order items (PO1s and PIDs), and totals (CTT). When using BizTalk messaging services to process EDI documents (X12 and/or EDIFACT), you use BizTalk Editor to create the specification for the body. If you want to generate an outbound document to EDI documents, you need to create an envelope that provides header and trailer information. In addition, as we mentioned in the last chapter, you also need to specify the selection criteria in the document definition. For inbound documents, however, BizTalk Server 2000 is able to retrieve the information from the EDI document itself. You don't need to specify an envelope for it. You do still need to specify selection criteria, though, so that the BizTalk messaging engine will know how to associate a document with the appropriate document definition.

Flat Files

BizTalk Server 2000 supports both delimited and positional flat files. It also supports flat files that are both delimited and positional.

In a delimited flat file, the fields of a record are separated by a specified character, called a delimiter—for example, a comma, tab, space, and so on. The records are separated by a different delimiter from the field delimiter, usually a carriage return (CR) or line feed (LF) character. The following is a sample delimited flat file that contains information taken from the Employees table of the Northwind database (a sample database that shipped with SQL Server 7.0 and 2000):

```
1,Davolio,Nancy
2,Fuller,Andrew
3,Leverling,Janet
4,Peacock,Margaret
5,Buchanan,Steven
6,Suyama,Michael
7,King,Robert
8,Callahan,Laura
9,Dodsworth,Anne
```

In this example, fields are separated by commas, and records are separated by carriage returns. Each record contains the ID, first name, and last name of an employee.

In a positional flat file, record fields are identified by a fixed length of characters. Records in a positional flat file are separated by an end-of-record terminator—for example, a carriage return. The following is a positioned version of the employee data you saw earlier:

```
1         Davolio   Nancy
2         Fuller    Andrew
3         Leverling Janet
4         Peacock   Margaret
5         Buchanan  Steven
6         Suyama    Michael
7         King      Robert
8         Callahan  Laura
9         Dodsworth Anne
```

Here, each record is terminated by a carriage return character. Each field in a record takes ten characters. For each employee record, the first ten characters represent the employee ID, the second ten characters represent the first name, and the last ten characters represent the last name. If the value of the field is less than ten characters, the rest will be filled with white spaces.

You can also mix the delimited and positional records together to construct a flat file which is again supported by BizTalk Server 2000. For instance, in a single file you can have delimited fields in some records and positional fields in other records.

The Structure of a Specification

Specifications are developed based on XML Data Reduced Schemas (or XDR Schemas, a functional subset of proposed XML Schemas proposed to W3C by Microsoft; see Appendix A for details). XDR schemas are used to define the structures and constraints (validation rules) for XML documents. In order to use the same semantics to define the structures and constraints for non-XML documents as well, BizTalk specifications are based on XDR schemas with some additions of BizTalk Server-specific XML elements and attributes (under the namespace of BizTalk Server).

Figure 4-2 is a screen shot of a partial BizTalk specification displayed in IE 5. It is a specification for a purchase order request. This particular specification defines the structure of a flat file format. Later in this section, we will show you how to create this specification.

As you can see in Figure 4-2, a specification starts with the standard XDR root element *Schema*, and defines three namespaces. The xml-data namespace and xml-datatypes are standard XDR namespaces, whereas the BizTalk Server namespace has been added to define the BizTalk Server-specific information inside the XDR document. (XML namespaces and XDR schemas are explained in greater detail in Appendix A). BizTalk Server-specific elements and attributes are prefixed with **b:** to indicate they belong to the BizTalk Server namespace. The rest of the elements and attributes are either prefixed with **d:** (under the xml-data namespaces) or no prefixes at all (under the default namespace). The entire document consists of *ElementType/element* and *AttributeType/*attributes elements. BizTalk-specific elements and attributes (b:RecordInfo, b:FieldInfo, etc.) are appended to these elements. For example, the *structure* attribute of the <b:RecordInfo> element specifies that delimited flat file.

A specification can be used to describe a number of document formats, including both XML and non-XML documents, as presented in the next section. BizTalk Server uses specifications to define both inbound documents and outbound documents. Later in this chapter, you will learn how to use BizTalk Mapper to create maps that instruct the BizTalk messaging engine to transform inbound documents to outbound documents if their formats are different.

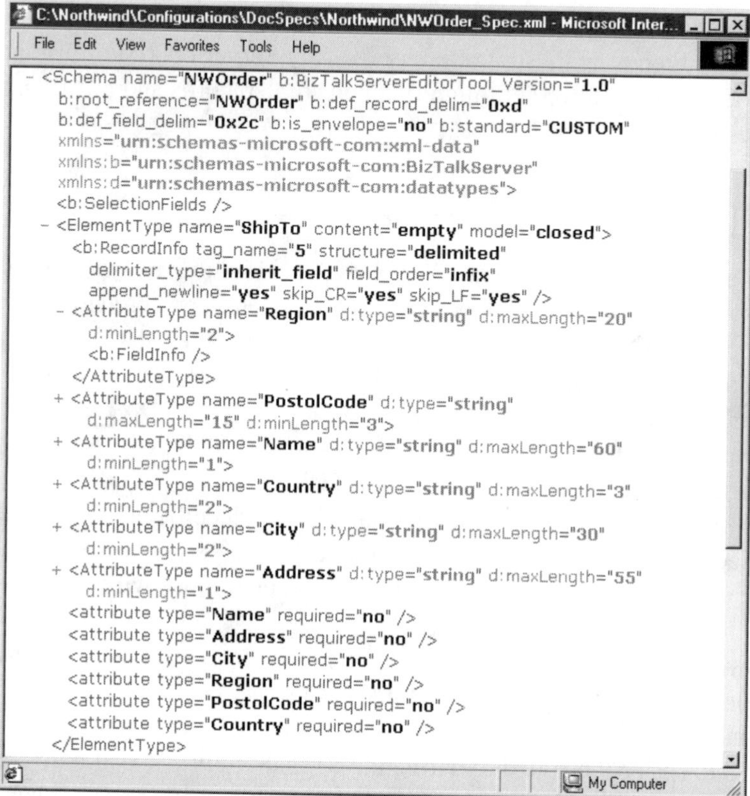


```
- <Schema name="NWOrder" b:BizTalkServerEditorTool_Version="1.0"
    b:root_reference="NWOrder" b:def_record_delim="0xd"
    b:def_field_delim="0x2c" b:is_envelope="no" b:standard="CUSTOM"
    xmlns="urn:schemas-microsoft-com:xml-data"
    xmlns:b="urn:schemas-microsoft-com:BizTalkServer"
    xmlns:d="urn:schemas-microsoft-com:datatypes">
    <b:SelectionFields />
  - <ElementType name="ShipTo" content="empty" model="closed">
      <b:RecordInfo tag_name="5" structure="delimited"
        delimiter_type="inherit_field" field_order="infix"
        append_newline="yes" skip_CR="yes" skip_LF="yes" />
    - <AttributeType name="Region" d:type="string" d:maxLength="20"
        d:minLength="2">
        <b:FieldInfo />
      </AttributeType>
    + <AttributeType name="PostolCode" d:type="string"
        d:maxLength="15" d:minLength="3">
    + <AttributeType name="Name" d:type="string" d:maxLength="60"
        d:minLength="1">
    + <AttributeType name="Country" d:type="string" d:maxLength="3"
        d:minLength="2">
    + <AttributeType name="City" d:type="string" d:maxLength="30"
        d:minLength="2">
    + <AttributeType name="Address" d:type="string" d:maxLength="55"
        d:minLength="1">
      <attribute type="Name" required="no" />
      <attribute type="Address" required="no" />
      <attribute type="City" required="no" />
      <attribute type="Region" required="no" />
      <attribute type="PostolCode" required="no" />
      <attribute type="Country" required="no" />
    </ElementType>
```

Figure 4-2 *A sample BizTalk specification for a flat file purchase order*

The BizTalk Editor

We have introduced BizTalk specifications; now it's time to use BizTalk Editor (one of the XML-based tools of BizTalk Server 2000) to actually create specifications that fit the needs of some of the specific file formats discussed earlier.

User Interface

Figure 4-3 is a screen shot of BizTalk Editor. Because the underlying specifications created by the BizTalk Editor are XML documents, you can view BizTalk Editor as a specific XML editor that can be used to create BizTalk-specific XML documents (specifications).

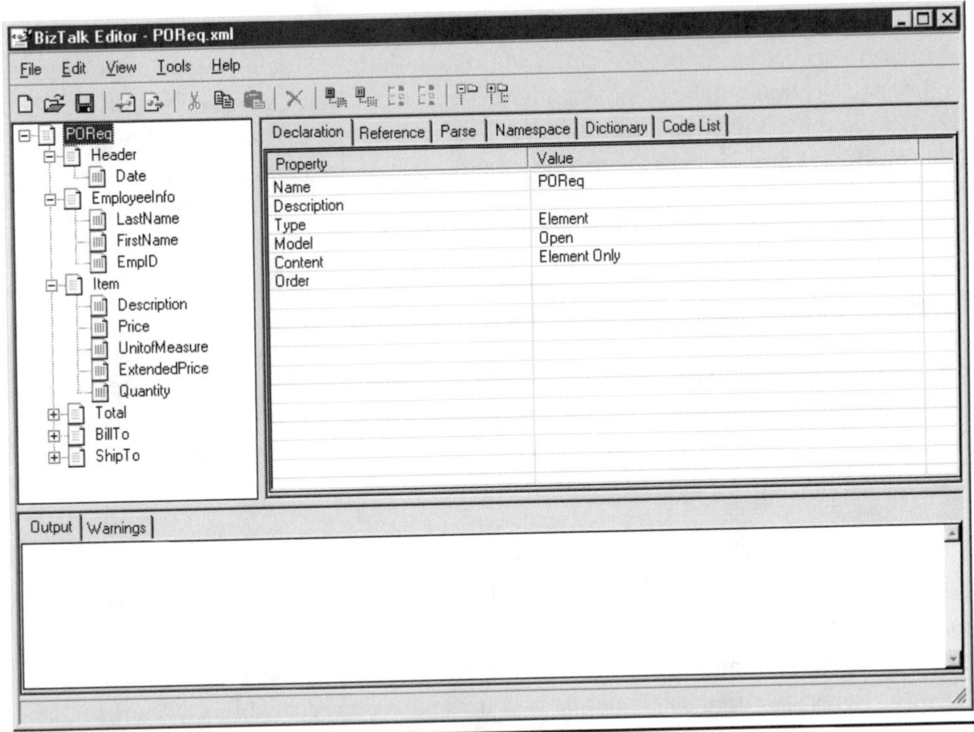

Figure 4-3 *The BizTalk Editor user interface*

As shown in Figure 4-3, BizTalk Editor consists of three panes. The left pane displays the hierarchical structure (called a tree structure) of the underlying specification document, consisting of records and fields. Figure 4-3 displays the structure of a specification for the purchase order request, taken from the BizTalk Server 2000 Tutorial, Module 2—Creating Specifications and Maps. As you can see, the specification tree consists of *records* and *fields*, represented by document icons with horizontal green lines and vertical blue lines, respectively. In the specification, a record is always an XML element, whereas a field can be either an element or an attribute. It is important to understand that records and fields in specifications are designed to work across formats, which means there isn't a one-to-one correlation between elements and attributes and records and fields because we need to handle element-only designs as well as element-attribute designs. In addition, neither the MSXML 3.0 parser nor BizTalk Server 2000 handles mixed-mode content because it's the middle ground between these two and is not a good design. You can use the left pane of BizTalk Editor to create, delete, or rename records and fields. You may also rearrange records and fields by way of drag-and-drop operations. You can even expand or collapse an element in the left pane. In Figure 4-3, the root element (POReq) and three of its child elements (Header, EmployeeInfo, and Item) are expanded, whereas the other elements are collapsed. By default, the new fields you inserted in the specification will be automatically set to attribute. You can change this behavior by clicking the Tools menu option and selecting Options. In the BizTalk Editor Options dialog box, select Create a new field as an element and click OK (see Figure 4-4). This will modify a value in the registry so BizTalk Editor knows what default type should be used for newly inserted fields. You can also change the type for the fields after they are inserted by manipulating the appropriate property in the right top pane, as you will see shortly.

A record can contain fields as well as child records. A field, on the other hand, cannot have any child records, even if the field is an element type. When designing a specification, you should be aware of a couple of aspects about both XML and the MSXML parser used by BizTalk Server 2000 in choosing between elements and attributes for a field:

- **Field ordering** In XML, the sequence of attributes that are not forced by either XDR schema or DTD (see Appendix A). If the ordering of fields is important, consider using elements instead of attributes.
- **Whitespace handling** By default, MSXML parser does not preserve whitespaces for fields specified as elements. If you want to preserve whitespaces for fields, set them as attributes instead of elements. This is especially important for positional flat files in which whitespaces play an important role in identifying and separating fields.

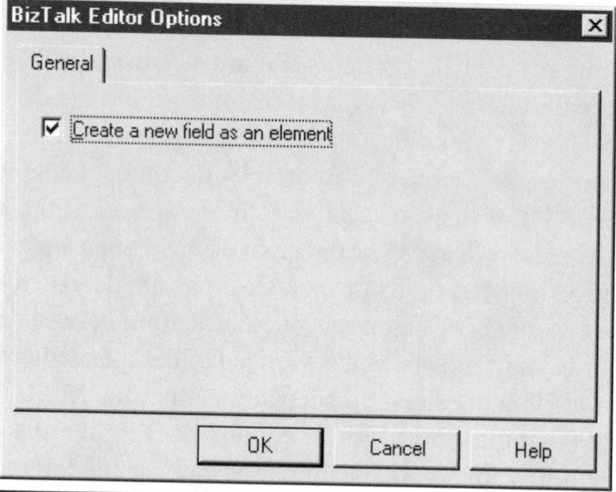

Figure 4-4 *Changing the default field type in BizTalk Editor*

The right top pane of BizTalk Editor is the place where you can set different properties for records and fields. It contains six tabs as shown in Figure 4-3. Depending on the type of specification you are working on (XML, EDI, or flat files) and the type node you are dealing with (record or field), the contents in these tabs vary. Some of the tabs may not be applicable to certain types of specifications. In this section, we will briefly introduce these tabs. Later in this chapter, we will give you more details as we create particular types of specifications.

The Declaration Tab

The information you specified in the Declaration tab defines the XML document for the specification. Most of the properties in this tab are directly mapped to the *ElementType* and *AttributeType* elements of XDR schema (see Appendix A if you are not familiar with XDR schema). According to the node type you are dealing with, appropriate properties are available. Additionally, the choices offered for these individual properties also vary, depending on the node type and specification.

For example, records are *Element Only* type elements. The available properties are Name, Description, Type, Model, Content, and Order, corresponding to the attribute of the ElementType element in XDR schema.

For attribute type fields, available properties may include Name, Description, Type, Data Type, Data Type Values, Minimum Length, Maximum Length, and Default Value. However, some of the properties may be disabled depending on the type of specification.

Available properties for element type fields include Name, Description, Type, Model, Content, Data Type, Data Type Values, Minimum Length and Maximum Length. The Content property is automatically set to *Text Only* and is a read-only property. This is because BizTalk Server 2000 does not support mixed-mode content, as explained earlier.

The Reference Tab

For root elements, the properties in this tab provide information about the characteristics of the specification document. The following table lists the available properties on the Reference tab regarding the different types of specifications:

Property	XML	Flat File (Delimited and Positional)	X12	EDIFACT
Specification Name	Available	Available	Available	Available
Standards Version	Available	Available	Available	Available

Property	XML	Flat File (Delimited and Positional)	X12	EDIFACT
Document Type	Available	Available	Available	Available
Version	Available	Available	Available	Available
Default Record Delimiter		Available		
Default Field Delimiter		Available		
Default SubField Delimiter		Available		
Default Escape Character		Available		
Code Page		Available		
Receipt	Available	Available	Available	Available
Envelope		Available	Default to No	Default to No
Target Namespace	Available	Available	Available	Available

Some of the properties in the preceding table are self-explanatory—for example, Specification Name, Receipt, Envelope, and Target Namespace. Other properties, like the Standard, Standards Version, Document Type, and Version properties, are primarily used to identify the standard information on which an X12 or EDIFACT specification is based. For example, the properties and their values in the following table specify an X12 4010 850 document, used as a purchase order:

Property	Value
Specification Name	X12_4010_850
Standard	X12
Standards Version	4010
Document Type	850
Version	1.0

The Default Record Delimiter, Default Field, Default SubField, Default Escape Character, and Code Page properties are specifically used by flat file specifications (delimited, positioned, or mixed). They provide some global constants for the parser and can be used in the Parse tab, as you will see shortly.

In case of records and fields, the properties on the Reference tab are a lot simpler. Available properties for records are the same across all types of specifications. There are only two of them: Minimum Occurrences and Maximum Occurrences. Most types of specifications have only one property available to their fields: Required, which has two possible values (Yes and No). The only exception is for positional fields, which support two additional properties: Start Position and End Position, that explain to the parser how to parse the record.

The Parse Tab

The Parse tab is only available for flat file specifications and will be disabled for other types of specifications. The properties on the Parse tab provide information to the parser about how to parse fields and records for flat files. We will discuss these properties in more detail later in this chapter as we create flat file specifications.

The Namespace Tab

The Namespace tab is where you can specify custom namespaces. The scope of custom namespaces is dependent on where you declare it. There are three predefined namespaces for every specification, as shown in Figure 4-5.

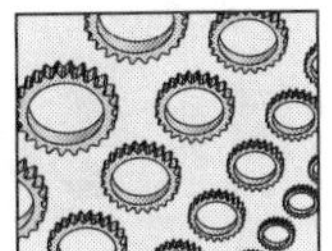

NOTE

See Appendix A for more information about XML namespaces.

The Dictionary Tab

The properties on the Dictionary tab provide a mechanism to identify the document, and specify routing information in the document itself. They also tell the parser in which field a specific piece of information is located.

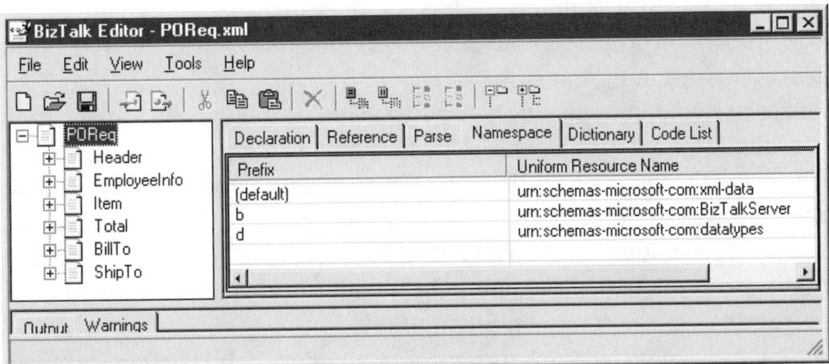

Figure 4-5 *Built-in namespaces for specifications*

As you may recall in the last chapter, we defined routing as a process in which the BizTalk messaging engine locates a specific channel during run-time to process a document. In order to locate a channel, three pieces of information are needed, a document definition, the source (organization or application) and the destination (organization or application).

You may also recall there are several ways in which routing information can be provided to the messaging engine:

- Passing it on as input parameters of the Submit or SubmitSync calls
- Specifying it in the receive definition
- Embedding the routing information in the document itself

You can also split the routing information between one or more of the locations listed in the bullet points. If identical information has been specified in more than one place, the information in the Submit or SubmitSync calls, or in the receive functions, will overwrite the information contained in the other documents.

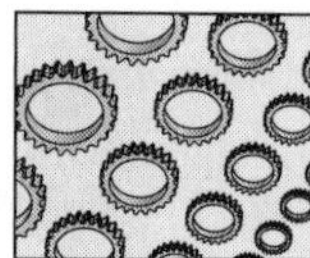

NOTE

Alternatively, you may include the name of the channel either as an input parameter in the Submit or SubmitSync calls or in the receive functions.

Figure 4-6 illustrates the Dictionary tab in the BizTalk Editor.

As shown in Figure 4-6, the Dictionary tab contains six properties. The Document Container Node property is used to identify the document and is only available for record nodes, including the root node. It is used in envelope specifications (i.e., the envelope property on the Reference tab is set to Yes when appropriate). By selecting the check box of this property, you specify that the node is the root node of the document contained in the envelope.

The other five properties on the Dictionary tab are used to specify routing information and are available only to field nodes. The Document Name property specifies the field containing the name of the document. The Source Type and Destination Type properties specify the fields holding the organization qualifier types for source and destination organizations, respectively. The Source Value and Destination Value properties specify the fields containing the organization identifier values for source and destination organizations, respectively.

After you have specified the appropriate properties on the Dictionary tab and saved the specification, the routing information will be saved as XPath expressions in the specification XML document (see Appendix B for more information about the XPath language).

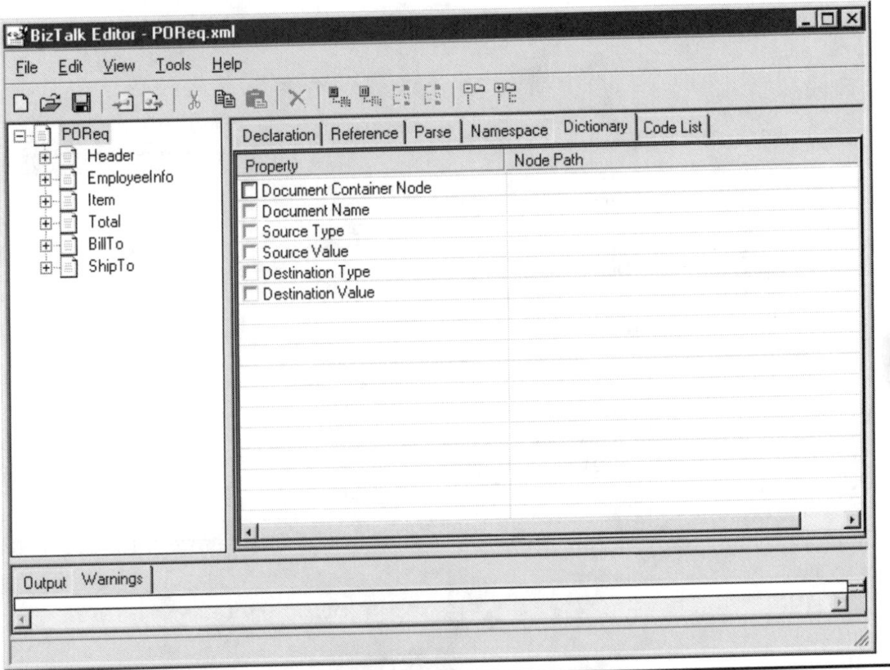

Figure 4-6 *The Dictionary tab in the BizTalk Editor*

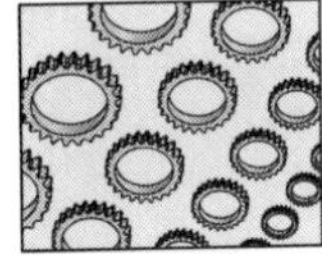

NOTE

Because the properties on the Dictionary tab contain routing information, it makes no sense to allow more than one field in the document to determine a single piece of routing information. As a result, after you have specified one property for a specific field, that property will be disabled for the rest of the fields in the document. If you want to change the selection you made, you have to deselect the field you selected earlier.

The Code List Tab

The Code List tab is specific to X12 and EDIFACT specifications only, being disabled for other types. Figure 4-7 shows the Code List tab for a customized X12 850 specification we will create later in this chapter.

As shown in Figure 4-7, the Code List tab provides a convenient means by which you can build an enumeration of acceptable values from a pre-defined list. In this case, the Code List displays all the available values for the BEG01 field of the BEG record. The values whose check boxes are selected will be added to the specification in syntax appropriate to the enumeration data type of XDR schema (see Appendix A for details regarding the XDR schema).

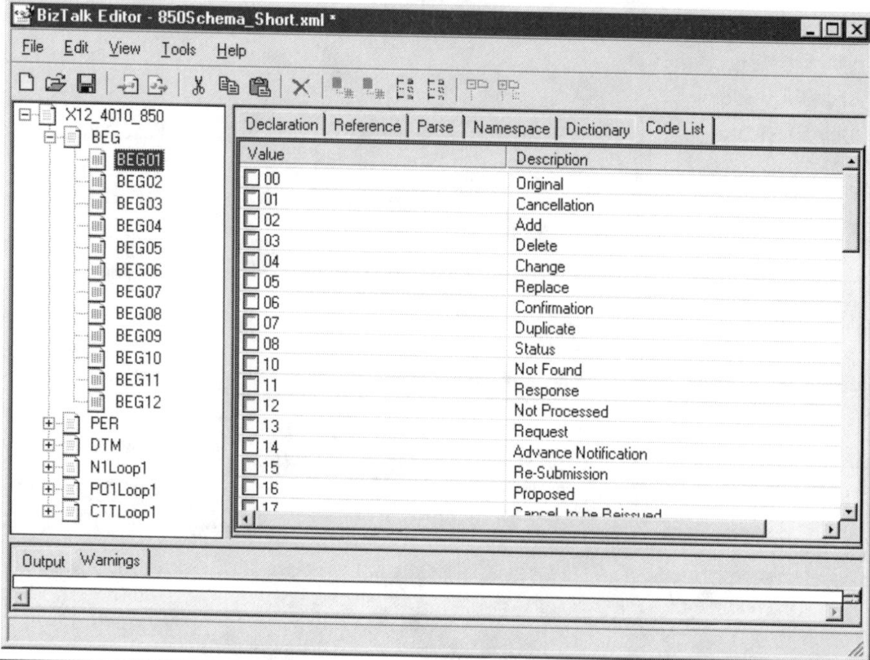

Figure 4-7 *The Code List tab*

The data in the Code List tab of the BizTalk Editor comes from an Access database, CodeListX12a.mdb, located under the <BizTalk Server installation folder>\XML Tools\Databases\CodeLists\ folder. Despite the name of the database, it actually contains code list tables for both X12 and EDIFACT standards.

The bottom pane in BizTalk Editor provides information that helps you debug and test your specifications.

Introducing WebDAV

BizTalk Server 2000 uses WebDAV (Web Distributed Authoring and Versioning) to manage its specifications and maps. WebDAV is an Internet Engineering Task Force (IETF) specification developed as an extension to HTTP 1.1, and provides the following benefits over traditional file management systems:

- **Resource protection** WebDAV provides a resource-locking mechanism to protect resources (e.g., files) from being overwritten by multiple clients.

- **Sophisticated data storage** WebDAV uses the collection object, which provides a means of organizing data more efficiently. A collection in WebDAV is similar to a system file folder. You can create, move, copy, or delete collections as well as files and other documents (such as e-mail) inside a collection.
- **Diversified document types** WebDAV uses XML as a means of storing and retrieving different types of data with unique properties.

By taking advantage of WebDAV, BizTalk Server 2000 provides enhanced protection for its specifications and maps. The specifications and maps you will save shortly using BizTalk Editor and Mapper via WebDAV will be stored under the <BizTalk Server installation folder>\BizTalkServerRepository\<DocSpecs or Maps folder> on the machine where BizTalk Server 2000 is installed. As you will see in the next chapter, the BizTalk Messaging Manager also uses WebDAV to retrieve the specifications and maps.

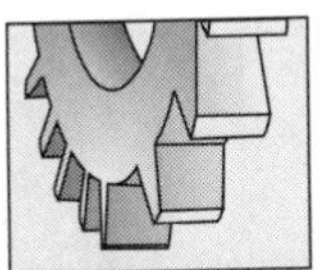

TIP

A full analysis of WebDAV is beyond the scope of this book. To find out more information about WebDAV, visit the IETF WebDAV working group's web site at: http://www.webdav.org.

CAUTION

Simply copying files or folders to the BizTalkServerRepository\DocSpecs or BizTalkServerRepository\Maps folder on the server may not guarantee their retrievability from BizTalk Editor, Mapper, or Messaging Manager. You should always use BizTalk Editor or Mapper to create folders, as well as to store and retrieve specifications and maps using the WebDAV repository.

To retrieve or store a specification in the WebDAV repository in BizTalk Editor, click the Retrieve From WebDAV or Store To WebDAV icon, respectively. Alternatively, you can select File | Retrieve From WebDAV, or File | Store To WebDAV from the menu options. BizTalk Maps works exactly the same way in dealing with WebDAV storage and retrieval. Figure 4-8 illustrates the default look of the Retrieve From WebDAV dialog box opened in BizTalk Editor.

As you can see in Figure 4-8, the filenames of some specifications are truncated. This could be a problem for two specifications with similar names. For example, we see two Employees_... icons but we cannot tell them apart. In this case, you may click the List View button at the top right corner of the dialog box to display the specification documents so they appear with smaller icons and their entire file names shown, as illustrated in Figure 4-9. Here we can see the two Employees_… files are

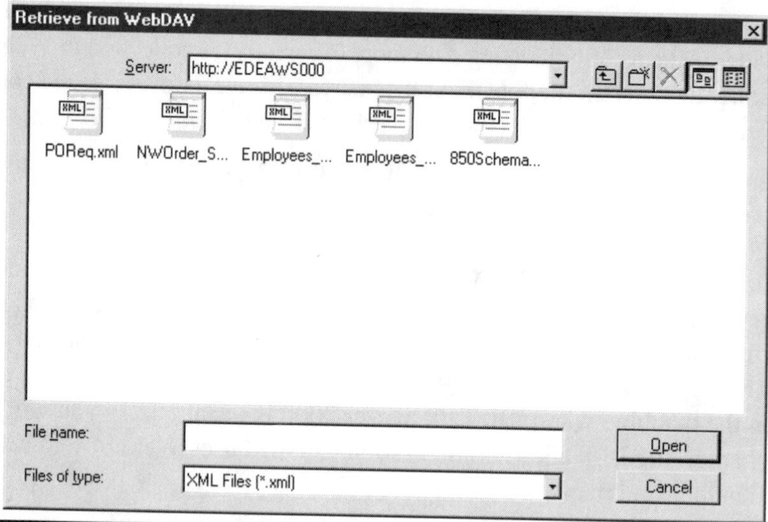

Figure 4-8 *The Retrieve From WebDAV dialog box of BizTalk Editor*

actually Employees_FlatFile.xml and Employees_CSV.xml. (We will create these two flat file specifications in just a moment.)

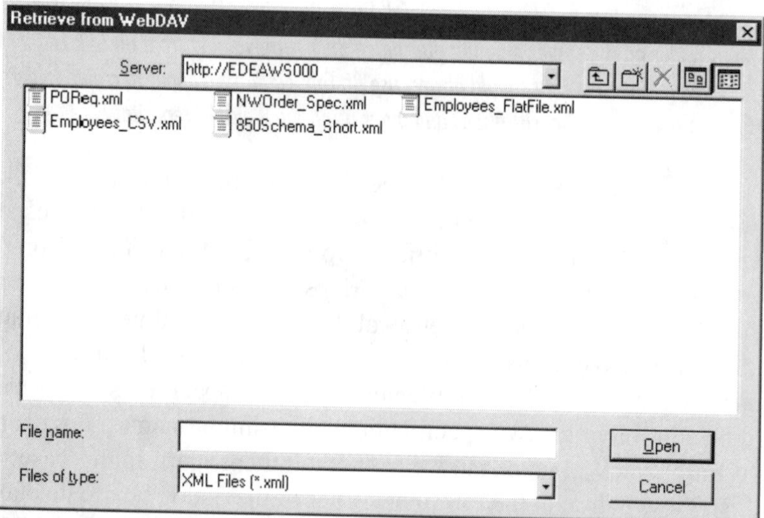

Figure 4-9 *The List View of the Retrieve From WebDAV dialog box*

Creating Specifications

By now, you are familiar enough with BizTalk Editor to put its various concepts into action. We will start off by creating specifications for all the different document types, including XML, flat files, and EDI documents. You can create a specification using BizTalk Editor in several different ways:

- Starting a blank specification from scratch—this method is especially suitable when creating new specifications for flat files.
- Importing from an existing XML document instance, a DTD, or an XDR schema and using it as a starting point. These methods only work for specifications of XML documents.

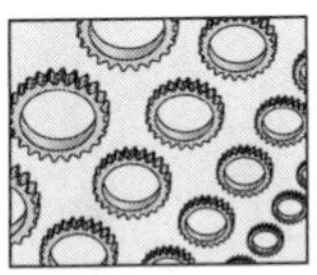

NOTE

When working with a DTD document, if your DTD contains references to external DTDs, you will have to incorporate them into the master DTD document (by copying and pasting, for example) before you can import the DTD document into a specification.

- Starting from one of the templates shipped with BizTalk Server 2000—BizTalk Server ships with the templates of some common documents, such as purchase order templates, invoice templates, and so on. These templates are available for XML, X12, and EDIFACT document formats and are located under the <BizTalk Server install folder>\XML Tools\Templates folder. Templates are especially useful in creating X12 and EDIFACT specifications, as well as common XML specifications.
- Using third party templates, or document specifications outsourced from biztalk.org.

Creating Specifications for XML Documents

Creating a specification for an XML document is straightforward. Because the specification structure is built on top of the XDR schema structure—which itself is a "specification" for XML documents—it defines the structure and validation rules for an XML document. As a result, a pure XDR schema is almost qualified to be a BizTalk specification (in some simple scenarios, it is a specification). Of course, you can also add some BizTalk Server-specific information to the specification, such as the routing information.

Module 2 of the BizTalk Server 2000 Tutorial shows you how to create specifications (and a map) for an XML document. We won't spend time here to discuss how to create specifications for an XML document. Read and follow the BizTalk Server 2000 Tutorial if you need to.

TIP

In addition to creating specifications, BizTalk Editor allows you to export the specification as an XDR schema using only the two base namespaces. The XDR schema you exported from BizTalk Editor removed all the BizTalk specific elements and attributes. You can use BizTalk Editor as a handy tool for creating an XDR schema, as shown in Figure 4-10. Additionally, BizTalk Server 2000 includes a utility by which you can convert an XDR schema to a W3C data schema (XSD). This utility is located under <BizTalk Server installation folder>\SDK\XSDConverter\ folder. The Readme.txt file under this folder contains instructions on how to use the utility.

Creating Specifications for Flat File Documents

Now let's see how to create specifications for flat file documents. First, we will create a specification for a delimited flat file, a purchase order. We will use an

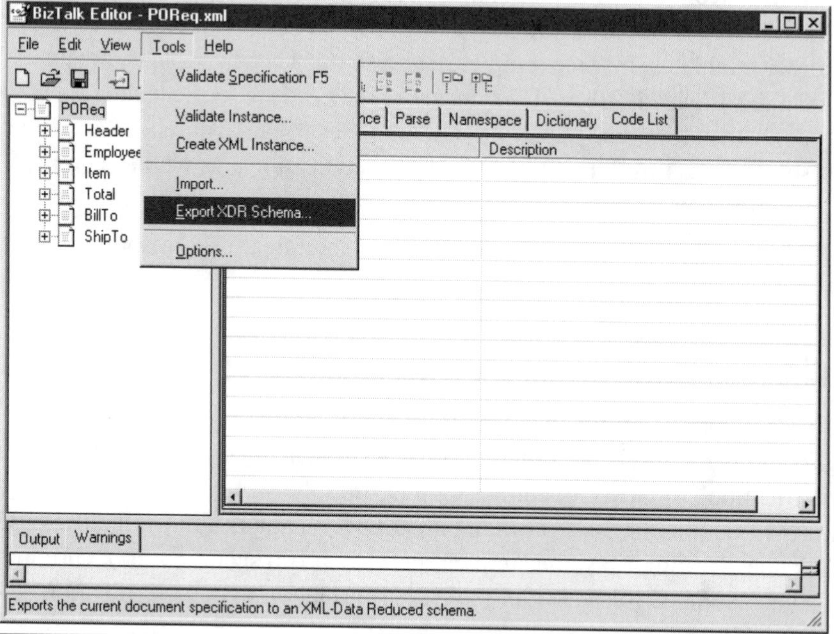

Figure 4-10 *Exporting a specification as an XDR schema*

instance of a data file created by retrieving data of order ID 10262 from the Northwind sample database shipped with SQL Server 7.0 or 2000. The sample data file, NWOrder_10262.dat, can be found on this book's web site. It looks like this:

```
110262,1996-07-22
28,Callahan,Laura
3Chef Anton's Gumbo Mix,21.35,36
3Uncle Bob's Organic Dried Pears,30,12
3Gnocchi di nonna Alice,38,24
4Rattlesnake Canyon Grocery,2817 Milton Dr.,Albuquerque,NM,87110,USA
5Rattlesnake Canyon Grocery,2817 Milton Dr.,Albuquerque,NM,87110,USA
```

The records in this sample data file are delimited by a carriage return character (CR), whereas a field in a record is delimited by commas. The first character of the first field in each record indicates the type of record. For example, 1 indicates the record is a header. A header contains an order ID and a date field. 2 indicates the record represents an employee. An employee record contains three fields, employee ID, last name, and first name. Records starting with 3 are order items. This particular order contains three items. Each item record consists of a product name, unit price, and the quantity ordered. 4 and 5 are Bill To and Ship To address records, respectively.

Knowing the data file's detailed structure information, we're ready to create a specification. Open the BizTalk Editor and select File | New from the menu options, or click the New button on the toolbar (the one with the empty document icon). Select Blank Specification in the New Document Specification dialog box and click OK. Now we have a blank specification with only the one record (the root) with the name BlankSpecification. Change it to NWOrder by single-clicking the root node and directly type **NWOrder** over it. The Name property on the Declaration tab and the Specification Name property on the Reference tab should both be changed to NWOrder now. Click the Reference tab. You will see that the Standard property is set to XML by default. For flat files we need to specify CUSTOM as the standard. To do this, click the Value column in the Standard property row and select CUSTOM from the drop-down list. You will receive a warning from the BizTalk Editor, as shown in Figure 4-11. This is because the type of specification determines what properties should be available, as discussed earlier in this chapter. Click Yes to dismiss the warning box and return to BizTalk Editor.

The record delimiter and field delimiter in our flat data file are carriage return and comma. On the Reference tab, specify "CR" and "," as the Default Record Delimiter and Default Field Delimiter, respectively. Now the Reference tab should look like that in Figure 4-12.

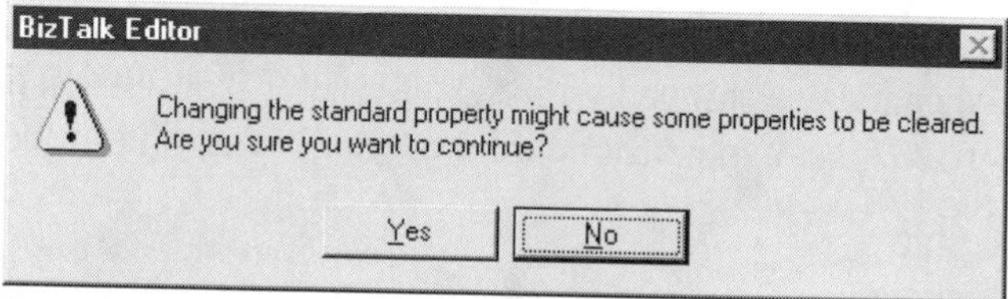

Figure 4-11 *The Warning dialog box of BizTalk Editor*

You may have noticed the Code Page property in Figure 4-12. This property is only available for flat file specifications on the root element. You can set the Code Page property to specify the language used in the document. We will live with the default value, Western-European (1252) for the Code Page property (default values remain blank in the grid). It is worth noting that XML documents are encoded in Unicode.

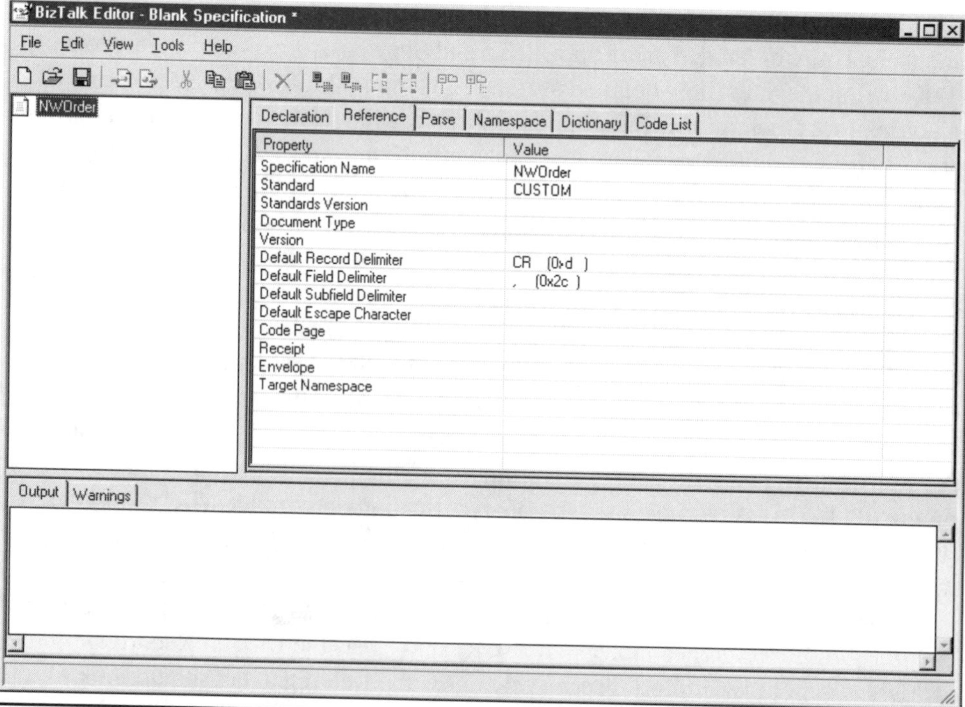

Figure 4-12 *Properties of the root element in the Reference tab*

Now click the Parse tab. The properties you specified in this tab provide information to the appropriate parsers in BizTalk Server 2000. Click the Value column of the Structure property and select Delimited. You will see another BizTalk Editor warning box, similar to the one in Figure 4-11, which appears for the same reason—click Yes to ignore it. Then set the Field Order property to Postfix. This will tell the BizTalk Server flat file parser that the record delimiters will appear at the end of each record.

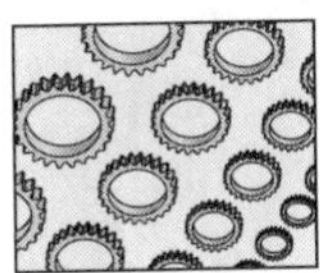

NOTE

An example of Postfix for the Field Order would be "1,2,3,"; the commas acting as field delimiters. Infix takes the form of "1,2,3", while Prefix would be ",1,2,3". A common error BizTalk developers make is forgetting to set the Field Order property (the default is Prefix) or setting it to a wrong value.

Also, set the Delimiter Type property to Default Record Delimiter so the parser will use the <CR> you specified in the Reference tab as the record delimiter. Now set three more properties as described in the following table and leave the rest of the properties to their defaults (leave them blank in the grid):

Property	Value	Comments
Append Newline	Yes	This will tell the BizTalk Server serializer to automatically append a new line character to the end of each record.
Skip Carriage Return	No	This property tells the BizTalk Server serializer to skip CR and LF characters in the file. Because CR acts as a record delimiter, this property should be set to No.
Skip Line Feed	Yes	Set this property to Yes. Because the record delimiter is CR, additional LF characters will be ignored by the BizTalk serializer. Setting this property is necessary because BizTalk can only handle single delimiters, and the second one will need to be skipped.

The Parse tab should now look like the one in Figure 4-13.

Now add a record under the root record by right-clicking the NWOrder node and selecting New Record. Set its properties according to the following:

Declaration Tab Properties:

Name = Header

Reference Tab Properties:

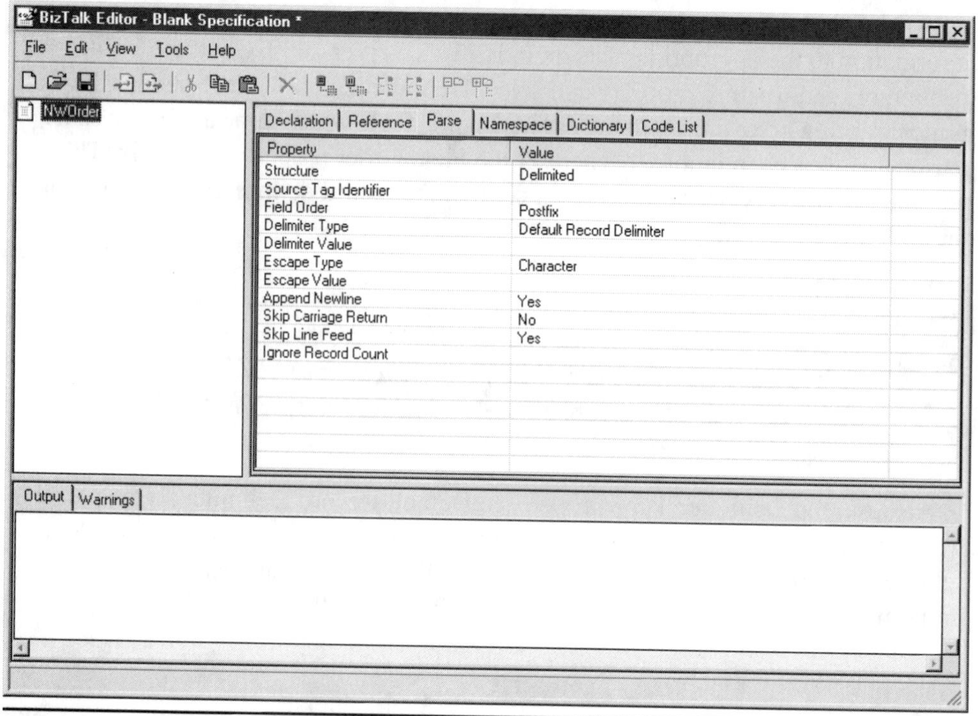

Figure 4-13 *The properties of the root element in the Parse tab*

Minimum Occurrence = 1

Maximum Occurrence = 1

Parse Tab Properties:

Structure = Delimited

Source Tag Identifier = 1

Field Order = Infix

Delimiter Type = Default Field Delimiter

Append New Line = Yes

Skip Carriage Return = Yes

Skip Line Feed = Yes

Notice that on the Parse tab we set the Source Tag Identifier property to 1, meaning it's the first character of the header record in the data file (as we explained earlier). We set the Field Order property to Infix, because the commas were placed between the fields.

Now we can add two fields to the new Header record. Right-click the Header record and select New Field. Repeat it to create another new field. Name the two new fields **OrderID** and **OrderDate**, respectively, and set the Required property on the Reference tab to Yes for both fields. Set the properties for these two fields on the Declaration tab as follows:

OrderID Properties:

Name = OrderID

Type = Attribute

DataType = String

Minimum Length = 1

Maximum Length = 10

OrderDate Properties:

Name = OrderDate

Type = Attribute

DataType = Date

In similar fashion, add the remaining records and fields to the specification and set the appropriate properties. The finished specification should look like the one in Figure 4-14.

To save the file to a disk drive, click the File menu and select Save As. Type **NWOrder_Spec.xml** as the filename and select a folder where you want to save the specification file. To store it to the BizTalk Server WebDAV repository, click the Store To WebDAV button on the toolbar and click the Add New Folder button (the second button to the right of the Server textbox on the Store To WebDAV dialog

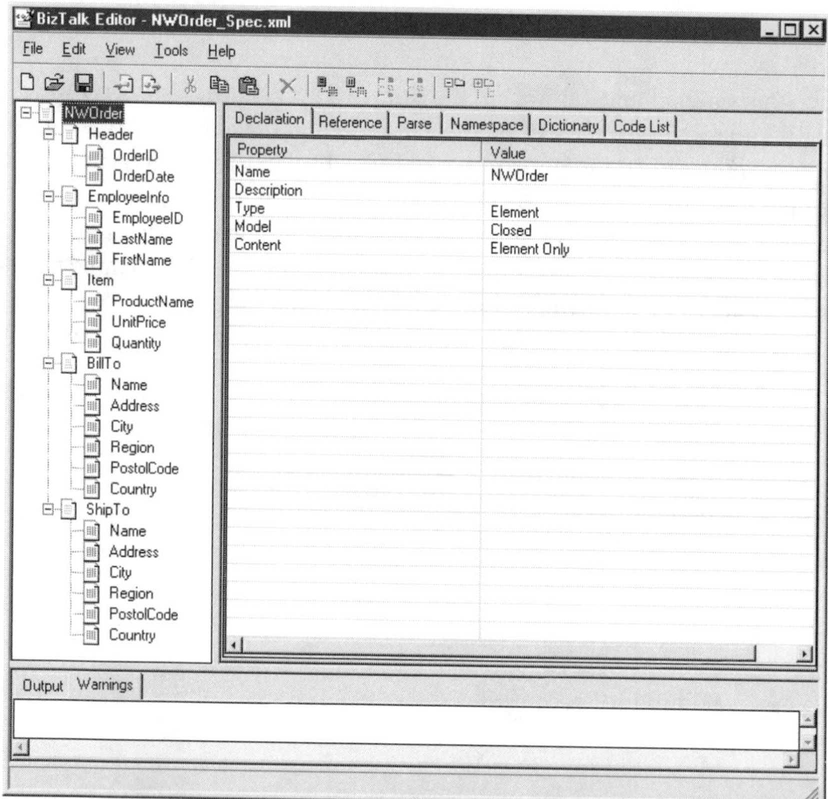

Figure 4-14 *The complete NWOrder flat file specification*

box) and name it **Northwind**. Click the newly created folder to open it, then click the Save button to save the file to the WebDAV repository.

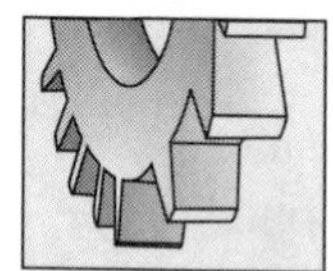

TIP

You can get the sample file, named NWOrder_Spec.xml, from this book's web site.

To test the specification, click the Tools menu and select Validate Instance. In the Validate Document Instance dialog box, select All Files (*.*) in the Files Of Type box and browse to the location where you saved the NWOrder_10262.dat file. Select the file and click Open. If everything went well, the message in the Warnings tab of the bottom pane in BizTalk Editor should state the document instance validation succeeded and will suggest you click the Output tab to view the generated XML instance. Figure 4-15 shows the intermediate XML version of the purchase order request on the Output tab.

If something went wrong, look at the messages displayed on the Warnings tab for information that can be used to help you troubleshoot the problem. For example, there are three ordered items in the data file; if you forgot to set the Maximum Occurrence property of the Item record to * (the default will be 1) and tried to validate the NWOrder_10262.dat file against the specification, you will get an error in the Warnings tab saying that "Additional data in the document instance was not parsed. Make sure that the document you want to validate contains only one document".

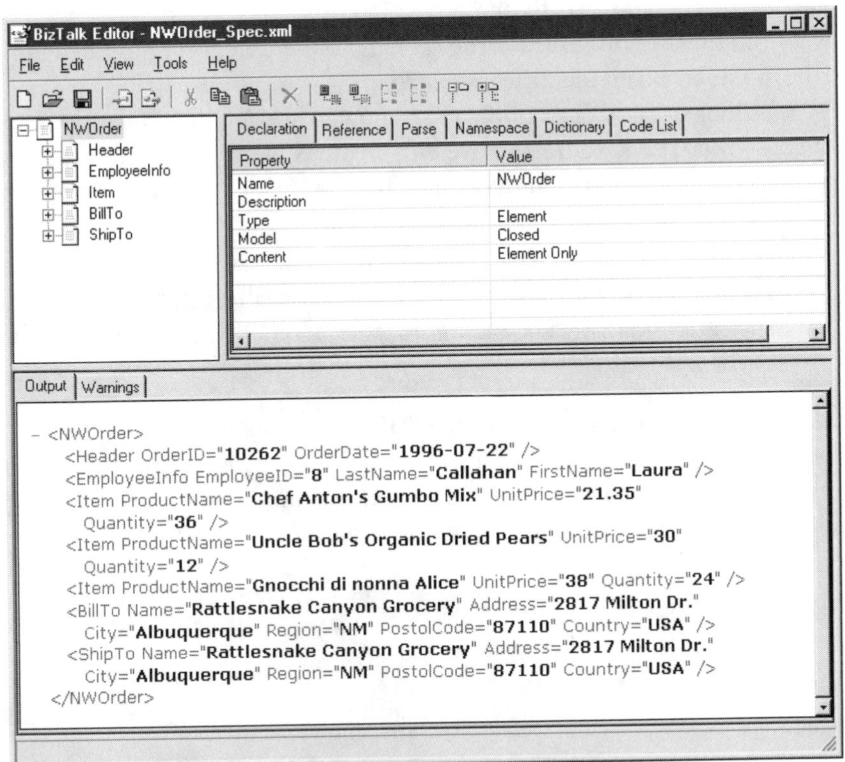

Figure 4-15 *The Output tab showing the generated XML instance after a successful validation*

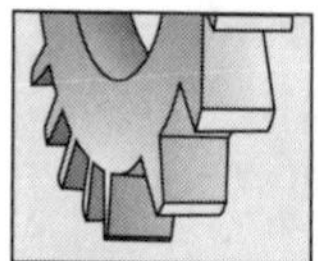

TIP

The validate document command is also useful when applied against document instances that have been dropped into the suspended queue for failing to be parsed. You can re-load and try to validate them in the BizTalk Editor, make changes and then re-validate until you have identified/fixed the problem.

The flat file purchase order request file contains irregular records (i.e., each type of record has different fields). In this case, you need to identify different records to the default record delimiter (CR) by other means. That's where the Source Tag Identifier property on the Parse tab comes in (see Figure 4-13). It provides additional information for the parser to identify specific record types.

There are other flat files in which the formats of records are uniform (i.e., each record in the file contains exactly the same kind of fields). The two Northwind employees flat files we discussed earlier belong to this category. For this kind of flat file, no Source Tag Identifier is needed.

Now, let's look at another example to see how to create a specification for a positional flat file. The specification we will create is based on the file structure of the positional Northwind employees data file you saw earlier in this chapter.

TIP

We have included both the delimited and positional Northwind employee files (employees.csv and employees.dat), and their specifications, in the source code of this chapter, which can be downloaded from this book's web site.

Open a new Blank Specification in BizTalk Editor and change the name of the root record to Employees_FlatFile. On the Reference tab, change the Standard property to CUSTOM and set CR as the Default Record Delimiter. Click the Parse tab and set the following properties, leaving defaults for the rest:

Property	Value
Standard	Delimited
Field Order	Postfix
Delimited Type	Default Record Delimiter

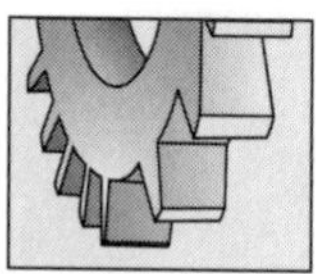

TIP

You may wonder why we set the properties for a positional flat file as the delimited type. This is because a positional record must always be a child of a delimited record. Records in a positional flat file are also separated by delimiters (or terminators).

Now create an Employee record under the root record and set its properties to match the following:

Reference Tab:

Minimum Occurrence = 0

Maximum Occurrence = *

Parse Tab:

Structure = Positional

We set the Structure property of the Employee record to Positional to tell the BizTalk flat file parser that the fields in a record should be identified by their positions. Let's go ahead and create three fields under the Employee record, EmployeeID, FirstName, and LastName. The Type properties for all fields are set to Attribute and the Required properties are set to Yes.

Next, we need to specify the position information (starting and ending positions) so the parser knows how to deal with the fields in a record as described in the following table. Recall that each field is exactly ten characters long.

Field	Start Position	End Position
EmployeeID	1	10
FirstName	11	20
LastName	21	30

There are two ways to specify position information:

1. Type in the values for the Start Position and End Position properties on the Reference tab, as specified in the preceding table.
2. Specify the Data Type property as String, and set the Maximum Length properties for each field to 10 on the Declaration tab. Next, right-click the Employee record and select Calculate Field Positions.

Now save the specification to WebDAV and name it **Employees_FlatFile.xml**. You can use the Employees.dat instance file to validate the specification, as shown in Figure 4-16. It is worth noting that as part of the validation, we parsed the file and converted it into XML.

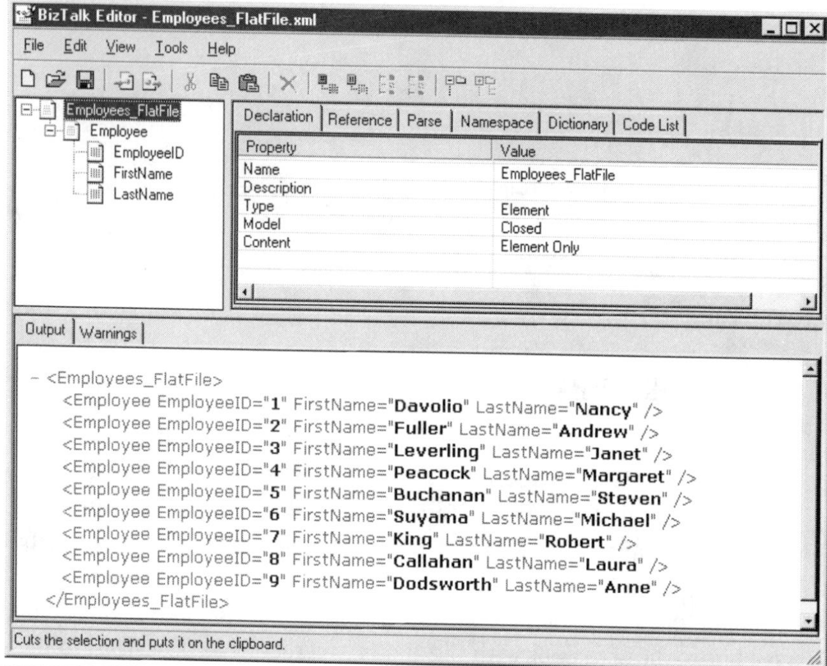

Figure 4-16 *Validating the Employees.dat instance against the positional flat file specification*

TIP

In the source code download for this chapter, we also included the specification file (Employees_CSV.xml) and the corresponding instant data file (Employees.csv) so you can practice creating and validating delimited flat files.

Creating Specifications for EDI Documents

To create a specification for an EDI (X12 or EDIFACT) document, start with one of the templates included in the BizTalk Server installation and then remove unused records and fields in it to fit the agreed document requirements between you and your business trading partner (in EDI, trading partners typically use only a subset of the overall functionality). You can also define your own EDI documents, or get them from a third party vendor or a public repository, such as www.xmledi-group.org. The templates contain the complete standard specifications, and are usually very lengthy (a typical X12 standard is longer than 200 printed pages).

In the following example, we will create a specification for an X12 850 purchase order document, of a type you saw earlier in this chapter (Figure 4-2).

Start the BizTalk Editor, click the File menu and select New. In the New Document Specification dialog box, double-click the X12 folder, then the 4010 folder. You should see dozens of templates available. Click the View List button if the template filenames were truncated. Select the 850Schema.xml file and click OK. The X12_4010_850 specification template will be loaded in BizTalk Editor. Before we start modifying the specification, save it to a local disk drive and name the file **850Schema_Short.xml** so it won't be inadvertently mixed up with the template itself.

After saving a copy of the template, remove all records except the ones that will be used. The finished specification should look like the one in Figure 4-17.

If you want to validate the specification, you need to create a subset of the EDI document by removing the header and trailer parts, and leaving only the body (refer to Figure 4-2). You also need to specify the appropriate delimiters as shown in Figure 4-18.

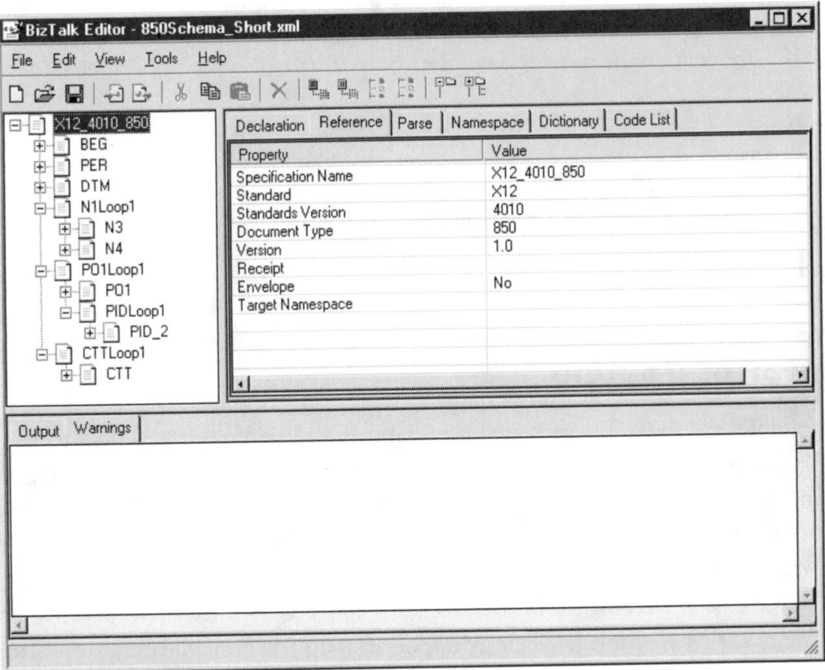

Figure 4-17 *An X12 4010 850 purchase order specification*

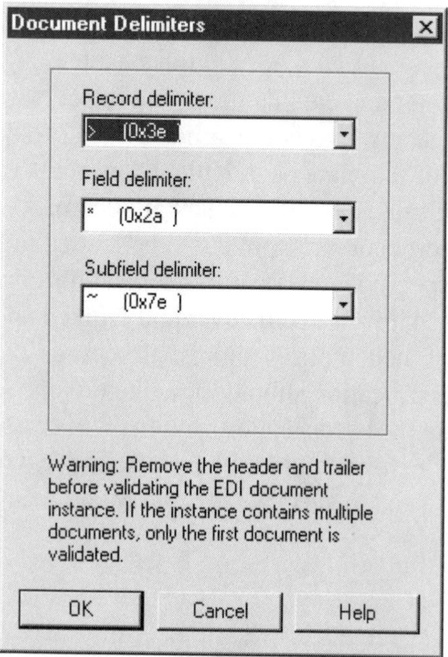

Figure 4-18 *Specifying document delimiters before validating an X12 specification*

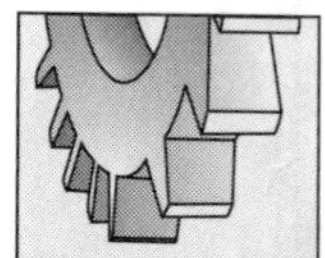

TIP

In addition to selecting the ones from the list, you can also type in other delimiters (e.g., 0x12—which is a non-printable character).

Chapter in Review

In this chapter, we have discussed specifications and demonstrated how to use BizTalk Editor to create specifications of different formats, including XML, flat files, and X12 formats. Specifications are extended XDR documents used to define the structure and validation rules for XML and non-XML documents used by BizTalk Server messaging services. Specifications are the basis for document definitions and in some cases, envelopes. In the next chapter, you will learn how to use another BizTalk Server XML tool, BizTalk Mapper, to map (or translate) one specification onto another.

CHAPTER

5

Mapping Specifications

IN THIS CHAPTER:

Introducing Maps and BizTalk Mapper

Links and Functoids

Creating Maps

Chapter in Review

In the last chapter, you learned what specifications are and how to create them in a variety of different formats using BizTalk Editor. In this chapter, you will learn how to use another important BizTalk Server XML tool—BizTalk Mapper—to create *maps* that translate the format of one specification (the source specification) to the format of the other specification (the destination specification).

Introducing Maps and BizTalk Mapper

Recall that in Chapter 3, we explained that when the inbound and outbound documents in a channel have different structures, you need a map to transform the structure of the inbound document to the outbound document. So, what is a map? What does it look like? And how does BizTalk Server 2000 use maps to perform transformations?

Maps

A map is an XML document that provides information regarding both source and destination specifications, as well as instructions on how to transform documents that meet source specifications into documents that meet the destination specifications.

The Structure of a Map

Figure 5-1 illustrates a high-level map displaying all the top-level elements, which in this rendering are collapsed.

As shown in Figure 5-1, a map is an XML document that contains a root element <mapsource>. The <srctree> and <sinktree> elements are embedded source and destination specifications, respectively. Figure 5-2 illustrates part of the embedded

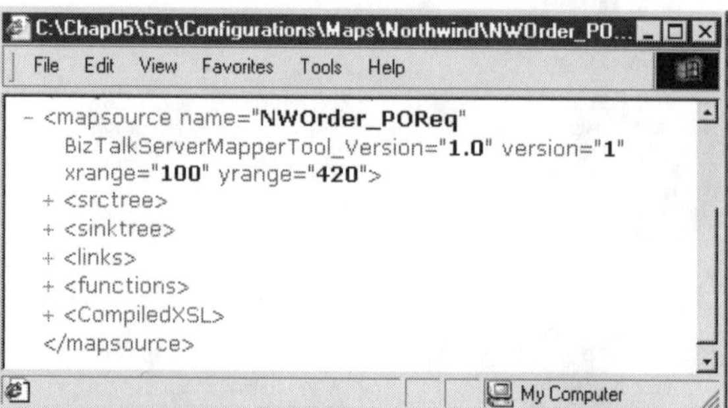

Figure 5-1 *A collapsed map displayed in Internet Explorer*

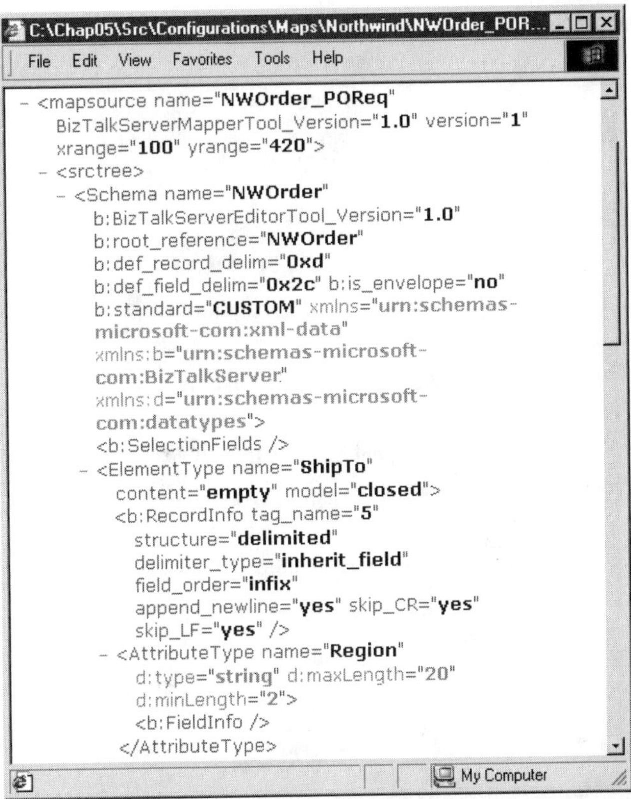

Figure 5-2 *The partially displayed source specification embedded in the map*

specification NWOrder, under the <Schema> element. Recall that this is a specification you created in the last chapter defining the structure of a flat file purchase order request using BizTalk Editor. The specification contains XDR elements (<Element>, <Attribute>, etc.), as well as elements under the BizTalk namespace (<b:RecordInfo>, <b:FieldInfo>, etc).

The <links> element and <functions> element contain <link> elements and <function> elements, respectively. The <link> elements store information about *links* whereas the <function> elements store information about *functoids*. Links and functoids are objects you created using BizTalk Mapper. The former define the relationships and correspondences between the nodes (elements and fields) of the source and destination specifications; the latter are built-in reusable functions that enable complex structural manipulation operations between nodes of source

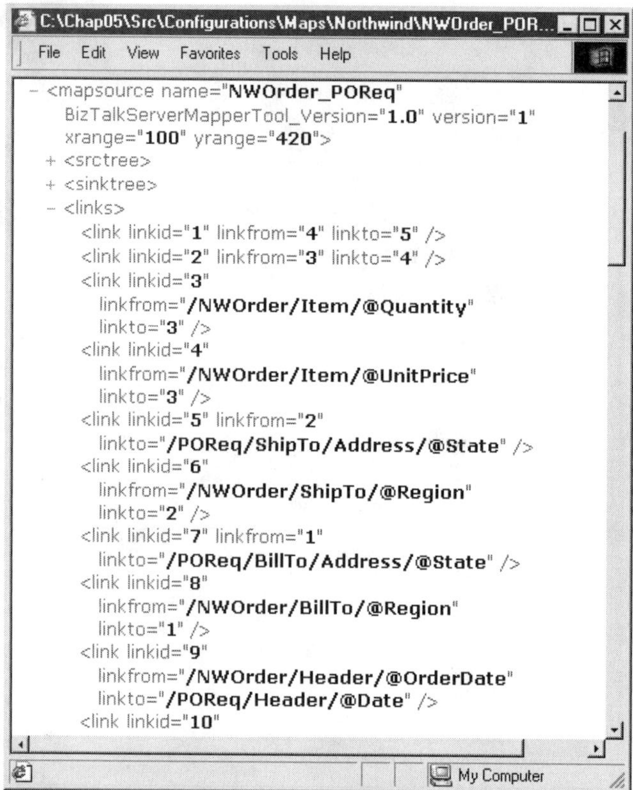

Figure 5-3 *The link elements in the map*

and destination specifications, as well as other functoids. We will discuss links and functoids in more detail later in this chapter. Figure 5-3 shows some expanded <link> elements, while Figure 5-4 displays some <function> elements.

The last top-level element in a map document is the <CompiledXSL> element, which encloses an embedded XSLT document, as shown in Figure 5-5. BizTalk Server maps rely on this embedded XSLT document to perform the transformation from the source specification to the destination specification. Everything above the <CompiledXSL> element in the map document contains information used by BizTalk Mapper to display the map graphically in its user interface, and to generate the embedded XSLT document, known as a compiled XSL document. During run time, the BizTalk Server 2000 messaging engine invokes the XSLT processor of the MSXML parser and uses this embedded XSL document to perform the transformation.

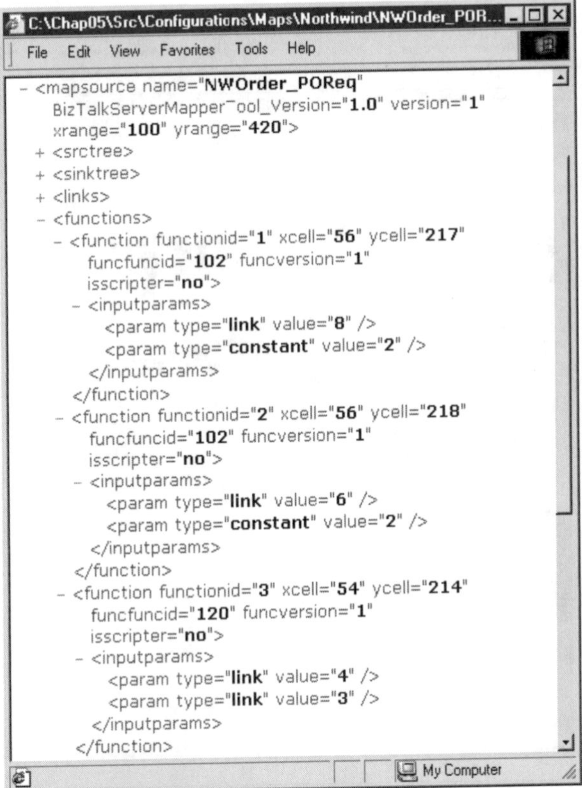

```
- <mapsource name="NWOrder_POReq"
    BizTalkServerMapperTool_Version="1.0" version="1"
    xrange="100" yrange="420">
  + <srctree>
  + <sinktree>
  + <links>
  - <functions>
    - <function functionid="1" xcell="56" ycell="217"
        funcfuncid="102" funcversion="1"
        isscripter="no">
      - <inputparams>
          <param type="link" value="8" />
          <param type="constant" value="2" />
        </inputparams>
      </function>
    - <function functionid="2" xcell="56" ycell="218"
        funcfuncid="102" funcversion="1"
        isscripter="no">
      - <inputparams>
          <param type="link" value="6" />
          <param type="constant" value="2" />
        </inputparams>
      </function>
    - <function functionid="3" xcell="54" ycell="214"
        funcfuncid="120" funcversion="1"
        isscripter="no">
      - <inputparams>
          <param type="link" value="4" />
          <param type="link" value="3" />
        </inputparams>
      </function>
```

Figure 5-4 *The function elements in the map*

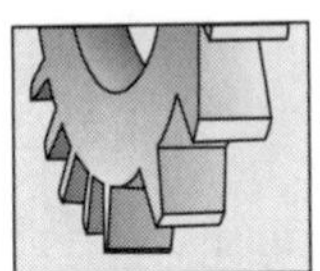

TIP

BizTalk Server 2000 stores maps in the Messaging Management Database (in the bts_xmlshare table of the InterchangeBTM database). During run time, the BizTalk messaging engine loads the map with an embedded XSLT document from the database, then stores the cache in memory, instead of reading the XSLT document from the file system, to improve performance.

The Mapping Process

It is important to understand that the product of the XSL Transformation (XSLT) process is an intermediate XML representation (as defined by the schema of the destination specification) and may or may not be in the native format required by the destination organization. BizTalk Server 2000 uses an appropriate serializer to translate the output document from this intermediate XML document to the required

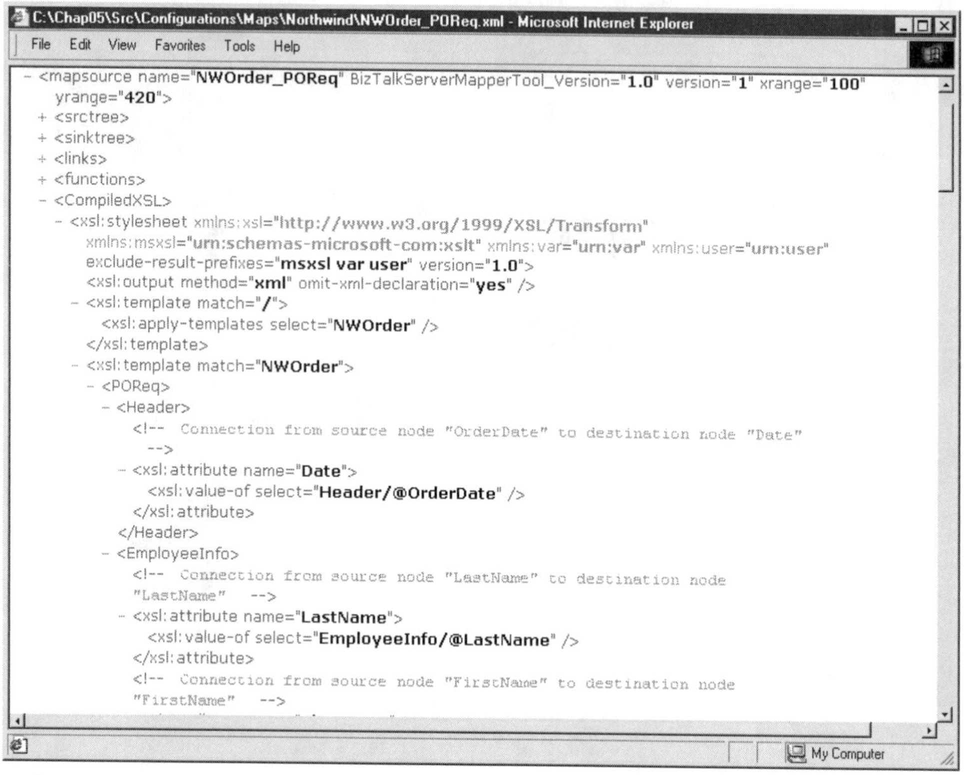

```
C:\Chap05\Src\Configurations\Maps\Northwind\NWOrder_POReq.xml - Microsoft Internet Explorer
File  Edit  View  Favorites  Tools  Help
- <mapsource name="NWOrder_POReq" BizTalkServerMapperTool_Version="1.0" version="1" xrange="100"
    yrange="420">
  + <srctree>
  + <sinktree>
  + <links>
  + <functions>
  - <CompiledXSL>
    - <xsl:stylesheet xmlns:xsl="http://www.w3.org/1999/XSL/Transform"
        xmlns:msxsl="urn:schemas-microsoft-com:xslt" xmlns:var="urn:var" xmlns:user="urn:user"
        exclude-result-prefixes="msxsl var user" version="1.0">
        <xsl:output method="xml" omit-xml-declaration="yes" />
      - <xsl:template match="/">
          <xsl:apply-templates select="NWOrder" />
        </xsl:template>
      - <xsl:template match="NWOrder">
        - <POReq>
          - <Header>
              <!-- Connection from source node "OrderDate" to destination node "Date"
                -->
            - <xsl:attribute name="Date">
                <xsl:value-of select="Header/@OrderDate" />
              </xsl:attribute>
            </Header>
          - <EmployeeInfo>
              <!-- Connection from source node "LastName" to destination node
              "LastName" -->
            - <xsl:attribute name="LastName">
                <xsl:value-of select="EmployeeInfo/@LastName" />
              </xsl:attribute>
              <!-- Connection from source node "FirstName" to destination node
              "FirstName" -->
My Computer
```

Figure 5-5 *The embedded XSLT document under the CompiledXSL element*

native format. BizTalk Server provides serializers for four known formats—XML, X12, EDIFACT, and flat file. To serialize the output file to other formats, you need to create custom serializers using the *IBizTalkSerializerComponent* interface. Similarly, if the native format of the inbound document submitted to BizTalk Server is not in an XML format, BizTalk Server uses an appropriate parser to parse the document into the intermediate XML document format (as defined by the schema of the source specification). Like in the serializing scenarios, if the native format of the inbound document does not fall into the four supported formats (XML, X12, EDIFACT and flat file), you need to create a custom parser using the *IBizTalkParser Component* interface. In addition, envelopes are needed in case of custom parsers and/or serializers. Figure 5-6 illustrates the process of how an inbound document is parsed, transformed, and serialized into the outbound document by BizTalk Server Messaging Services.

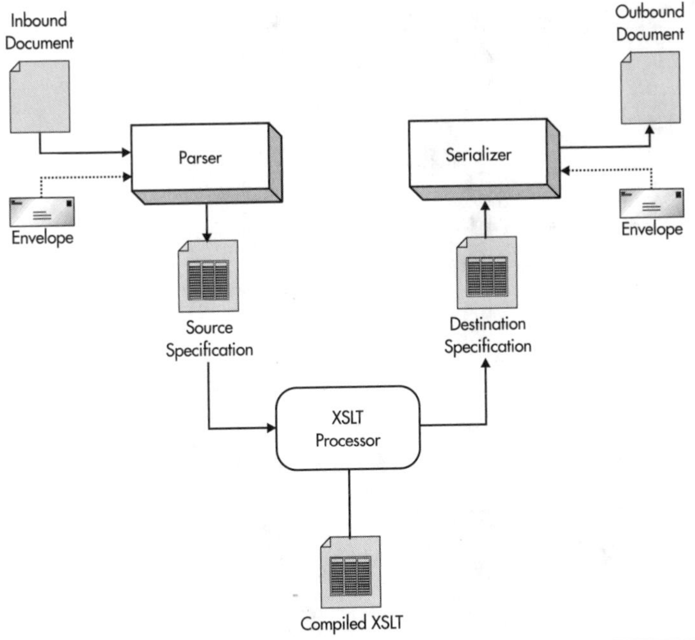

Figure 5-6 *The process of mapping*

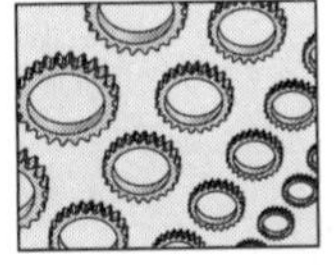

NOTE

We will discuss custom parsers and serializers in Chapter 11.

BizTalk Mapper

BizTalk Mapper is an XML tool provided in BizTalk Server 2000 that enables you to create and manipulate maps. Figure 5-7 is a screen shot of the BizTalk Mapper user interface. It displays the map document we saw in Figure 5-1. Later in this chapter, you will create this map. In the meantime, let's get familiar with the user interface of BizTalk Mapper.

As shown in Figure 5-7, the user interface of BizTalk Mapper consists of two major areas, an upper pane and a lower pane. On the left side of the upper pane is a tree view of the source specification created in the editor, which can be in any of the supported file formats (XML, flat file, X12, EDIFACT, and custom formats). In this example, the source specification is the NWOrder.xml specification you created in the last chapter. On the right side of the upper pane is a tree view of the destination

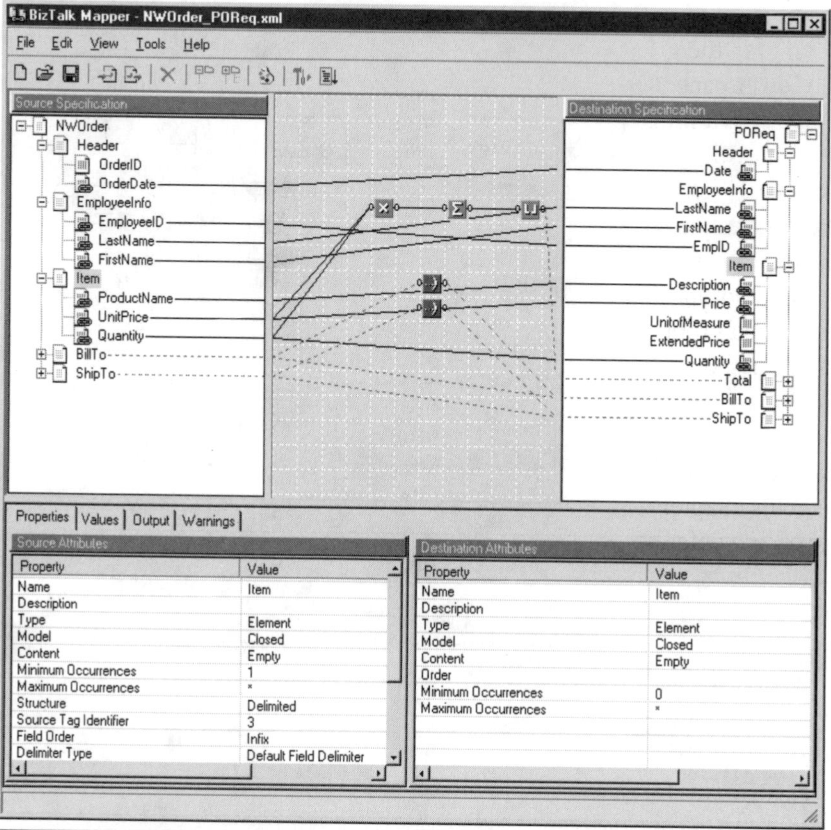

Figure 5-7 *The BizTalk Mapper user interface*

specification. Here we adapted the POReq.xml specification by changing the Maximum Occurrence property of the Item record from 1 to * to fit our needs (in our source specification, the corresponding Item record has the Maximum Occurrence property set to * to allow multiple items in a single order).

Between the two specifications is the mapping grid that graphically displays the structural data transformation between the two specifications. The mapping grid is also a spot where you can place functoids (you can see five functoids displayed in Figure 5-7). You can move around in the mapping grid by placing the mouse pointer close to one of the four edges where it will change to a big white arrow. Clicking and holding down the left mouse button will cause the mapping grid to move in the direction the big white arrow pointed to. You can also use Grid Preview to assist in navigation, which can be extremely helpful when you have many functoids. To use the Grid Preview, right-click anywhere in the mapping grid and select Grid Preview.

The Grid Preview window displays where functoids are located in the mapping grid. You can drag the green locator bar to a new location on the Grid Preview dialog box.

The lower pane in BizTalk Mapper consists of four tabs—Properties, Values, Output, and Warnings. On the Properties tab, two property grids are placed in parallel. They display the properties of the highlighted records and/or fields of the source and destination specifications, respectively.

The data displayed in the Properties tab of BizTalk Mapper is consolidated and abstracted information from the original specification you created in BizTalk Editor, which are appropriate for the purposes of mapping. They provide a convenient view of the related properties that help you identify the appropriate records and/or fields when you associate them together. These properties are read-only in BizTalk Mapper.

The Values tab contains two textboxes as shown in Figure 5-8. The Source Test Value box on the left side allows you to test the map by typing in some test values for different fields and checking the results on the Output tab (as we will demonstrate later in this chapter). The Destination Constant Value box on the right side allows you to assign default values (constants) to the fields of the outbound document. This box will only be enabled for those fields in the destination specifications that do not have any links or functoids associated with them, and whose Content property is set to Text Only in the destination specification. Just as you cannot add constant values to destination fields and records, neither can you create links to the fields or records that have constant values assigned to them. Because both links and constant values serve as the sources for destination fields and records, you cannot have both at the same time.

TIP

The values you typed in the Values tab of BizTalk Mapper will be saved under a <Value> element, and placed between the <srctree> and <sinktree> elements. The value you entered in the Source test value box will be stored under the <TestValues> subelements in the saved map. They won't go to the compiled XSLT stylesheet (the <CompiledXSL> element). The values you entered in the Destination constant value, on the other hand, will be stored under the <ConstantValue> subelement and likewise compiled in the <CompiledXSL> element.

Properties | Values | Output | Warnings

Source test value:

Destination constant value:

Figure 5-8 *The Values tab of BizTalk Mapper*

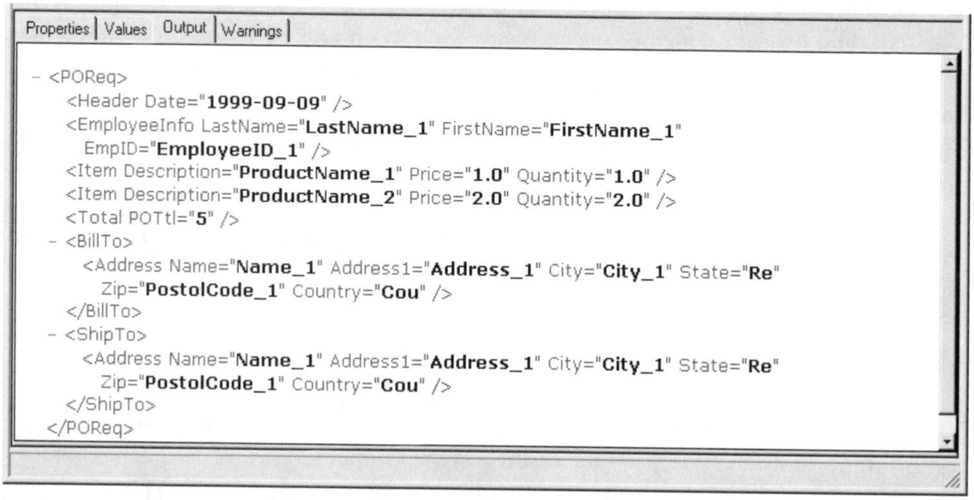

Properties | Values | Output | Warnings

```
- <POReq>
    <Header Date="1999-09-09" />
    <EmployeeInfo LastName="LastName_1" FirstName="FirstName_1"
      EmpID="EmployeeID_1" />
    <Item Description="ProductName_1" Price="1.0" Quantity="1.0" />
    <Item Description="ProductName_2" Price="2.0" Quantity="2.0" />
    <Total POTtl="5" />
  - <BillTo>
      <Address Name="Name_1" Address1="Address_1" City="City_1" State="Re"
        Zip="PostolCode_1" Country="Cou" />
    </BillTo>
  - <ShipTo>
      <Address Name="Name_1" Address1="Address_1" City="City_1" State="Re"
        Zip="PostolCode_1" Country="Cou" />
    </ShipTo>
  </POReq>
```

Figure 5-9 *The Output tab of BizTalk Mapper*

The Output tab will display either a compiled XSLT stylesheet of the map or an XML instance of the destination specification, depending on whether you are compiling or testing the map. Figure 5-9 illustrates an instance of the destination specification of a tested map.

The Warnings tab will report the results of testing or compiling the map. It is similar to the Warnings tab in BizTalk Editor you learned about in the last chapter.

Most of the buttons on BizTalk Mapper's toolbar are similar to those in BizTalk Editor. The unique buttons to BizTalk Mapper include View Functoid Palette (with a paint brush in the icon), Compile Map (with a hammer, a screw driver, and a small triangle in the icon) and Test Map (with a document and a down arrow in the icon). Clicking the View Functoid Palette button will open the Functoid Palette dialog with built-in functoids grouped into different tabs according to different categories as we will discuss shortly in this chapter. Clicking the Compile Map button causes the BizTalk Mapper to generate an XSLT stylesheet according to the instructions set in the upper pane of BizTalk Mapper, and displayed in Output tab stylesheet. This XSLT stylesheet is called the Compiled XSL stylesheet and will be embedded inside the <CompiledXSL> element of the saved map document (clicking the Save button will automatically trigger the same compilation process). The BizTalk Server messaging engine uses this compiled XSLT stylesheet to perform the transformation. The Warnings tab reports whether the compilation was successful and alerts you to any potential problems encountered during the compilation. These actions are also available from the menu options, such as View (Functoid Palette) and Tools (Compile Map or Test Map).

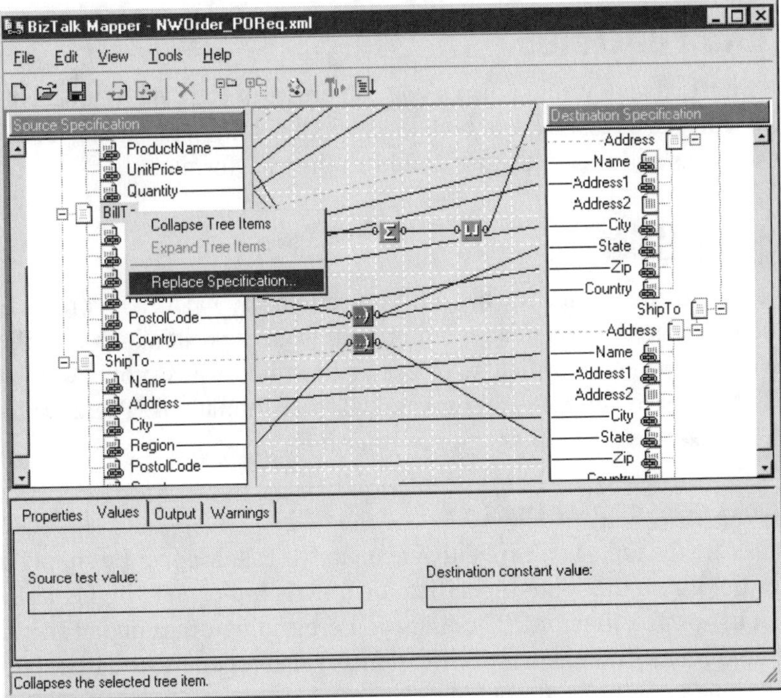

Figure 5-10 *Replace the source specification of the map*

You can update either the source or destination specification (or both) by right-clicking on the tree view of the specification you want to update and selecting Replace Specification… in the pop-up menu (see Figure 5-10). When you update the specifications, the Mapper uses built-in heuristics to determine which links you created are still valid.

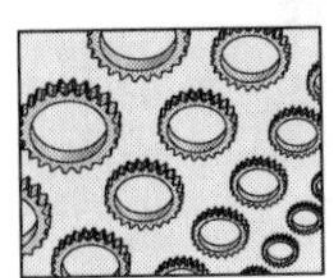

NOTE

BizTalk Mapper also allows you to export the compiled map as a stand-alone XSLT stylesheet. To do this, you must first compile the map and then select File/Save Compiled Map As. This feature alone can make the BizTalk Mapper a useful tool for generating XSLT stylesheets graphically and using them outside the BizTalk context (both BizTalk Editor and BizTalk Mapper are also available from the BizTalk JumpStart Kit version L MSDN download). You need to keep in mind a couple of constraints when using BizTalk Mapper in this manner, though. First, both the inbound and outbound documents must be in XML formats. Secondly, if functoids were used, the compiled XSLT stylesheet will only work under the MSXML parser, because functoids are VBScript code embedded in MSXML parser-specific <msxsl:script> elements.

Links and Functoids

Links and Functoids are visual objects you can create in BizTalk Mapper. In this section, we will take a close look at both links and functoids and explain how BizTalk Mapper uses links and functoids to accomplish the transformation.

Working with Links

A link is represented as a line in BizTalk Mapper, and connects a record or field from the source specification to a record or field from the destination specification. It can also connect a record or field to or from a functoid. A link provides information for BizTalk Mapper to generate appropriate XSL transformations. There are basically two types of links: (regular) *links* and *compiler links*.

Regular Links and Compiler Links

Regular links are the links you explicitly create in BizTalk Mapper by simply dragging a record or field from the source specification to a record or field in the destination specification—or to a functoid. The links you created by dragging a functoid to a record or field in the destination specification are also regular links. Regular links are simple value-copy links. By default, BizTalk Mapper copies the values of the source to the destination in a regular link. You can also force BizTalk Mapper to copy the name instead of the value of the source to the destination. You can do this in the Link Properties dialog box. To open the Link Properties dialog box, click a link (a solid black line) in the mapping grid to highlight it. Right-click the highlighted link and select Properties. The opened Link Properties dialog box will be defaulted to the General tab, as shown in Figure 5-11. The source and destination nodes connected by the link are displayed as XPath expressions.

Whenever you create a new regular link, BizTalk Mapper automatically generates a compiler link, also known as a *compiler directive link*. Compiler directives are BizTalk Mapper specific instructions that enable BizTalk Mapper to generate appropriate XSL statements in the compiled XSLT stylesheet. You can view and change compiler directives in the Compiler tab of the Link Properties dialog box, as shown in Figure 5-12.

You can select between Copy Value (Default) and Copy Name option boxes on the Source Specification Links frame to notify BizTalk Mapper as to whether you want the value or name of the source to be copied to the destination. There are three compiler directives in the destination specification links that we will explain later in this chapter when we discuss different mapping scenarios.

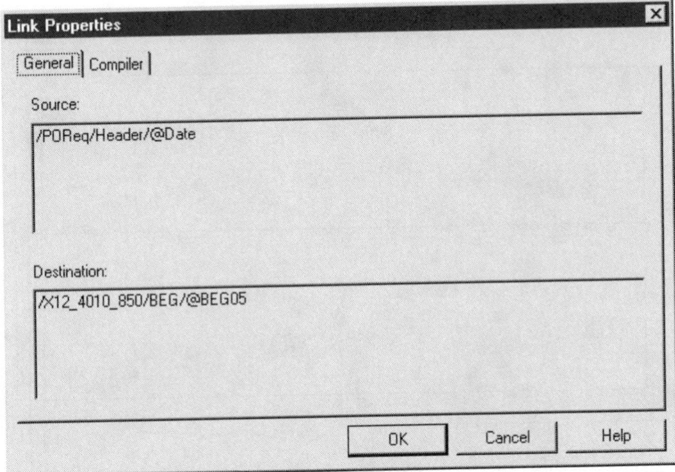

Figure 5-11 *The General tab of the Link Properties dialog box*

Setting BizTalk Mapper Options

You can set different options in BizTalk Mapper through the BizTalk Mapper Options dialog box. You can access this dialog box by selecting Tools | Options or right-clicking the mapping grid and selecting Options. The General tab of the

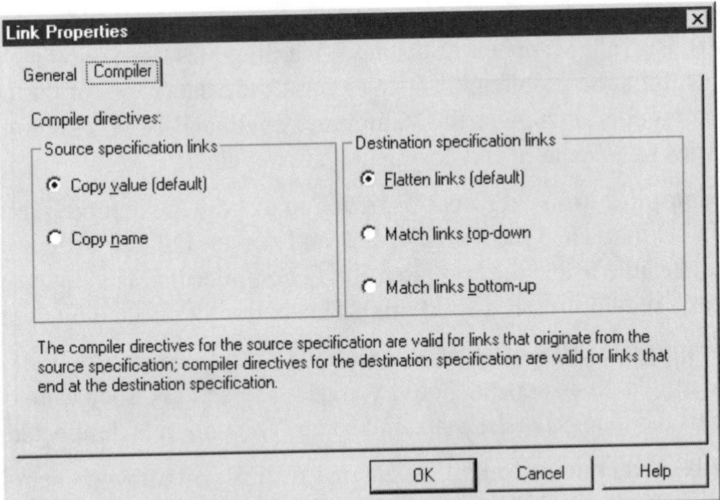

Figure 5-12 *The Compiler tab of the Link Properties dialog box*

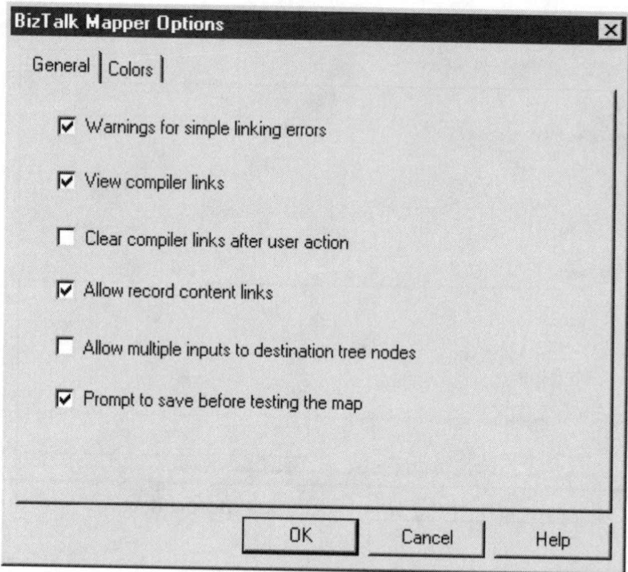

Figure 5-13 *The General tab of the BizTalk Mapper Options dialog box*

BizTalk Mapper Options dialog box contains the following options, as shown in Figure 5-13.

- **Warnings for simple linking errors** When this option is selected (the default), BizTalk Mapper will display a warning message if you try to create a link that might be problematic—for example, the data types of the source and destination don't match, or the Minimum Length and/or Maximum Length properties of the source and destination are not equal.
- **View compiler links** Select this option to display the compiler directive links. Note that when the compiler link and regular link are overlapped, you will not be able to see the compiler link (a compiler link is a dotted line, whereas a regular link is a solid line). This option is selected by default.
- **Clear compiler links after user action** Selecting this option will cause the compiler links to disappear should you take any actions, such as to compile the map, test the map, save the map, and so on. The option is deselected by default.
- **Allow record content links** Selecting this link will allow content links from records to functoids to be created. This option is deselected by default. Recall that in Chapter 4 we discussed that neither the MSXML 3.0 parser nor BizTalk Server 2000 handles mixed-mode content. If you have records that contain content, then you often need to map that content to another record.

- **Allow multiple inputs to destination tree nodes** Select this option to allow links to be created from multiple sources. You set this option only if you are sure the values of the multiple sources are mutually exclusive (i.e., if one of them can be evaluated to a non-null value, the rest must all be nulls). This option is deselected by default.
- **Prompt to save before testing the map** Selecting this option will cause BizTalk Mapper to remind you to save incremental updates to the map when testing it by clicking the Test Map button or the Tools | Test Map menu option. The option is selected by default

The Colors tab of the BizTalk Mapper Options dialog box allows you to set colors for selected objects in the mapping grid (links and functoids), compiler warnings, grid backgrounds and foregrounds, as well as lines used for links, as shown in Figure 5-14.

You might have noticed that there are four types of links referred to on the Colors tab of the BizTalk Mapper Options dialog box. We've already explained what compiler links are earlier in this chapter. The other three links on the Colors tab are referred to as regular links. You can use different colors to distinguish between those links that are completed (*fixed links*) and those being created (*elastic links*). *Partial links* are those links whose parent nodes are collapsed in the Mapper. If you set the same color for more than two of the eight options and click the OK button, BizTalk Mapper displays a warning message to remind you. You can restore colors to their default settings by clicking the Restore Default Colors button.

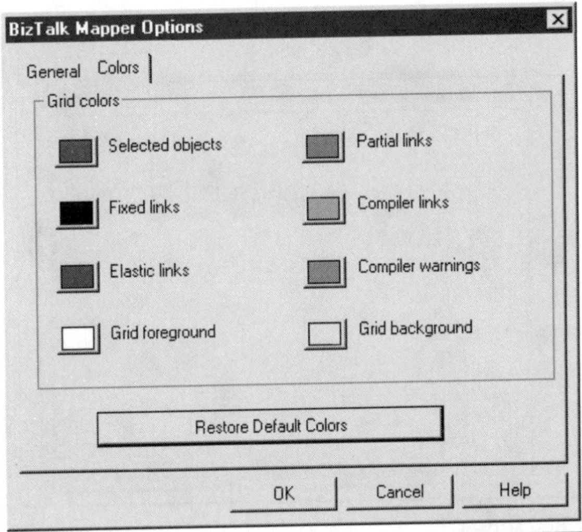

Figure 5-14 *The Colors tab on the BizTalk Mapper Options dialog box*

Working with Functoids

Whereas links in BizTalk Mapper provide a convenient way for copying data and defining the mapping structure between sources and destinations, there are situations in which you need to manipulate, aggregate, or perform complicated conversions to the data themselves. This is where functoids come into play. Functoids are mostly built-in functions written in VBScript and compiled to XSLT inside the MSXML specific <msxsl:script> elements. As you will learn shortly, BizTalk Mapper also allows you to write custom functoids in VBScript. In addition, BizTalk Server 2000 provides an open Functoid architecture enabling you to implement custom functoids as COM components (DLLs) and reuse them in any number of maps. You will learn how to create custom functoids in Chapter 11. In BizTalk Mapper, Functoids are implemented individual graphic objects in BizTalk Mapper and are available in the Functoid Palette (see Figure 5-15). The returned value of a functoid is outputted to the linked destination.

You can drag a functoid from the Functoid Palette, place it on the mapping grid and then link the appropriate functoid to the records or fields in the source and destination specifications. As we will explain shortly, some functoids can only be linked to records or fields of the destination specification.

To link a record or field from the source specification to a functoid, you simply drag the record or field from the source specification tree on the left side of the upper pane, then move your mouse pointer over the functoid you want to connect to and release it. When you start dragging the record or field, an elastic link will be created, starting from the dragging point. As soon as you release the mouse button, the link is changed to a fixed link and connected to the functoid.

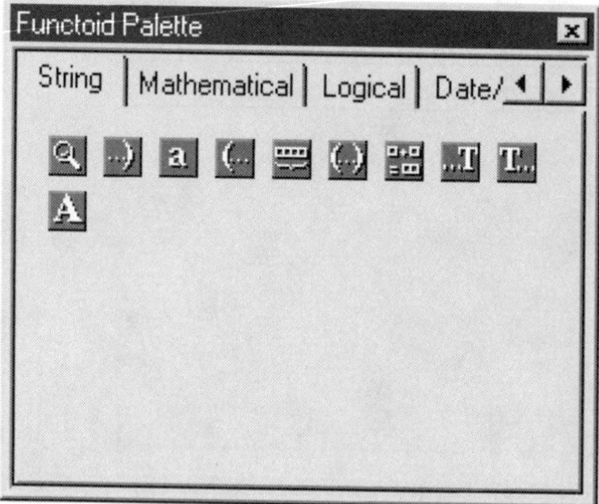

Figure 5-15 *The Functoid Palette*

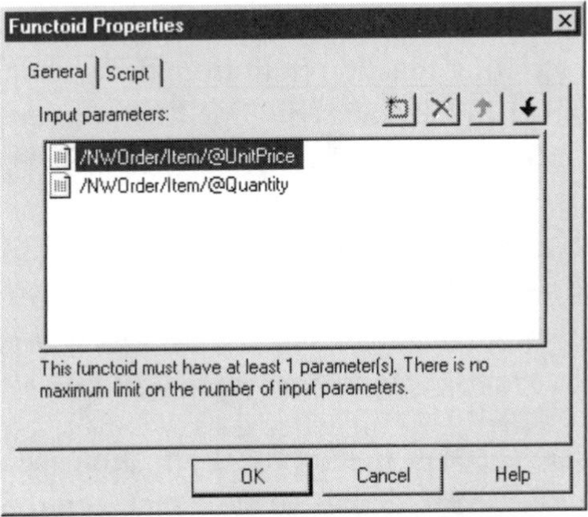

Figure 5-16 *The General tab of the Functoid Properties dialog box*

You can access the properties of a functoid by right-clicking a functoid and selecting Properties to display the Functoid Properties dialog box. The Functoid Properties dialog box has two tabs, as shown in Figures 5-16 and 5-17.

The General tab displays the record or fields from the source specification in the Input parameters list as XPath expressions, in the order these links were created. There are four buttons in the upper-right corner of the General tab that allow you to insert new input parameters (constants), delete existing parameters and reorder the links. The Script tab displays the actual VBScript code of the function the Functoid supports. If the script function has input parameters, their order will be the same as you set on the General tab. The scripts on the Script tab of the Functoid Palette are

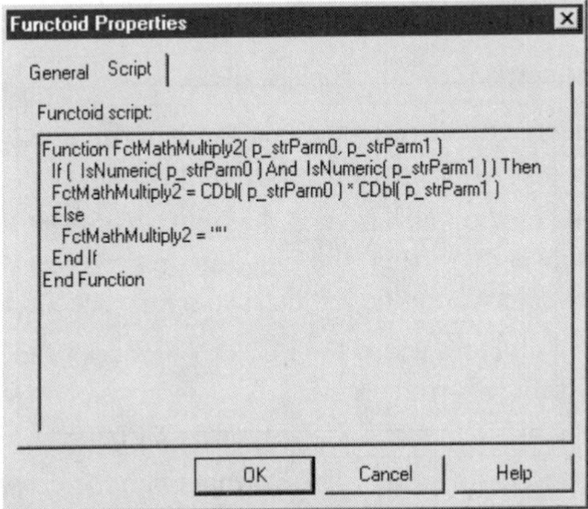

Figure 5-17 *The Script tab of the Functoid Properties dialog box*

read-only except for the *Scripting functoid* (to be discussed shortly), which allows you to write your own scripting function right from the Script tab. Functoids take the scripting support advantage of the underlying MSXML parser used by the BizTalk Server messaging engine to extend the functionality of XSLT transformations.

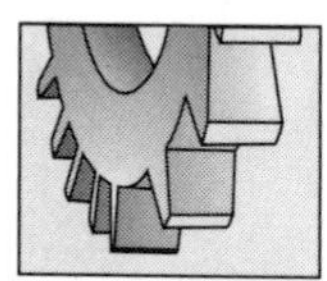

TIP

Due to the size of the area displayed in the Script tab, it is often hard to see the entire scripting code. You can copy the scripts and paste them to a text editor (such as Notepad) to study them. Understanding how a functoid is implemented will help you figure out how to use them.

To link a functoid to a record or field of the destination specification, click and hold the functoid and drag the elastic link to the target record or field and release it.

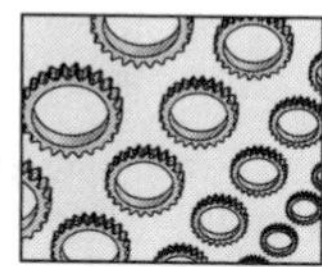

NOTE

If you click the functoid without holding the mouse button, you will select the functoid. You cannot link a selected functoid to a target record or field.

Functoids are grouped into nine tabs in the Functoids Palette according to different categories, including String, Mathematical, Logical, Date and Time, Conversion, Scientific, Cumulative, Database, and Advanced functoids. To identify each individual functoid, move your mouse pointer over a functoid, and a tooltip box will display the name of the functoid.

String Functoids

The functoids on the String tab of the Functoid Palette perform string manipulations. Their underlying scripting functions are described in Table 5-1 in the order they appear on the tab:

Functoid	Description
String Find	This functoid wraps the Instr() VBScript function. It returns the position of the second string in the first string.
String Left	This functoid is based on the Left() VBScript function. It returns a subset of a string (the first input parameter) with the number of characters from the left defined by the second input parameter.
Lowercase	This functoid wraps the LCase() VBScript function and converts a string to lowercase.
String Right	This functoid is based on the Right() VBScript function and returns a subset of a string (the first input parameter) with the number of characters from the right defined by the second input parameter.

Table 5-1 *Scripting Functions of Functoids on the Script Tab*

Functoid	Description
String Length	This functoid wraps the Len() VBScript function and returns the size of the string.
String Extract	This functoid extracts a subset of a string specified by the start and end positions of a string.
Concatenate	This functoid concatenates a series of input strings. It can grow or shrink automatically according to the number of input fields linked to the functoid.
String Left Trim	This functoid wraps the Ltrim() VBScript function and trims out the leading spaces of a string.
String Right Trim	This functoid wraps the RTrim() VBScript function and trims out the trailing spaces of a string.
Uppercase	This functoid wraps the UCase() VBScript function and converts a string to uppercase.

Table 5-1 *Scripting Functions of Functoids on the Script Tab* (continued)

Mathematical Functoids

The functoids on the Mathematical tab perform basic mathematical operations as described in Table 5-2.

Functoid	Description
Absolute Value	This functoid returns the absolute value of a number.
Integer	This functoid converts a number to an integer by returning its integer portion. For example, 1.9 will be converted to 1.
Maximum Value	This functoid returns the maximum value of a series of numeric values.
Minimum Value	This functoid returns the minimum value of a series of numeric values.
Modulo	This functoid returns the remainder of a number divided by an integer. It is based on the Mod() VBScript function.
Round	This functoid rounds a figure to a specified number of decimal places. It is based on the Round() VBScript function.
Square Root	This functoid returns the square root of a number. It is based on the Sqr() VBScript function.
Addition	This functoid returns the sum of a series of numbers.
Subtraction	This functoid subtracts one number from another.
Multiplication	This functoid multiplies two numbers.
Division	This functoid divides one number by another.

Table 5-2 *The Functoids on the Mathematical Tab*

Logical Functoids

The functoids on the Logical tab perform logical operations and return Boolean results (True or False). Most of them are very straightforward as summarized in Table 5-3. Logical functoids perform logical operations (greater than, less than, not equal to, and so on) and return True or False results. The outputs of these functoids are often used to make logic decisions rather than put the results directly into destination fields or records.

Functoids	Description
Greater Than (>)	These functoids compare two numbers and return Boolean results (True of False) based on the comparison. For example, if paramA>param B, the Greater Than, Greater Than or Equal To, and Not Equal functoids will return True, whereas the Less Than, Less Than or Equal To, and Equal will return False.
Greater Than or Equal To (>=)	
Less Than (<)	
Less Than or Equal To (<=)	
Equal (=)	
Not Equal (<>)	
Logical String	This functoid will return True if the input parameter is a string.
Logical Date	This functoid will return True if the input parameter is a date. It wraps the IsDate() VBScript function.
Logical Numeric	This functoid will return True if the input parameter is a numeric value. It wraps the IsNumeric() VBScript function.
Logical OR	This functoid returns the Logical OR of input parameters. For example, if either paramA or paramB is true or both of them are True, then the Logical OR functoid will return True. Otherwise it returns False.
Logical AND	This functoid returns the logic AND of input parameters. For example, only if both paramA and paramB are True will the functoid return True. Otherwise, it returns False.

Table 5-3 *The Functoids on the Logical Tab*

Functoid	Description
Add Days	This functoid adds a specific number of days to a date.
Date	This functoid returns the current date in YYYY-MM-DD format. It takes no input parameters.
Time	This functoid returns the current time in HH:MM:SS format. It takes no input parameters.
Date and Time	This functoid returns current date and time in YYYY-MM-DDTHH:MM:SS format. It also takes no input parameters.

Table 5-4 *The Functoids on the Date/Time Tab*

Date and Time Functoids

The functoids on the Date/Time tab are described in Table 5-4.

Conversion Functoids

There are four functoids on the Conversion tab that convert ASCII code from characters or vice versa and decimal to hexadecimal or decimal to octal values, as summarized in Table 5-5.

Scientific Functoids

The functoids on the Scientific tab resemble the buttons commonly seen on a scientific calculator and perform scientific calculations. They are either direct

Functoid	Description
ASCII from Character	This functoid wraps the ASC() VBScript function and returns a character's ASCII code.
Character from ASCII	This functoid wraps the Chr() VBScript function and returns a character from an ASCII code.
Hexadecimal	This functoid wraps the Hex() VBScript function and converts a decimal number to a hexadecimal number.
Octal	This functoid wraps the Oct() VBScript function and converts a decimal number to an octal number.

Table 5-5 *The Functoids on the Conversion Tab*

Functoid	Description
Arc Tangent	This functoid wraps the Atn() VBScript function and calculates the arc tangent of a number.
Cosine	This functoid wraps the Cos() VBScript function and calculates the cosine of a number.
Sine	This functoid wraps the Sin() VBScript function and calculates the sine of a number.
Tangent	This functoid wraps the Tan() VBScript function and calculates the tangent of a number.
Natural Exponential Function	This functoid wraps the Exp() VBScript function and calculates returns raised to a specified power.
Natural Logarithm	This functoid is based on the Log() VBScript function and calculates the e-based logarithm of a value.
10^X	This functoid calculates 10 raised to a specific number.
Common Logarithm	This functoid calculates a 10-based logarithm of a number.
X^Y	This functoid calculates a value raised to a specific power.
Base-Specified Logarithm	This functoid calculates a base-specific logarithm of a number.

Table 5-6 *The Functoids on the Scientific Tab*

wrappers of VBScript scientific functions or custom functions based on a basic VBScript scientific function. Table 5-6 describes them.

Cumulative Functoids

Functoids on the Cumulative tab perform aggregations as described in Table 5-7. Cumulative functoids work at the record level in the source specification. Those records whose Maximum Occurrences properties are set to a value greater than one, typically repeat many times in a document (for example, the Item records in our POReq.xml specification). BizTalk Mapper provides cumulative functoids that perform cumulative and aggregation operations (e.g., totals, averages, and so on) to simplify the mapping process.

Functoid	Description
Cumulative Sum	This functoid calculates the sum of all values for the connected fields by iterating over its parent record.
Cumulative Average	This function calculates the average of all values for the connected fields by iterating over its parent record.

Table 5-7 *The Functoids on the Cumulative Tab*

Functoid	Description
Cumulative Minimum	This functoid calculates the minimum of all values for the connected fields under a parent record.
Cumulative Maximum	This functoid calculates the maximum of all values for the connected fields under a parent record.
Cumulative String	This functoid concatenates strings of the connected fields by iterating over its parent record.

Table 5-8 *The Functoids on the Cumulative Tab* (continued)

Database Functoids

There are three functoids on the Database tab: Database Lookup, Value Extractor, and Error Return. You can store static data in a persistent database and look them up during run time using these database functoids instead of carrying static data into the inbound document.

These database functoids are usually used together to perform a database lookup. The Database Lookup functoid searches a specific database and returns a record (a serialized ADO recordset). The Database Lookup functoid takes exactly four input parameters: a connection string (the second parameter), the lookup database table (the third parameter), and a column name/value pair (the fourth and first parameter). You specify the third parameter by linking a field from the source specification to the functoid. You then define constants as the rest of the parameters and put them into the right order.

The Value Extractor is a downstream functoid of the Database Lookup. The Value Extractor string takes exactly two input parameters, a link from a Database Lookup functoid and a constant which defines the column name. It will retrieve the value of the specific column from the recordset and output it to either a field in the destination specification or another functoid.

The Error Return functoid is also a downstream functoid of the Database Lookup. It takes only one input parameter, a Database Lookup functoid, and will retrieve the error string encountered during the database lookup process. Then it will output this error string to a field of the destination specification. Figure 5-18 illustrates a possible use of the database functoid.

Suppose you have an Employees table that can be accessed from the BizTalk Server which stores employee ID, first name, last name, and so on. You can use a Database Lookup functoid and connect it to the EmployeeID field of the source specification. You then define the connection string that points to the database where the Employees table resides. You also specify Employee as the table name and EmployeeID as the column name in the functoid so the Database Lookup functoid will retrieve an employee record identified by the EmployeeID (see Figure 5-19).

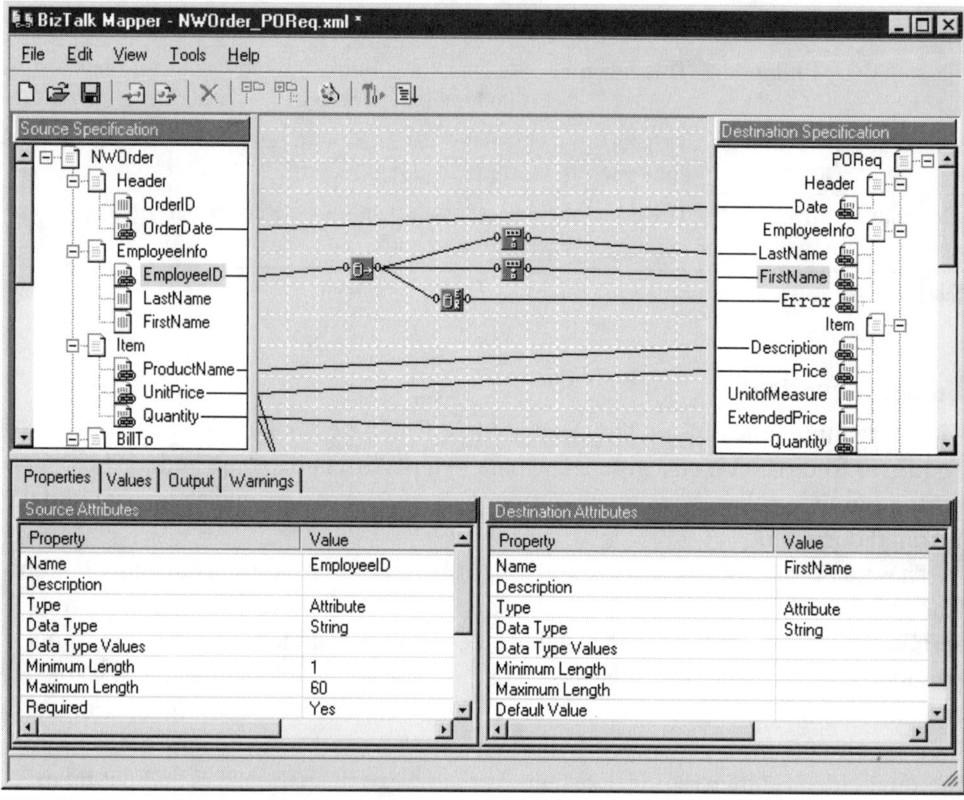

Figure 5-18 *Using database functoids in a map*

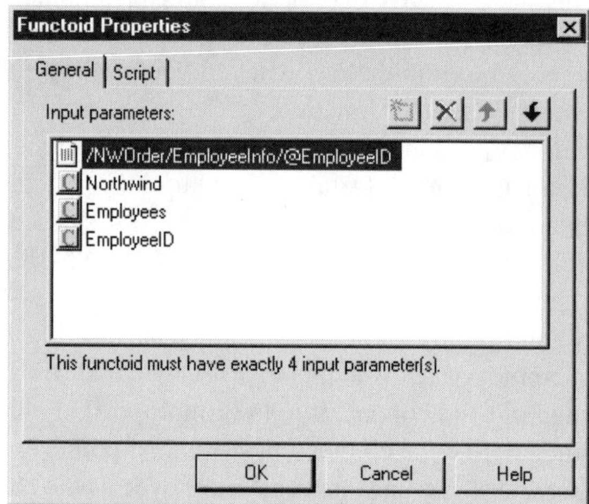

Figure 5-19 *Setting input parameters for the Database Lookup functoid*

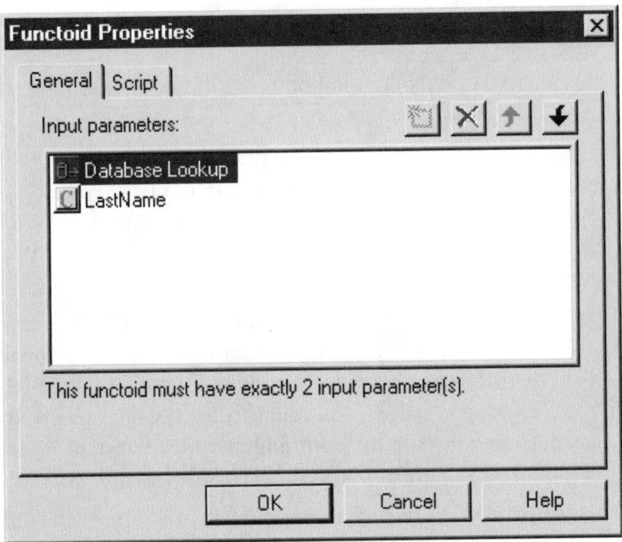

Figure 5-20 *Setting input parameters for a Value Extract functoid*

With the Database Lookup functoid in place, let's add two Value Extract functoids. Figure 5-20 illustrates the Value Extract functoid setup that retrieves the last name of the employee.

Using an Error Returned database functoid is most straightforward. You simply place an Error Returned functoid and link a Database Lookup functoid as the input, and a field in the destination specification as its output (such as the Error field in Figure 5-18).

Advanced Functoids

With the functoids on the Advanced tab of the Functoid Palette, you can do things like writing custom VBScript functions, mapping values, managing and extracting information from a record loop and so on. By using these functoids, you can create very advanced maps to handle fairly complicated mapping situations. Table 5-8 provides summarized information about the functoids on the Advanced tab. BizTalk Server 2000 documentation has detailed explanations on each of these functoids, with plenty of examples.

Functoid	Description
Scripting	This functoid enables you to write your own functions in VBScript if the built-in functoids cannot fit your needs. Before rolling out your own functions, though, I strongly recommend you study the scripting code of the built-in functoids. They demonstrate good scripting practices (especially from the perspective of writing functoids) and neat coding styles.

Table 5-8 *The Functoids on the Advanced Tab*

Functoid	Description
Record Count	This functoid counts the total number of records encountered.
Index	This functoid returns the value of a record or a field at a specified index. The Maximum Occurrence of the record (or the parent record if a field is used) is set to * in the source specification. For example, to return the price of the second item line, you can use an Index functoid linked to the Price field whose parent record is the Item record. You then add a constant as the second input parameter and set its value to 2.
Iteration	This functoid returns the iteration numbers in a source record whose Maximum Occurrence property is set to * in the source specification. There is a subtle difference between the Index functoid and the Iteration functoid. In the former, you *specify* (tell the functoid) which record (or field) in a loop you want to work with by assigning an index constant. In the latter, the functoid *identifies* (tells you) which record you are working on.
Value Mapping	This functoid takes two input parameters and returns the value of the second parameter if the value of the first parameter is True. This Value Mapping functoid provides some filtering capabilities. The Value Mapping functoid is usually used in conjunction with a logic functoid, such as an Equal functoid. For example, you can use several Equal-Value Mapping functoid pairs linked to the same source fields. According to evaluations of the Equal functoid (True or False), only one of the Value-Mapping results goes to the destination field.
Value Mapping (Flattening)	This functoid is similar to the Value Mapping functoid discussed previously. It also takes two input parameters, and if the value of the first parameter is True, it returns the second parameter. In addition, it flattens the source document hierarchy.
Looping	This functoid combines multiple records and/or fields from the source specification into a single record in the destination specification. For example, you can use the Looping functoid to map a flat schema to a Microsoft Commerce Server catalog.

Table 5-8 *The Functoids on the Advanced Tab* (continued)

Creating Maps

Now that you are armed with all the knowledge for creating maps using BizTalk Mapper, let's see some examples of mapping in action. In this section, we are going to create two maps, using the specifications you created in the last chapter. To work with these examples, download the source code for this chapter from this book's Web site. Open the NWOrder_Spec.xml specification in BizTalk Editor. Click the

Store To WebDAV button on the toolbar and create a Northwind folder in the Save To WebDAV dialog box. Open the Northwind folder and click the Save button. This specification will be saved under <BizTalk Server Installation Folder>\ BizTalk ServerRepository\DocSpecs\Northwind folder. Also save the POReq.xml and the 850Schema_Short.xml specifications to the Northwind WebDAV folder. Similarly, create another Northwind folder under <BizTalk Server Installation Folder>\ Biz TalkServerRepository\Maps and save two map files there, NWOrder_POReq.xml and POReq.xml_To_X12PO.xml.

Mapping Flat Files to XML

The first map you will create maps the NWOrder.xml flat file specification you generated in the last chapter to an XML purchase order request, the POReq.xml specification adapted from BizTalk tutorial (we changed the Maximum Occurrence property of the Item document to * to fit our needs).

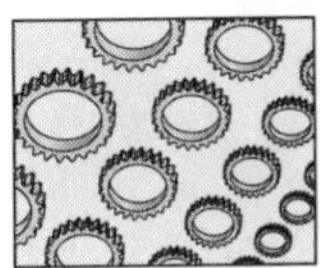

NOTE

If the formats of inbound and outbound documents are different, you must create a map for them even if their intermediate XML specifications are identical.

Launch the BizTalk Mapper and click the New button on the toolbar. In the Select Source Specification Type dialog box, click WebDAV Files. You should see the Retrieve Source Specification dialog box with two folders, Northwind and Microsoft, similar to the one in Figure 5-21

Click the Northwind folder to open it. You will see the three specifications you copied there a moment ago. Select NWOrder_Spec.xml and click Open. In the Select Destination Specification Type, select WebDAV Files and click OK. You will be brought to the Retrieve Destination Specification dialog box. Select POReq.xml and click Open. The BizTalk Mapper display will look like the one in Figure 5-22, loaded with the source specification in the upper-left pane and the destination specification in the upper-right pane. You are now ready to map these two specifications.

Creating Links

Expand appropriate records of both the source and destination specification trees and create links as shown in Table 5-9 (all the links use default compiler directives—i.e., Copy values for the source specification links, and Flatten links for the destination specification links).

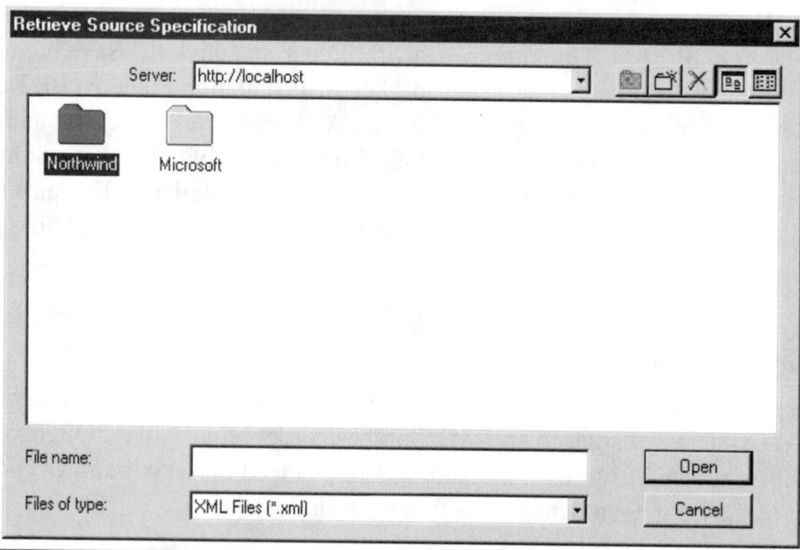

Figure 5-21 *The Retrieve Source Specification dialog box*

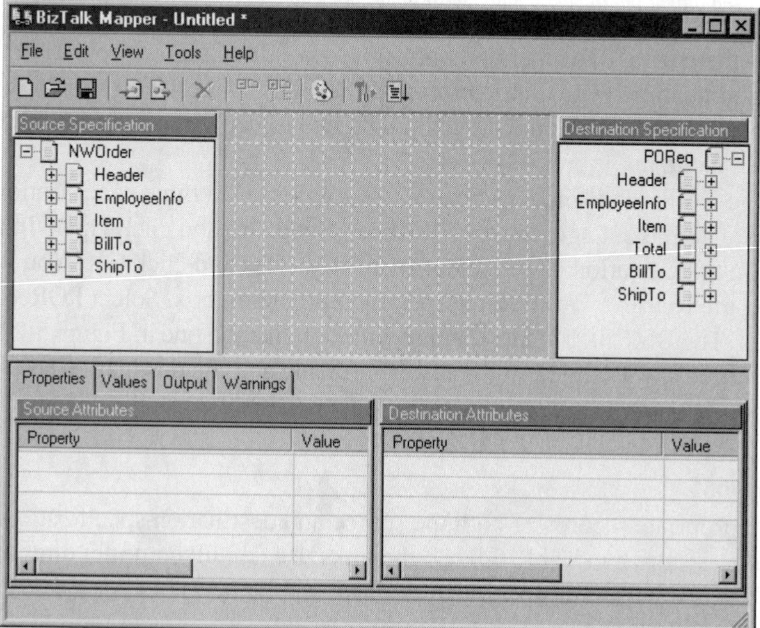

Figure 5-22 *BizTalk Mapper loaded with two specifications*

Source Record or Field	Destination Record or Field
Header/OrderDate	Header/Date
EmployeeInfo/EmployeeID	EmployeeInfo/EmpID
EmployeeInfo/LastName	EmployeeInfo/LastName
EmployeeInfo/FirstName	EmployeeInfo/FirstName
Item/ProductName	Item/Description
Item/UnitPrice	Item/Price
Item/Quantity	Item/Quantity
BillTo/Name	BillTo/Address/Name
BillTo/Address	BillTo/Address/Address1
BillTo/City	BillTo/Address/City
BillTo/PostalCode	BillTo/Address/Zip
BillTo/Country	BillTo/Address/Country
ShipTo/Name	ShipTo/Address/Name
ShipTo/Address	ShipTo/Address/Address1
ShipTo/City	ShipTo/Address/City
ShipTo/PostalCode	ShipTo/Address/Zip
ShipTo/Country	ShipTo/Address/Country

Table 5-9 *Links Using the Source and Destination Specification Trees*

Using Functoids

You may notice we have not created links between BillTo/Region and BillTo/ Address/ State or ShipTo/Region and ShipTo/State yet. This is because the BillTo/Region (or ShipTo/Region) field has a Maximum Length property of 20, longer than the Maximum Length property of the BillTo/Address/State (or ShipTo/Address/State) field which is 2, as shown in Figure 5-23.

If you directly map these fields, it may cause a mapping error in the run time if the values of the Region fields in the inbound document exceed 2 characters. In this situation, we can use simple string functoids—the String Left functoid—to solve the problem. Place a String Left functoid on the mapping grid and link the BillTo/Region to the functoid. Double-click the functoid to open the Functoid Properties dialog box. Add a constant 2 to the General tab, as shown in Figure 5-24.

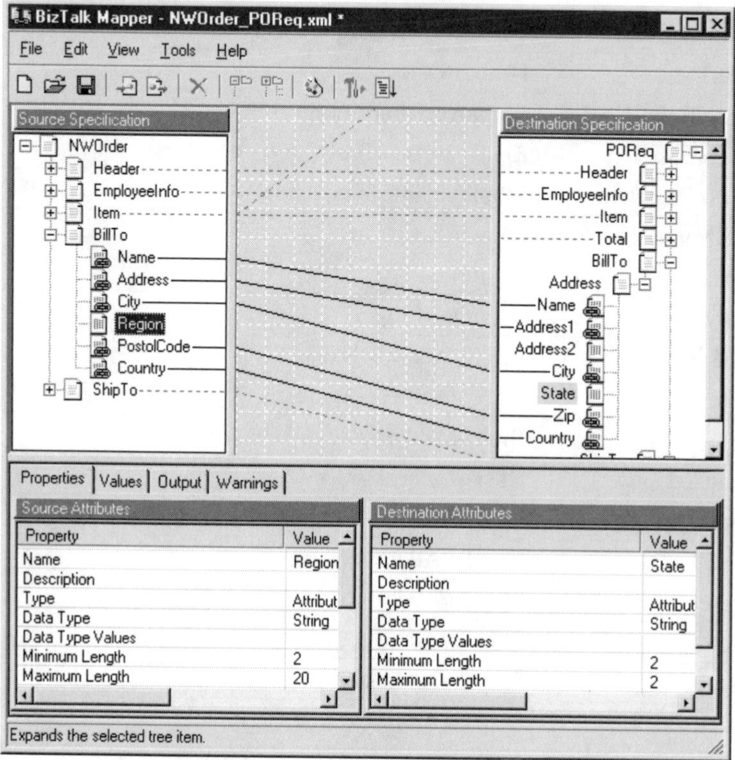

Figure 5-23 *The source field has more characters than the destination field*

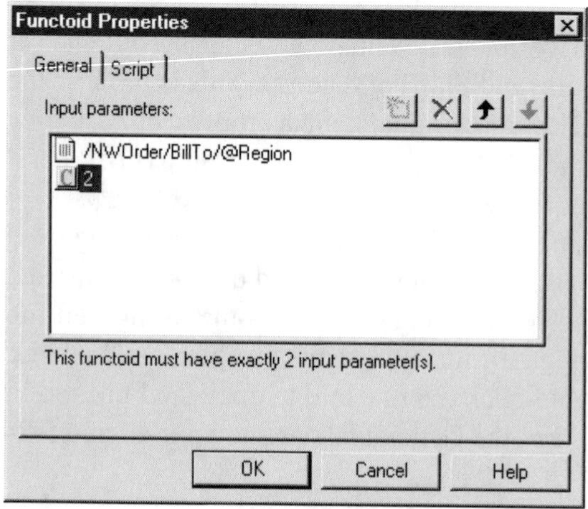

Figure 5-24 *Add a constant to restrict the characters of the source field*

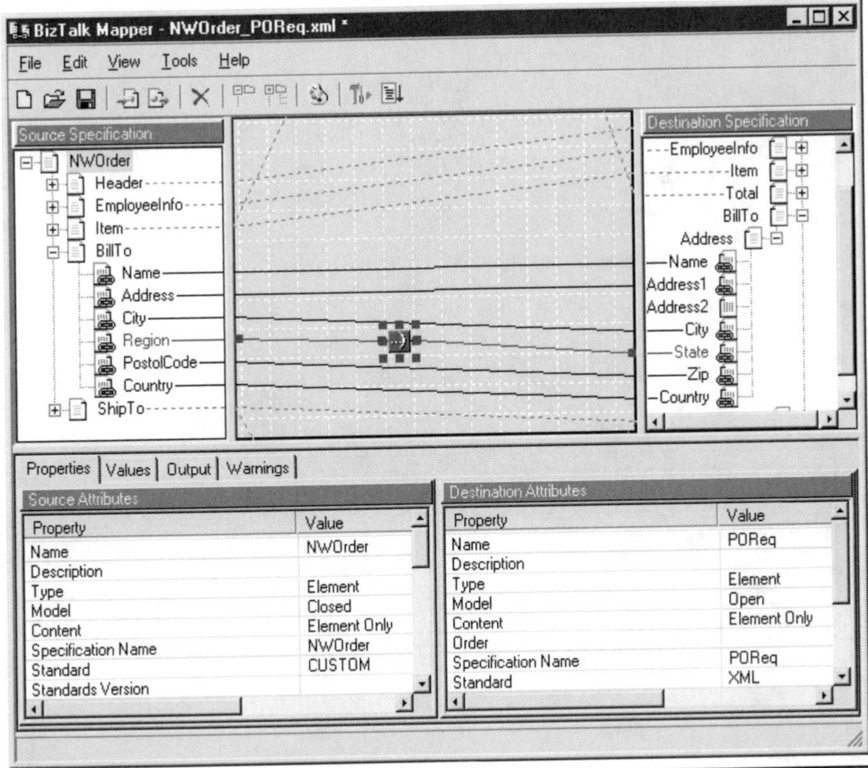

Figure 5-25 *A functoid is added to the map*

This will return only the first two characters of the BillTo/Region field. Click OK to dismiss the Functoid Properties dialog box. Deselect the functoid by clicking an area outside the functoid (you cannot link a selected functoid to a destination field or record). Now link the functoid to the BillTo/Address/State field in the destination specification. Your map should now look like the one in Figure 5-25.

Create another similar String Left functoid and link it to the ShipTo/Region and ShipTo/Address/State fields.

Notice in Figure 5-26 that in the destination specification, there is a Total/POTtl field which stores the total price of a purchase order request. We don't immediately have similar fields in the source specification document. However, we do have Item/UnitPrice and Item/Quantity fields in the source specification, and the Item record is a loop (i.e., its Maximum Occurrences property is set to *). Based on this information, we can use functoids again to resolve our problem. This time, we need tree functoids in a roll, as shown in Figure 5-26. Functoids used in this manner are referred to as *cascading functoids*.

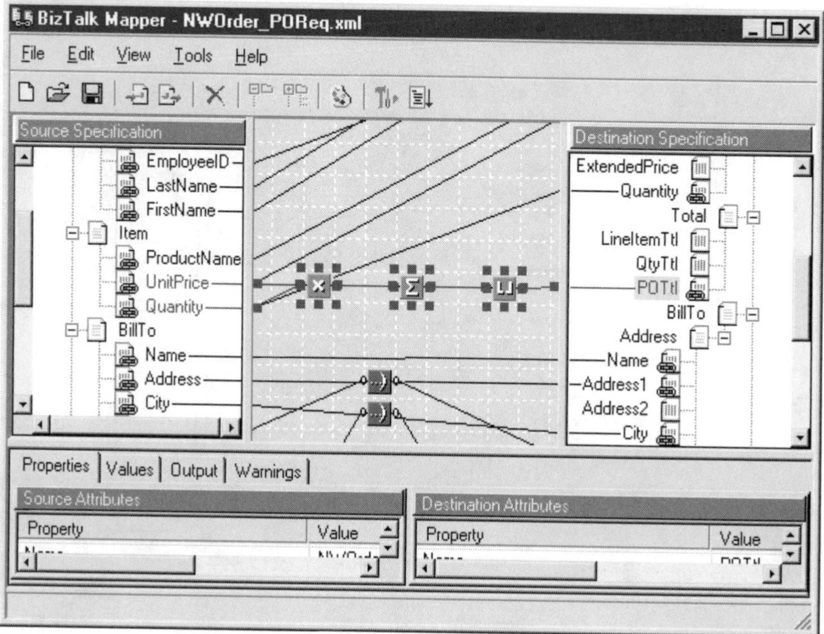

Figure 5-26 *Cascading functoids*

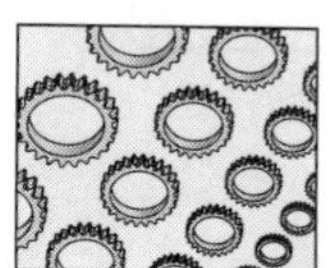

NOTE

Whereas cascading functoids add great flexibility to your mapping solutions, you should keep in mind that complex cascading functoids can result in reduced performance.

The first functoid is a Multiply functoid that returns the product of UnitPrice and Quantity. The second function, a Cumulative Sum functoid, will sum up the products generated by the multiple functoid for every Item record. The last functoid, the Round functoid, rounds the total value to the second decimal place. Figure 5-27 illustrates the Functoid Properties of the Cumulative Sum functoid with a constant of 2 to indicate the intended decimal place to round to.

Now you've completed your first map. Save it to the WebDAV repository by clicking the Store To WebDAV button on the toolbar of BizTalk Mapper. Browse to the Northwind folder and name the file NWOrder_POReq.xml, then click the Save button. BizTalk Mapper may ask if you want to overwrite an existing map since we copied one there earlier. Click Yes to save the map.

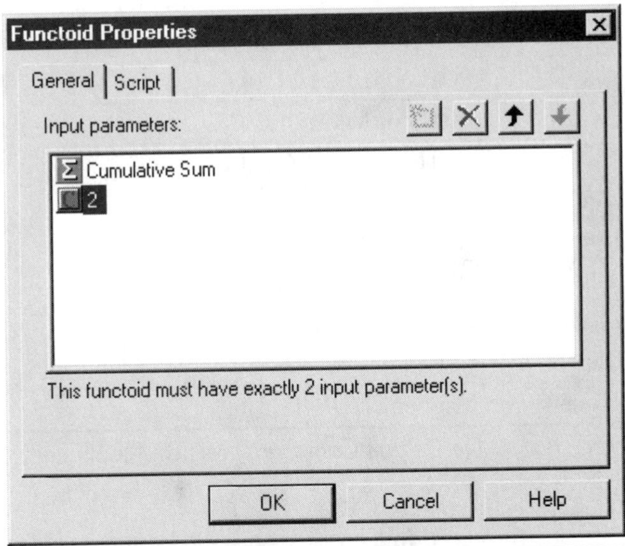

Figure 5-27 *The properties of the Cumulative Sum functoid*

Mapping XML to EDI X12

The second map you are going to create will map the POReq.xml specification to an EDI X12 purchase order specification you created in the last chapter— 850Schema_Short.xml.

Creating Links

First, open BizTalk Mapper and load the source and destination specifications. Then create the following links with default compiler directives, as shown in Table 5-10.

Source Record or Field	Destination Record or Field
Header/Date	BEG/BEG05
Item/Description	PO1Loop1/PIDLoop1/PID_2/PID05
Item/Price	PO1Loop1/PO1/PO104

Table 5-10 *Created Links to the Default Compiler Directives*

Source Record or Field	Destination Record or Field
Item/UnitofMeasure	PO1Loop1/PO1/PO103
Item/Quantity	PO1Loop1/PO1/PO102
Total/POTtl	CTTLoop1/CTT/CTT02
ShipTo/Address/Address1	N1Loop1/N3/N301
ShipTo/Address/Address2	N1Loop1/N3/N302
ShipTo/Address/City	N1Loop1/N4/N401
ShipTo/Address/State	N1Loop1/N4/N402
ShipTo/Address/Zip	N1Loop1/N4/N403
ShipTo/Address/Country	N1Loop1/N4/N404

Table 5-10 *Created Links to the Default Compiler Directives* (continued)

Now create a record-to-record link by dragging the Item record from the source specification tree and link it to the PO1Loop1 record in the destination specification tree. Right-click the link in the mapping grid and select Properties. Click the Compiler tab. Change the Destination Specification Links to Match Links Top-Down, as shown in Figure 5-28. Click OK to close the Link Properties dialog box.

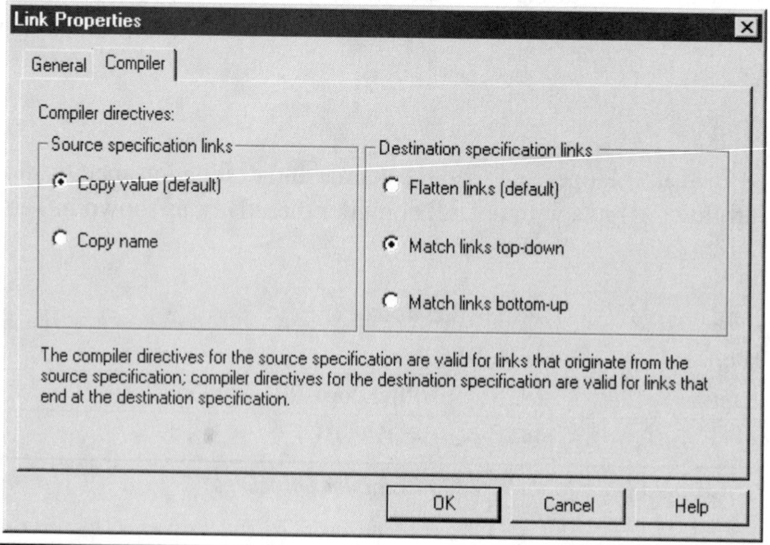

Link Properties

General | Compiler

Compiler directives:

Source specification links
- (•) Copy value (default)
- ( ) Copy name

Destination specification links
- ( ) Flatten links (default)
- (•) Match links top-down
- ( ) Match links bottom-up

The compiler directives for the source specification are valid for links that originate from the source specification; compiler directives for the destination specification are valid for links that end at the destination specification.

OK | Cancel | Help

Figure 5-28 *Create a top-down map*

In addition to the default, flatten links, BizTalk Mapper also supports two other link types: matching links top-down and matching links bottom-up (to handle node-hierarchy levels). In this example, both the source record (Item) and the destination record (PO1Loop1) are loops. The source specification has the following structure regarding the item records:

```
<Item Description = "Item1"
      Price = "P1"
      UnitofMeasure = "M1"
      Quantity = "Q1"/>
<Item Description = "Item2"
      Price = "P2"
      UnitofMeasure = "M2"
      Quantity = "Q2"/>
<Item Description = "Item3"
      Price = "P3"
      UnitofMeasure = "M3"
      Quantity = "Q3"/>
```

A flatten link will result in the POLoop1 structure like this:

```
<POLoop1>
  <PO1 PO102 = "Q1" PO103 = "M1" PO104="P1"/>
  <PO1 PO102 = "Q2" PO103 = "M2" PO104="P2"/>
  <PO1 PO102 = "Q3" PO103 = "M3" PO104="P3"/>
  <PIDLoop1>
    <PID_2 PID05 = "Item1"/>
    <PID_2 PID05 = "Item2"/>
    <PID_2 PID05 = "Item3"/>
  </PIDLoop1>
</POLoop1>
```

Whereas the specified POLoop1 structure should look like this:

```
<POLoop1>
  <PO1 PO102 = "Q1" PO103 = "M1" PO104="P1"/>
  <PIDLoop1>
     <PID_2 PID05 = "Item1"/>
  </PIDLoop1>
  <PO1 PO102 = "Q2" PO103 = "M2" PO104="P2"/>
  <PIDLoop1>
     <PID_2 PID05 = "Item2"/>
```

```
  </PIDLoop1>
  <PO1 PO102 = "Q3" PO103 = "M3" PO104="P3"/>
  <PIDLoop1>
     <PID_2 PID05 = "Item3"/>
  </PIDLoop1>
</POLoop1>
```

Specifying a Match Links Top-Down compiler directive for the destination specification links will result in the correct outbound document structure as defined by the destination specification.

Setting default values for outbound documents

Some of the required fields in the destination specification do not have corresponding fields in the source specification. We can use the Value tab of the lower pane in BizTalk Mapper to specify the following defaults for these required fields, as shown in Table 5-11.

Using Functoids

In this map, we will use three functoids. First, place a Date functoid in the mapping grid and link it to the DTM/DTM02 field in the destination specification. It will set the date when the document is being mapped as the date for the purchase order in the destination document.

Now place a Record Count functoid in the mapping grid and link the Item record from the source specification to the functoid. Then link the functoid to the CTT/CTT01 field in the destination specification (the Number of Line Items field). Because the Item is a loop record, the Record Count functoid will count the number of line items and insert the result in the destination field.

Finally, place a Concatenate functoid in the mapping grid and link the EmployeeIn fo/LastName and EmployeeInfo/FirstName fields from the source specification to

Destination Field	Default Value
BEG/BEG01	00
BEG/BEG02	SA
BEG/BEG03	123456789
PER/PER01	SA
DTM/DTM01	118
PO1Loop1/PIDLoop1/PID-2/PID01	F

Table 5-11 *Default Values on the Value Tab*

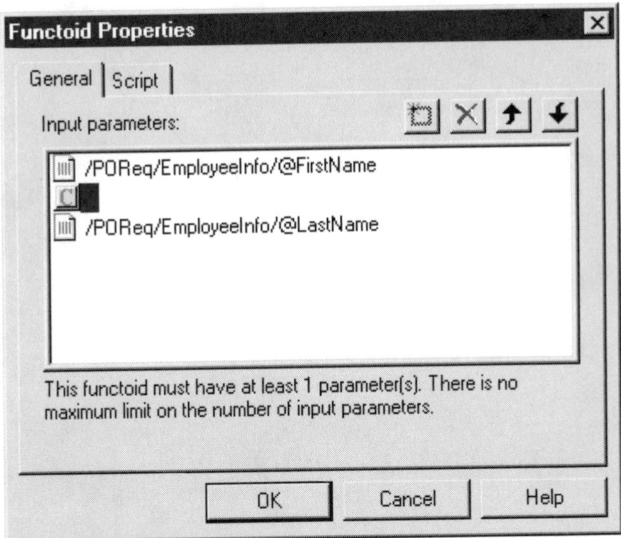

Figure 5-29 *Using a Concatenate functoid*

the functoid. Add a constant as a whitespace and rearrange the input parameters so the Functoid Properties dialog box will look like the one in Figure 5-29.

This functoid will return a string FirstName+Space+LastName (for example, "John Smith"). Click OK to close the Functoid Properties dialog box and link the functoid to the PER/PER02 field in the destination specification.

Now you've completed the XML POReq to X12 PO map. Save it to WebDAV as POReq_To_X12PO.xml.

Now that we have demonstrated how to map a flat file to XML and XML to EDI, you can always create maps that link a flat file to a flat file, XML to XML, EDI to EDI, and so on. There is no limitation regarding which format can be mapped to which format, as long as you create specifications (using BizTalk Editor) for the source and destination documents.

Chapter in Review

In this chapter, we have discussed the mapping process of BizTalk Server 2000 Messaging Services. We explained what a map is and introduced BizTalk Mapper, an XML tool that enables you to create maps graphically. We also discussed the concepts of links, functoids, and their significance in constructing a map. Finally, we used two examples to demonstrate how to create maps using BizTalk Mapper in different mapping scenarios.

CHAPTER

6

Managing BizTalk Server Messaging Services

IN THIS CHAPTER:

In Chapter 3, we introduced the architecture of BizTalk Messaging Services and explained the concepts of BizTalk Server 2000 messaging managing objects such as organizations, channels and messaging ports, distribution lists, document definitions, and envelopes. In Chapter 4 and 5, we discussed specifications and maps and showed you how to create them using BizTalk Editor and BizTalk Mapper. In this chapter, we will teach you how to leverage the knowledge and techniques you learned in the past three chapters to build sophisticated messaging solutions using the BizTalk Messaging Manager.

We will also explain the different types of receipts and how you can leverage the built-in receipt processing functionality of BizTalk Server 2000 to improve the reliability of your messaging solutions.

In addition, we will discuss the BizTalk Messaging Configuration Model and show you how to use it to automate the management of BizTalk Messaging Configuration objects.

The best way to master a technology is through practice. To help you get the most out of BizTalk Server 2000 Messaging Services and learn how to configure and manage these services using BizTalk Messaging Manager as well as other BizTalk Server 2000 tools, it will be necessary to utilize everything you've learned so far to build a complete, end-to-end, BizTalk Server messaging application. This sample application will help you better understand a variety of BizTalk messaging objects (first explained in Chapter 3) and show you how and when to use them in real-world scenarios. The primary tool necessary in building a BizTalk Server 2000 messaging application is the BizTalk Messaging Manager.

Using BizTalk Messaging Manager

BizTalk Messaging Manager is a custom web-browser application through which you can create, delete, and manage BizTalk messaging objects. Messaging objects play an important role in BizTalk Server 2000 messaging services, providing configuration information to the BizTalk Server 2000 messaging engine that include the messaging formats of both inbound and outbound documents, processing rules (validation and transformation), transport services, and so on. A typical BizTalk Server 2000 messaging application may contain messaging objects like those shown in Figure 6-1.

Depending on the complexity of your application, you may use more or fewer messaging objects than that illustrated in the figure (which first appeared in Chapter 3 as Figure 3-4; we've reprised it here to refresh your memory).

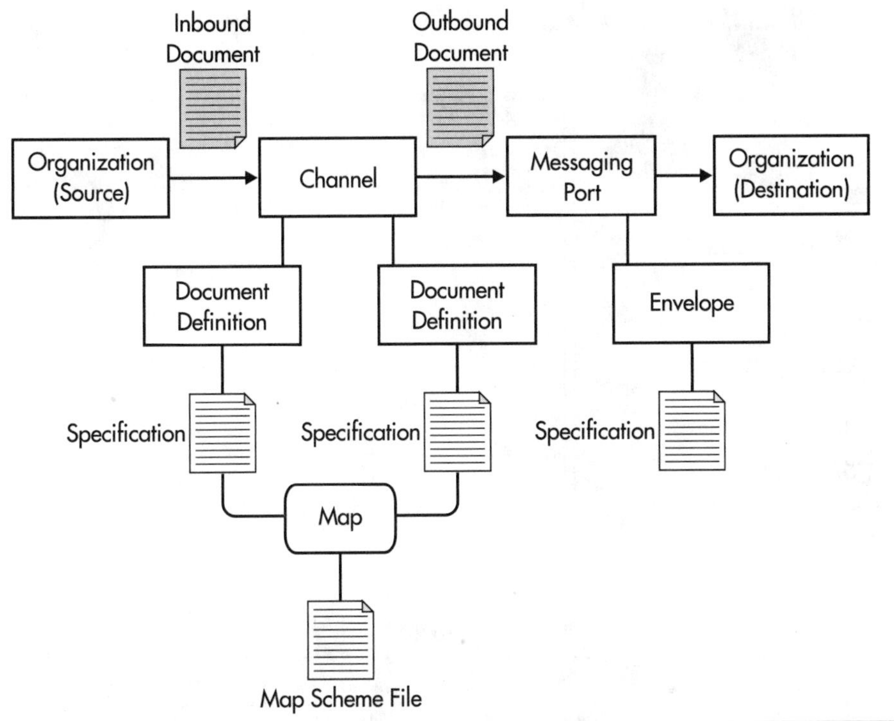

Figure 6-1 *Messaging objects in a typical BizTalk Server 2000 messaging application*

The BizTalk Messaging Manager User Interface

Figure 6-2 is a screen shot of the BizTalk Messaging Manager. The user interface of BizTalk Messaging Manager consists of two frames. The frame on the left enables you to search for various messaging objects.

Searching

To specify a particular category of objects you want to search, click one of the hyperlink-like items on the bottom-left list. As soon as you click a particular item in the list, its color changes from blue to gray. The search textboxes and other controls on the upper-left also change accordingly, allowing you to define the appropriate search criteria. After you type your search criteria into the appropriate places, click the Search Now button. The search results will be displayed in the right frame.

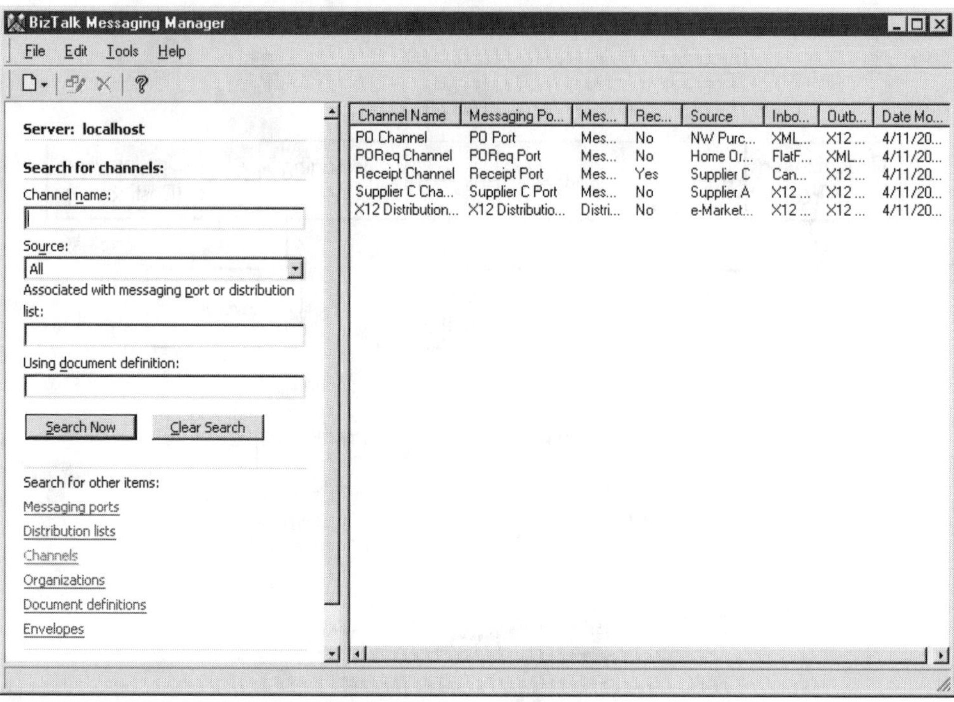

Figure 6-2 *BizTalk Messaging Manager user interface*

BizTalk Messaging Manager allows you to use the following four wildcards in your search criteria:

Wildcard	Description	Example
%	Any string of zero or more characters.	To find a channel that starts with the characters *PO*, use *PO%*. In this situation, both the *PO Channel* and *POReq Channel* will be returned.
_(underscore)	Any single character. It serves as a place holder.	_ C _ will return the *Supplier C Channel* (as shown in Figure 6-2).
[ ]	Any single character within the specified range ([x-z]) or set ([xyz]). This is an inclusive wildcard.	Both [xyz] and [x-z] will return the *X12 Distribution Channel* (as shown in Figure 6-2).
[^]	Any single character *not* within the specified range ([^x-z]) or set ([^xyz]). This is an exclusive wildcard.	Specify [^x]% should exclude the *X12 Distribution Channel* from the display shown in Figure 6-2.

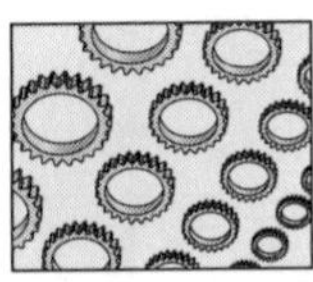

NOTE

You may notice that the wildcards described in the preceding table are exactly the same as those used in SQL Server. In fact, they are the same wildcards used in Transact SQL (TSQL) as well. This is because BizTalk Server 2000 uses SQL Server to store messaging objects in the InterchangeBTM database. Although the [^] wildcard doesn't work in BizTalk Messaging Manager, it does work in SQL Query Analyzer. (For example, "SELECT id, name FROM bts_channel WHERE name LIKE '[^x]%'" will exclude the X12 Distribution Channel from the result set, whereas specifying [^x]% in the Channel name search criteria will return the X12 Distribution Channel as one of the channels.)

If you didn't specify any search criteria, as shown in Figure 6-2, all the messaging objects of a particular category (channels in this case) will be displayed. If you click the Clear Search button, both the search criteria on the left frame and the results displayed in the right frame will be cleared.

Managing Remote Servers

By default, the BizTalk Server to which the BizTalk Messaging Manager connects is the local server (displayed as "localhost" in Figure 6-2). You can also configure BizTalk Messaging Manager to any servers on which you have permissions, meaning you can manage messaging objects residing on remote servers. To connect to a specific server, select Tools | Options and type the server name into the Name Of BizTalk Server To Connect To box (shown in Figure 6-3).

A Sample Messaging Application

In this sample application, a fictitious online food retailer sends its orders via an online marketplace. The marketplace distributes the orders to a group of selected individual suppliers, some of whom may use other suppliers (a supplier chain) to fill the orders.

The Business Scenario

Northwind Traders, Inc. is a retailer who sells food on the Web using an online marketplace, called e-MarketPlace, to get its orders filled. Figure 6-4 illustrates its high-level process flow.

When Northwind Traders receives an order from one of its customers via the Internet, its legacy ERP application generates a flat file purchase order request, which is then submitted to the BizTalk Server. BizTalk Server converts it to an XML document and forwards the XML purchase order request to the Purchase Department

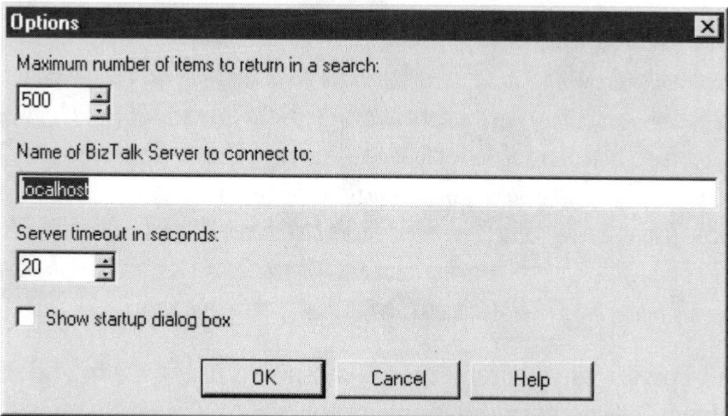

Figure 6-3 *Specifying a BizTalk Server you want to connect to*

(Step 1). From there, the Purchase Department further converts the XML purchase order request into the EDI X12 format and forwards it to e-MarketPlace (Step 2).

e-MarketPlace, one of Northwind Trader's direct suppliers, contacts individual suppliers to acquire the goods. e-MarketPlace and its suppliers all use X12 EDI standards for their document formats. When e-MarketPlace receives the X12 purchase order from the Purchase Department of Northwind Traders, it distributes the order to two of its suppliers, Supplier A and B, each supplier taking care of part of the order (Step 3).

Supplier A, in turn, uses Supplier C to provide the food it requires (Step 4).

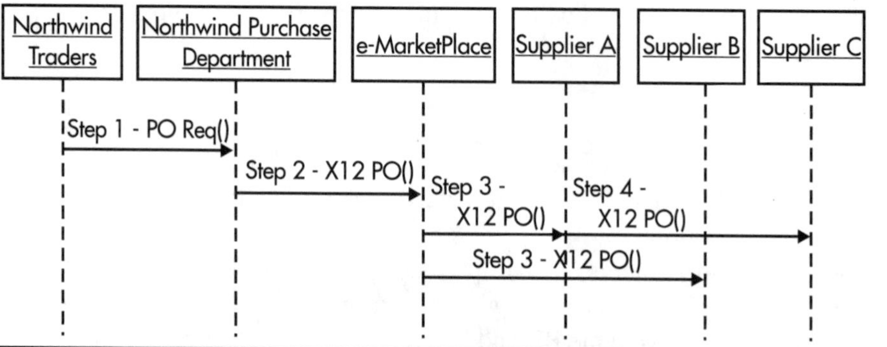

Figure 6-4 *The process flow of the sample messaging application*

Your job as a BizTalk developer is to build a complete messaging solution using BizTalk Messaging Manager and other BizTalk Server tools to meet the online transaction business requirement of this fictitious food retailer.

Prerequisites

There are several prerequisites you need to set up to work with this sample application:

1. Open Windows Explorer and create a folder, C:\Northwind\ with the following six sub folders: e-Market, Receipt, ReliableReceipt, Supplier A, Supplier B, and Supplier C.
2. Open the Computer Management MMC snap-in from Start | Programs | Administrative Tools. In the tree-view on the left side, expand the Services and Applications node, and then the Messaging Queuing node. Right-click the Private Queues node and select New | Private Queue. Type **POReqInbox** (Note: As mentioned in Chapter 3, Message Queue names are case-sensitive, even though they appear in Computer Management in lowercase) in the Name textbox of the Queue Name dialog box (as shown in Figure 6-5). This will create a private queue in Messaging Queuing Service (formally known as MSMQ).
3. Copy the TransportPOReq.asp from this chapter's source code, available at this book's web site, and download it to C:\Northwind. Expand the Internet Information Services node in the Computer Management snap-in, right-click the Default Web Site node and then select New | Virtual Directory. Click Next on the Welcome To Virtual Directory Creation Wizard screen. Type **Northwind** in the Alias: textbox on the Virtual Directory Alias screen and click Next. On the Web Site Content Directory screen, type **C:\Northwind** or click the Browse button and select C:\Northwind and click Next. Leave the

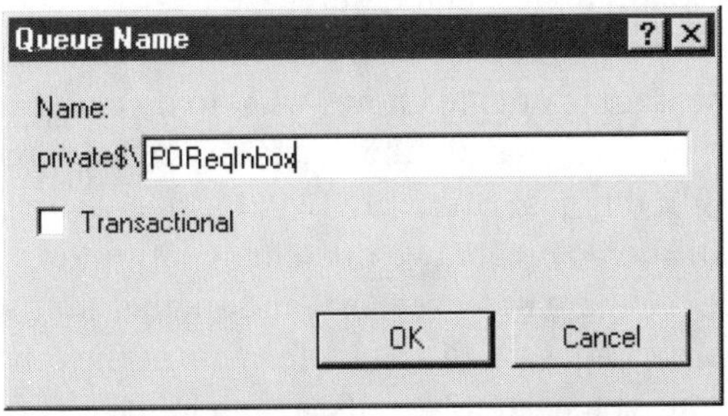

Figure 6-5 *Creating a private queue in Messaging Queuing Service*

default selections in place on the Access Permissions screen and click Next. Click Finish on the last screen to dismiss the Virtual Directory Creation Wizard.

4. Next, we'll use some of the specifications and maps you created in Chapter 4 and 5 along with some other specifications and maps shipped with BizTalk Server 2000. Save three specifications you created in Chapter 4, NWOrder_Spec.xml, POReq.xml, and 850Schema_Short, to <BizTalk Installation Folder>**DocSpecs**\Northwind through WebDAV (see Chapter 4 for instructions). Also open 997Schema.xml, found in <BizTalk Installation Folder>\XML Tools\Templates\X12\4010 folder, and save it to <BizTalk Installation Folder>\DocSpecs\Northwind using WebDAV. In addition, if you haven't done them in Chapter 5 yet, save two maps you created in Chapter 5, NWOrder_POReq.xml and POReq_To_X12PO.xml, to <BizTalk Installation Folder>**Maps**\Northwind (see Chapter 5 for instructions).

Converting Flat Files to XML PO Reqs

In the first step, you need to enable Northwind Traders to submit a flat file purchase order request from its legacy ERP system to the BizTalk Server, convert it to XML format, and send it to the Purchase Department.

Before you start building a messaging application using BizTalk Messaging Manager, you need to identify what messaging objects to create. First, ask: What relationships and dependencies exist between these messaging objects?

Recall that in Chapter 3 we introduced the concept of Home Organization and explained that it represents your organization. Here we will treat Northwind Traders as the Home Organization. In addition, we will use a VBScript application (which is a stub for a real application, such as an ERP application) to submit the flat file purchase order to BizTalk Server. Therefore, we need to create an application in the Home Organization to represent this VBScript program. The destination of the purchase order request is the Purchase Department of Northwind Traders. You need to create an organization to represent the Purchase Department.

At minimum, you need to create at least one channel and one messaging port so the BizTalk Server messaging engine knows what to do about the documents you submitted to it. In the channel, specify the document definitions for inbound and outbound documents. In this case, there are two document formats involved (flat file and XML), so you should create two document definitions, one for the inbound document (the flat file purchase order request) and another for the outbound document (the XML purchase order request). Since the formats of the inbound and outbound documents are different, you need to specify a map in the channel to help the transformation. The source of the channel will be the application of the Home

Organization. In addition, for the flat file inbound document format, you need to create an envelope and specify that envelope, either in the receiving function or in the input parameters of the Submit (or SubmitSync) method call, depending on the method you use to submit the document to BizTalk Server. Using an envelope (defined in the BizTalk Editor) in this manner will notify BizTalk Server which parser should be launched to parse the inbound document, and how to handle the semantics of that specific format.

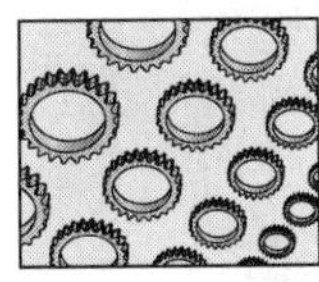

NOTE

In this sample application, we submit the document to BizTalk Server using VBScript code to demonstrate how to create and use the application object in BizTalk Messaging Manager. Due to the performance, and tightly coupled issues associated with the Submit and SubmitSync methods (as mentioned in Chapter 3), I strongly recommend you use receive functions (file or Messaging Queuing) in a production environment.

In the messaging port, you need to specify the transport protocol, the address, as well as the destination organization or application. In this case, you will use HTTP as the transport protocol and specify the Purchase Department as the destination organization.

Figure 6-6 illustrates the messaging objects, their relationships, and other related information.

TIP

Before you start creating messaging objects and setting their relationships in BizTalk Messaging Manager, draw a diagram like the one shown in Figure 6-6 on a whiteboard or a piece of paper to display the messaging objects and their relationships to one another. In a complicated messaging solution, you will end up creating a lot of messaging objects. Without a clear roadmap, it will become very difficult to manage as the number of messaging objects grows. A diagram can also be very helpful when you want to write a program to automate the creation of messaging objects through the BizTalk Messaging Configuration Object Model (something you will learn later in this chapter).

Having the roadmap in place, we are ready to start creating messaging objects using BizTalk Messaging Manager. Let's start with organizations and applications. Open BizTalk Messaging Manager and click the Organizations item in the left frame. Type **Home** as the search criteria, then click the Search Now button. Home Organization (Default) should appear in the right frame. Double-click Home Organization and select the Identifier tab on the Organization Properties dialog box that appears. You will need a more descriptive name for Northwind Traders instead of the default name (Home Organization). The Identifiers tab is where you can create

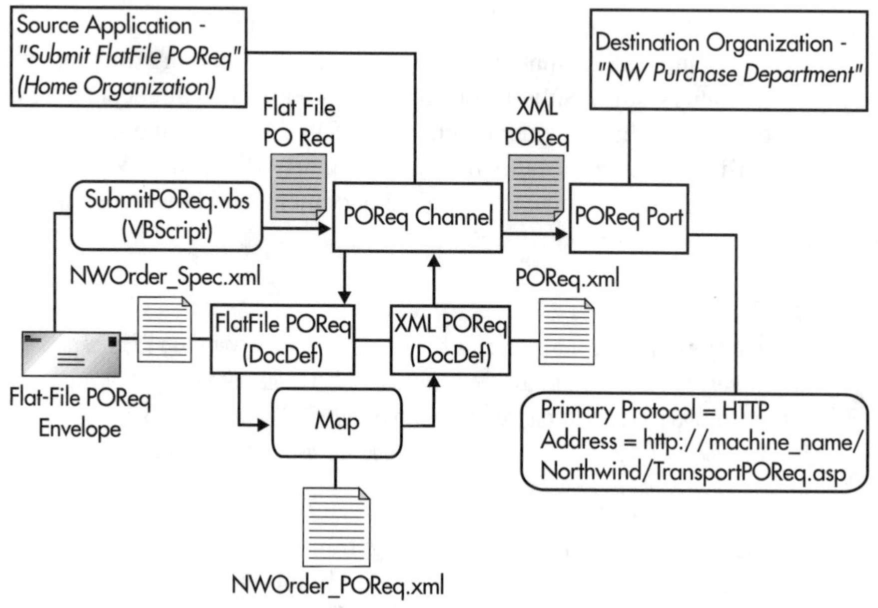

Figure 6-6 *The messaging objects for processing the flat file purchase order request*

aliases for the organizations. Click the Add button and set the properties in the Identifier Properties dialog box to those shown in Figure 6-7.

You also need to create an application to represent the VBScript program that submits the flat file purchase order request to BizTalk Server. Switch to the Applications tab, click Add, and type **Submit FlatFile POReq** as the application name in the Application Properties dialog box, then click OK. Click OK to dismiss the Organization Properties box.

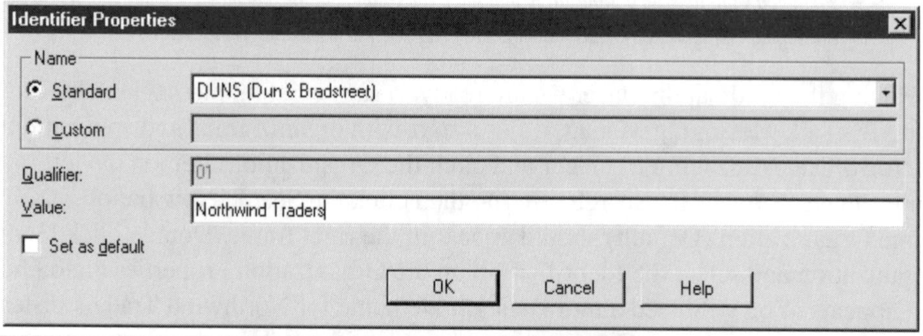

Identifier Properties
Name
Standard DUNS (Dun & Bradstreet)
Custom
Qualifier: 01
Value: Northwind Traders
Set as default
OK Cancel Help

Figure 6-7 *Creating an alias for the Home Organization*

Next, you need to create an organization to represent the Purchase Department of Northwind Traders. Right-click the white area in the right frame and select New Organization. Alternatively, you may select File | New | Organization from the menu option or press CTRL-G. On the General tab, type **NW Purchase Department** as the Organization name. This will use the default organization qualifier, OrganizationName, as discussed in Chapter 3. The default organization qualifier is usually good enough for organizations that send and/or receive XML and flat file documents. This OrganizationName qualifier (sixteen characters long), however, is considered too long in scenarios that involve EDI (X12 or EDIFACT) documents. For example, in X12 document headers, the organization qualifiers (sender and receiver) are limited to two characters, whereas the values are limited to fifteen characters. Later, the Purchase Department of Northwind Traders will need to submit an X12 purchase order to e-MarketPlace, which means you will have to use a shorter identifier. Throughout this chapter, you will stick to the standard organization identifier, DUNS (Dun & Bradstreet), for the alternative organization identifier. So, click the Identifier tab, and set the properties for the Purchase Department of Northwind Traders to those shown in Figure 6-8.

Now you need to create two document definitions, one for a flat file and the other for an XML document. The processes of creating document definitions for flat file and XML documents are the same. In BizTalk Messaging Manager, select File | New | Document Definition (or press CTRL-D). On the General tab of the New Document Definition dialog box, type FlatFile POReq in the Document Definition Name textbox. Select the Document specification check box and click the Browse button. Navigate to the Northwind WebDAV folder and select NWOrder_Spec.xml. The New Document Definition dialog box should look like the one in Figure 6-9. The Global Tracking tab enables you to specify document level tracking options that you will see in Chapter 8. The Selection Criteria tab enables you to specify selection

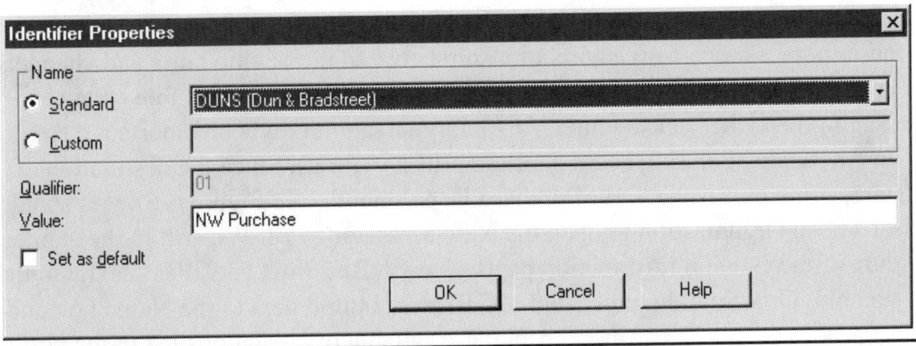

Figure 6-8 *Specifying an alternative organization identifier*

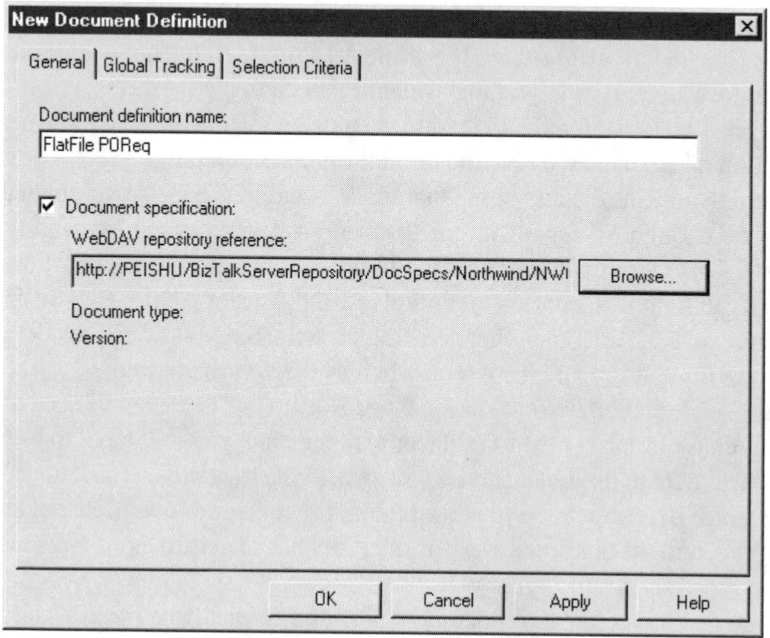

Figure 6-9 *Creating a document definition for a flat file document*

criteria for EDI documents (X12 or EDIFACT). We introduced selection criteria in Chapter 3 and will teach you how to use them later in this chapter when creating document definitions for X12 EDI documents. Click OK to dismiss the dialog box.

Similarly, create a document specification named "XML POReq" and point to the POReq.xml in the Northwind WebDAV folder.

Now that we have organizations (or applications) and document definitions in place, it's time to create the two most important messaging objects: messaging ports and channels. You need to create a messaging port first before creating a channel because there is a one-to-many relationship between messaging ports and channels. To create a messaging port in BizTalk Messaging Manager, select File | New | Messaging Port, then select either To An Organization (keyboard shortcut CTRL-R) or To An Application (keyboard shortcut SHIFT-CTRL-R). Since the destination of the messaging port is the "NW Purchase Department" (see Figure 6-6), you should select To An Organization to open the New Messaging Port Wizard. In the Name textbox of the General Information page, type **POReq Port** and click Next. On the Destination Organization page, click the Browse button next to the Name box and select NW Purchase Department from the Available organizations list in the pop-up Select An Organization dialog box. Click the Browse button next to the Address box in the Primary Transport frame to open the Primary Transport dialog box and select

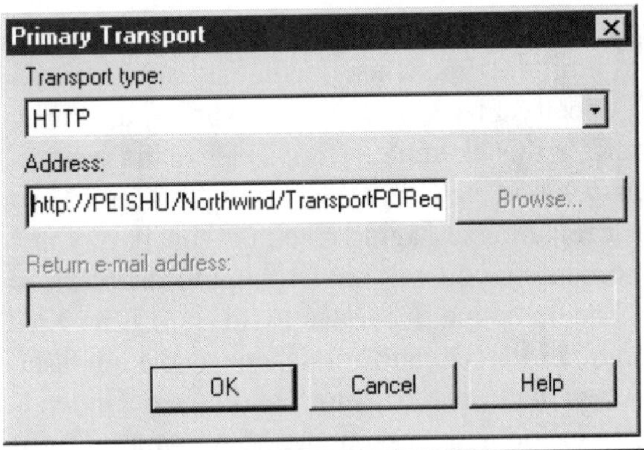

Figure 6-10 *Specifying the primary transport for a port*

HTTP as the Transport type. Next, type **http://*MachineName*/Northwind/TransportPOReq.asp**, as shown in Figure 6-10.

Click OK to dismiss the Primary Transport dialog box. The New Messaging Port Wizard should now look like the one in Figure 6-11.

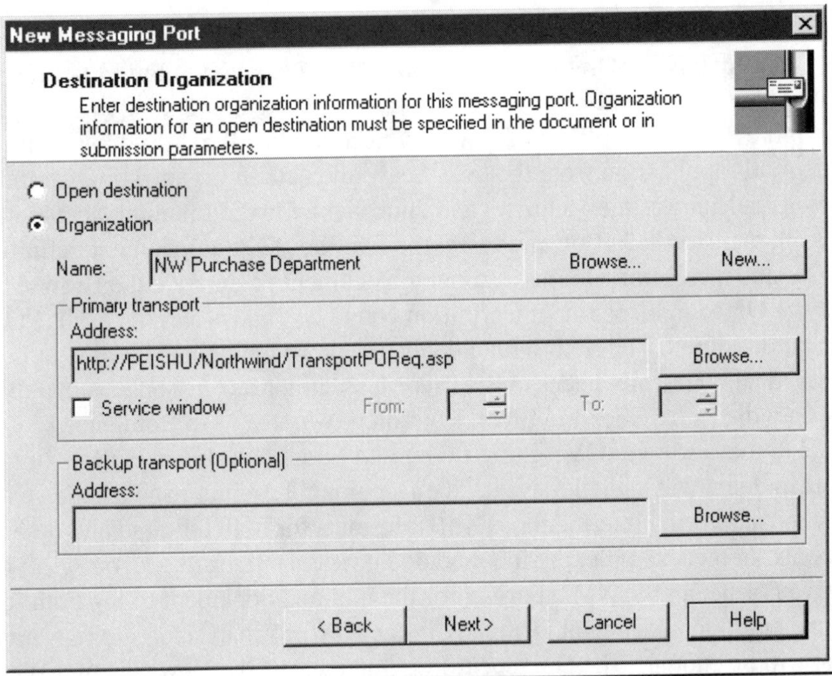

Figure 6-11 *The Destination Organization page of the New Messaging Port dialog box*

As shown in Figure 6-11, you may specify a service window (in hours) for the primary transport to limit the time when documents can be transported. In addition, you may optionally specify a backup transport to use as an alternative should the primary transport fail. In this example, you will leave the service window and the backup transport unspecified, and click Next. You don't need an envelope for the port at this point (for reliable messaging receipt at this port, you will need to use a reliable envelope, something you will see later in this chapter), so leave the envelope information blank. The outbound document to this port is an XML document, so the default organization qualifier (OrganizationName as the qualifier) would be fine in this case. Click Next on the Envelope Information page. On the Security Information page, you can specify encoding, encryption, and signature information to secure the messaging in BizTalk Server 2000, as detailed in the Microsoft white paper, "Using Certificates with Microsoft® BizTalk™ Server 2000" which can be downloaded from the BizTalk Server 2000 web site at **http://www.microsoft.com/BizTalk**. In this example, you don't use securities. The Create A Channel For This Messaging Port check box is marked by default. You can specify From An Application (which we used to create the application "Submit FlatFile POReq" in the Home Organization earlier) as the channel type (the default) and click the Finish button. This will dismiss the New Messaging Port Wizard and open the New Channel Wizard, as shown in Figure 6-12.

Type **POReq Channel** in the General Information page of the New Channel Wizard, and click Next. On the Source Application page, the Submit FlatFile POReq application should be selected in the Name box automatically (if you created more than one application, you may need to click the drop-down button and select this application from the list). Leave the default organization identifier (OrganizationName as the qualifier) and click Next. On the Inbound Document page, click the Browse button and select the FlatFile POReq document definition. Click OK and then Next. On the Outbound Document page, click the Browse button next to the Outbound Document Definition Name box and select the XML POReq document definition. The Map Inbound Document To Outbound Document box will be checked automatically because BizTalk Messaging Manager detects that their formats are different. Click the Browse button next to the Map Reference box, navigate to the Northwind WebDAV folder and select NWOrder_POReq.xml as the map document and click Next. The Document Logging page enables you to specify the native and intermediate (XML) formats for both inbound and outbound documents. In this example, the inbound document is a flat file, so you select both In Native Format and In XML Format for the inbound document to log both formats. Since the outbound document is already in the XML format, selecting In Native Format will be enough. The Document Logging page of the New Channel Wizard looks like the one in Figure 6-13.

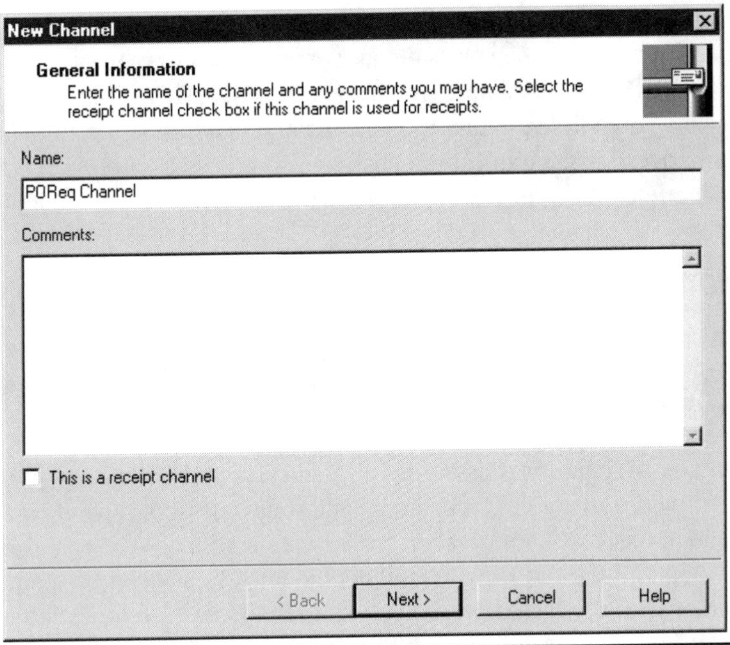

Figure 6-12 *Specifying a name for a new channel*

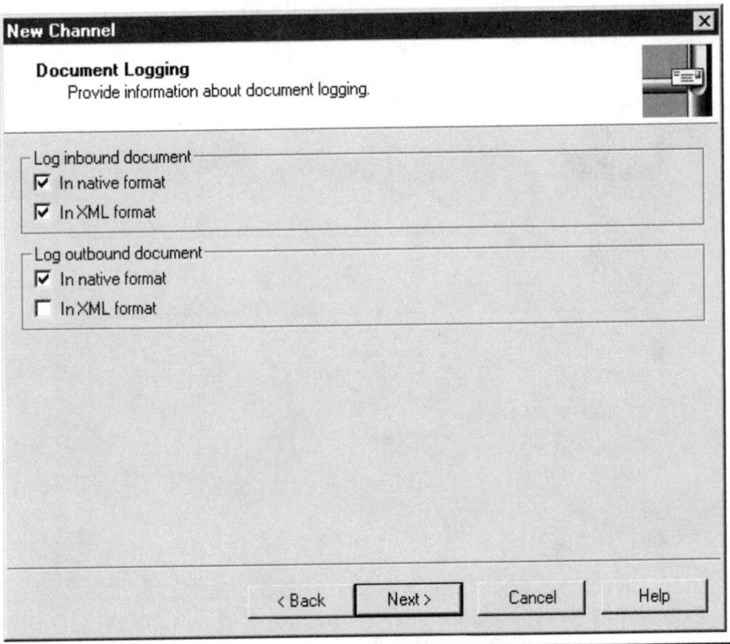

Figure 6-13 *Specifying document logging options in a channel*

On the Advanced Configuration page, the last page of the New Channel Wizard, you may specify retry options, such as number of retries and retry intervals (in minutes). For an X12 or EDIFACT document, you also need to specify a group control number (something else you will learn later in this chapter). In addition, the Advanced button enables you to override the transport or envelope component settings for a messaging port or distribution list. In this example, leave the defaults and click the Finish button to create the channel.

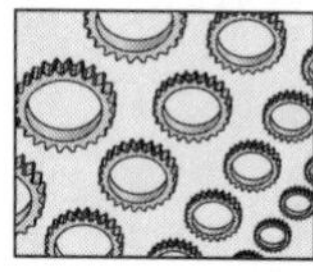

NOTE

Depending on the specific transport types, each of the built-in transports has a page with various settings on it. For example, the HTTP transport has a properties page for proxy, a user/password for client certificates, and so on.

Now that you have built a messaging infrastructure that will accept a flat file document, convert it to an XML document and transport it to a specified address (an ASP page in this case). Remember, earlier we mentioned that you also need a reliable envelope for the flat file inbound document. Click New | Envelope from the menu option of BizTalk Messaging Manager. In the New Envelope dialog box, type **FlatFile POReq Envelope**. Select FLATFILE from the Envelope Format drop-down list. Check the Envelope Specification box and click the Browse button. Navigate to the Northwind WebDAV folder and select NWOrder_Spec.xml (this is the specification for the inbound document). The New Envelope dialog box should look like the one in Figure 6-14.

Figure 6-14 *Creating an envelope for the flat file inbound document*

The ASP page, TransportPOReq.asp (located at C:\Northwind\) receives the XML purchase order request document from the POReq Port messaging port and sends the message to the private queue, POReqInbox (that you created earlier), in the Messaging Queuing Services.

```
<%
Option Explicit
Dim oStream, oQueueInfo, oQueue, oMessage

Const MQ_SEND_ACCESS = 2
Const MQ_DENY_NONE = 0

On Error Resume Next

If Request.totalBytes = 0 then
    Response.Write "No Data Posted From BizTalk Server. Could Not Process"
    Err.Raise vbObjectError+ 101,, _
               "No Data Posted From BizTalk Server. Could Not Process"
    Response.End
End If

Set oStream = CreateObject("ADODB.Stream")
oStream.Open
oStream.Type = 1
oStream.Write Request.BinaryRead(Request.TotalBytes)
oStream.Position = 0
oStream.Type = 2
oStream.Charset ="us-ascii"

Set oQueueInfo = Server.CreateObject("MSMQ.MSMQQueueInfo")
oQueueInfo.FormatName = "DIRECT=OS:.\private$\POReqInbox"
Set oQueue = oQueueInfo.Open(MQ_SEND_ACCESS, MQ_DENY_NONE)
Set oMessage = Server.CreateObject("MSMQ.MSMQMessage")
oMessage.Label = "POReq"
oMessage.Body = oStream.ReadText
oMessage.Send oQueue

Set oStream = Nothing
Set oQueueInfo = Nothing
Set oQueue = Nothing
Set oMessage = Nothing

If Err <> 0 then
```

```
        Response.Write "Error Occurred.  Could Not Process"

        Err.Raise Err.Number,, "Error Occurred.  Could Not Process"

        Response.End

    End If
%>
```

After declaring object variables and Messaging Queuing constants, the ASP page checks to see if there is any data being submitted by testing the TotalBytes property of the Request object. Then it creates an ADO stream object and copies the data from the request object to the stream object:

```
Set oStream = CreateObject("ADODB.Stream")
oStream.Open
oStream.Type = 1
oStream.Write Request.BinaryRead(Request.TotalBytes)
oStream.Position = 0
oStream.Type = 2
oStream.Charset ="us-ascii"
```

After calling the Open method of the stream object, the ASP page sets the Type property to 1 (adTypeBinary). Then it calls the Write method of the stream object to copy the binary read from the Request object. After that, it sets the position to the beginning of the stream and sets the Type property of the stream to 2 (adTypeText). It also sets the Charset property of the stream object to "us-ascii". At this point, you are ready to read the text contents of the stream data and send it to the queue:

```
Set oQueueInfo = Server.CreateObject("MSMQ.MSMQQueueInfo")
oQueueInfo.FormatName = "DIRECT=OS:.\private$\POReqInbox"
Set oQueue = oQueueInfo.Open(MQ_SEND_ACCESS, MQ_DENY_NONE)
Set oMessage = Server.CreateObject("MSMQ.MSMQMessage")
oMessage.Label = "POReq"
oMessage.Body = oStream.ReadText
oMessage.Send oQueue
```

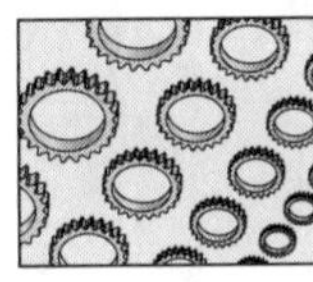

NOTE

In Windows 2000 Message Queuing Services, public queues are those published in Active Directory and can be accessed anywhere in the Active Directory forest. Private queues are not published in Active Directory and can only by accessed by Message Queuing applications that know the full pathname or format name of the queue. Public queues are persistent. Private queues, on the other hand, are light-weighted and more suitable for offline operations where the directory services may not be available.

After completing the job, the ASP page cleans up the objects from memory. If any error occurs during the process, it reports them.

```
Set oStream = Nothing
Set oQueueInfo = Nothing
Set oQueue = Nothing
Set oMessage = Nothing

If Err <> 0 then

    Response.Write "Error Occurred. Could Not Process"

    Err.Raise Err.Number,, "Error Occurred. Could Not Process"

    Response.End

End If
```

In the VBScript program, SubmitPOReq.vbs submits the flat file purchase order request, NWOrder_10262.dat, to the BizTalk Server through the Submit method of the IInterchange interface, as illustrated in the following:

```
Dim oInterchange, FSO, strFilePath
Const cChannel = "POReq Channel"
Const cEnvelope = "FlatFile POReq Envelope"
Const cFileToSubmit = "NWOrder_10262.dat"

On Error Resume Next
```

```
Set FSO = CreateObject("Scripting.FileSystemObject")
strFilePath = FSO.GetAbsolutePathName(cFileToSubmit)

Set oInterchange = CreateObject("BizTalk.Interchange")
oInterchange.Submit 1, _
                   , _
                   , _
                   , _
                   , _
                   , _
                   , _
                   cChannel,_
                   strFilePath, _
                   cEnvelope, _
                   False

If err = 0 Then
  wscript.echo "Document has been successfully submitted!"
Else
  wscript.echo err.description
End if
```

As we mentioned before, the preceding code is for demonstration purposes only. You should avoid using the IInterchange interface in a production environment. Use receive functions (file or Messaging Queuing) instead in a production environment.

Now, copy both SubmitPOReq.vbs and NWOrder_10262.dat to the C:\Northwind folder. The content for NWOrder_10262.dat looks like this:

```
110262,1996-07-22
28,Callahan,Laura
3Chef Anton's Gumbo Mix,21.35,36
3Uncle Bob's Organic Dried Pears,30,12
3Gnocchi di nonna Alice,38,24
4Rattlesnake Canyon Grocery,2817 Milton Dr.,Albuquerque,NM,87110,USA
5Rattlesnake Canyon Grocery,2817 Milton Dr.,Albuquerque,NM,87110,USA
```

Double-click SubmitPOReq.vbs from Windows Explorer. You should see a confirmation message from the Windows Script Host, stating the document was successfully submitted.

If you check the POReqInbox queue from the Computer Management MMC snap-in, you should see a message labeled "POReq" in the queue (as shown in Figure 6-15). To manually remove the message from the queue, right-click the

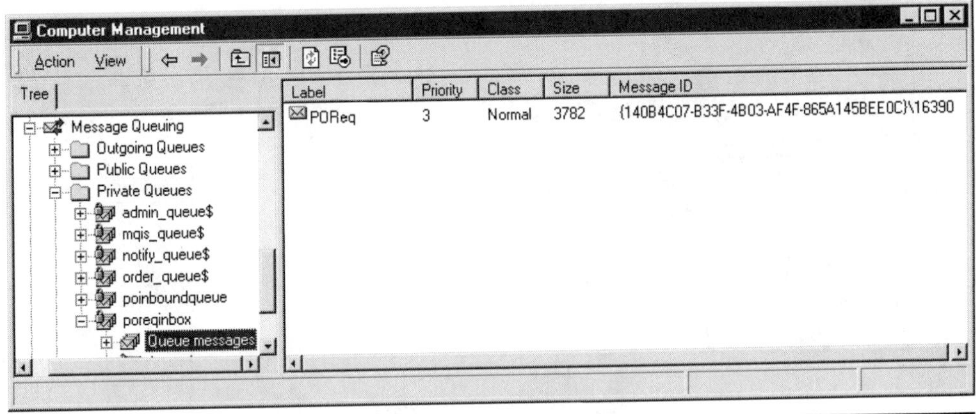

Figure 6-15 *Viewing the POReq document in the Messaging Queuing queue*

Queue Messages node and select All Tasks | Purge. Select Yes when asked if you're sure you want to delete all the messages in the queue.

Converting XML PO Reqs to X12 PO

In the next step (Step 2), you will create messaging objects and other necessary applications for the Purchase Department of Northwind Traders to convert the received XML purchase order request to an X12 purchase order and to transport it to e-MarketPlace. Figure 6-16 illustrates the BizTalk messaging solution you need to build in this step.

As you can see from Figure 6-16, some of the messaging objects are the same as the ones you used in Step 1. Others are new messaging objects you need to create in this step.

One of the new messaging objects is the destination organization. Use BizTalk Messaging Manager to create an organization named "e-MarketPlace" and add an alternate identifier with the following properties:

Name: e-MarketPlace

Standard - DUNS (Dun & Bradstreet)

Qualifier: 01

Value: e-Market

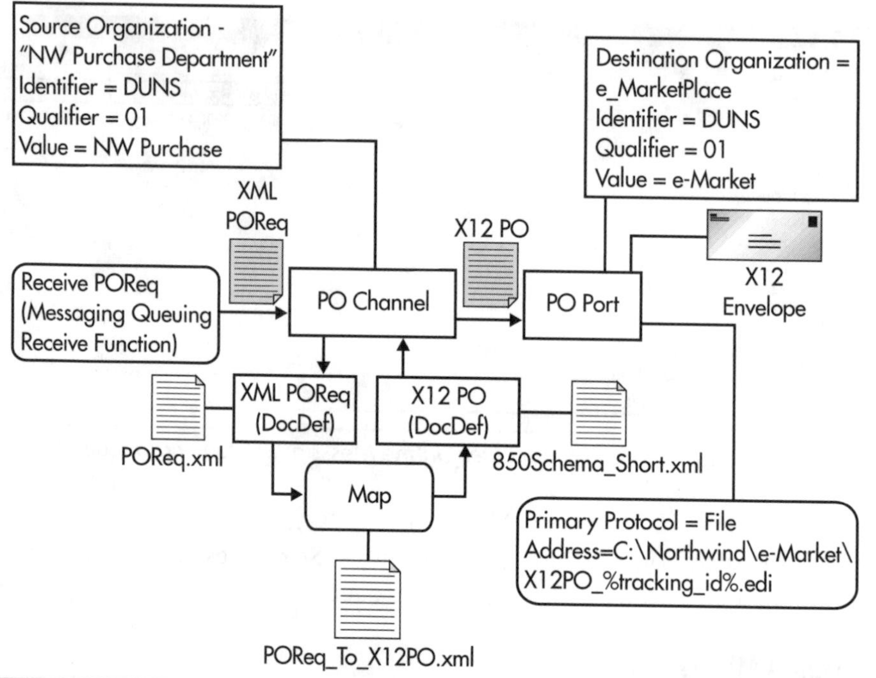

Figure 6-16 *Converting an XML purchase order request to an X12 purchase order and transporting it to the marketplace*

As we explained earlier, you need the shorter version qualifier for organizations when dealing with EDI documents.

You also need an X12 envelope for the messaging port so the BizTalk messaging engine knows to launch the X12 serializer to serialize the document from the intermediate XML format to the X12 EDI format. Create a new envelope in BizTalk Messaging Manager, type **X12 Envelope** as the Envelope Name and select X12 as the Envelope Format, as shown in Figure 6-17.

Create a document definition for the X12 purchase order named **X12 PO** and point to the specification 850Schema_Short.xml in the Northwind WebDAV folder (see Figure 6-18).

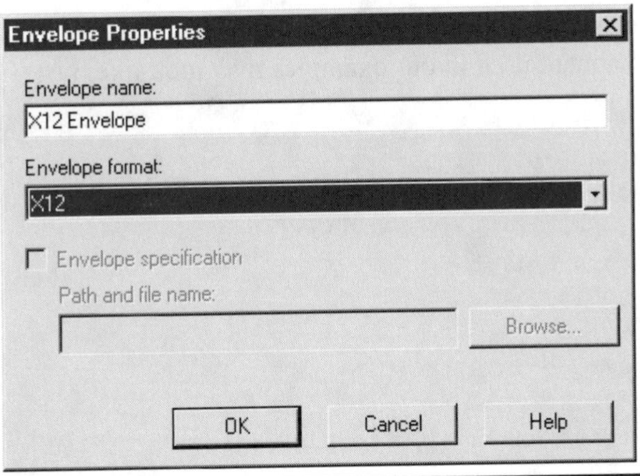

Figure 6-17 *Creating an X12 envelope*

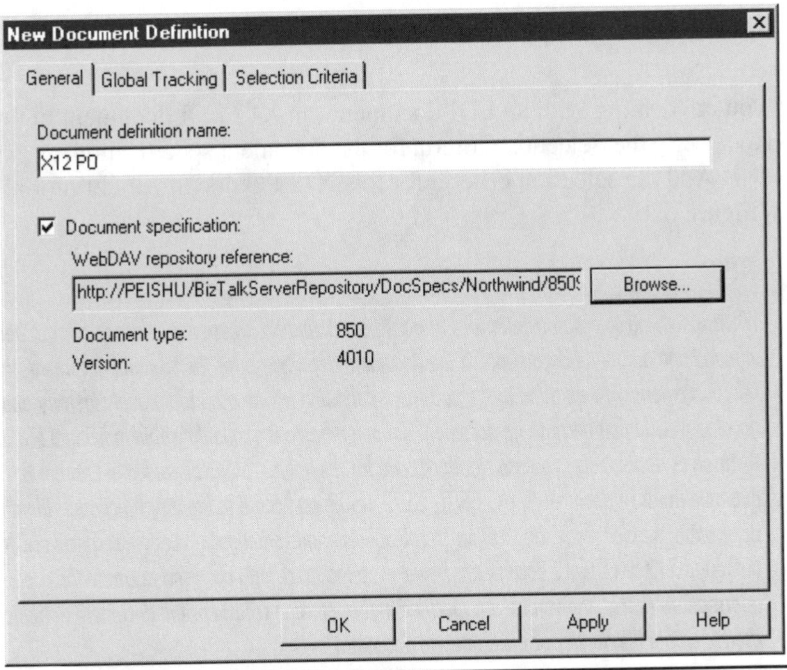

Figure 6-18 *Creating a document definition for the X12 purchase order*

Recall that this is one of the specifications you created in Chapter 4. An instance of an X12 PO document used in our examples may look like this:

```
ISA*00*          *00*          *01*NT Traders     *01*Supplier B     *
010323*0053*U*00400*000001003*0*P*>~
  GS*PO*NW Traders*Supplier B*20010323*0053*1002*X*4010~
    ST*850*0001~BEG*00*SA*123456789**19960722~
      PER*SA*Laura Callahan~
      DTM*118*20010323~
      N3*2817 Milton Dr.~
      N4*Albuquerque*NM*87110*USA~
      PO1**36**21.35~
      PID*F****Chef Anton's Gumbo Mix~
      PO1**12**30~
      PID*F****Uncle Bob's Organic Dried Pears~
      PO1**24**38~
      PID*F****Gnocchi di nonna Alice~
    CTT*3*2040.6~SE*14*0001~
  GE*1*1002~
IEA*1*000001003~
```

Since you are dealing with an EDI document (an X12 EDI document in this case), you need to specify the Selection Criteria for the document specification, as explained in Chapter 3. Add the selection criteria for this X12 PO document definition, as shown in Figure 6-19.

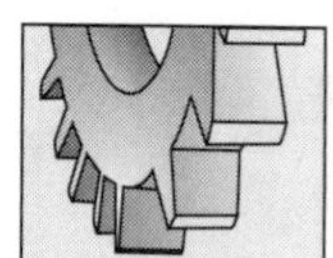

TIP

When specifying selection criteria for EDI document definitions, there is a subtle difference between inbound and outbound documents. If the document definition is for the inbound document, then the selection criteria you specified in the document definition will be used to uniquely identify and select a document definition because no document definition name is available within individual EDI documents themselves. In this case, you use standard code for the values, as we discussed in Chapter 3. For example, for X12 documents, use GS01, GS02, GS03, and GS08 to identify functional_identifier, application_sender_code, application_receiver_code, and standards_version, respectively. In case of outbound X12 or EDIFACT documents, however, selection criteria are used to create the group header information. That is, the values you specified in the selection criteria of the document definition will be used to create the header of the outbound document.

Now it's time to create the messaging port and the channel. In BizTalk Messaging Manager, create a messaging port (To An Organization) named **PO Port** and click Next. In the Destination Organization page of the New Messaging Port Wizard,

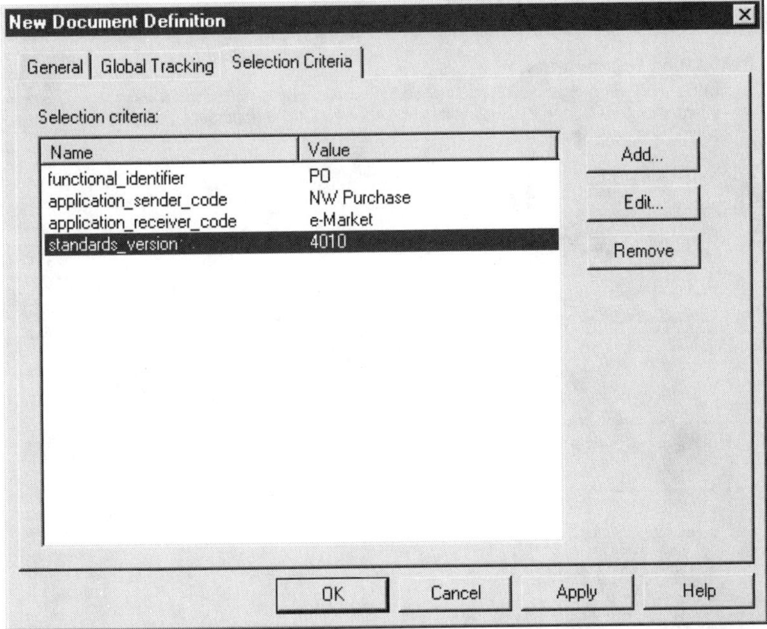

Figure 6-19 *Selection criteria for the X12 purchase order document definition*

select e-MarketPlace as the destination organization and HTTP as the file transport type. Type **file://C:\Northwind\e-Market\X12PO_%tracking_id%.edi** for the address of the primary transport, as shown in Figure 6-20.

Click Next on the Envelope Information page of the New Messaging Port Wizard, and select X12 Envelope from the drop-down box. When you use an X12 document, you need to specify appropriate delimiters. Delimiters indicate the characters used to separate the records and fields of the envelope and the documents contained in the envelope. Click the Delimiters button, and type appropriate characters for Component Element Separator, Element Separator, and Segment Terminator, as shown in Figure 6-21.

Click OK to return to the Envelope Information page. Type **1001** in the Interchange Control Number box. When you select an envelope with an X12 or EDIFACT format, you must also specify an interchange control number. An interchange control number is used to identify and track documents processed using the messaging port. The interchange control number is incremented with each use of the envelope and messaging port. The default Organization Identifier uses the OrganizationName

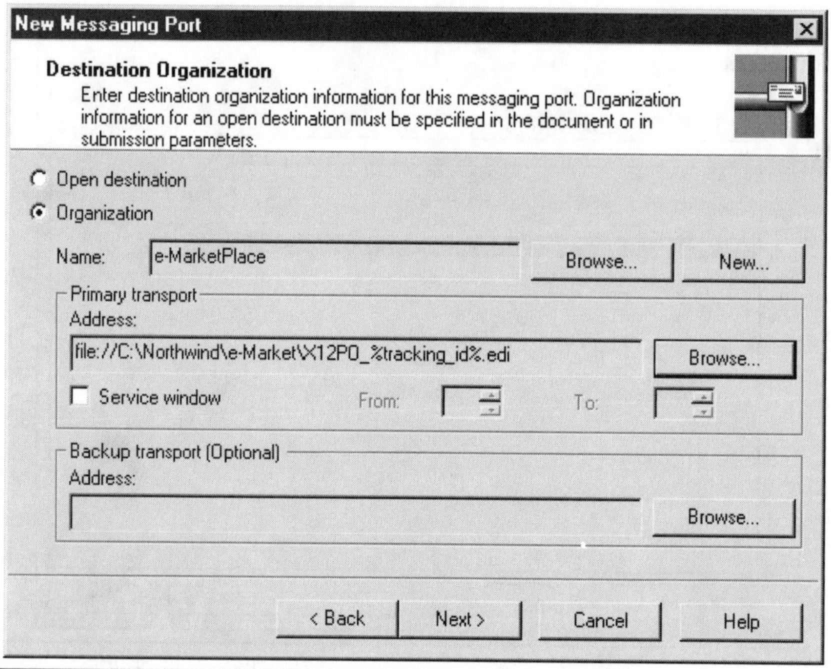

Figure 6-20 *Specifying the destination organization and transport protocol address*

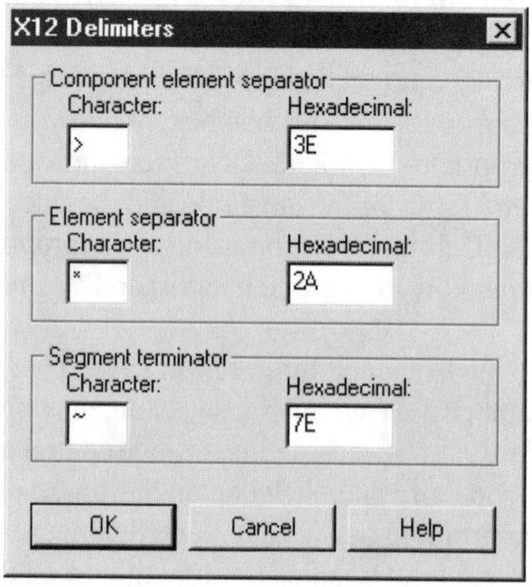

Figure 6-21 *Specifying X12 delimiters*

as the qualifier. For X12 documents, you need to select a shorter qualifier to identify the destination organization. To do this, select DUNS (Dun & Bradstreet) from the drop-down box, as shown in Figure 6-22. Click Next.

On the Security Information page of the New Messaging Port Wizard, select From An Organization as the Channel Type, and click Finish. This will launch the New Channel Wizard. Type **PO Channel** in the Name box of the General Information page of the New Channel Wizard, and click Next. In the Source Organization page of the New Channel Wizard, select NW Purchase Department as the source organization and select DUNS (Dun & Bradstreet) / NW Purchase as the organization identifier (because X12 documents require shorter organization identifiers), as shown in Figure 6-23.

Click Next, select XML POReq as the inbound document definition on the Inbound Document page. Click Next, select X12 PO as the outbound document definition on the Outbound Document page and specify POReq_To_X12PO.xml as the map from the Northwind WebDAV folder. Click Next. In the Document Logging page, select In Native Format for the inbound document and both In Native Format and In XML Format for the outbound document. Click Next. On the Advanced Configuration page, type **1001** as the group control number (note that here you

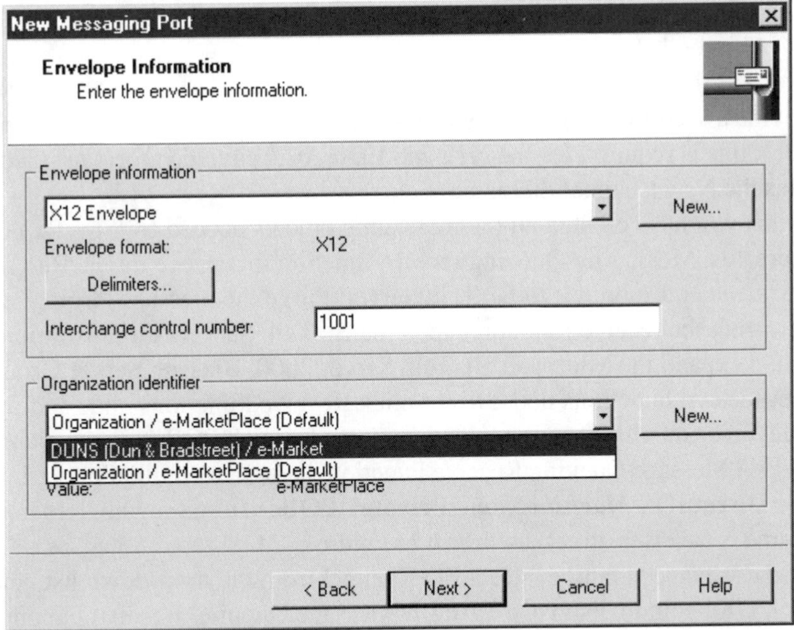

Figure 6-22 *Selecting a shorter qualifier to identify the destination organization*

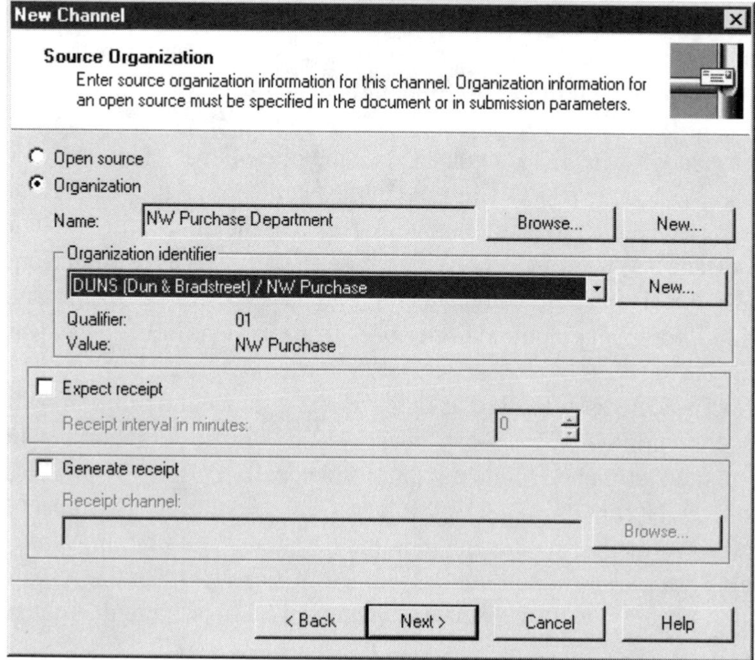

Figure 6-23 *Specifying the source organization for the channel*

only provide a seed for the group control number; it will automatically increment over time); this is required for the X12 and EDIFACT envelope formats. Click OK to dismiss the New Channel dialog box.

Now that you have created all the messaging objects needed for Step 2. You will need to create a Messaging Queuing receive function to retrieve the POReq message from the queue and submit it to BizTalk Server. Purge the messages from the queue before creating the receive function. Open the BizTalk Server Administration MMC snap-in and expand the Microsoft BizTalk Server 2000, BizTalk Server Group to show the Receive Functions node. Right-click Receive Functions node and select New | Message Queuing Receive Function. Type Receive POReq in the Name box of the Add A Message Queuing Receive Function dialog box. In the Polling Location box, type **Direct=OS:*MachineName*\Private$\POReqInbox** (again, remember the queue name is case-sensitive), as shown in Figure 6-24.

Click the Advanced button, select PO Channel from the drop-down list, and click OK. Click OK again to dismiss the Add A Message Queuing Receive Function dialog box.

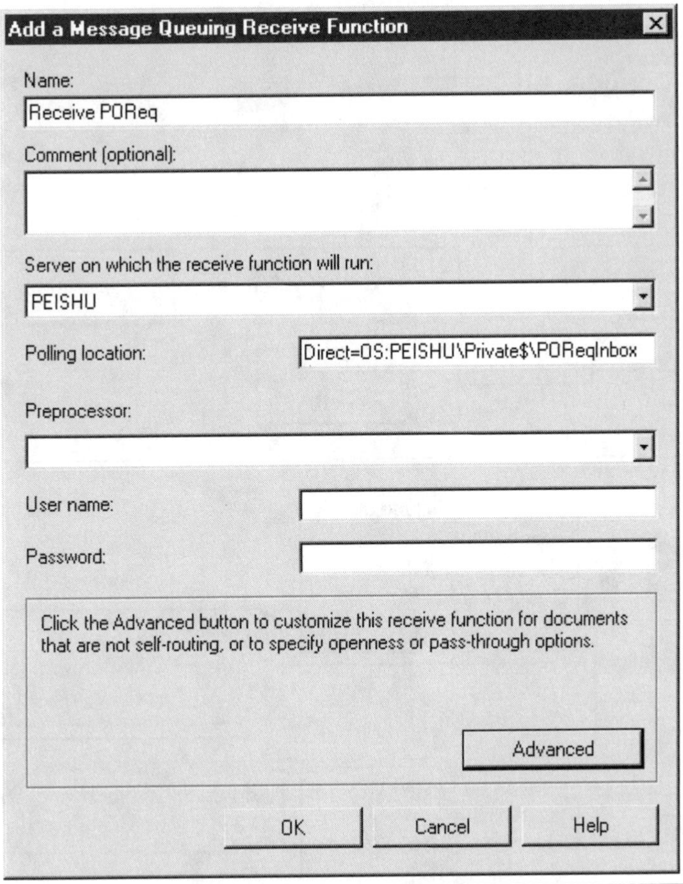

Add a Message Queuing Receive Function	
Name:	Receive POReq
Comment (optional):	
Server on which the receive function will run:	PEISHU
Polling location:	Direct=OS:PEISHU\Private$\POReqInbox
Preprocessor:	
User name:	
Password:	

Click the Advanced button to customize this receive function for documents that are not self-routing, or to specify openness or pass-through options.

Advanced

OK Cancel Help

Figure 6-24 *Creating a Messaging Queuing receive function*

Now, if you run the SubmitPOReq.vbs again, the generated POReq message will be gone from the POReqInbox queue in the Messaging Queuing Service and an X12 purchase order document should be found in the C:\Northwind\e-Market folder. You can open the generated X12 document in Notepad to check its content.

Using Distribution Lists

In this section, you will create messaging objects and necessary applications for the e-MarketPlace organization (Step 3), including a distribution list. In addition, you will build the messaging solution for Supplier C (Step 4). Figure 6-25 illustrates the messaging solutions for Step 3 and Step 4.

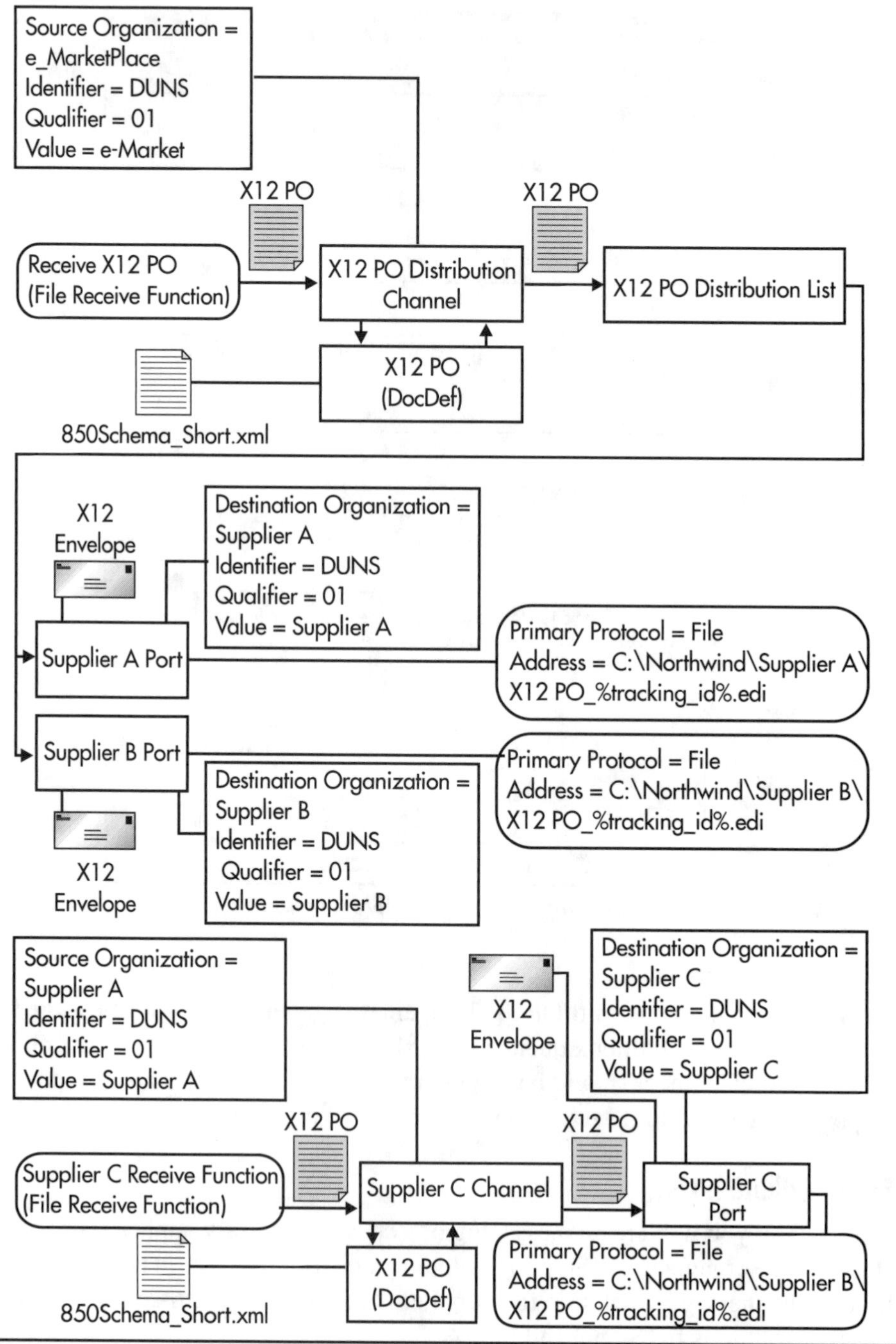

Figure 6-25 *Messaging solutions for e-MarketPlace and its suppliers*

As you can see from Figure 6-25, you can reuse most of the "auxiliary" messaging objects (document definitions, envelopes, and so on) you built in previous sections. Now, create three organizations in BizTalk Messaging Manager.

Organization for Supplier A:

Name: Supplier A

Standard - DUNS (Dun & Bradstreet)

Qualifier: 01

Value: Supplier A

Organization for Supplier B:

Name: Supplier B

Standard - DUNS (Dun & Bradstreet)

Qualifier: 01

Value: Supplier B

Organization for Supplier C:

Name: Supplier C

Standard - DUNS (Dun & Bradstreet)

Qualifier: 01

Value: Supplier C

Now, let's create the primary messaging objects for e-MarketPlace, including a channel, a distribution list, and two messaging ports. First, you need to create the messaging ports. Secondly, you must create the distribution list and add the messaging ports to it. Finally, you should create the channel for the distribution list.

Creating messaging ports for Supplier A and B is very similar to creating the messaging port for e-MarketPlace (the PO Port), including selecting the X12 envelope, specifying delimiters, and setting interchange control numbers. The only difference is on the last page of the New Messaging Port Wizard, the Security Information page: unselect the Create A Channel For This Messaging Port check box. Messaging ports for Supplier A and B are used by the distribution list, not by channels. The messaging port properties for Supplier A are:

Name: Supplier A Port

Destination Organization:

Name: Supplier A

Primary Transport Address (File):

file://C:\Northwind\Supplier A\X12PO_%tracking_id%.edi

Envelope: X12 Envelope

Delimiters: >, *, ~

Interchange control number: 1001

(Destination Organization)

Identifier: DUNS (Dun & Bradstreet)

Qualifier: 01

Value: Supplier A

The messaging port properties for Supplier B are:

Name: Supplier B Port

Destination Organization:

Name: Supplier B

Primary Transport Address (File):

file://C:\Northwind\Supplier B\X12PO_%tracking_id%.edi

Envelope: X12 Envelope

Delimiters: >, *, ~

Interchange Control Number: 1001

(Destination Organization)

Identifier: DUNS (Dun & Bradstreet)

Qualifier: 01

Value: Supplier B

Now you can create the distribution list that distributes the documents from the X12 PO Distribution Channel to two messaging ports, Supplier A Port and Supplier B Port. In BizTalk Messaging Manager, select File | New | Distribution List from the menu options (or use the CTRL-T keyboard shortcut). In the New Distribution List dialog box, type **X12 PO Distribution List** in the Distribution List Name box. Double-click Supplier A Port and Supplier B Port in the Available Messaging Ports list on the left and make them appear in the Selected Messaging Ports list on the right, as shown in Figure 6-26. Click OK to dismiss the New Distribution List dialog box.

Click Distribution Lists Searching Item in the left frame of the BizTalk Messaging Manager and click the Search Now button. The X12 PO Distribution List you just created should appear in the right frame. Right-click X12 PO Distribution List and select New Channel | From An Organization. This will launch the New Channel Wizard. You can create a channel for the distribution list according to the following properties:

Name: X12 PO Distribution Channel

Source Organization:

Name: e-MarketPlace

Identifier: DUNS (Dun & Bradstreet)

Qualifier: 01

Value: e-Market

Inbound Document: X12 PO

Outbound Document: X12 PO

Document Logging: Check all options

Group Control Number: 1001

Since the inbound and outbound documents are the same, there is no need for a map. Note that we are reusing the document definition, X12 PO, here to simplify the demonstration. In the real world, you should create individual document definitions for each channel since the source and destination entities are not the same.

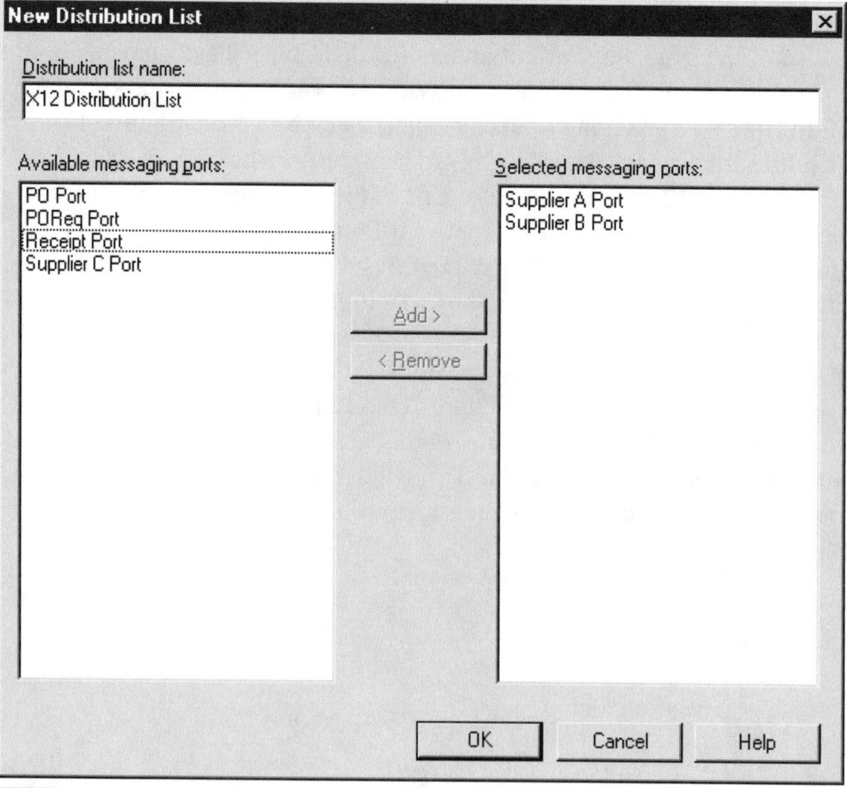

Figure 6-26 *Creating a distribution list*

To complete the messaging solution for e-MarketPlace, you also need to create a file receive function in the BizTalk Server Administration snap-in, with the following properties:

Name: Receive X12 PO

Protocol: File

Polling Location: C:\Northwind\e-Market\

File Types To Poll For: *.EDI

Channel Name: X12 PO Distribution Channel

This file receive function will retrieve the X12 purchase order generated in Step 2 from the C:\Northwind\e-Market folder and submit it to BizTalk Server (to the X12 PO Distribution Channel).

Supplier A relies on Supplier C to fill its goods orders. Now, you can create a messaging port and channel for Supplier C, according to the following properties:

Messaging port properties for Supplier C:

Name: Supplier C Port

Destination Organization:

Name: Supplier C

Primary Transport Address (File):

file://C:\Northwind\Supplier C\X12PO_%tracking_id%.edi

Envelope: X12 Envelope

Delimiters: >, *, ~

Interchange Control Number: 1001

(Destination Organization)

Identifier: DUNS (Dun & Bradstreet)

Qualifier: 01

VALUE

Supplier CNote: Choose Creating A Channel From An Organization at the end of the Messaging Port Wizard.

Channel properties for Supplier C:

Name: Supplier C Channel

Source Organization:

Name: Supplier A

Identifier: DUNS (Dun & Bradstreet)

Qualifier: 01

Value: Supplier A

Inbound Document: X12 PO

Outbound Document: X12 PO

Document Logging: Check all options

Group Control Number: 1001

Now, create a file receive function to complete Step 4:

Name: Supplier C Receive Function

Protocol: File

Polling Location: C:\Northwind\Supplier A\

File Types To Poll For: *.EDI

Channel Name: Supplier C Channel

This file receive function will retrieve the X12 purchase order from Supplier A at the C:\Northwind\Supplier A\ folder and submit it to BizTalk Server (to the Supplier C Channel).

Now, if you run the SubmitPOReq.vbs script, you should find two X12 PO EDI documents, one at C:\Northwind\Supplier B and another at C:\Northwind\Supplier C. There should be no files at C:\Northwind\e-Market, nor at C:\Northwind\Supplier A, because they were picked up by the receiving functions and submitted to BizTalk Server.

Processing Receipts

When business partners exchange documents with each other, it is sometimes desirable for the destination entity to generate an acknowledgement of receipt. BizTalk Server 2000 provides sophisticated built-in mechanisms for handling receipts of both EDI documents (X12 or EDIFACT) and XML documents based on the BizTalk Framework 2.0 (although how these are handled is completely different in each case). In addition, for custom document formats, BizTalk Server 2000 provides an IBizTalkCorrelation interface so you can create receipt correlator components to correlate documents, groups of documents, and interchanges with their receipts.

In this section, you will learn how to process receipts for X12 documents by using channels. You will also learn how to configure BizTalk Server 2000 to automatically process receipts by using reliable messaging, which uses the BizTalk Framework 2.0. We'll explain the IBizTalkCorrelation interface later in Chapter 11.

Using Channels

For processing EDI (X12 or EDIFACT) documents, BizTalk Server 2000 uses channels. The information in BizTalk Server 2000 online documentation regarding processing EDI receipts using channels is overwhelming and somewhat misleading. It mixes the procedures necessary for processing receipts with those used for (business) document processing. In fact, to process receipts for X12 or EDIFACT documents, you need to perform the following steps:

1. Create a messaging port / channel pair and other related messaging objects for delivering receipts, including:
   - A messaging port that transmits the receipt to its recipient (i.e., the sender of the original business document).
   - An associated channel for processing the receipt. This channel is referred to (marked) as a *receipt channel.*

- Document definitions for the receipts. These are optional if you only use the BizTalk Canonical Receipt generated by the BizTalk Server.
- A map that transforms the receipts from canonical format to other desired formats. This is also optional if you only use the BizTalk Canonical Receipt.

2. Configure existing channels for generating and receiving receipts:
   - Mark the channel that receives the business document as "Generate receipt," and specify which receipt channel you wish to deliver the receipt. When the business documents arrive at a channel marked "Generate receipt," BizTalk Server issues a canonical receipt according to a predefined specification (CanonicalReceipt.xml) stored in the Microsoft WebDAV folder.
   - Mark the channel that sends the original business document as "Expecting receipt." This configuration causes BizTalk Server to correlate the receipt with the appropriate channel, and then log the receipt document in the tracking database.

Assume that Supplier A requires that Supplier C send an acknowledgement of receipt regarding an X12 purchase order. Let's see how you add receipt-processing functionality to the messaging application you built in previous sections of this chapter by following the simple steps outlined in the preceding bullet points. Figure 6-27 shows what you'll need to build.

At first glance, Figure 6-27 may seem complicated, but it really isn't! If you take a closer look, the only new elements are the receipt channels, messaging ports, and related messaging objects located in the lower part of the diagram. The rest of the messaging objects are ones you built in previous sections (like those shown in Figure 6-25). As a matter of fact, we even simplified the diagram by taking out Supplier B and any related messaging objects since they have nothing to do with receipt processing. We also highlighted the existing channels that need to be configured to support processing receipts, in addition to the receipt channel and messaging port.

Creating Messaging Ports, Channels, and Related Messaging Objects

First, let's build a messaging system that processes and delivers the receipts. The system will include a messaging port, a channel, and related messaging objects, such as document definitions, a map, and source and destination organizations.

As shown in Figure 6-27, the source and destination organizations of the receipt channel and messaging port are the reverse of the source and destination organizations for Supplier C. So, you don't need to create any organizations.

You do need two document definitions for the receipts, though, one for the canonical receipt and another for the X12 receipt. To create the document definition for the canonical receipt, select New | Document Definition from the menu options in BizTalk Messaging Manager. Type **Canonical Receipt** as the document

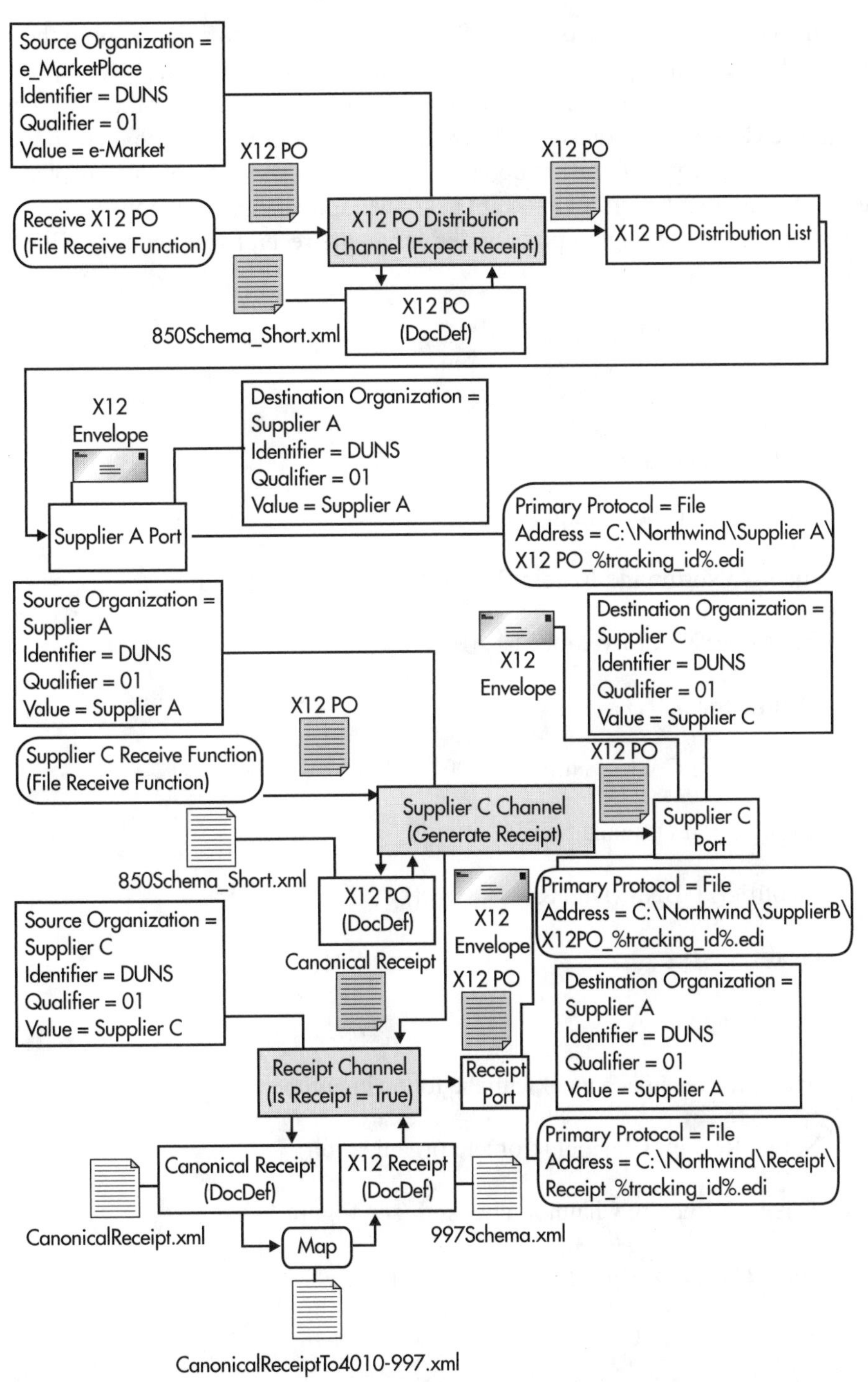

Figure 6-27 *Processing receipts for X12 PO documents*

definition name. Select the Document Specification check box and point to the CanonicalReceipt.xml specification found in the Microsoft WebDAV folder of the BizTalk Server 2000 repository. Create the document definition for the X12 receipt, name it **X12 Receipt** and point to the 997Schema.xml specification from the Northwind WebDAV repository that you set up in the Prerequisites section of this chapter. The 997 Schema.xml is an X12 receipt acknowledgment specification.

Now, create the messaging port for delivering the receipt with the following properties:

Name: Receipt Port

Destination Organization:

Name: Supplier A

Primary Transport Address (File):

file://C:\Northwind\Receipt\Receipt_%tracking_id%.edi

Envelope: X12 Envelope

Delimiters: >, *, ~

Interchange Control Number: 1001

(Destination Organization)

Identifier: DUNS (Dun & Bradstreet)

Qualifier: 01

Value: Supplier A

Then create the receipt channel with the following properties:

Name: Receipt Channel (from an organization)

This Is A Receipt Channel: **checked** (see Figure 6-28)

Source Organization:

Name: Supplier C

Identifier: DUNS (Dun & Bradstreet)

Qualifier: 01

Value: Supplier C

Inbound Document: Canonical Receipt (Alternatively, you can also use BizTalk Canonical Receipt)

Outbound Document: X12 Receipt

Map Reference: CanonicalReceiptTo4010-997.xml (found in the Microsoft WebDAV repository that shipped with BizTalk Server 2000)

Document Logging: Check all options

Group Control Number: 1001

Note the following facts for the receipt channel:

On the General Information page of the New Channel Wizard, make sure the This Is A Receipt Channel check box is selected (as shown in Figure 6-28).

Configuring Existing Channels for Generating and Receiving Canonical Receipts

To complete receipt processing, you also need to configure two existing channels. As you saw earlier in Figure 6-27, the Supplier C Channel is the channel that generates the canonical receipt, and the X12 PO Distribution Channel is the channel that expects receipts. To configure these channels, open BizTalk Messaging Manager and click Channels from the search items list in the left frame. Click the Search Now button to display all the channels. Double-click Supplier C Channel from the result list to open the Channel Properties Wizard. Click Next to go to the Source Organization page. Select Generate Receipt check box and the Browse button next to the Receipt Channel box should become enabled. Click the Browse button to open the Select a Receipt Channel dialog box. The receipt channel you created earlier should appear in the Available Receipt Channels list, as shown in Figure 6-29.

TIP

To make a channel appear in the Select A Receipt Channel dialog box, two conditions must be met. First, the receipt channel must be marked as a receipt channel, as shown in Figure 6-28. Secondly, the source and destination organizations of the receipt channel must be the exact opposite of the port associated with the channel that generates the receipt. For example, the source and destination organizations of the Receipt Channel are exactly the opposite of the Supplier C Channel, as shown in Figure 6-27.

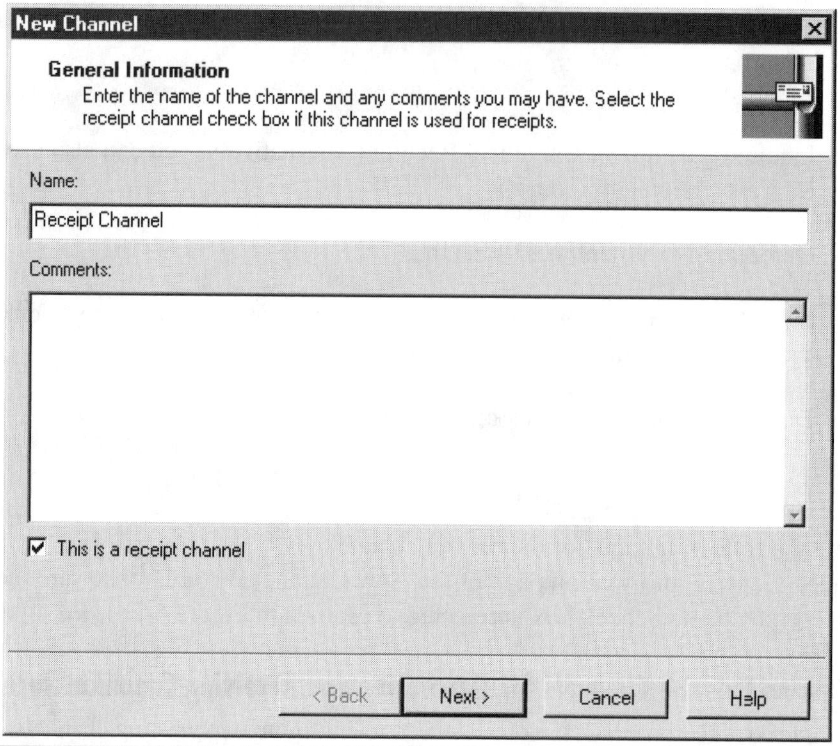

Figure 6-28 Creating a receipt channel

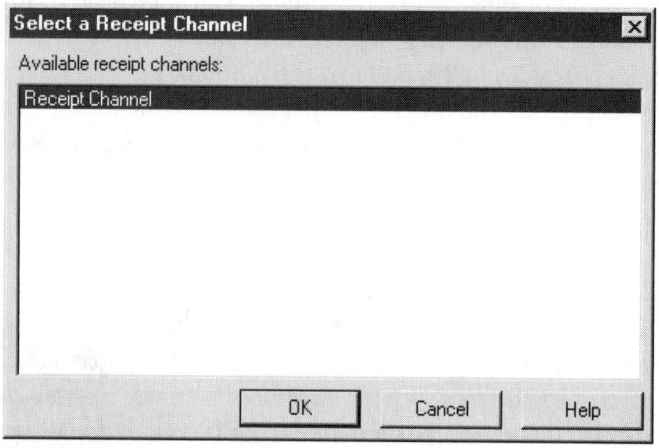

Figure 6-29 Selecting a receipt channel

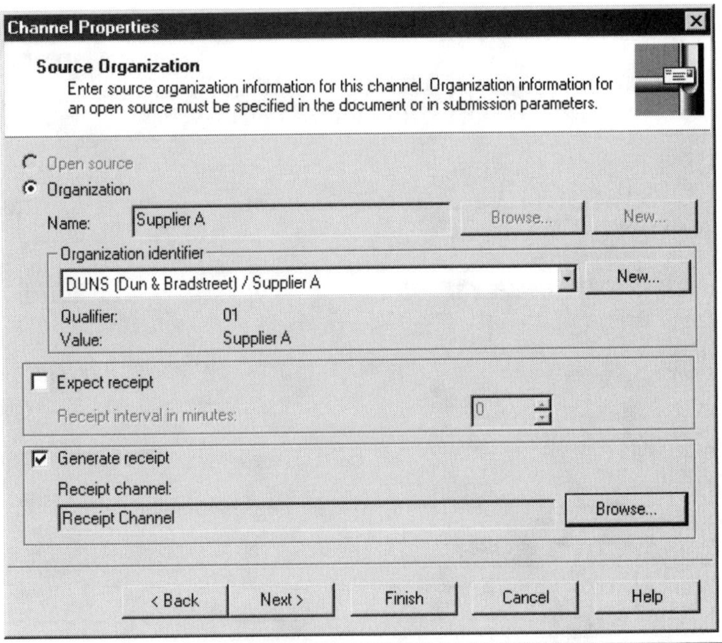

Figure 6-30 *Configuring the existing channel to generate canonical receipts*

Click OK to dismiss the Select A Receipt Channel dialog box. The Channel Properties Wizard should now look like the one in Figure 6-30.

Click Finish to dismiss the Channel Properties Wizard. You're done with this channel. Now, double-click the X12 PO Distribution Channel to open the Channel Properties Wizard and click Next. In the Source Organization page, select the Expect Receipt check box as shown in Figure 6-31, click Finish and you're done.

That's it! Now you have everything set for generating and processing receipts using channels. To test it out, run the SubmitPOReq.vbs again. This time, in addition to the X12 documents received in C:\Northwind\Supplier B and C:\Northwind\Supplier C folders, you should also find an EDI (X12) receipt document in the C:\Northwind\Receipt folder, as shown in Figure 6-32.

Figure 6-33 illustrates how the receipt looks in Notepad (we've slightly reformatted the receipt by removing some whitespaces and appropriately indenting the records to improve readability). It's basically an X12 version of the canonical receipt.

The receipt is also logged into the BizTalk Server Tracking database and can be viewed in the BizTalk Document Tracking tool, as shown in Figure 6-34 and 6-35. You will learn about the BizTalk Document Tracking tool in Chapter 8. To open

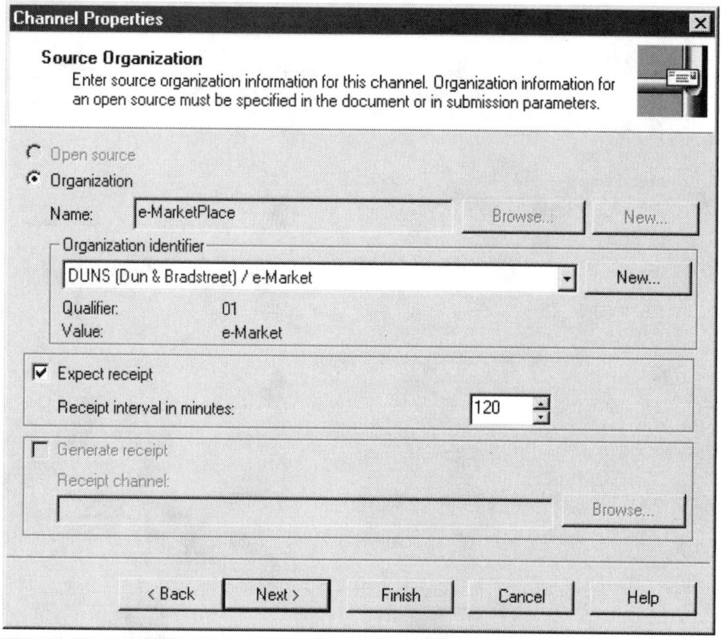

Channel Properties

Source Organization

Enter source organization information for this channel. Organization information for an open source must be specified in the document or in submission parameters.

Open source
Organization
Name: e-MarketPlace
Browse... New...
Organization identifier
DUNS (Dun & Bradstreet) / e-Market
New...
Qualifier: 01
Value: e-Market
Expect receipt
Receipt interval in minutes: 120
Generate receipt
Receipt channel:
Browse...
< Back Next > Finish Cancel Help

Figure 6-31 *Configuring the existing channel to expect receipts*

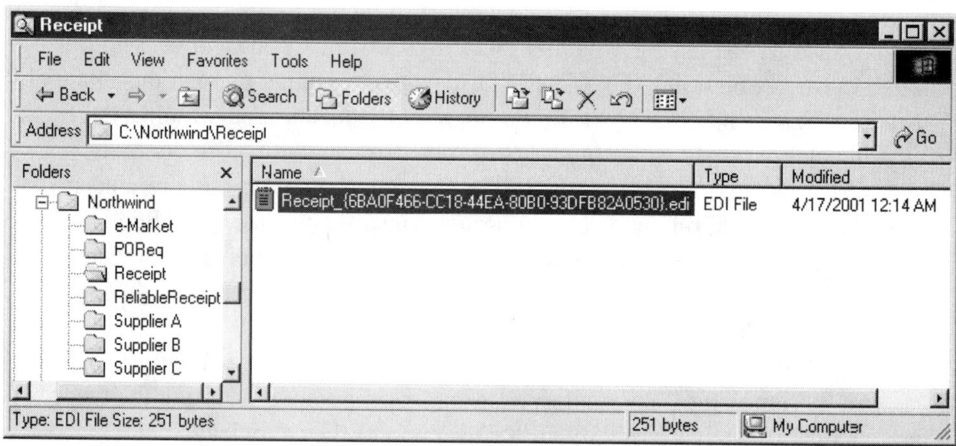

Figure 6-32 *An X12 receipt has been generated*

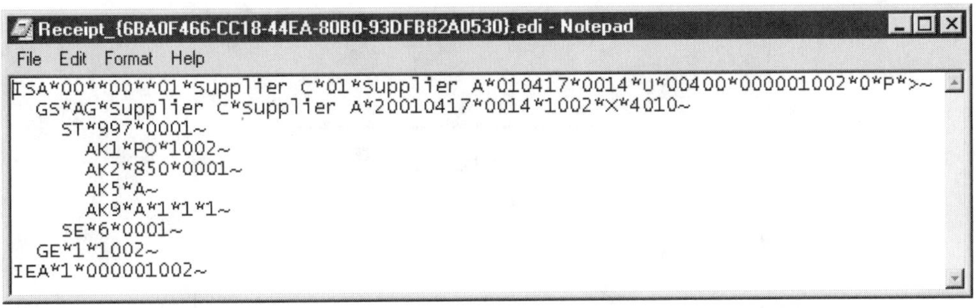
Receipt_{6BA0F466-CC18-44EA-80B0-93DFB82A0530}.edi - Notepad
File Edit Format Help
ISA*00**00**01*Supplier C*01*Supplier A*010417*0014*U*00400*000001002*0*P*>~
GS*AG*Supplier C*Supplier A*20010417*0014*1002*X*4010~
ST*997*0001~
AK1*PO*1002~
AK2*850*0001~
AK5*A~
AK9*A*1*1*1~
SE*6*0001~
GE*1*1002~
IEA*1*000001002~

Figure 6-33 *The content of the X12 receipt*

this tool, click Start | Program Files | Microsoft BizTalk Server 2000 | BizTalk Document Tracking.

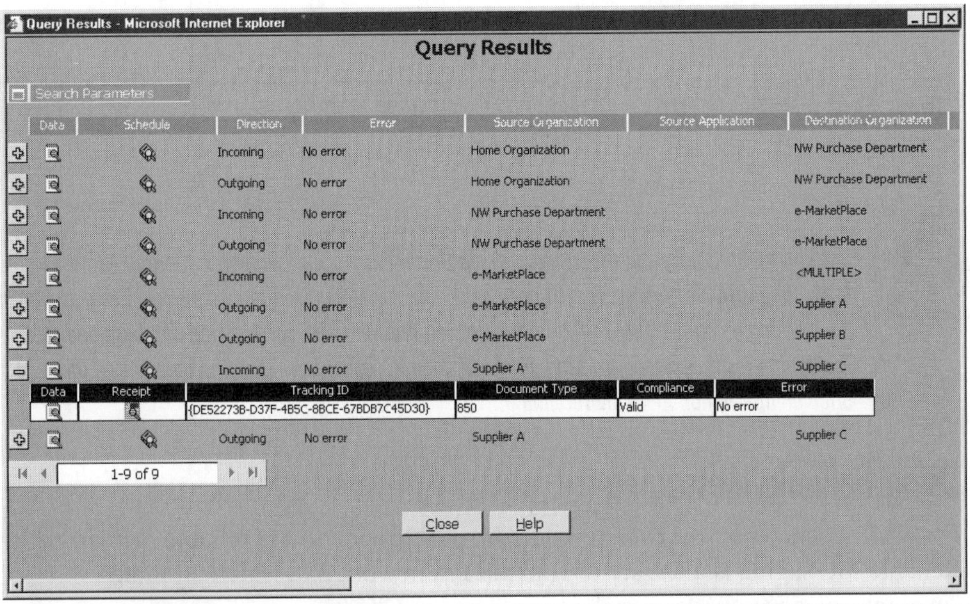
Query Results - Microsoft Internet Explorer
Query Results
Search Parameters
Data
Schedule
Direction
Error
Source Organization
Source Application
Destination Organization
Incoming No error Home Organization NW Purchase Department
Outgoing No error Home Organization NW Purchase Department
Incoming No error NW Purchase Department e-MarketPlace
Outgoing No error NW Purchase Department e-MarketPlace
Incoming No error e-MarketPlace <MULTIPLE>
Outgoing No error e-MarketPlace Supplier A
Outgoing No error e-MarketPlace Supplier B
Incoming No error Supplier A Supplier C
Data Receipt Tracking ID Document Type Compliance Error
{DE52273B-D37F-4B5C-8BCE-67BDB7C45D30} 850 Valid No error
Outgoing No error Supplier A Supplier C
1-9 of 9
Close
Help

Figure 6-34 *The receipt has been logged into the tracking database with other business documents*

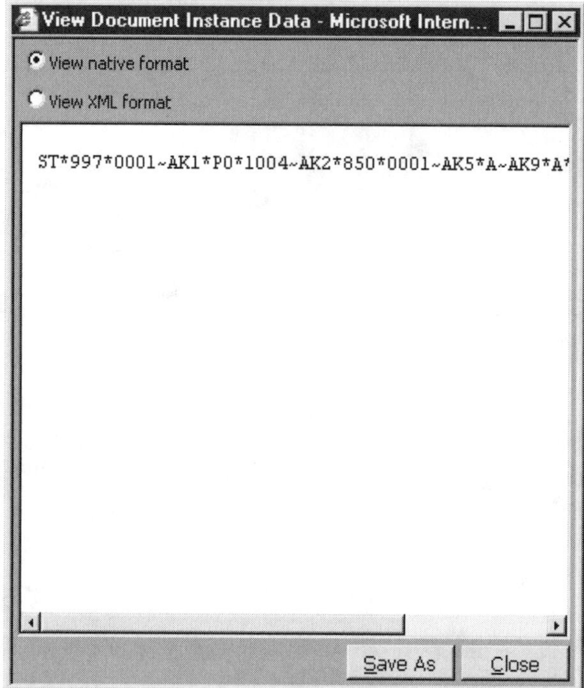

Figure 6-35 *A detailed view of the receipt in its native format*

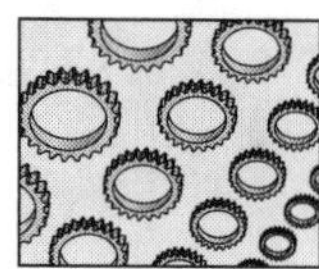

NOTE

It is important to point out that using a single Document Tracking Database (default name InterchangeDTA) for processing EDI documents and correlating return receipts requires a lookup in the tracking database. That is, if you send from a machine with one tracking database and receive it at another with a second tracking database, then BizTalk Server won't be able to find the original information to do the receipting.

Using Reliable Messaging

For XML documents, BizTalk Server 2000 enables you to use reliable messaging. Reliable Messaging is a feature of BizTalk Framework 2.0, which promotes "guaranteed once only delivery," as explained in Chapter 1. In this section, you will configure the messaging system in the Northwind Traders organization to use reliable messaging.

To process receipts using reliable messaging, you need to do the following:

- Create a reliable envelope
- Associate the reliable envelope with a messaging port
- Configure the BizTalk server group by specifying a reply-to URL address

When you associate a reliable messaging envelope to a messaging port and specify the reply-to URL address for the BizTalk Server group, BizTalk Server will wrap the outbound document into a BTF 2.0 envelope (which is built inside a SOAP envelope) to create the outbound interchange, inserting the reply-to URL into the header of the outbound interchange. BizTalk Server will then place the original interchange into the Retry queue (in contrast with normal documents) and resubmit the original interchange according to the retry counts and intervals specified in the channel's Retry options until it receives the receipt. When the destination system (which must also use BizTalk Server for reliable receipt messaging) receives an interchange with a reliable messaging format, it uses a set of hidden system messaging objects, including a special document definition (named Reliable Messaging Acknowledgement), a channel (named the Reliable Messaging Acknowledgement Channel), and messaging port (named the Reliable Messaging Acknowledgement Port) to process and transport a receipt to the source system. You cannot view these system messaging objects in BizTalk Messaging Manager, nor can you create messaging objects using these reserved system names.

Configuring the Source System

To demonstrate how to use reliable messaging to handle receipts, let's use the messaging systems you created earlier in this chapter for the Northwind Traders organization. Figure 6-36 illustrates both the source system and the destination system. It is basically a combination of Figure 6-6 and 6-16, with the exception that a reliable envelope is added to the messaging port of the source system, POReq Port.

First, let's create a reliable envelope. In BizTalk Messaging Manger, create a new envelope and name it **Reliable Envelope**. Select RELIABLE as the Envelope format (shown in Figure 6-37). Click OK.

Now, you must associate this reliable envelope to the messaging port. Double-click the POReq Port messaging port in BizTalk Messaging Manager and move it to the Envelope Information page in the Messaging Port Properties Wizard. Select the Reliable Envelope you just created from the Envelope Information drop-down list (as shown in Figure 6-38). Click Finish to dismiss the Messaging Port Properties Wizard.

In the last step, you need to specify the reply-to URL address for the BizTalk Server group that expects the receipts. To do this, open the BizTalk Server Administration snap-in and expand Microsoft BizTalk Server 2000. Right-click the

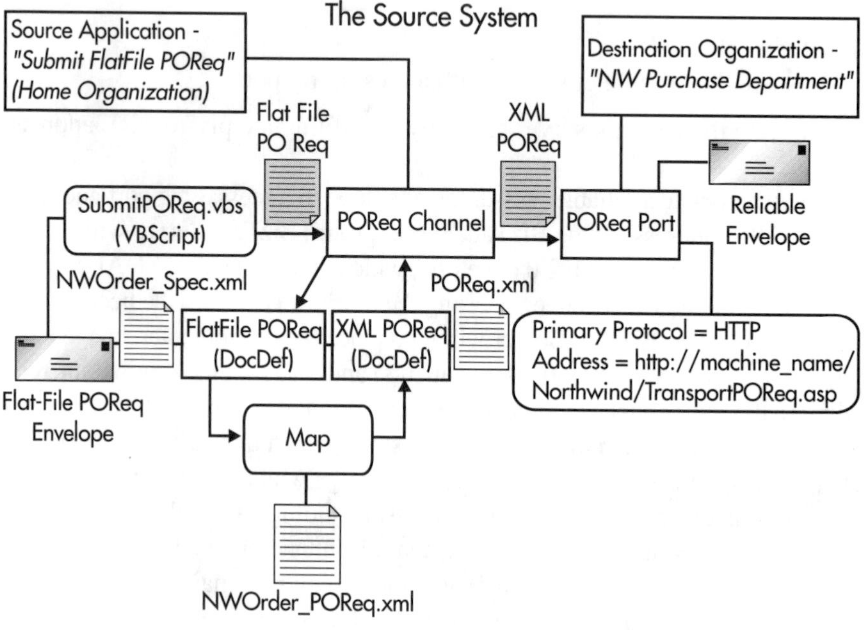

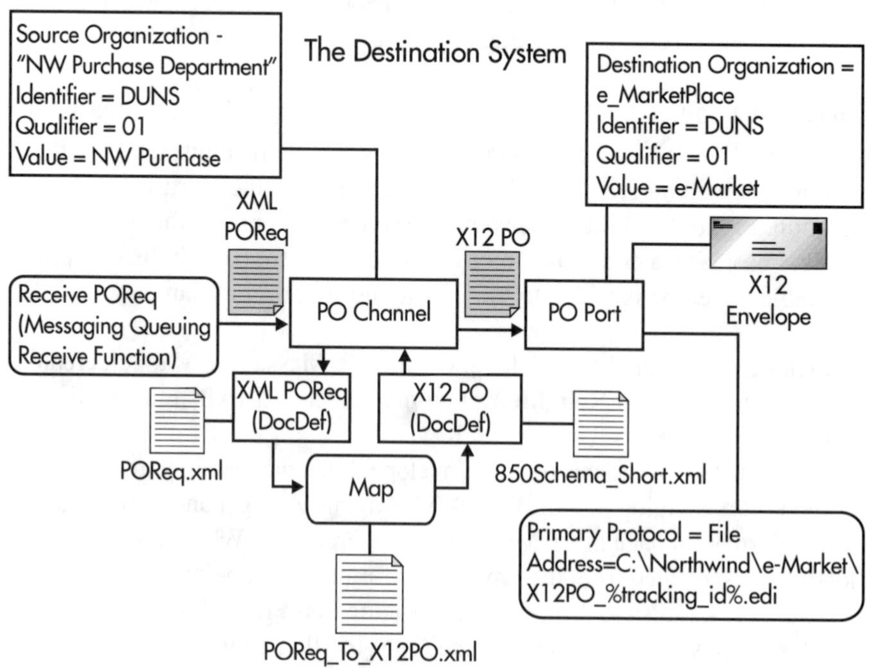

Figure 6-36 *Processing receipts using reliable messaging*

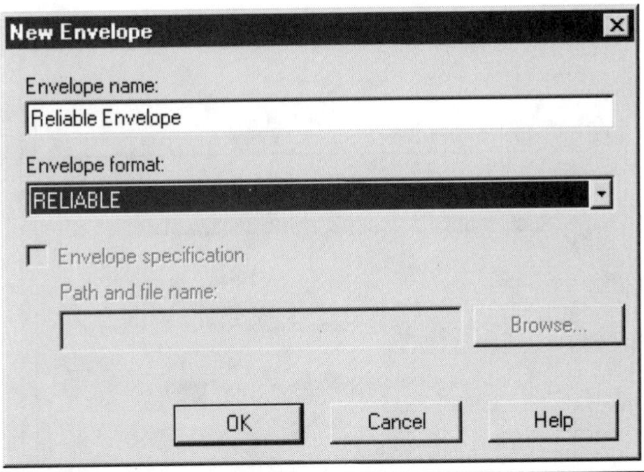

Figure 6-37 *Creating a reliable envelope*

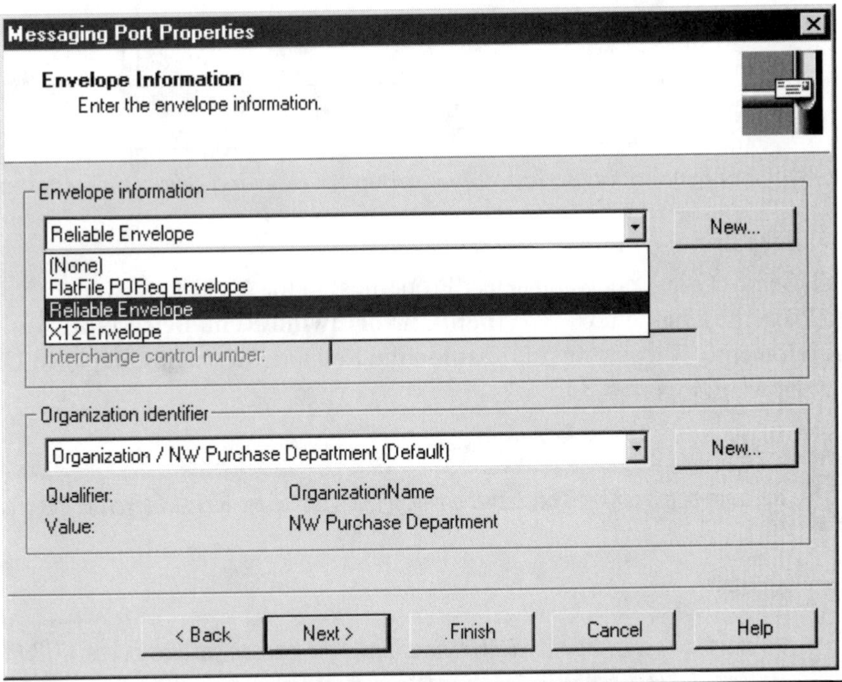

Figure 6-38 *Associating the reliable envelope to the messaging port*

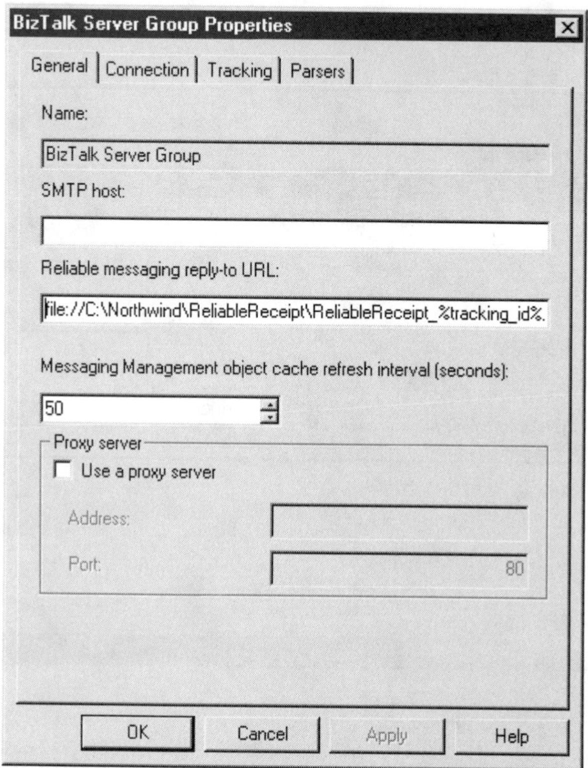

Figure 6-39 *Configuring the BizTalk Server group for receiving reliable messaging receipts*

BizTalk Server Group node and select Properties. In the BizTalk Server Group Properties dialog box, type **file://C:\Northwind\ReliableReceipt\ReliableReceipt_%tracking_id%.xml** in the Reliable Messaging Reply-to URL box, as shown in Figure 6-39.

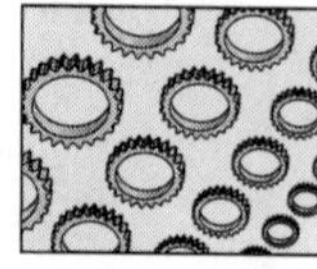

NOTE

The scope of this setting is per server group. It will affect all the BizTalk Servers in this group.

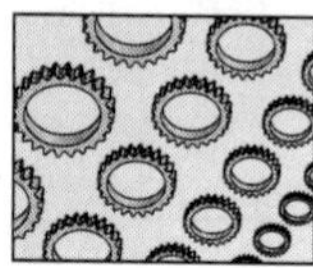

NOTE

We used the File Transport Protocol (FTP) here. Other valid transport protocols include: HTTP, HTTPS, Messaging Queuing, and SMTP. You can use the same protocols as those used in messaging ports.

Now, the system is ready to handle receipts using reliable messaging. If you run the SubmitPOReq.vbs script again, you will get a reliable messaging receipt in the C:\Northwind\ReliableReceipt\ folder. Figure 6-40 illustrates the reliable messaging receipt in IE 5.

Configuring the Destination System for SMTP Transports

As we just demonstrated, you usually do not need to further configure a destination system to handle reliable messaging receipts, as long as it uses BizTalk Server 2000. If the SMTP protocol is specified as the reply-to URL address in the source system, however, you must configure the destination system. If you specified an SMTP reply-to address, you must also configure the "Home Organization" of the destination system by specifying a value for the Reliable Messaging Acknowledgement SMTP From Address (as illustrated in Figure 6-41).

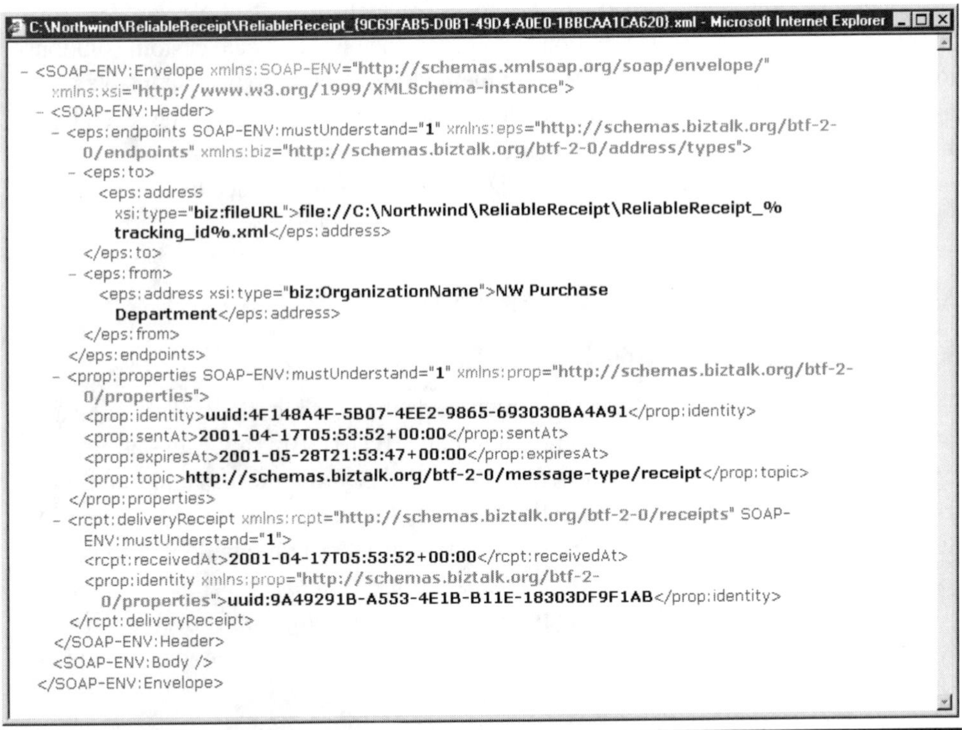

C:\Northwind\ReliableReceipt\ReliableReceipt_{9C69FAB5-D0B1-49D4-A0E0-1BBCAA1CA620}.xml - Microsoft Internet Explorer


```
- <SOAP-ENV:Envelope xmlns:SOAP-ENV="http://schemas.xmlsoap.org/soap/envelope/"
   xmlns:xsi="http://www.w3.org/1999/XMLSchema-instance">
  - <SOAP-ENV:Header>
    - <eps:endpoints SOAP-ENV:mustUnderstand="1" xmlns:eps="http://schemas.biztalk.org/btf-2-
        0/endpoints" xmlns:biz="http://schemas.biztalk.org/btf-2-0/address/types">
      - <eps:to>
          <eps:address
            xsi:type="biz:fileURL">file://C:\Northwind\ReliableReceipt\ReliableReceipt_%
            tracking_id%.xml</eps:address>
        </eps:to>
      - <eps:from>
          <eps:address xsi:type="biz:OrganizationName">NW Purchase
            Department</eps:address>
        </eps:from>
      </eps:endpoints>
    - <prop:properties SOAP-ENV:mustUnderstand="1" xmlns:prop="http://schemas.biztalk.org/btf-2-
        0/properties">
        <prop:identity>uuid:4F148A4F-5B07-4EE2-9865-693030BA4A91</prop:identity>
        <prop:sentAt>2001-04-17T05:53:52+00:00</prop:sentAt>
        <prop:expiresAt>2001-05-28T21:53:47+00:00</prop:expiresAt>
        <prop:topic>http://schemas.biztalk.org/btf-2-0/message-type/receipt</prop:topic>
      </prop:properties>
    - <rcpt:deliveryReceipt xmlns:rcpt="http://schemas.biztalk.org/btf-2-0/receipts" SOAP-
        ENV:mustUnderstand="1">
        <rcpt:receivedAt>2001-04-17T05:53:52+00:00</rcpt:receivedAt>
        <prop:identity xmlns:prop="http://schemas.biztalk.org/btf-2-
          0/properties">uuid:9A49291B-A553-4E1B-B11E-18303DF9F1AB</prop:identity>
      </rcpt:deliveryReceipt>
    </SOAP-ENV:Header>
    <SOAP-ENV:Body />
  </SOAP-ENV:Envelope>
```


Figure 6-40 *A reliable messaging receipt*

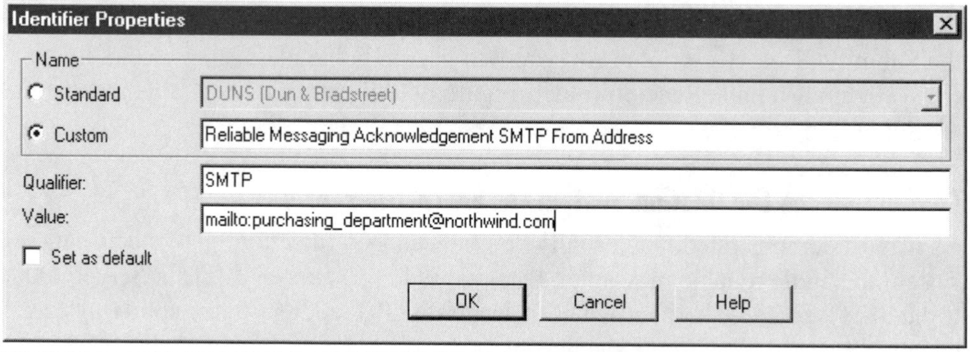

Figure 6-41 *Configuring the destination system for reliable messaging using SMTP*

Custom Receipt Processing

In previous sections, you learned how to process receipts in BizTalk Server 2000 for EDI and XML documents. In addition to this, you can always create custom solutions to process receipts. When you use custom methods, you will also be responsible for assuring the correlation of the receipts with the original interchange. If the receipt recipient uses BizTalk Server 2000, you can use the IBizTalkCorrelation interface to simplify the tasks. We will discuss the IBizTalkCorrelation interface later in Chapter 11.

Using the BizTalk Messaging Configuration Object Model

BizTalk Server 2000 stores the messaging objects metadata in the BizTalk Messaging Management Database (default name InterchangeBTM). BizTalk Messaging Manager is a browser-like user interface that enables you to access and manipulate BizTalk messaging objects graphically. BizTalk Server also provides a Messaging Configuration Object Model, a series of COM interfaces that enable you to access BizTalk messaging objects programmatically.

In this section, we will introduce the BizTalk Messaging Configuration Object Model and show you how to use these COM APIs in VBScript language to create the messaging objects.

Introducing the BizTalk Messaging Configuration Object Model

The BizTalk Messaging Configuration Object Model consists of a little more than a dozen COM interfaces. Here we will introduce the seven basic, yet most important, BizTalk Messaging Configuration objects, derived from corresponding underlying interfaces. Later, we will use these basic BizTalk configuration objects to create messaging objects used in previous sections of this chapter.

The BizTalkConfig Object

The BizTalkConfig object is the top-level BizTalk messaging configuration object which can be used to create and retrieve other BizTalk messaging objects, such as organizations, document definitions, envelopes, channels, and messaging ports.

The following code segment illustrates how to create an instance of the BizTalkConfig object:

```
Dim oBizTalk
Set oBizTalk = CreateObject("BizTalk.BizTalkConfig")
```

The BizTalkConfig object supports a series of *CreateXXX* methods that create other BizTalk messaging objects, such as *CreateOrganization*, *CreateDocument*, *CreateChannel*, *CreatePort* and so on, as illustrated in the following code snippet.

```
Set oBizTalk = CreateObject("BizTalk.BizTalkConfig")
Set oOrg = oBizTalk.CreateOrganization
Set oChannel = oBizTalk.CreateChannel
Set oPort = oBizTalk.CreatePort
Set oPortGroup = oBizTalk.CreatePortGroup
Set oDoc = oBizTalk.CreateDocument
Set oEnvelope = oBizTalk.CreateEnvelope
```

To retrieve other BizTalk messaging objects through the BizTalkConfig object, use its corresponding collections, such as Organizations, Channels, Ports, and so on. These collections return an ADO recordset object that contains the corresponding messaging object data stored in the BizTalk Messaging Management Database. You can iterate through the resulting ADO recordset to enumerate the related messaging objects in the database to find the one you are interested in. The following sample code searches the organizations collection to find the name of the Home Organization:

```
Dim oBizTalk, rsOrganizations
Set oBizTalk = CreateObject("BizTalk.BizTalkConfig")
Set rsOrganizations = oBizTalk.Organizations
'Loop through the organizations collection to find
'the Home Organization, report its name.
Do Until rsOrganizations.EOF
    If rsOrganization.Fields("defaultflag").Value = -1 Then
        wscript.echo "Name of the Home Organization = " & _
            rsOrganizations.Fields("name").Value
        Exit Do
    End If
    rsOrganization.MoveNext
Loop
```

Other Important BizTalk Messaging Configuration Objects

The following table lists six basic, yet very important, BizTalk messaging configuration objects and their corresponding messaging objects in BizTalk Messaging Manager.

Messaging Configuration Object	BizTalk Messaging Manager Object
BizTalkChannel	Channel
BizTalkDocument	Document Definition
BizTalkEnvelope	Envelope
BizTalkOrganization	Organization
BizTalkPort	Messaging Port
BizTalkPortGroup	Distribution List

All of the messaging configuration objects are derived from the *IBizTalkBase* interface which supports the following common methods:

Method	Description
Clear	Clears the object in memory and resets the default values. You can call this method prior to reusing an object. For example, oOrganization.Clear.
Load	Loads a new object in memory; takes the handle of the object as an input parameter. For example, oOrganization.Load lOrgHandle.

Method	Description
LoadByName	Loads a new object in memory; takes the name of the object as the input parameter. For example, oOrganization.LoadByName "e-MarketPlace".
Remove	Removes the object from the database; takes the name as the input parameter. For example, oOrganization.Remove "e-MarketPlace".
Save	Saves the object to the database. For example, oOrganization.Save.

In addition to the common methods derived from the IBizTalkBase interface just described, each individual messaging configuration object supports its own set of properties and unique methods.

The properties of each messaging configuration object are roughly equivalent to the available options found in the corresponding configuration wizard in BizTalk Messaging Manager. For example, the BizTalkChannel object has properties such as *InputDocument*, *OutputDocument*, *MapReference*, and so on.

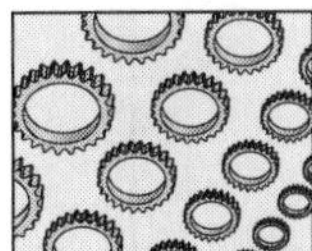

NOTE

Localhost doesn't work in the port references for transports. You need to put in the actual machine name.

In the next subsection, we are going to demonstrate how to use various BizTalk messaging configuration objects, their properties, and methods to create messaging objects used in previous sections of this chapter.

Automating BizTalk Messaging Solutions

Included in the sample code download of this chapter is a VBScript file, Config.vbs, that creates the entire messaging infrastructure used in the Northwind Traders example, using the BizTalk Messaging Configuration Object Model. You can use the cscript.exe command line utility that comes with Windows Script Host (automatically installed with Windows 2000) to execute this script file so the messaging objects used in this chapter can be created. To do this, click Start | Run and type **cmd** to open the DOS screen. Navigate to the folder where the config.vbs file resides and type the following line:

```
cscript config.vbs //nologo
```

After the execution of the script file, the DOS screen should look like the one in Figure 6-42 (You can also double-click the config.vbs file in Windows Explorer to execute it).

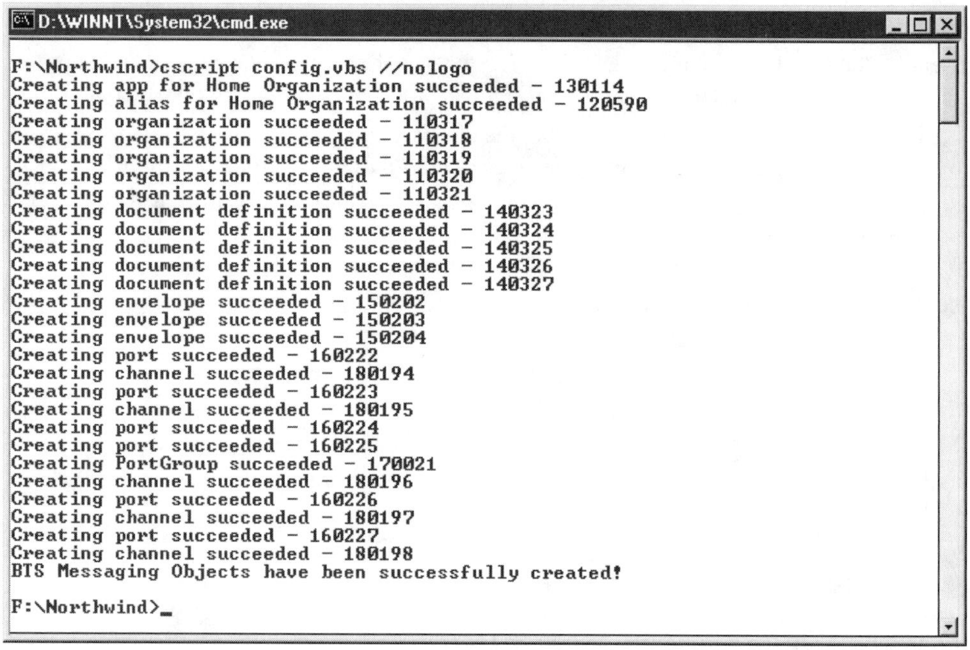

```
D:\WINNT\System32\cmd.exe

F:\Northwind>cscript config.vbs //nologo
Creating app for Home Organization succeeded - 130114
Creating alias for Home Organization succeeded - 120590
Creating organization succeeded - 110317
Creating organization succeeded - 110318
Creating organization succeeded - 110319
Creating organization succeeded - 110320
Creating organization succeeded - 110321
Creating document definition succeeded - 140323
Creating document definition succeeded - 140324
Creating document definition succeeded - 140325
Creating document definition succeeded - 140326
Creating document definition succeeded - 140327
Creating envelope succeeded - 150202
Creating envelope succeeded - 150203
Creating envelope succeeded - 150204
Creating port succeeded - 160222
Creating channel succeeded - 180194
Creating port succeeded - 160223
Creating channel succeeded - 180195
Creating port succeeded - 160224
Creating port succeeded - 160225
Creating PortGroup succeeded - 170021
Creating channel succeeded - 180196
Creating port succeeded - 160226
Creating channel succeeded - 180197
Creating port succeeded - 160227
Creating channel succeeded - 180198
BTS Messaging Objects have been successfully created!

F:\Northwind>_
```

Figure 6-42 *Using a VBScript file to automatically create messaging objects*

The entire script file runs more than a dozen pages. Next, we'll discuss the programming flow and some typical code examples to demonstrate the most important techniques used in the script.

The first part of the script file contains constant declarations, messaging configuration object declarations, and global handle declarations, followed by the object creation code you saw earlier:

```
Set oBizTalk = CreateObject("BizTalk.BizTalkConfig")
Set oOrg = oBizTalk.CreateOrganization
Set oChannel = oBizTalk.CreateChannel
Set oPort = oBizTalk.CreatePort
Set oPortGroup = oBizTalk.CreatePortGroup
Set oDoc = oBizTalk.CreateDocument
Set oEnvelope = oBizTalk.CreateEnvelope
```

The messaging configuration objects created here are reusable, thanks to the Clear method of the IBizTalkBase interface from which they derive.

The next block of code calls a helper function, *DeleteBTSMessagingObjects* to delete the objects in case they already exist, passing the object variable and the name of the object to be deleted:

```
DeleteBTSMessagingObjects oChannel, cPOReqChannel
DeleteBTSMessagingObjects oChannel, cPOChannel
DeleteBTSMessagingObjects oChannel, cX12DistributionListChannel
DeleteBTSMessagingObjects oChannel, cSupplierCChannel
DeleteBTSMessagingObjects oChannel, cReceiptChannel
DeleteBTSMessagingObjects oPort, cPOReqPort
DeleteBTSMessagingObjects oPort, cPOPort
DeleteBTSMessagingObjects oPort, cReceiptPort
DeleteBTSMessagingObjects oPortGroup, cX12DistributionList
DeleteBTSMessagingObjects oPort, cSupplierAPort
DeleteBTSMessagingObjects oPort, cSupplierBPort
DeleteBTSMessagingObjects oPort, cSupplierCPort
DeleteBTSMessagingObjects oEnvelope, cFlatFilePOReqEnvelope
DeleteBTSMessagingObjects oEnvelope, cX12Envelope
DeleteBTSMessagingObjects oEnvelope, cReliableEnvelope
DeleteBTSMessagingObjects oDoc, cFlatFilePOReqDocDef
DeleteBTSMessagingObjects oDoc, cXMLPOReqDocDef
DeleteBTSMessagingObjects oDoc, cX12PODocDef
DeleteBTSMessagingObjects oDoc, cX12ReceiptDocDef
DeleteBTSMessagingObjects oDoc, cCanconicalReceiptDocDef
DeleteBTSMessagingObjects oOrg, cNWPurchaseOrg
DeleteBTSMessagingObjects oOrg, cEMarketOrg
DeleteBTSMessagingObjects oOrg, cSupplierAOrg
DeleteBTSMessagingObjects oOrg, cSupplierBOrg
DeleteBTSMessagingObjects oOrg, cSupplierCOrg
```

This is similar to the Drop Transact SQL statement you used prior to a Create statement (Create Table, Create Proc, and so on). Please notice the sequence of object deletions here. Recall that in Chapter 3 we discussed the dependencies between BizTalk messaging objects. When you create or delete messaging objects in code, you are restricted by these dependencies. You must create the depending objects first, before creating the dependent objects. In contrast, you must first delete the dependent objects before deleting the depending objects. In the previous code, we delete the objects in the following order: channels, messaging ports, distribution lists, envelopes, document definitions, and organizations. The following is the DeleteBTSMessagingObjects helper function.

```
Sub DeleteBTSMessagingObjects(oObject, Name)
    On Error Resume Next
    ' Load the object by calling the LoadByName method of the
    'IBizTalkBase interface
    oObject.LoadByName Name
    If err = 0 Then
        oObject.Remove
        if err <> 0 then
            WScript.echo err.description
        end if
    ElseIf err <> -1061154302 Then
        WScript.echo "DeleteBTSMessagingObjects()-" & Name & " Error: " & _
                      err.description
        Exit Sub
    Else
        'Ignore the "Object not found" error
        err.Clear
    End If
End Sub
```

This function calls the LoadByName method of the IBizTalkBase interface. If the object does not exist, an "Object not found" error (-1061154302) will be returned. This error can be ignored for our purposes, since we simply want to make sure no identical objects exist prior to their creation. If no error is returned (i.e., the object is found), we use a Remove method to delete the object from the database. When other errors are encountered, we report the error and exit the function.

The next two lines of code call two other helper functions to remove the Application object as well as the alias from the Home Organization.

```
RemoveAppForHomeOrg oOrg, cHomeOrgApp1
RemoveAKAForHomeOrg oOrg, cHomeOrgAKA1
```

The reason for using different functions rather than the DeleteBTSMessagingObjects function you saw earlier has to do with the Home Organization. First, you cannot delete the Home Organization. Therefore, you cannot remove its applications and alias simply by deleting the organization itself, as you would with a regular organization. Secondly, applications and aliases are secondary objects of organizations; they are not derived from the IBizTalkBase interface and therefore cannot be removed by a Remove method. The following is the *RemoveAppForHomeOrg* function.

```
Function RemoveAppForHomeOrg(oOrg,AppName)
  Dim rsApps
```

```
  oOrg.Load 110001 'Load the Home Organization
  set rsApps = oOrg.Applications
  do until rsApps.EOF
    If rsApps.Fields("name") = AppName Then
      oOrg.RemoveApplication(rsApps.Fields("id").value)
      oOrg.Save
      exit do
    end if
    rsApps.MoveNext
  loop
  set rsApps = Nothing
End Function
```

This function loads the Home Organization and returns the Applications collection to an ADO recordset. It then loops through the collection, finds the matching application by its name and deletes the application from the database by calling the *RemoveApplication* method of the Organization object. The *RemoveAKAForHomeOrg* function works similarly, as illustrated in the following.

```
Function RemoveAKAForHomeOrg(oOrg,AKAName)
  Dim rsAKAs
  oOrg.Load 110001 'Load the Home Organization
  Set rsAKAs = oOrg.Aliases
  do until rsAKAs.EOF
    if rsAKAs.Fields("id").value > 120002 and _
      rsAKAs.Fields("value").value = AKAName then
      'excluding the default Home org and reliable msg ack.
      oOrg.RemoveAlias(rsAKAs.Fields("id").value)
      oOrg.Save
      exit do
    end if
    rsAKAs.MoveNext
  loop
  Set rsAKAs = Nothing
End Function
```

The remaining junk code performs the major tasks: creating the messaging objects for this chapter. Each object is created in a similar pattern, as demonstrated by the following pseudo code.

```
Call the Clear method to remove the object in memory
Set appropriate properties for the object
```

```
Create the secondary objects of this object if necessary
Set appropriate properties for the secondary objects if necessary
Call the Save method to save the object into the database and store
the handle to a variable for later use.
```

A typical example is the creation of the messaging port, Receipt Port, as illustrated next.

```
' Call the Clear method to remove the object in memory
oPort.Clear
' Set appropriate properties for the object
oPort.Name = cReceiptPort
oPort.DestinationEndPoint.Organization = gSupplierAHandle
oPort.DestinationEndPoint.Alias = lESupplierAAKA
oPort.Envelope = gX12EnvelopeHandle
' Create the secondary object
Set oPort.Delimiters = CreateObject("Commerce.Dictionary")
' Set appropriate properties for the secondary object
oPort.Delimiters.subfield_delim = ">" 'chr(62)
oPort.Delimiters.field_delim = "*" 'chr(42)
oPort.Delimiters.record_delim = "~" 'chr(126)
oPort.PrimaryTransport.Type = BIZTALK_TRANSPORT_TYPE_FILE
oPort.PrimaryTransport.Address = cReceiptAddress
oPort.ControlNumberValue = "1001"
' Call the Save method to save the object into the database and
' store the handle to a variable for later use.
gReceiptPortHandle = oPort.Create
```

Some objects don't have secondary objects, so their creation is more straightforward, as demonstrated by the following sample code, which creates the Receipt Channel.

```
oChannel.Clear
oChannel.Name = cReceiptChannel
oChannel.IsReceiptChannel = 1
oChannel.InputDocument =gCanConicalReceiptDocHandle
oChannel.OutputDocument = gX12ReceiptDocHandle
oChannel.MapReference = "http://" & gHostName &
"/BizTalkServerRepository/Maps/Microsoft/CanonicalReceiptTo4010-997.xml"
oChannel.Port = gReceiptPortHandle
oChannel.SourceEndPoint.Organization = gSupplierCHandle
oChannel.SourceEndPoint.Alias = lESupplierCAKA
oChannel.ControlNumberValue = "1001"
oChannel.LoggingInfo.LogNativeInputDocument = True
```

```
oChannel.LoggingInfo.LogNativeOutputDocument = True
oChannel.LoggingInfo.LogXMLInputDocument = True
oChannel.LoggingInfo.LogXMLOutputDocument = True
gReceiptChannelHandle = oChannel.Create
```

Chapter in Review

In this chapter, you learned how to use the BizTalk Messaging Manager tool to create and manage messaging objects by creating a real-world messaging application. Two major transport protocols were used in the example, HTTP and File. Other protocols, such as Messaging Queuing and SMTP, although not demonstrated in the example, are also easy to use. Employing them is simply a matter of selecting the protocol type from the option drop-down box and typing in a valid URL address. The Application Interchange Component (AIC) protocol was not used because it will be covered in Chapter 11 of this book (where we discuss how to extend the functionality of BizTalk Server 2000). So far, you've created several receive functions, including both File and Messaging Queuing to transfer the document from one stage to another.

You've also learned how to handle receipts in different scenarios, using the sophisticated receipt processing mechanisms provided by BizTalk Server 2000.

In addition, we've introduced the BizTalk Messaging Configuration Object Model and demonstrated how to use it to create the messaging objects used in this chapter.

PART III

Bizlet—BizTalk Server 2002

OBJECTIVES

- To master the BizTalk Server Administration MMC snap-in
- To manage BizTalk Server databases
- To learn about BizTalk Server WMI programming

CHAPTER 7

BizTalk Server Administration

IN THIS CHAPTER:

The BizTalk Server Administration Tool

Managing BizTalk Server Databases

Administrating BizTalk Server Programmatically

Chapter in Review

BizTalk Server 2000 is a comprehensive product, consisting of a suite of tools and services. BizTalk applications are typically deployed in highly distributed environments. As a result, the administration of BizTalk Server 2000 involves many areas, including administrating the server itself (server administration), managing BizTalk databases (database administration), managing XLANG schedules (application administration), managing messaging objects (messaging objects administration), tracking documents, and so on.

In the last chapter, you learned to create and manage messaging objects through both BizTalk Messaging Manager and the BizTalk Messaging Configuration Object Model. In the next chapter, you'll learn how to track documents and interchanges in BizTalk Server 2000. XLANG schedule and BizTalk Orchestration will constitute topics in Part IV of this book.

In this chapter, we will focus our discussion on server administration. You will learn to use the BizTalk Server Administration MMC snap-in to manage BizTalk servers and *server groups*, receive functions, and queues. You will also learn how to manage BizTalk databases (messaging management, shared queue and tracking databases). In addition, you will learn how to programmatically administrate BizTalk Server through the WMI APIs.

The BizTalk Server Administration Tool

BizTalk Server Administration is an administration tool implemented as a Microsoft Management Console (MMC) snap-in. Figure 7-1 is a screen shot of the BizTalk Server Administration tool.

As illustrated in Figure 7-1, BizTalk Server Administration has a look typical of an MMC snap-in. In the left pane of the BizTalk Server Administration is a tree view with different nodes organized in a hierarchy. In the right pane is a list view that displays appropriate properties of a particular node selected in the tree view. Using BizTalk Server Administration, you can manage BizTalk servers and server groups, queues and receiving functions. The integrated Event Viewer provides help in troubleshooting.

Managing Server Groups and Servers

Typical EAI and B2B integration scenarios usually involve a large volume of document exchanges. Multiple servers and databases are often used to improve performance and scalability. The BizTalk Server Administration tool provides a

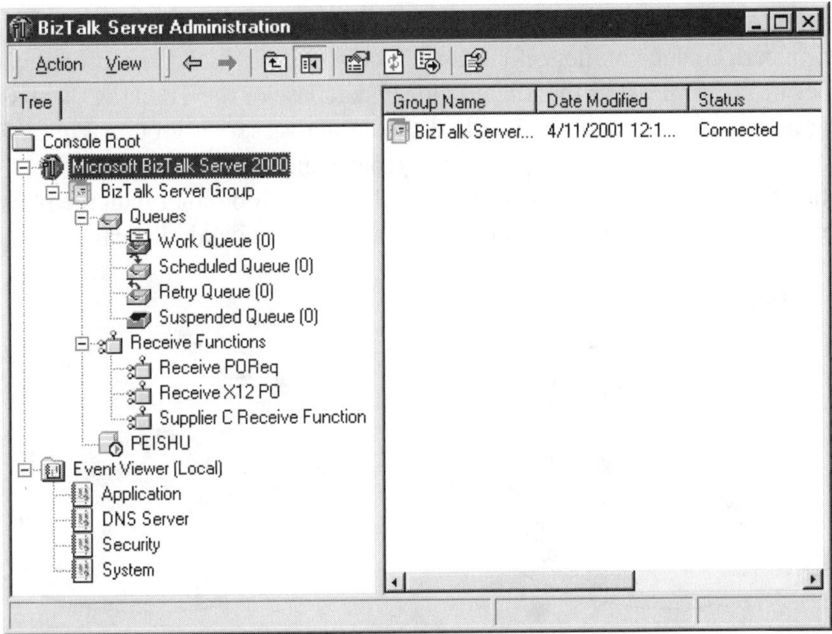

Figure 7-1 *BizTalk Server Administration graphic user interface*

centralized management environment enabling you to manage BizTalk server groups as well as individual servers.

Relationships

A server group is a collection of individual BizTalk servers that is centrally managed, configured, and monitored. By grouping individual servers into server groups you can increase the performances and provide a level of redundancy and fault tolerance. Servers in the same server group can share some common resources, such as a Shared Queue database, a Tracking Database, an XLANG database, and so on, as well as required components for processing documents and interchanges such as transport components, application integration components (AICs), and others.

The BizTalk Messaging Management database, however, is a global database that is sharable across multiple server groups so you can remotely administer each server and group from the BizTalk Server Administration tool. Using only one central BizTalk Messaging Management database also enables servers in multiple server groups to use the same configuration information so they can be configured as redundant server and/or server groups in order to improve performance and scalability. Additionally, the BizTalk Messaging Management database won't become a performance bottleneck because it only stores the configuration metadata and doesn't grow as fast as the Shared Queue database or the Tracking database, making it ideal as a globally accessible database across server groups. Figure 7-2 illustrates a potential relationship between groups and servers.

Notice that Figure 7-2 describes the logical relationship rather than the physical relationship. In a physical deployment, you can use individual, dedicated server

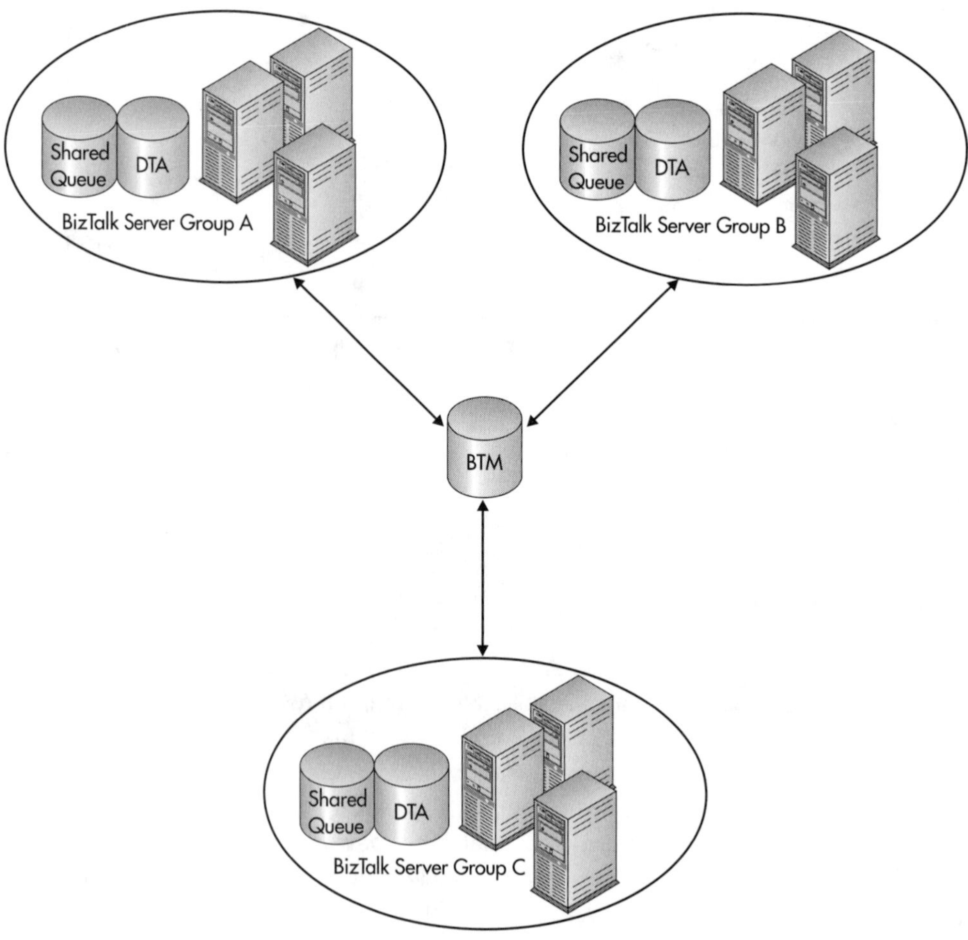

Figure 7-2 *Logical configuration of groups and servers*

machines to host each database (as shown in Figure 7-2), or you can combine some of the databases in a single server machine. How you want to do it depends on the performance and scalability requirements, as well as the availability of hardware and software (licenses).

To specify the global BizTalk Messaging Management database, right-click the Microsoft BizTalk Server 2000 nóde in the BizTalk Server Administration snap-in and select Properties. In the Microsoft BizTalk Server 2000 Properties dialog box, you can specify the name of the Messaging Management database, the name of the SQL Server, its username, and password, as shown in Figure 7-3.

Managing Groups

Using the BizTalk Server Administration snap-in, you can add, delete, and configure server groups. You can also monitor the status of a server group.

To add a server group, right-click the Microsoft BizTalk Server 2000 node and select New Group. In the New Group dialog box, specify the name of the group, as well as the connection information for the Tracking and Shared Queue databases (as shown in Figure 7-4).

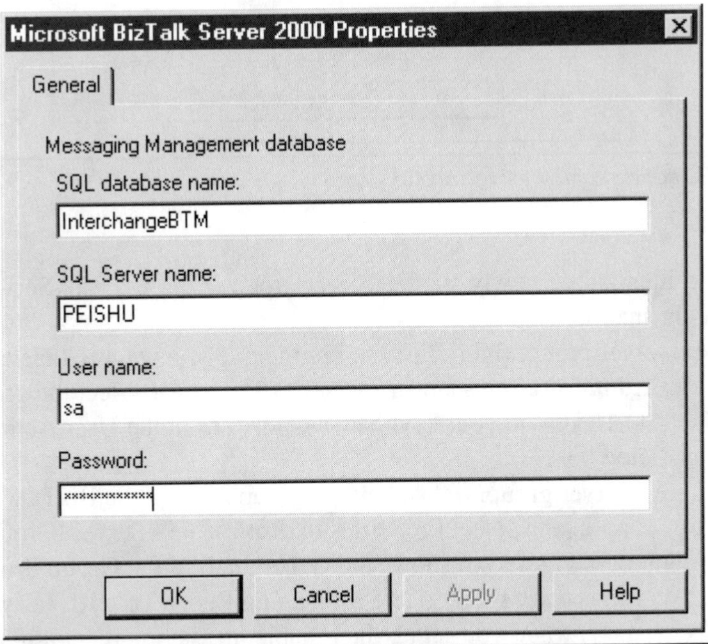

Figure 7-3 *Configuring the global Messaging Management database*

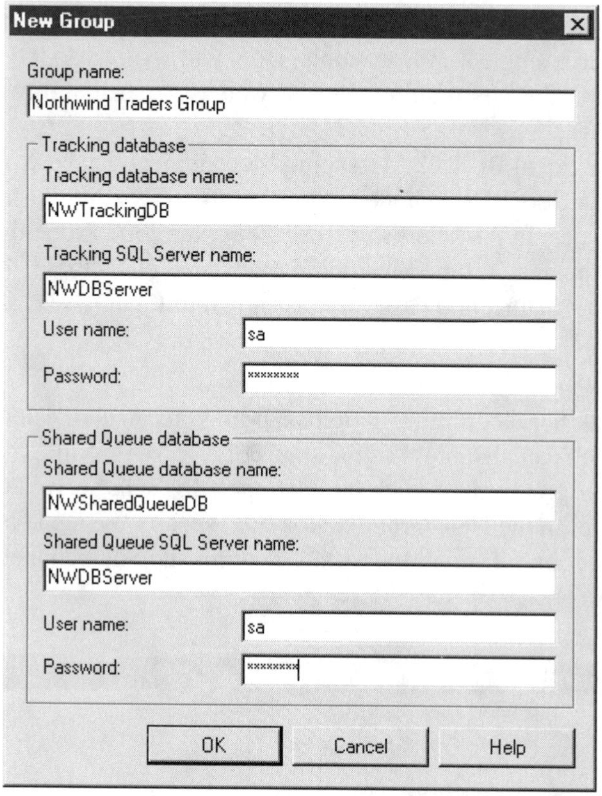

Figure 7-4 *Creating a new server group*

Figure 7-5 illustrates a newly created server group in the BizTalk Server Administration snap-in.

To delete a server group, right-click the group node you want to delete in the BizTalk Server Administration snap-in and select Delete (or select the group node and press the DELETE key on your keyboard). Click Yes in the User Action Confirmation dialog box.

To configure a server group, right-click the group node in the BizTalk Server Administration snap-in and select Properties to display the <Server_Group_Name> Properties dialog box. Figure 7-6 shows the General tab of the Group Properties dialog box. You can specify the Reliable Messaging Reply-To URL (as you did in the last chapter) when you set up the reliable messaging receipt in the Northwind Traders example. If SMTP protocol is used for reliable messaging receipt (that is, the reply-to URL is specified as something like

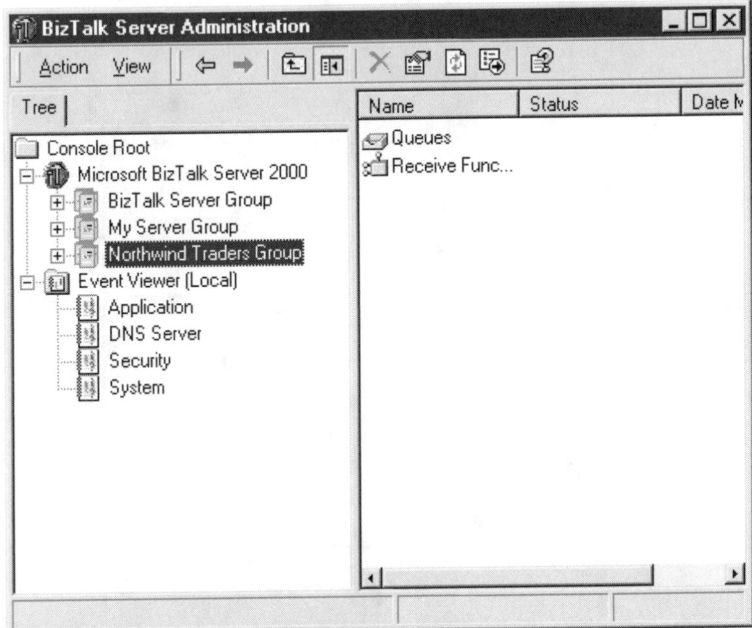

Figure 7-5 *A new server group is created*

"mailto:purchasing@northwind.com"), you must type in the name of the SMTP server (for example, the name of your exchange server) in the SMTP Host box.

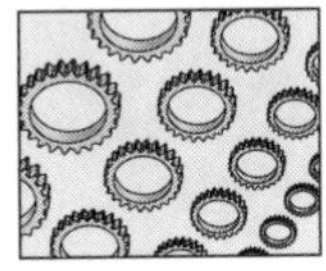

NOTE

When BizTalk Server is started, BizTalk Server creates an administration cache in its memory to store all items in the BizTalk Server Administration, such as server groups, server group properties, channels, ports, document definitions, envelopes, receive functions, connections to the Shared Queue and Tracking databases, and so on. By default, the refresh interval for the administration case is set to 50 seconds so that if you change the general properties for a server group, such as the SMTP host or the reliable messaging reply-to URL, the changes are picked up within 50 seconds. You may fine-tune the cache refresh interval to a value that fits your specific business need.

TIP

In a development environment, you usually set the refresh interval for the cache at a lower value (for example, 5 seconds to make sure the changes made are quickly picked up). In a production environment, however, you will need to reset the refresh interval to a higher value to improve performance.

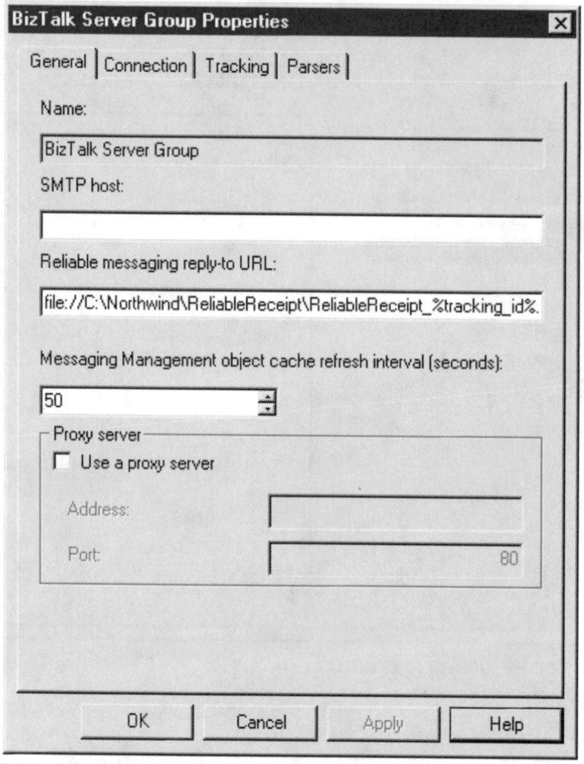

Figure 7-6 *The General tab of the Group Properties dialog box*

If you want to configure BizTalk Server to connect to the Internet through a proxy server, you can select the Use A Proxy Server checkbox and specify the IP address and port number of the proxy server.

In the Connection tab of the Group Properties dialog box, you can specify the connection information for the Tracking and Shared Queue databases for the group, as shown in Figure 7-7.

The Tracking tab of the Group Properties dialog box enables you to specify document tracking options (a topic discussed in the next chapter). Already, you've seen the discussion of the Parsers tab in the Group Properties dialog box in Chapter 3 (refer to Figure 3-14).

You can also monitor the status of server groups in the BizTalk Server Administration by clicking the Microsoft BizTalk Server 2000 node. The list view

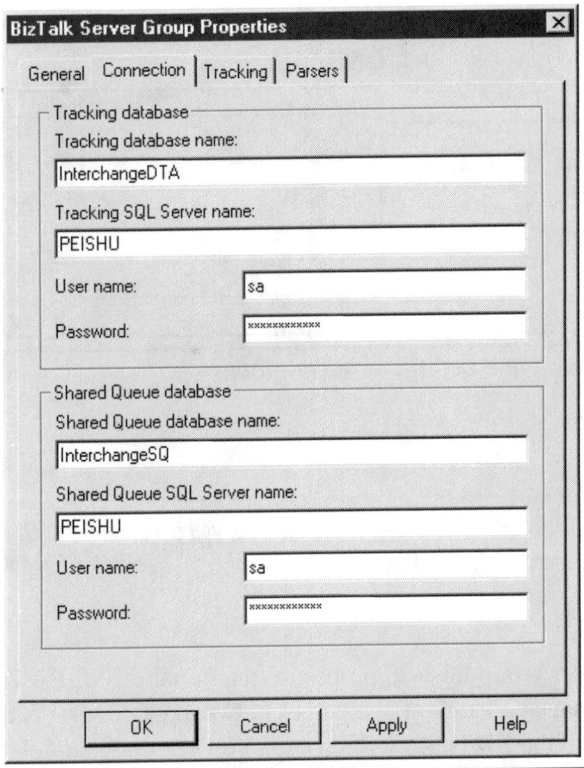

Figure 7-7 *The Connection tab of the Group Properties dialog box*

in the right pane will display the group names, as well as the date modified and statuses of all the server groups (shown in Figure 7-8).

Figure 7-8 shows the statuses of both server groups as *connected*, indicating they are connected to their own Tracking and Shared Queue databases. Other possible statuses include:

- **Tracking connection failed** Indicates the group is not connected to the Tracking database.
- **Shared Queue connection failed** Indicates the group is not connected to the Shared Queue database.
- **Tracking and Shared Queue connections failed** Indicates the group is neither connected to the Tracking database nor the Shared Queue database.

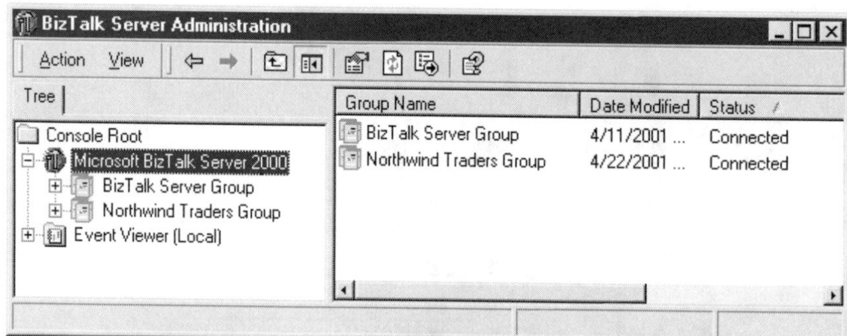

Figure 7-8 *Monitoring the statuses of server groups*

TIP

In cases where these error messages are received, you can check your SQL connections using the Enterprise Manager or the SQL client network tool.

Managing Servers

A server in a server group hosts appropriate functionalities of BizTalk Messaging Services and manages document exchanges between other servers and applications that are external to the BizTalk server group. You can add and delete servers in a server group. You can also set all the servers in a group to use the exact same configuration, or configure some servers in a group to perform dedicated tasks, such as receiving documents.

To add a server to a server group, right-click the server group and select New | Server. Type a name for the server in the Add A BizTalk Server dialog box and click OK (see Figure 7-9). The server must have BizTalk Server 2000 installed and must

Figure 7-9 *Adding a new server to the server group*

be connected in the network and accessible from the computer where you are running the BizTalk Server Administration snap-in.

To delete a server from the server group, right-click the server node in BizTalk Server Administration and select Delete. Click Yes in the User Action Confirmation dialog box.

To configure a server, right-click the server node in the BizTalk Server Administration snap-in and select Properties to open the *<Server_Name>* Properties dialog box, as shown in Figure 7-10.

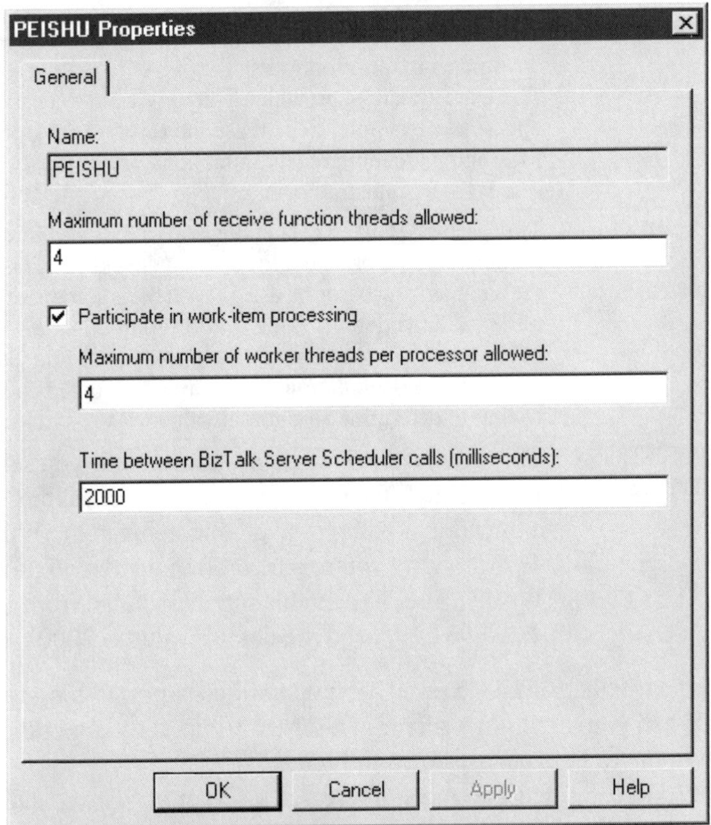

Figure 7-10 *The server Properties dialog box*

In the server Properties dialog box, you can specify the following properties:

Properties	Description
Maximum number of receive function threads allowed	This property is set on a per-processor basis. You may increase this number to increase the throughput of the receive functions on the server. For a BizTalk server that is configured to receive and process documents or just process documents, set this property to 1. If a BizTalk server is configured to just receive documents without processing them, set this property to 4 to optimize throughput. Acceptable numbers range from 1 to 128, where the default value is 4.
Participate in work-item processing	This checkbox determines whether the BizTalk server processes documents in the Work queue (as we will explain shortly). There are situations in which you may want to turn off this option (for example, to increase the receiving performance for Messaging Queuing receive functions, or to specify a dedicated server for administrative tasks).
Maximum number of worker threads per processor allowed	This property will only become available if you selected the Participate In Work-item Processing checkbox. This property is set on a per-processor basis. Acceptable numbers range from 1 to 128 and the default value is 4. Keep in mind that a high number may increase the throughput, but it could also cause performance degradation. You may need some benchmark testing to determine an optimal value.
Time between BizTalk Server Scheduler calls (milliseconds)	This property only becomes available if you selected the Participate In Work-item Processing checkbox. There is a thread that polls for available items in the Work queue. This property controls how often the thread polls the Work queue. Acceptable numbers range from 1 to 4,294,967,295, and the default value is 2000.

You can also use the BizTalk Server Administration snap-in to monitor the status of a server. When you highlight a server in a server group, its status is displayed in the list view of the right pane, as shown in Figure 7-11.

Figure 7-11 indicates that the status of a selected server is *running*. Other possible server statuses include:

- **Access denied** Indicates you do not have Windows 2000 Administrator privileges on the server.
- **Error** Indicates the BizTalk server has been removed from the group.

- **Stopped** Indicates if the server has stopped.
- **Unknown** Indicates if a server in a server group is unavailable for an unknown reason. This is usually caused by loss of connection to the server.

Managing Queues

The queues in the BizTalk Server Administration snap-in are logical representations of underlying tables in the Shared Queue database. When a document is submitted to BizTalk Server, either through its receive functions or submitted asynchronously through the Interchange COM interface, it is stored in the Shared Queue database until it is completely processed. There are four types of queues you can manage using the BizTalk Server Administration snap-in: the *Work queue*, the *Scheduled queue*, the *Retry queue,* and the *Suspended queue*. These queues enable you to determine the processing stages of documents and identify possible causes in the event of processing failures.

Managing the Work Queue

The Work queue contains documents that are currently being processed by the BizTalk Server. Documents in the Work queue are processed upon their arrival, therefore they won't sit in the Work queue for long. You rarely see documents in the Work queue unless you are continually processing a large volume of files.

You can move a document from the Work queue to the Suspended queue, where the document can then be deleted, resubmitted, or retransmitted to the Work queue to complete its processing.

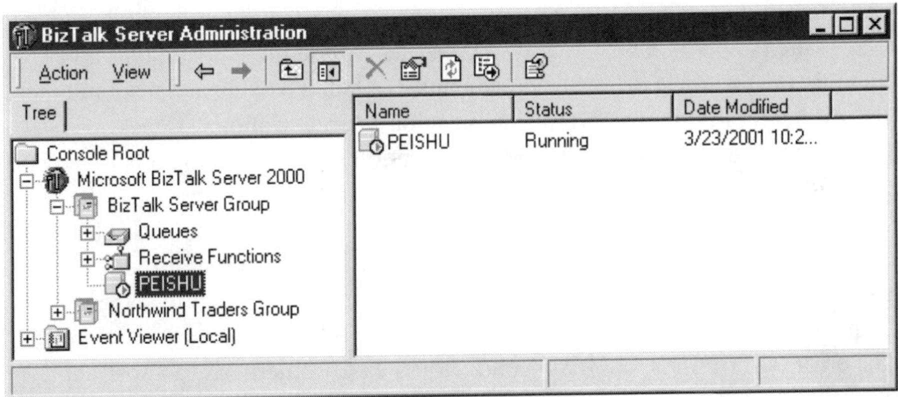

Figure 7-11 *Monitoring the status of a server*

To move a document to the Suspended queue, select the Work queue node, right-click the document you want to move in the list view, and select Move To Suspended Queue.

Managing the Scheduled Queue

The Scheduled Queue contains documents that have been processed by the BizTalk Server and are awaiting transmission according to the Service window property you specified in the messaging port.

As in the Work queue, you can move documents from the Scheduled queue to the Suspended queue.

Managing the Retry Queue

The Retry queue contains two types of documents: documents that are being resubmitted for delivery, and documents that have been sent to trading partners but are waiting for reliable messaging receipts. You cannot distinguish these two types of transmissions. As you learned in the last chapter, you can determine the retry behavior by specifying the retry counts (number of retries) and retry interval in the Advanced Configuration page of the Channel Wizard.

You can select any documents in this queue and move them to the Suspended queue.

Managing the Suspended Queue

The Suspended queue contains documents that have failed processing for some reason (for example, parsing errors, serialization errors, failed transmissions, missing channels, and so on).

You can delete any documents in the Suspended queue. You may also resubmit or retransmit most documents in the Suspended queue, with the exception of documents that have failed to parse. You can write an interface to edit these documents and resubmit them. You must delete the documents that failed parsing and resubmit them to BizTalk Server through the original application or organization.

The Suspended queue also provides information that can help you troubleshoot BizTalk Server errors and processing issues. For example, you can view the error descriptions by right-clicking a document in the Suspended queue and selecting View Error Description. You may also view either the document or the interchange by right-clicking the document in the Suspended queue and selecting View Document or View Interchange.

The error descriptions in the Suspended queue are sometimes too abstract and generic; you may also use the integrated Event Viewer to further diagnose the problem.

To use the Event Viewer for troubleshooting, click the Application node of the Event Viewer in BizTalk Messaging and then double-click an item in the list view in the right pane to bring up the Event Properties (the Description area usually contains detailed information about the error).

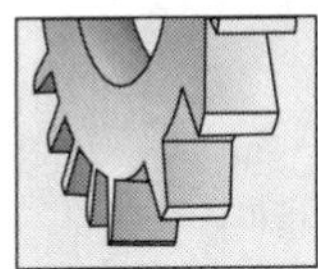

TIP

The Event Viewer can be so crowded it becomes difficult to identify the errors you are interested in. You can set a specific filter in the Event Viewer to display only those related items. To do this, right-click the Application node under Event Viewer and select Properties. Click the Filter tab. The source for BizTalk Server-related issues is usually marked as "BizTalk Server," and their types are either "Error" or "Warning." For example, the Filter properties illustrated in Figure 7-12 will help narrow down events when it comes to BizTalk Server-related warnings and errors.

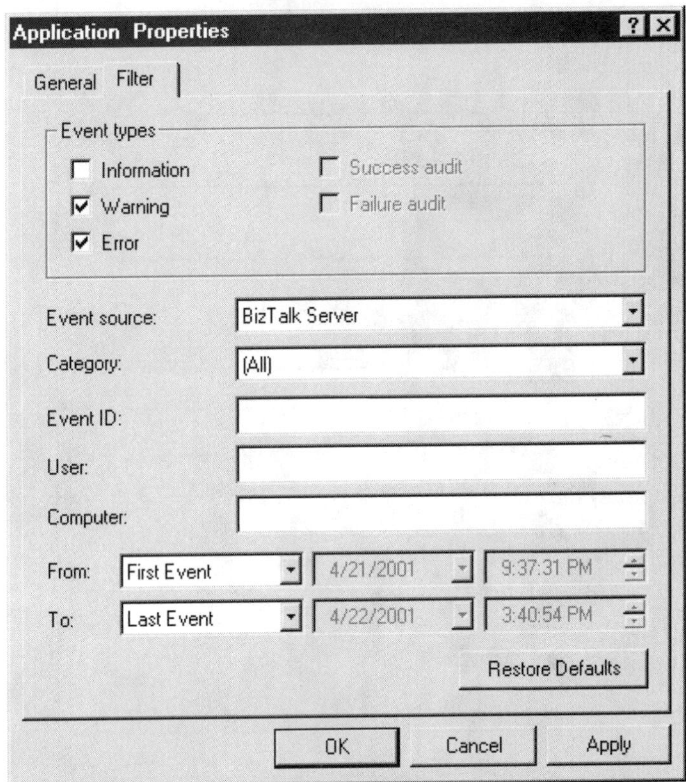

Figure 7-12 *Setting the Filter in the Event Viewer to display BizTalk Server-related warnings and errors*

Managing Receive Functions

You've learned how to create receive functions for both File and Messaging Queuing types by using BizTalk Server Administration in previous chapters. Another way you can disable a receive function is to select the Disable Receive Function checkbox in the General tab of its Properties dialog box (as shown in Figure 7-13). When you select this checkbox, the system will display a User Action Confirmation dialog box warning you that disabling this receive function will cause any documents dropped off at this receive location (a file share or a message queue) to be rendered incapable of pick up. Click Yes to confirm your intention.

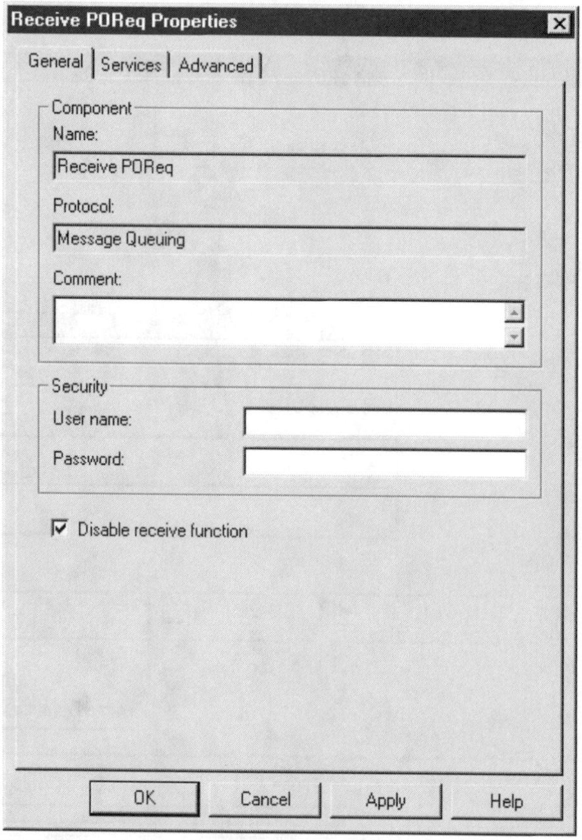

Figure 7-13 *Disabling a receive function*

Managing BizTalk Server Databases

BizTalk Server Messaging Services uses three SQL Server databases: the BizTalk Messaging Management database, the Tracking database, and the Shared Queue database.

The BizTalk Messaging Management database stores both administration objects, such as group and server settings and receive functions, as well as messaging configuration objects, such as channels, messaging ports, and so on. The administration objects can be accessed and managed through either the BizTalk Server Administration snap-in or WMI APIs, as you will learn later in this chapter. The messaging configuration objects can be accessed and managed through either BizTalk Messaging Manager or the BizTalk Messaging Configuration Object Model COM API, as you learned in the last chapter. In most cases, the BizTalk Messaging Management database is globally available to multiple server groups.

The Tracking database provides a log of all interchanges, documents, and receipts processed by BizTalk Server, and the Shared Queue database holds documents while they are being processed or waiting to be processed, provided you have set the appropriate tracking options, as you will learn in the next chapter. Documents are later removed after they have been processed. The scope of Tracking and Shared Queue databases are server groups. They are accessible only within each server group.

Managing the BizTalk Messaging Management Database

Using the BizTalk Server Administration snap-in and other tools, you can change the BizTalk Messaging Management database, remove servers from a BizTalk Management database and move servers between BizTalk Messaging Management databases.

Configuring the BizTalk Messaging Management Database

You can configure the BizTalk Messaging Management database during or after the installation of the BizTalk servers.

During installation you can configure all servers to point to a central BizTalk Messaging Management database. In this way, every time you open the BizTalk Server Administration snap-in, the servers under the Microsoft BizTalk Server 2000 node point to the same BizTalk Messaging Management database, and can be centrally managed. Usually, you don't need to change the configuration that was set up during installation.

Under certain circumstances, however, changing the BizTalk Messaging Management database to a different database may become necessary. For example, you may want to take the production database server offline for maintenance. In this case, you can replicate the production BizTalk Messaging Management database to another server and then use the BizTalk Server Administration snap-in to configure all the server groups to point to the central BizTalk Messaging Management database in a new location. In this way, you can keep downtime to a minimum.

Depending on the frequency requirement of your maintenance schedule, you may need to use a dedicated server that is configured exactly the same way as the production database server that hosts the BizTalk Messaging Management database. You can periodically replicate the BizTalk Messaging Management database to this backup database, and once you need to take the production database offline, you can easily switch over to the backup server and use it as the new production database server. After you perform maintenance on the previous database production server, you can use it as the backup server (that is, you reverse the rolls of production-backup servers). This active-passive server pair strategy can maximize the availability of your BizTalk servers.

Removing Servers from a BizTalk Messaging Management Database

You can remove a server from the central BizTalk Messaging Management database. To do this, right-click the server in its server group and select Delete (or select the server and press the DELETE key on your keyboard). Click Yes in the Confirm User Action dialog box.

Moving Servers Between BizTalk Messaging Management Databases

You can add a new server to the central BizTalk Messaging Management database by running the BizTalk Server 2000 Database Setup Wizard, BTSsetupDB.exe, found in the <BizTalk Server Install>\Setup\ folder. You then select an existing database on the Configure A BizTalk Messaging Management database page in the Setup Wizard.

CAUTION

If you attempt to add a remote server to an existing BizTalk Messaging Management database and the server was originally in a different BizTalk Messaging Management database, you will get an error in the Windows 2000 Event Log, stating that a new instance of the WMI class "MicrosoftBizTalkServer_Server" cannot be created in the BizTalk Server WMI provider. It also indicates that the server may already belong to a different BizTalk Server installation.

Managing the Tracking Database

All servers in a server group share a single Tracking database. (For EDI scenarios, you need to have a single DTA for receipt processing to work even across Server Groups). The Tracking database stores activity information about documents in BizTalk Server, and then tracks the status of the documents as they move through the server. In the next chapter, you will learn to use the BizTalk Document Tracking tool to query the Tracking database and to examine transmission times, receipt responses, and other document aspects. You can configure the server group to point to a specific Tracking database in the Connection tab of the server group Properties dialog box, as shown earlier in Figure 7-7.

As you will see in the next chapter, you can configure tracking options at the global level through the Properties dialog box of a BizTalk Server group. You can also specify other tracking options at the channel and document levels.

Keep in mind, the Tracking database can grow in size very quickly. To help you maintain it, BizTalk Server 2000 provides a TSQL script file, DTA_SampleJobs.sql, found in the <BizTalk Server Install>\SDK\Messaging Samples\SQLServerAgentJobs\ folder. This script creates two SQL Server Agent jobs. One job purges older records in the dta_debugdoc_data table and keeps the size of the table at 25000 records. Another job monitors records in the dta_outdoc_details table and marks those records whose waiting periods timed-out before receiving receipts as expired. The Readme.txt document, found in the same folder, contains detailed information about the two SQL Server Agent jobs.

Should the Tracking database become corrupted or damaged, you can manually restore the Tracking database by doing the following:

1. Create a new database in SQL Server Enterprise Manager.
2. Open the SQL Server Query Analyzer and execute, in the following order, five TSQL scripts, all found in the <BizTalk Server Install>\Setup folder: BTS_Tracking_Schema.sql, BTS_Reporting.sql, BTS_Tracking_Logic.sql, BTS_WorkflowEvents.sql, and BTS_WorkflowSchema.sql.
3. If the name of the Tracking database you specified in Step 1 is different than the Tracking database name prior to the restoration, you need to configure the server group to point to the new Tracking database using the Connection tab of the server group Properties dialog box, as shown earlier in Figure 7-7.

CAUTION

To keep from losing data, always back up the data before manually restoring the Tracking database.

Managing the Shared Queue Database

All servers in a server group share a single Shared Queue database. The Shared Queue database stores all documents and interchanges submitted to the servers until they are processed.

You can configure the server group to point to a specific Shared Queue database in the Connection tab of the server group Properties dialog box, as shown earlier in Figure 7-7. In addition, if the Shared Queue database becomes corrupted or damaged, you can manually restore the Shared Queue database by creating a new database in the SQL Server Enterprise Manager and executing two TSQL scripts in the SQL Server Query Analyzer, BTS_Core_Schema.sql, and BTS_Core_Logic.sql.

CAUTION

To prevent losing data, always back up the data before manually restoring the Shared Queue database.

Administrating BizTalk Server Programmatically

BizTalk Server 2000 exposes a set of *Windows Management Instrumentation* (*WMI*) APIs that enables you to programmatically access all the administration objects and functionalities available in the BizTalk Server Administration snap-in. As a matter of fact, the BizTalk Server Administration snap-in itself uses WMI APIs to access and manipulate administration objects stored in the BizTalk Messaging Management database. You can use the WMI API to manage servers, server groups, Shared Queues, receive functions, and so on.

In this section, we will introduce the WMI from BizTalk Server 2000 and its Scripting APIs. We will use some sample code to demonstrate how to use BizTalk Server WMI Scripting APIs, as well as show how to use the IInterchange COM interface in order to work with the Suspended queue.

Using BizTalk Server WMI APIs

Windows Management Instrumentation (WMI) is Microsoft's implementation of *Web-Based Enterprise Management* (*WBEM*) on the Windows platform (Windows NT and Windows 2000). WBEM is an industry initiative, managed by the *Desktop Management Task Force* (*DMTF*). It establishes management infrastructure standards and provides a way to combine information from various hardware and software management systems. In addition, it can access data from a variety of underlying technologies and platforms, and then present that data in a consistent fashion.

WMI in BizTalk Server 2000

Microsoft WMI is a WBEM-compliant implementation that provides a consistent and richly descriptive model of the configuration, status, and operational aspects of Windows NT 4.0 (SP4+) and Windows 2000 platforms. When used in conjunction with other management services provided in Windows NT and Windows 2000, such as Microsoft Management Consoles (MMCs), WMI can simplify the task of developing well-integrated management applications, providing scalable, effective enterprise management solutions.

BizTalk Server 2000 uses the WMI layer to encapsulate administrative functions that support the management of systems in an enterprise. Figure 7-14 illustrates the WMI architecture in BizTalk Server 2000.

WBEM uses a three-tiered approach for collecting and distributing data based on the *Common Information Model* (*CIM*) schema. In the BizTalk Server 2000 WMI architecture (as shown in Figure 7-14), the middle tier is the executable process, WinMgmt.exe, that provides all of the WMI functionality.

The CIM-compliant object repository provides a standard mechanism for storing object definitions. A standard protocol (for example, COM/DCOM in this case) is used for obtaining and disseminating management data. The BizTalk Server WMI Provider functions as the data access API for accessing the underlying instrumentation data (the back-end or data tier, referred to as managed objects in WBEM terminology). The CIM Object Manager is a key component in the BizTalk Server 2000 WMI architecture. It provides a collection and manipulation point for managed objects.

The CIM Object Manager gathers management information from the BizTalk Server WMI provider and makes it available to management applications (the front-end or presentation tier) through appropriate APIs. For example, the BizTalk

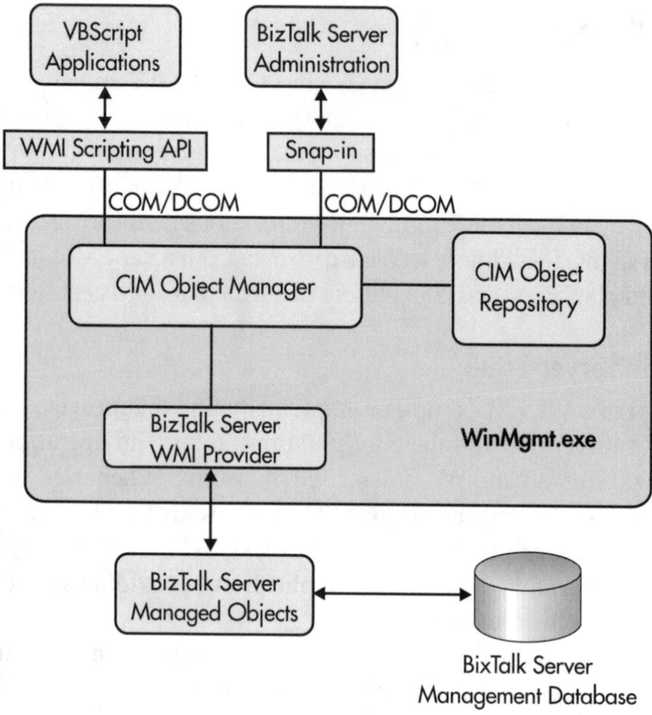

Figure 7-14 *The BizTalk Server 2000 WMI architecture*

Server Administration snap-in accesses the BizTalk Server administration information through appropriate COM interfaces. BizTalk Server 2000 also provides a Scripting WMI interface for you to access its management information using scripting languages, such as VBScript.

BizTalk Server 2000 Namespaces and Classes

In WMI, managed objects, also referred to as *classes*, are grouped into individual distinct logical groups, called *namespaces*. All the namespaces on a given computer are under a top-level system namespace, known as the *root namespace*. For example, the namespace of BizTalk Server 2000 is defined as "MicrosoftBizTalkServer". A valid namespace reference for BizTalk Server 2000 would be "root/MicrosoftBizTalkServer". The following table summarizes the managed objects (classes) under BizTalk Server 2000's namespace.

Class Name	Description
MicrosoftBizTalkServer_Group	This class represents the BizTalk Server groups you saw in the BizTalk Server Administration snap-in.
MicrosoftBizTalkServer_ GroupServer	This class is an association class that allows you to retrieve all the servers in a group. The *Antecedent* property references the properties of the BizTalk Server group, for example, "\\Machine_Name\ Root\MicrosoftBizTalkServer: MicrosoftBizTalkServer_Server.Name = "Machine_Name". The *Dependent* property references the properties of the server associated with the BizTalk Server group, for example, "MicrosoftBizTalkServer_ Group = "BizTalk Server Group".
MicrosoftBizTalkServer_Queue	This class is abstract, and serves only as a base for new classes. It should not be implemented.
MicrosoftBizTalkServer_ WorkQueue	This class represents a Work queue from the BizTalk Server Administration snap-in.
MicrosoftBizTalkServer_ ScheduledQueue	This class represents a Scheduled queue from the BizTalk Server Administration snap-in.
MicrosoftBizTalkServer_ RetryQueue	This class represents a Retry queue from the BizTalk Server Administration snap-in.
MicrosoftBizTalkServer_ SuspendedQueue	This class represents a Suspended queue from the BizTalk Server Administration snap-in.
MicrosoftBizTalkServer_ ReceiveFunction	This class represents receive functions (File or Messaging Queuing) from the BizTalk Server Administration snap-in.
MicrosoftBizTalkServer_ GroupReceiveFunction	This class is an association class that allows you to retrieve all the receive functions in a group. Similar to the MicrosoftBizTalkServer_ServerGroup class, this class also supports two properties, Antecedent and Dependent. The former references the properties of the BizTalk Server group, whereas the latter references the properties of the receive function associated with the BizTalk Server group.
MicrosoftBizTalkServer_Server	This class represents servers from the BizTalk Server Administration snap-in.
MicrosoftBizTalkServer_MgmtDB	This class represents the BizTalk Messaging Management database.

Class Name	Description
DocSuspendedEvent	This class represents events raised by documents sent to the Suspended queue.
InterchangeProvError	This class represents error information returned by the interchange provider when creating class instances.

Each class in the previous table supports a set of properties (and possibly methods) appropriate to the managed object the class represents.

TIP

*For detailed properties and methods about these classes, refer to the Windows Management Instrumentation in the BizTalk Server 2000 Help File (BTSwmi.chm), which is downloadable from the Microsoft BizTalk Server production site at **http://www.microsoft.com/BizTalk**, under Product Documentations. This help file provides a complete BizTalk Server 2000 WMI API reference.*

Programming WMI Scripting API in BizTalk Server 2000

The Windows Management Instrumentation (WMI) Scripting API consists of nineteen objects that can be used to develop management applications using programming languages, such as Visual Basic, and scripting languages, such as VBScript and Microsoft JScript. In this subsection, we will introduce the most important and frequently used WMI scripting objects and demonstrate how to use these WMI scripting objects along with the classes of BizTalk Server namespace to create management applications for BizTalk Server 2000. We will use VBScript in the code examples.

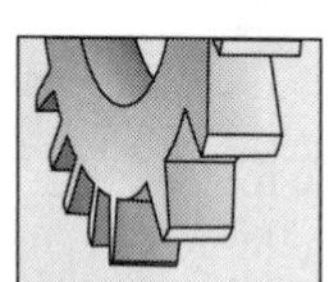

TIP

*For detailed information about WMI programming, refer to the Platform SDK documentation on the MSDN online Library at **http://msdn.microsoft.com/library**. Under Platform SDK Documentation/Management Services/Windows Management Instrumentation/WMI Application Programming, look for the Scripting API and WMI Reference.*

The root WMI scripting object is the *SWbemLocator* object that represents a connection to a namespace on a local or remote host computer (all the WMI scripting objects use the naming convention SWbemXXX to reflect SWBM where XXX stands for the actual object name). The program ID (ProgID) of the SWbemLocator is *WbemScripting.SWbemLocator*. The SWbemLocator object supports a single method, *ConnectServer,* which takes up to six optional input parameters. The method returns a SWbemServices object that will be discussed shortly. The following

VBScript code segment demonstrates how to create an instance of the SWbemLocator object and connect to the BizTalk Server 2000 namespace:

```
Dim oLocator, oServices
Set oLocator = CreateObject("SWbemScripting.SWbemLocator")
Set oServices = oLocator.ConnectServer(Server_Name, _
                "root/MicrosoftBizTalkServer")
```

If you don't specify the server name in the ConnectServer method, it will default to the local computer. For example:

```
Set oServices = oLocator.ConnectServer(, _
                "root/MicrosoftBizTalkServer")
```

The SWbemServices object supports eighteen methods. For demonstration purposes we will only introduce three of the most important methods of this object: *Get*, *ExecQuery*, and *Delete*.

The Get method of the SWbemServices object uses an *object path* to return a *SWbemObject* object which represents a specific managed object, such as a receive function. To specify an object path, use its class name, such as MicrosoftBizTalkServer_ReceiveFunction, and an appropriate property such as *Name* to establish a search criterion. For example, the following code example demonstration shows how to get an SWbemObject object that represents the "Receive PO Req" receive function you created in the last chapter:

```
Dim oReceiveFunction 'A SWbemObject representing a receive function
Dim sObjectPath
'......
sObjectPath = "MicrosoftBizTalkServer_ReceiveFunction.Name = " _
            & chr(34) & "Receive PO Req" & chr(34)
Set oReceiveFunction = oServices.Get(sObjectPath)
```

Similarly, the Delete method of the SWbemServices object uses an object path to specify a specific object to be deleted. To delete the "Receive PO Req" receive function, for example, you can use the following scripting code:

```
Dim sObjectPath
'......
sObjectPath = "MicrosoftBizTalkServer_ReceiveFunction.Name = " _
            & chr(34) & "Receive PO Req" & chr(34)
oServices.Delete(sObjectPath)
```

The ExecQuery method of the SWbemServices object returns an *SWbemObjectSet* object which is a collection of *SWbemObject* objects. The method takes a WMI Query Language (WQL) statement as the input parameter. WQL is a subset of the standard ANSI SQL language, with minor semantic changes to support WMI. The following code sample, taken from a sample scripting file for this chapter, ListReceiveFunctions.vbs, uses the ExecQuery method of the SWbemServices object to return a collection of the receive functions, then iterates through the collection to report the name and protocol type (File or Messaging Queuing) of each individual receive function in the collection:

```
Dim oLocator
Dim oServices
Dim oReceiveFunctions
Dim oReceiveFunction
Dim sWQL, sProtocolTYpe

On Error Resume Next
sWQL = "Select * from MicrosoftBizTalkServer_ReceiveFunction"

Set oLocator = CreateObject("WbemScripting.SWbemLocator")
Set oServices =
oLocator.ConnectServer(,"root/MicrosoftBizTalkServer")
Set oReceiveFunctions = oServices.ExecQuery(sWQL)
For each oReceiveFunction in oReceiveFunctions
  Select Case oReceiveFunction.ProtocolType
    Case 1
      sProtocolType = "File Receive Function"
    Case 2
      sProtocolType = "Messaging Queuing Receive Function"
  End Select
  wscript.echo oReceiveFunction.Name & " - " & sProtocolType
Next

Set oLocator = Nothing
Set oServices = Nothing
Set oReceiveFunction = Nothing
Set oReceiveFunctions = Nothing
If err <> 0 Then
  wscript.echo err.description
End If
```

The WQL statement used in the preceding example is "Select * from MicrosoftBizTalkServer_ReceiveFunction", which is very similar to a standard SQL statement. Figure 7-15 illustrates the output of this code, which lists the three receive functions we created in the last chapter.

TIP

For a complete WQL language reference, refer to the MSDN online library at ***http://msdn.microsoft.com/library****, under Platform SDK Documentations/Management Services/Windows Management Instrumentation/WMI Development Environment/WMI Query Language.*

The SWbemObject object supports a few dozen methods. Here, for demonstration purposes, we will discuss the three most important ones: *SpawnInstance_*, *Put_*, and *Delete_*. You might have noticed the trailing underscore ("_") used in each of the methods. This is a naming convention for all the generic methods that belong to the SWbemObject object. It is used to differentiate them from the dynamic WMI methods and properties, such as those supported in the classes of the BizTalk Server namespace.

The SpawnInstance_ method creates a new instance of a class, and the Delete_ method deletes the current class or instance and causes the underlying object to be removed from the BizTalk Messaging Management database. Neither of these two methods require input parameters.

Depending on the wbemChangeFlag enumeration, the output of the Put_ method varies. For example, to create a new object, you call the Put_ method and pass 2 as the input parameter (wbemChangeFlagCreateOnly). To update changes to an object, you call the Put_method and pass 1 (wbemChangeFlagUpdateOnly).

The following VBScript sample, taken from the source code of this chapter, CreateReceiveFunction.vbs, demonstrates how to use the WMI scripting API and BizTalk Server WMI classes to create the Messaging Queuing receive function, Receive PO Req, you used in the last chapter.

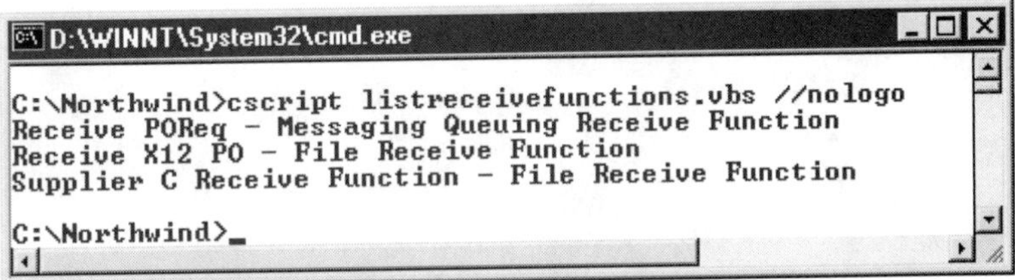

Figure 7-15 *Listing receiving functions*

```
Dim oLocator
Dim oServices
Dim oReceiveFunction
Dim oReceiveFunctionInstance

On Error Resume Next

Set oLocator = CreateObject("WbemScripting.SWbemLocator")
Set oServices = oLocator.ConnectServer(,"root/MicrosoftBizTalkServer")
Set oReceiveFunction =
oServices.Get("MicrosoftBizTalkServer_ReceiveFunction")
Set oReceiveFunctionInstance = oReceiveFunction.SpawnInstance_

If Not oReceiveFunctionInstance Is Nothing Then
  With oReceiveFunctionInstance
    .Name = "Receive POReq"
    .GroupName = "BizTalk Server Group"
    .ProcessingServer = "PEISHU" 'Change this to reflect your server name
    .ProtocolType = 2 'Messaging Queuing Receive Function
    .PollingLocation = "Direct=OS:.\Private$\POReqInbox"
    .OpennessFlag = 1 'BIZTALK_OPENNESS_TYPE_NOTOPEN
    .ChannelName = "PO Channel"
    .Put_ (2) 'wbemChangeFlagCreateOnly
  End With
Else
  wscript.echo "Creating Receive Function instance error!"
  wscript.quit
End If

Set oLocator = Nothing
Set oServices = Nothing
Set oReceiveFunction = Nothing
Set oReceiveFunctionInstance = Nothing
If Err.Number = 0 Then
  wscript.echo "Receive Function - Receive POReq has " & _
               "been successfully created!"
Else
  wscript.echo Err.Description
End If
```

This sample code also illustrates typical steps taken to create a new BizTalk Server administration object using WMI, as explained in the following:

1. Create an instance of the SWbemLocator object.
2. Call the ConnectServer method of the SWbemLocator object to the BizTalk server and return an SWbemServices object.
3. Call the Get method of the SWbemServices object to create a SWbemObject object.
4. Call the SpawnInstance_ method of the SWbemObject object to create a new instance of the class.
5. Set up properties for the class instance.
6. Call the Put_ method and passing parameter 2 (wbemChangeFlagCreateOnly) to create the new class and save it to the BizTalk Messaging Management database.

The example also demonstrated the error handling techniques in VBScript. An "On Error Resume Next" statement sets up the in-line error handling style. By the end of the code execution, you change the *Number* property of the *Err* object and report the error peacefully.

A Receive Function Utility

You can use the knowledge you learned in this chapter to create a utility that exports existing receive functions from the local BizTalk Server and exports them to a VBScript file. Then you can use the exported VBScript file to deploy these receive functions to another BizTalk Server. The source code for this utility is illustrated in the following example (The file, ReceiveFunctions.vbs, can be downloaded from this book's Web site):

```
Dim oLocator, oServices, oReceiveFunctions, oReceiveFunction
Dim sWQL, sProtocolTYpe
Dim oXML, oXSL, oRoot, oNodeReceiveFunction, oNode
Dim oFSO, oFile, sScript

On Error Resume Next

Set oXML = CreateObject("MSXML2.DOMDocument")
oXML.async = False

Set oRoot = oXML.CreateElement("BizTalkReceiveFunctions")
oXML.appendChild oRoot

sWQL = "Select * from MicrosoftBizTalkServer_ReceiveFunction"
```

```
Set oLocator = CreateObject("WbemScripting.SWbemLocator")
Set oServices =
oLocator.ConnectServer(,"root/MicrosoftBizTalkServer")
Set oReceiveFunctions = oServices.ExecQuery(sWQL)

If oReceiveFunctions.count = 0 Then
   WScript.Echo "No receive functions to export"
   WScript.Quit
End If

For each oReceiveFunction in oReceiveFunctions
  Set oNodeReceiveFunction =
oXML.CreateElement("BizTalkReceiveFunction")
  oRoot.appendChild oNodeReceiveFunction

  Set oNode = oXML.CreateElement("Name")
  oNode.Text = oReceiveFunction.Name & ""
  oNodeReceiveFunction.appendChild oNode

  Set oNode = oXML.CreateElement("Comment")
  oNode.Text= oReceiveFunction.Comment & ""
  oNodeReceiveFunction.appendChild oNode

  Set oNode = oXML.CreateElement("ProtocolType")
  oNode.Text= oReceiveFunction.ProtocolType & ""
  oNodeReceiveFunction.appendChild oNode

  'Set oNode = oXML.CreateElement("ProcessingServer")
  'oNode.Text= oReceiveFunction.ProcessingServer & ""
  'oNodeReceiveFunction.appendChild oNode

  Set oNode = oXML.CreateElement("GroupName")
  oNode.Text= oReceiveFunction.GroupName & ""
  oNodeReceiveFunction.appendChild oNode

  Set oNode = oXML.CreateElement("FileNameMask")
  oNode.Text= oReceiveFunction.FileNameMask & ""
  oNodeReceiveFunction.appendChild oNode

  Set oNode = oXML.CreateElement("PollingLocation")
  oNode.Text= oReceiveFunction.PollingLocation & ""
  oNodeReceiveFunction.appendChild oNode
```

```
Set oNode = oXML.CreateElement("PreProcessor")
oNode.Text= oReceiveFunction.PreProcessor & ""
oNodeReceiveFunction.appendChild oNode

'Set oNode = oXML.CreateElement("Username")
'oNode.Text= oReceiveFunction.Username & ""
'oNodeReceiveFunction.appendChild oNode

'Set oNode = oXML.CreateElement("Password")
'oNode.Text= oReceiveFunction.Password & ""
'oNodeReceiveFunction.appendChild oNode

Set oNode = oXML.CreateElement("OpennessFlag")
oNode.Text= oReceiveFunction.OpennessFlag & ""
oNodeReceiveFunction.appendChild oNode

Set oNode = oXML.CreateElement("IsPassThrough")
oNode.Text= oReceiveFunction.IsPassThrough & ""
oNodeReceiveFunction.appendChild oNode

Set oNode = oXML.CreateElement("EnvelopeName")
oNode.Text= oReceiveFunction.EnvelopeName & ""
oNodeReceiveFunction.appendChild oNode

Set oNode = oXML.CreateElement("ChannelName")
oNode.Text= oReceiveFunction.ChannelName & ""
oNodeReceiveFunction.appendChild oNode

Set oNode = oXML.CreateElement("DocumentName")
oNode.Text= oReceiveFunction.DocumentName & ""
oNodeReceiveFunction.appendChild oNode

Set oNode = oXML.CreateElement("SourceID")
oNode.Text= oReceiveFunction.SourceID & ""
oNodeReceiveFunction.appendChild oNode

Set oNode = oXML.CreateElement("SourceQualifier")
oNode.Text= oReceiveFunction.SourceQualifier & ""
oNodeReceiveFunction.appendChild oNode

Set oNode = oXML.CreateElement("DestinationID")
oNode.Text= oReceiveFunction.DestinationID & ""
oNodeReceiveFunction.appendChild oNode
```

```
    Set oNode = oXML.CreateElement("DestinationQualifier")
    oNode.Text= oReceiveFunction.DestinationQualifier & ""
    oNodeReceiveFunction.appendChild oNode

    Set oNode = oXML.CreateElement("DisableReceiveFunction")
    oNode.Text= oReceiveFunction.DisableReceiveFunction & ""
    oNodeReceiveFunction.appendChild oNode

Next

Set oXSL = CreateObject("MSXML2.DOMDocument")
oXSL.async = False
oXSL.Load "ReceiveFunctions.xsl"
sScript = oXML.TransformNode(oXSL)

Set oFSO = CreateObject("Scripting.FileSystemObject")
Set oFile = oFSO.CreateTextFile("ReceiveFunctionsImports.vbs",True)
oFile.WriteLine sScript
oFile.Close


Set oLocator = Nothing
Set oServices = Nothing
Set oReceiveFunction = Nothing
Set oReceiveFunctions = Nothing
Set oXML = Nothing
Set oXSL = Nothing
Set oRoot = Nothing
Set oNode = Nothing
Set oNode1 = Nothing
Set oFSO = Nothing
Set oFile = Nothing
If err <> 0 Then
  wscript.echo err.description
Else
  wscript.echo "Receive Functions have been successfully exported!"
End If
```

This script retrieves the receive functions from the local BizTalk database through WMI, as you learned earlier in this chapter. Then it stores the information about receive functions in an XML DOM object in memory. The XML document is shown in Figure 7-16.

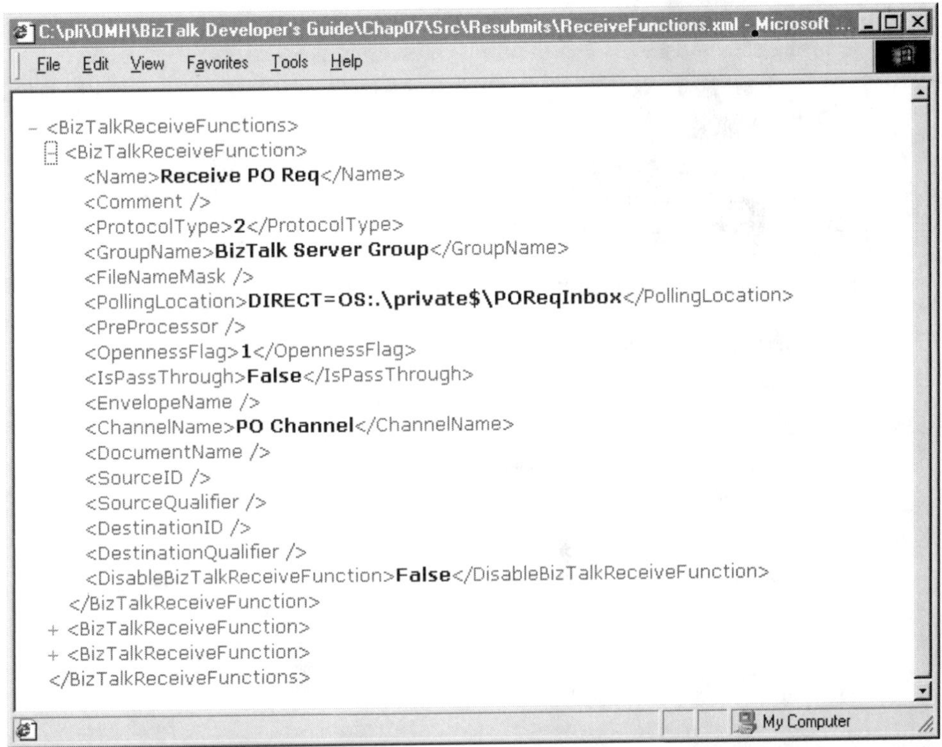

Figure 7-16 *Receive functions are stored in an XML document*

Then the script loads an XSLT stylesheet and transforms the XML document to another scripting file, ReceiveFunctionsImport.vbs, and persists this file to the desk.

The XSLT stylesheet looks like this:

```
<?xml version="1.0"?>
<xsl:stylesheet xmlns:xsl="http://www.w3.org/1999/XSL/Transform" version="1.0">
<xsl:output method="text"/>
<xsl:template match="/">
Dim oLocator, oServices, oReceiveFunction, oReceiveFunctionInstance
Dim oNetwork, gHostName

On Error Resume Next

Set oNetwork = CreateObject("Wscript.Network")
gHostName = oNetwork.ComputerName

Set oLocator = CreateObject("WbemScripting.SWbemLocator")
```

```
Set oServices = oLocator.ConnectServer(,"root/MicrosoftBizTalkServer")
Set oReceiveFunction = oServices.Get("MicrosoftBizTalkServer_ReceiveFunction")
<xsl:for-each select="//BizTalkReceiveFunction">
<xsl:text>
Set oReceiveFunctionInstance = oReceiveFunction.SpawnInstance_

If Not oReceiveFunctionInstance Is Nothing Then
    With oReceiveFunctionInstance</xsl:text>
  <xsl:for-each select="*">
   <xsl:if test="string-length()>0">
      <xsl:choose>
        <xsl:when test = "name()='Name'
                                 or name()='Comment'
                                 or name()='GroupName'
                                 or name()='FileNameMask'
                                 or name()='PollingLocation'
                                 or name()='PreProcessor'
                                 or name()='EnvelopeName'
                                 or name()='ChannelName'
                                 or name()='DocumentName'
                                 or name()='SourceID'
                                 or name()='SourceQualifier'
                                 or name()='DestinationID'
 or name()='DestinationQualifier'">
          .<xsl:value-of select="name()"/> = "<xsl:value-of select="."/>"</xsl:when>
        <xsl:otherwise>
          .<xsl:value-of select="name()"/> = <xsl:value-of select="."/>
        </xsl:otherwise>
      </xsl:choose>
   </xsl:if>
  </xsl:for-each>
<xsl:text>
          .ProcessingServer=gHostName
          .Put_ (2) 'wbemChangeFlagCreateOnly
    End With
End If
Set oReceiveFunctionInstance = Nothing
</xsl:text>
</xsl:for-each>
<xsl:text>

Set oLocator = Nothing
Set oServices = Nothing
Set oReceiveFunction = Nothing
Set oReceiveFunctionInstance = Nothing
If Err = 0 Then
  Wscript.Echo "Receive Functions have been successfully created!"
```

```
Else
  Wscript.Echo Err.Description
End If
</xsl:text>
</xsl:template>
</xsl:stylesheet>
```

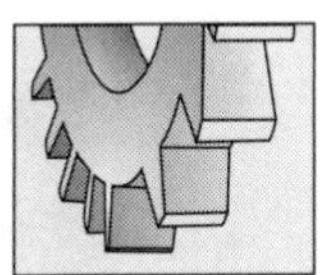

TIP

In case you aren't familiar with XSLT, Appendix B of this book covers it comprehensively.

The following is a sample script file automatically generated by the receive function utility. You can use this script to regenerate three receive functions (on another BizTalk Server) that you created in Chapter 6.

```
Dim oLocator, oServices, oReceiveFunction, oReceiveFunctionInstance
Dim oNetwork, gHostName

On Error Resume Next

Set oNetwork = CreateObject("Wscript.Network")
gHostName = oNetwork.ComputerName

Set oLocator = CreateObject("WbemScripting.SWbemLocator")
Set oServices =
oLocator.ConnectServer(,"root/MicrosoftBizTalkServer")
Set oReceiveFunction =
oServices.Get("MicrosoftBizTalkServer_ReceiveFunction")

Set oReceiveFunctionInstance = oReceiveFunction.SpawnInstance_

If Not oReceiveFunctionInstance Is Nothing Then
    With oReceiveFunctionInstance
          .Name = "Receive PO Req"
          .ProtocolType = 2
          .GroupName = "BizTalk Server Group"
          .PollingLocation = "DIRECT=OS:.\private$\POReqInbox"
          .OpennessFlag = 1
          .IsPassThrough = False
          .ChannelName = "PO Channel"
          .DisableReceiveFunction = False
          .ProcessingServer=gHostName
          .Put_ (2) 'wbemChangeFlagCreateOnly
```

```
    End With
End If
Set oReceiveFunctionInstance = Nothing

Set oReceiveFunctionInstance = oReceiveFunction.SpawnInstance_

If Not oReceiveFunctionInstance Is Nothing Then
    With oReceiveFunctionInstance
           .Name = "Receive X12 PO"
           .ProtocolType = 1
           .GroupName = "BizTalk Server Group"
           .FileNameMask = "*.EDI"
           .PollingLocation = "C:\Northwind\e-Market\"
           .OpennessFlag = 1
           .IsPassThrough = False
           .ChannelName = "X12 Distribution Channel"
           .DisableReceiveFunction = False
           .ProcessingServer=gHostName
           .Put_ (2) 'wbemChangeFlagCreateOnly
    End With
End If
Set oReceiveFunctionInstance = Nothing

Set oReceiveFunctionInstance = oReceiveFunction.SpawnInstance_

If Not oReceiveFunctionInstance Is Nothing Then
    With oReceiveFunctionInstance
           .Name = "Supplier C Receive Function"
           .ProtocolType = 1
           .GroupName = "BizTalk Server Group"
           .FileNameMask = "*.EDI"
           .PollingLocation = "C:\Northwind\Supplier A\"
           .OpennessFlag = 1
           .IsPassThrough = False
           .ChannelName = "Supplier C Channel"
           .DisableReceiveFunction = False
           .ProcessingServer=gHostName
           .Put_ (2) 'wbemChangeFlagCreateOnly
    End With
End If
Set oReceiveFunctionInstance = Nothing

Set oLocator = Nothing
```

```
Set oServices = Nothing
Set oReceiveFunction = Nothing
Set oReceiveFunctionInstance = Nothing
If Err = 0 Then
  Wscript.Echo "Receive Functions have been successfully created!"
Else
  Wscript.Echo Err.Description
End If
```

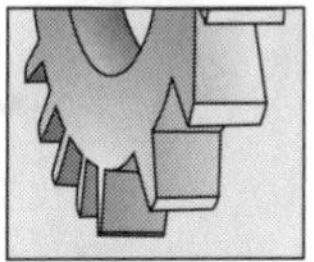

TIP

Use the appendix of the Windows Management Instrumentation in the BizTalk Server 2000 Help File. The Solution Library contains plenty of Visual Basic code samples employing BizTalk WMI to manage BizTalk Server 2000 administration objects, including the BizTalk Messaging Management database, documents, groups, servers, queues, and receive functions.

Chapter in Review

In this chapter, you learned how to use the BizTalk Server Administration MMC snap-in to manage BizTalk Server 2000 administration objects, including server groups, servers, queues, receive functions, and the BizTalk Messaging Management database. You also learned how to configure and administrate the SQL Server databases for BizTalk Messaging Services, including the BizTalk Messaging Management database, the Shared Queue database, as well as the Tracking database. In addition, you learned how to use the BizTalk Server WMI API to programmatically manage administration objects. In Part IV of this book, you will learn how to administrate BizTalk Server 2000 Orchestration and XLANG schedules.

CHAPTER

8

Tracking Interchanges and Documents

IN THIS CHAPTER:

Seting Up Tracking Options

Understanding the Tracking Database

Using BizTalk Document Tracking

Chapter in Review

When you exchange electronic data with your business partners, for numerous reasons (such as legal data retaining requirements and audit trails), your organization and/or your trading partner track the electronic interchanges and documents exchanged. In addition, if the captured data is stored in a well-organized manner (for example, if it's stored in a Relational Database Management System (RDBMS) such as SQL Server database), you can easily develop a custom analytical application to perform trends. Finally, logged data provides a valuable resource to troubleshooting.

BizTalk Server 2000 has built-in support for tracking interchanges and documents, or portions thereof. In this chapter, you will learn what document tracking options are available and how to set them up. Then you will learn about the internals of the BizTalk Tracking database, and explore how data are interchanged and documents are logged. Finally, you will learn how to use the BizTalk Document Tracking Web tool query, the BizTalk Tracking database.

Setting up Tracking Options

In BizTalk Server 2000, you can configure document tracking options at three different levels. You can enable and disable document tracking, and determine what to track in a BizTalk server group. You can choose specific data fields to track using a document definition, and make this option globally available to all the channels that employ this document definition. The tracking fields specified in a document definition are thus referred to as *global tracking fields*. In addition, you can also select the tracking fields in individual channels. The tracking fields specified in channels override the global tracking fields specified in document definitions.

Setting up Server Group Tracking Options

To set tracking options for a BizTalk server group, open the BizTalk Server Administration snap-in. Right-click the server group for which you want to set up tracking options, then select Properties. Click the Tracking tab to set the tracking options (as shown in Figure 8-1), which is comprised of the following check boxes:

- **Enable document tracking** This option determines whether BizTalk Server should track interchanges and/or documents at all. By default, the check box is checked, meaning document tracking is automatically enabled during the

BizTalk Server 2000 installation. When you unselect this check box, a User Action Confirmation dialog box will warn you that documents now passing through BizTalk server will not be tracked if you disable document tracking. Answering Yes to the dialog box will disable BizTalk Tracking for all the servers in the server group. Disabling this option will cause the remaining options (check boxes) to be unavailable. In most cases, you need to enable document tracking. There are a few circumstances, however, where disabling document tracking may be desirable. For instance, when you are handling large documents, you may want to disable document tracking to improve performance.

- **Log incoming interchange** When this option is selected (by default), BizTalk server will log metadata for the incoming interchanges. Interchange metadata includes source and destination organization information, document type (the Document Type property you set for the specification in BizTalk Editor, as shown in Figure 8-2), date and time the interchange was processed by BizTalk server, document count, error information, and so on.

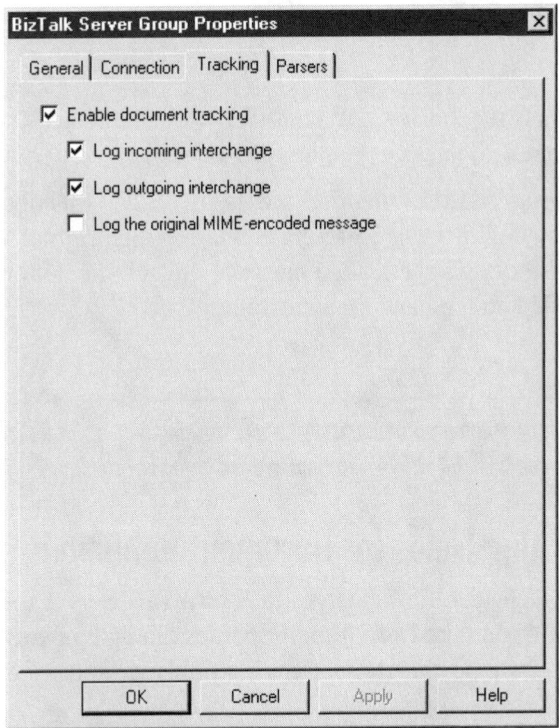

Figure 8-1 *Setting up tracking options for a BizTalk server group*

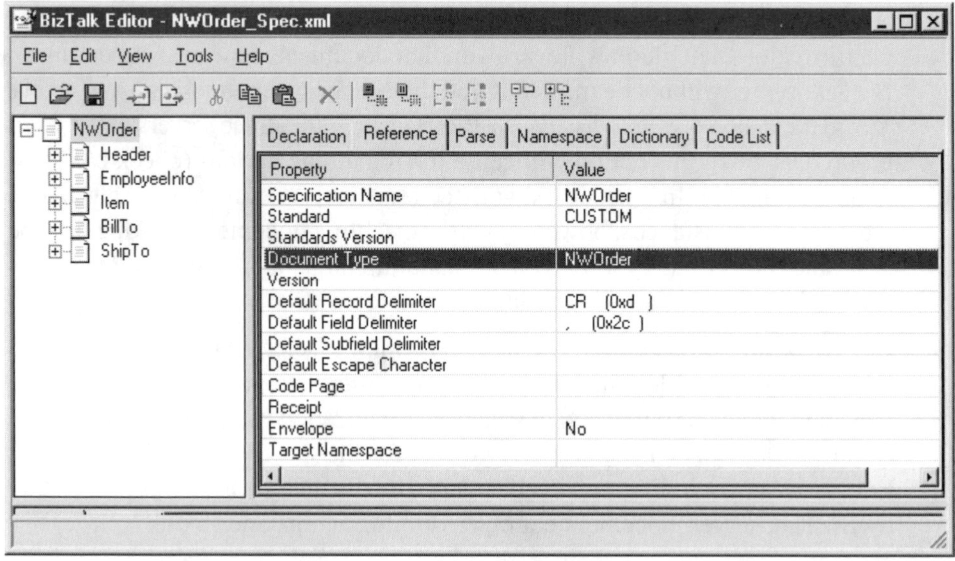

Figure 8-2 *The Document Type property of a specification**Log outgoing interchange***

- **Log outgoing interchange** When this option is selected (by default), BizTalk server will log metadata for the outgoing interchanges.
- **Log the original MIME-encoded message** When this option is selected (deselected by default), BizTalk server will log the original MIME- (Multiple Internet Mail Extension) encoded message. Select this option when you have MIME-encoded attachments in a message.

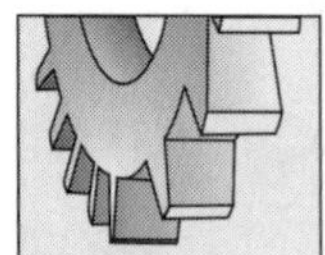

TIP

Alternatively, you can programmatically specify tracking options for a BizTalk server group using the BizTalk Server 2000 WMI API, as you learned in the last chapter.

Specifying Tracking Fields for Document Definitions

You can choose which specific fields you want BizTalk Server to track in the Global Tracking tab of the Document Definition Properties dialog box in BizTalk Messaging Manager. Figure 8-3 shows the global tracking fields we specified for the FlatFile POReq document definition you created in Chapter 6.

To specify a field to track, expand the tree view on the left under Specification fields to display the fields, highlight the field you want to track and click one of the top

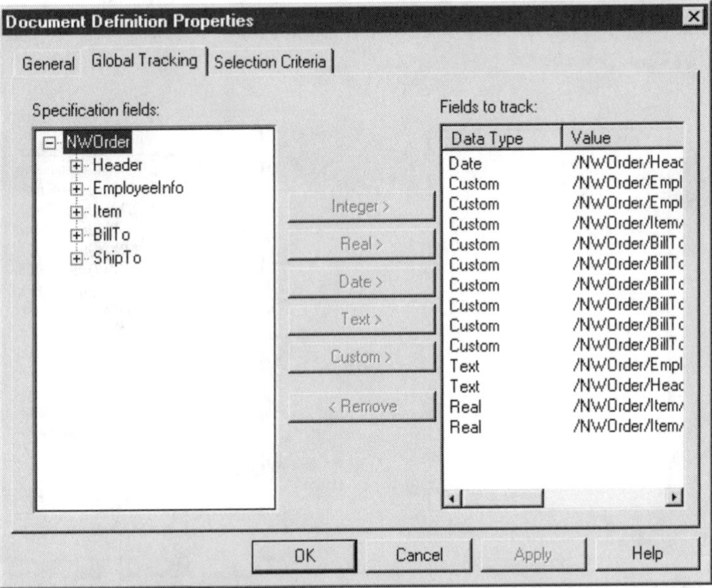

Figure 8-3 *Specifying global tracking fields for a document definition*

five buttons in the middle (See Figure 8-4). A new entry will be created in the list view on the right under Fields To Track. Each entry has two columns, the first column displays the data type you specified for the field and the second column displays an XPath expression that identified the fields to track in the document.

There are five data types for the fields and thus five corresponding buttons on the Global Tracking tab of the Document Definition Properties dialog box: Integer, Real, Date, Text, and Custom. For each document definition, you can assign up to two fields for Integer, Real, Date, and Text data types, and an unlimited number of fields for Custom data types. Values tracked for fields assigned as Integer, Real, Date, and Text data types are stored in individual fields in the Tracking database. Fields using the Custom data type are all grouped into a single XML string and stored together in a single field in the Tracking database, whereas the other fields are normalized (we will discuss the Tracking database later in this chapter). Subject to the availability of a specific data type (i.e., if a specific data type has already been assigned to two fields, it becomes unavailable), an appropriate button is enabled for a selected field with the same data type chosen as that in the specification. For example, if you select the

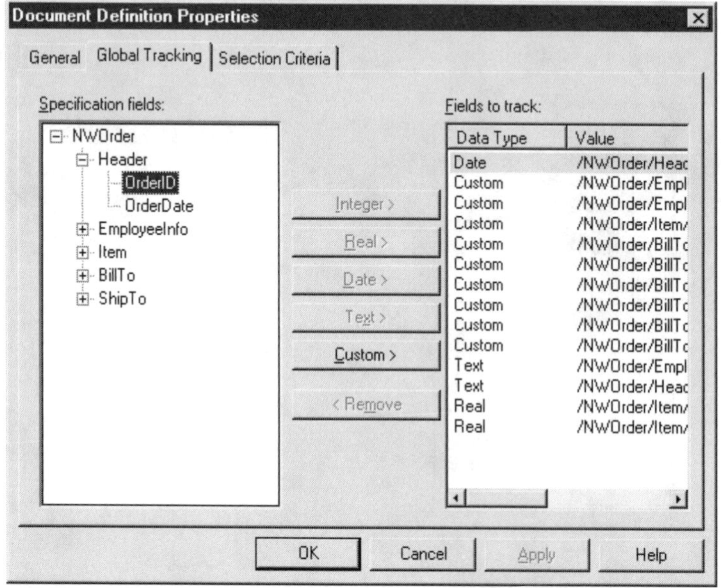

Figure 8-4 *Selecting a field to track*

OrderID field, which is specified as the Text data type in the specification, the Text > button will become enabled, assuming no other two fields have already been assigned as the Text data type. The Custom > button, on the other hand, is always enabled because it applies to any data type. The following table outlines the tracking fields we specified in Figure 8-3 and 8-4.

Tracking Field	Data Type	Value (XPath Expression)
OrderID	Text	/NWOrder/Header/@OrderID
OrderDate	Date	/NWOrder/Header/@OrderDate
EmployeeID	Text	/NWOrder/EmployeeInfo/@EmployeeID
LastName	Custom	/NWOrder/EmployeeInfo/@LastName
FirstName	Custom	/NWOrder/EmployeeInfo/@FirstName
ProductName	Custom	/NWOrder/Item/@ProductName
UnitPrice	Real	/NWOrder/Item/@UnitPrice
Quantity	Real	/NWOrder/Item/@Quantity
Name	Custom	/NWOrder/BillTo/@Name

Tracking Field	Data Type	Value (XPath Expression)
Address	Custom	/NWOrder/BillTo/@Address
City	Custom	/NWOrder/BillTo/@City
Region	Custom	/NWOrder/BillTo/@Region
PostalCode	Custom	/NWOrder/BillTo/@PostalCode
Country	Custom	/NWOrder/BillTo/@Country

In addition to using BizTalk Messaging Manager, you can also programmatically specify the global tracking fields for a document definition using the BizTalk Messaging Configuration Object Model (BizTalk Messaging COM APIs). The following code segment demonstrates how to set the tracking fields for the FlatFile POReq document definition in VBScript:

```
'............
oDoc.Clear
oDoc.Name = cFlatFilePOReqDocDef
oDoc.Reference = "http://" & gHostName _
                          &
"/BizTalkServerRepository/DocSpecs/Northwind/NWOrder_Spec.xml"

' Setting tracking fields, starting with known data types -
' Two Text fields, one Date field, and two Real fields
Set oDoc.TrackFields = CreateObject("Commerce.Dictionary")
oDoc.TrackFields.s_value1 = "/NWOrder/Header/@OrderID"
oDoc.TrackFields.s_value2 = "/NWOrder/EmployeeInfo/@EmployeeID"
oDoc.TrackFields.d_value1 = "/NWOrder/Header/@OrderDate"
oDoc.TrackFields.r_value1= "/NWOrder/Item/@UnitPrice"
oDoc.TrackFields.r_value2= "/NWOrder/Item/@Quantity"

' Then we work on the Custom fields
Set oDoc.TrackFields.x_custom_search = CreateObject("Commerce.SimpleList")
oDoc.TrackFields.x_custom_search.Add "/NWOrder/EmployeeInfo/@LastName"
oDoc.TrackFields.x_custom_search.Add "/NWOrder/EmployeeInfo/@FirstName"
oDoc.TrackFields.x_custom_search.Add "/NWOrder/Item/@ProductName"
oDoc.TrackFields.x_custom_search.Add "/NWOrder/BillTo/@Name"
oDoc.TrackFields.x_custom_search.Add "/NWOrder/BillTo/@Address"
oDoc.TrackFields.x_custom_search.Add "/NWOrder/BillTo/@City"
oDoc.TrackFields.x_custom_search.Add "/NWOrder/BillTo/@Region"
oDoc.TrackFields.x_custom_search.Add "/NWOrder/BillTo/@PostalCode"
oDoc.TrackFields.x_custom_search.Add "/NWOrder/BillTo/@Country"

gFlatFilePOReqDocHandle = oDoc.Create
'............
```

As just shown, we basically added two blocks of code in the original code by creating FlatFile POReq document definitions. We have five fields with known data types (two Text, one Date, and two Real data types). As we mentioned earlier, in one single document, you can assign up to two of each known data type, such as Integer, Text, Date, and Real. To assign known data types to fields, you first create an instance of the *Commerce.Dictionary* object and assign it to the *TrackFields* property of the BizTalkDocument object:

```
Set oDoc.TrackFields = CreateObject("Commerce.Dictionary")
```

Then you can appropriate properties of the TrackFields property:

```
oDoc.TrackFields.s_value1 = "/NWOrder/Header/@OrderID"
oDoc.TrackFields.s_value2 = "/NWOrder/EmployeeInfo/@EmployeeID"
oDoc.TrackFields.d_value1 = "/NWOrder/Header/@OrderDate"
oDoc.TrackFields.r_value1 = "/NWOrder/Item/@UnitPrice"
oDoc.TrackFields.r_value2= "/NWOrder/Item/@Quantity"
```

For each known data type, there are two properties for the TrackFields property: s_value1 and s_value2 for two Text fields, i_value1 and i_value2 for two Integer fields, d_value1 and d_value2 for two Date fields, r_value1 and r_value2 for two Real fields, respectively. In the previous code sample, we only used five of these properties.

Next, you assign the Custom data types for the remaining fields. To do this, create a *Commerce.SimpleList* object and assign it to the *x_custom_search* property of the TrackFields property:

```
Set oDoc.TrackFields.x_custom_search = _
    CreateObject("Commerce.SimpleList")
```

Then, call the Add method to assign the Custom data type to each field:

```
oDoc.TrackFields.x_custom_search.Add "/NWOrder/EmployeeInfo/@LastName"
oDoc.TrackFields.x_custom_search.Add "/NWOrder/EmployeeInfo/@FirstName"
oDoc.TrackFields.x_custom_search.Add "/NWOrder/Item/@ProductName"
oDoc.TrackFields.x_custom_search.Add "/NWOrder/BillTo/@Name"
oDoc.TrackFields.x_custom_search.Add "/NWOrder/BillTo/@Address"
oDoc.TrackFields.x_custom_search.Add "/NWOrder/BillTo/@City"
oDoc.TrackFields.x_custom_search.Add "/NWOrder/BillTo/@Region"
oDoc.TrackFields.x_custom_search.Add "/NWOrder/BillTo/@PostalCode"
oDoc.TrackFields.x_custom_search.Add "/NWOrder/BillTo/@Country"
```

Specifying Tracking Fields for Channels

The tracking fields specified in a document definition are globally available to all channels that use this document definition. You can also specify tracking fields in each individual channel. If you specify tracking fields in a channel, the global tracking fields will be ignored. To specify the tracking fields in a channel, double-click a channel in BizTalk Messaging Manager to open up the Channel Wizard. Go to the Inbound Document page and select Track inbound document. The Track Inbound Document button will be enabled (as shown in Figure 8-5).

Click the Tracking button to open the Tracking For Inbound Document dialog box, as illustrated in Figure 8-6.

As you can see in Figure 8-6, the Global tracking fields you specified in the document definition appear in the upper part of the dialog box. In this dialog box, you can specify the tracking fields just as you did on the Global Tracking tab of the Document Definition Properties dialog box (shown in Figure 8-4).

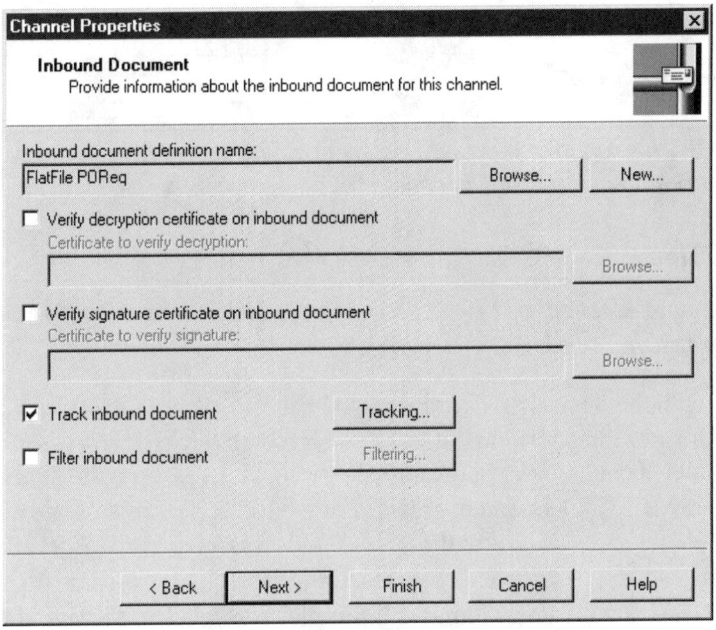

Figure 8-5 *Enabling field tracking in a channel*

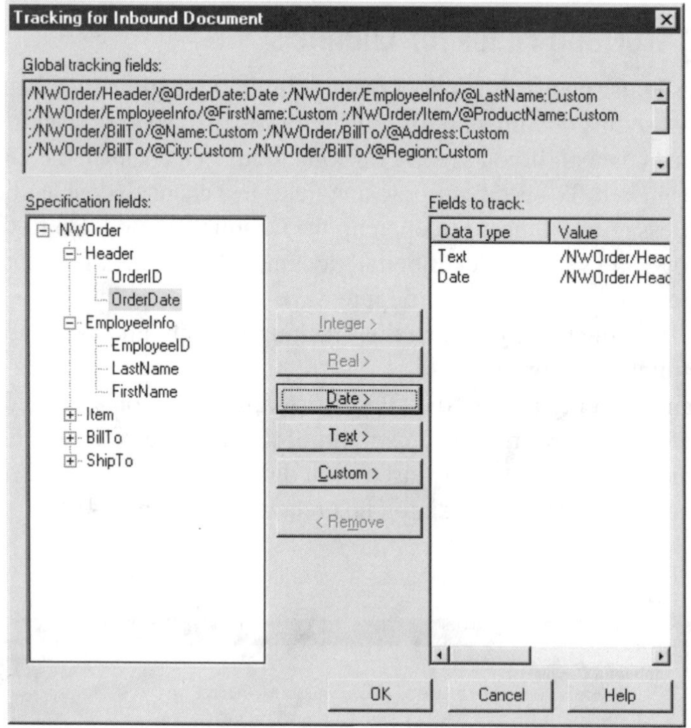

Figure 8-6 *The Tracking For Inbound Document dialog box, where you can specify tracking fields for the channel*

NOTE

As we mentioned earlier, if you specify any tracking fields in a channel, all the global tracking fields will be ignored.

Also, as with the document definition, you can programmatically specify tracking fields in a channel. This time, you work with the *TrackFields* property of the BizTalkChannel object in exactly the same way you used the TrackFields property of the BizTalkDocument object. For example, you first create a Commerce. Dictionary object and assign it to the TrackFields property of the BizTalk Channel object. Then you assign known data types to the fields using s_value1, s_value2, and so on. Next, you create a Commerce.SimpleList object and assign it to the x_ custom_search property of the TrackFields property. Finally, you call the Add method of the x_custom_search property and assign the Custom data type for the fields.

In addition to specifying tracking fields, in the Document Logging page of the Channel Wizard, you can choose whether you want the document (incoming and/or outgoing) to be logged in either its native format, the intermediate XML format, or both, as shown in Figure 8-7 (see Chapter 6 for more information on how to use the Channel Wizard).

Understanding the Tracking Database

As you've seen in previous chapters, BizTalk Server 2000 uses a SQL Server database to store tracking data, called the Tracking database (it's sometimes referred to as a Data Tracking Activity (DTA) database with the default name InterchangeDTA). All servers in a server group share the same Tracking database.

There are, in total, twenty-three tables in the Tracking database. These tables can be grouped into five categories: metadata tables, dynamic data tables, static lookup tables, XLANG schedule-related tables, and miscellaneous tables. BizTalk Server 2000

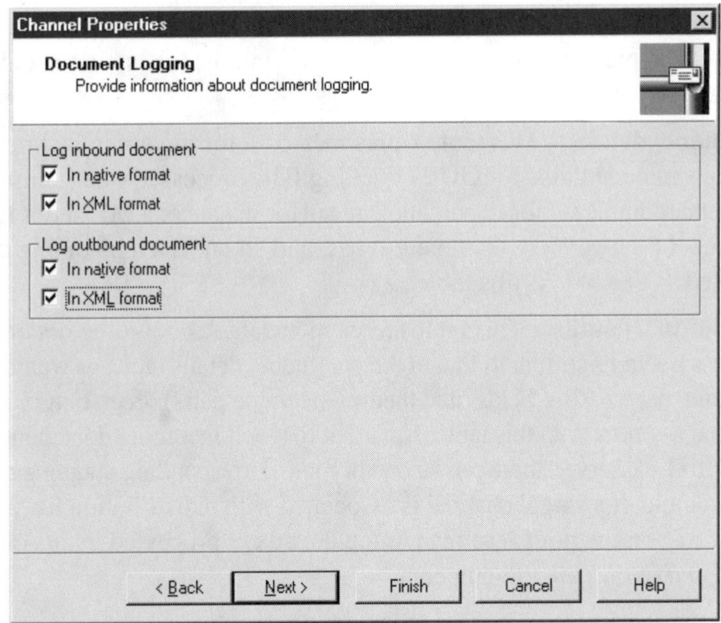

Figure 8-7 *Specifying document logging formats*

online documentation contains detailed information about the table schema and data dictionary of the Tracking database. In this section, we will introduce and discuss the tables in the Tracking database, and explain how and where the information for interchanges and documents are stored.

Metadata Tables

Information about source and destination organizations, document types, interchange processed timestamps, document counts, errors, and so on, are referred to as metadata in BizTalk Server messaging services. There are three tables that store metadata information for interchanges, as well as incoming and outgoing documents. These include:

- **dta_interchange_details** This table stores metadata for interchanges. (An interchange, by definition, contains one or more documents.) Each interchange is stored as one row in this table. The value of the nDirection column indicates whether a particular interchange is incoming (1) or outgoing (0). Other columns in this table include those pertaining to error codes, source and destination organizations/applications, document types, document counts, interchange control IDs, receipt statuses, processed timestamps, times interchanges were sent, and so on.
- **dta_indoc_details** This table stores metadata for incoming documents. Its columns include those for GUID tracking IDs, processed timestamps, the code and version numbers for document syntax (for instance, XML and X12), release numbers of the version, document types, and so on. Each incoming document is stored as one row in this table.
- **dta_outdoc_details** This table stores metadata for outgoing documents, and includes columns similar to that in the dta_indoc_details table, as well as columns regarding the tracking fields (and their name-value pairs). Each outgoing document is stored as one row in this table. Note that for each incoming document submitted to the BizTalk Server, there can be one or more corresponding outgoing documents. For example, if a single channel is associated with a distribution list that consists of five messaging ports, each incoming document processed in this channel will result in five outgoing documents.

Dynamic Data Tables

There are nine tables that store supporting data for interchanges and/or documents:

- **dta_custom_field_names** This table stores the tracking fields of known data types (Integer, Text, Real, and Date) that you defined in the document definitions and/or channels. Each row stores one tracking field. The name and the value pairs for each specified field are stored in the dta_outdoc_details table. The columns for tracking name fields (nRealName1, nRealName2, nIntName1, nIntName2, and so on) in the dta_outdoc_details correspond to the nNameKey values of related rows in the dta_custom_field_names table. In other words, there is a one-to-many relationship between the dta_outdoc_detail table and the dta_custom_field_names table.
- **dta_debugdoc_data** This table stores the interim XML format of incoming and outgoing documents, as specified in the Document Logging page of the channel (see Figure 8-7) or through the BizTalk Messaging COM APIs. It has a one-to-one relationship with the dta_indoc_details table and a one-to-many relationship with the dta_outdoc_details table.
- **dta_document_data** This table stores the contents of incoming and outgoing documents as binary large objects (BLOBs). It has a one-to-one relationship with both the dta_indoc_details and dta_outdoc_details tables.
- **dta_group_details** This table contains group data for X12 and EDIFACT documents, such as functional group IDs, group control numbers, and so on. It provides parsers, serializers, and receipt correlators, along with document format information within an interchange. This table has a one-to-many relationship with both the dta_indoc_details and dta_outdoc_details table. It also has a many-to-one relationship with the dta_interchange_details table.
- **dta_interchange_data** This table stores incoming and outgoing interchanges and any response documents returned to the IInterchange::SubmitSync calling application. It has a many-to-one relationship with the dta_interchange_details table.
- **dta_MIME_data** This table stores MIME-encoded interchanges. The MIME–data, with attachments, is stored as BLOB data in the table.
- **dta_routing_details** This table stores information regarding all the channel-messaging port combinations, including source and destination organizations/applications, channel GUIDs, and messaging port GUIDs. For each messaging port you created in the BizTalk Messaging Management database (through BizTalk Messaging Manager or BizTalk Messaging COM APIs), there is a corresponding row in this table. Storing repeated or mirrored information in the Tracking database avoids across-database dependency on the BizTalk Messaging Management database. This table has a one-to-many relationship with the dta_outdoc_details table.

- **dta_group_correlation_keys** This table stores the group correlation keys that help identify possible group candidates during receipt correlation.
- **dta_interchange_correlation_keys** This table stores the interchange correlation keys that help identify possible interchange candidates during receipt correlation.

Static Lookup Tables

The following tables store static lookup data that are referred in the dynamic data tables through foreign keys to provide cross-references. There are seven of them.

- **dta_ack_status_values** This table enumerates possible receipt status values, such as None, Pending, Overdue, Accepted, Accepted with errors, and Rejected.
- **dta_blobtype_values** This table stores the BLOB types, Unknown or XMLDOM Loadable.
- **dta_data_level_values** This table lists possible data level values used in BizTalk Server, such as Interchange, Group, Incoming Document, and Outgoing Document.
- **dta_direction_values** This table stores direction lookup values, 1 for incoming, and 0 for outgoing.
- **dta_error_message** This table enumerates error messages that provide descriptive information about the nature of encountered errors during BizTalk Server messaging processes. Possible error messages include: "No error", "A custom component could not be called.", "The interchange could not be parsed.", "The specified channel does not exist.", "The interchange could not be serialized.", "The interchange could not be encoded.", "The interchange could not be signed.", "The interchange could not be encrypted.", "The transmission attempt failed (a retry is pending).", "The last transmission attempt failed.", "The document could not be parsed.", "The document could not be validated.", "A valid channel could not be found.", "The document could not be mapped.", "A valid messaging port could not be found.", and "The document could not be serialized."
- **dta_transport_type_values** This table stores possible transport type values, including None, HTTP, SMTP, DCOM, App Integration, FTP, Message Queuing, File, Fax, HTTPS, Open Destination, Loopback, and Orchestration Activation.
- **dta_validity_values** This table stores possible validity values, including Not valid, Valid, and Pass-through.

XLANG Schedule-related Tables

There are two tables involving XLANG schedule-related data. They include:

- **dta_wf_EventData** This table stores monitored COM+ events fired by an XLANG schedule.
- **dta_wf_WorkFlowEvent** This table stores one row for each property logged in relation to a monitored COM+ event fired by an XLANG schedule. It has a many-to-one relationship with the dta_wf_EventData table.

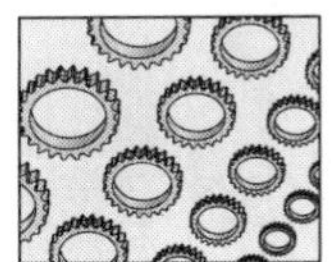

NOTE

These tables are only filled when the workflow audit sample is running. The workflow audit sample can be found under the <BizTalk Server 2000 Installation Folder>\SDK\XLANG Samples\WorkFlowAudit folder. XLANG schedules will be explained in Chapter 9 and 10 of this book.

Miscellaneous Tables

The last two tables in the Tracking database are:

- **dta_ui_codepage_charset** This table stores the system code pages for character encoded data (for example, iso-8859-1, euc-jp, big5, and so on). It is also a static table.
- **dta_ui_user_queries** This table stores advanced queries you created and saved while using the BizTalk Document Tracking Web tool (which will be explained in the next section).

Using BizTalk Document Tracking

In previous sections, you learned how to set up document tracking options using both the BizTalk Server Administration snap-in and the BizTalk Messaging Manager tool (or through the BizTalk Messaging COM APIs). You also learned about the table schemas of the BizTalk Tracking database and how and where interchanges and document tracking take place. In this section, you will learn how to use the BizTalk Document Tracking tool to query the database in order to see what's happening during the BizTalk messaging process.

Introducing the BizTalk Document Tracking User Interface

BizTalk Document Tracking is implemented as a web application that utilizes technologies such as Active Server Pages (ASP), HTML, and ActiveX Control (Office Controls). It can be accessible through Internet Explorer 5 or later. Figure 8-8 is a screen shot of the BizTalk Document Tracking user interface when it is launched.

You must belong to the BizTalk Server Report Users group on the server to access BizTalk Document Tracking. To add a user to the BizTalk Server Report Users group, open the Computer Management MMC snap-in on the server, expand System Tools, Local Users And Groups, and select Groups. You should see a BizTalk Server Report Users group displayed in the list view on the right pane, as shown in Figure 8-9.

Double-click the BizTalk Server Report Users listing to open its properties dialog box (see Figure 8-10). Click the Add button to add a user to the group.

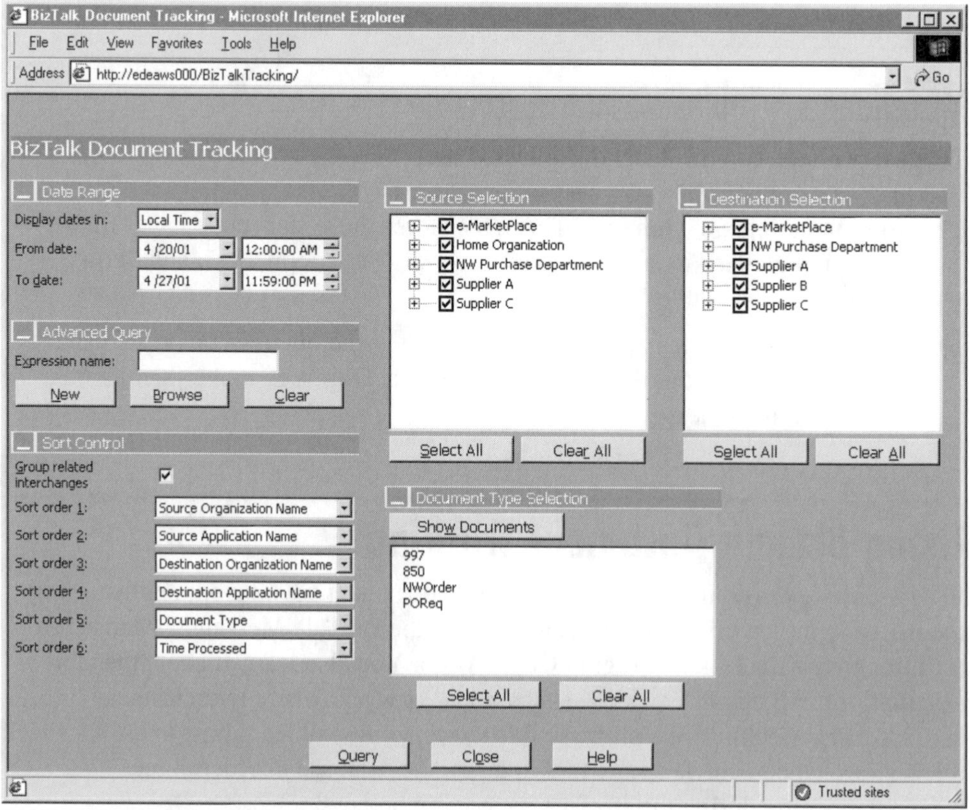

Figure 8-8 *The BizTalk Document Tracking Web application*

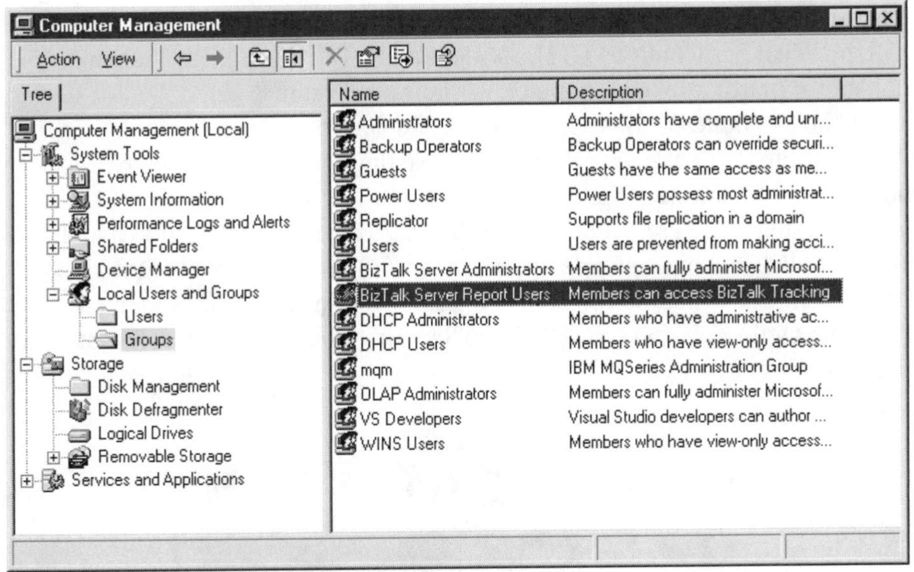

Figure 8-9 *The BizTalk Server Report Users group*

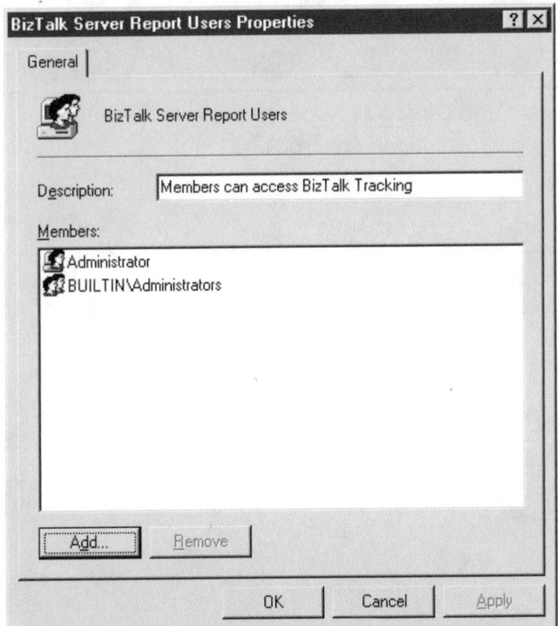

Figure 8-10 *Adding users to the BizTalk Server Report Users group*

The first time you open BizTalk Document Tracking, you may be prompted to install the Windows Common Controls and the BizTalk Document Tracking Installation Control to your computer, as shown in Figure 8-11.

Click the Continue button to install the listed controls.

You may also get a warning message box stating that the page you tried to access is on another domain (See Figure 8-12).

As suggested in Figure 8-12, to avoid this message box, you need to add the URL of the BizTalk Tracking web application to the Trusted Sites zone on the IE 5 or later browser. To do this, select Tools | Internet Options on the IE 5 menu to open the Internet Options dialog box. Click the Security tab and select the Trusted Sites icon as shown in Figure 8-13.

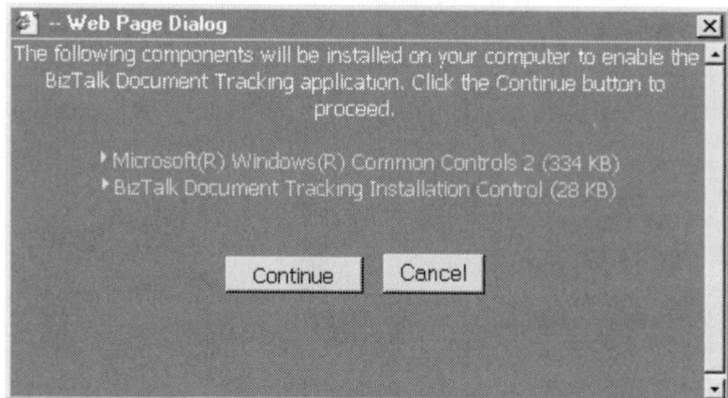

Figure 8-11 *The Web Page Dialog prompts you to install computer controls upon first opening BizTalk Document Tracking*

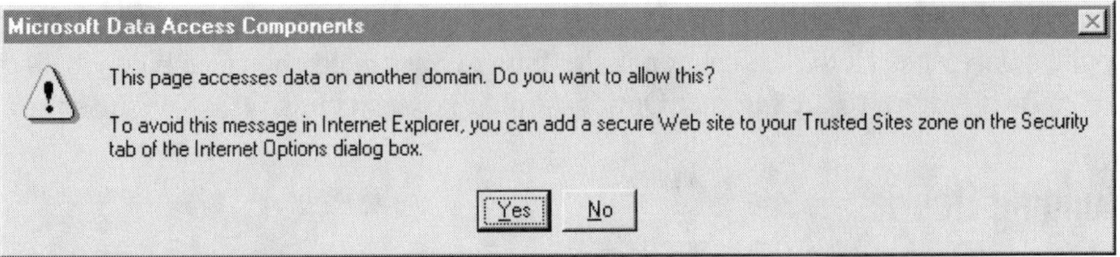

Figure 8-12 *A warning message that suggests you set your Trusted Sites Zone in Internet Explorer*

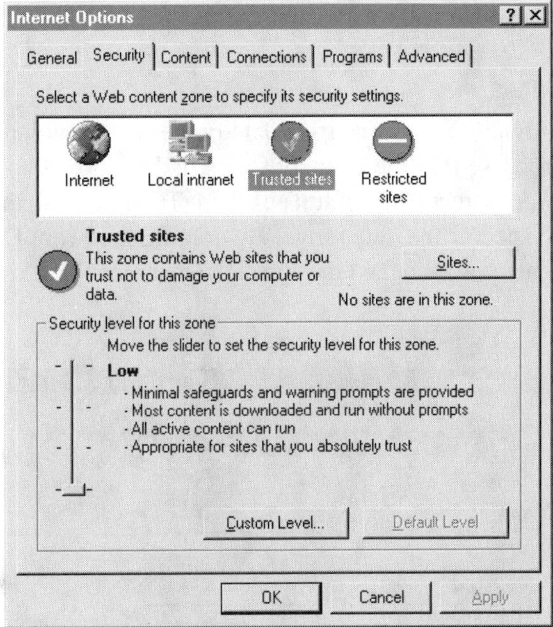

Figure 8-13 *Accessing the Trusted Sites Zone in Internet Explorer*

Click the Sites button and type the URL of the BizTalk Document Tracking Web application, then click the Add button in the Trusted Sites dialog box (see Figure 8-14). Click OK to return to the Internet Options dialog box and click OK to dismiss it.

Building Queries

As you saw in Figure 8-8, the BizTalk Document Tracking tool consists of six working areas that enable you to specify the date ranges, select source and destination organizations/applications, sort the query results, build advanced queries, and specify appropriate document types. Using these working areas, you can define and customize your query for specific interchanges and documents.

Specifying Date Range

In the Date Range area, you can specify a date range within which interchanges and documents were processed. In the Display Dates In drop-down box, you can decide whether to use the local time (the default) or the UTC time. Use the From Date and To Date controls to specify the date range. By default, the From Date will be set to midnight of the date you launched the BizTalk Document Tracking tool, and the

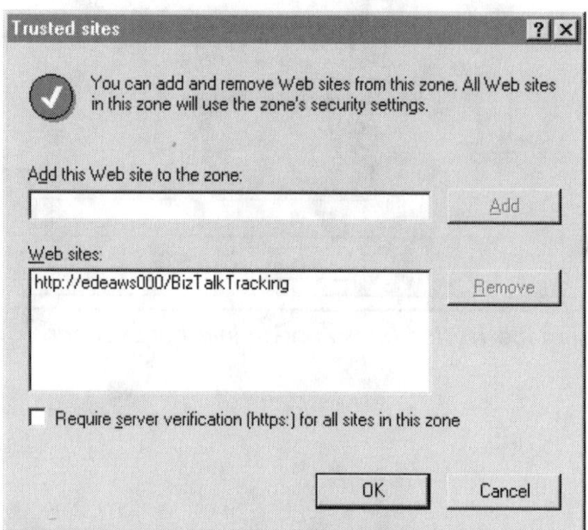

Figure 8-14 *Add a web site to the Trusted Sites Zone*

To Date will be set at one minute to midnight one week from the date you launched BizTalk Document Tracking.

Specifying Sources and Destinations

You can specify the source and destination in the Source Selection and Destination Selection areas, respectively. For example, to query the interchanges/documents processed in Step 1 of the Northwind Traders example in Chapter 6, you may select the Submit FlatFile POReq application of the Home Organization as the source, and NW Purchase Department as the destination, as shown in Figure 8-15.

The Select All and Clear All buttons allow you to select or deselect all the sources and destinations.

Specifying Document Types

Clicking the Show Documents button in the Document Type Selection area will cause the document types that meet the query criteria you specified, such as Date Range, Source Selection, Destination Selection, and so on, to be displayed. Figure 8-16 contains the Show Documents results based on the query criteria defined in Figure 8-15. It displays the NWOrder (the flat file purchase order) and the POReq (the XML purchase order request) documents which are the incoming and outgoing documents for the source and destination specified in Figure 8-15.

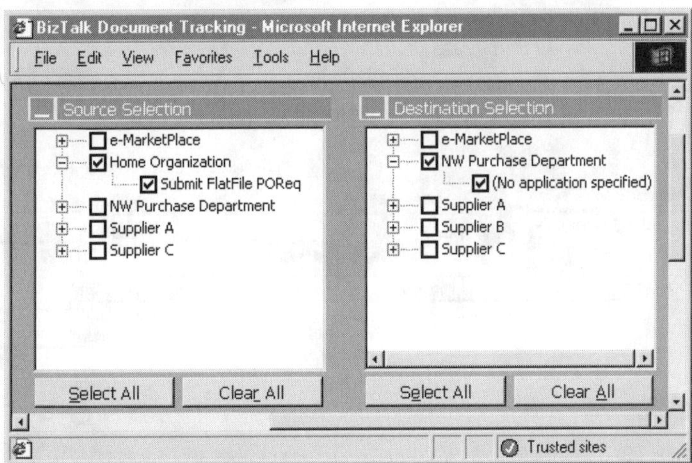

Figure 8-15 *Specifying source and destination*

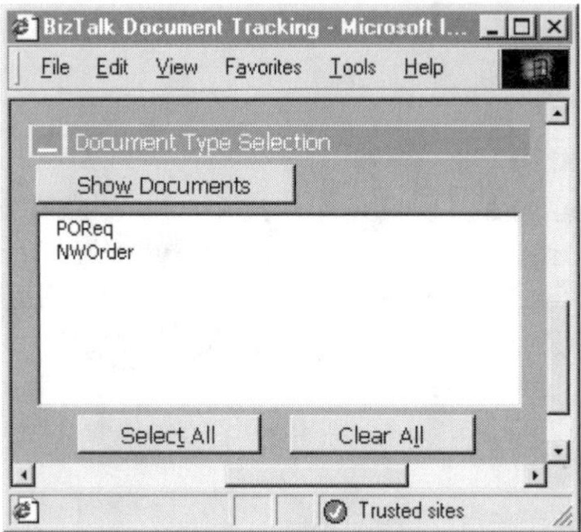

Figure 8-16 *Displaying matching document types*

Using Advanced Queries

The Advanced Query working area allows you to query expressions based on predefined tracking fields in document definitions and/or channels. Clicking the New button will open the Advanced Query Builder window as shown in Figure 8-17.

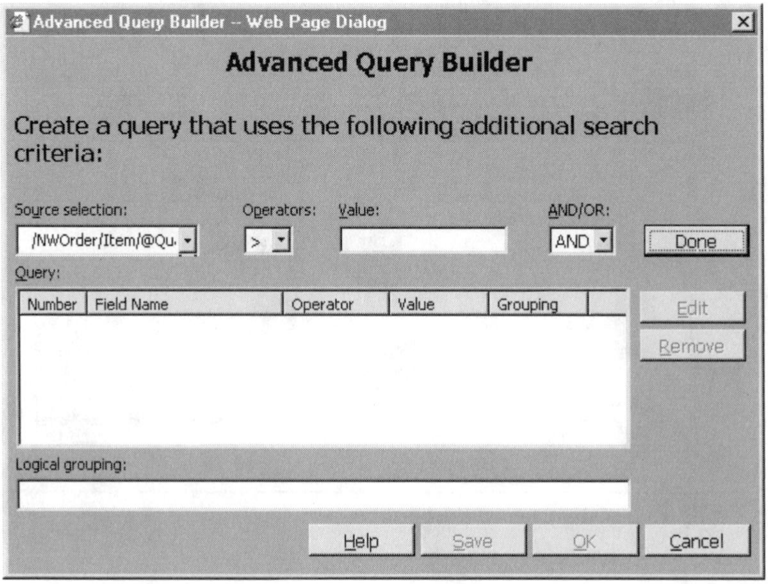

Figure 8-17 *The Advanced Query Builder*

The Source Selection drop-down list contains the XPath expressions that correspond to the predefined tracking fields. By selecting a source, specifying one of the operators (>, <, =, and !=), and typing a value, you can build simple expressions using this rudimentary query builder. Clicking the Done button will add the new query expression to the Query list. The Done button will then change to a New button allowing you to add new expressions. The AND/OR operators, meanwhile, enable you to specify the logical grouping (AND and OR). For example, you may want to query the POReq documents processed by a user with an employee ID of 8 where the Order ID of the document is 123456789. Figure 8-18 illustrates how to build an advanced query for this.

This query contains two expressions, 1 and 2, as displayed in the Query list in Figure 8-18. The Logical Grouping shows "1 AND 2", indicating the query is a combination of two query expressions, both of which must be met.

Click the Save button on the Advanced Query Builder and type a name, **ByEmployeeAndOrderID**, in the pop-up box (see Figure 8-19), then click OK. A new advanced query will show up in the Expression Name box of the Advanced Query area (see Figure 8-20). Advanced query expressions are saved in the dta_ui_user_queries table in the BizTalk Tracking database.

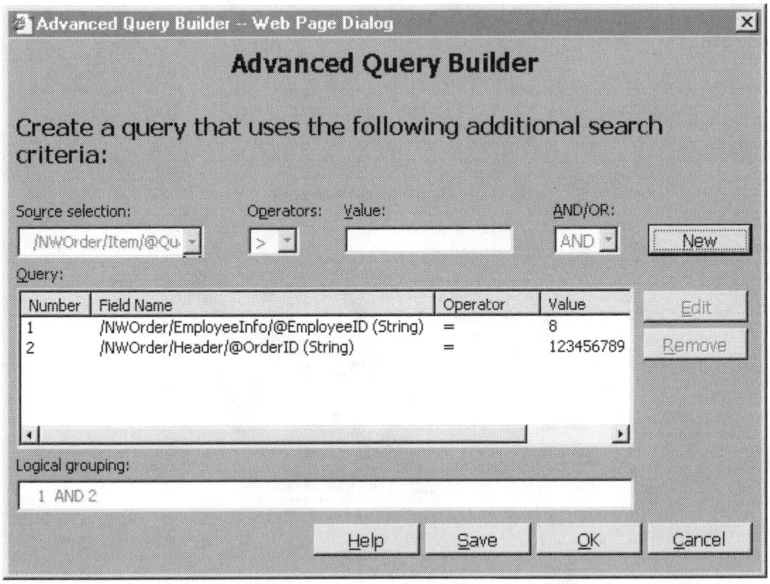

Figure 8-18 *Building an advanced query*

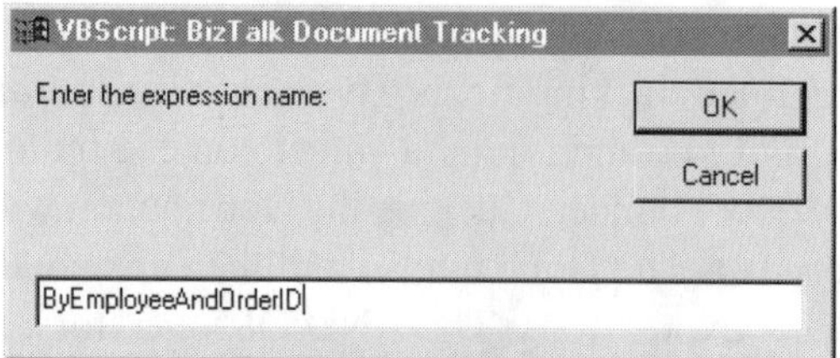

Figure 8-19 *Specifying a name for the advanced query*

To specify a different query, click the Browse button to display the Advanced Queries - Web Page Dialog box (see Figure 8-21). The three buttons on the right of the dialog box allow you to edit an existing query, create a new query, or delete an existing query.

To clear the Expression Name box in the Advanced Query area, click the Clear button (see Figure 8-20).

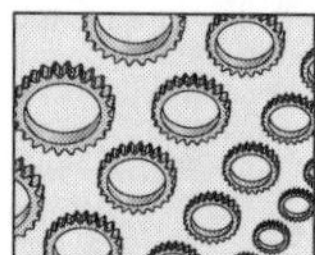

NOTE

Unless you have defined appropriate tracking fields either in the document definitions or in the channels, you will not be able to build advanced queries.

Specifying Sorting Orders

In the Sort Control area, you can specify up to six sorting orders, including sorting by source and destination organizations/applications, document type, and the time processed (as shown in Figure 8-22). You can enable or disable the sorting by toggling the Group Related Interchanges check box.

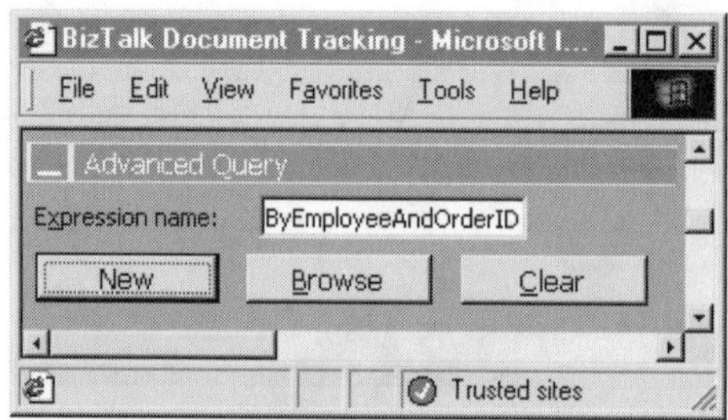

Figure 8-20 *A new advanced query is built*

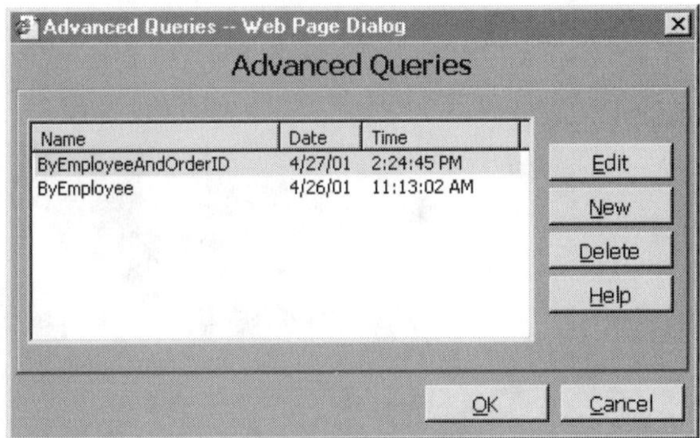

Figure 8-21 *The Advanced Queries - Web Page Dialog*

Viewing Query Results

Selecting the appropriate document types in the Document Type Selection area (of the BizTalk Document Tracking user intefare) and clicking the Query button displays the Query Results page.

Viewing Interchanges

By default, the Query Results page displays the collapsed interchange, as shown in Figure 8-23.

Figure 8-22 *Grouping and sorting the query results*

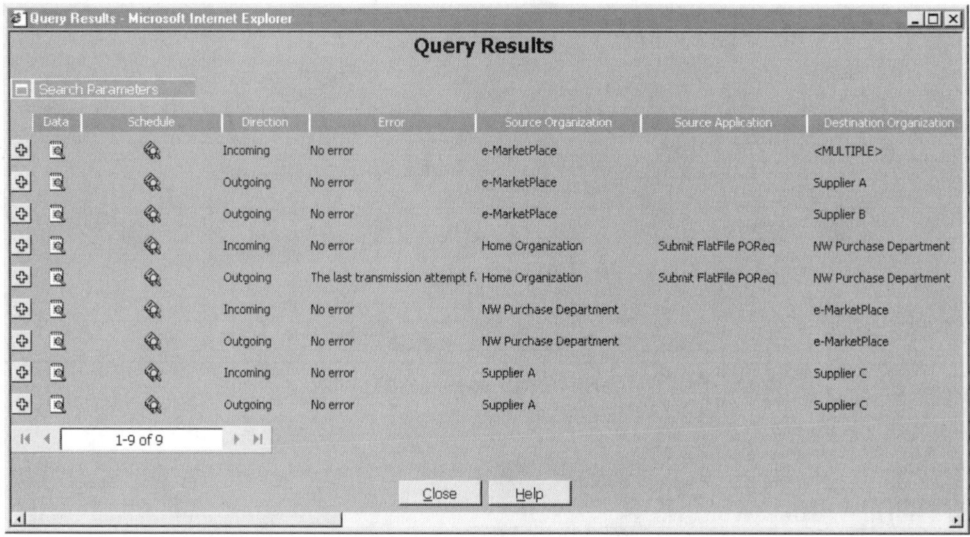

Figure 8-23 *The default display of the Query Results page*

Clicking the icon (a document with a magnifier) in the Data column brings up the View Interchange Data window that displays the interchange in its native format, as displayed in Figure 8-24.

The Schedule column allows you to view related XLANG schedules, if any (you will learn about XLANG schedules and BizTalk Orchestration services later in this book). The Direction column indicates whether an interchange is incoming or outgoing. The Error column, meanwhile, displays related errors as detailed in the dta_error_message table (as we explained earlier).

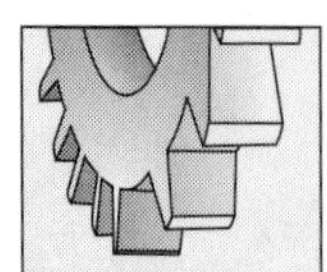

TIP

Since the contents of the error may be truncated in the Query Results window, you can view the entire error message by moving the mouse pointer to the texts in the error column and then stopping. A yellow ToolTip-like box will then display the complete error message (as shown in Figure 8-25).

Other columns for interchanges include source and destination organization/application names, qualifiers, identifiers, time processed and time sent, document type, document count, control ID, receipt status, and so on. You can use the horizontal scroll bar on the bottom of the Query Results table to view the columns on the right side.

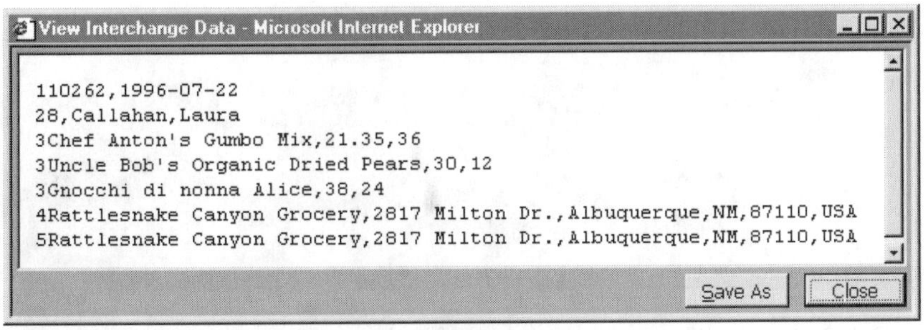

View Interchange Data - Microsoft Internet Explorer

```
110262,1996-07-22
28,Callahan,Laura
3Chef Anton's Gumbo Mix,21.35,36
3Uncle Bob's Organic Dried Pears,30,12
3Gnocchi di nonna Alice,38,24
4Rattlesnake Canyon Grocery,2817 Milton Dr.,Albuquerque,NM,87110,USA
5Rattlesnake Canyon Grocery,2817 Milton Dr.,Albuquerque,NM,87110,USA
```

Save As | Close

Figure 8-24 *The View Interchange Data window*

Viewing Documents

To display incoming and outgoing documents, click the plus sign icons on the left side of the appropriate interchanges to expand the interchanges (as shown in Figure 8-26).

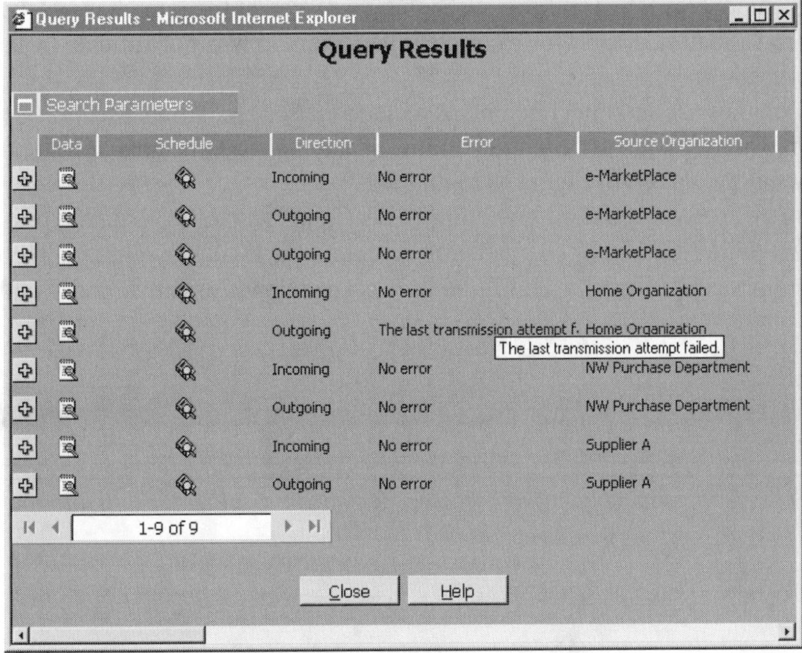

Figure 8-25 *Displaying the complete error message*

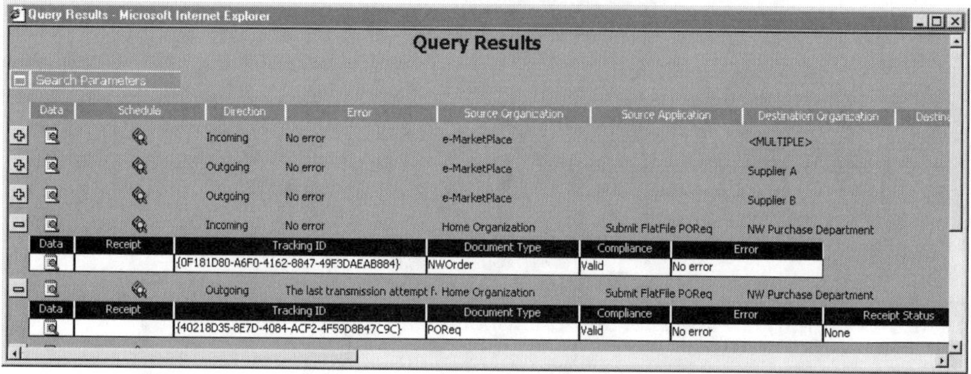

Figure 8-26 *Displaying documents under appropriate interchanges*

The columns for incoming documents include Date, Receipt, TrackingID, Document Type, Compliance, and Error (see Figure 8-25). Note the error displayed at the document level is not the same as that displayed at the interchange level. These are validation errors (for example, the document was not validated against its specification).

The columns for outgoing documents include the same columns used for incoming documents, along with additional columns displaying receipt status and tracking information (as shown in Figure 8-26 and 8-27).

If you've specified custom searching fields (fields with custom data types) in the document definition and/or channel, you can view the results by clicking the icon in the Custom Search column (see Figure 8-27). The View Custom Search Field Data

Query Results - Microsoft Internet Explorer

Real 1	Real 2	Integer 1	Integer 2	Date 1	Date 2	String 1	String 2	Custom Search
21.35	36			7/22/96		10262	8	

Figure 8-27 *Additional columns in outgoing documents display tracking information*

window will appear and display the data for these custom search fields (as illustrated in Figure 8-28). You can save the result as an XML document by clicking the Save As button and specifying a filename.

In addition, you can view the document in either its native format (see Figure 8-29) or the interim XML format (see Figure 8-30), provided you specified the appropriate document tracking options in the channel.

Viewing Receipts

If you used channels to process receipts, you will be able to view the receipts in the Query Results page. Recall that in the Northwind sample application in Chapter 6, Supplier A expected receipts from Supplier C and you configured the appropriate channels to process the receipts. Figure 8-31 illustrates the incoming document between Supplier A (the source) and Supplier C (the destination).

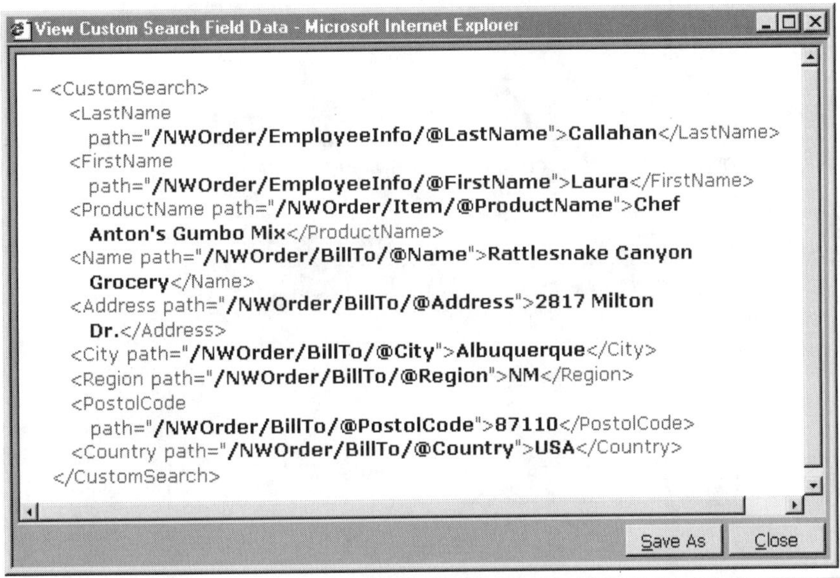

```
- <CustomSearch>
    <LastName
      path="/NWOrder/EmployeeInfo/@LastName">Callahan</LastName>
    <FirstName
      path="/NWOrder/EmployeeInfo/@FirstName">Laura</FirstName>
    <ProductName path="/NWOrder/Item/@ProductName">Chef
      Anton's Gumbo Mix</ProductName>
    <Name path="/NWOrder/BillTo/@Name">Rattlesnake Canyon
      Grocery</Name>
    <Address path="/NWOrder/BillTo/@Address">2817 Milton
      Dr.</Address>
    <City path="/NWOrder/BillTo/@City">Albuquerque</City>
    <Region path="/NWOrder/BillTo/@Region">NM</Region>
    <PostolCode
      path="/NWOrder/BillTo/@PostolCode">87110</PostolCode>
    <Country path="/NWOrder/BillTo/@Country">USA</Country>
  </CustomSearch>
```

Figure 8-28 *The View Custom Search Field Data window*

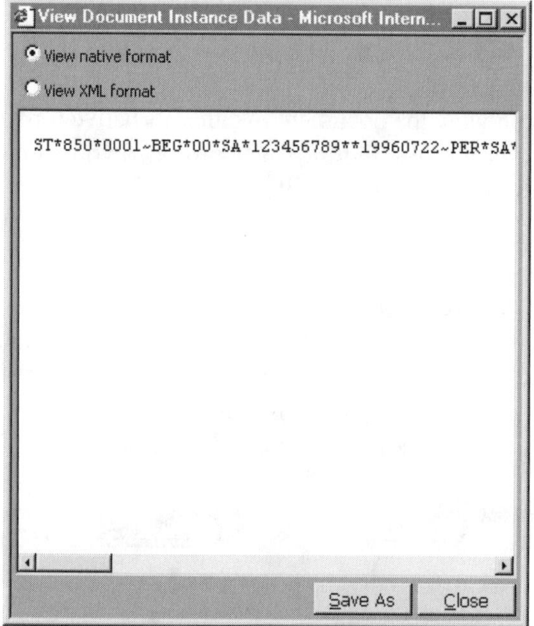

Figure 8-29 *Viewing an X12 document in its native format*

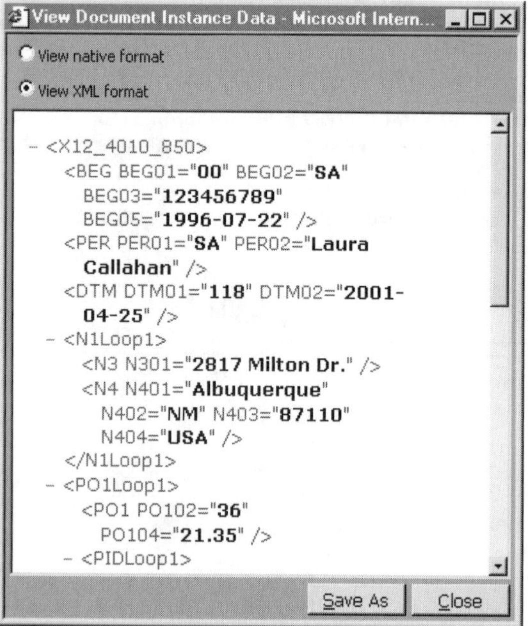

Figure 8-30 *Viewing the same X12 document in the interim XML format*

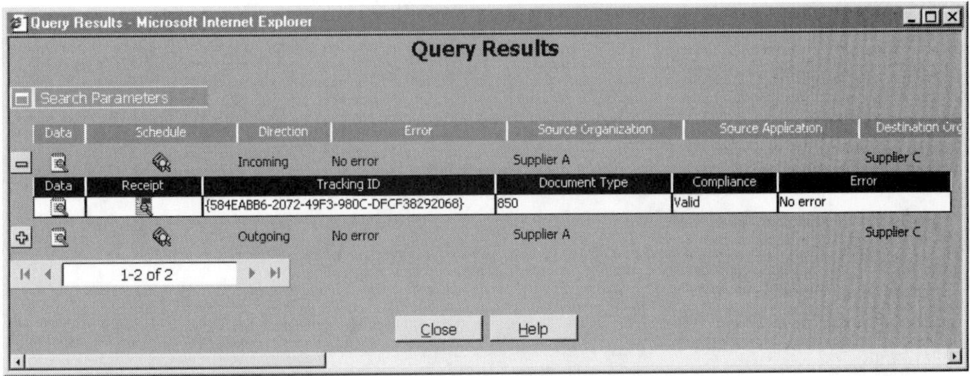

Figure 8-31 *An incoming document that has a receipt associated with it*

As you can see in Figure 8-31, there is an icon in the Receipt column. Clicking this icon will bring up another Query Results window that treats the receipt document as an outgoing document with the source and destination revised (as shown in Figure 8-32).

You can then view the contents of the receipt document the same way you did regular interchanges and documents.

Chapter in Review

In this chapter, you learned how to use the BizTalk Server Administration snap-in and the BizTalk Messaging Manager (or the BizTalk Messaging COM APIs) to configure different options for tracking interchanges and documents processed by the BizTalk Messaging engine. You also learned the table schemas of the BizTalk Tracking database and how to use the BizTalk Document Tracking tool to query the Tracking database for information about interchanges, documents, and receipts.

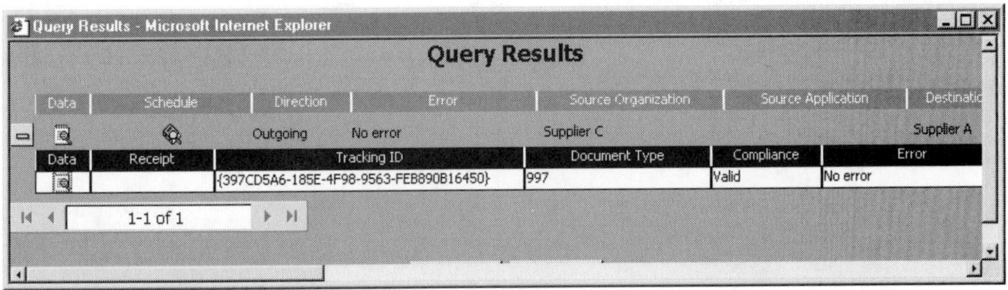

Figure 8-32 *A Query Results window that displays the receipt document*

PART

IV

BizTalk Server 2000 Orchestration Services

OBJECTIVES

- Mastering BizTalk Server 2000 Orchestration Services
- To understand BizTalk Server 2000 Orchestration Services
- To learn how to use BizTalk Orchestration Designer to create XLANG schedules
- To learn how to integrate BizTalk Orchestration and Messaging Services
- To learn how to manage long-running transactions, debugging, and error-handling

CHAPTER

9

Orchestrating Business Processes

IN THIS CHAPTER:

Introducing BizTalk Orchestration

Using BizTalk Orchestration Designer

Chapter in Review

In previous chapters, you have learned how to use BizTalk Server 2000 Messaging Services to solve EAI and B2B problems, including defining business document specifications, mapping different document formats, processing flat file and EDI documents, and using different transports to exchange documents within and between business entities. You've also learned how to use BizTalk administration and tracking tools to manage BizTalk Server, Server Groups, and track business documents. In Part IV of this book, you will learn about another very important feature of BizTalk Server 2000—the Orchestration Services.

In this chapter, you will learn the fundamentals of BizTalk Server 2000 Orchestration Services and how to use BizTalk Orchestration Designer to develop orchestration applications, referred to as *XLANG schedules*, something you'll learn more about later in this chapter. You will also learn how to invoke and manage instances of XLANG schedules. In Chapter 10, you will learn how to use the built-in feature of BizTalk Server 2000 Orchestration Services to manage long-running transactions, debugging, and error handling.

Introducing BizTalk Orchestration

In this section, we will look at the challenges and issues that EAI and B2B system integrators and developers have been facing to give you an idea why you need BizTalk Orchestration.

The Challenges

The problem domain in a typical EAI and B2B integration challenge can be abstracted into two distinct layers. On the surface is a communication layer that requires an infrastructure enabling discrete systems to speak to one another. In other words, the infrastructure in the communication layer is responsible for effectively exchanging business documents both within and between business entities. It must address issues such as document validation, format translation, schema transformation, reliable and secure delivery, and so on. As you've seen in previous chapters of this book, BizTalk Server 2000 Messaging Services provides a robust infrastructure that addresses all the challenges involved in the communication layer, including document validation, mapping, receipt handling, and transporting, using a variety of protocols, such as HTTP, across the Internet.

Having a solid communication infrastructure alone, however, is not enough. For every business document exchanged, there must be corresponding business processes that need to take place before and after the exchange of the document. Consider an example in which a buyer submits a purchase order to a supplier. You can use

BizTalk Server 2000 Messaging Services to handle the transmission of the purchase order document between the buyer and the supplier. You must also prepare the purchase order that may involve approving the purchase order and selecting an appropriate supplier. On the supplier side, someone must also take care of the processing of a received purchase order, which may involve processes for fulfilling the purchase order, checking inventory levels, arranging shipping, notifying the buyer regarding availability of goods, sending invoices to the buyer, and so on.

A business process is a set of steps that collectively performs a specific business function which may or may not involve manual interactions. For example, approving a purchase order might require a pair of human eyes to review the order. On the other hand, a process that can make efficient decisions based strictly on data calculation pertaining to a document is an example of an automatic process.

Prior to BizTalk Server 2000, few tools and products had really attempted to tackle the issues involved in automating processes. There is no easy way to describe and represent business processes in a consistent manner. System integrators and developers usually ended up spending a lot of time writing custom code in order to address problems and facilitate the communication layer. A typical custom solution often involved building blocks (usually implemented as components) and plumbing code that glued everything together to represent an entire process. As one might expect, there are a number of difficulties associated with this custom-built approach:

- Writing custom code to automate processes, especially plumbing code, has traditionally been problematic and time-consuming.
- Solutions based on custom code are usually inflexible and do not scale well. Adding a new business partner often involves writing code to model new processes or modify existing ones, both time-consuming. The more partners that are added to the picture, the more static your custom solution will become and the more difficult it will be to propagate modifications and enhancements throughout the process.
- Business processes, especially those that cross organizational boundaries, such as sending a purchase order or waiting for an invoice, could take days or even months to complete. In case something goes wrong, appropriate actions must take place to restore the process to its previous state. Writing custom code to address a long-running process like this usually involves state management, status correlation, and complex transaction handling. Writing this kind of code is extremely challenging and requires hard-core skills.

Because of these problems, a second layer is needed in the integration problem domain—the business orchestration layer.

The Solution—BizTalk Orchestration

BizTalk Server 2000 Orchestration Services provides a set of tools and services that address all the issues involved in the orchestration layer, including various features such as dynamic processes binding, states management, the handling of long-running transactions, and separating the definition of business processes from their implementation.

Separating Process Definitions from Implementations

BizTalk Orchestration Designer, a tool of BizTalk Server 2000, enables business analysts or system architects and application developers both working on the same design environment.

As shown in Figure 9-1, on the Business Process page, business analysts or system architects can model a business process by drawing a flowchart diagram on the left half of the design page using the flowchart shapes from the Flowchart stencil on the left. After the modeling is completed, application developers can implement the process by using available implementation shapes from the Implementation stencil on the right and linking each of the implementation shapes to the appropriate Action shapes in the flowchart. In addition, application developers also need to specify appropriate data flows by using the message shapes on the Data tab of BizTalk Orchestration Designer, as you will see later in this chapter.

The beauty here is that the definition of the business process is completely independent of the underlying implementation. In other words, developers can choose different ways to implement the sample process defined by the business process (the flowchart in this case). They can easily swap implementation technologies

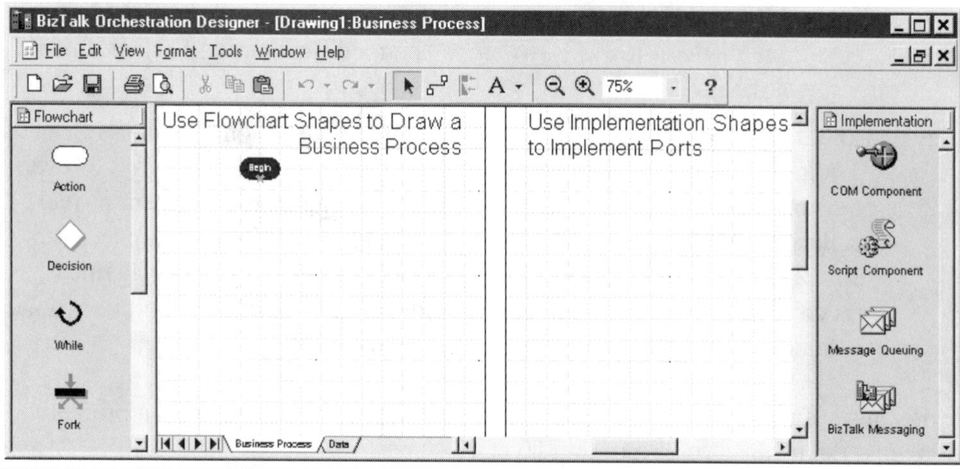

Figure 9-1 *The design environment of BizTalk Orchestration Designer*

used on the right side of the design page without altering the flowchart on the left, the definition of a business process. This separation of business process definition from its implementation provides a great flexibility that enables system integrators to rapidly define, implement, and alter the implementation of business processes in response to quick changes in business and market environments.

Dynamic Process Binding

BizTalk Server 2000 Orchestration Services provides an infrastructure that enables dynamic process binding based on the content of the business documents, similar to the self-routing capability provided by BizTalk Server 2000 Messaging Services. This greatly improves the scalability. For example, you can design a single purchase order process in BizTalk Orchestration Designer and dynamically choose a supplier in the run-time, based on the information provided in the purchase order document itself. In this way, you may add as many suppliers as you wish without having to change the purchase order process orchestration application.

State Management

When you use BizTalk Server 2000 Orchestration Services, each business process is implemented as a BizTalk Orchestration Services-specific XML application, known as an XLANG schedule. Each running instance of an XLANG schedule consumes a certain amount of system resources such as memory, CPU time, and so on. In a real world scenario, you could have thousands of XLANG schedule instances running simultaneously. Some of these instances may take a long time to complete (days, weeks, or even months). Keeping all instances alive for such lengthy stretches requires a lot of system resources, something which may cause the system to eventually crash.

BizTalk Server 2000 Orchestration Services provides a sophisticated *dehydration/rehydration* mechanism to cope with this problem. The XLANG Scheduler Engine monitors all the running instances of XLANG schedules. When it detects that an instance of an XLANG schedule is waiting for a message to arrive for an extended time period (more than 180 seconds, for example) and that there are no other activities going on within the schedule, it will *dehydrate* the XLANG instance—i.e., it will persist all the instance-specific states to the persistent database (an SQL Server database with the default name XLANG) and remove the instance from memory (assuming no stateful components support the IPersistStream or IpersistStreamInit interfaces). When the expected message finally arrives, the XLANG Scheduler Engine will *rehydrate* the previously dehydrated schedule instance—i.e., reinstantiates the instance in the memory and restores its states from the persistent database.

The dehydration/rehydration feature of BizTalk Server 2000 Orchestration Services provides a very efficient state and resource management mechanism.

Long-running Transactions

Another very powerful feature of BizTalk Server 2000 Orchestration Services is its built-in capability for managing complex transactions, including short-lived, COM+ transactions, nested transactions, and long-running transactions that last for days, weeks or even months. The transaction management feature of BizTalk Server 2000 Orchestration Services is one of the topics of the next chapter.

Using BizTalk Orchestration Designer

BizTalk Orchestration Designer is a great tool with which you can build XLANG schedules that orchestrate your business processes. In this section, you'll become familiar with BizTalk Orchestration Designer. Then you will work through a series of XLANG schedule examples, each of which is designed to address some specific feature of BizTalk Server 2000 Orchestration Service.

As mentioned earlier, creating an XLANG schedule involves two distinct steps, defining a business process, and implementing the process using available implementation technologies.

Defining and Implementing a Business Process

BizTalk Orchestration Designer is actually a custom Visio application. As a result, defining a business process in BizTalk Orchestration Designer is not altogether different from any other graphic design software—you simply drag some predefined shapes from the Flowchart stencil and drop them on the flowchart design page (the left side of the XLANG schedule drawing), then connect these shapes to create a complete graphic representing the business process.

Using Flowchart Shapes

BizTalk Orchestration Designer provides nine design shapes, as illustrated in Figure 9-2. The Begin shape is automatically placed on the design page when you open a new BizTalk orchestration Designer instance. The other flowchart shapes are available through the Flowchart stencil.

The flowchart shapes enable business analysts and system architects to model both simple and complex business processes, including decision branching, looping, concurrency and synchronization, and transactions. The following table briefly

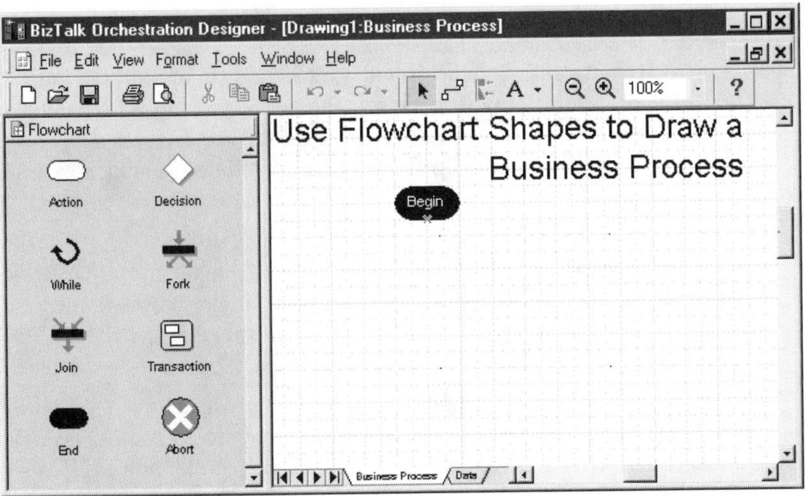

Figure 9-2 *Flowchart shapes*

describes these flowchart shapes. Later in this chapter, you will learn how to use these flowchart shapes through a series of examples.

Flowchart Shape	Description
Begin	The Begin shape indicates the beginning of the XLANG schedule drawing. The Begin shape is automatically placed on the page whenever you open BizTalk Orchestration Designer. It is not available from the Flowchart stencil. You can move the Begin shape, but you cannot delete or resize it. Neither can you add another Begin shape to the design page. The Begin shape has some transaction-related properties that will be outlined in the next chapter.
End	The End shape indicates the completion of one process flow. One XLANG schedule drawing may contain one or more End shapes.
Action	Each Action shape in an XLANG schedule drawing represents one step in the entire workflow. After business analysts or system architects complete the business process drawing, the developers need to bind all the actions in an XLANG schedule drawing to appropriate technology implementations through *ports*, as you will see later in this chapter.

Table 9-1 *Flowchart Shape and Descriptions*

Flowchart Shape	Description
Decision	The Decision shape provides a mechanism of multiple logic branching similar to the switch/case blocks in C/C++ language or the Select Case… blocks in Visual Basic. The decision shape uses one or more *rules* to represent the conditions for each branch. A rule is a VBScript expression. You will learn how to create rules for Decision and While shapes later in this chapter.
While	The While shape provides a looping mechanism similar to the While… loop in most programming languages. As in the case of the Decision shape, you need to define a rule that specifies the criterion regarding whether the looping should continue or terminate.
Fork	A Fork shape branches out from one process flow into multiple, parallel process flows. You can have up to 64 parallel process flows from a single Fork shape. All of these parallel process flows must end with either a Join shape or an End shape.
Join	In contrast to the Fork flow, the Join shape combines multiple process flows into a single process flow. You can connect up to 64 process flows to a Join shape. The Join shape has a Join type property which can be either AND (the default) or OR, as you will see later in this chapter.
Transaction	The Transaction shape enables you to place actions into a single unit of work. Either all of these actions take place or none of them takes place. You will learn more about transactions and Transaction shapes in the next chapter.
Abort	The Abort shape is used inside a transaction shape, causing the transaction to abort and trigger the compensating and/or exception processes to roll back the transaction.

Table 9-1 *Flowchart Shape and Descriptions* (continued)

Using Implementation Shapes

Out of the box, BizTalk Orchestration Designer provides four implementation shapes, as illustrated in Figure 9-3.

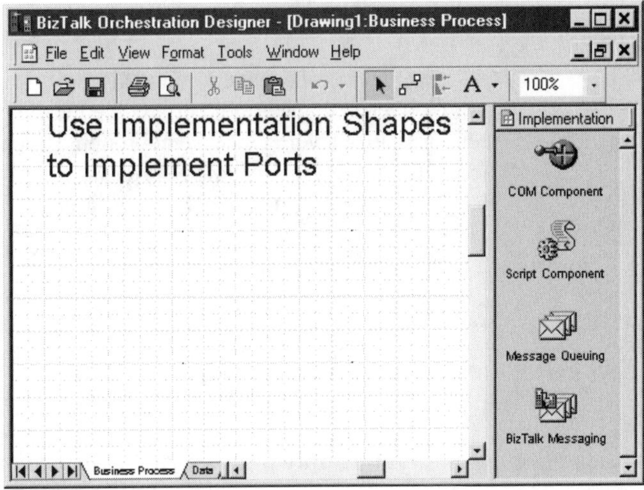

Figure 9-3 *The implementation shapes*

The following table briefly describes these four implementation shapes. Later in this chapter, you'll learn how to use each of them to create various XLANG schedules.

Implementation Shape	Description
COM Component	The COM Component shape enables you to implement business processes using COM components (ActiveX DLLs created in Visual Basic, Visual C++, and so on). In addition to implementing business logics for the actions in the business process flow, COM components provide a means by which you can easily create a wrapper object for proprietary APIs, such as IBM.
Script Component	The Script Component shape enables you to use Windows Script Components to implement business processes. Windows Script Components are COM components written in scripting language and XML. Script components provide an alternate way of quickly creating a COM component. If you are not familiar with Windows Script Components, Appendix D of this book has everything you need to know to create script components.

Table 9-2 *The Four Implementation Shapes*

Implementation Shape	Description
Message Queuing	Message Queuing shapes represent Microsoft Messaging Queuing queues that can send or receive messages. Message Queuing shapes leverage the asynchronous processing of Microsoft Messaging Queuing Services, formerly known as Microsoft Message Queue Server or MSMQ.
BizTalk Messaging	BizTalk Messaging shapes represent BizTalk Server Messaging Services. You can use BizTalk Server Messaging Services to send and receive messages.

Table 9-2 *The Four Implementation Shapes* (continued)

To use implementation shapes, you simply drag a shape from the Implementation stencil and place it on the right side of the design page of the BizTalk Orchestration Designer. As soon as you place the implementation shape on the design page, an appropriate binding wizard appears and helps you set the appropriate properties for the implementation shape. At the end of this process, a *port* will be created automatically, with the name you specified in the wizard. It is important to understand that the ports (called *implementation ports*) discussed here are totally different from the messaging ports you read about in previous chapters. As you may recall, a messaging port in BizTalk Messaging Services defines a set of properties that directs how documents are enveloped, secured, and transported to a designated destination organization or application. An implementation or orchestration port, on the other hand, is a named location in an XLANG schedule used to bind an action to a specific implementation. The location is uniquely identified by the name of the port. So don't confuse implementation ports with messaging ports.

After you have placed an appropriate implementation shape and configured the properties of the port, you need to connect it to a specific action shape.

Using Communication Shapes

Having drawn the process diagram (the flowchart), selected appropriate technical implementations, and connected them together, you need to specify the data flow for the messages. You do this in the Data page, which can be accessed by clicking the Data tab of the BizTalk Orchestration Designer.

Figure 9-4 illustrates the Data page of a simple XLANG schedule example that you will see later in this chapter. As you will note, there are three types of shapes in the Data page (referred to as *communication shapes*) described in the table that follows.

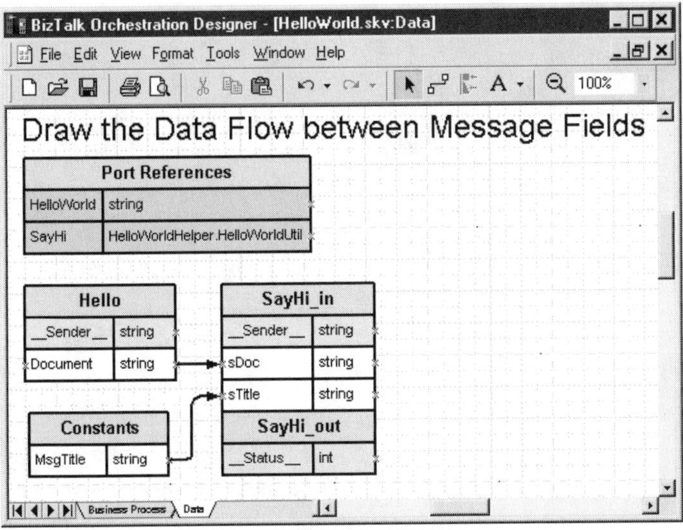

Figure 9-4 *The communication shapes*

Communication Shapes	Description
Port References	The Port References shape is a table that lists all the implementation ports in the Business Process page of the BizTalk Orchestration Designer. Every time you add a new implementation shape on the design page, a new port is automatically created and a new entry is automatically added to the Port References shape. The entries in the Port References shape can be served as either origins or destination of messages.
Message	Every time you connect an action shape to an implementation port, a message shape will be automatically created in the Data page. For the ports that are bound to Message Queuing or BizTalk Messaging shapes, the name of the message shapes are the name of the messages you specified in the Binding Wizard. For the ports that are bound to COM components or script components, the message shapes are split into two parts, representing the input (calls) and output (returns), respectively. The input part of the message uses the name of the method with a suffix _in. The output part of the message also uses the name of the method, but with a suffix _out.
Constants	The Constants shape provides a place where you can define constants. The constants you defined in the Constants shape are initialized when the XLANG schedule starts.

Table 9-3 *Communications Shapes*

You can define the data flow by connecting appropriate fields between the communication shapes.

Each message on the Data page has a set of system fields, as described in Table 9-4.

Orchestration in Action

In this section, you will see a series of examples showing how to create XLANG schedules in different business scenarios.

Getting Started

In this example, you will create a simple XLANG schedule that receives a message from a preexisting Messaging Queuing queue and then extract the contents of the message and display it in a message box. This example illustrates how to create a simple process which uses only two action shapes. It also demonstrates how to use Messaging Queuing and COM component implementation technologies. Figure 9-5 illustrates the completed XLANG schedule.

The process of this example only contains two actions. When you open BizTalk Orchestration Designer, a Begin shape is automatically created and placed at the upper-left of the design page. Drag an action shape to the design page and name it **Get Greeting**. Drag another action shape under the first and name it **Say Hi**. Drag an End shape under the second action shape. Now, connect all the flowchart shapes, as shown on the left side in Figure 9-5.

System Field	Description
__Sender__	For incoming messages, this field contains the identifier of the sender. For outgoing messages, it stores Null. This field appears at the top row of a message in yellow color. The name of the field has two leading underscores and two trailing underscores.
__Status__	This field only appears in the _out part of the message for COM or Script components, and is highlighted in yellow. It stores the HRESULT of method calls. The name of the field has two leading underscores and two trailing underscores.
__Exist__	This field is hidden in the message shapes on the Data page but is available in the Field drop-down list in the Expression Assistant of the Rule Properties dialog box. You can use this field to test the existence of incoming or outgoing messages. The name of the field has two leading underscores and two trailing underscores.
Document	This field only appears (in white) in the message shapes for Messaging Queuing or BizTalk Messaging messages. It stores the body of an XML message.

Table 9-4 *System Fields*

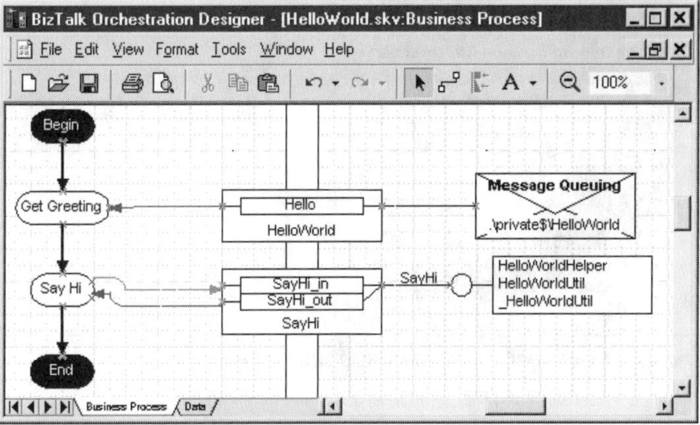

Figure 9-5 *A simple XLANG schedule example*

Now that you have defined the business process, it is time to implement it. The first action receives a message from a Messaging Queuing Queue, so you need to drag a Message Queuing shape from the Implementation stencil and place it to the right of the Get Greeting action shape. As soon as you release the mouse button, the Message Queuing Binding Wizard appears. In the first page of the wizard, specify a name for the port which will be used to link your implementation to an action in the flowchart. In this case, name the port **HelloWorld**, as shown here.

The second page of the Message Queuing Binding Wizard asks you whether you want to create a static queue or a dynamic queue (see Figure 9-6).

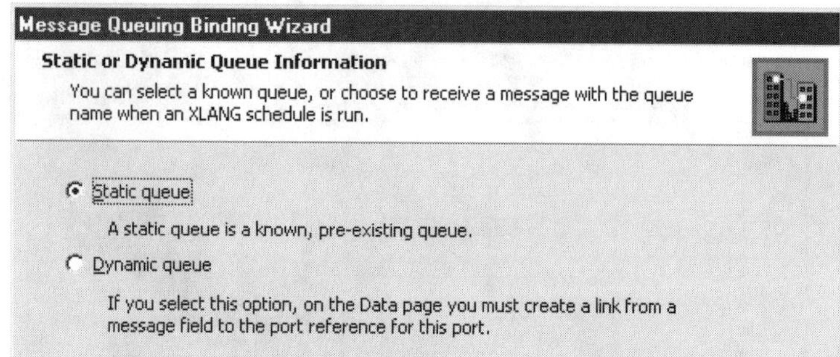

Figure 9-6 *Choosing between a static queue and a dynamic queue*

A static queue is a queue that is known at design time, whereas a dynamic queue is a queue not known at design time, while the actual queue path is provided in the run time as the field of a message. When a dynamic queue is selected, you need to specify which message field contains the queue path by connecting the field of the appropriate message shape to the port field of the Port References communication shape that implements the dynamic port. In this example, you select a static queue and click Next.

TIP

In the case of BizTalk Messaging implementation shapes, you can specify whether to use static or dynamic channels. Using a dynamic channel is very similar to using a dynamic queue, as described in the previous paragraphs.

In the next page, Queue Information, you can specify whether to create a new queue for every XLANG schedule instance (referred to as a per-instance queue) or to use a preexisting queue. You will learn how to use a per-instance queue shortly. For now, select Use A Known Queue For All Instances and name the queue **.\private$\HelloWorld**, as shown in Figure 9-7 (this private queue can be created by running the accompanied batch file, setup.cmd, located in the \Orchestration\HelloWorld folder of the downloaded code). Click Next.

In the last page of the Message Queuing Binding Wizard, you can specify if the queue should be secured and whether it is transactional. In this example, you use the default settings, as shown in Figure 9-8. Click the Finish button to close the wizard. The design page should now look like that in Figure 9-9.

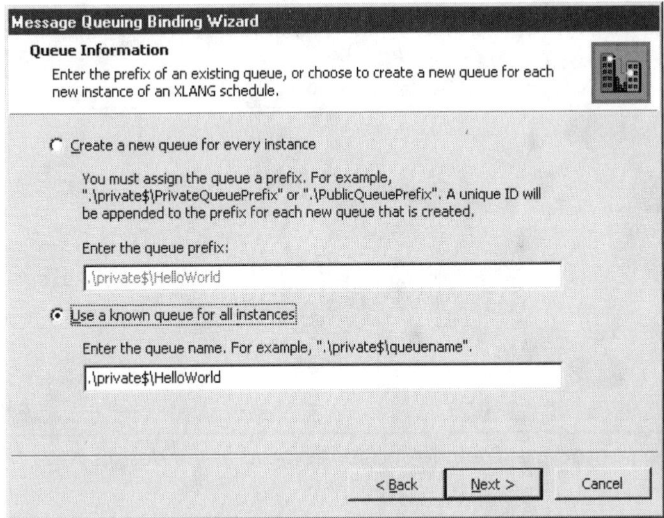

Figure 9-7 *Selecting between a per-instance queue and a preexisting queue*

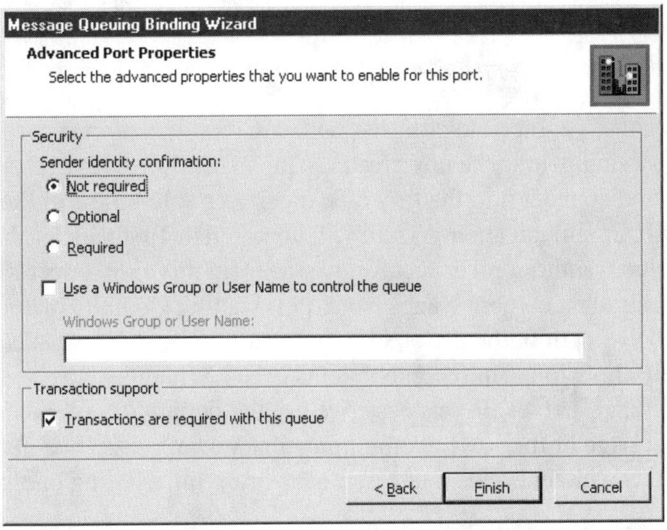

Message Queuing Binding Wizard

Advanced Port Properties

Select the advanced properties that you want to enable for this port.

Security

Sender identity confirmation:

Not required

Optional

Required

Use a Windows Group or User Name to control the queue

Windows Group or User Name:

Transaction support

Transactions are required with this queue

< Back | Finish | Cancel

Figure 9-8 *Specifying security and transactional properties for the queue*

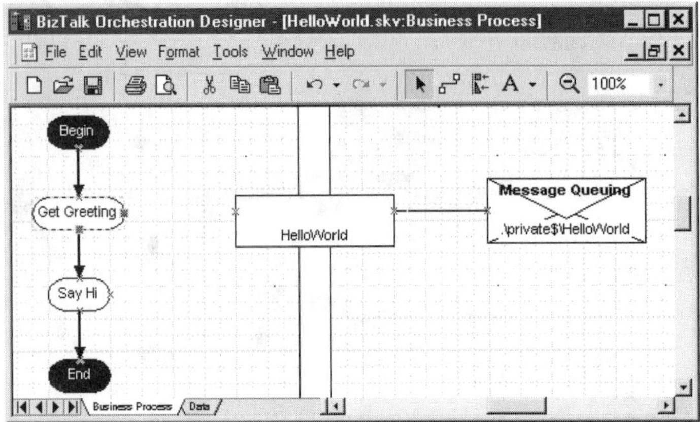

Figure 9-9 *The Messaging Queuing shape is placed in the design page*

CAUTION

By default the Message Queuing Binding Wizard will specify the queue to be transactional (which is recommended in most scenarios); it is not mandatory, however. When you create a new queue in the Computer Management MMC snap-in, the queue you created will not be transactional by default. It is important the transactional property of the queue and the implementation port match. Otherwise, an error will occur.

In the next step, you need to connect the Get Greeting action to the HelloWorld port. To do this, simply drag the tiny green square on the right edge of the Get Greeting action shape and connect it to the tiny blue cross on the left edge of the HelloWorld port. The XML Communication Wizard will appear. The first page of the wizard asks you whether you want to send or receive messages. In this case, select Receive because the port is going to receive messages from a Messaging Queuing queue. When you select the Receive option, the textbox on the bottom of the wizard is enabled. Here you can specify how long (in seconds) the XLANG Scheduler Engine should wait before the message arrives. In this case, we use the default (0 seconds). Click Next.

On the next page of the XML Communication Wizard, specify a name for the message. You can either create a new message or use an existing one. Since you have not created any messages in this XLANG schedule yet, you can only create a new message at this point. Type **Hello** as the message name (see Figure 9-10) and click Next.

On the next page of the wizard, you need to specify whether you want to receive an XML message or a string message from the queue. In this example, you will receive an XML message. So, select Receive XML messages from the queue (the default) and click Next. Now you need to specify a Message type for the message. The message type you specified here will be used to identify the messages from the Queue, so messages can be selectively picked up. The XLANG Scheduler Engine will first compare the message type to the label of the queue. If the message type and the label of the queue do not match and the message is an XML message, the XLANG Scheduler Engine will further compare the message type to the root element of the XML document. To reduce the matching time and optimize performance, if possible, you should try to use the same text for the message type, the label of the queue (the default label of a queue is its name), and the root element of the XML. In this

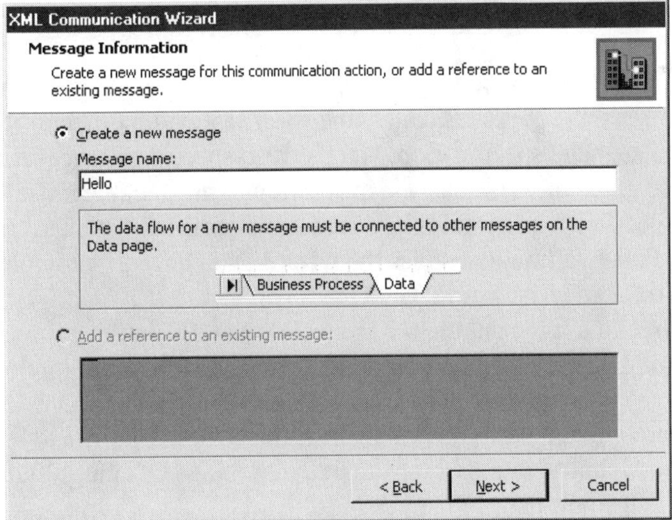

Figure 9-10 *Specifying a name for the new message*

example, type **Hello** as the message type and click Next. (Note that the MSMQ label is case-sensitive.)

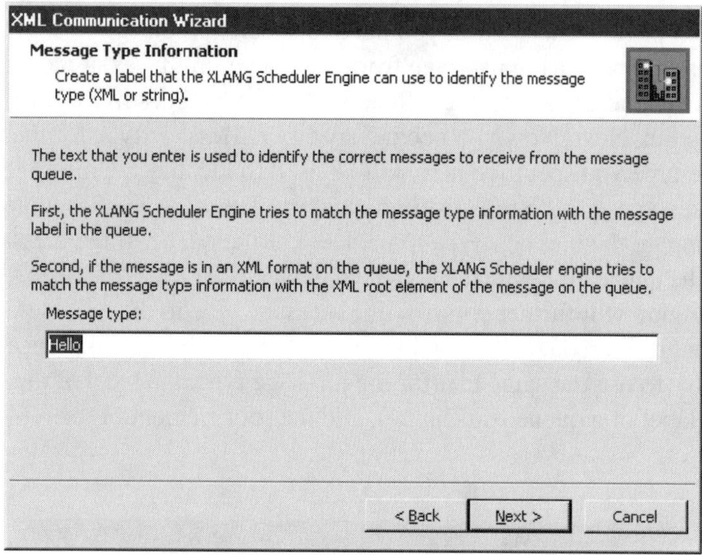

On the last page of the wizard, you can choose an optional message specification so you can validate the message against the specification (another optional function). If you select a message specification, you can also specify message fields and make them available in the message shapes, in addition to the document itself. You will learn to use specifications in XLANG schedules later in this chapter; for now, just click the Finish button to dismiss the wizard. You have just completed the implementation of the first action, Get Greeting.

Now it's time to implement the second action, Say Hi. In this instance, you will use a COM component. Drag a COM component shape from the Implementation stencil and place it to the right of the Say Hi action shape. The COM Component Binding Wizard will appear. The first page of the wizard asks you to specify a name for the new port, similar to the first page of the Message Queuing Binding Wizard. Type **SayHi** as the port name and click Next.

On the second page of the COM Component Binding Wizard, you specify how the COM component should be initialized, as shown in Figure 9-11. You will have three options.

In the case of COM components (as well as Script components), the static or dynamic communications are a little different than the static or dynamic queues or channels discussed earlier. Unlike Message Queuing or BizTalk Messaging,

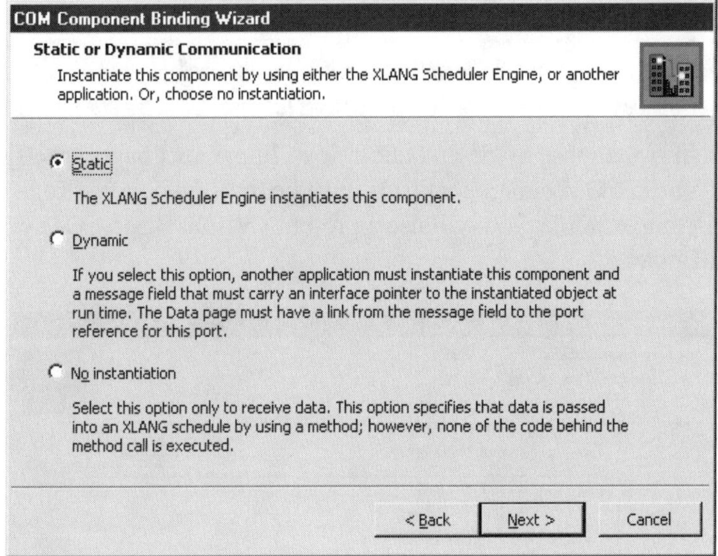

Figure 9-11 *Specifying how to initialize the COM component*

no matter which option you choose (Static, Dynamic, or No Instantiation), you must always specify the interface and methods information for a COM component, as you will see shortly. These options actually specify how a COM component should be initiated (as described in the following table).

Options	Description
Static	This is the default option. The XLANG Scheduler Engine instantiates the COM component.
Dynamic	When you select the Dynamic option, the object will not be instantiated by the XLANG Scheduler Engine. Instead, it will be instantiated by an external application (a Visual Basic application, for example) before the process flows into the port that implements this COM component. In this case, the object reference must be sent to the XLANG schedule by means of a message field. You need to connect the appropriate message field to the port field (in the Port References shape) on the Data page.
No Instantiation	If this option is selected, the object will not be instantiated at all. No methods will be called, either. The XLANG Scheduler Engine intercepts both the method request and response from the COM component. In this case, the COM component (or more accurately, the methods implemented in the COM component) will serve as message stubs.

TIP

The Static, Dynamic, and No Instantiation options are also available for Script components. They work exactly the same for COM components (as described in the previous table).

In this example, choose Static and click Next. In the next page, specify the class information of the COM component (this must be registered in the Registry using regsvr32). In this example, you will use a pre-built Visual Basic COM component, HelloWorldHelper.dll.

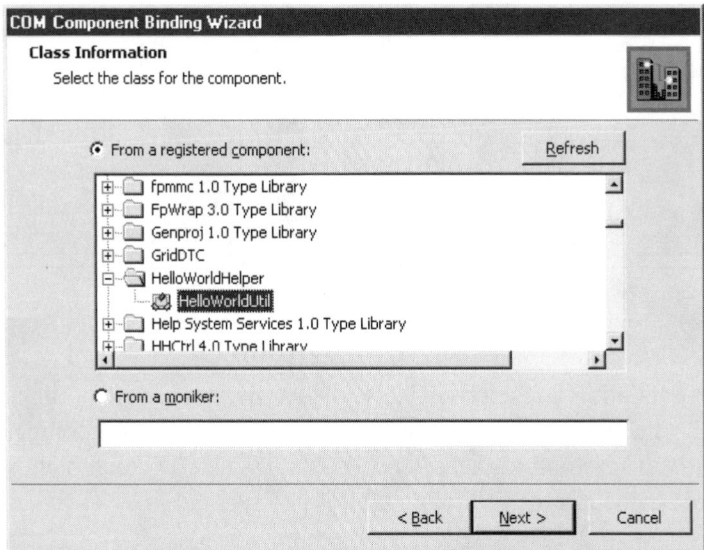

Click Next. The last page of the COM Component Binding Wizard allows you to specify security, transaction support, state management properties, and error handling options. You will see why and how to use the state management support later in this chapter. Transactions and error handling will be discussed in the next chapter. For now, just leave the defaults and click Finish. The COM component implementation shape and a corresponding port shape should appear in the design page.

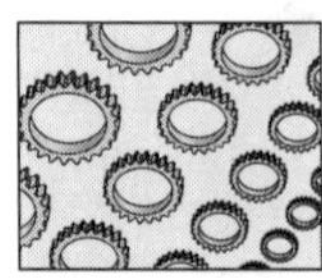

NOTE

If the interface of your COM component has more than one method, you will see an additional page before the last page, allowing you to specify which methods should be made available in the XLANG schedule.

Now, let's connect the Say Hi action shape to the SayHi COM component port. When you connect these two shapes, you will see the Method Communication Wizard, similar to the XML Communication Wizard shown earlier when you connected the Get Greeting action to the HelloWorld port. On the first page, select Initial A Synchronous Method Call and click Next. On the following page, Message Information, select Create A New Message, then click Next. The last page of the Method Communication Wizard is shown in Figure 9-12, and allows you to specify which method you want to call. In this case, there is only one method, SayHi. Click Finish. Now your XLANG scheduler drawing should look something like that in Figure 9-5.

Now that you have defined the business process and bound the actions to appropriate implementations, the last step in creating an XLANG schedule is to direct the data flow. Click the Data tab in the BizTalk Orchestration Designer. You should see the communication shapes (messages, constants, and port references) shown previously in Figure 9-4, with the exception being that none of the shapes is connected. First,

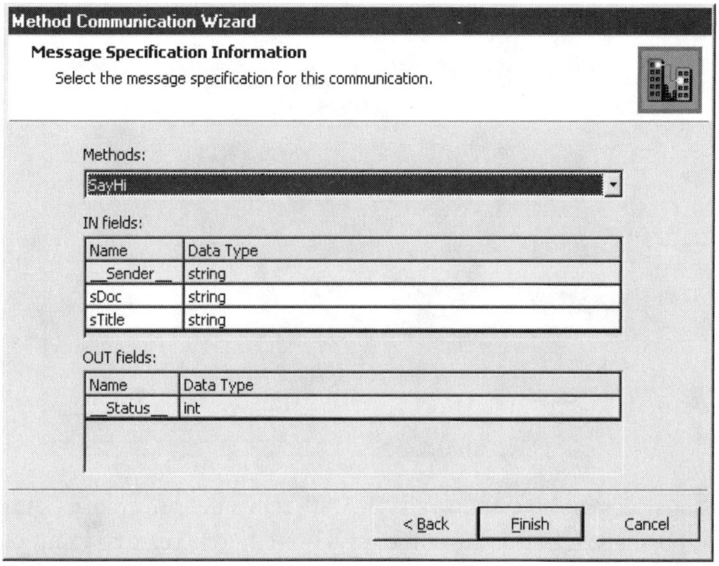

Figure 9-12 *Specifying a method to be called*

you'll need to create a constant. To create a new constant, right-click the Constants shape and select Properties. In the Constants Message Properties dialog box, click the Add button. Another dialog box, Constant Properties will appear. Type **MsgTitle** as the name. Select String as the data type and type **Hello World Demo** in the Value box. Click OK to return to the Constants Message Properties dialog box. Click OK.

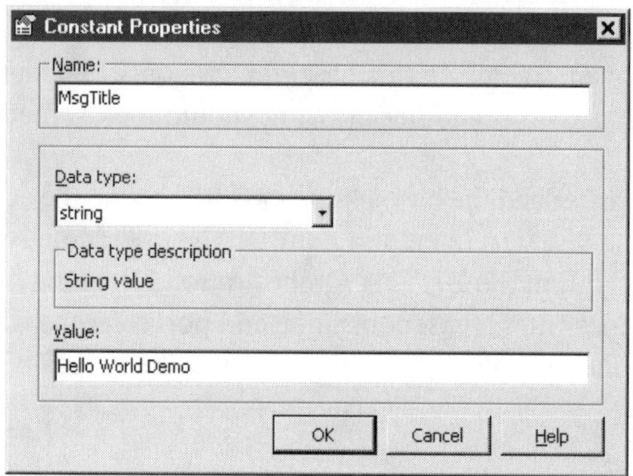

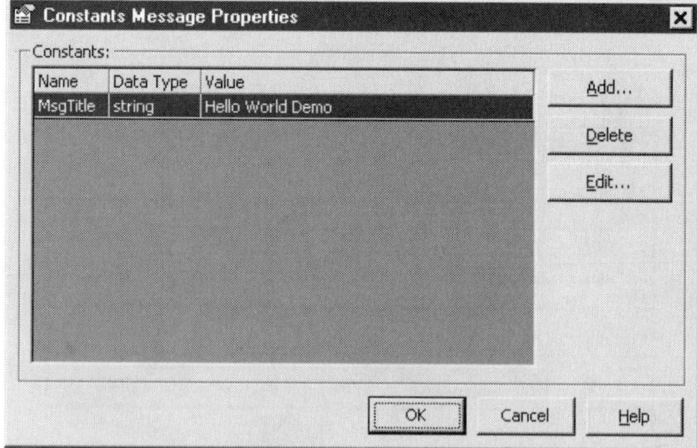

The last step necessary in creating an XLANG schedule is to connect the appropriate communication shapes. In this case, the SayHi method takes two input parameters. So, you need to connect the Document field from the Hello message and the MsgTitle constant you created earlier with the corresponding fields (sDoc and sTitle, respectively) in the SayHi_in message (as shown in Figure 9-4).

Now save the XLANG schedule drawing by clicking File and then Save Drawing1.skv, and typing **HelloWorld.skv** in the File name box of the Save XLANG Schedule Drawing As dialog box. You can save a schedule drawing at any time, since it is simply a Visio drawing with a .skv extension.

Having completed the XLANG schedule drawing (i.e., defined and implemented the business process and connected the data flows), you can now compile the XLANG schedule drawing into an XLANG schedule—an XML file with an .skx extension. In this case, select File | Make XLANG HelloWorld.skx from the menu option. In the Save XLANG Schedule To dialog box, you can specify where you want to save the file to, and change the file name if you like. Clicking the Save button will start the compilation process.

That's all it takes to create an XLANG schedule. Now, let's set up a test harness so we can see the XLANG schedule in action. You will need to create a private Messaging Queuing queue, named HelloWorld, and mark it as transactional. You can do this either in the Computer Management console or through script code. The sample code accompanying this chapter provides a setup.cmd batch file (under the \Orchestration\HelloWorld folder of the downloaded code) which calls the CreateQueues.vbs to create the queue, and also registers the COM component for the Say Hi action. You can simply double-click the setup.cmd file from Windows Explorer to set up the environment for this example. To test the XLANG schedule, navigate to the \HelloWorld\Apps folder and double-click the HelloWorld.vbs file. You should next see a message box which says Hello, World!

The HelloWorld.vbs script code does two things: sends a transactional message to the HelloWorld private queue, and invokes the HelloWorld.skx XLANG schedule, as illustrated in the following:

```
Dim oQInfo, oQ, oMsg
Dim sPath, oSked

Const MQ_SEND_ACCESS         = 2
Const MQ_DENY_NONE           = 0
Const MQ_SINGLE_MESSAGE      = 3

On Error Resume Next

Set oQInfo = CreateObject("MSMQ.MSMQQueueInfo")
oQInfo.PathName = ".\Private$\HelloWorld"
Set oQ = oQInfo.Open(MQ_SEND_ACCESS,MQ_DENY_NONE)
If oQ.IsOpen Then
```

```
  Set oMsg = CreateObject("MSMQ.MSMQMessage")
  oMsg.Label = "Hello"
  oMsg.Body = "<Hello>Hello, world!</Hello>"
  oMsg.Send oQ, MQ_SINGLE_MESSAGE
  oQ.Close
End If

Set oMsg = Nothing
Set oQ = Nothing
Set oQInfo = Nothing

If Err <> 0 Then
  WScript.Echo "Queue Error: " & vbCrLf & Err.Description
  WScript.Quit
End If

sPath = WScript.ScriptFullName
sPath = Mid(sPath, 1, InStrRev(sPath, "\"))
Set oSked = GetObject("sked:///" & sPath & "HelloWorld.skx")

If Err <> 0 Then
  WScript.Echo "XLANG Schedule Error: " & vbCrLf & Err.Description
End If
```

The message you sent is an XML string: <Hello>Hello, world!</Hello>. When the XLANG schedule is invoked, it receives this message from the queue and passes it along as the parameter of the `SayHi` method of the COM object: `HelloWorldHelper.HelloWorldUtil`. The `SayHi` method extracts the contents of the XML string and displays it in a message box. The following is the implementation of the SayHi method:

```
Public Sub SayHi(ByVal sDoc As String, ByVal sTitle As String)
    On Error GoTo SayHi_Err
    Dim sHello As String
    Dim oXML As Object
    Set oXML = CreateObject("MSXML2.DOMDocument")
    oXML.async = False
    oXML.loadXML sDoc
    sHello = oXML.documentelement.selectSingleNode("//Hello").Text
    MsgBox sHello, vbOKOnly, sTitle
    Exit Sub
SayHi_Err:
    Err.Raise Err.Number
End Sub
```

In the first code listing of HelloWorld.vbs, the line that invokes the XLANG schedule looks like this:

```
Set oSked = GetObject("sked:///" & sPath & "HelloWorld.skx")
```

It calls the `GetObject()` method and passes a "sked" moniker, then returns an `IWFWorkflowInstance` object. This is one way of invoking an XLANG schedule using the moniker syntax. Later in this chapter, you will see another.

A complete sked moniker syntax looks like this:

sked://[ComputerName][!BizTalkServerGroupName][/FilePath][/PortName]

The ComputerName and BizTalkServerGroupName arguments are optional. If you omit them, the local machine and the default BizTalk Server Group will be assumed. You can also specify the port name (which is case-sensitive) when you invoke an XLANG schedule. The file path is the path of the XLANG schedule (.skx) file.

This example is simple, in terms of the business process model. It does, however, illustrate the complete process of creating an XLANG schedule. It also demonstrates how to use COM Components and Message Queuing implementations in an XLANG schedule.

Using Per-Instance Queues

This example is transformed from the HelloWorld example by simply replacing the preexisting permanent queue with a per-instance queue. The process of creating this XLANG schedule is almost exactly the same as that used for the HelloWorld XLANG schedule, with one exception. On the third page of the Message Queuing Binding Wizard, instead of selecting Use A Known Queue For All Instances, you must select Create A New Queue For Every Instance and type **.\private$\HelloWorld** in the queue prefix box, as shown in Figure 9-13.

When you specify a per-instance queue in an XLANG schedule, you don't have to (and shouldn't have to) create the queue by yourself. Instead, a temporary queue will be created by the XLANG Scheduler Engine every time a new instance of the XLANG schedule is instantiated. This temporary queue will be assigned a unique name, which is a combination of the prefix you specified in the Message Queuing Binding Wizard and a GUID. The lifetime of a per-instance queue is the same as that of the XLANG schedule.

Save the new XLANG schedule drawing as HelloWorld_PerInstanceQ.skv and compile it as HelloWorld_PerInstanceQ.skx. You can test this XLANG schedule by running the HelloWorld_PerInstanceQ.vbs script file (also located in the Orchestration\

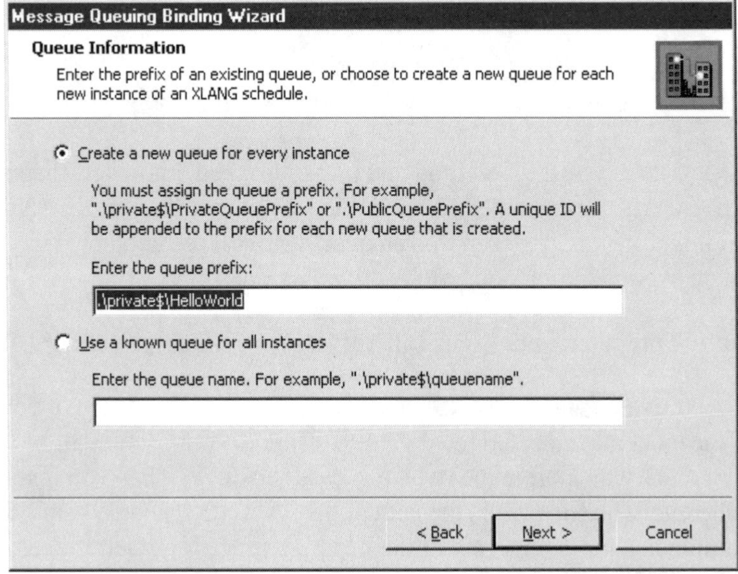

Figure 9-13 *Specifying a per-instance queue*

HelloWorld\Apps folder). You will first see a message box displaying the name of the per-instance queue.

If you leave the message box (don't click OK) and go to the Computer Management console, you should see the per-instance queue.

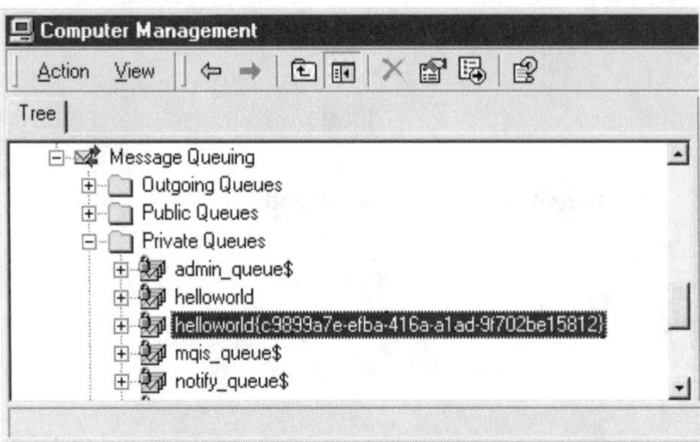

Now, switch back to the dialog box and click OK to dismiss it. Another dialog box should appear that says Hello, World! Clicking OK on the second dialog box will end the XLANG schedule. If you look in the Computer Management console now, you will find the per-instance queue has gone.

The HelloWorld_PerinstanceQ.vbs is almost the same as the HelloWorld.vbs. The only difference is that instead of passing the XML string to a preexisting queue, .\private$\HelloWorld, the script first gets the name of the per-instance queue by calling the `FullPortName` method of the `IWFWorkflowInstance` object, then it passes it to the PathName property of the `MSMQQueueInfo` object, as shown in the following:

```
Set oSked = GetObject("sked:///" & sPath & "HelloWorld_PerInstanceQ.skx")
sQPath = oSked.FullPortName("HelloWorld")
WScript.Echo sQPath
...
Set oQInfo = CreateObject("MSMQ.MSMQQueueInfo")
oQInfo.PathName = sQPath
...
```

Per-instance queues are a powerful mechanism for returning messages to the save running instance of an XLANG schedule which sent the original messages out. You will learn more about this later in the chapter in an example that integrates BizTalk Orchestration Services with BizTalk Messaging Services.

Making Decisions

In this example, you will learn how to use the Decision shape to create a simple XLANG schedule that simulates a purchase order approval process. The completed XLANG schedule drawing is shown in Figure 9-14.

When the XLANG schedule starts, the ReceivePOReq action waits for a message from a static, preexisting queue, .\private$\ReceivePOReq. The Count Items action then calls the CountItems methods of the Script Component (POReqUtil.wsc) which counts the number of line items in the purchase order request document. Then the process flows into a Decision shape which checks the item count returned from the Count Items action. If the item count is less then three, the process flows into the Approval action, which calls the Approval method of the POReqUtil.wsc Script component. Otherwise, the process flows into the Denial action, which calls the Denial method of the Script component. Both the Approval and Denial methods display a message box, indicating whether the purchase order has been approved or denied, along with the document body itself. Figure 9-15 illustrates the data flow of the ApprovePOReq XLANG schedule.

The implementation of this XLANG schedule is pretty straightforward, using a private queue and a Script component. The binding process for the Script component is similar to that for the COM component, with only one small difference in the

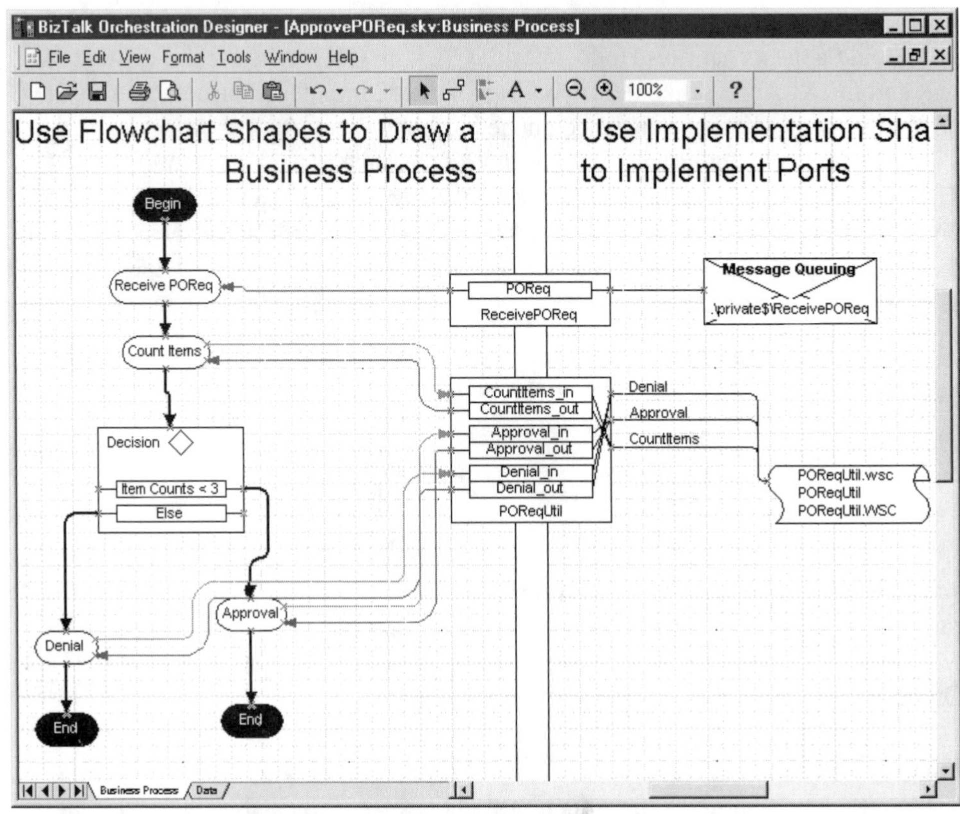

Figure 9-14 *The ApprovePOReq XLANG schedule drawing*

component selection step. Instead of selecting a registered type library, as in the case of the COM component, you need to specify the physical path of the Script component.

Script Component Binding Wizard

Specify the Script File

Enter the path to the Windows Script component (.wsc) file.

C:\Orchestration\ApprovePOReq\Components\POReqUtil.wsc

Browse...

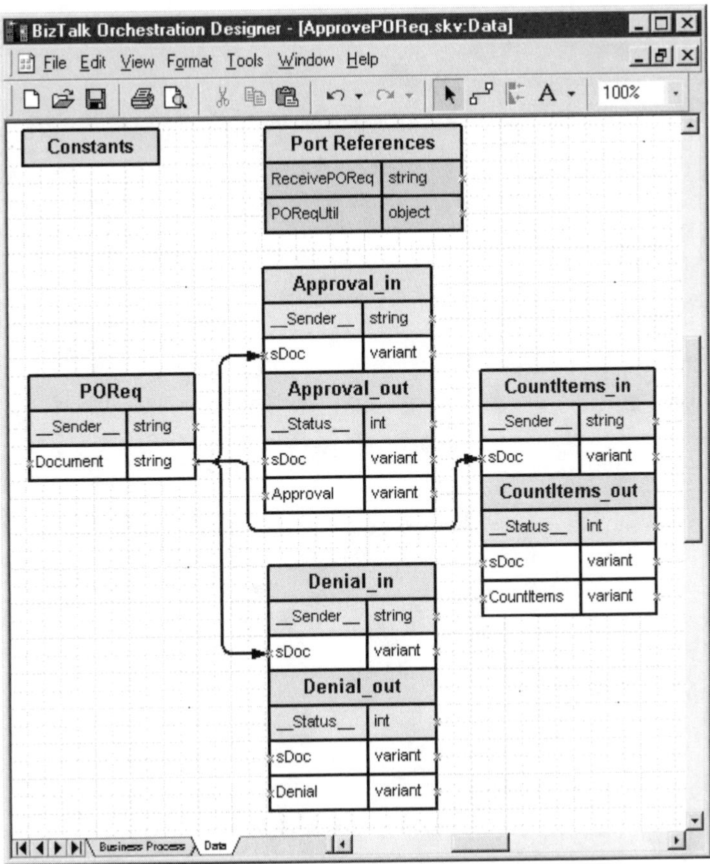

Figure 9-15 *The data flow of the ApprovePOReq XLANG schedule*

The Script Component implements three methods: CountItems, Approval, and Denial (as described previously). The following are the VBScript codes for these three methods:

```
Function CountItems(ByVal sDoc)
  Dim oXML, iCountItems

  On Error Resume Next
  Set oXML = CreateObject("MSXML2.DOMDocument")
  oXML.async = False
  oXML.LoadXML sDoc
  iCountItems =  oXML.documentElement.selectNodes("//Item").length
```

```
  If Err = 0 Then
    CountItems = iCountItems
  Else
    CountItems = 0
    Err.Raise Err.Number
  End If
End Function

Sub Approval(ByVal sDoc)
  Dim oXML

  Set oXML = CreateObject("MSXML2.DOMDocument")
  oXML.async = False
  oXML.LoadXML sDoc

  Msgbox "The following POReq document has been approved:" & _
         vbCRLF & vbCRLF & oXML.XML

End Sub

Sub Denial(ByVal sDoc)
  Dim oXML

  Set oXML = CreateObject("MSXML2.DOMDocument")
  oXML.async = False
  oXML.LoadXML sDoc

  Msgbox "The following POReq document has been denied:" & _
         vbCRLF & vbCRLF & oXML.XML

End Sub
```

Now, let's see how to define a rule for the Decision shape. After you place a Decision shape in the design page, double-click the shape to open up the Decision Properties dialog box. Next, click the Add button to open the Rule Properties dialog box. Type **Item Counts < 3** in the Rule name box. You can optionally type in some texts in the Rule description box to document the rule. Click inside the Script Expression box. This will enable the Message and Field drop-down boxes of the Expression Assistant down at the bottom. Select CountItems_out from the Message drop-down list and CountItems from the Field drop-down list, then click the Insert button. You will notice "CountItems_out.CountItems" appears in the Script expression box. Click to the right of the texts and type **<3** so the Rule Properties box looks like that in Figure 9-16.

Figure 9-16 *Creating a rule for the Decision shape*

Click OK to return to the Decision Properties dialog box, which should now look like this:

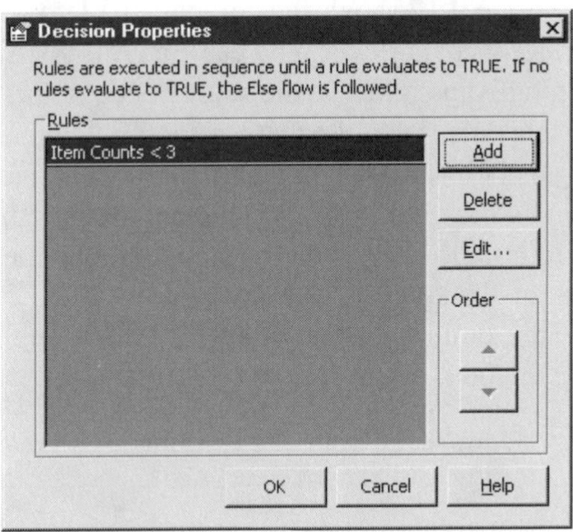

You can add more rules to a Decision shape. The rules will be evaluated in the order from top to bottom. You can click the arrow buttons in the Order area to rearrange the order of rules. In this example, you use only one rule. Click OK to close the dialog box. The source code for this example is located under the \Orchestration\ApprovePOReq folder. To set up the testing environment, double-click the setup.cmd batch file to create the queue and register the Script component. To remove it, double-click the remove.cmd file. Under the \Orchestration\ApprovePOReq\Apps folder, find two VBScript files, POReqApproval.vbs and POReqDenial.vbs. The former will submit POReq_Approval.xml (a purchase order request that contains two line items) and start the XLANG schedule. Whereas, the latter will submit POReq_Denail.xml (a purchase order request that contains three line items) and also start the XLANG schedule. The following illustration shows a message box that is the result of running the POReqApproval.vbs file.

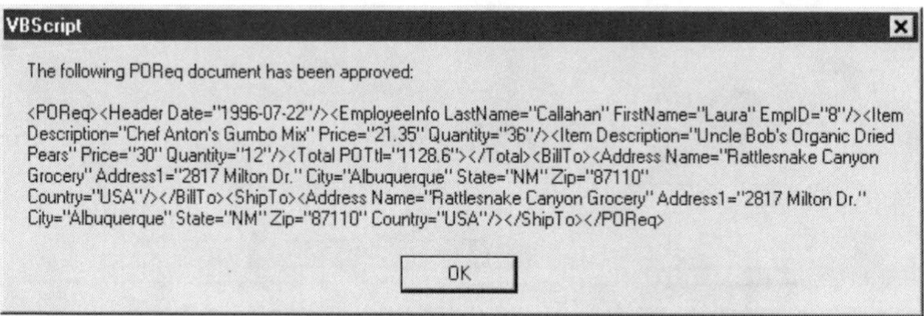
VBScript
The following POReq document has been approved:
<POReq><Header Date="1996-07-22"/><EmployeeInfo LastName="Callahan" FirstName="Laura" EmpID="8"/><Item Description="Chef Anton's Gumbo Mix" Price="21.35" Quantity="36"/><Item Description="Uncle Bob's Organic Dried Pears" Price="30" Quantity="12"/><Total POTtl="1128.6"></Total><BillTo><Address Name="Rattlesnake Canyon Grocery" Address1="2817 Milton Dr." City="Albuquerque" State="NM" Zip="87110" Country="USA"/></BillTo><ShipTo><Address Name="Rattlesnake Canyon Grocery" Address1="2817 Milton Dr." City="Albuquerque" State="NM" Zip="87110" Country="USA"/></ShipTo></POReq>
OK

Looping

In this example, you will learn how to use the While shape to implement loops. You will also learn how to maintain states inside the While shape, as well as inside the COM component. Figure 9-17 shows the completed XLANG schedule drawing and Figure 9-18 illustrates its data flows. You can find this XLANG schedule in the Orchestration\Looping\Apps folder in the source code of this chapter.

When the XLANG schedule starts, the Get Doc action will call the `GetDoc` method of the LoopingHelper.LoopingUtil COM component, passing in the path of the Items.xml document, which is a POReq document that has three line items. The `GetDoc` method will return the item count (as an output parameter) and the content of the Items.xml file as an XML string. The source code of the COM component can be found in the \Orchestration\Looping\LoopingUtil folder. The following code illustrates the `GetDoc` method:

```
Public Function GetDoc(ByVal sPath As String, _
                       ByRef lItemCount As Integer) As String
    Dim oXML As Object
    On Error GoTo GetDoc_Err
```

```
    Set oXML = CreateObject("MSXML2.DOMDocument")
    oXML.async = False
    oXML.Load App.Path & "\" & sPath
    lItemCount = oXML.documentElement.selectNodes("//Item").length
    GetDoc = oXML.xml
    Set oXML = Nothing
    Exit Function
GetDoc_Err:
    Err.Raise Err.Number
End Function
```

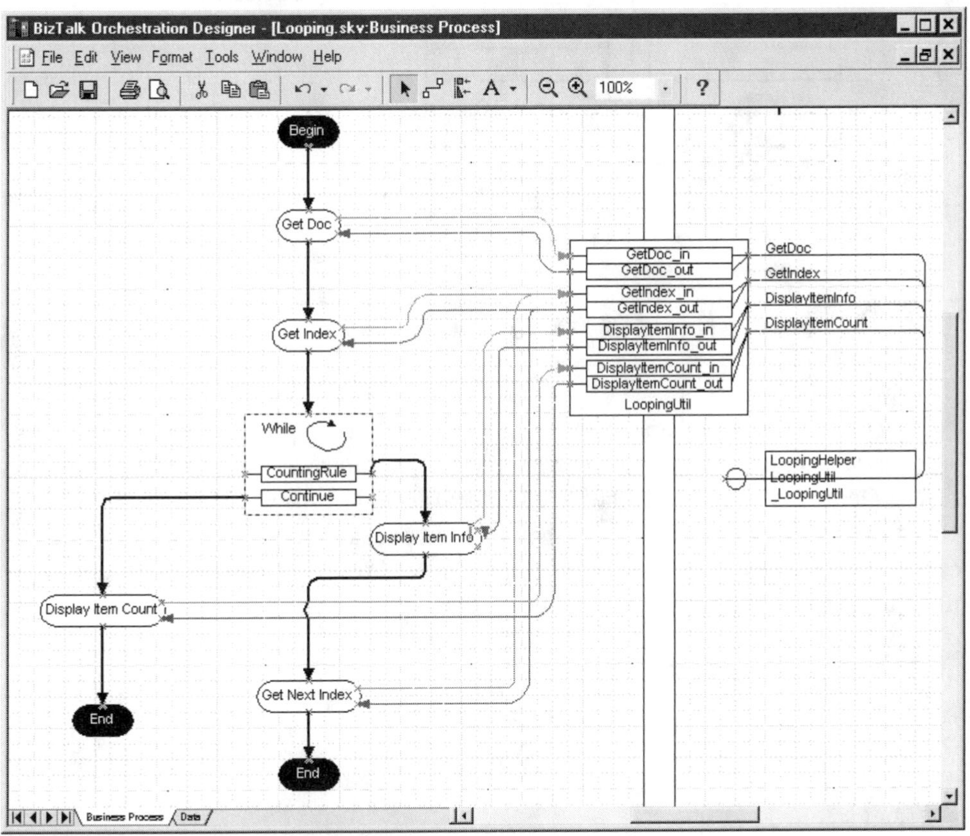

Figure 9-17 *A looping XLANG schedule drawing*

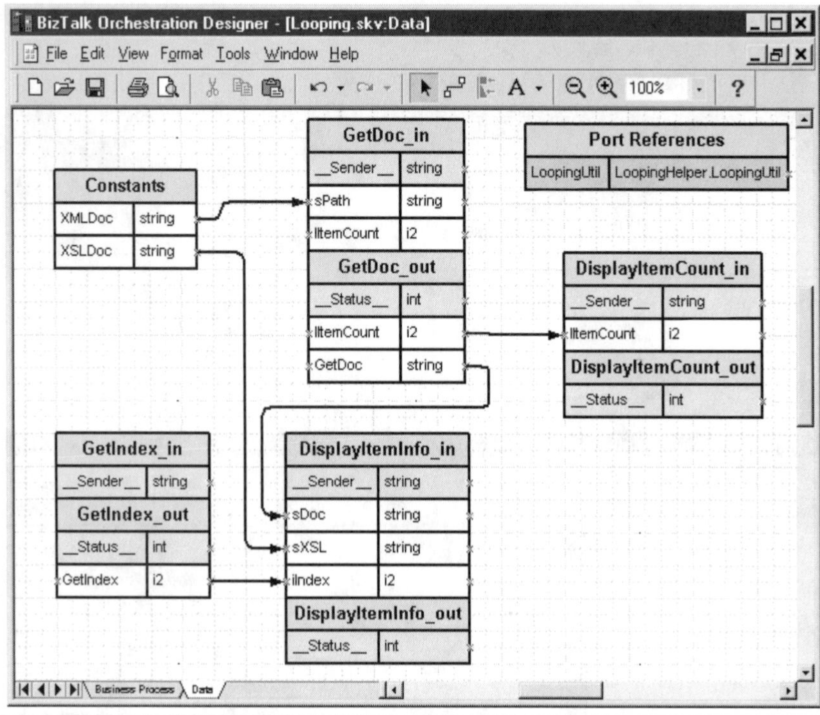

Figure 9-18 *The data flows of the looping XLANG schedule*

Notice that the second parameter, ItemCount, is defined by the reference ByRef, so it is an output parameter. It will be the criterion that determines if the loop should continue.

The Get Index action calls the `GetIndex` method of the COM component, which does two things: increments the index by one, and returns the value of the current index. The index is stored in a module level private variable, m_iIndex, as illustrated in the following code segment:

```
Private m_iIndex As Integer
...
Public Function GetIndex() As Integer
    GetIndex = m_iIndex
    m_iIndex = m_iIndex + 1
End Function
```

The value of m_iIndex needs to be persisted so the next time the `GetIndex` method gets called, it will return the correct index number. To make a variable in the COM persistent, you can specify the State Management Support property as either

"Holds state, but doesn't support persistence" or "Holds state, but does support persistence" in the Advanced Port Properties page of the COM Component Binding Wizard. The difference between these two options is whether the state is held in the memory (the former option) only, or persisted to a database (the latter option). For demonstration purposes, select "Holds state, but doesn't support persistence" (in a production environment, you should select "Holds state, but does support persistence" so the instance of the XLANG schedule can be dehydrated), as shown in Figure 9-19.

The process then flows into a While shape, which has only one rule. To add a new rule to a While shape, right-click the shape and select Add Rule… The same Rule Properties dialog box will appear that was used to define the rules for the Decision shape. During the business modeling stage, you don't need to fill up the Script Expression for the rule. You can simply give the rule a descriptive name, like "CountingRule". You can also add a description for the rule that can help when you build the expression later. In this case, the rule requires that if the value of the current item index is less then the total number of items (the item count), the process will flow to the Display Item Info action, followed by the Get Next Index action, and the loop continues. Otherwise, the process will flow to the Display Item Count and then terminate. The Display Item Info action calls the `DisplayItemInfo` method and the Display Item Count calls the `DisplayItemCount` method of the COM component. The Get Next Index action calls the `GetIndex` method in every loop, which returns the current item index number, and increments by one, as you saw

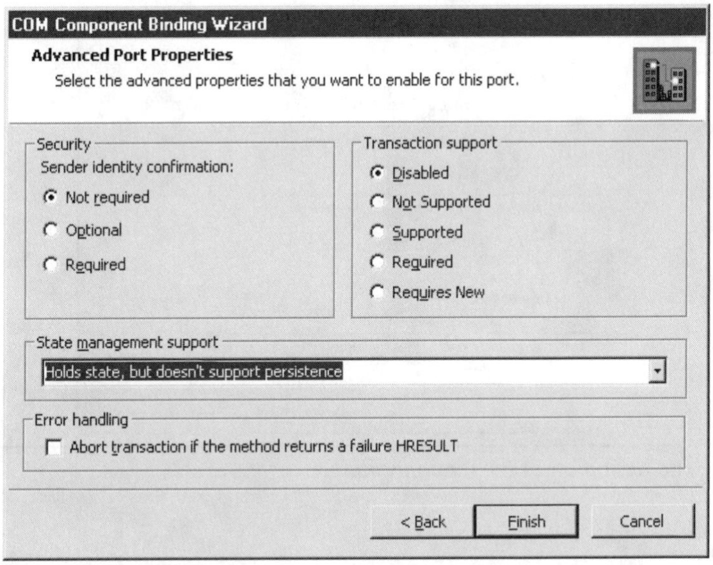

Figure 9-19 *Specifying the state management options for a COM component*

earlier. There are a couple of things you need to understand here. First, following the Get Next Index action, the flow will go back to the top of the While shape, but below the Get Index shape. Secondly, the value of the index inside the While shape needs to be persistent in order for the rule to work. This can be achieved by setting the State Persistence property to Yes.

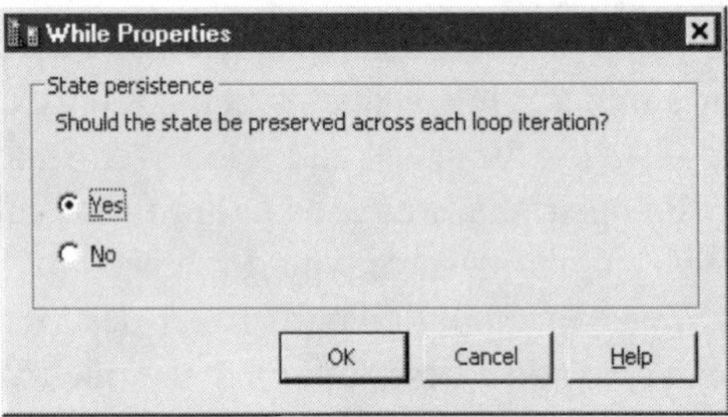

Figure 9-20 shows what the rule looks like.

Rule Properties
Rule name:
CountingRule
Rule description:
When the current item index is less than the total item count, the process flows to the Display Item Info action. Otherwise, it flows to the Display Item Count action.
Script expression:
If this script expression evaluates to TRUE, the connection from this rule is followed. Expressions can be combined with logical operators.
Valid expressions must be written in the following form:
message1.field1 > 50
GetIndex_out.GetIndex < GetDoc_out.lItemCount
Expression assistant
Message:
Constants
Field:
[__Exists__]
Insert
OK
Cancel
Help

Figure 9-20 *The definition of the CountingRule*

The following code listing illustrates the implementation of the `DisplayItemInfo` method:

```
Public Sub DisplayItemInfo(ByVal sDoc As String, _
                           ByVal sXSL As String, _
                           ByVal iIndex As Integer)
    Dim oXML    As Object
    Dim sXPath  As String
    Dim oItem   As Object
    Dim oXSL    As Object
    Dim sMsg    As String

    On Error GoTo GetItemInfo_Err

    Set oXML = CreateObject("MSXML2.DOMDocument")
    oXML.async = False
    oXML.LoadXML sDoc

    sXPath = "//Item[" & CStr(iIndex) & "]"
    Set oItem = oXML.documentElement.selectSingleNode(sXPath)
    Set oXSL = CreateObject("MSXML2.DOMDocument")
    oXSL.async = False
    oXSL.Load App.Path & "\" & sXSL
    sMsg = oItem.transformnode(oXSL)
    MsgBox sMsg, , "Looping Demo"
    Exit Sub
GetItemInfo_Err:
    Err.Raise Err.Number
End Sub
```

The `DisplayItemInfo` method takes three input parameters: the content of the Items.xml document (as an XML string), an XSL stylesheet (which we will discuss shortly), and the index number. It first loads the XML string to a DOMDocument object, then calls the selectSingleNode, using an XPath expression "//Item[index]" to return the specified Item node. For example, the first item, indicated by the XPath expression "//Item[1]", will return the following <Item> element:

<Item Description="Chef Anton't Gumbo Mix" Price="21.35" Quantity="36"/>

The DisplayItemInfo method then loads an XSL stylesheet whose contents are listed in the following:

```
<xsl:stylesheet xmlns:xsl="http://www.w3.org/1999/XSL/Transform" version="1.0">
<xsl:output method="text"/>
<xsl:template match = "Item">
  <xsl:text>  Item name: </xsl:text>
    <xsl:value-of select ="@Description"/>
  <xsl:text>
  Price: $</xsl:text><xsl:value-of select ="@Price"/>
  <xsl:text>
  Quantity: </xsl:text><xsl:value-of select ="@Quantity"/>
</xsl:template>
</xsl:stylesheet>
```

Next, the DisplayItemInfo method applies the preceding stylesheet to the <Item> element node, which will generate the formatted message and display it in a message box.

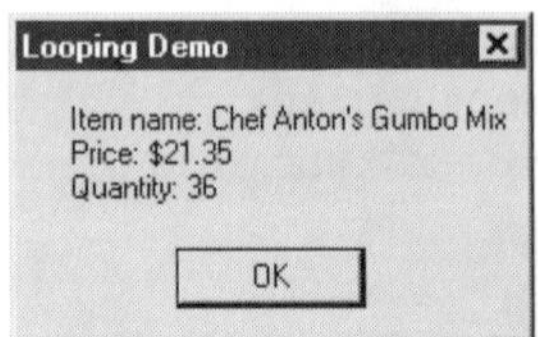

When the item index reaches the item count, the loop will stop and the process will flow to the Display Item Count action. Now, the DisplayItemCount method simply displays the item count:

```
Public Sub DisplayItemCount(ByVal lItemCount As Integer)
    MsgBox CStr(lItemCount) & " items found in the document." _
           , , "Looping Demo"
End Sub
```

CAUTION

Whereas the While shape provides a convenient way for building looping logics, you need to be careful not to inadvertently create infinite loops that can cause the process to never flow to the next action, thereby making the XLANG schedule run forever. As in this example, if you forget to add a Get Net Index action shape, you will create an infinite loop.

Integrating BizTalk Services

You can integrate BizTalk Orchestration Services and Messaging Services to take advantage of both, building complete EAI and B2B integration solutions (which is the most common case). In this section, you will see two examples that integrate BizTalk Services.

In the first example, you will add an automatic approval process for the Northwind purchase department. For demonstration purposes, use the same simple rule you used in the ApprovePOReq XLANG schedule earlier in this chapter (only those purchase order requests with less than three line items will be approved).

Recall that in Chapter 6 you learned that when the Northwind purchase department receives a purchase order request, it simply converts the request to an X12 EDI purchase order document, and forwards it to the e-MarketPlace which will distribute the X12 PO to its associated suppliers. In the real world, however, every purchase order has to be approved inside the buyer organization before it can be submitted to the supplier. You can use an XLANG schedule to orchestrate the approval business process and integrate it seamlessly into the messaging flow you built in Chapter 6. The completed XLANG schedule drawing for approving the PO request looks like the one in Figure 9-21. This XLANG schedule drawing, NWPOReqApproval.skv, can be found in the \Orchestration\Northwind\Apps folder.

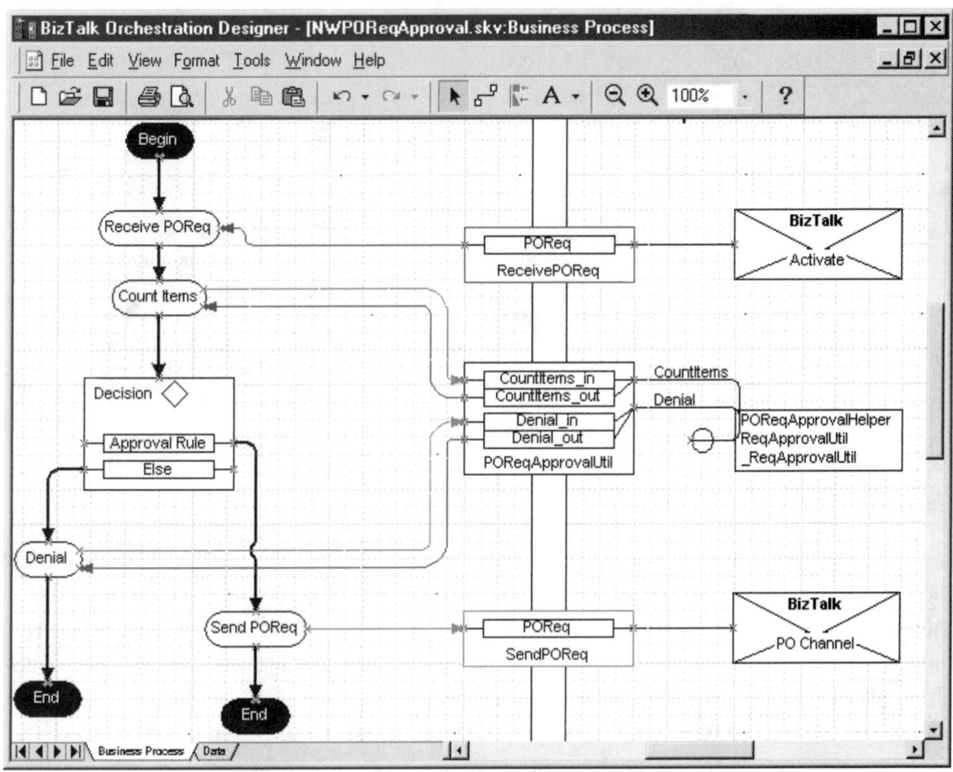

Figure 9-21 *The PO XLANG schedule for the Northwind purchase department*

As you can see in Figure 9-34, there are two BizTalk Messaging shapes in this XLANG schedule. The upper one receives the POReq document from BizTalk Messaging Services (as you may recall, this document is from the Northwind Home Organization) and the bottom one sends the approved PO back to BizTalk Messaging Services through the PO Channel.

The orchestration itself is very straightforward and similar to the one you built earlier, so we won't waste time discussing how to use the Decision shape, create rules, or bind COM components. Rather, we will focus on those two BizTalk Messaging shapes. The first BizTalk Messaging shape does two things. In addition to receiving documents from the BizTalk Messaging Services, it also invokes the XLANG schedule instance—another way of starting an XLANG schedule—in response to a message that arrives from the BizTalk Messaging Service.

To use a BizTalk Messaging shape in this way, drag a BizTalk Messaging shape from the Implementation stencil and place it on the design page as close to the corresponding action shape as possible. The BizTalk Messaging Binding Wizard launches, which has three pages. On the first page of the wizard, you specify the name of the implementation port, which is "ReceivePOReq" in this case. On the second page of the wizard, you select Receive to notify BizTalk Orchestration Services that this port is expected to receive messages from BizTalk Messaging Services. On the last page of the wizard, you need to specify that you want the BizTalk Messaging Services to activate (invoke) a new instance of this XLANG schedule in response to an arrived message.

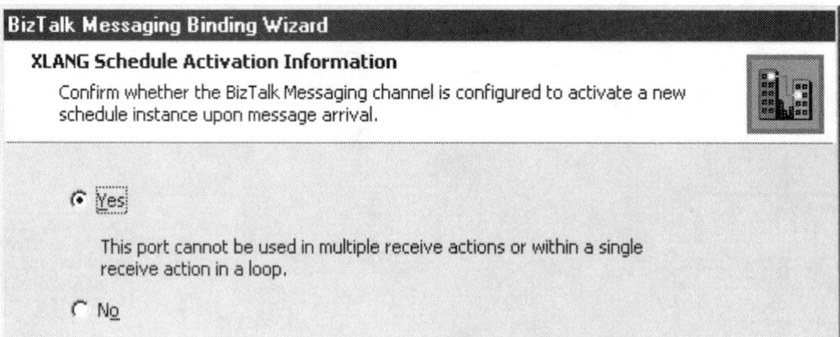

Click Finish to dismiss the BizTalk Messaging Binding Wizard. You will see that the word "Active" appears in the BizTalk Messaging shape. You also need to alter the messaging port POReq Port so it will activate the XLANG schedule and redirect the message to the schedule instance. To do this, drop and then re-create the involved channel-messaging port pair, POReq Channel and POReq Port, since BizTalk Messaging Manager won't allow you to change the destination of the port after it is built. To activate an XLANG schedule instance from a messaging port, you need to select the New XLANG Schedule option in the Messaging Port Properties dialog box, specify the path of the schedule (.skx) file and the name of the implementation port, as shown in Figure 9-22. You must spell the name exactly as it is spelled in the orchestration schedule.

The second BizTalk Messaging shape sends a message to a messaging channel. To configure this port, drag a BizTalk Messaging shape from the Implementation stencil and place it to an appropriate location on the design page. Name the port **SendPOReq** and click Next. In the second binding step, select Send and click Next. In the last step, select Static Channel option and type **POReq Channel** as the channel name (shown in Figure 9-23). Click Finish. You don't need to do anything special to the POReq Channel to receive the message from BizTalk Orchestration Services.

Figure 9-24 illustrates the data flows of this XLANG schedule.

The COM component, POReqApprovalHelper.dll, is a VB COM object. It supports two methods, CountItems and Denial. The former returns the number of items it finds in the POReq document and later saves the denied POReq document to a location specified by the filename, which is defined in the DeniedDoc constant as shown in the data flow diagram in Figure 9-24. We specified the value of the constant as

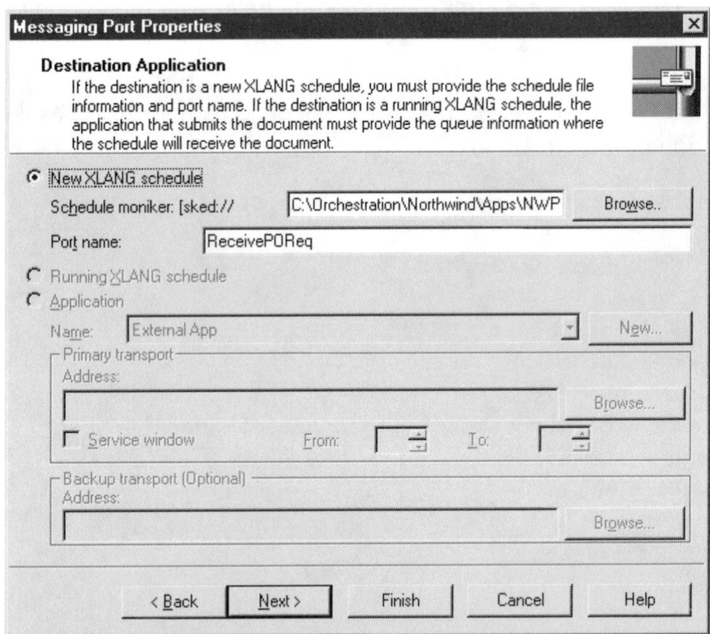

Figure 9-22 *Specifying a new XLANG schedule and port in the Messaging Port Wizard*

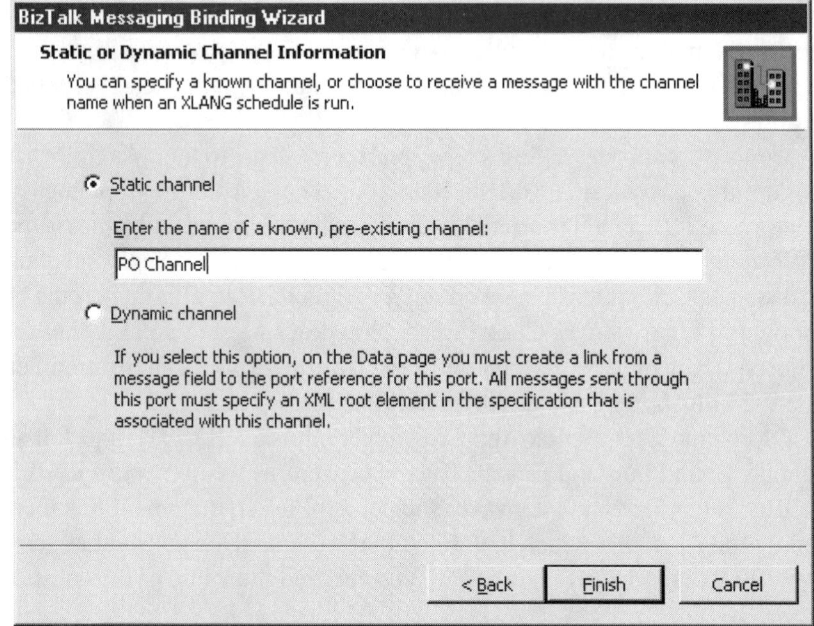

Figure 9-23 *Configuring the BizTalk Messaging shape to send a message to a channel*

"C:\Northwind\POReq_Denial". The following code listing illustrates the implementation of these methods:

```
Public Function CountItems(ByVal sDoc As String) As Long
  Dim oXML, iCountItems
  On Error GoTo CountItems_Err

  Set oXML = CreateObject("MSXML2.DOMDocument")
  oXML.async = False
  oXML.LoadXML sDoc
  iCountItems = oXML.documentElement.selectNodes("//Item").length
  CountItems = iCountItems
  Exit Function
CountItems_Err:
  Err.Raise Err.Number
End Function

Public Sub Denial(ByVal sDoc As String, ByVal sPath As String)
```

```
  Dim oXML
  On Error GoTo Denial_Err

  Set oXML = CreateObject("MSXML2.DOMDocument")
  oXML.async = False
  oXML.LoadXML sDoc
  oXML.Save sPath
  Exit Sub
Denial_Err:
  Err.Raise Err.Number
End Sub
```

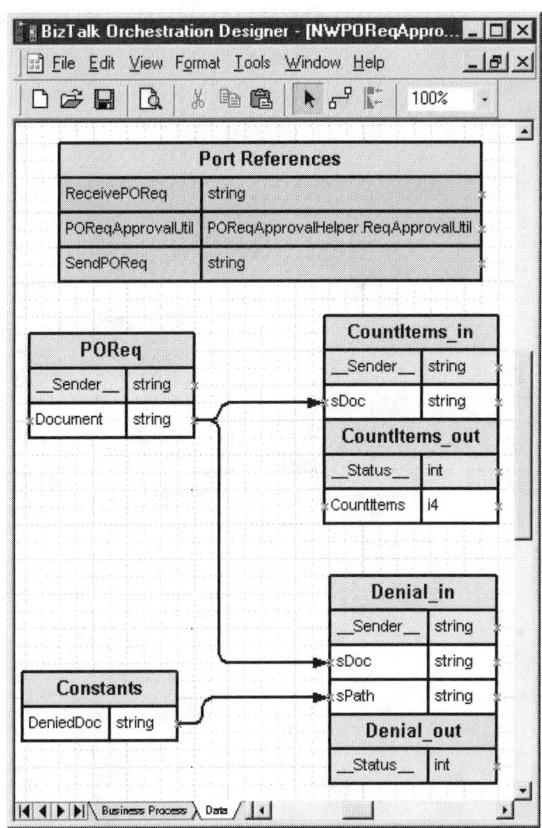

Figure 9-24 *The data flows of the NWPOReqApproval XLANG schedule*

In this example, you've seen how easily you can use BizTalk Orchestration Services to automate a business process and integrate it into an existing messaging solution. To test the changes you just made, find the two VB script files, SubmitPOReq_Approval.vbs and SubmitPOReq_Denial.vbs in the \Orchestration\Northwind\Apps folder. The former will submit a POReq document that contains only two items, so it will pass through the entire messaging system (see Chapter 6 for details). The latter will submit a POReq document that contains three items, so it will be denied by the XLANG schedule. In this case, you will find the POReq_Denial.xml document in the C:\Northwind folder.

In the next example, you will discover another way to integrate BizTalk services, this time by sending a message from an XLANG schedule to BizTalk Messaging Services through a channel, having an external application process the message, and sending the result back to the same XLANG schedule (which sent the original message).

Figure 9-25 describes the message flow of this sample application. A VBScript file, Integration.vbs sends a purchase order document to the private queue, PO, and

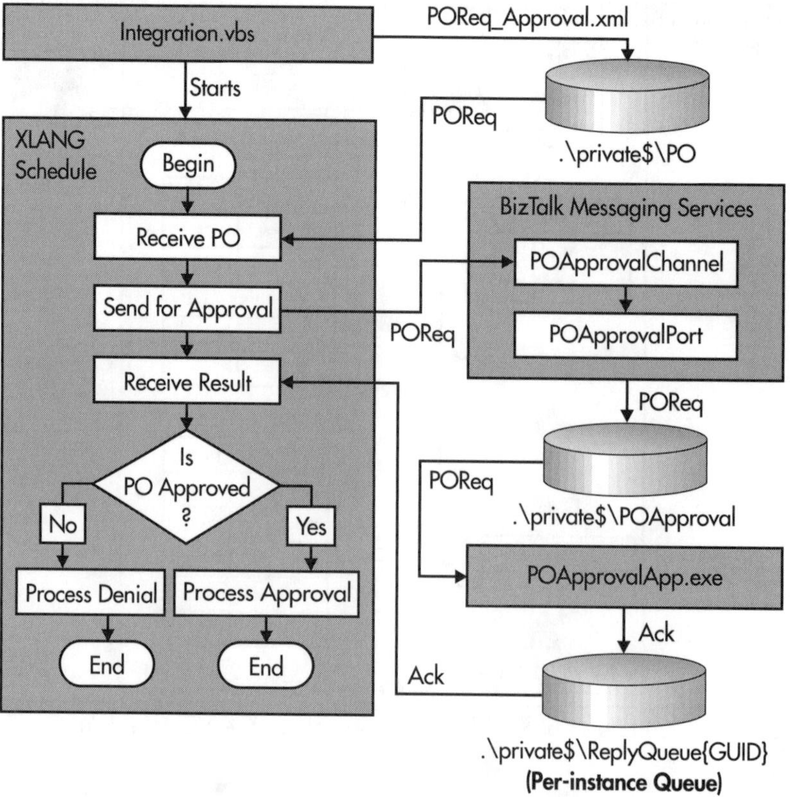

Figure 9-25 *The message flow of the sample application*

starts an XLANG schedule instance. The first action, Receive PO, will receive the purchase order documents from the private queue, then flow to the next action, which will send it to BizTalk Messaging Services through the channel, POApprovalChannel. The associated messaging port, POApprovalPort then transports the purchase order document to another private queue, POApproval. This queue is monitored by a VB application, POApprovalApp.exe, which allows you to approve or deny the purchase order request, then generates an acknowledgement document. This acknowledgement document is then sent back to the same XLANG schedule that sent the original POReq document, this time by way of a per-instance queue specified in the XLANG schedule.

Figure 9-26 illustrates the XLANG schedule drawing of this sample application.

At this point in the chapter, you should be pretty comfortable with the techniques used in the schedule. We do, however, want to discuss a couple of key points. The

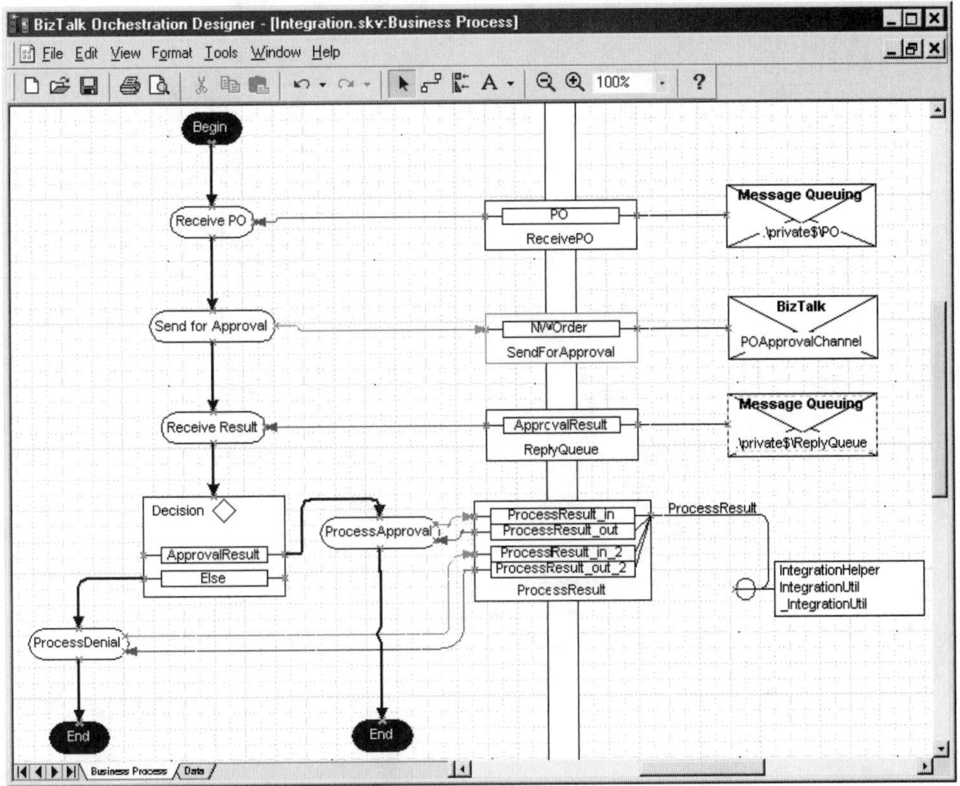

Figure 9-26 *The XLANG schedule drawing of the sample application*

techniques you used here that make it possible for an external application to send the message back to the same XLANG schedule are:

- Using a per-instance queue, with a prefix ReplyQueue
- Enclosing the actual per-instance queue name inside the purchase order document that is sent out. This is done by connecting the ReplyQueue field in the Port References shape to the ReplyQueue field of the outgoing message, NWOrder, as shown in Figure 9-27.

In order to make the ReplyQueue field available in the message shape on the Data page, you must create a specification for the message, NWOrder, using BizTalk Editor. You need to add a ReplyQueue field (as an Element instead of Attribute) in the specification, PO_Spec.xml. When you configure the message through the XML

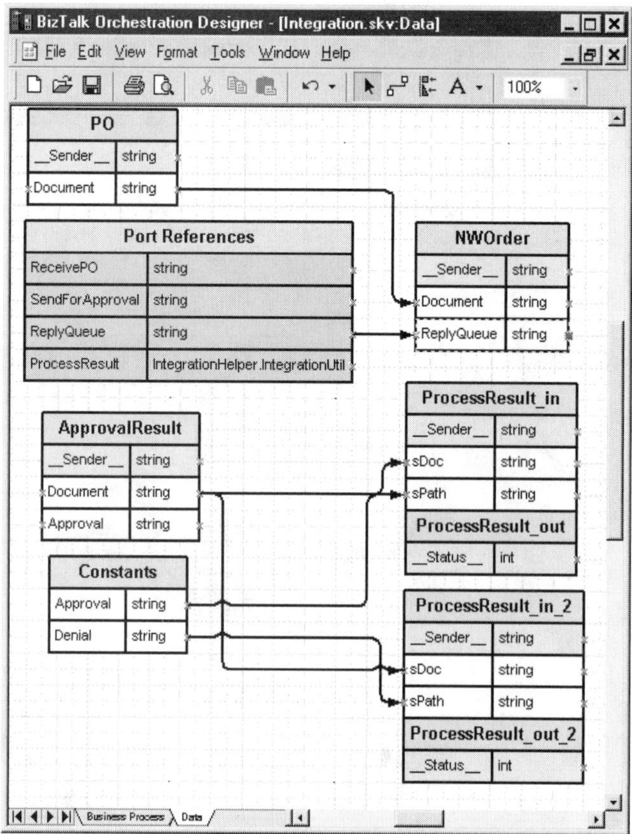

Figure 9-27 *The data flow of the sample XLANG schedule*

Communication Wizard in BizTalk Orchestration Designer, you can select the specification in the Message Specification box and click the Add button. The Field Selection dialog box appears. Select ReplyQueue (which can have any name and be in any position in the document) in the Select Node tree view, and its XPath expression will be displayed in the Node Path box. You can modify both the Field Name and Node Path when necessary.

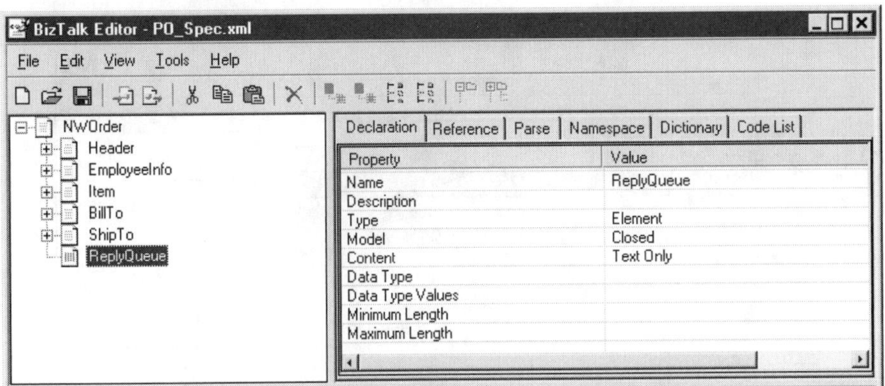

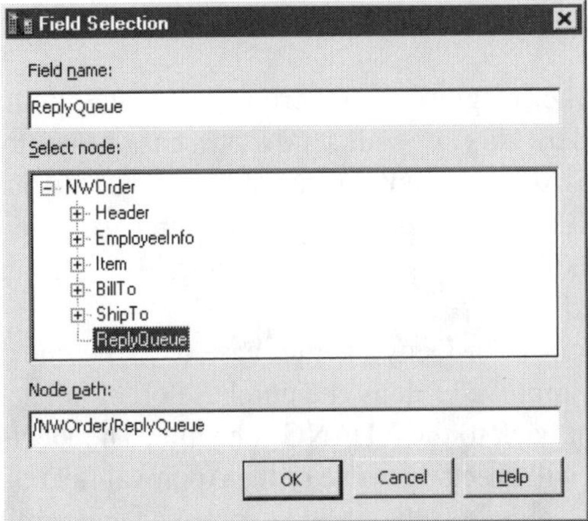

Click OK to dismiss the Field Selection dialog box and return to the XML Communication Wizard, which now looks like the one in Figure 9-28.

To set up this sample, run the batch file, setup.cmd in the \Orchestration\Integration folder. To run this sample application, first start the POApproveApp.exe, located in the \Orchestration\Integration\External App folder. Once started, the application will receive an event whenever a new message arrives in the queue the application is monitoring—in this case, the POApproval queue. The main display area will show the message "Waiting for the next PO document…"

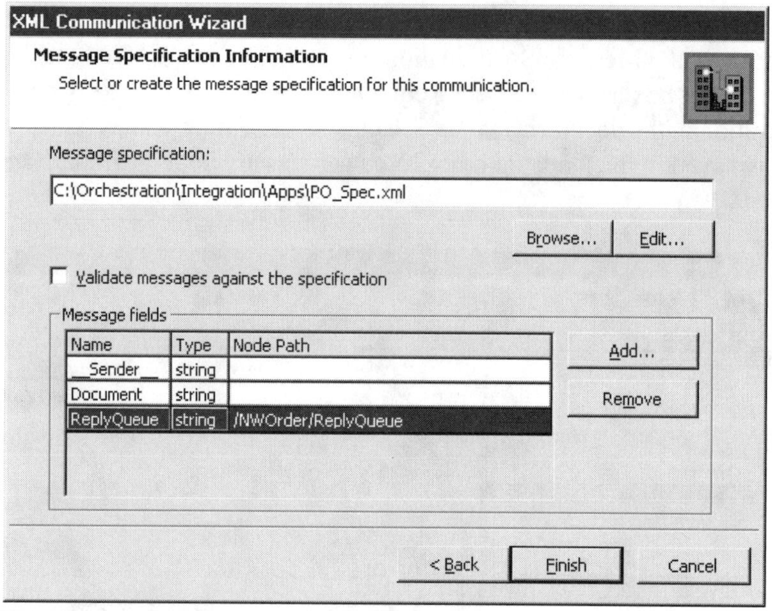

Figure 9-28 *The ReplyQueue field is available in the Message fields list*

Now you can run the Integration.vbs script file, located in the \Orchestration\Integration\Apps folder. This app will send a purchase order document to the PO queue and start an XLANG schedule instance. After a confirmation message indicating the XLANG schedule has started, the purchase order document will appear in the main display area (as shown in Figure 9-29), where the ReplyQueue element is highlighted.

You can either Approve or Deny the purchase order by clicking the appropriate button. Whether you approve or deny the purchase order, an acknowledgement document will be sent back to the XLANG schedule. The Decision shape has a rule, ApprovalRule, which will check the value of the Approval field of the acknowledgement document. If the value equals 1, the order is approved and will be redirected to the Approval folder under the \Orchestration\Integration\Components folder. If the value of the Approval field is 0, the order is denied and redirected to the Denial folder. The acknowledgement document for an approved purchase order looks like this:

```
<POAck OrderID = "10262">
  <Approval>1</Approval>
</POAck>
```

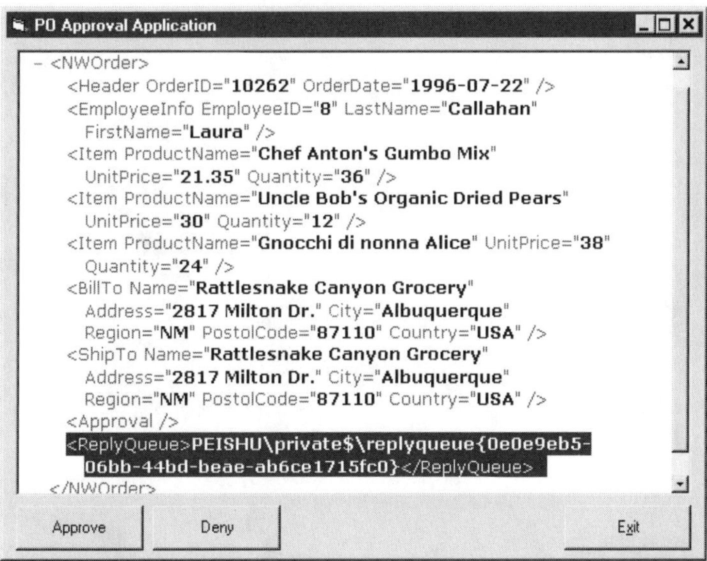

Figure 9-29 *The purchase order document appears in the PO Approval Application*

Chapter in Review

In this chapter, you learned about BizTalk Server 2000 Orchestration Services. You also learned how to create XLANG schedules using BizTalk Orchestration Designer. Finally, you worked through many examples demonstrating how to use BizTalk Orchestration Services to solve a variety of orchestration problems, including how to use different flowchart shapes, implementation shapes, and how to integrate BizTalk Orchestration Services with BizTalk Message Services to build powerful integration solutions. In the next chapter, you will learn more advanced BizTalk Orchestration techniques, including how to manage long-running, distributed transactions, and how to manage and debug XLANG schedules and handling errors.

CHAPTER

10

Advanced XLANG Schedules

IN THIS CHAPTER:

Managing Transactions

Exception Handling

Debugging XLANG Schedules

Chapter in Review

In the last chapter, you learned the fundamentals of BizTalk Server 2000 Orchestration Services, including how to use different flowchart shapes to define business processes in various scenarios, as well as how to utilize available implementation technologies and bind them to the business processes to create a BizTalk Orchestration solution: XLANG schedules. In this chapter, you will learn some more advanced BizTalk Orchestration features, including how to use BizTalk Orchestration Services to manage transactions, especially long-running transactions, how to handle exceptions in your XLANG schedules and how to debug your XLANG schedules.

Managing Transactions

In this section, we will introduce you to transaction concepts. We will discuss distributed transactions, COM+ transactions, and long-running transactions—the fundamentals on which the transaction supports of BizTalk Orchestration Services are based.

Introducing Transactions

In the real world, you deal with transactions all the time. Consider a scenario in which you transfer $100 from a savings account to a checking account. This money transfer process involves two actions, withdrawing money from the savings account and depositing money to the checking account. There must be a mechanism that ensures either both actions (withdrawal and deposit) succeed or none of them do. You don't want to see a situation in which the withdrawal action succeeds but the deposit action fails; otherwise your $100 would vanish into thin air. On the other hand, the bank would be mortified if the opposite scenario occurred, costing them the $100 instead. The mechanism that guarantees this all-or-nothing outcome is called a *transaction*. A transaction constitutes a series of actions that are grouped into a logical unit of work, essentially a single, atomic operation. As illustrated in the money transfer example, there can be only two possible outcomes of a transaction: either all actions are completed successfully, or none are.

The ACID Properties

A typical transaction can be characterized by four attributes—*Atomicity*, *Consistency*, *Isolation,* and *Durability*, or ACID for short—as described below:

- **Atomicity** A transaction must be an atomic, single unit of work in which all or none of the individual actions are completed.

- **Consistency** The state of data must be consistent before and after the transaction. In the money transfer scenario, both the checking and savings accounts should have new balances after a successful transaction. If the transaction failed, the balances of both accounts should remain unchanged.
- **Isolation** Concurrent transactions should be isolated from one another. One transaction should not be able to view or change data being modified by other transactions, and vice versa. Concurrent individual transactions should appear to be serialized.
- **Durability** A transaction must be durable. Changes to the data after a committed transaction must persist in a permanent data store and should survive system failures.

Isolation is usually implemented by applying locks to database tables to a certain degree, referred to as the *isolation level*. Table 10-1 describes isolation levels defined in the ANSI SQL-92 specification, in order of increasing restrictiveness.

Increasing the restiveness of the isolation level will certainly improve the data integrity, but at the cost of degrading the concurrency and throughput.

Distributed Transactions and MS DTC

Most relational databases support some sort of transaction mechanism for updating data across multiple tables, such as the *BEGIN TRANS…COMMIT/ROLLBACK* SQL Server TSQL statement and the *BeginTrans*, *CommitTrans*, and *RollbackTrans*

Isolation Level	Description
Read Uncommitted	A transaction can read transient data of another current transaction before that transaction commits. This is the least restrictive isolation level and is sometimes referred to as a *dirty read*. Results from dirty reads are unreliable.
Read Committed	A transaction cannot read the data of another transaction until that transaction is committed. This is the default isolation behavior of SQL Server.
Repeatable Read	A transaction cannot read the data of another transaction during the entire transaction lifetime.
Serializable	This is similar to Repeatable Read in which unrepeatable reads are avoided. In addition, this isolation level further prevents *phantom reads*. Phantom reads occur when a row that belongs to a range of rows being read by a transaction is inserted or deleted by another concurrent transaction. This is the most restrictive isolation level.

Table 10-1 *Isolation Levels Defined in the ANSI SQL-92 Specification*

methods of the ADO connection object. These database-oriented transactions are usually implemented by a so-called *write-ahead* mechanism using a transaction log. The snapshot of the data before the transaction was written to the transaction log before the data was updated. If everything went well, the transaction committed and the updates were made permanent in the database. Should anything go wrong, however, the data would be restored to their values prior to the updating, using the snapshot saved in the transaction log.

Whereas write-ahead type transactions work fine within the scope of a single database on a single machine, they won't work in the distributed scenarios in which updates involve multiple databases residing across multiple machines. To cope with the distributed transaction, a two-phase commit protocol (or 2-pc protocol) is usually used. In the two-phase commit architecture, each transaction participant is referred to as a *transaction manager*, or TM. There is also a special TM responsible for coordinating the rest of the TMs. As its name implies, the protocol operates on voting bases which involves two distinct phases:

- Phase one is the preparation phase in which each individual TM reports to the coordinating TM to indicate its readiness for committing the overall transaction, at which time it also indicates its vote regarding its own transaction outcome (success or failure).
- In phase two, the coordinating TM instructs all the participating TMs to commit the transaction, as long as they all agree (vote) to do so, or abort the transaction if at least one TM disagrees.

Microsoft Distributed Transaction Coordinate, or *MS DTC* for short, is just such a coordinating transaction manager. MS DTC was originally shipped with SQL Server 6.5 and is now an integral part of the Windows 2000 operating system. By using MS DTC, you can manage transactions across multiple transactional databases and resources.

COM+ Transactions

Microsoft Transaction Server, or MTS, is now one of the core COM+ Services, enabling you to manage transactions, including distributed transactions at the COM component level. It enables each COM component to participate in distributed transactions managed by MS DTC. COM+ transactions use the context concept (a wrapper object) that enables you to enlist COM components in an existing transaction, allowing each participating COM component to vote whether to commit or abort the transaction. In addition, COM+ enables you to specify the transactional attributes of your COM components installed in COM+ Applications (formerly known as MTS packages), using the Component Services MMC snap-in, as shown in Figure 10-1.

Table 10-2 describes the transactional attributes supported in COM+ transactions.

Transactions in B2B Scenarios

COM+ or DTC transactions are short-lived. Short-lived transactions imbibe all four characteristics of the ACID property.

In B2B integration scenarios (and in some EAI scenarios as well) in which transaction participants are physically distributed across the Internet around the world, transactions typically take an indefinite period of time to complete (measured in days, weeks, or even months), due to the latency inherited from the Internet. Any attempt to lock database tables or other resources would be impractical for long-running transactions (highly distributed transactions that last days, weeks, or months). As a result, long-running transactions must sacrifice the Isolation characteristic of the ACID property and use other mechanisms to compensate for data integrity issues. Nevertheless, long-running transactions typically include several ACID transactions.

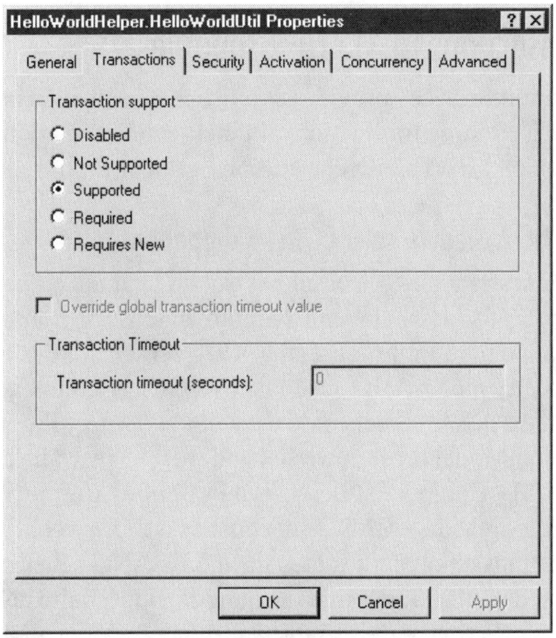

Figure 10-1 *Configuring the transactional attributes of a COM component*

Transactional Attributes	Description
Disabled	The COM+ transaction support is disabled for this component. When Disable is selected, the COM component is treated as if it was not installed in the COM+ application (known as the *unconfigured* COM component in COM+). The COM component may or may not participate in transactions, depending on the transactional status of its caller.
Not Supported	The COM component does not support transactions, regardless of the transactional status of its caller.
Supported	If the caller is transactional, the COM component will be enlisted in the existing transaction context. Otherwise, the COM component won't participate in transactions.
Required	If the caller is transactional, the COM component will be enlisted in the existing transaction context. Otherwise, the COM component will start a new transaction context.
Requires New	The COM component will always start a new transaction context, regardless of the transactional context of its caller.

Table 10-2 *Transactional Attributes Supported in COM+ Transactions*

Managing Transactions in XLANG Schedules

BizTalk Orchestration Services provides sophisticated semantics that support both short-lived and long-running transactions. In this section, you will learn how to use the features available in BizTalk Orchestration Services to manage transactions.

Treating the XLANG Schedule as a COM+ Component

BizTalk Server Orchestration Services allows you to treat the entire XLANG schedule as a COM+ component so it can be enlisted into an existing transactional context of a calling COM component. In this case, the XLANG schedule is invoked by a COM component. To specify an XLANG schedule as a COM+ component, right-click the Begin shape in the XLANG schedule drawing and select Properties. Then click the Transaction Model drop-down list and select Treat The XLANG Schedule As A COM+ Component (as shown in Figure 10-2).

When you elect to treat an XLANG schedule as a COM+ component, you can further specify the transactional attributes for the XLANG schedule by selecting Not Supported (the default), Supported, Required, and Requires New, as described earlier in this chapter. Note that the Disabled attribute does not apply in this situation, so it is not available in the Transaction Activation drop-down list (as shown in Figure 10-2).

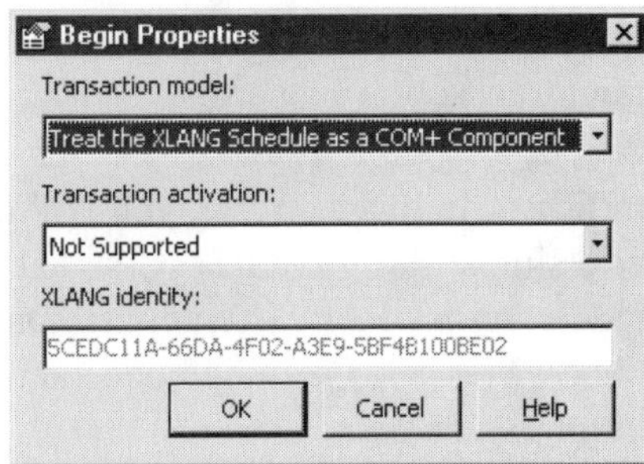

Figure 10-2 *Specifying the transaction model for an XLANG schedule*

The default transaction model of the XLANG schedule is Include Transactions Within The XLANG Schedule (not shown in Figure 10-2) that enables you to use transaction shapes and associated mechanisms in your XLANG schedules, as will be described shortly.

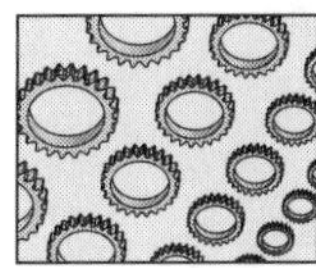

NOTE

Whereas treating the entire XLANG schedule as a COM+ component gives you the option to invoke an XLANG schedule from a COM component and enlist the running instance of the XLANG schedule into the existing transaction context of the calling COM component, this approach also has several limitations. First, you cannot use transaction shapes in an XLANG schedule drawing which is configured to be treated as a COM+ component. Thus, you will not be able to take advantage of the sophisticated transaction management provided by BizTalk Orchestration Services. Secondly, using the Fork shape in the XLANG schedule will be limited to a single stream of execution. Keep these guidelines in mind when deciding whether to use an XLANG schedule in this manner.

You may have noticed that in Figure 10-2, there is a third property, XLANG Identity. This is a read-only property that is a GUID generated by BizTalk Orchestration Designer. The XLANG Identity property can be used to uniquely identify an XLANG schedule drawing (the .skv file) and correlate it with the XLANG schedule it generates (the .skx file). Whenever you make changes in the XLANG schedule drawing, a new GUID (XLANG identity) is generated automatically. Every instance of the same XLANG schedule has an identical XLANG identity and individual GUID ID.

Using Transactions in XLANG Schedules

The default Transaction Model property of the Begin shape, Include Transactions Within The XLANG Schedule, enables you to use transaction shapes inside an XLANG schedule drawing to manage sophisticated transactions, including short-lived (or DTC-style), long-running, and nested transactions. In this section, you will create three XLANG schedules and learn how to use the transaction shapes in XLANG schedules to handle different transaction scenarios.

Short-lived, DTC-style Transactions In this exercise, you will learn how to use the Transaction shape to create a simple short-lived, DTC-style transaction. The business process this XLANG schedule describes is extremely simple. It receives a purchase order document from an inbox Message Queuing queue and places it into an outbox queue for another application to pick up.

Open the BizTalk Orchestration Designer and draw two Action shapes, Receive POReq and Send PO, and an End shape in the flowchart design area and connect them together. Then drag a Transaction shape and place it to enclose the two Action shapes. Double-click the Transaction shape to bring up the Transaction Properties dialog box and set the name of the Transaction shape to DTCTransaction (as shown in Figure 10-3).

As you may have noticed in Figure 10-3, the Type property of a Transaction shape allows you to specify if the transaction is a short-lived, DTC-style transaction, a long-running transaction, or a timed transaction (a variation of a long-running transaction). In this example, you choose the default: short-lived, DTC-style transaction.

In the Transaction Options area, you can specify the timeout value (the Timeout property that is only available for short-lived and timed transaction types), and retry options. For retry options, you can specify how many times (the Retry Count property) and how frequent (the Backoff Time property) you want to retry. Note that the backoff value is exponential. The formula you use to determine the backup value (in seconds)

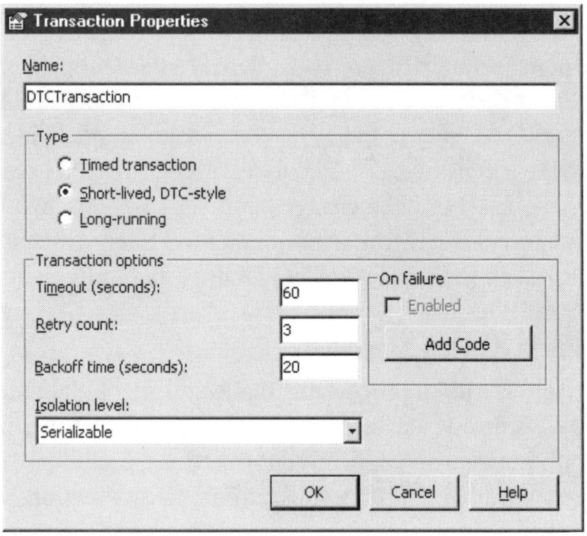

Figure 10-3 *Naming the transaction shape*

is B**R (B raised to the power of R), where B represents the Backoff Time property, and R is the value of the current retry count. For example, if the Retry Count property is set to 3 and the backoff time is set to 2, the transaction action will retry in intervals of 2, 4, and 8 seconds, respectively. If the backoff time of a specific transaction retry attempt (determined by the B**R formula) is greater than 180 seconds, the XLANG schedule instance will be dehydrated to the persistence database immediately.

The Isolation Level drop-down list allows you to specify an appropriate isolation level to control the balance between concurrency and throughput. The default is set to be Serializable. Isolation is not practical for long-running transactions and thus the Isolation Level options are not available for timed and long-running transaction types.

Click OK to return to the design page. The flowchart diagram should look like the one in Figure 10-4. Note that the color of a short-lived Transaction shape (including the Action shapes it encloses) is gray.

Don't be fooled by Figure 10-4 into thinking the transaction is completely configured. Not just yet! If you take a closer look at Figure 10-4, you will find that connections are made between the Begin shape and the Receive POReq Action shape, and between the Send PO Action shape and the End shape. They are not connected to the Transaction shape at all. To appropriately configure the Transaction shape, you need to connect it to appropriate Action shapes. First, you need to delete the connections from the Begin shape to the Receive POReq Action shape and from the Send PO shape to the End shape. You then connect the *outer shapes* (the Begin End shapes in this case) to the boundaries of the Transaction shape, as shown in Figure 10-5. Note that in Figure 10-5

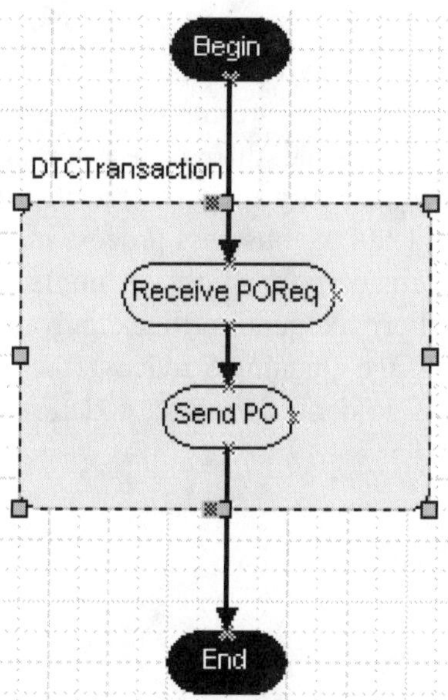

Figure 10-4 *A transaction shape is added to the XLANG schedule drawing*

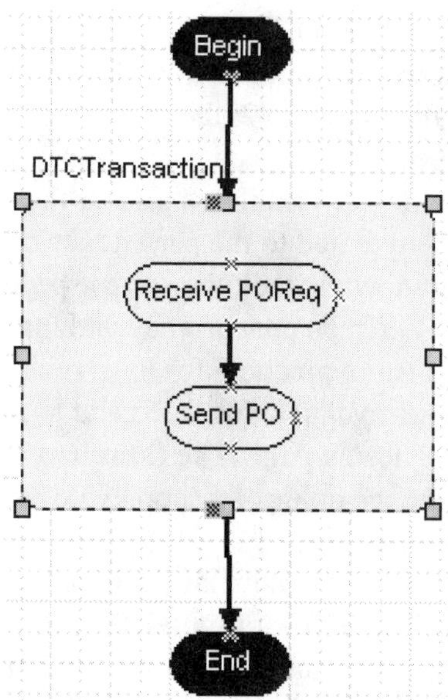

Figure 10-5 *Connecting the outer shapes to a Transaction shape*

the arrows from the Begin shape to the End shape are connected to the central green dots on the top and bottom of the Transaction shape. There are also two dark green dots positioned next to the central dots used to connect the Transaction shape to the Begin and End shapes. These two dots are used to connect to the *inner shapes* (the Receive POReq and Send PO Action shapes, in this case). The completed connections should look like those in Figure 10-6. Can you tell the difference between Figures 10-4 and 10-6? In Figure 10-6, the Action shapes are connected to the Transaction shape, whereas in Figure 10-4 they are not. This small difference is very important! It will decide whether your XLANG schedule really supports transactions or not.

Now that you have completed the business process modeling, it is time to bind the process to appropriate implementations. In this example, you bind the Action shapes to preexisting, transactional private queues (to take advantage of the transactional feature from Microsoft Message Queuing Services) (the setup.cmd batch file, found in the \BTS_Transaction\DTC folder in the source code, will create the queues for you), as shown in Figure 10-7.

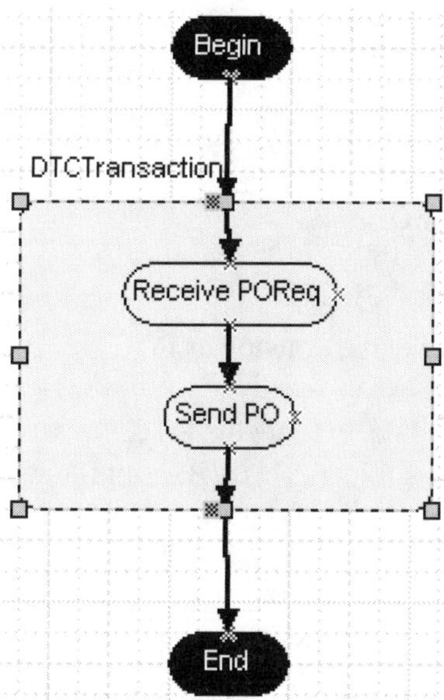

Figure 10-6 *An appropriately connected Transaction shape*

To complete the XLANG schedule drawing, don't forget to connect the appropriate messages in the Data page, as shown in Figure 10-8.

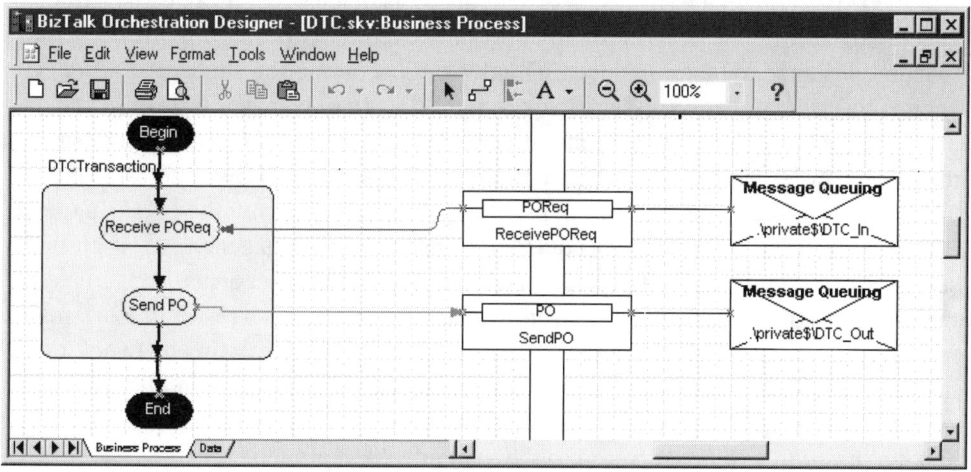

Figure 10-7 *The actions are bound to the queues*

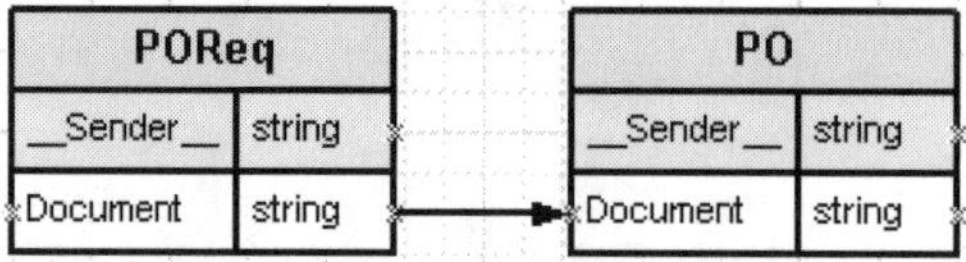

Figure 10-8 *Connecting the messages*

Now save the XLANG schedule drawing as DTC.skv and compile it into an XLANG schedule executable, DTC.skx.

To test this XLANG schedule, execute the DTC.vbs script file, found in the \BTS_Transaction\DTC\Apps folder. This VBScript file will place a POReq document into the DTC_In queue (don't forget the case-sensitivity of queue names) and starts an instance of the DTC.skx XLANG schedule. After doing this, you should find that DTC_In is empty and DTC_Out has a PO message, exactly as you would expect.

You may wonder what this XLANG schedule really has to do with transactions, and why you should bother using the Transaction shape at all. If everything were as perfect as what was shown the example, you wouldn't need to. But in the real world, there is always the unexpected. For instance, what happens if the DTC_Out queue is located on another machine not currently available? Worse yet, what if the DTC_Out queue is accidentally deleted for some reason? In such cases, the Transaction shape will instruct the XLANG engine to take a rollback action. The schedule will first pick up (de-queue) the message that arrives in the DTC_In queue and try to place it in the DTC_Out queue. If the DTC_Out queue is deleted, a system error will be generated, causing the transaction to abort (and eventually prompting the XLANG schedule instance to be terminated). Thanks to the Transaction shape, the XLANG engine will put the same message back in the DTC_In queue as if it were never picked up in the first place. To demonstrate this, delete the DTC_Out queue from the Computer Management MMC snap-in and execute the DTC.vbs script again.

The first action, Receive POReq, picked up the message from the DTC_In queue. Because the DTC_Out queue was deleted, a system error was generated when the second action, Send PO, tried to place a message in the DTC_Out queue. This triggered the rollback action because a Transaction shape was used. As a result, the original message will be sent back to the DTC_In queue. You can verify this by checking the DTC_In queue in the Computer Management MMC snap-in. In addition, the system error will be logged into the Windows Event Log, as shown in Figure 10-9, and the message will be delivered to the xlang.deadletter queue.

Long-running Transactions As we mentioned earlier, isolation is impractical for long-running transactions since it requires locking database resources. First, remote databases in a typical long-running transaction process are not always visible to all

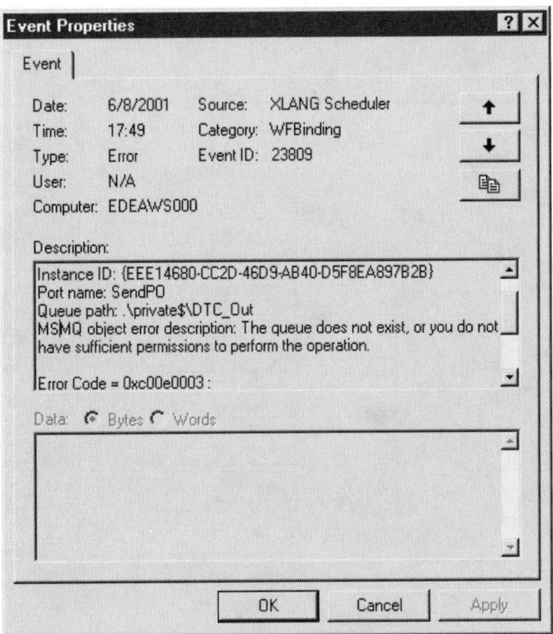

Figure 10-9 *A system error is recorded in the Event Log*

participants. Secondly, even locking local databases for a long period of time will consume significant memory resources, which could become a bottleneck. BizTalk Server 2000 Orchestration Services provides built-in semantics for managing long-running transactions, including sacrificing isolation from the ACID properties (BizTalk Server only supports Atomicity, Consistency, and Durability for long-running transactions) and adding additional design pages in XLANG schedule drawings for dealing with failures and performing compensation actions.

In addition, BizTalk Orchestration Services supports an additional variation of long- running transactions, Timed transaction, in which you can specify a timeout parameter used to trigger appropriate actions, failure recoveries, and/or compensations.

In this section, you will create an XLANG schedule that uses a long-running Transaction shape. You will learn how to use Timed transactions (which are specific instances of a long-running transaction) in the next section as you learn how to use nested transactions. The Business Process page of the completed XLANG schedule drawing is illustrated in Figure 10-10.

When the XLANG schedule starts, the first action, Receive POReq, receives a POReq document from the POReq_In message queue. Then the second action, AskForApproval, invokes a Windows script component, asking for approval. The script component simply displays a message box, asking the user whether to approve

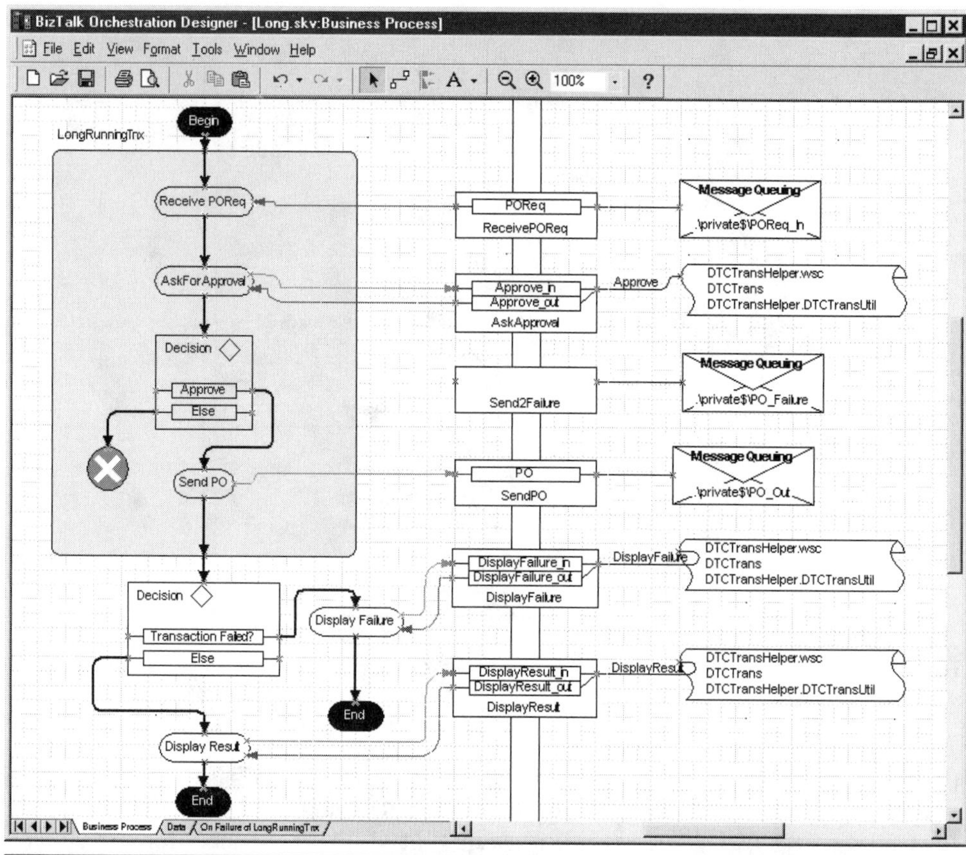

Figure 10-10 *The XLANG schedule drawing for a long-running transaction*

or deny the request. This simulates a purchase order approval process which can take an indefinite time to complete. Following the second action is a Decision shape, which checks whether the request was approved or denied. If the request was approved, the process will flow to the Send PO action which sends a PO document to the PO_Out message queue. Should the request be denied, an Abort shape is used to abort the transaction. Up to this point, everything, including three Action shapes, one Decision shape, and one Abort shape, is enclosed in a long-running Transaction shape, denoted by the color of yellow. Figure 10-11 illustrates its Properties page.

As you can see in Figure 10-11, the Type of Transaction shape is set to Long-running. The Isolation level has been disabled. In the On Failure section, the caption of the Add Code command button changes (it happens as soon as you click the Add Code button) to Delete Code and the Enabled box is checked. When you return to the BizTalk Orchestration Designer, a new design page will be inserted in the XLANG

Transaction Properties

Name:
LongRunningTnx

Type
Timed transaction
Short-lived, DTC-style
Long-running

Transaction options
Timeout (seconds): 60
Retry count: 0
Backoff time (seconds): 20
Isolation level:
Serializable

On failure
Enabled
Delete Code

OK Cancel Help

Figure 10-11 *The Transaction Properties page of a long-running transaction*

drawing, with a name of On Failure Of Name_of_the_Transaction_Shape. The name of the Transaction shape in this example is LongRunningTnx; therefore the new page inserted into the XLANG schedule drawing will have the caption of On Failure Of LongRunningTnx, as shown in Figure 10-12.

By inserting this On Failure page in the same XLANG schedule drawing, BizTalk Orchestration enables you to handle transactional failures the same way you handle normal business processes. In addition, BizTalk Orchestration coordinates the business

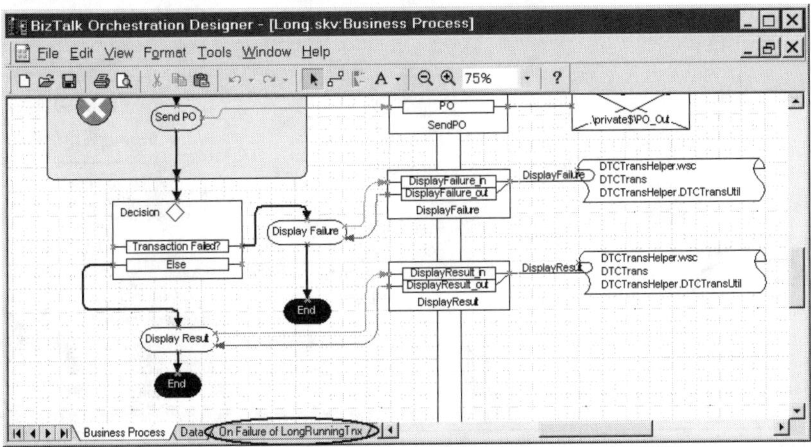

Figure 10-12 *An On Failure page is inserted into the XLANG drawing*

process with the failure handling process. When the transaction is aborted (in this case, the Abort shape is encountered), the flow branches to the On Failure page where you can define a custom solution for handling the failure using the same techniques you do for normal business processes. Figure 10-13 illustrates the On Failure page of the example. It uses a single Action shape, Send To Failure, to send the PO to the PO_Failure message queue. You can have another application monitor the PO_Failure queue and take appropriate actions accordingly.

All flowchart shapes (including Transaction shapes) and implementation shapes are available in the On Failure page, just as they are in the Business Process page. In addition, the implementation ports will appear in both the Business Process page and the On Failure page. The Data page is shared by messages on both the Business Process page and the On Failure page (you'll be shown the Data page from this example in just a moment).

It is important to understand that when the transaction is completed (whether committed or aborted), the flow will always return to the point that connects to the downstream action shapes. In this example, if the transaction request is approved, the Decision shape will flow to the Send PO Action shape, which sends the PO to the PO_Out message queue. In case the request is denied, the Abort shape is encountered, which will trigger the process defined in the On Failure Of LongRunningTnx page (see Figure 10-13) which sends the PO to the PO_Failure queue. In either case, the process will flow to the second Decision shape shown in Figure 10-10.

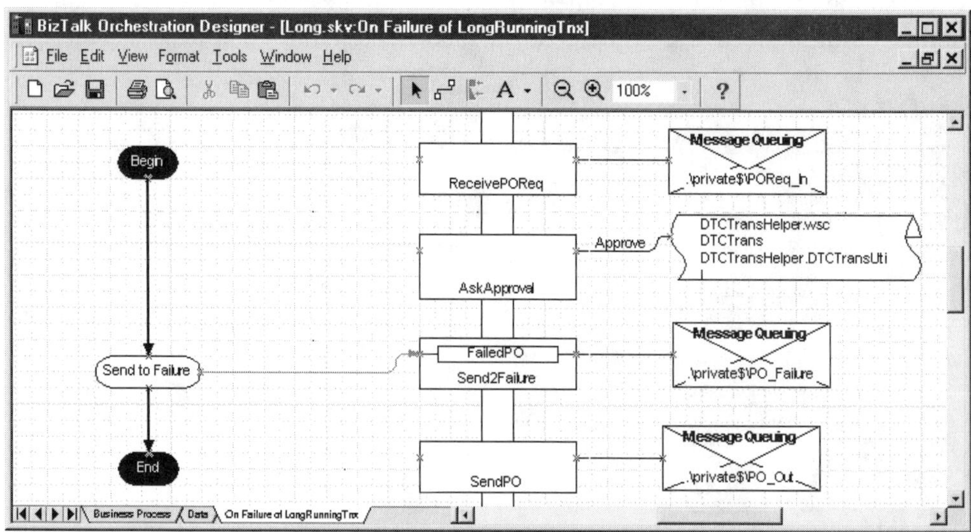

Figure 10-13 *Using the On Failure page to handle transaction failures*

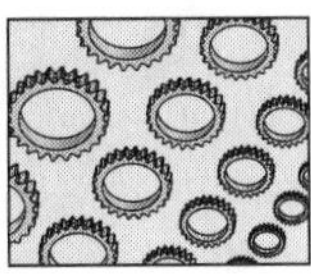

NOTE

The failure here refers to the transaction failure or abortion. If a failure occurs, the transaction aborts but the XLANG schedule continues to run until all the processes following the Transaction shape are completed. If a non-trappable system failure is encountered (for example, it's discovered a message queue doesn't exist) within the transaction, the On Failure page will not be triggered and the XLANG schedule terminates immediately.

Because the Transaction shape will flow to the sample downstream Action shape regardless of the transaction outcome (committed or aborted), you often need to test the transaction outcome after the Transaction shape so you can act accordingly. In this example, you use another Decision shape that tests whether the transaction is aborted by checking the existence of a message in the PO_Failure queue. It then directs the flow of process to either the Display Failure action or the Display Result action, depending on the result of the rule defined in the Decision shape (FailedPO.[__Exists__]). You can also test the HRESULT of COM components.

Figure 10-14 illustrates the message flows in the Data page of this example.

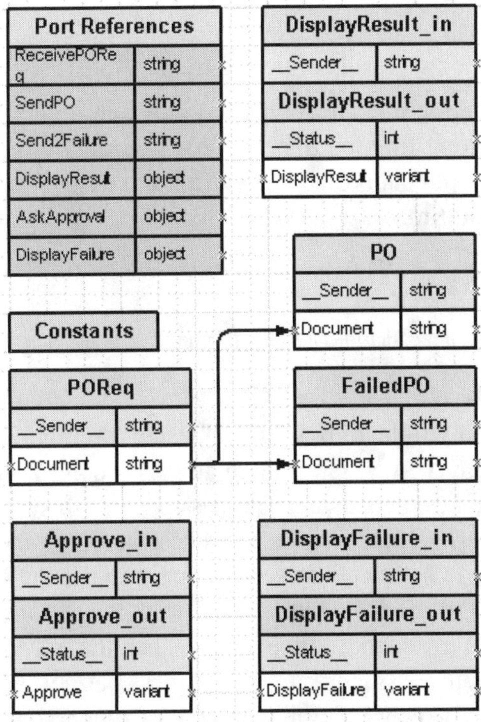

Figure 10-14 *The message flow of the long-running transaction example*

You can find the XLANG schedule drawing and compiled XLANG schedule files (Long.skv and Long.skx, respectively) under the \BTS_Transaction\Long\Apps folder of the source code for this chapter. The Windows script component used in this example, DTCTransHelper.wsc is located in the \BTS_Transaction\Long\Components folder. The setup.cmd batch file, found in the \BTS_Transaction\Long folder will create three message queues and register the script component for this example (the remove.cmd batch file will do the opposite, deleting queues and unregistering script components).

To test this example, execute the VBScript file, Long.vbs in the \BTS_Transaction\Long\Apps folder. You will see a dialog box, asking if you want to approve the PO. If you click Yes, you will see another message box, confirming that the transaction succeeded. In this case, you should find the PO message in the PO_Out message queue, and no message in the PO_Failure queue.

If you chose No when you were asked if you wanted to approve the PO, you will see another message box, stating the transaction failed. This time, you will find there is a PO message in the PO_Failure queue and no message in the PO_Out queue.

Nested Transactions BizTalk Server 2000 Orchestration Services also supports nested transactions, with the following limitations:

1. There can only be two levels of nested transactions.
2. The outer transaction must be a type of long-running or timed transaction (a variation of the long-running transaction). The inner transaction, though, can be any of three types supported by BizTalk Orchestration Services (short-lived, long-running, and timed).

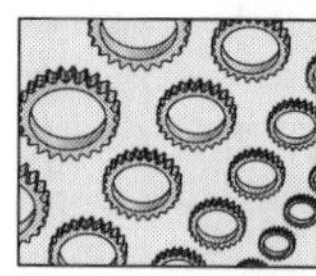

NOTE

You can compose many short-lived transactions inside a single, long-running transaction.

In this example, you will learn how to use nested transactions in BizTalk Orchestration Designer. You will also learn how to use the Timed transaction.

Figure 10-15 illustrates the Business Process page of this example.

As shown in Figure 10-15, the business process itself is very simple. The XLANG schedule waits for the PO request message to arrive in the POReq_In message queue and then sends the PO to the PO_Out queue. These two actions are wrapped into a short-lived, DTC-style transaction, InnerTrans. Then the XLANG schedule waits for an acknowledgement message from the business partner in the Ack_In message queue. This action can take an indefinite amount of time to complete, so the entire process is a good candidate for a long-running transaction, OuterTrans.

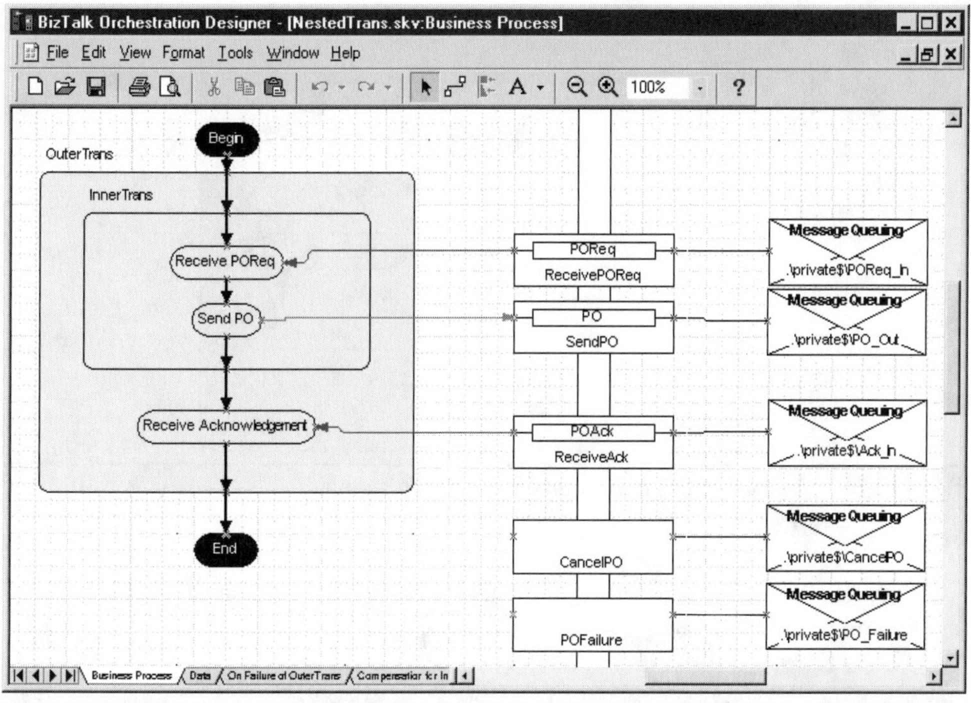

Figure 10-15 *A nested transaction*

Let's first look at the properties of the OuterTrans Transaction shape, as shown in Figure 10-16.

As you can see in Figure 10-16, for the outer transaction (the OutTrans shape in Figure 10-15), the Short-lived, DTC-style transaction type is disabled because it is not supported in outer transactions. In this example, you choose the Timed Transaction type and set the Timeout variable to 20 seconds for the purpose of demonstration. In a real-world scenario, the time should be set for much longer, essentially a more reasonable window within which the acknowledgement message could be expected. The color of a Timed transaction shape is blue.

In addition, the retry parameters are not available either. The options in the On Failure section indicate that an On Failure page is inserted into the XLANG schedule drawing to provide custom processes necessary for dealing with failures of this outer transaction. In this case, an On Failure Of OuterTrans page is inserted, as shown in Figure 10-17. As you can see, it is similar to the On Failure page of the long-running transaction example in the last section. The Notify ProcessPO Failure action will send the PO message to the PO_Failure queue.

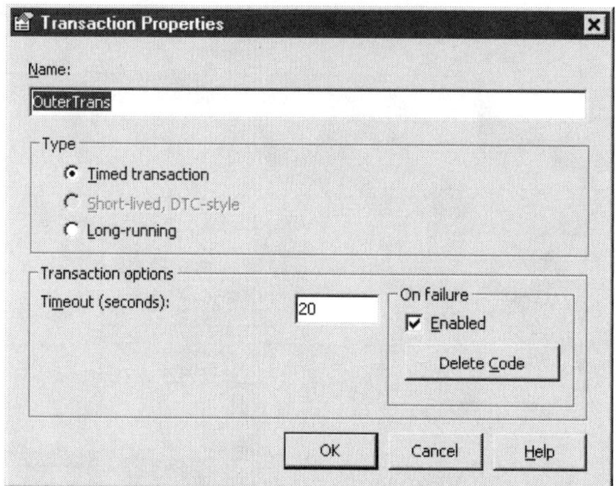

Figure 10-16 *The properties of an outer Transaction shape*

Now, let's look at the properties of the nested, inner Transaction shape, InnerTrans, as shown in Figure 10-18.

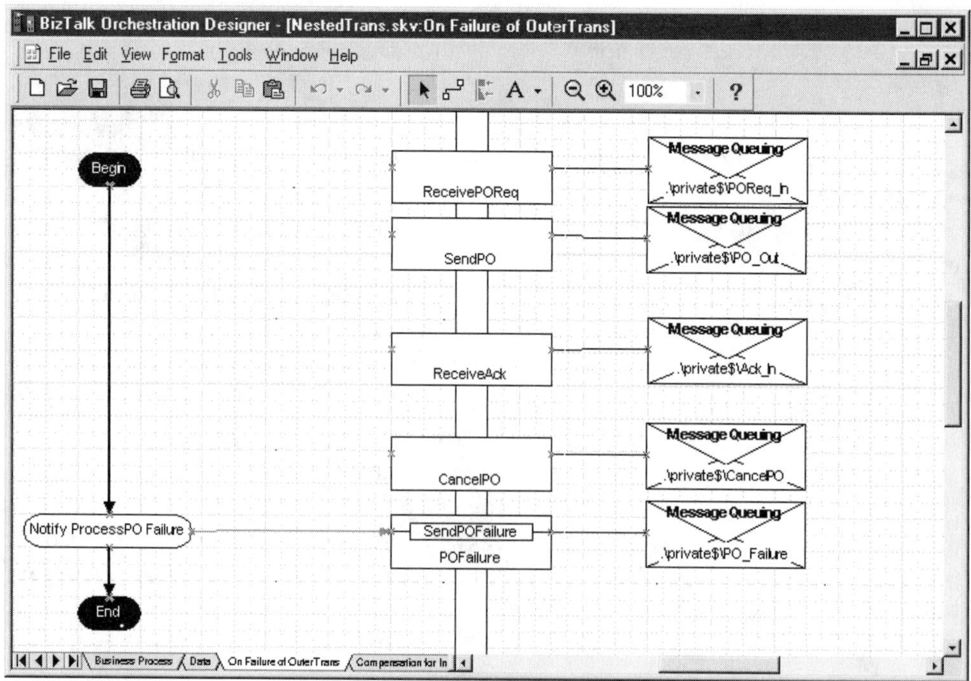

Figure 10-17 *The On Failure page for the outer transaction*

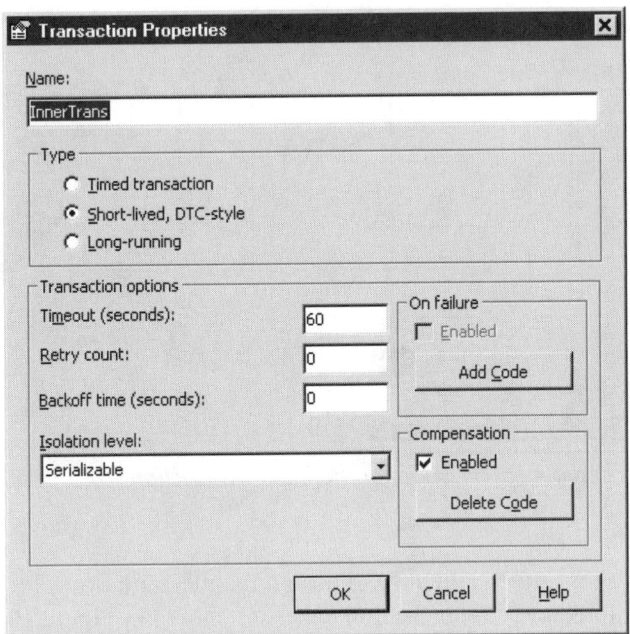

Figure 10-18 *The properties of the nested, inner Transaction shape*

As you can see in Figure 10-18, the transaction type is set to Short-lived, DTC-style. You may have also noticed in Figure 10-18 that right below the On Failure option, there is a new option, Compensation, which is next to the On Failure section. The Compensation option is only available for nested, inner transactions. By enabling this option, a new page, Compensation For Name_of_the_nested_transaction will be inserted into the XLANG schedule drawing, as shown in Figure 10-19. You can use this page to design a process to perform actions that will compensate the committed nested inner transaction in case the outer transaction fails. The action you want to take in this example is simple. As shown in Figure 10-20, you send a cancellation message to the CancelPO message queue, which can be picked up by an external application and delivered to the business partner.

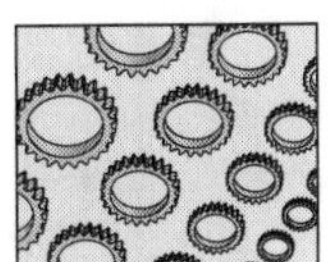

NOTE

A failure of the inner transaction does not cause a failure of the outer transaction. To keep the process from continuously flowing to the outer transaction should a failure occur in the inner transaction, you can use the decision shape at the exit point of the inner transaction. If no error occurs in the inner transaction, the process will continue to flow in the outer transaction. Otherwise, end the entire process.

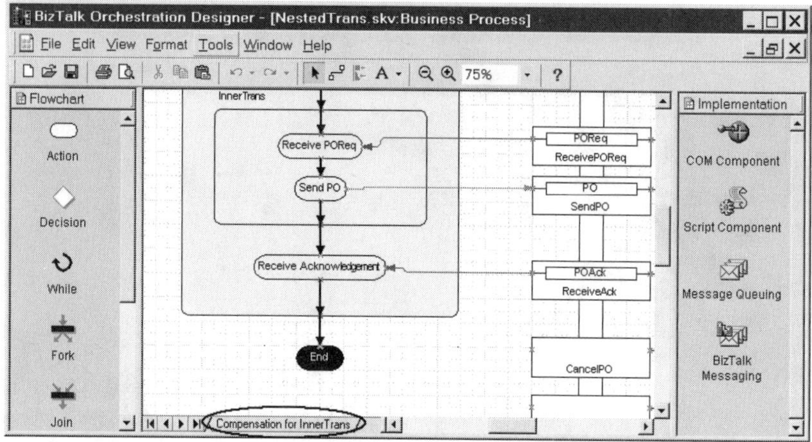

Figure 10-19 *A compensation page for the inner transaction*

Again, you use a single Data page to design the message flows for the Business Process, On Failure, and Compensation pages, as shown in Figure 10-21.

The XLANG schedule drawing and executable files (NestedTrans.skv and NestedTrans.skx, respectively) can be found in the \BTS_Transaction\Nested\Apps

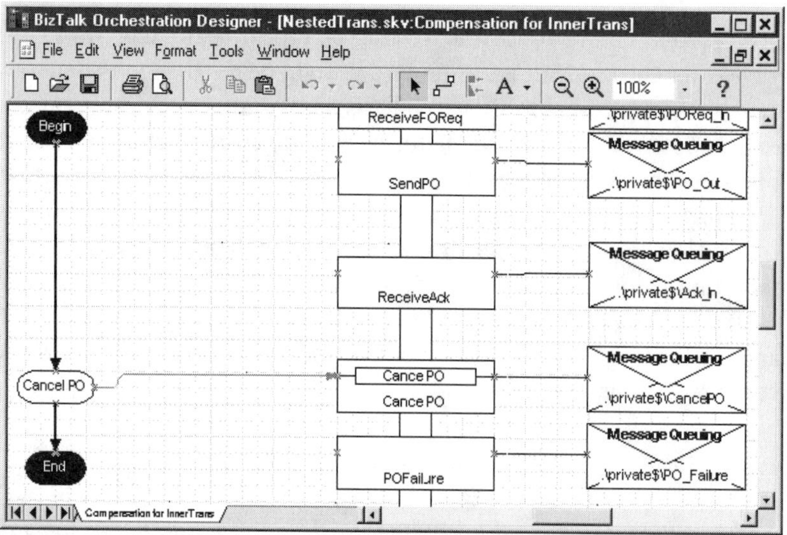

Figure 10-20 *The compensating action: Sending a cancellation message*

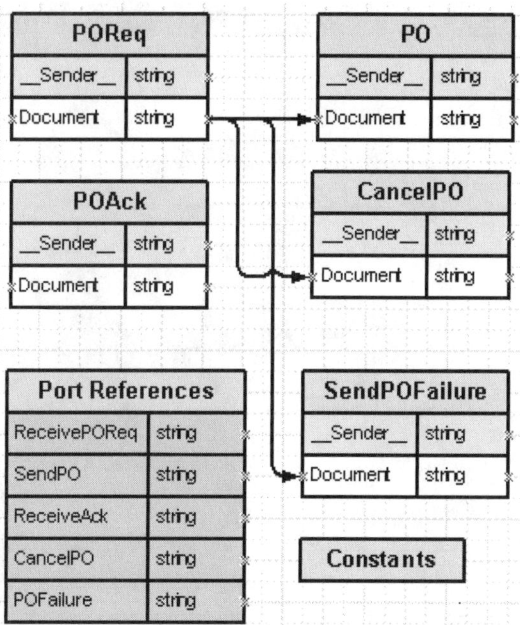

Figure 10-21 *The data flow of the nested transaction example*

folder. To set up this example, you can run the setup.cmd batch file, located in the \BTS_Transaction\Nested folder. (It is recommended you run the remove.cmd from the last example before running the setup.cmd, mostly because some of the queue names are shared between these two examples.)

Before starting the test, you need to enable the Journal for the Ack_In and POReq_In message queues. When messages arrive in these queues, the actions in the XLANG schedule will pick them up. So, by the end of the process, you can't see any messages left in these queues. You will have no idea whether the message arrived or not. The journaling feature of Microsoft Messaging Queuing Services, on the other hand, enables you to keep a copy of the messages that arrived and were picked up by other applications. To enable the journal, right-click the queue in the Computer Management MMC snap-in and select Properties. Check the Enabled box in the Journal section, as shown in Figure 10-22.

In the \BTS_Transaction\Nested\Apps folder, execute the VBScript file, NestedTrans.vbs, which will send a POReq message to the POReq_In message queue and kick up an instance of the NestedTrans.skx XLANG schedule. After

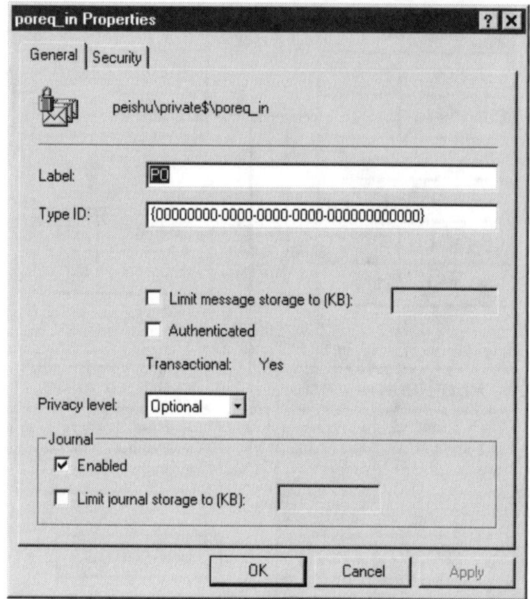

Figure 10-22 *Enabling the journal for a message queue*

waiting more than 20 seconds, check the message queues and you should find the following messages in corresponding queues:

Message Queue	Finding
Ack_In (Journal Messages)	No messages. There is no external application that sends messages to this queue during this test.
CancelPO	A PO message. Recall that when the nested, inner transaction is aborted (if the acknowledgment message dose not arrive within the timeout window), the Cancel PO action on the Compensation for InnerTrans page will send a PO message to the CancelPO queue.
PO_Failure	A PO message. Recall that the Notify ProcessPO Failure action on the On Failure Of OuterTrans page will send a PO message to the PO_Failure queue. In this test, it is caused by the timeout.
PO_Out	A PO message. Because the nested, inner transaction successfully committed. The message was sent to the PO_Out queue. In the real world, there should be another application that monitors and processes the messages in the PO_Out queue.
PO_In (Journal Messages)	A PO message, indicating the PO message arrived and was picked up.

Now, delete all the messages from the appropriate queues by right-clicking the Queue Messages node in the appropriate queue in the Computer Management MMC snap-in and choose, All Task | Purge… | Let's take another test. Run the NestedTrans.vbs script again, but this time run the SendAck.vbs script immediately (must be run within 30 seconds). If you check the message queues, you will find the following this time:

Message queue	Finding
Ack_In (Journal Messages)	A POAck message, indicating the POAck message arrived and was picked up.
CancelPO	No message. Everything went fine.
PO_Failure	No message. Everything went fine.
PO_Out	A PO message. Because the nested, inner transaction successfully committed. The message was sent to the PO_Out queue. In the real world, there should be another application that monitors and processes the messages in the PO_Out queue.
PO_In (Journal Messages)	A PO message, indicating the PO message arrived and was picked up.

Let's take a moment to summarize how the failures and compensations are handled for nested transactions in an XLANG schedule. When the inner transaction is committed, the changes made become permanent. If the outer transaction failed afterwards, the process defined in the On Failure page of the outer transaction will be executed to deal with failures of the outer transaction (there is no auto-rollback, however, because it is already committed). In addition, the process defined in the Compensation page for the inner transaction will also be triggered. You can define appropriate actions on this page to compensate for the committed transactions (for example, to simulate a rollback or report the overall outcome of the entire nested transaction). Notice that the Compensation page of the inner transaction is triggered by the failure of the outer transaction. You may also enable an On Failure page for the inner transaction (not used in this example) to handle the failures related to the inner transaction. It is important to understand that even though the inner transaction failed (aborted), the process will still flow to the downstream Action shape of the inner Transaction shape (in this example, the Receive Acknowledgement action). Unless an un-trappable system error occurs, the XLANG schedule instance won't be terminated. To prevent the XLANG schedule from continuing to flow when the inner transaction has failed, you can use a Decision shape between the inner Transaction shape and its immediate downstream Action shape to test the results of the inner transaction. Should the inner transaction fail, you can direct the flow to an appropriate Action shape that will force the XLANG schedule to terminate earlier.

Exception Handling

In addition to the transaction failure handling and compensation techniques you learned in previous sections of this chapter, you need to also deal with non-transactional related exceptions. These include exceptions caused by system errors or application designs.

Causes of Exceptions

XLANG errors fall into the following three categories, in order of increasing severity:

- Trappable Errors
- Errors that terminate XLANG schedule instances
- Errors that cause the XLANG Scheduler Engine to fail

Trappable Errors

Errors that can be trapped by the XLANG Scheduler Engine include COM errors and transaction abortions.

Transaction-related COM errors can be handled using techniques you learned in the previous sections, by employing On Failure and/or Compensation pages. You need to enable the error handling for a COM component or a script component so the transaction will be aborted should a COM error occur. You can do this on the last page of the COM or Script Component Binding Wizard by checking the Abort transaction if the method returns a failure HRESULT. Figure 10-23 illustrates the last page of the Script Component Binding Wizard for the AskForApproval action of the long-running example.

For non-transaction-related COM errors, you can use the logic branching technique. For example, the Display Item Count action in the Looping XLANG schedule drawing you saw in the last chapter, the DisplayItemCount of a COM component. The method call could be failed. Figure 10-24 illustrates a possible solution that tests for the COM error and action accordingly.

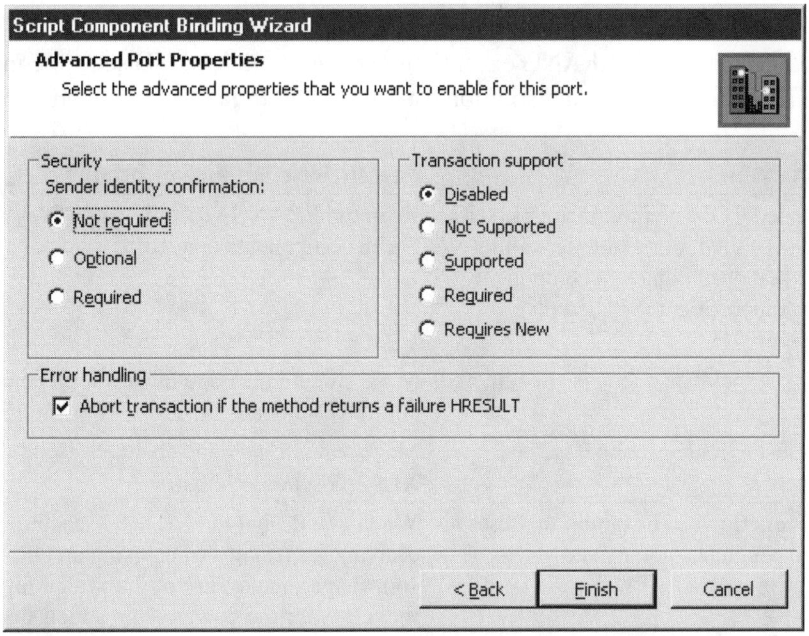

Script Component Binding Wizard

Advanced Port Properties

Select the advanced properties that you want to enable for this port.

Security
Sender identity confirmation:
(•) Not required
( ) Optional
( ) Required

Transaction support
(•) Disabled
( ) Not Supported
( ) Supported
( ) Required
( ) Requires New

Error handling
[x] Abort transaction if the method returns a failure HRESULT

< Back | Finish | Cancel

Figure 10-23 *Enable error handling for a script component in a transaction*

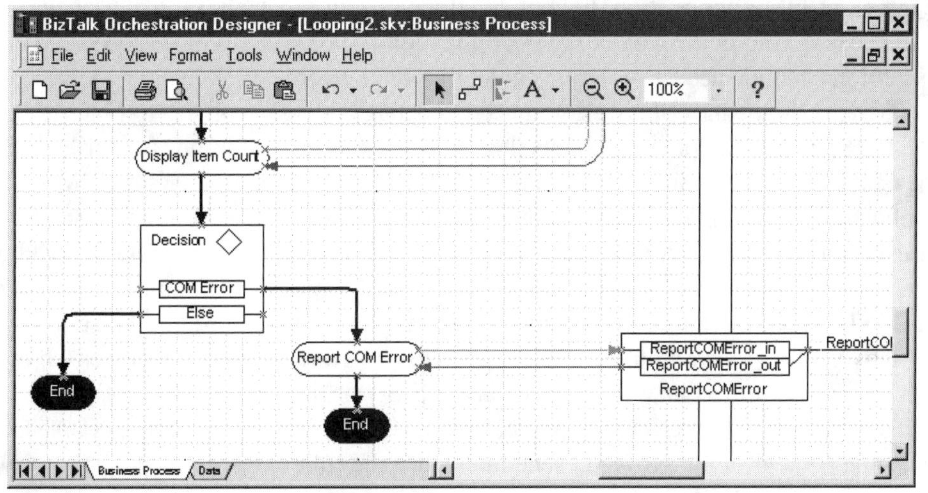

Figure 10-24 *Using logical branching to handle non-transactional COM errors*

Errors that Terminate XLANG Schedules

The second category of XLANG exceptions can cause the XLANG schedule instance to terminate. Their causes and solutions are described in the following table:

Cause of the Error	How to Avoid this Kind of Error
An outdated COM method in an XLANG schedule is called. For example, calling a GUID that doesn't have a component instance supporting it installed on the machine.	Keep the XLANG schedule and COM and/or Script components in sync.
A non-exist message queue is encountered.	Make sure all message queues used in an XLANG schedule exist.
A non-exist message channel is encountered.	Make sure all message channels used in an XLANG schedule exist.
The process flows to an action that uses a message which has not arrived yet.	When you design the XLANG schedule drawing (especially when using an OR Join shape), make sure of the availability of messages for the downstream action shapes.

Errors that Stop the XLANG Scheduler Engine

Exceptions in this category are not trappable and can cause the XLANG Scheduler Engine (a COM+ application) to shut down which can cause all XLANG schedule instances running in the same COM+ application to fail. Causes of these system exceptions include access violations and other fatal errors.

To avoid these kinds of errors, you need to debug and test your XLANG schedules and COM and/or Script components thoroughly, using the techniques described in the next section. In addition, it is recommended that you create separate COM+ applications for each XLANG schedule (or group of XLANG schedules) instead of using the default XLANG Scheduler COM+ application (the XLANG Scheduler Engine). A COM+ application is the Windows 2000 equivalent of an MTS package in Windows NT. Among other things, it provides a host for the running instance of ActiveX dlls (each running COM+ application will appear in the Processes tab of the Task Manager as entry, DllHost.exe (in MTS world, this was Mtx.exe)).

To create a Custom COM+ application to host instances for a specific XLANG schedule (or a group of XLANG schedules), use the following steps:

1. Create a COM+ application as a Server application, using the Component Services MMC snap-in.
2. Import appropriate COM+ component(s) into the COM+ application.

3. Specify that the COM+ application you created will be used as an XLANG Scheduler Engine by checking the This Application Is A Host For XLANG Schedule Instances check box on the XLANG tab of the property page of the COM+ application.
4. Create a DSN that points to the hydration SQL Server database (default name XLANG).

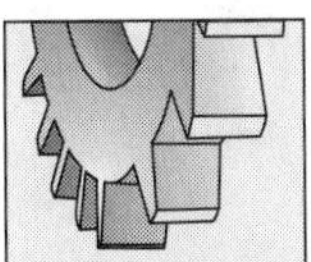

TIP

To learn more about COM+ applications, you can read Visual Basic and COM+ Programming By Example from Que.

To invoke an XLANG schedule inside a custom XLANG Scheduler Engine, use the moniker syntax. For example, if the COM+ application you created previously is named "My XLANG Scheduler", the moniker syntax will look like this:

Set oSked = GetObject("sked://!My XLANG Scheduler/ScheduleFileName.skx")

Debugging XLANG Schedules

Debugging an XLANG schedule is a complicated process. You need to use a variety of tools and techniques to thoroughly debug and test your XLANG schedules before rolling them out into production.

Using XLANG Event Monitor

BizTalk Server 2000 ships with a tool called XLANG Event Monitor (XLANGMon.exe), located in the <BizTalk Server Install>\SDK\XLANG Tools folder. This tool enables you to trace all events generated by running XLANG schedule instances in real time. You can use the XLANG Event Monitor to monitor running instances of XLANG schedules, track events, and to start and terminate XLANG schedule instances. You can also save the tracked events of instance to a file for later analysis.

The Readme.htm file, located in the same folder as the XLANG Event Monitor contains detailed information about how to use XLANG Event Monitor.

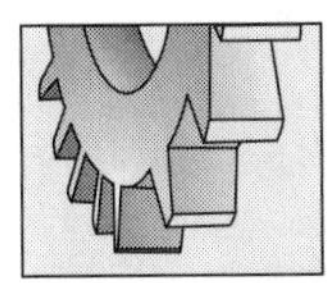

TIP

To make the XLANG Event Monitor functional, you need to have the Windows 2000 Service Pack 2 and BizTalk Server 2000 Service Pack 1 installed on your machine, You can download Windows 2000 Server service packs from the http://www.Microsoft.com/windows web site. BizTalk Server 2000 Service Pack 1 is available at http://www.microsoft.com/biztalk.

Using Event Log

Windows Event Log can be used as a convenient troubleshooting and debugging tool. The errors logged in the Event Log often provide supplemental information that can be used, along with other debugging tools, to help you pinpoint causes of problems. Look in the Application folder for BizTalk Server, XLANG Scheduler, and other sources for help in resolving problems.

Using Message Queuing

In addition to the journaling feature, in some cases (an invalid XML message, for example) BizTalk Orchestration Services may create private dead letter queues labeled Name_of_XLANG_Scheduler.DeadLetter (e.g., My XLANG Scheduler.DeadLetter). Remember that the name of the queue is case-sensitive, even though it appears in the Computer Management MMC snap-in in lower case.

Debugging COM Components

You can also set stop points inside your Visual Basic COM component to debug the same while the XLANG schedule instance is running. To enable this integrated debugging, you need to create a symbolic file (a .pdb file) when you compile your COM component into a DLL file. To do this, check the Create Symbolic Debug Info box on the Compile tab of the property page of your COM component Visual Basic project.

In addition, you can use Visual C++ IDE to debug your COM components by attaching it to the XLANG COM+ process ID and setting break points in your component.

Chapter in Review

In this chapter, you learned how to design XLANG schedules to handle transactions, including short-lived transactions, long-running transactions, and timed transactions. In addition, you learned how to handle different exceptions in your XLANG schedules, as well as how to debug and troubleshoot them.

PART

V

Extending BizTalk Server 2000

OBJECTIVES

- Building custom components to extend BizTalk Server 2000
- Integrating BizTalk Server 2000 with Commerce Server 2000

CHAPTER

11

Building Custom Components

IN THIS CHAPTER:

In previous chapters of this book, you learned about all the out-of-the-box features of BizTalk Server 2000. This knowledge, along with the various techniques discussed, will help you develop BizTalk solutions that can meet more than 95 percent of your integration needs (both EAI and B2B). In some instances, you may want to extend the functionalities provided in the BizTalk Server 2000 product box in order to solve specific problems. First, you may wish to increase your skills by extending the development environment of certain BizTalk Server tools, such as BizTalk Mapper. Secondly, you may need to preprocess a document before submitting it to BizTalk Server. For example, the file you received in a File receive function may be compressed in a binary format to reduce its size and quicken its transmission over the Internet. If so, you'll need to decompress the file first, and then submit it to BizTalk Server. Finally, you may want to send a document from BizTalk Server to a legacy line-of-business (LOB) application. Or perhaps you want to use some special transport protocols not directly supported in BizTalk Server 2000.

Fortunately, BizTalk Server 2000 provides an open architecture and the necessary infrastructure you need to extend its functionality by developing custom components to address these special requirements previously mentioned. In this chapter, you will learn how to leverage the extensible infrastructure of BizTalk Server 2000 to build custom components that meet your special needs. Specifically, you will learn how to build custom functoids to extend the functionality of BizTalk Mapper. You will also learn how to build preprocessors to handle special documents prior to their submission to BizTalk Server, as well as how to build so-called Application Integration Components (AIC or BizTalk Adapters) to extend BizTalk Server so it can speak to your legacy LOB applications or third-party products.

In Chapter 12, you will learn how to integrate BizTalk Server 2000 with Microsoft Commerce Server 2000 to build end-to-end e-Commerce solutions.

Building Custom Functoids

Recall that in Chapter 5, you learned that BizTalk Mapper is a great mapping tool which enables you to map the documents from one format (the inbound document format) to another format (the outbound document format) through drag-and-drop operations. For an efficient BizTalk Mapper user, creating a complex map takes about a couple of hours. Whereas, for a hardcore XSLT developer, creating an XSLT stylesheet that transforms a document to EDI format by hand typically takes a couple of days. In addition, BizTalk Mapper leverages an important technology to manage complex structural manipulation and mapping: functoids. Functoids are reusable functions implemented as a combination of XLST and scripting languages (currently VBScript), that leverage the support for the <msxsl:script> element in the Microsoft XSLT processor (which comes with MSXML 3.0 parser). BizTalk Mapper provides build-in functoids for string manipulation, mathematical calculation, logical reasoning, data/time conversion, character/numerical conversion, scientific calculation, cumulative aggregation, database accessing, and other complex operations. These built-in functoids are usually more than enough in most circumstances.

If you occasionally need some functionality not provided by the built-in functoids, you can use the *Scripting functoid*, found in the Advanced tab of the Functoid Palette to create per-link-based functions to fit your needs. Though powerful, these Scripting functoids have some shortcomings. First of all, they are not reusable—either inside or outside the map. To use even the same function provided by one Scripting functoid in a map, you have to create another Scripting functoid and rewrite the same script code by copying and pasting it. (It must have a different name though, as required by the uniqueness rule for functoid/function names.) Moreover, the Scripting functoids are not portable—they can not be used outside the BizTalk Mapper development instance in which they were created (without copying from the XLST file). If you find you are frequently writing the same sort of Scripting functoids over and over again, consider converting it to a custom functoid so it can be reused like any other built-in functoid.

BizTalk Server 2000 provides a necessary infrastructure for you to build custom functoids that can be plugged into the BizTalk Mapper development environment as if they were built-in functoids. In this section, you will start with an understanding of the required COM interface every custom functoid must implement. Then you will learn about the semantics of creating a custom functoid by implementing a single yet useful functoid that can extract the filename out of a valid path name from a field in the inbound document.

Understanding the IFunctoid Interface

A custom functoid is a COM component that implements a special interface—the *IFunctoid* interface. In Visual C++, you can directly implement the IFunctoid interface. In a higher-level language, such as Visual Basic, you can use the *CannedFunctoid* object equivalent. The IFunctoid interface or the Canned Functoid object is defined in the Microsoft BizTalk Server Canned Functoids 1.0 Type Library, CannedFunctoids.dll, located in the <BizTalk Server Installation>\XML Tools\ folder.

The custom functoid you created must register its *class identifier* (or *CLSID*) under a well-known *category identifier* (or *CATID*) in order for your custom functoid to be recognized by BizTalk Mapper. The IFunctoid interface or the CannedFunctoid object exposes specific properties and methods that determine the characteristics and behaviors of the custom functoid you want to create. In addition, the IFunctoid interface or the CannedFunctoid object defines four specific enumerations that determine what kind of connections to the functoid are allowed, which Functoid Palette tab the functoid will appear on, how it handles input parameters, which scripting language is supported, and so on.

Properties

The IFunctoid interface or the CannedFunctoid object supports two properties: *FunctionsCount* and *Version*.

The FunctionsCount Property Each custom functoid object you implement can support multiple functions. The FunctionsCount property returns a Long that indicates the number of functions implemented by a functoid. This is a read-only property.

The Version Property The Version property returns a Long that contains the custom functoid version. This is also a read-only property.

Methods

The IFunctoid interface or the CannedFunctoid object supports three methods: *GetFunctionParameter*, *GetFunctionDescripter*, and *GetScriptBuffer*.

The GetFunctionParameter Method The GetFunctionParameter method returns the connection-type bit flags (indicated by the CONNECTION_TYPE enumeration as we will explain shortly) for the specified parameter. The Visual Basic function stub of the GetFunctionParameter looks like this:

```
Public Function CannedFunctoid_GetFunctionParameter (
    ByVal funcId As Long, _
    ByVal lParameter As Long) As Long
```

Table 11-1 describes the parameters of the GetFunctionParameter method.

The GetFunctionDescripter Method The GetFunctionDescripter method retrieves information about a specific functoid. It returns a Long that contains the function identifier. The Visual Basic function stub of the GetFunctionDescripter looks like this:

```
Public Function CannedFunctoid_GetFunctionDescripter ( _
        ByVal lIndex As Long, _
        pFuncCategory As FUNC_CATEGORY, _
        pScriptCategory As SCRIPT_CATEGORY, _
        pFuncType As FUNC_TYPE, _
        pbstrName As String, _
        pbstrTooltip As String, _
        plBitmapID As Long, _
        plParmCount As Long) As Long
```

The GetFunctionDescripter method takes eight parameters, as described Table 11-2.

In the GetFunctionDescripter method, the first parameter, lIndex, is the only input parameter, denoted by the *ByVal* keyword. The rest of the parameters are all output parameters. You use them to instruct BizTalk Mapper as to what it should do about your custom functoid.

The GetScriptBuffer Method The GetScriptBuffer method returns a String containing the actual script code that implements a function for the functoid. The Visual Basic function stub of the GetScriptBuffer looks like this:

```
Public Function CannedFunctoid_GetScriptBuffer ( _
        ByVal cFuncId As Long, _
        ByVal lInputParameters As Long) As String
```

Enumerations

Table 11-3 describes the parameters of the GetScriptBuffer method.

Parameter	Description
funcId	A Long that contains the function identifier. Function identifiers from 0 to 1000 are reserved for built-in functions in the BizTalk Mapper. User-defined functions (custom functions) should use function identifiers 1001 and above.
lParameter	A Long that contains the function parameter number. For output parameters, a value of -1 is used.

Table 11-1 *Input parameters of the GetFunctionParameter method*

Parameter	Description
LIndex	A Long that specifies the index number of the function.
PfuncCategory	A value that specifies flags as indicated by a FUNC_CATEGORY enumeration for this function. As we will explain shortly, the FUNC_CATEGORY bit flag determines which tab your functoid will appear on in the Functoid Palette.
PscriptCategory	A value that specifies flags as indicated by a SCRIPT_CATEGORY enumeration for this function (as we will explain shortly in this chapter). Currently BizTalk Server 2000 only supports VBScript as the scripting language for functoid, so you must set its value to SCRIPT_CATEGORY_VBSCRIPT.
PfuncType	A value that specifies flags as indicated by a FUNC_TYPE enumeration for this function (to be explained shortly in this chapter).
PbstrName	A String that contains the function name. This name will be displayed as the first part of the tool tip when you move the mouse over the functoid icon in the Functoid Palette (prior to a colon). For example, *Function Name*: Tool tip text.
PbstrTooltip	A String that contains the contents of the tool tip. It will be displayed as the second part in the tool tip when you move the mouse over the functoid in the Functoid Palette (after a colon). For example, Function Name: *Tool tip text.*
PlBitmapID	A Long that contains the bitmap identifier of the bitmap used for the custom functoid icon displayed in the mapping tool. This is the value of the ID of the bitmap resource file you included in your VB or VC++ IDE.
PlParmCount	A Long that contains the number of parameters implemented by the function.

Table 11-2 *Input parameters of the GetFunctionDescripter method*

The Microsoft BizTalk Server Canned Functoids 1.0 Type Library defines four types of functoid enumerations that provide possible values of properties and parameters: CONNECTION_TYPE, FUNC_CATEGORY, FUNC_TYPE, and SCRIPT_CATEGORY.

CONNECTION_TYPE The value of the CONNECTION_TYPE enumeration determines what kind of objects (fields, records, other functoids, none, and so on) are allowed to be connected to the functoid, as described in Table 11-4.

Parameter	Description
CfuncId	A Long that contains the function identifier. Function identifiers from 0 to 1000 are reserved for built-in functions in the BizTalk Mapper. User-defined functions (custom functions) should use function identifiers 1001 and above.
lParameter	A Long that indicates the number of connected input parameters for the specified function.

Table 11-3 *Input parameters of the GetScriptBuffer method*

Enumeration Constant	Value	Description
CONNECT_TYPE_NONE	0	You cannot connect anything to this functoid.
CONNECT_TYPE_FIELD	1	You can connect fields to this functoid.
CONNECT_TYPE_RECORD	2	You can connect records to this functoid.
CONNECT_TYPE_RECORD_CONTENT	4	You can connect record contents to this functoid.
CONNECT_TYPE_FUNC_STRING	8	You can connect the functoids in the String tab of the Functoid Palette to this functoid.
CONNECT_TYPE_FUNC_MATH	16	You can connect the functoids in the Mathematical tab of the Functoid Palette to this functoid.
CONNECT_TYPE_FUNC_DATACONV	32	You can connect the functoids in the Conversion tab of the Functoid Palette to this functoid.
CONNECT_TYPE_FUNC_DATETIME_FMT	64	You can connect the functoids in the Date/Time tab of the Functoid Palette to this functoid.
CONNECT_TYPE_FUNC_SCIENTIFIC	128	You can connect the functoids in the Scientific tab of the Functoid Palette to this functoid.
CONNECT_TYPE_FUNC_BOOLEAN	256	You can connect the functoids in the Logical tab (that return boolean values) of the Functoid Palette to this functoid.

Table 11-4 *The CONNECTION_TYPE enumeration*

Enumeration Constant	Value	Description
CONNECT_TYPE_FUNC_SCRIPTER	512	You can connect a Scripting functoid in the Advanced tab of the Functoid Palette to this functoid.
CONNECT_TYPE_FUNC_COUNT	1024	You can connect a Record Count functoid in the Advanced tab of the Functoid Palette to this functoid.
CONNECT_TYPE_FUNC _INDEX	2048	You can connect an Index functoid in the Advanced tab of the Functoid Palette to this functoid.
CONNECT_TYPE_FUNC_CUMULATIVE	4096	You can connect the functoids in the Cumulative tab of the Functoid Palette to this functoid.
CONNECT_TYPE_FUNC_VALUE_MAPPING	8192	You can connect Value Mapping and Value Mapping (Flattening) functoids in the Advanced tab of the Functoid Palette to this functoid.
CONNECT_TYPE_FUNC_LOOPING	16384	You can connect a Looping functoid in the Advanced tab of the Functoid Palette to this functoid.
CONNECT_TYPE_FUNC_ITERATION	32768	You can connect an Iteration functoid in the Advanced tab of the Functoid Palette to this functoid.
CONNECT_TYPE_FUNC_DBLOOKUP	65526	You can connect a Database Lookup functoid in the Database tab of the Functoid Palette to this functoid.
CONNECT_TYPE_FUNC_DBEXTRACT	131072	You can connect a Value Extractor functoid in the Database tab of the Functoid Palette to this functoid.
CONNECT_TYPE_ALL	–1	You can connect any objects (fields, records, other functoids, and so on) that are appropriate to this functoid.
CONNECT_TYPE_ALL_EXCEPT_RECORD	-3	You can connect any objects *except for records* to this functoid.

Table 11-4 *The CONNECTION_TYPE enumeration(4)* (continued)

FUNC_CATEGORY The value of the CONNECTION_TYPE enumeration determines what specific type your functoid belongs to. Its value also determines which Functoid Palette tab your functoid icon will be displayed on. Table 11-5 describes the FUNC_CATEGORY enumeration.

Enumeration Constant	Value	Description
FUNC_CATEGORY_STRING	3	The functoid belongs to the string category and appears on the String tab in the Functoid Palette.
FUNC_CATEGORY_MATH	4	The functoid belongs to the mathematical category and appears on the Mathematical tab in the Functoid Palette.
FUNC_CATEGORY_DATACONV	5	The functoid belongs to the data conversion category and appears on the Conversion tab in the Functoid Palette.
FUNC_CATEGORY_DATETIME_FMT	6	The functoid belongs to the date/time category and appears on the Date/Time tab in the Functoid Palette.
FUNC_CATEGORY_SCIENTIFIC	7	The functoid belongs to the scientific category and appears on the Scientific tab in the Functoid Palette.
FUNC_CATEGORY_BOOLEAN	8	The functoid belongs to the boolean category and appears on the Logical tab in the Functoid Palette.
FUNC_CATEGORY_SCRIPTER	9	The functoid belongs to the script category and appears on the Advanced tab in the Functoid Palette.
FUNC_CATEGORY_COUNT*	10	The functoid belongs to the count category and appears on the Advanced tab in the Functoid Palette.
FUNC_CATEGORY_INDEX	11	The functoid belongs to the index category and appears on the Advanced tab in the Functoid Palette.
FUNC_CATEGORY_CUMULATIVE	12	The functoid belongs to the cumulative category and appears on the Cumulative tab in the Functoid Palette.
FUNC_CATEGORY_VALUE_MAPPING*	13	The functoid belongs to the value mapping category and appears on the Advanced tab in the Functoid Palette.
FUNC_CATEGORY_LOOPING*	14	The functoid belongs to the looping category and appears on the Advanced tab in the Functoid Palette.
FUNC_CATEGORY_ITERATION*	15	The functoid belongs to the iteration category and appears on the Advanced tab in the Functoid Palette.

Table 11-5 *The FUNC_CATEGORY enumeration*

Enumeration Constant	Value	Description
FUNC_CATEGORY_DBLOOKUP	16	The functoid belongs to the database lookup category and appears on the Database tab in the Functoid Palette.
FUNC_CATEGORY_DBEXTRACT	17	The functoid belongs to the value extractor category and appears on the Database tab in the Functoid Palette.
FUNC_CATEGORY_UNKNOWN	31	The category of the functoid is unknown.

* These category enumeration values are not supported in the current release of BizTalk Server 2000.

Table 11-5 *The FUNC_CATEGORY enumeration (continued)*

FUNC_TYPE The values of the FUNC_TYPE enumeration indicate the type of functions your functoid supports, as described in Table 11-6.

SCRIPT_CATEGORY The last enumeration, SCRIPT_CATEGORY, specifies which script language is used to implement the functions (described next in Table 11-7). The current release of BizTalk Server 2000 only supports VBScripts (SCRIPT_CATEGORY_VBSCRIPT) in its mapping engine (the compiler used by the Mapper).

Creating a Sample Functoid

In this section, you will create a sample functoid in Visual Basic, using the theory you learned in previous sections. The sample functoid you are going to implement extracts the filename from a given path name in the input field or record and outputs the filename to the output field or record. It is adapted from the sample date conversion functoid example of BizTalk Server 2000 SDK, found in <BizTalk Server Installation>\SDK\Messaging Samples\SampleFunctoid folder.

Enumeration Constant	Value	Description
FUNC_TYPE_STD	1	The function takes a fixed number of input parameters.
FUNC_TYPE_VARIABLEINPUT	2	The function can take a variable number of input parameters.
FUNC_TYPE_SCRIPTER	3	The function allows users to edit the script code.

Table 11-6 *The FUNC_TYPE enumeration*

Enumeration Constant	Value	Description
SCRIPT_CATEGORY_VBSCRIPT	0	Your functoid function is implemented in VBScript.
SCRIPT_CATEGORY_JSCRIPT	1	Your functoid function is implemented in JScript (note that JScript is a Microsoft scripting language similar to JavaScript but with subtle differences).
SCRIPT_CATEGORY_XSLSCRIPT	2	Your functoid function is implemented in XSLT. Currently this option is not available in BizTalk Server 2000.

Table 11-7 *The SCRIPT_CATEGORY enumeration*

Creating a custom functoid in Visual Basic involves the following steps:

1. Creating an in-process COM component (COM DLL) that implements the properties and methods of the CannedFunctoid interface.
2. Appropriately register (and add the category ID) to the COM component that implements the CannedFunctoid interface so it can be recognized by BizTalk Mapper at design time.
3. Test your custom functoid in BizTalk Mapper.

Creating the Custom Functoid COM Component

Creating the custom functoid COM Component involves setting up the development environment and implementing the CannedFunctoid interface.

Setting up the Development Environment First, you need to set up your development environment by doing the following:

1. Start a new ActiveX DLL project in Visual Basic 6.0 and naming the project *SampleFunctoid.*
2. Change the name of the class to *PathToFile*.
3. Set a reference in the VB project to Microsoft BizTalk Server Canned Functoids 1.0 Type Library by browsing to the CannedFunctoids.dll file, located in the <BizTalk Server Installation>\XML Tools\ folder, as shown in Figure 11-1.

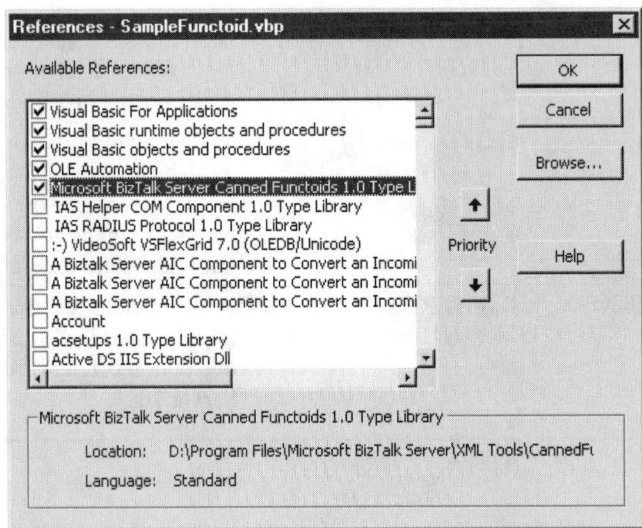

Figure 11-1 *Setting a reference to the CannedFunctoids type library*

Implementing the CannedFunctoid Interface In the General Declaration section of the class module (PathToFile.cls), add the following code:

```
Option Explicit
Implements CannedFunctoid
```

The *Implements* keyword makes the stubs of all the properties and methods available in the Visual Basic IDE (introduced in previous sections). We will discuss the code implementation of these stubs in a moment. First, we have to clear out a few things.

Following the Implements line of code, you define four constants that defines the ProgID, version of the functoid, maximum number of input parameters, and total number of functions:

```
Const PROGID = "SampleFunctoid.PathToFile"
Const VER = 1                   ' Version is 1
Const iMAX_PARAMS_c = 1         ' Max number of input parameters
Const CFUNCTOID = 1             ' Total number of functoids
```

In this particular example, the ProgID of your functoid is SampleFunctoid.PathToFile. The functoid starts with Version 1. You implement only one functoid in the component that takes a single input parameter.

The next block of constants defines the functoid identifier, the name and contents of the ToolTip, help information, bitmap identifier, the name and data type of the output parameter, the name, data type, and number of input parameters, and so on.

```
Const FUNCID_PATHTOFILE = 1010 ' Functoid identifier
Const FUNCNAME_PATHTOFILE = "Get File Name"
Const FUNCTOOLTIP_PATHTOFILE = _
      "Returns the file name given its path name"
Const FUNCHELP_PATHTOFILE = "This functoid requires one input " _
    & "parameter. The resulting output can be copied to multiple " _
    & "fields in the Destination Specification tree. This " _
    & "functoid converts a path name to a file name. " _
    & "For example: from C:\Northwind\PO.xml to PO.xml"
Const BITMAP_PATHTOFILE = 101
Const OUTPARAMTYPE_PATHTOFILE = "String"
Const OUTPARAMNAME_PATHTOFILE = "File name from path"
Const CINPUT_PATHTOFILE = 1
Const INPARAMTYPE_PATHTOFILE1 = "String"
Const INPARAMNAME_PATHTOFILE1 = "PathName"
```

The SCRIPTBUFFER_PATHTOFILE constant that follows hosts the entire script code of the function that the custom functoid will expose:

```
Const SCRIPTBUFFER_PATHTOFILE = _
    "Function FctFileName(p_strPath)" & vbNewLine _
    & "  Dim sPath, sFile" & vbNewLine _
    & "  On Error Resume Next" & vbNewLine _
    & "  sPath = StrReverse(p_strPath)" & vbNewLine _
    & "  sFile = Left(sPath,Instr(sPath,Chr(92))-1)" & vbNewLine _
    & "  sFile = StrReverse(sFile)" & vbNewLine _
    & "  If Err <> 0 Then" & vbNewLine _
    & "    FctFileName = ""Invalid path name""" & vbNewLine _
    & "  Else" & vbNewLine _
    & "    FctFileName = sFile" & vbNewLine _
    & "  End If" & vbNewLine _
    & "End Function " & vbNewLine
```

Next, you define a User Defined Type (UDT), FUNCTOIDINFO, to hold the structured data for the functoid:

```
Public Type FUNCTOIDINFO
    funcType As FUNC_TYPE                          'Type
    funcCatagory As FUNC_CATEGORY                  'Category
```

```
    scriptCatagory As SCRIPT_CATEGORY               'Script category
    funcId As Long                                  'FuncID
    funcName As String                          'Function Name
    tooltip As String                           'Function Tooltip
    helpFile As String                          'Helpfile
    bitMap As Long                              'Bitmap
    scriptBuffer As String                      'Script buffer
    outparamType As String                      'Output parameter type
    outparamName As String                      'Output argument name
    outparamConn As Long                        'Output argument
                                                'connection type
    cInput As Long                              'No of input args
    inputParamType(iMAX_PARAMS_c) As String     'Input parameter type
    inputParamName(iMAX_PARAMS_c) As String     'Input parameter name
    inputParamConn(iMAX_PARAMS_c) As Long       'Input parameter
                                                'connection type
End Type
```

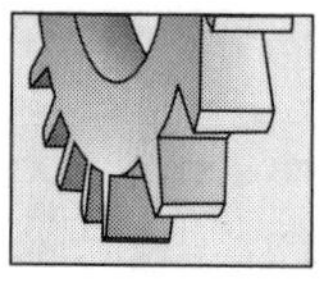

TIP

You should thoroughly test the script function using a stand-alone VBScript .vbs file before incorporating it into the functoid component. In this way, you can easily debug the function itself without complicating other issues associated with the functoid component.

Finally, you declare an array variable of type FUNCTOIDINFO, module level variables for holding the number of functions the functoid supports, and the version number of the functoid.

```
Private mvarFunctoid() As FUNCTOIDINFO
Private mvarFunctionsCount As Long
Private mvarVersion As Long
```

These module level variables are initialized in the *Initialize* event of the PathToFile class module:

```
Private Sub Class_Initialize()
    mvarFunctionsCount = CFUNCTOID
    mvarVersion = VER
    Call FunctoidInit(mvarFunctoid())
End Sub
```

Here is the code of the *FunctoidInit* helper function that initializes the array:

```
Private Sub FunctoidInit(functoid() As FUNCTOIDINFO)
    ReDim functoid(mvarFunctionsCount)
    functoid(0).funcType = FUNC_TYPE_STD
    functoid(0).funcCatagory = FUNC_CATEGORY_STRING
    functoid(0).scriptCatagory = SCRIPT_CATEGORY_VBSCRIPT
    functoid(0).funcId = FUNCID_PATHTOFILE
    functoid(0).funcName = FUNCNAME_PATHTOFILE
    functoid(0).tooltip = FUNCTOOLTIP_PATHTOFILE
    functoid(0).helpFile = FUNCHELP_PATHTOFILE
    functoid(0).bitMap = BITMAP_PATHTOFILE
    functoid(0).scriptBuffer = SCRIPTBUFFER_PATHTOFILE
    functoid(0).outparamType = OUTPARAMTYPE_PATHTOFILE
    functoid(0).outparamName = OUTPARAMNAME_PATHTOFILE
    functoid(0).outparamConn = CONNECT_TYPE_ALL
    functoid(0).cInput = CINPUT_PATHTOFILE
    functoid(0).inputParamType(0) = INPARAMTYPE_PATHTOFILE1
    functoid(0).inputParamName(0) = INPARAMNAME_PATHTOFILE1
    functoid(0).inputParamConn(0) = CONNECT_TYPE_ALL
End Sub
```

As you can see, the array is initialized with some of the constants you defined at the top, as well as some enumeration constants we discussed earlier in this chapter.

Now let's look at how the properties and methods of the CannedFunctoid interface are implemented, starting with the two properties, Version and FunctionsCount. The implementation of these two read-only properties are very straightforward:

```
Public Property Get CannedFunctoid_Version() As Long
    CannedFunctoid_Version = VER
End Property

Public Property Get CannedFunctoid_FunctionsCount() As Long
    CannedFunctoid_FunctionsCount = mvarFunctionsCount
End Property
```

Next, let's see the implementation of the three methods of the CannedFunctoid interface. Here is the GetFunctionDescripter function:

```
Public Function CannedFunctoid_GetFunctionDescripter( _
    ByVal lIndex As Long, _
    pFuncCategory As FUNC_CATEGORY, _
    pScriptCategory As SCRIPT_CATEGORY, _
    pFuncType As FUNC_TYPE, _
```

```
    pbstrName As String, _
    pbstrTooltip As String, _
    plBitmapID As Long, _
    plParmCount As Long) As Long

    If lIndex < 0 Or lIndex >= mvarFunctionsCount Then
        Err.Raise 5
        Exit Function
    End If

    pFuncCategory = mvarFunctoid(lIndex).funcCatagory
    pScriptCategory = mvarFunctoid(lIndex).scriptCatagory
    pFuncType = mvarFunctoid(lIndex).funcType
    pbstrName = mvarFunctoid(lIndex).funcName
    pbstrTooltip = mvarFunctoid(lIndex).tooltip
    plBitmapID = mvarFunctoid(lIndex).bitMap
    plParmCount = mvarFunctoid(lIndex).cInput

    CannedFunctoid_GetFunctionDescripter =
mvarFunctoid(lIndex).funcId
End Function
```

Information such as the function category, script category, type and name of the function, ToolTip, bitmap, input parameter count, and so on are communicated to BizTalk Mapper by means of output parameters. The function returns the value of the function identifier.

Next, the GetFunctionParameter function returns the Connect Type for a functoid parameter for the given input function identifier and parameter:

```
Public Function CannedFunctoid_GetFunctionParameter( _
    ByVal funcId As Long, _
    ByVal lParameter As Long) As Long

    Dim i As Long
    Dim bValid As Boolean
    bValid = False

    If lParameter < -1 Or _
       lParameter > iMAX_PARAMS_c - 1 Then
        Err.Raise 5
        CannedFunctoid_GetFunctionParameter = _
            CONNECT_TYPE_NONE
```

```
    Else
        For i = 0 To mvarFunctionsCount - 1
            If mvarFunctoid(i).funcId = funcId Then
                bValid = True
                Exit For
            End If
        Next
        If bValid = False Then
            Err.Raise 5 'Invalid procedure call or argument
            CannedFunctoid_GetFunctionParameter = _
                CONNECT_TYPE_NONE
        Else
            CannedFunctoid_GetFunctionParameter = _
                GetConnectType(i, lParameter)
        End If
    End If
End Function
```

If everything goes fine, the GetFunctionParameter calls a helper function *GetConnectType* to get the Connect Type. The GetConnectType function looks like this:

```
Private Function GetConnectType( _
    ByVal ind As Long, _
    ByVal lParameter As Long) As Long
        If lParameter = -1 Then
        GetConnectType = mvarFunctoid(ind).outparamConn
    Else
        GetConnectType = mvarFunctoid(ind).inputParamConn(lParameter)
    End If
End Function
```

Depending on whether the parameter being passed is an input or output parameter, the GetConnectType returns the Connect Type information accordingly.

Finally comes the GetScriptBuffer function, which submits the script code to BizTalk Mapper by calling the *GetScriptBuffer* helper function:

```
Public Function CannedFunctoid_GetScriptBuffer( _
    ByVal cFuncId As Long, _
    ByVal lInputParameters As Long) As String

    Dim i As Long
    Dim bValid As Boolean
    bValid = False
```

```
    For i = 0 To mvarFunctionsCount - 1
        If mvarFunctoid(i).funcId = cFuncId Then
            bValid = True
            Exit For
        End If
    Next
    If bValid = False Then
        Err.Raise 5
        CannedFunctoid_GetScriptBuffer = ""
    Else
        CannedFunctoid_GetScriptBuffer = GetScriptBuffer(i,
lInputParameters)
    End If
End Function
```

The GetScriptBuffer helper function simply returns the script buffer for the appropriate function (you only implemented one script function in this example):

```
Private Function GetScriptBuffer( _
    ByVal ind As Long, _
    ByVal lInputParameters As Long) As String

    GetScriptBuffer = mvarFunctoid(ind).scriptBuffer
End Function
```

Before you can compile your source code, you also need to include the bitmap file in your project that will show up in the Functoid Palette as a small icon. You can include the bitmap as a resource file as shown in Figure 11-2 (it is a 16×16 .bmp file).

Registering the Custom Functoid COM Component

In order for BizTalk Mapper to recognize that your custom COM component is in fact a functoid, you will first need to register your COM DLL by executing the Regsvr32.exe (this step can be skipped if you compile the DLL from inside Visual Basic, which takes care of registering the COM DLL automatically). Then you also need to include a specific category ID, or CATID, subkey under the Implemented Categories subkey of the CLSID of your component. The CATID for functoids is {2560F3BF-DB47-11D2-B3AE-00C04F72D6C1}, as shown in Figure 11-3.

To facilitate this registry setting process, a registry importing file, SampleFunctoid.reg, is included in this chapter's source code (located in the \Functoid folder). Its contents look like this:

```
Windows Registry Editor Version 5.00
[HKEY_CLASSES_ROOT\CLSID\{4476D504-D098-445C-89C9-6341C74F653F}\Imple
mented Categories\{2560F3BF-DB47-11d2-B3AE-00C04F72D6C1}]
```

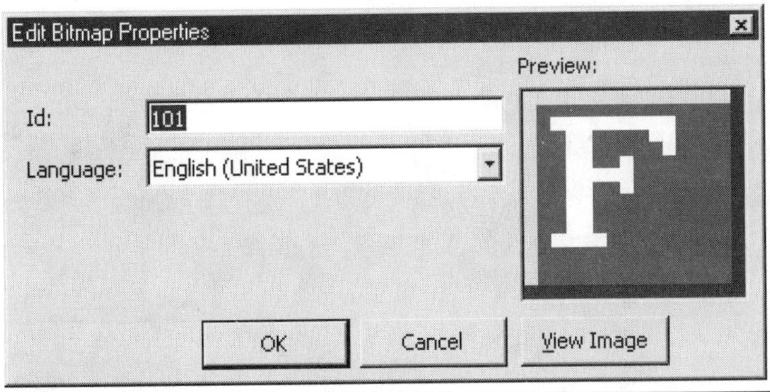

Edit Bitmap Properties

Preview:

Id: 101

Language: English (United States)

OK Cancel View Image

Figure 11-2 *Including the bitmap as a resource file*

The first highlighted GUID is the CLSID of your COM DLL that implements the CannedFunctoid interface. The second GUID is the aforementioned CATID. By double-clicking on this .reg file, the CATID will be automatically written in under the Implemented Categories subkey of the CLSID.

To create a .reg file for a different custom functoid COM component, simply replace the CLSID in the preceding .reg file with the CLSID of your COM component and save the .reg file under a different name. You can find the CLSID under the HKEY_CLASS_ROOT\ProgID\Clsid key.

Testing Your Custom Functoid

Having created and appropriately registered your custom functoid component, you can now open BizTalk Mapper. If you click the View Functoid Palette button on the toolbar, you should see that a new "F" functoid has been added to the String tab. If you move the mouse over the new functoid, the ToolTip should be displayed (as shown in Figure 11-4).

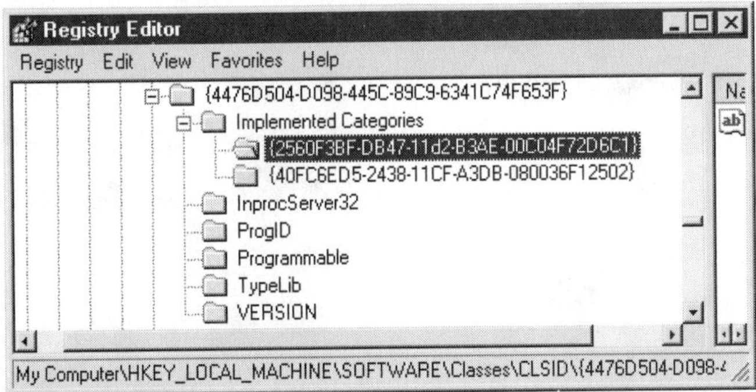

Figure 11-3 *Including a special CATID for the custom functoid component*

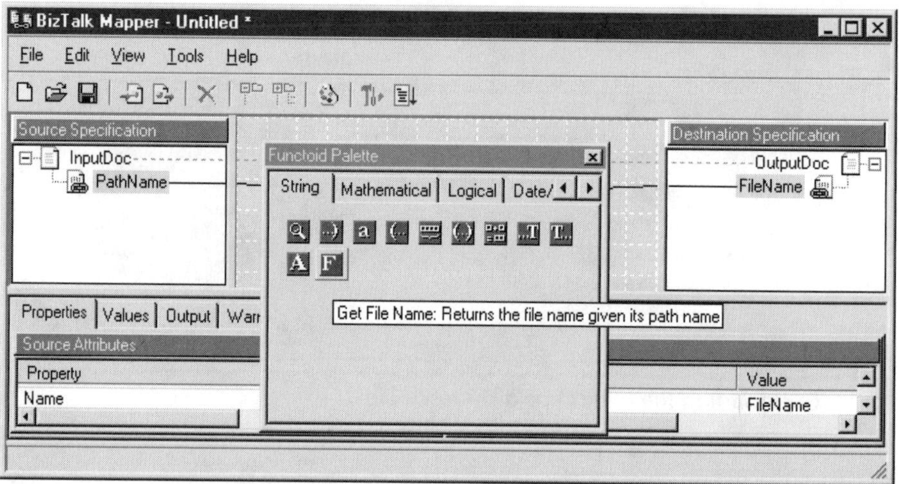

Figure 11-4 *Your custom functoid is displayed in the Functoid Palette*

To help test your custom functoid, we have provided two simple schemas—InDocSchema.xml and OutDocSchema.xml—located under the \Functoid folder. You can load these schemas into BizTalk Mapper by clicking the New button and selecting Local Files for both source and destination specifications, then pointing to the right schemas. The BizTalk Mapper design environment should now resemble the one in Figure 11-5.

As you can see in Figure 11-5, the source and destination specifications are extremely simple—both contain a single node under a root node. An instance of the source specification may look like this:

```
<InputDoc>
  <PathName>C:\Program Files\Microsoft BizTalk Server\
    BizTalkServerRepository\DocSpecs\CommonPO.xml
  </PathName>
</InputDoc>
```

While an instance of the destination specification would look like the following:

```
<OutputDoc>
  <FileName>CommonPO.xml</FileName>
</OutputDoc>
```

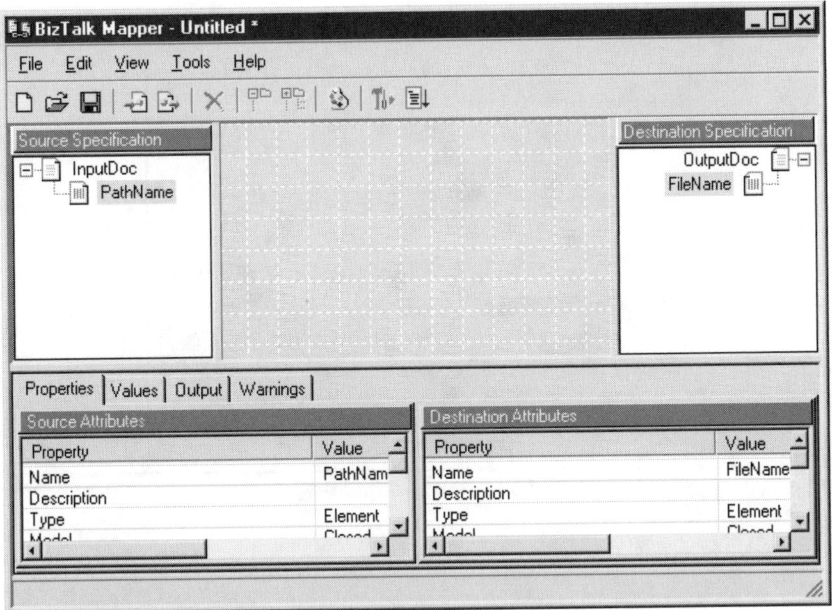

Figure 11-5 *Loading two schemas into BizTalk Mapper*

Now, open the Functoid Palette if it is closed and drag an "F" functoid from the String tab onto the grid area of BizTalk Mapper. Double-click the functoid to bring up its Functoid Properties page. Click the Script tab. It should display the script function you implemented in the custom functoid component, FctFileName, as shown in Figure 11-6.

Now close the Functoid Properties dialog box. Connect the PathName record in the source specification to the functoid, and then connect the functoid to the FileName record in the destination specification. You are now ready to test your functoid. Click the Values tab in the lower pane of BizTalk Mapper, then type in a path name in the Source test value box such as C:\Program Files\Microsoft BizTalk Server\BizTalkServerRepository\DocSpecs\CommonPO.xml. Click Tools, Test Map, and answer No in the confirmation dialog box when asked to save changes to the map source. The Output tab of the lower pane of BizTalk Mapper should now look like the one in Figure 11-7. This is exactly what you expected.

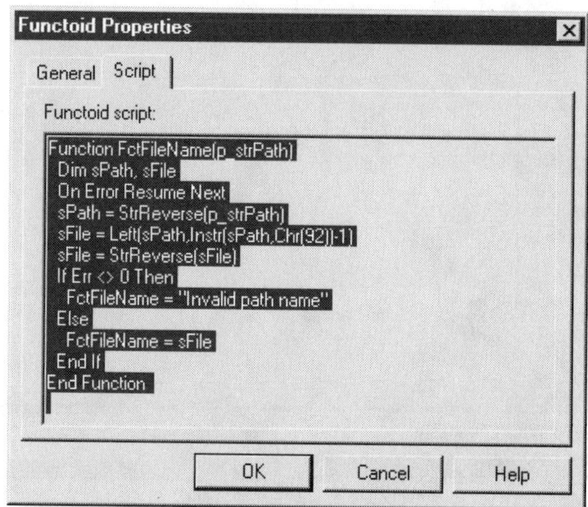

Figure 11-6 *The script function of your custom functoid*

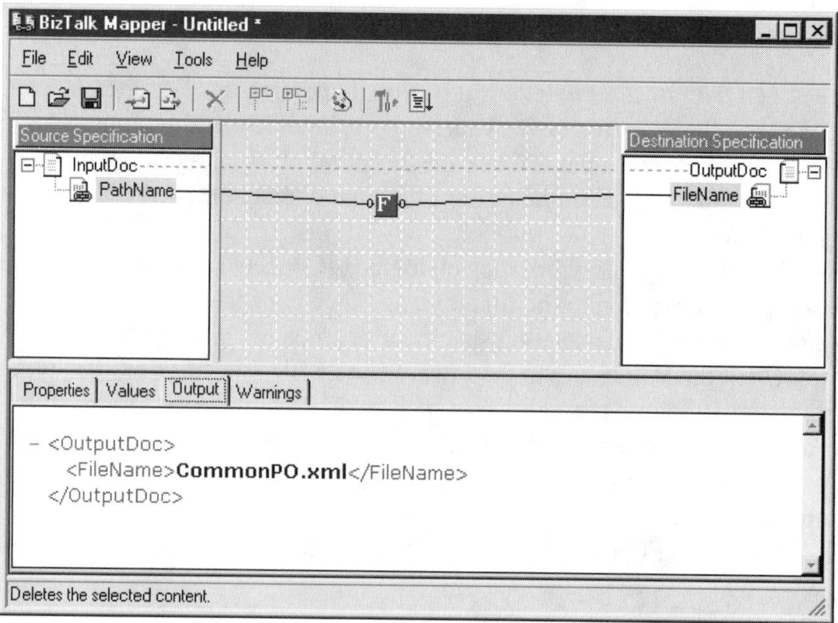

Figure 11-7 *The testing result of your custom functoid*

Building Custom Preprocessors

Recall that in Chapter 3 we briefly mentioned you can choose to specify a custom preprocessor in a receive function to handle some preliminary processes to the inbound document before submitting it to BizTalk Server, such as unzipping a compressed document, or performing whatever actions are appropriate to the document. In this section, you will learn how to create a custom preprocessor in Visual Basic and use it in a Messaging Queuing receive function to fix an ill-formed XML document into a well-formed one and then submit it to BizTalk Server. Similar to creating a custom functoid, to implement a custom preprocessor in Visual Basic, you need to create a COM component that implements a specific interface, IBTSCustomProcess, which is defined in the Microsoft BizTalk Server Application Interface Components 1.0 Type Library, btscomplib.tlb, located in the <BizTalk Server Installation>\ folder.

The IBTSCustomProcess Interface

The IBTSCustomProcess is a simple COM interface that has only two methods: *SetContext* and *Execute*.

The SetContext Method

When a document is received by a receive function that has a preprocessor specified, the SetContext method is called first, followed by an *IBTSCustomProcessContext* object, as illustrated in the following Visual Basic function stub:

```
Private Sub IBTSCustomProcess_SetContext( _
        ByVal pCtx As BTSComponentsLib.IBTSCustomProcessContext)
```

The IBTSCustomProcessContext object has nine properties that give you an opportunity to retrieve appropriate context information or receive function-related properties—those properties that are available in the Advanced tab of the Properties dialog box of a receive function. Table 11-8 describes the properties of the IBTSCustomProcessContext object.

You can retrieve a channel property using this syntax:

```
strPropertyName = pCtx.PropertyName
```

For example:

```
strChannelName = pCtx.ChannelName
strDestID = pCtx.DestID
......
```

Property	Data Type	Description
ChannelName	String	The name of the channel.
DestID	String	The value of the destination organization qualifier.
DestQualifier	String	The type of the destination organization qualifier.
DocName	String	The name of the inbound document definition.
EnvelopeName	String	The name of the envelope used with the inbound document.
Openness	Long	The openness flag.
PassThrough	Long	The pass-through flag.
SourceID	String	The value of the source organization qualifier.
SourceQualifier	String	The type of the source organization qualifier.

Table 11-8 *The properties of the IBTSCustomProcessContext object*

The Execute Method

The Execute method is called followed by the call to the SetContext method. Its stub in Visual Basic looks like this:

```
Private Sub IBTSCustomProcess_Execute( _
        ByVal vDataIn As Variant, _
        ByVal nCodePageIn As Long, _
        ByVal bIsFilePath As Boolean, _
        nCodePageOut As Variant, _
        vDataOut As Variant)
```

As you can see, the Execute method takes three input parameters (denoted by the ByVal keywords) and two output parameters (as described in Table 11-9).

Creating a Custom Preprocessor

Now let's create a simple custom preprocessor for a Messaging Queuing receive function. The original document received by the Message Queuing receive function looks like this:

```
<PO Id ="10001">
<Item id="001" qty="10" price="15"/>
<Item id="002" qty="5" price="20"/>
</PO>
<PO Id ="10002">
<Item id="003" qty="15" price="3.99"/>
```

Parameter	Data Type	Description
vDataIn	Variant	An input parameter that contains the data being received by the receive function. Depending on the type of the receive function, it could be the name of the file path (for File receive function) or the document itself (in the case of a Message Queuing receive function). You use this parameter to get the input document data.
nCodePageIn	Long	An input parameter that contains the code page of the input data (indicating the character set and keyboard layout used on a computer).
bIsFilePath	Boolean	A flag that indicates the type of the receive function—True for the File receive function; False for the Message Queuing receive function.
nCodePageOut	Variant	An output parameter that contains the code page of the output data (indicating the character set and keyboard layout used on a computer).
vDataOut	Variant	An output parameter that contains the output data. You use this parameter to send the document back to BizTalk Server.

Table 11-9 *The parameters of the Execute method*

```
<Item id="004" qty="20" price="12.99"/>
</PO>
```

It is a master purchase order document that contains two individual purchase orders. Whereas each <PO> node is a well-formed XML document, the structure of the entire document violates the rule of being a well-formed XML document because of the lack of a single root element. To fix it, you simply use a preprocessor that prepares the document by wrapping it under a single root XML element, <PurchaseOrders>, so the new document becomes a well-formed XML document before being submitted to BizTalk Server.

Setting up the Development Environment

Start a new Visual Basic ActiveX DLL project and name the project and class module *SamplePreProcessor* and *PreProcessor*, respectively. Set project references to the following type libraries:

- The Microsoft BizTalk Server Application Interface Components 1.0 Type Library
- The Microsoft ActiveX Data Objects 2.6 Library

- The Microsoft XML v3.0
- The Microsoft Scripting Runtime

Implementing the IBTSCustomProcess Interface

In the General Declaration section of the class module, add the following lines:

```
Option Explicit
Implements IBTSCustomProcess
```

The implements keyword makes the method stubs of the IBTSCustomProcess available to the class module. In this example, you are not going to code the SetContext method, but you still need to implement an empty function to comply with the COM interface rule so it looks like this:

```
Private Sub IBTSCustomProcess_SetContext( _
    ByVal pCtx As _
    BTSComponentsLib.IBTSCustomProcessContext)
    'Do nothing
End Sub
```

The majority of the code goes to the Execute method:

```
Private Sub IBTSCustomProcess_Execute( _
    ByVal vDataIn As Variant, _
    ByVal nCodePageIn As Long, _
    ByVal bIsFilePath As Boolean, _
    nCodePageOut As Variant, _
    vDataOut As Variant)

    Dim oXML As New MSXML2.DOMDocument
    Dim sPO As String
    On Error Resume Next
    If bIsFilePath = False Then
       sPO = "<PurchaseOrders>" & vbNewLine _
           & vDataIn & vbNewLine _
           & "</PurchaseOrders>"

        oXML.async = False
        oXML.loadXML sPO
        vDataOut = oXML.xml
        If Err <> 0 Then
```

```
            Err.Raise vbObjectError + 1, _
            "BTSCustomProcess_Execute", _
            "Unable to load the document"
        End If
    Else
        Err.Raise vbObjectError + 2, _
          "BTSCustomProcess_Execute", _
          "This BTSCustomProcess may only " & _
          "be used for MSMQ receive functions"
    End If
End Sub
```

The method first tests the bIsFilePath flag to make sure the document is received by a Message Queuing receive function and then concatenates a starting tag <PurchaseOrders>, the original document, and an ending tag </PurchaseOrders> to a well-formed XML document. Next, the method tries to load the new document into a DOMDocument object to ensure the document is indeed well-formed. If the loading process succeeds, the XML string of the document is passed back to BizTalk Server via the vDataOut output parameter.

Registering the Preprocessor Component

The registration process for a preprocessor component is similar to that of a custom functoid component—you first need to register the COM component that implements the IBTSCustomProcess interface and then include a specific CATID -{20E8080F-F624-4401-A203-9D99CF18A6D9} under the CLSID of the COM component. Again, this can be achieved by creating a reg file like the following:

```
Windows Registry Editor Version 5.00
[HKEY_CLASSES_ROOT\CLSID\{CCE67D0F-4370-405D-859D-F7C29DE74DD1}\Implemented
Categories\{20E8080F-F624-4401-A203-9D99CF18A6D9}]
```

The first GUID is your CLSID and the second GUID is the CATID for preprocessor components.

Testing Your Preprocessor Component

In the source code of this chapter, you can find a VBScript file, PreprocessorBTMSetup.vbs, located in the \Preprocessor sub folder. This file will create necessary messaging objects for you to test your preprocessor component.

Next, you need to create a transactional private queue, Northwind_PO, and a Message Queuing receive function with the following properties:

Name: Receive PO Docs
Polling location: Direct=OS:.\private$\Northwind_PO

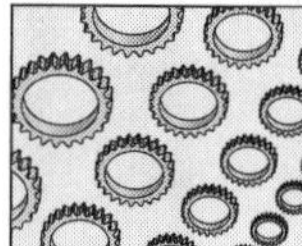

NOTE

Make sure that BTM has access to the Message Queuing private queues by adding the BTM user permissions, or if you're lazy, just set the permissions to Everyone Full.

Preprocessor: **SamplePreProcessor.Preprocessor**
Openness: Not open
Envelope name: <None>
Channel name: PO Channel

Finally, you need to create a folder C:\Northwind for the messaging port to transport the final PO document.

You can run another VBScript file, SendPO2Q.vbs, also located in the \Preprocessor folder. This script file sends the aforementioned ill-formed master purchase order to the private queue, Northwind_PO, which will be picked up by the receive function. The preprocessor will be invoked upon the arrival of the document and a preprocessed purchase order document will be sent to the PO Channel, then transported to C:\Northwind folder by the messaging port, PO Port. The final PO looks like the one in Figure 11-8, exactly as you expected.

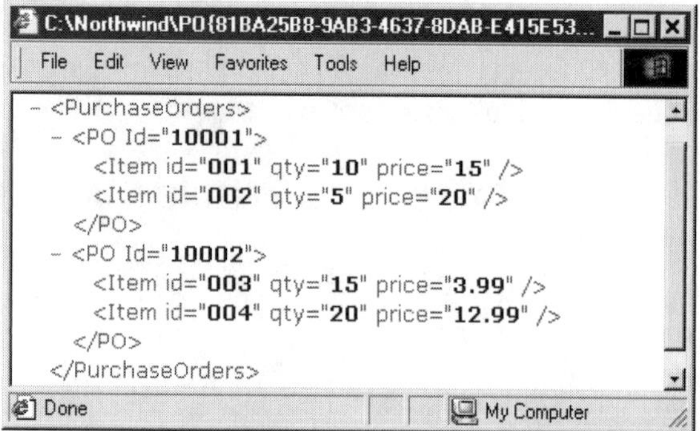

Figure 11-8 *The final purchase order document*

Building Application Integration Components

As you learned in previous chapters, BizTalk Server 2000 Messaging Services supports a series of transport protocols for transmitting the documents to the destinations, including Files, HTTP/HTTPS, Message Queuing, SMTP, and so on. For transmitting documents to destinations using other protocols or proprietary APIs, BizTalk Server supports an open architecture by means of *Application Integration Components* or AICs. AICs are special COM components that implement specific COM interfaces which can be invoked by messaging ports to extend BizTalk Server Messaging Services. AICs are also known as *BizTalk Adapters*. By using an appropriate adapter, you can extend the reach of BizTalk Server to virtually any system and application, such as line-of-business (LOB) systems, legacy systems, third-party ERP systems, and so on.

Depending on your flexibility, functionality, and simplicity, you can use three types of BizTalk AIC components or adapters, including:

- Lightweight AIC components
- Pipeline AIC components
- Scriptor AIC components.

Building a Lightweight AIC Component

Lightweight AIC components are COM components that implement a simple interface, *IBTSAppIntegration*, which is also provided in the Microsoft BizTalk Server Application Interface Components 1.0 Type Library (btscomplib.tlb).

The IBTSAppIntegration Interface

The IBTSAppIntegration interface has only one method, *ProcessMessage*, which takes a string input parameter—the content of the outbound document, such as the following:

```
Private Function IBTSAppIntegration_ProcessMessage( _
ByVal bstrDocument As String) As String
```

And returns it as a response string.

Creating an FTP Adapter

Sending documents out using FTP (File Transfer Protocol) is not directly supported in BizTalk Server 2000. Using the AIC approach, you can easily build an FTP adapter that can be plugged into BizTalk Server Messaging Services as if it were a native transport protocol for you to FTP documents to your trading partners.

To build an FTP Adapter (AIC) in Visual Basic, you first need to create an ActiveX DLL project, let's call it *AIC_FTP,* and change the name of the class module to *FTPAdapter.* Of course, you need to set a reference in your project to the Microsoft BizTalk Server Application Interface Components 1.0 Type Library.

To do FTP in Visual Basic, you can leverage the WinInet APIs, as documented in a Microsoft Knowledge Base article, *Q175179 - Sample: VBFTP.EXE: Implementing FTP Using WinInet API from VB.* Should you need to add a standard module, WININET.Bas can be downloaded from this KB article's Web page. This WININET.Bas contains the necessary API declarations and constants you can use in the class module. As you may have already realized, writing an FTP adapter is really just writing a COM-based WinInet API wrapper.

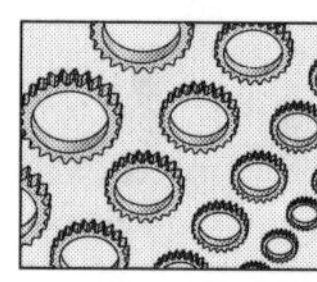

NOTE

WinInet is a client-side dll that is neither thread-safe nor server-side optimized. This FTP adapter is for demonstration purposes and will generally work fine under low load but will start to experience failures under high load. Companies such as www.xceedsoft.com have created thread-safe, MTA FTP AICs for production environments.

In the General Declaration area of your class module, add the following lines of code:

```
Option Explicit
Dim bActiveSession As Boolean
Dim hOpen As Long, hConnection As Long
Dim dwType As Long
Implements IBTSAppIntegration
```

The first few lines declare module level variables for tracking the session, connections, and so on. The Implements keyword of the last line makes the methods of the IBTSAppIntegration interface available in the class module. In this case, it's the ProcessMessage method, whose implementation looks like this:

```
Private Function IBTSAppIntegration_ProcessMessage( _
    ByVal bstrDocument As String) As String

    Dim oXML As New MSXML2.DOMDocument
    Dim sFTPServer As String
```

```
    Dim sUID As String
    Dim sPWD As String
    Dim sLocalDIR As String
    Dim sRemoteDIR As String
    Dim oHeader As Object
    Dim oChild As Object
    On Error GoTo ProcessMessage_Err

    oXML.async = False
    oXML.loadXML bstrDocument

    sFTPServer = oXML.selectSingleNode("//FTP/@Server").nodeValue
    sUID = oXML.selectSingleNode("//FTP/@UID").nodeValue
    sPWD = oXML.selectSingleNode("//FTP/@PWD").nodeValue
    sLocalDIR = oXML.selectSingleNode("//FTP/@LocalDIR").nodeValue
    sRemoteDIR = oXML.selectSingleNode("//FTP/@RemoteDIR").nodeValue

    Set oHeader = oXML.selectSingleNode("//Header")
    Set oChild = oXML.selectSingleNode("//FTP")
    oHeader.removeChild oChild
    oXML.save sLocalDIR

    If OpenConnection(sFTPServer, sUID, sPWD) Then
        If Upload(sLocalDIR, sRemoteDIR) Then
            CloseConnection
        End If
    End If

    IBTSAppIntegration_ProcessMessage = "ack"
    Exit Function
ProcessMessage_Err:
    Err.Raise Err.Number, Err.Source, Err.Description
End Function
```

This function assumes there is an <FTP> element somewhere in the document that provides login and other information about the FTP server such as the name of the server, the user ID and password, the location of the file you want to upload (FTP), the remote location where you want to upload the file, and so on, in forms of XML attributes. The function loads the file into a DOMDocument object and retrieves appropriate information from the <FTP> node, storing them in local variables:

```
On Error Resume Next
oXML.loadXML bstrDocument
sFTPServer = oXML.selectSingleNode("//FTP/@Server").nodeValue
```

```
sUID = oXML.selectSingleNode("//FTP/@UID").nodeValue
sPWD = oXML.selectSingleNode("//FTP/@PWD").nodeValue
sLocalDIR = oXML.selectSingleNode("//FTP/@LocalDIR").nodeValue
sRemoteDIR = oXML.selectSingleNode("//FTP/@RemoteDIR").nodeValue
```

It then removes the <FTP> node (since it only provides FTP-related transmission information and is not needed by the document recipient) and saves the manipulated XML document in a local location specified by the LocalDIR XML attribute:

```
Set oHeader = oXML.selectSingleNode("//Header")
Set oChild = oXML.selectSingleNode("//FTP")
oHeader.removeChild oChild
oXML.save sLocalDIR
```

Next, the function calls several helper functions to open a connection to the FTP site, upload the document, and close the connection. If everything goes fine, an "ack" string will be returned (otherwise an error will be raised):

```
If OpenConnection(sFTPServer, sUID, sPWD) Then
    If Upload(sLocalDIR, sRemoteDIR) Then
        CloseConnection
    End If
End If

If Err <> 0 Then
    IBTSAppIntegration_ProcessMessage = "nack"
Else
    IBTSAppIntegration_ProcessMessage = "ack"
End If
```

Three helper functions, *OpenConnection*, *Upload*, and *CloseConnection* are illustrated next. They call appropriate WinInet API functions to do the actual work. (For more information about WinInet APIs and how to use them in VB, read the KB article mentioned earlier.)

```
Private Function OpenConnection(ByVal Server, _
    ByVal User, ByVal Password) As Boolean

    On Error GoTo OpenConnection_Err
    If Not bActiveSession And hOpen <> 0 Then
        hConnection = InternetConnect(hOpen, Server, _
            INTERNET_INVALID_PORT_NUMBER, _
```

```
        User, Password, INTERNET_SERVICE_FTP, 0, 0)
        If hConnection = 0 Then
            bActiveSession = False
            OpenConnection = False
            Exit Function
        Else
            bActiveSession = True
            OpenConnection = True
       End If
    End If
    Exit Function
OpenConnection_Err:
        If hConnection Then InternetCloseHandle hConnection
        If hOpen Then InternetCloseHandle hOpen
        Err.Raise Err.Number
End Function
Private Function Upload(ByVal szFileLocal, _
    ByVal szFileRemote) As Boolean

    Dim bRet As Boolean
    Dim szTempString As String
    Upload = False
    If bActiveSession Then
        bRet = FtpPutFile(hConnection, szFileLocal, _
            szFileRemote, dwType, 0)
        If bRet = False Then
            Upload = False
            Exit Function
        End If
    Else
        Upload = False
        Exit Function
    End If
    Upload = True
End Function

Private Sub CloseConnection()
    bDirEmpty = True
    If hConnection <> 0 Then InternetCloseHandle hConnection
    hConnection = 0
    bActiveSession = False
End Sub
```

In addition, you add the following code to the *Initialize* and *Terminate* events of your class module to take care of the opening and closing of an FTP session:

```
Private Sub Class_Initialize()
    hOpen = InternetOpen(scUserAgent, _
        INTERNET_OPEN_TYPE_DIRECT, _
        vbNullString, vbNullString, 0)
End Sub

Private Sub Class_Terminate()
    If hConnection <> 0 Then InternetCloseHandle (hConnection)
    If hOpen <> 0 Then InternetCloseHandle (hOpen)
    hConnection = 0
    hOpen = 0
    If bActiveSession Then TreeView1.Nodes.Remove txtServer.Text
    bActiveSession = False
End Sub
```

Now you can compile the AIC component and appropriately register it so it can be recognized by BizTalk Server Messaging Services.

There are two ways in which you can register an AIC component. In the first method, you create a .reg file, as you did for custom functoid components or preprocessor components. This time, though, you need to include two CATIDs so your .reg file looks like this:

```
Windows Registry Editor Version 5.00
[HKEY_CLASSES_ROOT\Your_CLSID\AIC_CLSID\Implemented Categories\{5C6C30E7-
C66D-40e3-889D-08C5C3099E52}]
[HKEY_CLASSES_ROOT\Your_CLSID\AIC_CLSID\Implemented Categories\BD193E1D-
D7DC-4b7c-B9D2-92AE0344C836}]
```

The first CATID identifies the component as a BizTalk Server component (CATID_BIZTALK_COMPONENT). The second CATID identifies the component as an AIC (CATID_BIZTALK_AIC).

Another method of registering an AIC component is to create a COM+ Application to host your component. This approach is easier and provides fault isolation, because if the AIC fails, only the COM+ application that hosts the component will be affected, as opposed to the .reg approach where the AIC component is running at the process address of BizTalk Server Messaging Services. In this example, you create a COM+ application in the Component Services MMC snap-in and name it *BTS Adapters*. You then install the AIC_FTP.dll into the COM+ application and you're done.

Testing Your FTP Adapter

To test your FTP adapter, you need to set up a few things. First, you need to create an FTP site. To do this, open the Computer Management MMC snap-in by right-clicking the My Computer icon on the desktop and selecting Manage. Expand the Services and Applications node and then the Internet Information Services node to display the Default FTP Site. Right-click the Default FTP Site and select New | Virtual Directory. Name the Alias *AIC*, and set the path to C:\AIC (you need to create this folder on the C: drive first). Set Read and Write permissions for this virtual directory and close the Virtual Directory Creation Wizard. The Computer Management MMC snap-in should now look something like Figure 11-9.

Next, you need to set up BizTalk Messaging objects. You can reuse the organizations and document definitions you created earlier for the preprocessor component by adding a messaging port and a channel. Create a messaging port using BizTalk Messaging Manager and name it *AIC Port*. Select PO Destination as the destination organization for the messaging port. Click the Browse button next to the Primary transport address box and choose Application Integration Component from the Transport type drop-down box in the Primary Transport dialog box. Click the Browser button. You should see the AIC_FTP FTP Adapter in the Available components list on the Select A Component dialog box (shown in Figure 11-10). Click OK and then OK again to dismiss the dialog boxes.

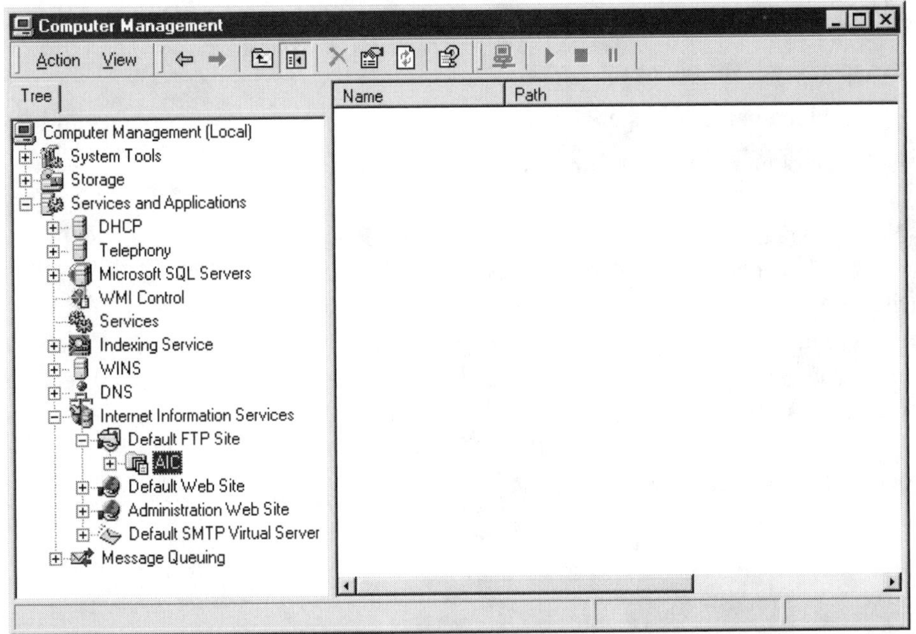

Figure 11-9 *Creating a virtual FTP site*

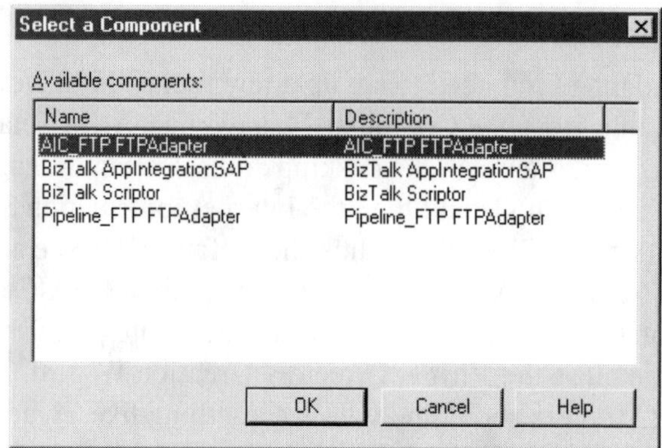

Figure 11-10 *Selecting the AIC component for the messaging port*

Next, create a channel, *AIC Channel*, for the messaging port, AIC Port. Select Northwind as its source organization and PO as the document definition for both the inbound and outbound documents.

Finally, you need to create a File receive function with the following properties:

- Name: Receive PO for AIC
- Polling location: C:\Northwind\AIC_In (you need to create this folder)
- File types to poll for: *.xml
- Openness: Not open
- Envelope name: <None>
- Channel name: AIC Channel

Now you are ready to test your FTP Adapter AIC component. Locate the PO.xml file in \AICs\Lightweight folder and open it in Notepad. Change the UID and PWD attributes so they reflect the logon ID and password of the FTP server, respectively. Save PO.xml and copy it to C:\Northwind\AIC_In. It will disappear a few seconds later. If you check the C:\AIC folder (the folder to which the FTP virtual directory points), you will find a PO.xml. If you open it in IE 5, it should look like the one in Figure 11-11. As you can see, the <FTP> element was removed (by the ProcessMessage method).

C:\AIC\PO.xml - Microsoft Internet Explorer
File Edit View Favorites Tools Help
- <POReq>
<Header Date="1996-07-22" />
<EmployeeInfo LastName="Callahan" FirstName="Laura" EmpID="8" />
<Item Description="Chef Anton's Gumbo Mix" Price="21.35" Quantity="36" />
<Item Description="Uncle Bob's Organic Dried Pears" Price="30" Quantity="12" />
<Total POTtl="1128.6" />
- <BillTo>
<Address Name="Rattlesnake Canyon Grocery" Address1="2817 Milton Dr." City="Albuquerque" State="NM" Zip="87110" Country="USA" />
</BillTo>
- <ShipTo>
<Address Name="Rattlesnake Canyon Grocery" Address1="2817 Milton Dr." City="Albuquerque" State="NM" Zip="87110" Country="USA" />
</ShipTo>
</POReq>
Done
My Computer

Figure 11-11 *A PO.xml document is uploaded to the FTP server*

Building a Pipeline AIC Component

As you can see in the preceding example, although simple to implement, the lightweight AIC isn't very flexible. Because the ProcessMessage method only accepts one input parameter (which is the document itself) in order to pass protocol-specific information, such as FTP server, login name, password, and so on, you have to either hardcode this configuration information in the component or include the information in the document as you did in the preceding example. It would be nice if there was a mechanism that enabled you to communicate this kind of information through configuration rather than coding. Fortunately, the Pipeline AIC component infrastructure enables you to do exactly that.

The IPipelineComponent and IPipelineComponentAdmin Interfaces

BizTalk Server 2000 supports the *IPipelineComponent* interface and its accompanying *IPipelineComponentAdmin* interface; both are inherited from Microsoft Site Server Commerce Edition 3.0 and now Microsoft Commerce Server 2000 (a topic of the next chapter). In Commerce Server, a pipeline is a software infrastructure that defines a business process as a series of stages linked together in a linear manner to complete a specific task. Each stage in a pipeline can be associated with one or more pipeline components (COM DLLs that implemented the IPipelineComponent and IPipelineComponentAdmin interfaces). You can use selected pipeline components to assemble an order processing process, using the Commerce Server Pipeline Editor. Figure 11-12 illustrates a Retailing Purchase pipeline, the Commerce Server Pipeline Editor, in which the pipe segments represent stages where the values stand for components.

Think of a pipeline as a conceptually simplified XLANG schedule drawing. By using the same interfaces defined in the Microsoft Commerce 2000 Default Pipeline Components Type Library, pipecomplib.tlb, you can use the power of the configuration-based programming model.

The IPipelineComponent supports two methods: *EnableDesign* and *Execute*.

The EnableDesign method determines whether the component will be in design mode or execute mode, based on the Boolean flag being passed in:

```
Private Sub IPipelineComponent_EnableDesign(ByVal fEnable As Long)
```

The Execute method functions like the ProcessMessage method in lightweight AIC components. Its VB stub looks like this:

```
Private Function IPipelineComponent_Execute( _
        ByVal pdispOrder As Object, _
        ByVal pdispContext As Object, _
        ByVal lFlags As Long) As Long
```

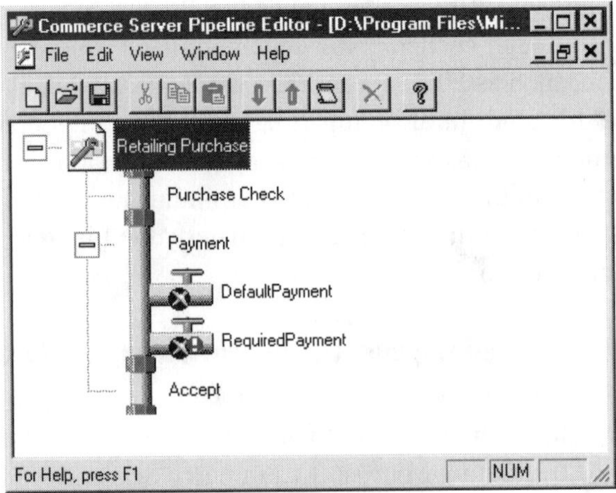

Figure 11-12 *The Commerce Server Pipeline Editor*

It gives you an opportunity to process the outbound document and to retrieve source and destination organizations, the name of the inbound document, and the document tracking ID, all through the first input parameter, *pdispOrder*, a Dictionary object that stores configuration information in a name-value pair, as described in Table 11-10.

In addition, you can add the ResponseField key to the Dictionary object to pass back a text-based response to an application when the original document is submitted to BizTalk Server using the SubmitSync method of the IInterchange interface. But, as we mentioned earlier in this book, this is strongly discouraged because the SubmitSync method is a blocking call and will kill the scalability of your applications.

The second parameter of the Execute method, *pdispContext*, is not used in the current release of BizTalk Server 2000, and the third parameter, lFlags, is reserved.

The IPipelineComponentAdmin interface supports two methods: *GetConfigData* and *SetConfigData*.

The GetConfigData method returns a Dictionary object that contains the configuration data for the component to be used, displaying these values:

- Private Function IPipelineComponentAdmin_GetConfigData() As Object

The SetConfigData method, on the other hand, takes a Dictionary object as an input parameter, enabling the user interface to write the updated value from the property page to the component:

- Private Sub IPipelineComponentAdmin_SetConfigData(ByVal pDict As Object)

Field Name	Description
Working_Data	The outbound document.
Src_ID_Type	The type of the source organization qualifier. For example, OrganizationName.
Src_ID_Value	The value of the source organization qualifier. For example, Northwind.
Dest_ID_Type	The type of the destination organization qualifier. For example, OrganizationName.
Dest_ID_Value	The value of the destination organization qualifier. For example, PO Destination.
Document_Name	The name of the inbound document. For example, PO.
Tracking_ID	The document tracking ID. It is a GUID.

Table 11-10 *Properties of the Dictionary object - pDispOrder*

It is important to understand when which method should be called.

During run time, BizTalk Server Messaging Services will first call the IPipelineComponentAdmin_SetConfigData to give you an opportunity to save the configuration data to the component. Then the IPipelineComponent_Execute method is called, enabling you to process the outbound document.

During design time, when you click the Advanced button to open the Overwrite Messaging Port Defaults dialog box and then click the Properties button, the following two methods will be called in the specified order, prior to the display of the properties page:

1. IPipelineComponent_EnableDesign
2. IPipelineComponentAdmin_GetConfigData.

The former enables you to specify the execution mode for the pipeline component: design mode or execution mode. The latter enables you to populate the Dictionary with configuration data stored in the component for display in the property page.

After you have filled up the property page and click OK, the following three methods will be called in the order specified:

1. IPipelineComponentAdmin_SetConfigData
2. IPipelineComponent_EnableDesign
3. IPipelineComponentAdmin_GetConfigData

The first method call enables you to save the configuration data collected from the property page to the component. The second method call gives you another opportunity to switch the execution mode (for example, if you set it to design mode in the previous step, you can switch it back to the execution mode again). The last method call gives you a second chance to retrieve the configuration data.

Creating an FTP Adapter as a Pipeline AIC Component

Now let's see how you can implement an enhanced FTP adapter as a Pipeline AIC Component. This time, you will take the FTP configuration data (server name, logon information, and so on) out of the document and provide a property page for the user to configure necessary data in the design time.

Start a new Visual Basic ActiveX DLL project, and name the project and class module *Pipeline_FTP* and *FTPAdapter*, respectively. You need to set references in the project to both the Microsoft Commerce 2000 Core Components Type Library

(MscsCore.dll) and the Microsoft Commerce 2000 Default Pipeline Components Type Library (pipecommpps.dll). Each is located in the \Program Files\Common Files\Microsoft Shared\Enterprise Servers\Commerce folder. In this particular example, you also set a reference to Microsoft XML 3.0 parser.

Next, add the WININET.Bas standard module that you used in the lightweight FTP AIC component.

Afterward, add the following lines in the General Declaration section of the class module in order to implement both pipeline interfaces and declare the module level variables for holding the configuration data.

```
Dim bActiveSession As Boolean
Dim hOpen As Long, hConnection As Long
Dim dwType As Long

Implements IPipelineComponentAdmin
Implements IPipelineComponent

Private m_sFTPServer As String
Private m_sUID As String
Private m_sPWD As String
Private m_sLocalDIR As String
Private m_sRemoteDIR As String
```

You are not going to use the EnableDesign method in this example, but you still have to include a stub in your class module to fully implement the IPipelineComponent interface:

```
Private Sub IPipelineComponent_EnableDesign(ByVal fEnable As Long)
    'Do nothing
End Sub
```

Now, implement the Execute method as follows:

```
Private Function IPipelineComponent_Execute( _
    ByVal pdispOrder As Object, _
    ByVal pdispContext As Object, _
    ByVal lFlags As Long) As Long

    Dim oXML As New MSXML2.DOMDocument
    Dim sFTPServer As String
    Dim sUID As String
    Dim sPWD As String
```

```
    Dim sLocalDIR As String
    Dim sRemoteDIR As String
    Dim sTrackingID As String

    On Error GoTo Execute_Err

    oXML.async = False
    oXML.loadXML pdispOrder("working_data")

    sFTPServer = m_sFTPServer
    sUID = m_sUID
    sPWD = m_sPWD
    sLocalDIR = m_sLocalDIR
    sRemoteDIR = m_sRemoteDIR

    oXML.Save sLocalDIR

    sTrackingID = pdispOrder("Tracking_ID")
    sRemoteDIR = Left(sRemoteDIR, InStr(sRemoteDIR, "/")) _
               & sTrackingID _
               & Mid(sRemoteDIR, InStr(sRemoteDIR, "/") + 1)

    If OpenConnection(sFTPServer, sUID, sPWD) Then
        If Upload(sLocalDIR, sRemoteDIR) Then
            CloseConnection
        End If
    End If

    'return success
    IPipelineComponent_Execute = 0
    Exit Function

Execute_Err:
    IPipelineComponent_Execute = 2 'Serious Error Occurred
    Err.Raise Err.Number, Err.Source, Err.Description
End Function
```

Although it seems long, the implementation of the Execute method is actually pretty straightforward. The function first loads the document to a DOMDocument object (notice that the document is stored in a Dictionary object):

```
oXML.async = False
oXML.loadXML pdispOrder("working_data")
```

The function then assigns the configuration data from module level variables to local variables. The module level variables were populated as IPipelineComponentAdmin_SetConfigData methods (as we will explain shortly in this chapter) using the values collected from the properties page during the design time.

```
sFTPServer = m_sFTPServer
sUID = m_sUID
sPWD = m_sPWD
sLocalDIR = m_sLocalDIR
sRemoteDIR = m_sRemoteDIR
```

Next, the function retrieves the tracking ID and concatenates it into the filename to make it unique when it is uploaded to the FTP server.

```
sTrackingID = pdispOrder("Tracking_ID")
sRemoteDIR = Left(sRemoteDIR, InStr(sRemoteDIR, "/")) _
           & sTrackingID _
           & Mid(sRemoteDIR, InStr(sRemoteDIR, "/") + 1)
```

The rest of the code is almost identical to that of the ProcessMessage method in the AIC component. The three helper methods, OpenConnection, Upload, and CloseConnection are the same as in the AIC component. You also add the same code to the Initialize and Terminate events of the class module.

Next, implement the IPipelineComponentAdmin_GetConfigData, populating the Dictionary object with the data stored in the module level variables:

```
Private Function IPipelineComponentAdmin_GetConfigData() As Object
    Dim objectConfig As New CDictionary

    objectConfig.Value("FTP_Server") = m_sFTPServer
    objectConfig.Value("UserID") = m_sUID
    objectConfig.Value("Password") = m_sPWD
    objectConfig.Value("Local_Dir") = m_sLocalDIR
    objectConfig.Value("Remote_Dir") = m_sRemoteDIR

    Set IPipelineComponentAdmin_GetConfigData = objectConfig
End Function
```

Here is how these module level variables get their value, through the IPipelineComponentAdmin_SetConfigData method:

```
Private Sub IPipelineComponentAdmin_SetConfigData( _
    ByVal pDict As Object)
```

```
    ' set m_sFTPServer
    If Not IsNull(pDict("FTP_Server")) Then
        m_sFTPServer = CStr(pDict("FTP_Server"))
    End If
    If m_sFTPServer = "" Then
            m_sFTPServer = "Localhost"
    End If
    ' set m_sUID
    If Not IsNull(pDict("UserID")) Then
        m_sUID = CStr(pDict("UserID"))
    End If
    If m_sUID = "" Then
            m_sUID = "Administrator"
    End If
    ' set m_sPWD
    If Not IsNull(pDict("Password")) Then
        m_sPWD = CStr(pDict("Password"))
    End If
    If m_sPWD = "" Then
            m_sPWD = ""
    End If
    ' set m_sLocalDIR
    If Not IsNull(pDict("Local_Dir")) Then
        m_sLocalDIR = CStr(pDict("Local_Dir"))
    End If
    If m_sLocalDIR = "" Then
            m_sLocalDIR = "C:\Temp\PO.xml"
    End If
    ' set m_sRemoteDIR
    If Not IsNull(pDict("Remote_Dir")) Then
        m_sRemoteDIR = CStr(pDict("Remote_Dir"))
    End If
    If m_sRemoteDIR = "" Then
            m_sRemoteDIR = "AIC/PO.xml"
    End If

End Sub
```

To implement the GUI interface of the property page, BizTalk Server 2000 provides specific semantics by means of a pair of ASP pages. You need to create two ASP pages and place them in the <BizTalk Server Installation>\MessagingManager\pipeline folder.

Keep in mind, the ASP pages must follow a predefined naming convention. In this example, the two ASP pages are named Pipeline_FTP_FTPAdapter.asp and Pipeline_FTP_FTPAdapter_post.asp, respectively. As you can see, your first page takes a slightly modified ProgID—the dot in the ProgID was replaced with an underscore. The second filename is the name of the first file plus an _post. The first ASP page must include two include files, pe_edit_header.asp and pe_edit_footer.asp, along with a number of *InputText* calls, passing the properties names. For each property, you will need to call the InputText function once:

```
<!--#INCLUDE FILE="pe_edit_header.asp" -->
<%
  call InputText("FTP_Server")
  call InputText("UserID")
  call InputText("Password")
  call InputText("Local_Dir")
  call InputText("Remote_Dir")
%>
<!--#INCLUDE FILE="pe_edit_footer.asp" -->
```

The second ASP page also needs to contain a pair of include files, pe_global_edit.asp and pe_post_footer.asp. It then calls the GetInputText for each property, as illustrated in the following:

```
<!--#INCLUDE FILE="pe_global_edit.asp" -->
<%
  call GetInputText("FTP_Server", 0, bufsize_medium)
  call GetInputText("UserID", 0, bufsize_medium)
  call GetInputText("Password", 0, bufsize_medium)
  call GetInputText("Local_Dir", 0, bufsize_medium)
  call GetInputText("Remote_Dir", 0, bufsize_medium)
%>
<!--#INCLUDE FILE="pe_post_footer.asp" -->
```

Registering and Testing Your Pipeline FTP Adapter

The registration process of a Pipeline component is the same as that for the AIC component. You simply install the Pipeline_FTP.dll into the FTP Adapters COM+ application. Before you can test your pipeline FTP Adapter, you will need to set up a pair of messaging ports and channels, as well as a File receive function.

First, create a messaging port and name it *Pipeline AIC Port*. Select PO Destination as its destination organization. Specify Application Integration Component and the primary transport and select Pipeline_FTP FTP Adapter in the Available Components list on the Select A Component dialog box.

Next, create a channel, *Pipeline AIC Channel,* for the messaging port Pipeline AIC Port. Select Northwind as its source organization and PO as the document definition for both the inbound and outbound documents. In the Advanced Configuration page of the Channel Wizard, click the Advanced button to display the Overwrite Messaging Port Defaults dialog box. Click the Properties button and the Pipeline_FTP FTPAdapter Properties dialog box appears, displaying all the configuration fields you implemented in the pipeline component, as well as a pair of ASP pages (shown in Figure 11-13). Change the appropriate fields to reflect the FTP configuration settings of your FTP server.

Finally, create a File receive function with the following properties:

- Name: Receive PO for Pipeline
- Polling location: C:\Northwind\Pipeline_In (you need to create this folder)
- File types to poll for: *.xml
- Openness: Not open
- Envelope name: <None>
- Channel name: Pipeline AIC Channel

To test the pipeline AIC adapter, copy the file PipelinePO.xml, located in the \AICs\Pipeline folder, to the C:\Northwind\Pipeline_In folder. A few seconds later, a {GUID}PO.xml document should appear in the FTP site (C:\AIC).

Using Scriptor AIC Components

In addition to lightweight and pipeline AIC components, BizTalk Server 2000 also supports a third option for you to write AIC components: Scriptors. BizTalk Scriptor

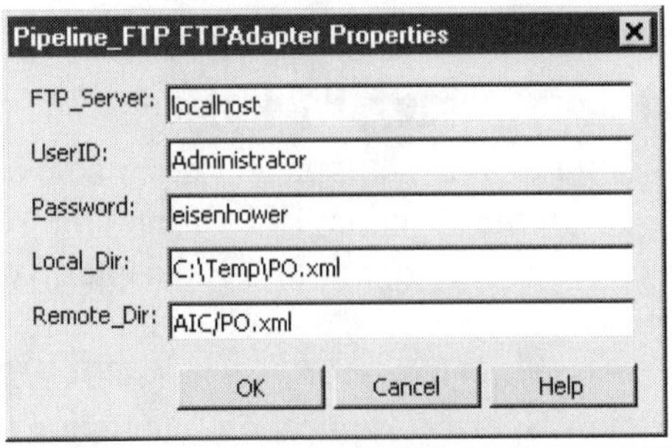

Figure 11-13 *The properties page allows you to specify configuration data for the pipeline component*

is a framework that enables you to write AIC components in scripting language (currently VBScript or JScript). These are most familiar to users of Commerce Server 2000 because the interface is identical.

In the Messaging Port Wizard, when you select Application Integration Component as the transport protocol (either primary or secondary), you'll see a BizTalk Scriptor component in the Available components list of the Select a Component dialog box (as shown in Figure 11-14). Select it and click OK to dismiss the dialog box.

After you have selected BizTalk Scriptor as the AIC component, you can create a new channel to use it. Navigate to the Advanced Configuration page of the Channel Wizard and click the Advanced button. You should see the Override Messaging Port Defaults dialog box (like that in Figure 11-15).

Click the Properties button and you will see the BizTalk Scriptor Properties page (shown in Figure 11-16).

As you can see in Figure 11-16, you can modify the skeleton code in the Script edit box if you choose the Internal option (the default). Alternatively, you can specify an external script file. Either way, you must implement the *MSCSExecute* function, and, optionally, the *MSCSOpen* and *MSCSClose* (you have to scroll down in the edit box to see it) functions.

You can also specify configuration data by entering the name-value pairs in the Configuration editor box in the following format:

```
name1 = value1; name2 = value2; ...
```

The MSCSOpen and MSCSClose methods provide a place for you to put initialization and clean-up code appropriate for your component. The MSCSExecute method is similar to the IPipelineComponent_Execute method. The *orderform* parameter is a Dictionary object and is equivalent to the pDispOrder parameter.

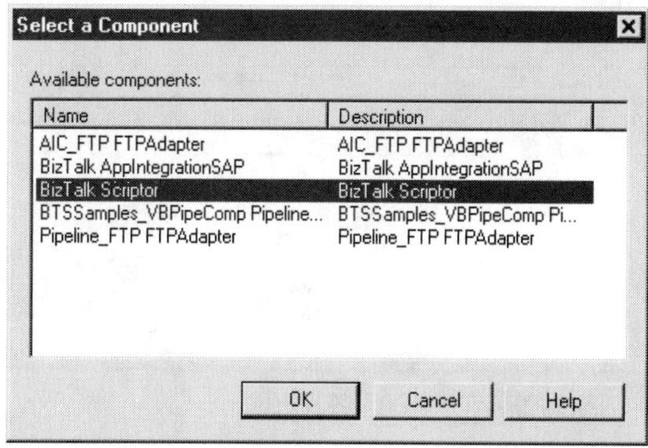

Figure 11-14 *Selecting a Scriptor component*

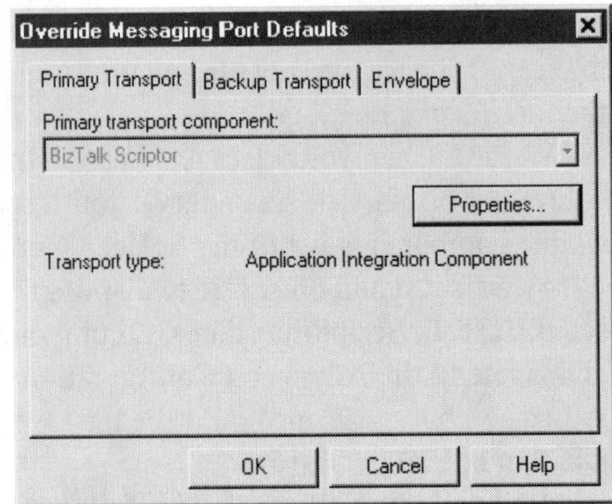

Figure 11-15 *An Overwrite Messaging Port Defaults dialog box is a messaging port that uses a Scriptor*

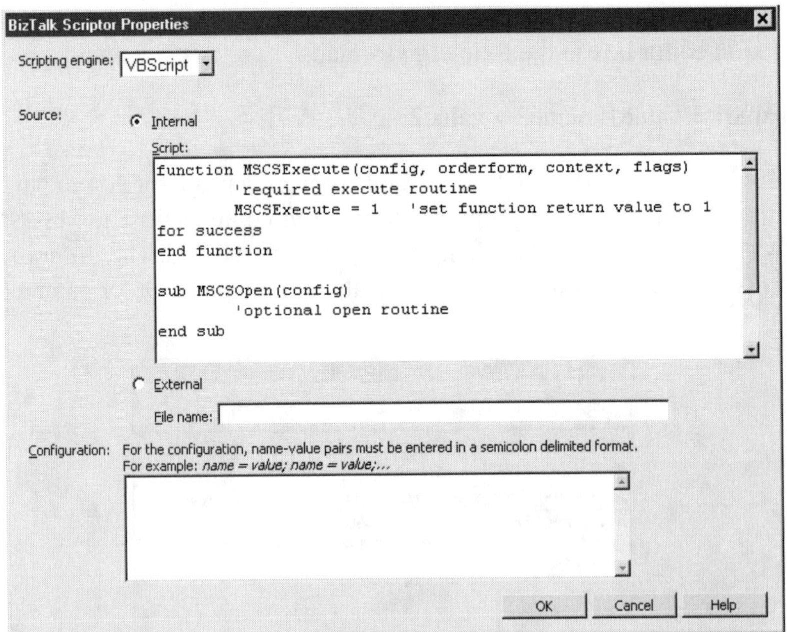

Figure 11-16 *The BizTalk Scriptor Properties page*

Similarly, the *context* and *flags* parameters are equivalent to pDispContext and lFlags, respectively. There is an additional parameter in the Scriptor, though: *config*. The config parameter is also a Dictionary object that enables you to retrieve user-defined properties entered in the Configuration edit box, for example:

```
sName1 = config.name1
sName2 = config.name2
......
```

Chapter in Review

In this chapter, you learned how to create custom components to extend BizTalk Server 2000 Messaging Services. First, you discovered how to create a custom functoid to speed up the map development for meeting your specific business needs. Second, you learned how to create a simple preprocessor to perform preliminary processing prior to submitting the document to BizTalk Server. Finally, you found out how to create an Application Integration Component using three different techniques: lightweight AIC components, pipeline AIC components, and Scriptor AIC components.

CHAPTER 12

Integrating with Commerce Server

IN THIS CHAPTER:

Introducing Microsoft Commerce Server 2000

Integrating BizTalk Server and Commerce Server

Chapter in Review

Microsoft Commerce Server 2000, another important member of the Microsoft .NET Servers family, provides a scalable platform framework and infrastructure to make the building of e-commerce Web sites for online businesses easy. Primarily a business-to-consumer (B2C) product, Commerce Server ships with a lot of out-of-the-box features that enable you to quickly develop effective and function-rich web site storefronts. Commerce Server 2000 also provides some business-to-business (B2B) support, such as its partner management features. In addition, using its highly extensible architecture and native support for integrating with BizTalk Server 2000, you can leverage the powerful B2B integration capabilities of BizTalk Server to streamline business partner integration for Commerce Server, such as catalog exchanges and order forms management.

In this chapter, we will introduce you to Microsoft Commerce Server 2000, from a BizTalk developer's perspective. Then we'll show you how to automate a product catalog integration using BizTalk Server 2000. Next, we will demonstrate how to configure Commerce Server and BizTalk Server to support order forms integration. The purpose of this chapter is not about trying to help you master Commerce Server 2000. Rather, what we are trying to achieve here is to help you, a BizTalk developer, to understand the fundamentals of Commerce Server 2000 (especially those features related to the integration of BizTalk Server 2000). After finishing this chapter, you should be well on your way to building seamless integration solutions for Commerce Server and BizTalk Server that will support a broad spectrum of e-commerce businesses.

Introducing Microsoft Commerce Server 2000

In this section, we will give you a quick, high-level overview of Microsoft Commerce Server 2000. We will introduce the major systems that comprise Commerce Server 2000, as well as its tools and solution sites, and briefly walk you through the relevant parts of the tutorials that ship with Commerce Server 2000. These steps will help you get familiar with the catalog management functionality of Commerce Server 2000 and set up an environment for you to practice the examples later in this chapter.

Commerce Server 2000 Features Overview

Microsoft Commerce Server 2000 provides a scalable e-commerce platform for you to quickly develop powerful and effective e-commerce storefronts. Commerce Server is a comprehensive product which consists of five core systems for managing all the aspects of a typical e-commerce web site. Commerce Server also provides site management and administration tools for both business managers and system administrators to manage core systems, applications, databases, and web servers. In addition, Commerce Server Solutions Sites offers lots of out-of-the-box, ready to use features, not to mention solutions that will significantly reduce the time and efforts of your development team when building powerful, function-rich e-commerce web sites.

Commerce Server Systems

Commerce Server 2000 offers its features and functionalities through the following five systems:

- **Product Catalog System** The Product Catalog System enables you to manage product catalogs. Using the Product Catalog System, you can create, update, and delete product catalogs. You can also import and/or export product catalogs in XML or CSV formats. In addition, you can add integrated search capabilities, manage special pricing and discounts, and identify best-selling products. In addition, you can leverage the B2B integration power of BizTalk Server 2000 to exchange catalogs with third-party vendors, as you will learn later in this chapter.
- **Profiling System** The Profiling System enables you to manage millions of users and/or organizations, and permit users to manage their own profile information and research the status of their orders. You can use the Profiling System to monitor users' online shopping habits and display targeted information (such as custom catalogs) to appropriate users accordingly. In addition, you can use the Profiling System to create advertising, discount, and direct mail campaigns to target specific user groups.
- **Business Analytics System** The Business Analytics System enables you to import large amounts of site usage data collected from different data sources and drop them into the Commerce Server Data Warehouse. From there, you can utilize the Analytical Services of Microsoft SQL Server 2000 (or the OLAP Services of Microsoft SQL Server 7.0) and the reporting capabilities of Commerce Server 2000 to analyze the site's effectiveness, identify specific groups of users, analyze hidden trends and new customer segments, provide intelligent cross-selling, and dynamically recommend products to users as they navigate your site.
- **Targeting System** The Targeting System enables you to provide personalized buying experience with targeted merchandising, deliver context-driven contents to the users, predictive capabilities to your web site,

and target ads or discounts to users of a specific profile as well as create and schedule campaigns for competing customers to ensure that these competing ads will never show on the same page at the same time. In addition, you can use the Targeting System to charge your advertising customers based on the number of ad requests or clicks they want their ads to receive, or based on the page on which they want to display their ad.

- **Business Process Pipelines System** The Business Process Pipelines System enables you to customize your business processes, such as the ordering, targeting, and merchandising processes. You can also use the serial Business Process Pipelines system to define and link together the stages of a business process (thus the name Process Pipeline).

Site Management and Administration Tools

Commerce Server 2000 provides tools for both business managers and system administrators to manage their site and system resources, including the Business Desk and Commerce Server Manager.

Business Desk Business Desk (sometimes referred to as BizDesk) is a site management tool that business managers use to manage and analyze their web sites as well as to access all five systems of Commerce Server 2000. Business Desk includes two parts: the Business Desk application and the Business Desk Client. A Business Desk application is a set of server-side application components and ASP pages that reside on the web server (Windows 2000 Server) and provide functionalities for you to configure, manage, and analyze the web site. The Business Desk client is a client-side GUI interface that can be installed on any computer running IE 5.5 or later. You use the Business Desk client to access the Business Desk applications on the server. Figure 12-1 is a screen shot of the Business Desk client.

The Commerce Server Manager The Commerce Server Manager is an administration tool that system administrators use to manage resources, sites, applications, and web servers. Like the BizTalk Administrator, the Commerce Server Manager is also implemented as an MMC snap-in (as shown in Figure 12-2).

Solution Sites

Commerce Server 2000 provides three prepackaged reference sites, known as Solution Sites, that provide an integrated set of features like merchandising, catalog display, customer service, and order capture and receipt. You can leverage the comprehensive e-commerce functionalities provided in Solution Sites and use them as a starting

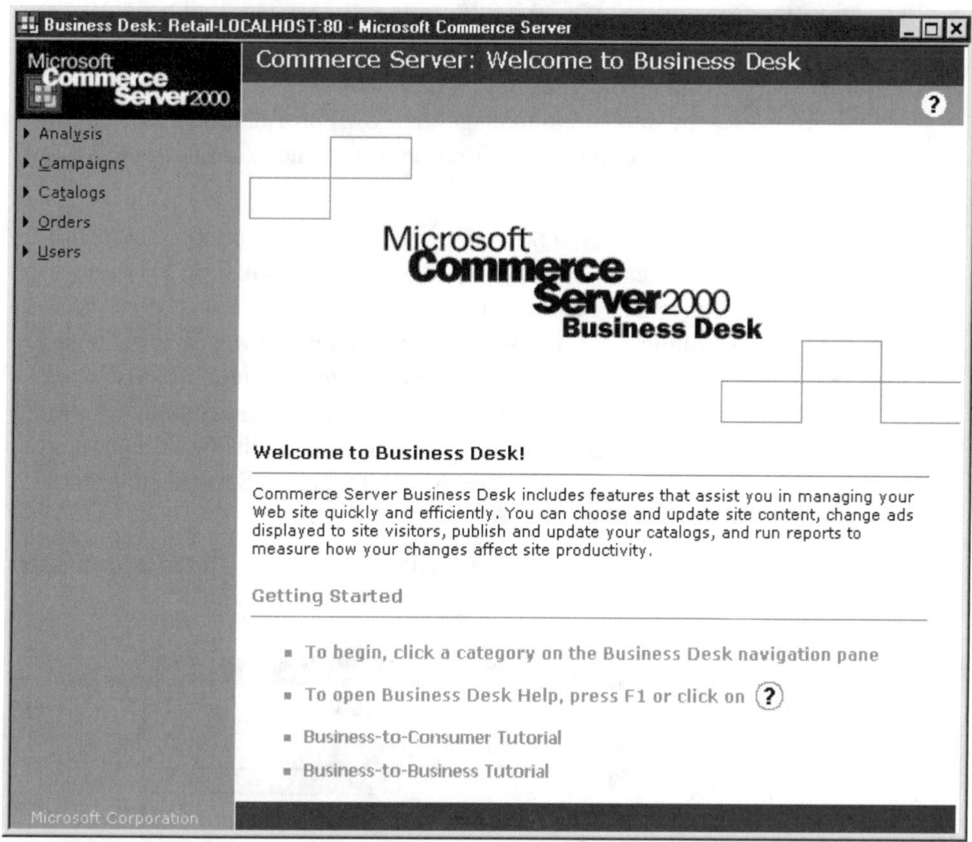

Figure 12-1 *The Business Desk client*

point for developing your own web sites. You can also add functionalities that are specific to your business.

Commerce Server 2000 includes three Solution Sites, and provides a Blank Solution Site right out-of-the-box. In addition, you can download two other Solution Sites, the Retail Solution Site, the Supplier Solution Site, and the Sweet Forgiveness Solution Site from Commerce Server's web site at http://www.microsoft.com/CommerceServer.

- **The Blank Solution Site** The Blank Solution Site includes all the basic Commerce Server resources you can use as a starting point for developing your own custom site.

- **The Retail Solution Site** The Retail Solution Site provides all the B2C functionalities, including personalization, merchandising, catalog search, customer service, and business analytics. The customer service functionality enables users of your web site to manage their own profiles and check their order status. You will use the Retail Solution Site in the examples in this chapter.
- **The Supplier Solution Site** The Supplier Solution Site, on the other hand, offers more B2B features such as purchase order and requisition handling, XML-based catalog updates and exchange, and trading partner self-service. You can use this Solution Site as a starting point to build a web site that requires more B2B functionalities. Of course, to fully realize B2B integrations, you can leverage the power of BizTalk Server 2000. Be aware that the Supplier Solution Site uses Active Directory Services for managing user authentication and group access permissions. You need to enable Active Directory Services in order to use the Supplier Solution Site.
- **The Sweet Forgiveness Solution Site** The multicurrency, international site.

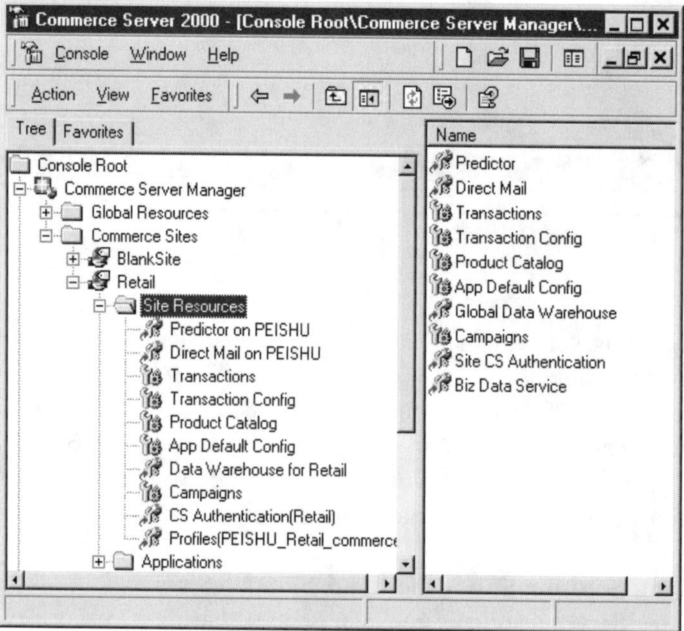

Figure 12-2 *The Commerce Server Manager*

Using Commerce Server 2000

In order to follow the examples in this chapter, you will need to install Commerce Server 2000 and the Retail Solution Site, set up its Business Desk and perform some tasks described in the Business Desk Tutorial of the Commerce Server 2000 product documentation.

Setting Up Commerce Server 2000

Installing Commerce Server 2000 is not extremely difficult. To ensure the installation process is as pleasant as possible, read the installation documentation, "Installing Commerce Server 2000," a Microsoft Word document (Installation_Guide.doc), downloadable from Commerce Server 2000's web site.

After successfully installing Commerce Server 2000, you need to download the Retail Solution Site (available at http://www.microsoft.com/commerceserver/solutionsites) and then unpack it. Refer to the Installation Guide for instructions regarding unpacking the Retail Solution Site. You will also need to set up the Business Desk for the Retail Solution Site.

Using the Business Desk Tutorial

The Commerce Server product documentation contains two Business Desk tutorials—the Business-to-Consumer Tutorial and the Business-to-Business Tutorial—located under Commerce Server 2000, Working with Business Desk, Business Desk Tutorial. These tutorials provide an excellent means of getting familiar with the Business Desk and Commerce Server 2000. In addition, as a prerequisite for working with BizTalk integration examples later in this chapter, you will need to follow some exercises described in the Business-to-Consumer Tutorial. At minimum, you need to complete the following two tutorial exercises:

- Adding a Shipping Method and a Tax Rate
- Adding a User with a New Profile

Integrating BizTalk Server and Commerce Server

Commerce Server 2000 offers many built-in functionalities that facilitate the integration with BizTalk Server, including supports for catalog integration, order forms integration, and order integration scenarios.

Integrating Catalogs Using BizTalk Server

In this section, you will build an automatic process that imports a third-party catalog into the Retail web site managed by Commerce Server 2000, using BizTalk Server.

Solution Overview

To integrate a third-party catalog into Commerce Server, you first need to transform the structure of the third-party catalog into a Commerce Server 2000 catalog schema. Then you can import the converted catalog file into Commerce Server either manually, by using the Catalog Editor module of the Business Desk as you learned in previous sections of this chapter, or automatically, by calling the *ImportXML* method of the *CatalogManager* COM object exposed by Commerce Server 2000. In this example, you will use the mapping feature of BizTalk Server 2000 Messaging Services to transform the third-party catalog into a Commerce Server 2000 catalog schema. BizTalk Server 2000 Orchestration Services then automates the importing process of the catalog, using an XLANG schedule. Finally, you will verify the results using the Retail Solution Site.

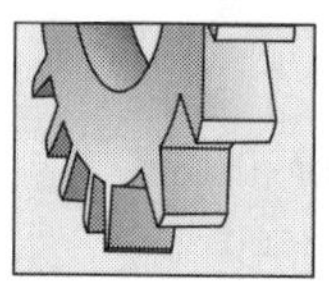

TIP

You can also download Commerce Server Service Pack 1 with the updated 1.5 version of the commerce catalog XML schema, available from the Microsoft Commerce Server web site at http://www.microsoft.com/CommerceServer.

The Commerce Server Catalog Schema

To import a catalog in XML format into Commerce Server, it must comply with the Commerce Server 2000 catalog schema, defined in an XDR schema document, CatalogXMLSchema.xml, located in the root directory of the Commerce Server installation folder (for example, C:\Program Files\Microsoft Commerce Server). If the original catalog (either in XML format or any other format) does not meet the schema constraint of Commerce Server 2000, it must first be converted (transformed) into a structure defined by the Commerce Server 2000 catalog schema. The structure of the Commerce Server 2000 catalog looks like this:

```
<MSCommerceCatalogCollection>
   <CatalogSchema>
      <AttributeDefinition name DataType Id />
      <PropertiesDefinition>
         <Property name DataType MinValue MaxValue DisplayName id
                  AssignAll DefaultValue DisplayInProductsList
```

```
                  DisplayOnSite ExportToDW IncludeInSpecSearch
                  IsFreeTextSearchable />
            <PropertyValue DisplayName />
         </Property>
      </PropertiesDefinition>
     <Definition Name DefinitionType properties variantProperties />
   </CatalogSchema>
   <Catalog catalogName description locale startDate endDate
           productIdentifier productVariantIdentifier currency>
      <Category name Definition isSearchable id parentCategories
               listprice>
         <Field fieldID fieldValue />
         <Relationship name description relation />
      </Category>
      <Product definition listprice id parentCategories
pricingCategory>
         <Field fieldID fieldValue />
         <ProductVariant Id>
            <Field fieldID fieldValue />
         </ProductVariant>
         <Relationship name description relation />
      </Product>
   </Catalog>
</MSCommerceCatalogCollection>
```

As you can see, right under the root element, *MSCommerceCatalogCollection*, there are two XML elements, *CatalogSchema* and *Catalog*. The former defines the Metadata of the catalog, namely property definitions and product definitions—those you defined in previous sections of this chapter in the Catalog Designer module of the Business Desk. The latter contains the contents of the actual data of the catalog (i.e., the categories and products)—those you created in the Catalog Editor module of the Business Desk earlier in this chapter. Both the CatalogSchema and the Catalog elements contain other child elements that are documented in details in the online product documentation of Commerce Server 2000, under Commerce Server 2000, Programmer's Reference, Catalog XML Structures.

Not every element or attribute in the Commerce Server 2000 catalog schema is mandatory. For the sake of simplicity, in this example, we are going to use the bare-bone catalog schema, utilizing only the required elements and attributes. To create a BizTalk specification for this bare-bone schema, open BizTalk Editor. Select Tools | Import… to open the Select Import Module dialog box. Select XDR Schema and click OK. Navigate to the Commerce Server catalog schema document,

CatalogXMLSchema.xml, and click the Open button in the Import XDR Schema dialog box. The schema should be imported into the BizTalk Editor now. You may receive a dozen warnings on the Warnings tab of the lower pane of the BizTalk Editor. These warnings are caused by the unspecified Content models for the elements in the original Commerce Server 2000 catalog schema. You can fix them by highlighting the appropriate element node in BizTalk Editor and specifying Element Only as the Content property in the Declaration tab of BizTalk Editor. To create the specification for our example, remove those optional elements and/or attributes so the completed schema will look something like Figure 12-3.

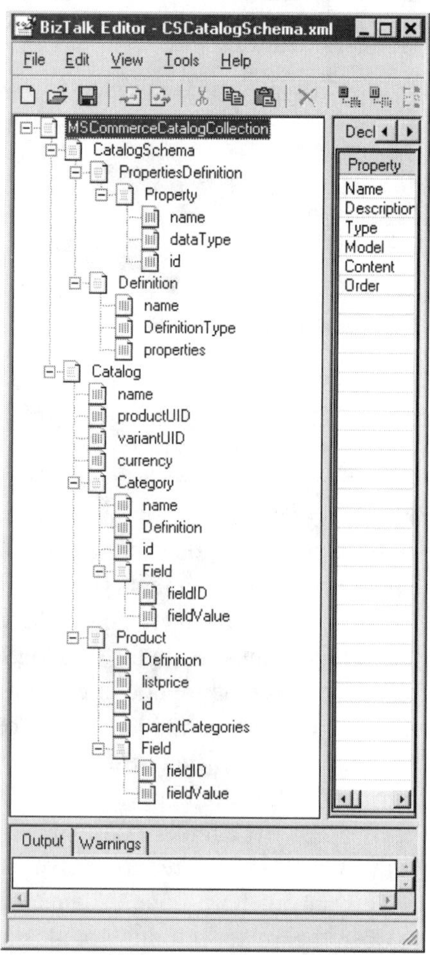

Figure 12-3 *A bare-bone Commerce Server catalog schema*

Save this specification to the BizTalk Server WebDAV repository by selecting Store To WebDAV… from the File menu option, then selecting the Microsoft folder, naming the specification CSCatalogSchema.xml, and clicking OK.

The Third-party Catalog Schema

The third-party catalog you are going to use in this example is an XML document created using a subset of data from the Northwind SQL Server sample database. The Categories and Products table in the Northwind database provides a perfect way for demonstrating how you can create a catalog file that can be converted to the Commerce Server catalog schema. Figure 12-4 shows the table schemas of these tables.

Based on the table schemas of the Categories and Products table, you can create an instance of an XML catalog document like the following:

```
<NWCatalog name="Foods" id="NW_CategoryID">
  <Fields>
    <Field name="Name" dataType="string" id="1"/>
    <Field name="Description" dataType="string" id="2"/>
    <Field name="NW_CategoryID" dataType="number" id="3"/>
    <Field name="NW_ProductID" dataType="number" id="4"/>
    <Field name="NW_QuantityPerUnit" dataType="string" id="5"/>
    <Field name="NW_UnitPrice" dataType="money" id="6"/>
  </Fields>
  <Categories>
    <Category name="Beverages" id="1"
       description="Soft drinks, coffees, teas, beers, and ales"/>
    <Category name="Condiments" id="2"
       description="Sweet and savory sauces, relishes, spreads, and seasonings"/>
  </Categories>
  <Products Definition="NW_Food">
    <Product name="Chai"
             comment="Best selling beverage"
             categoryid="1"
             id="1"
             QantityPerUnit="10 boxes x 20 bags"
             price="18"/>
    <Product name="Aniseed Syrup"
             comment="Best selling condiment"
             categoryid="2"
             id="2"
             QantityPerUnit="12 - 550 ml bottles" price="10"/>
  </Products>
</NWCatalog>
```

As you can see in the catalog document, we divided the file into three sections. The *Fields* section contains the Metadata of the catalog, a list of *Field* elements that

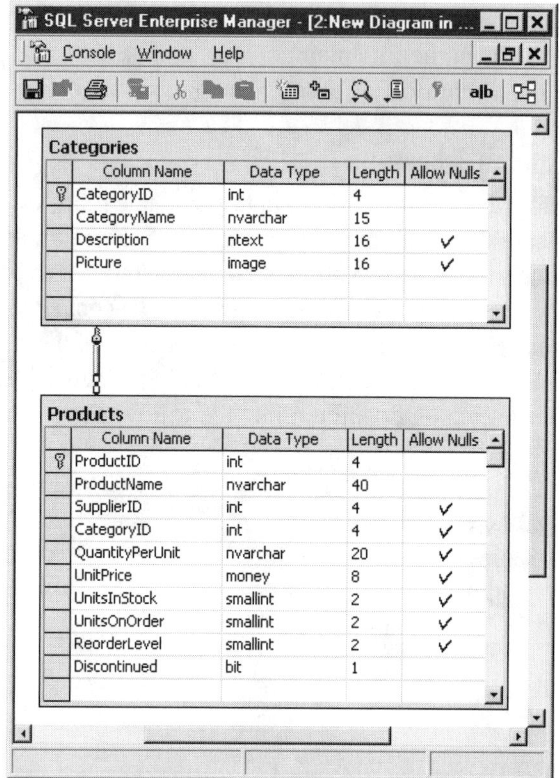

Figure 12-4 *The schemas of categories and product tables*

describes the column name, and data types (in terms of Commerce Server data types as specified in the product documentation). The Categories and Products section contains the data from the Categories and Products database tables, respectively.

The process of creating a specification for this catalog is pretty straightforward. Open the BizTalk Editor and select Tools | Import… Choose Well-Formed XML Instance in the Select Import Module dialog box and click OK. In the Import Well-Formed XML Instance dialog box, browse to NWCatalog.xml file in the Sample Data folder of the source code for this chapter (downloadable from this book's web site). Now the catalog document instance should be imported into the BizTalk Editor (and resemble the one in Figure 12-5).

Save the specification to the Microsoft BizTalk WebDAV repository, as you did for the Commerce Server catalog schema, and name the file NWCatalogSchema.xml.

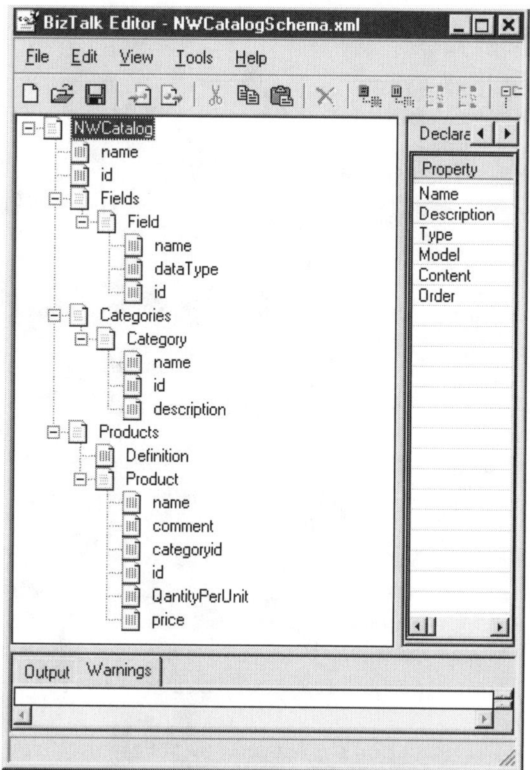

Figure 12-5 *The specification for the sample catalog schema*

Mapping Catalog Schemas

Now you need to map the NWCatalogSchema.xml to CSCatalogSchema.xml. The map can be found in the Maps folder of the source code, NW2CS_Catalog.xml. You can open it in BizTalk Mapper and study it. When you are finished, store it to the Microsoft BizTalk WebDAV repository the same way you did the specifications. Figure 12-6 is a screen shot of the map in BizTalk Editor.

For the most part, the map is fairly straightforward. The trickiest part is mapping the products from the original catalog to the Commerce Server catalog. The products in the source catalog look like the following (a flat model):

```
<Product name="Chai"
            comment="Best selling beverage"
            categoryid="1"
            id="1"
```

```
              QantityPerUnit="10 boxes x 20 bags"
              price="18"/>
<Product name="Aniseed Syrup"
              comment="Best selling condiment"
              categoryid="2"
              id="2"
              QantityPerUnit="12 - 550 ml bottles" price="10"/>
......
```

Whereas the Products section in the Commerce Server catalog resemble the following:

```
<Product Definition="NW_Food" listprice="18" id="Product1"
parentCategories="Category1">
  <Field fieldID="CatalogProperty1" fieldValue="Chai" />
  <Field fieldID="CatalogProperty2" fieldValue="Best selling
beverage" />
  <Field fieldID="CatalogProperty3" fieldValue="1" />
  <Field fieldID="CatalogProperty4" fieldValue="1" />
  <Field fieldID="CatalogProperty5" fieldValue="10 boxes x 20 bags"
/>
  <Field fieldID="CatalogProperty6" fieldValue="18" />
</Product>
<Product Definition="NW_Food" listprice="10" id="Product2"
parentCategories="Category2">
  <Field fieldID="CatalogProperty1" fieldValue="Aniseed Syrup" />
  <Field fieldID="CatalogProperty2" fieldValue="Best selling
condiment" />
  <Field fieldID="CatalogProperty3" fieldValue="2" />
  <Field fieldID="CatalogProperty4" fieldValue="2" />
  <Field fieldID="CatalogProperty5" fieldValue="12 - 550 ml bottles"
/>
  <Field fieldID="CatalogProperty6" fieldValue="10" />
</Product>
......
```

To map a flat structure into a hierarchical one, you need to use a Looping functoid, available in the Advanced tab of the Functoid Palette (revisit Chapter 5 if you need to refresh BizTalk maps and functoids).

Building the BizTalk Messaging Infrastructure

With the specifications and map in place, now it's time to create the BizTalk Messaging infrastructure in order to perform the transformation. You can do this in BizTalk Messaging Manager.

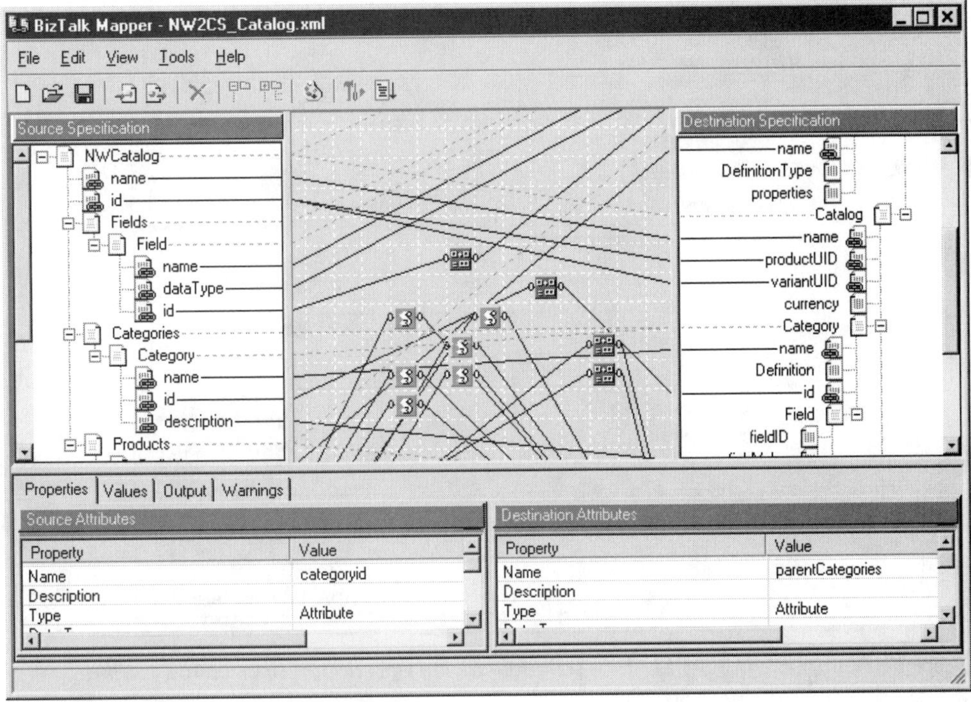

Figure 12-6 *The map in BizTalk Mapper*

Open the BizTalk Messaging Manager, create an organization, naming it, naturally enough, "Northwind." This is the source organization of the channel you are going to create shortly. You will use an XLANG schedule (which will be created in the next section of this chapter) as the destination, so there is no need to create a destination organization here. Otherwise, you might want to create a destination organization named Retail to represent the Retail solution web site managed by Commerce Server.

Next, you need to create two document definitions—Commerce Catalog and NW Catalog—which point to CSCatalogSchema.xml and NWCatalogSchema.xml you stored in the Microsoft BizTalk WebDAV repository, respectively.

Following this, you can create the messaging port, Port To Commerce Server Catalog. Select New Messaging Port To An Application. In the Destination Application page of the Messaging Port Wizard, select New XLANG Schedule and specify the Schedule moniker and Port name, as shown in Figure 12-7.

Accept the default values for the rest of the properties in the Messaging Port Wizard. In the last page of the wizard, specify Creating A New Channel From An Organization.

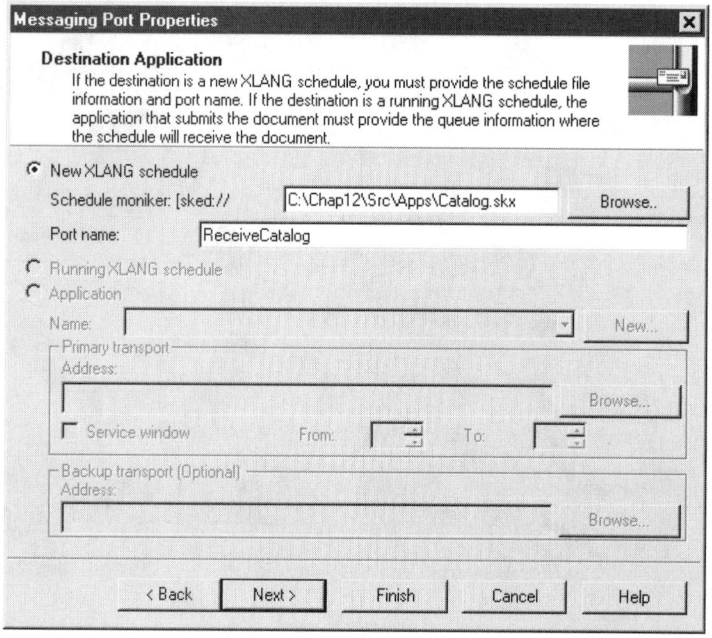

Figure 12-7 *Specifying an XLANG schedule as the destination application for the messaging port*

Finally, you can create the channel, Channel To Commerce Server Catalog. Specify Northwind as the source organization. Then choose NW Catalog and Commerce Catalog as the inbound and outbound document definitions, respectively. Specify NW2CS_Catalog.xml as the map. Accept the default values for the rest of the properties in the Channel Wizard and click Finish.

In addition, you need to create the file receive function, Receive NW Catalog, pulling the source catalog file from C:\Catalogs\In folder (you need to create a C:\Catalogs\In folder and a C:\Catalogs\Out folder for this example) and submitting it to channel, using the BizTalk Server Administration MMC snap-in (shown in Figure 12-8).

Creating an XLANG Schedule for Importing the Catalog

The XLANG Schedule you will create is shown in Figure 12-9.

It receives the Catalog from BizTalk Messaging Services and saves it to a permanent file in the desk (C:\Catalogs\Out) by calling the SaveCatalog method of the Catalog.Importer Windows script component. Finally, it calls the ImportCatalog method of the same script component to import the catalog into Commerce Server. The XLANG schedule drawing and executable, Catalog.skv and Catalog.skx, can be

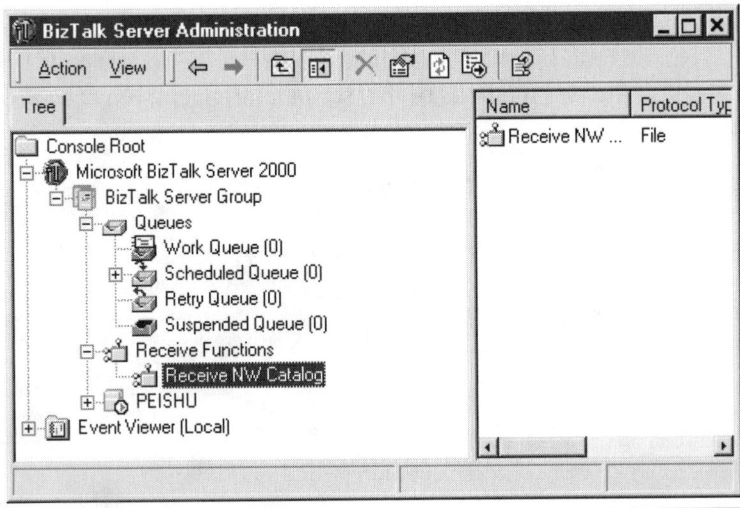

Figure 12-8 *Creating a file receive function*

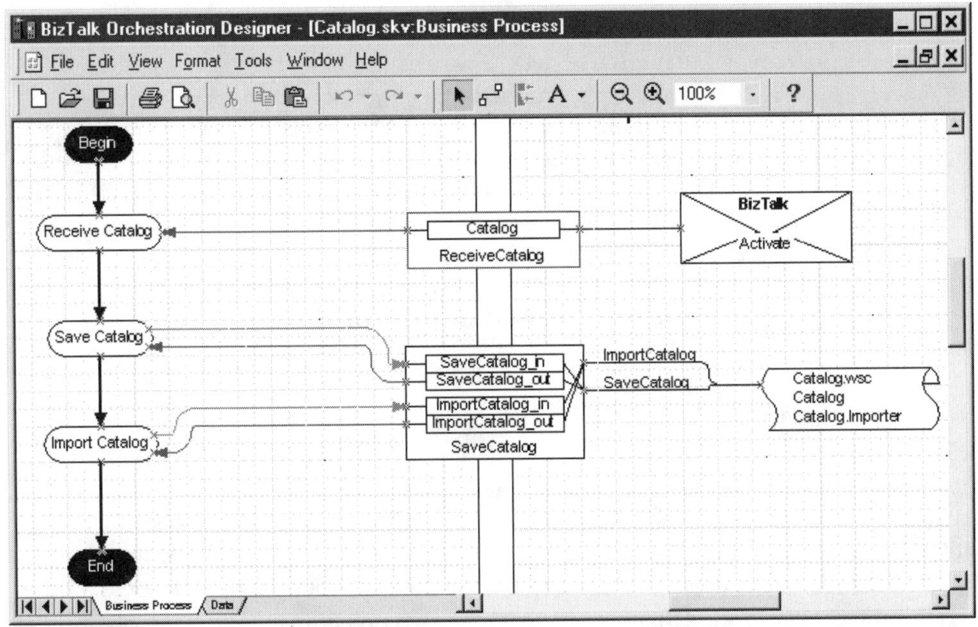

Figure 12-9 *The XLANG schedule drawing*

found in the Apps folder of the source code. The Windows script component, Catalog.wsc, can be found in the Components folder of the source code (you need to register it first). The two methods of this script component, *SaveCatalog* and *ImportCatalog*, are illustrated next:

```
Sub SaveCatalog(sCatalog, sFileName)
  Dim oXML
  Set oXML = CreateObject("MSXML2.DOMDocument")
  oXML.async = False
  oXML.LoadXML sCatalog
  oXML.Save sFileName
End Sub

Sub ImportCatalog(sFileName)
  Dim oAppConfig, oOptionsDictionary, oCatalogManager

  On Error Resume Next
  Set oAppConfig = CreateObject("Commerce.AppConfig")
  oAppConfig.Initialize "Retail"
  Set oOptionsDictionary = oAppConfig.GetOptionsDictionary("")

  Set oCatalogManager = CreateObject("Commerce.CatalogManager")
'//Note: if your CS2K and BizTalk box are not
'// on the same machine, you can export a proxy or better still
'//transfer the file and pick it up or call a Web Service or do
'//whatever is appropriate.
  oCatalogManager.Initialize
oOptionsDictionary.s_CatalogConnectionString, True
  oCatalogManager.ImportXML sFileName, True, True
If Err = 0 Then
  MsgBox "Catalog has been successfully imported!"
Else
  MsgBox Err.Description
End If
End Sub
```

The SaveCatalog is extremely simple—it loads the Catalog XML document into the DOM document object and calls the Save methods of the DOM document object to save the file to the desk. The ImportCatalog method, though, may deserve a little extra explanation. Notice that we have created two object instances here, one for the *AppConfig* object and the other for the CatalogManager object. The AppConfig object provides an interface for retrieving site configuration settings from the site configuration store. The *Initialize* method of the AppConfig object establishes a connection to the site whose name is passed on as the input parameter (in this case, the Retail Solution Site). Next, the *GetOptionsDictionary* method call of the AppConfig retrieves a *Dictionary* object that contains the site configuration information. Note that you always pass an empty string, "", when you call the GetOptionsDictionary method of the AppConfig object. You can use the Dictionary object to create, store, and retrieve name/value pairs in the system memory. The *s_CatalogConnectionString* property of the Dictionary object stores the connection string to the Commerce Server Catalog database and is passed to the Initialize method call of the CatalogManager object. The second Boolean parameter of the Initialize method of the CatalogManager object indicates whether the first parameter is an ADO connection string (True) or a site name (False). After the CatalogManager object is initialized, you can call the ImportXML method to import the catalog XML document to Commerce Server. The ImportXML method takes three import parameters. The first parameter is the name of the catalog XML file. The second parameter is a Boolean flag that indicates whether to update the existing catalog (True for incremental update) or replace the existing catalog with the imported file (False). The last input parameter determines whether the update should be executed synchronously (True) or asynchronously (False).

Figure 12-10 shows the message flow on the Data page.

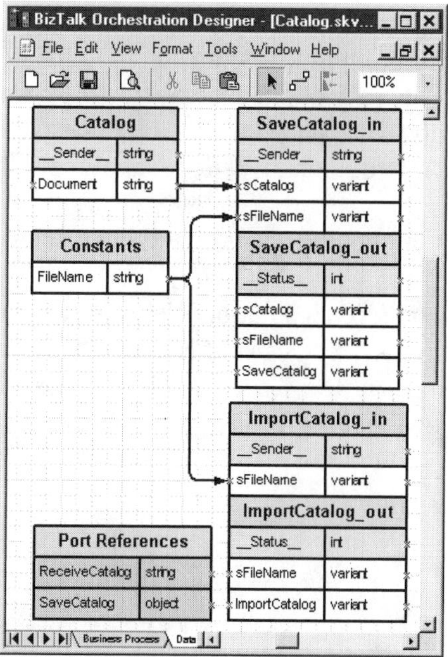

Figure 12-10 *The message flow of the XLANG schedule*

Testing the Solution

If you haven't created the C:\Catalogs\In and C:\Catalogs\Out folders yet, it is time to do so. The C:\Catalogs\In folder is monitored by the receive function, Receive NW Catalog, that you created earlier in this chapter. To start your test, copy the NWCatalog.xml file, located in the Sample Data folder to the C:\Catalogs\In folder. The receive function will pick up the file and submit it to BizTalk Server through the channel, Channel To Commerce Server Catalog, where the catalog document is transformed from its original format into the Commerce Server 2000 Catalog schema format. The channel then forwards the outbound document in Commerce Server schema format to the messaging port which in turn instantiates an instance of the XLANG schedule, Catalog.skx, and submits the converted document to the implementation port (not a messaging port) ReceiveCatalog. The XLANG scheduler engine then follows the process flow defined in the schedule and calls the SaveCatalog method of the script component Catalog.Importer which saves the converted catalog in the C:\Catalogs\Out folder. The next action of the XLANG schedule calls the ImportCatalog method of the script component, which in turn calls the ImportXML method of the CatalogManager object, as you saw earlier in this chapter. The ImportXML call will import the XML catalog document into the Commerce Server 2000 database. By the end of this process, you will see a message box, indicating that the catalog has been successfully imported. If you open the BizDesk for the Retail Solution Site, you should see that a new catalog, Foods, appears in the Catalog Editor module (as shown in Figure 12-11).

Clicking the Refresh catalog icon on the tool bar (the right-most icon) will cause the newly imported catalog to be published on the Retail Solution Site. Figure 12-12 shows that a new product definition, NW_Food, appears in the Catalog Designer module of the BizDesk.

Figure 12-13 shows that there are four new property definitions imported into the catalog.

Now you can log in to the Retail solution Web site at http://YourServerName/Retail. You can either generate a new login or use the login you created in the Tutorial, say Joe Visitor. After a successful login, if you click the Catalog hyperlink, the Foods catalog you imported should appear in the list, as shown in Figure 12-14.

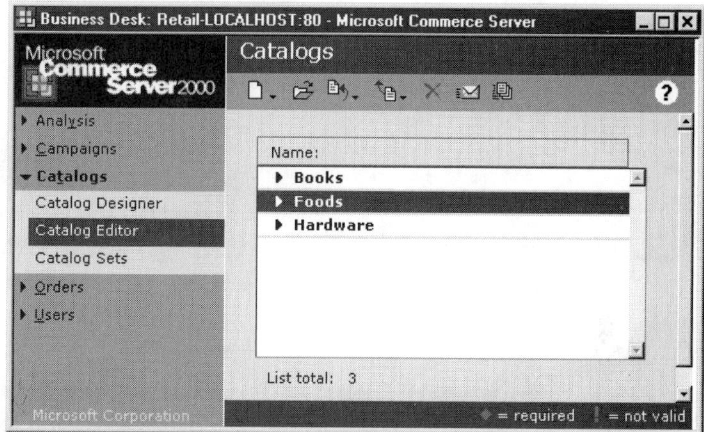

Figure 12-11 *A new catalog, Foods, appears in the Catalog Editor module of the Retail BizDesk*

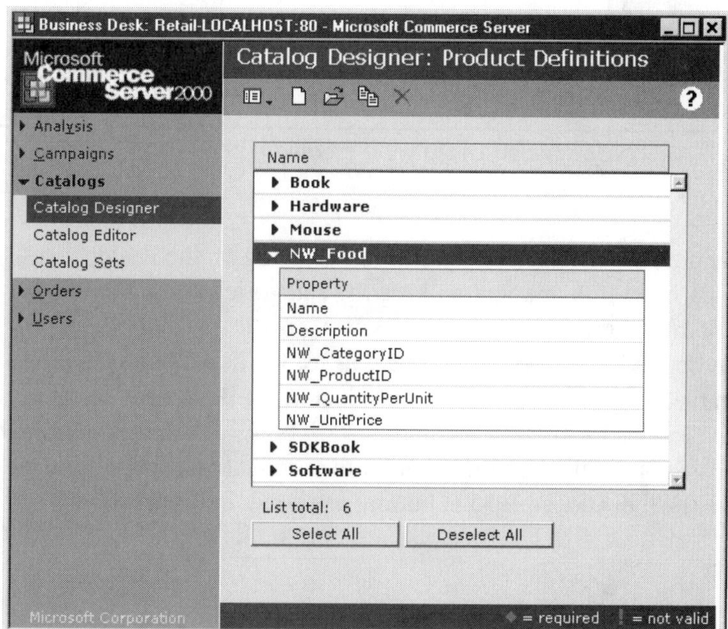

Figure 12-12 *A new product definition was created*

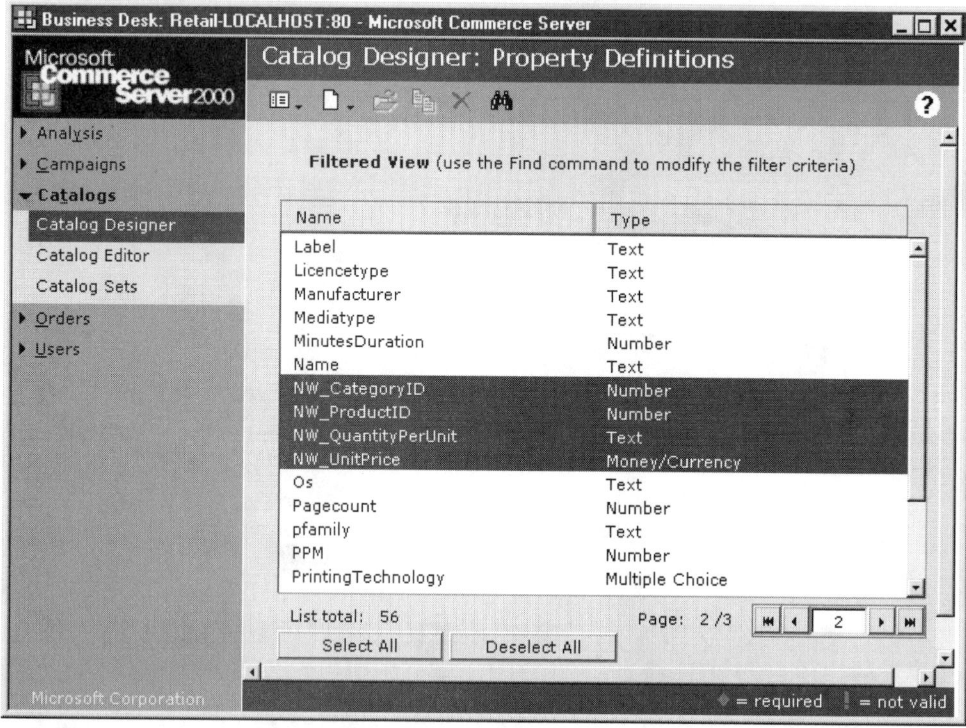

Figure 12-13 *New property definitions were created*

You may now choose foods from this new catalog on the Retail site. Click the Foods catalog hyperlink and you will see the categories under the Foods catalog (as shown in the Figure 12-15).

Click on the Beverages hyperlink, you will see the list of products in this category. In this example, you only imported one product in the Beverages category, Chai, as shown in the Figure 12-16.

To order this product, click the name of the product and specify the quantity you want, then click the Add To Basket button, as shown in Figure 12-17.

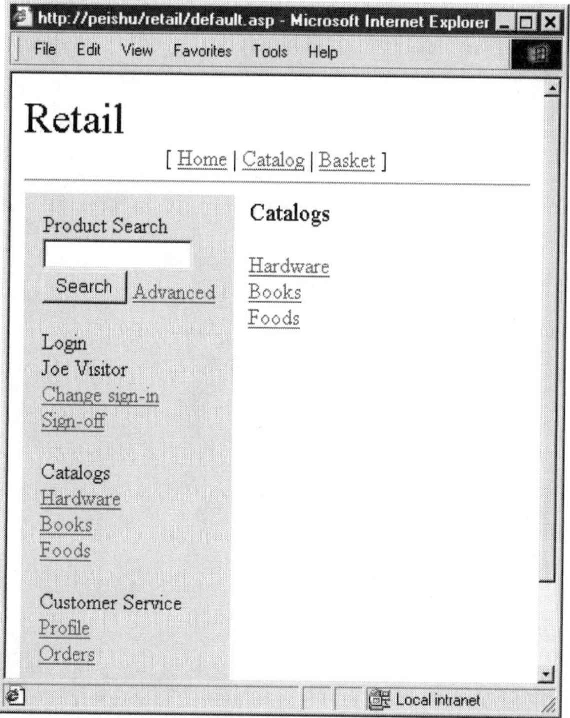

Figure 12-14 *The Foods catalog shows up in the Retail solution web site*

Follow the same process to add an Aniseed Syrup product to the Basket from the Condiments category. Click the Basket to see a list of products you tried to order (as shown in Figure 12-18).

Click the Check-out button and fill in the address and credit information on the next two pages. You should see an order summary page which displays the shipping and billing address, products you wanted to order, the sub-total, shipping and handling charges, taxes, order total, and so on, as shown in Figure 12-19.

Clicking the Check-out button on the order summary page will bring you to the order confirmation page (shown in Figure 12-20).

Figure 12-15 *Categories in the Foods catalog*

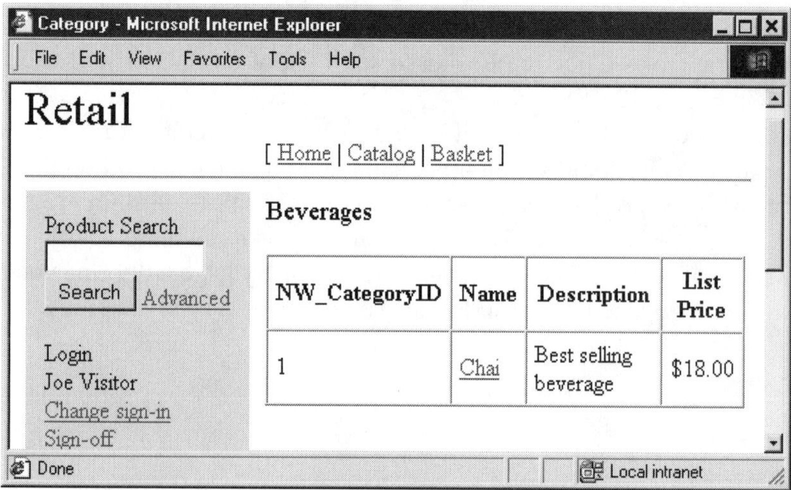

Figure 12-16 *Products in the Beverages category*

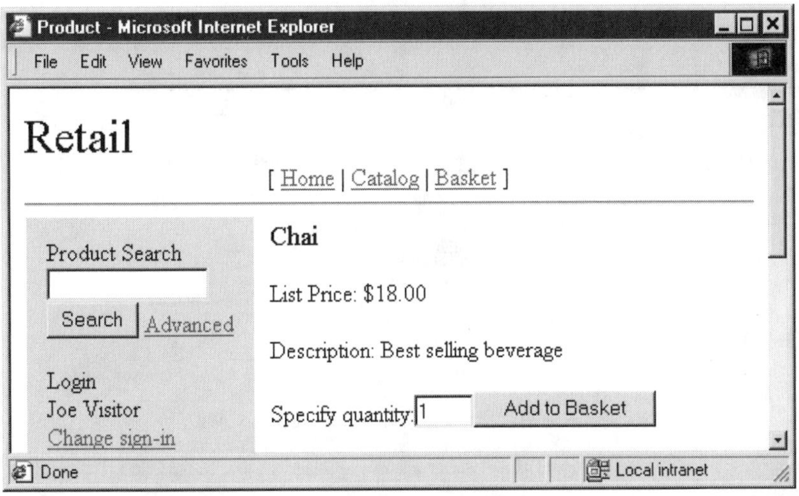

Figure 12-17 *Adding a product to the shopping basket*

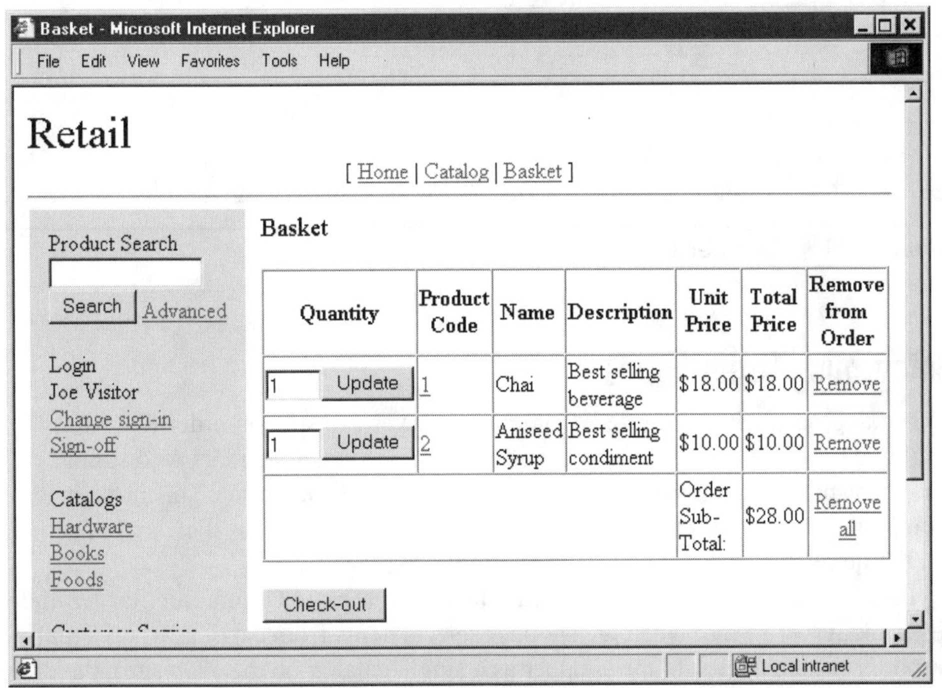

Figure 12-18 *Viewing your shopping basket*

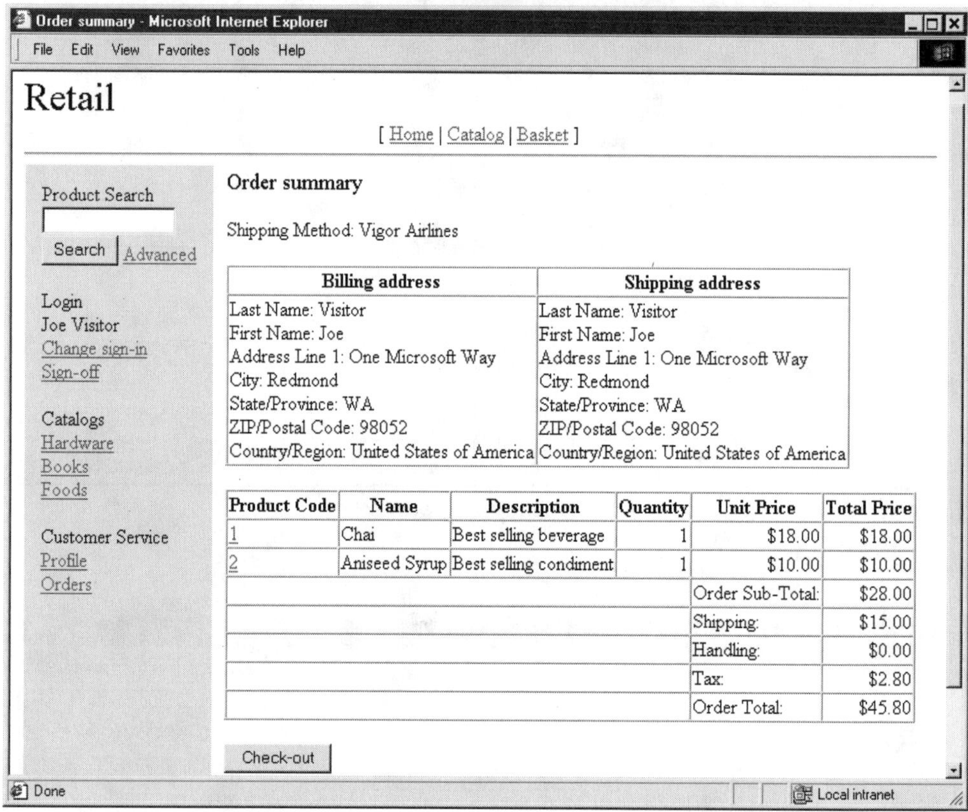

Figure 12-19 *The order summary page*

Integrating Order Forms

When appropriately configured, Commerce Server can split an order form into multiple purchase orders and then send them to individual vendors who supply the corresponding items in the order form, using BizTalk Server. This process is completely transparent to the shopper on the web site. As far as they are concerned, all the items they ordered come from a single catalog.

In this section, we will demonstrate how to integrate Commerce Server and BizTalk Server so that when the shopper selects items from catalogs of different vendors (which appear to the shopper as a single catalog on the Web site), the order form will be automatically divided up into individual purchase orders and submitted to appropriate vendors.

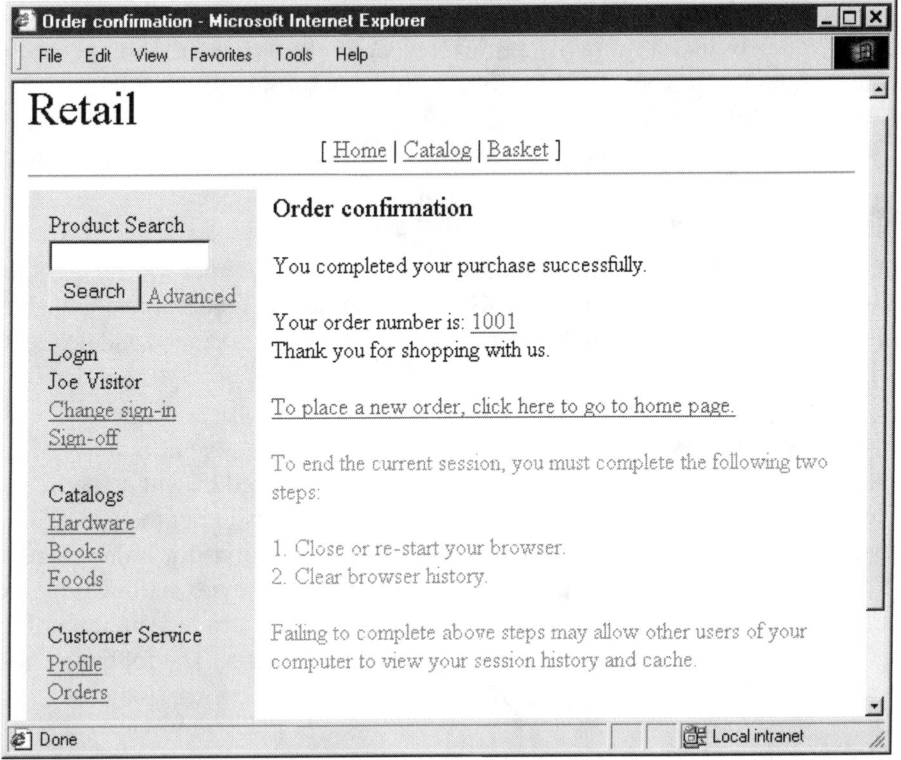

Figure 12-20 *The order confirmation page*

Solution Overview

To integrate order forms, you need to perform the following tasks:

- Configure Commerce Server and BizTalk Server to enable integration
- Associate vendors to appropriate catalogs to build a foundation for splitting purchase orders
- Optionally, customize the default ASP page that ships with the solution site to optimize the performance and improve scalability

In this example, you will configure the Retail Solution Site, along with the two catalogs that you can import from the Tutorial folder of the Commerce Server 2000 CD: the Books catalog and the Hardware catalog. You will create two fictitious organizations BookSupplier.com and HardwareSupplier.com to represent the vendors who provide these two catalogs, respectively. When an online customer selects both books and computer hardware products from the Retail Solution Site and checks out, the order form will be automatically split into two purchase orders and submitted to BizTalk Server, which then sends them to the appropriate vendors.

Configuring Commerce Server and BizTalk Server

First, you need to configure Commerce Server to enable the order form integration. Additionally, you need to create BizTalk Server messaging objects to both enable the association of vendors with the appropriate catalogs (the next step) and deliver the purchase orders to the vendors.

Configuring Commerce Server To configure Commerce Server, open Commerce Server Manager and expand Commerce Sites, then Retail, followed by Site Resources. Right-click App Default Config node and select Properties… Set the following properties on the Properties tab to enable BizTalk Integration (for order forms):

You can also access the App Default Config properties you set in Commerce Manager programmatically, by calling the GetOptionsDictionary method of the AppConfig object, passing an empty string as input parameter. The following table summarizes the corresponding properties of the returned Dictionary object:

Creating BizTalk Server Messaging Objects First, you need to create the following folders in the C:\ root directory:

C:\BookSupplier\PO_In
C:\BookSupplier\PO_Out
C:\HardwareSupplier\PO_In
C:\HardwareSupplier\PO_Out

Now, create two file receive functions—Receive Book PO and Receive Hardware PO—pointing to the C:\BookSupplier\PO_In and C:\HardwareSupplier\PO_In folders, respectively. Set the file masks for both receive functions as *.xml.

Next, rename the Home Organization "Retailer" and add an alias for it with Custom Identifier as "PO," Qualifier as "PO," and Value as "Retailer."

Then copy the POSchema.xml from the \Inetpub\wwwroot\Retail folder to <BizTalk Server Installation>\BizTalkServerRepository\DocSpecs\Microsoft folder.

Property	Description	Set The Value To...
BizTalk Catalog Doc Type	The name of the document definition you will create in BizTalk Messaging Manager for the catalog document. (We are not using this property in this example.)	Catalog
BizTalk Options	A flag that indicates whether BizTalk integration for order forms is enabled. (Set it to 1 to enable integration, and 0 to disable it.)	1
BizTalk PO Doc Type	The name of the document definition you will create in BizTalk Message Manager for the purchase order document.	PO
BizTalk Source Org Qualifier	The qualifier of the organization alias you will set in BizTalk Messaging Manager that represents the web site hosting the catalog.	PO
BizTalk Source Org Qualifier Value	The value of the qualifier of the organization alias you will set in BizTalk Messaging Manager that represents the web site hosting the catalog.	Retailer
BizTalk Submit Type	The value that corresponds to the BIZTALK_OPENNESS_TYPE enumeration. (Note that the explanation about this value in the Commerce Server product document is incorrect.)	1 (Not open)

Table 12-1 *Setting App Default Config properties to enable BizTalk integration*

Finally, create the rest of the BizTalk Server messaging objects (as illustrated in Figure 12-21).

App Default Config Property	Corresponding Dictionary Object Property
BizTalk Catalog Doc Type	S_BizTalkCatalogDocType
BizTalk Options	i_BizTalkOptions
BizTalk PO Doc Type	S_BizTalkOrderDocType
BizTalk Source Org Qualifier	S_BizTalkSourceQualifierID
BizTalk Source Org Qualifier Value	S_BizTalkSourceQualifierValue
BizTalk Submit Type	S_BizTalkSubmittypeQueue

Table 12-2 *App Default Config properties in the returned Dictionary object of the GetOptionsDictionary method*

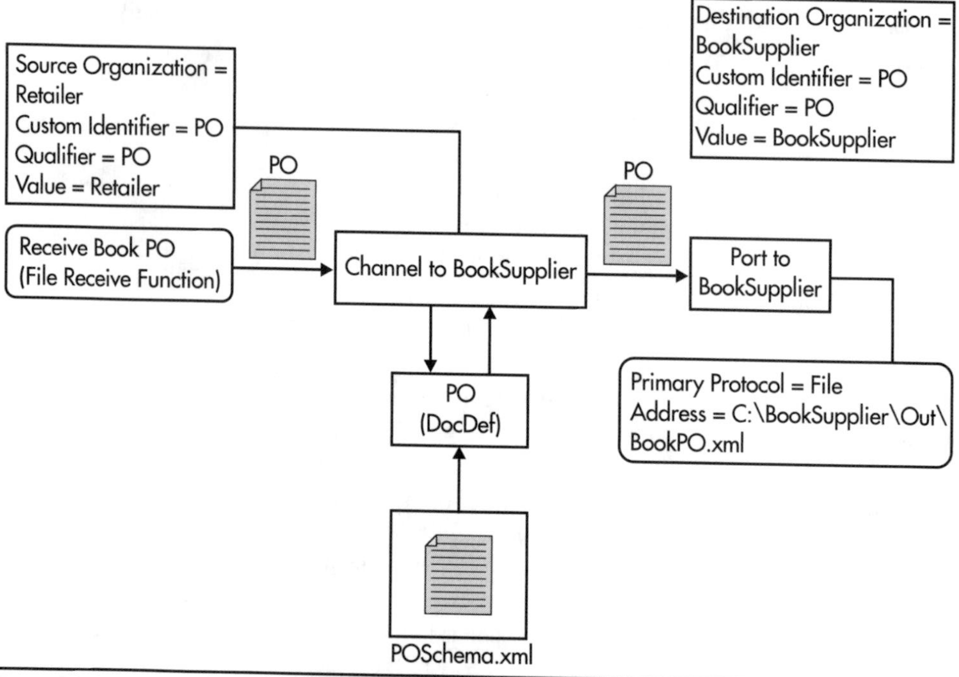

Figure 12-21 *BizTalk messaging objects for processing book purchase orders*

Similarly, create appropriate BizTalk Server messaging objects (as shown in Figure 12-22).

The purpose here is to demonstrate the integration of Commerce Server and BizTalk Server. For the sake of simplicity, you do not have to map the transformation of the purchase orders.

Associating Vendors with Catalogs

After you configured the Commerce Server and created and configured appropriate organizations in BizTalk Messaging Manager, you can associate a vendor with the appropriate catalog, using the Catalog Editor module of BizDesk. For example, to associate the BookSupplier to the Books catalog, open the BizDesk for the Retail solution site and expand Catalogs. Click Catalog Editor. Select Foods from the Catalogs list and click the Open icon on the toolbar. On the Catalog Properties page, click the … button next to the Vendor ID text box and you will see BookSupplier and HardwareSupplier in the pop-up box. Select BookSupplier and click OK. The Vendor ID property of the Books catalog is BookSupplier. In a similar manner, associate the Vendor ID of the Hardware catalog with HardwareSupplier.

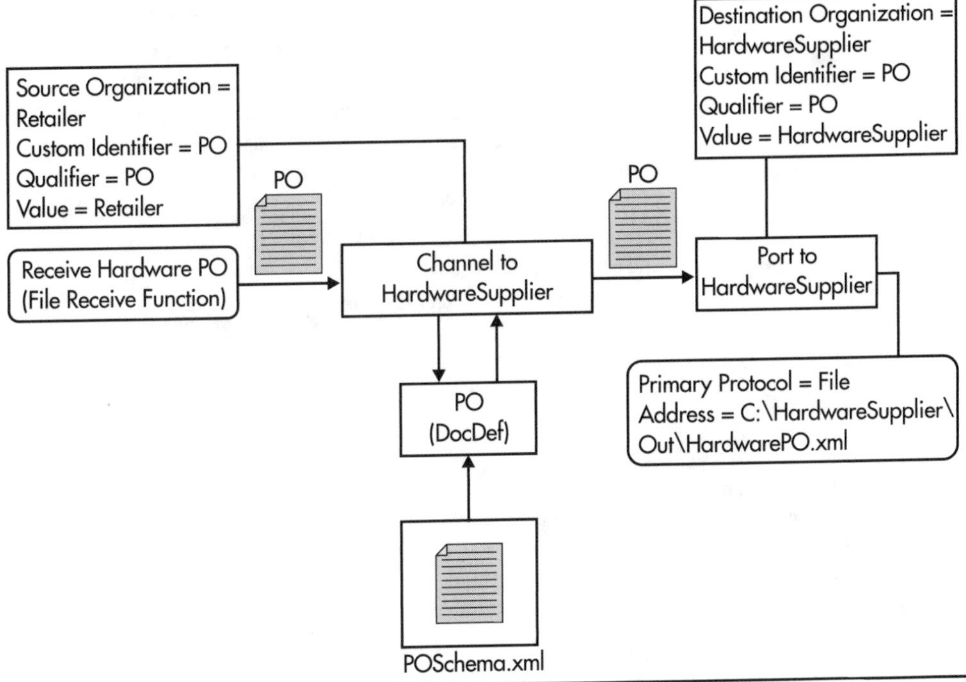

Figure 12-22 *BizTalk messaging objects for processing hardware purchase orders*

By assigning Vendor IDs to appropriate catalogs, you can identify the vendor of any given product in any order and thus make dividing up the order by its respective vendor possible (as we will explain next).

Modifying the Default ASP Page

Dividing up purchase orders and submitting them to the appropriate vendors through BizTalk Server is handled by the *InvokeBizTalk* function in the Payment.asp page, located in the \Include section of the Retail Solution Site virtual site folder. The following code listing illustrates how it works.

```
Sub InvokeBizTalk(ByVal mscsOrderGrp)
    Dim sOrderName, mscsOrderForm, oVendor, sXML
    Dim sVendorQualID, sVendorQualValue

    If dictConfig.i_BizTalkOptions = 1 Then
        For Each sOrderName In mscsOrderGrp.Value.OrderForms
            Set mscsOrderForm = _
```

```
                    mscsOrderGrp.Value(ORDERFORMS).Value(sOrderName)
                For Each oVendor In mscsOrderForm.value("_vendors")
                    If StrComp(oVendor.vendorID, DEFAULT_ORDERFORM, _
                                                 vbTextCompare) <> 0 Then
                        sXML = GetXMLForVendorItems(mscsOrderForm, oVendor)
                        sVendorQualID = _
                               mscsOrderForm.items( _
                                    oVendor.itemindexes(0)).vendor_qual)
                        sVendorQualValue = _
                               mscsOrderForm.items( _

oVendor.itemindexes(0)).vendor_qual_value
                        Call SubmitUsingBizTalk(sXML, oVendor.vendorID, _
                                                      sVendorQualID, _
                                                    sVendorQualValue)
                    End If
                Next
            Next
        End If
End Sub
```

The first thing the InvokeBizTalk function does is check to see if the BizTalk integration is enabled. If it is, then the function loops through the OrderForms collection for the given OrderGroup. For each order form in the collection, an inner nested For loop retrieves individual Vendor IDs, excluding the default order form that belongs to the Home organization (for example, if the user also selected the products from the Foods catalog whose Vendor ID is not associated with any vendors and yet is the default to the site host), because you don't want to send a purchase order for your own products. For each qualified vendor, the inner loop calls the *GetXMLForVendorItems* function, defined in the same ASP page (payment.asp), as we will explain shortly. The GetXMLForVendorItems function takes the order form and the vendor objects as the input parameters and returns an XML string, which is a subset of the original order form containing only items from the particular vendor. The next few lines of code retrieves the qualifier ID and value for the vendor organization. The last line of code in the inner loop calls the *SubmitUsingBizTalk* function that submits the separated purchase order to the BizTalk Server for processing.

The following code lists the GetXMLForVendorItems method:

```
Function GetXMLForVendorItems(ByVal mscsOrderForm, ByVal oVendor)
    Dim oXMLTransforms, oXMLSchema, oOrderFormXML, oXMLDoc
    Dim oNode, oAttribute
```

```
    Dim sFilePath

    Set oXMLTransforms = _
        Server.CreateObject("Commerce.DictionaryXMLTransforms")
    sFilePath = Server.MapPath("\" & MSCSAppFrameWork.VirtualDirectory) _
              & "\poschema.xml"
    Set oXMLSchema = oXMLTransforms.GetXMLFromFile(sFilePath)
    Set oOrderFormXML = _
      oXMLTransforms.GenerateXMLForDictionaryUsingSchema _
          (mscsOrderForm, oXMLSchema)
    Set oXMLDoc = Server.CreateObject("MSXML.DOMDOCUMENT")
    oXMLDoc.loadXML oOrderFormXML.xml
    For Each oNode In oXMLDoc.documentElement.childNodes
        If (oNode.nodeName = "Items") Then
            For Each oAttribute In oNode.Attributes
                If (oAttribute.nodeName = "vendorid") Then
                    If Not(oAttribute.nodeValue = oVendor.vendorID) Then
                        oNode.parentNode.removeChild oNode
                    End If
                    Exit For
                Else
                End If
            Next
        End If
    Next
    GetXMLForVendorItems = oXMLDoc.xml
End Function
```

The GetXMLForVendorItems function does the following:

1. Creates an instance of the *DictionaryXMLTransforms* object and then loads the POSchema.xml to a schema object by calling the GetXMLFromFile method of the DictionaryXMLTransforms object.
2. Calls the *GenerateXMLForDictionaryUsingSchema* method of the schema object which parses the order form into XML documents with the schema defined in POSchema.xml and returns a DOMDocument object.
3. Loads the XML contents of the order form to another declared DOMDocument object and manipulates it by traversing the DOM tree and removing all items whose value for the *vendorid* attributes are not those of the vendor of interest.
4. The resulting XML document is returned as a string.

The SubmitUsingBizTalk function looks like this:

```
Function SubmitUsingBizTalk(ByVal sXML, ByVal sVendorName, _
                            ByVal sDestQualID, ByVal sDestQualValue)
    Dim sSubmitType, sDocName
    Dim sSourceQualID, sSourceQualValue
    Dim oDBConfig, oOrg, sID, sName, sDef, oRes
    Dim oInterchange

    sSubmitType = dictConfig.s_BizTalkSubmittypeQueue
    sDocName = dictConfig.s_BizTalkOrderDocType
    sSourceQualID = dictConfig.s_BizTalkSourceQualifierID
    sSourceQualValue = dictConfig.s_BizTalkSourceQualifierValue

    Set oInterchange = Server.CreateObject("BizTalk.Interchange")
    oRes = oInterchange.Submit(sSubmitType, _
                               sXML, _
                               sDocName, _
                               sSourceQualID, _
                               sSourceQualValue, _
                               sDestQualID, _
                               sDestQualValue)
End Function
```

After variable declarations, the first block of code retrieves the appropriate application using a dictionary object (as explained earlier in this chapter). Then the function creates an instance of the Interchange object (which implements the IInterchange interface) and calls its Submit method to send the purchase order to BizTalk Server. Recall that according to the routing rules you learned earlier in this book, if the document definition, source and destination information are provided (as input parameters in this case), the BizTalk Server can find the correct channel without specifying the name of the channel. The problem with this approach is that the Submit method is not efficient, and remote DCOM calls are tightly coupled. A more appropriate approach would be using receive functions. In this example, you will use the file receive functions you created earlier to submit purchase order to the BizTalk Server. To use these receive functions, you need to modify the InvokeBizTalk method so it now looks like this:

```
Sub InvokeBizTalk(ByVal mscsOrderGrp)
    Dim sOrderName, mscsOrderForm, oVendor, sXML
    Dim sVendorQualID, sVendorQualValue
    Dim sVendorID, oXMLPO
    If dictConfig.i_BizTalkOptions = 1 Then
```

```
        For Each sOrderName In mscsOrderGrp.Value.OrderForms
            Set mscsOrderForm = _
                mscsOrderGrp.Value(ORDERFORMS).Value(sOrderName)
            For Each oVendor In mscsOrderForm.value("_vendors")
                If StrComp(oVendor.vendorID, DEFAULT_ORDERFORM, _
                                            vbTextCompare) <> 0 Then
                    sVendorID = oVendor.VendorID
                    sXML = GetXMLForVendorItems(mscsOrderForm, oVendor)
                    '//sVendorQualID = _
                    '//      mscsOrderForm.items( _
                    '//           oVendor.itemindexes(0)).vendor_qual)
                    '//sVendorQualValue = _
                    '//      mscsOrderForm.items( _
                    '//
oVendor.itemindexes(0)).vendor_qual_value
                    '//Call SubmitUsingBizTalk(sXML, oVendor.vendorID, _
                    '//                                 sVendorQualID, _
                    '//                              sVendorQualValue)
                    Set oXMLPO = CreateObject("MSXML2.DOMDocumnet")
                    oXMLPO.async = False
                    oXMLPO.LoadXML sXML
                    oXMLPO.Save "C:\" & sVendorID & "\PO_In\PO.xml"
                    Set oXMLPO = Nothing
                End If
            Next
        Next
    End If
End Sub
```

TIP

You can also do this by writing to a Message Queue which has the benefit of being transactional in most cases.

The inserted code in the preceding code listing is in bold. For comparison purposes, we commented out the original code instead of deleting them. What the new code does is create a DOMDocument object and load the XML purchase order to the DOM tree, saving it to an appropriate file folder according to the Vendor ID. You used a convention of C:\<VendorID>\PO_In when you created the file folders. These In folders are monitored by appropriate receive functions so that as soon as you save the PO document in an appropriate folder, as indicated in the previous code, it is picked up by the corresponding receive function and submitted to BizTalk Server for processing.

Testing the Solution

If you log in to the Retail Solution Site, order items from both the Books and Hardware catalogs, then check out all the way until you see the confirmation page, you should find the following files in the corresponding folders:

C:\BookSupplier\PO_Out\BookPO.xml
C:\HardwareSupplier\PO_Out\HardwarePO.xml

You may also want to use the BizTalk Document Tracking tool to verify the document exchange flows (as discussed in Chapter 8).

Chapter in Review

In this chapter, you learned about the integration features of Commerce Server 2000 and how it relates to BizTalk Server 2000. Particularly, you found out how to automate the integration of third-party catalogs with your web site, using BizTalk Server. You also learned how to integrate order forms so that when a customer submits an order containing items from different suppliers (or vendors), it is transparently divided up into several purchase order documents and sent to individual suppliers through the gateway established by BizTalk Server. You can also combine the catalog integration and order form management features to build complete integration solutions using Commerce Server and BizTalk Server.

PART

VI

Building Vertical Market Solutions Using BizTalk Server Accelerators

OBJECTIVES

- To learn BizTalk Server Accelerator for RosettaNet
- To understand BizTalk Server Accelerator for HIPAA
- To introduce Partner Interface Processes (PIPs) and the RosettaNet Implementation Framework (RNIF)
- To learn to use BizTalk Server Accelerator for RosettaNet to develop solutions using PIPs in RNIF

CHAPTER 13

BizTalk Server Accelerator for RosettaNet

IN THIS CHAPTER:

RosettaNet and the BizTalk Accelerator

Chapter in Review

Microsoft has developed a BizTalk Server Accelerator strategy to facilitate B2B integrations for vertical markets. A BizTalk Server Accelerator is an industry-specific collection of resources (XLANG schedules, document specifications, maps, adapters, parsers, serializers, tools, and so on) that can be used to accelerate the design and deployment of industry-specific BizTalk solutions. As of this writing, Microsoft has announced two vertical industry-focused BizTalk Server Accelerators, one for the Information Technologies (IT) industry (RosettaNet) and another for the health care industry (HIPAA). By the time you read this text, both of them should be released. In Part VI of this book, you will learn how to use BizTalk Server Accelerator for RosettaNet (this chapter) and BizTalk Server Accelerator for HIPAA (the next chapter) to develop BizTalk solutions for the IT and health care industries.

RosettaNet and the BizTalk Accelerator

RosettaNet (www.rosettanet.org) is a consortium of leading Information Technology (IT), Electronic Components (EC), and Semiconductor Manufacturing (SM) companies whose mission is to develop, implement, and promote open electronic business standards. In this section, we will introduce Partner Interface Processes and the RosettaNet Implementation Framework. We will then present BizTalk Server Accelerator for RosettaNet, showing you what tools and resources are available in the Accelerator so you understand how they can help develop RosettaNet Implementation Framework-compliant applications. Finally, we will explain how to install BizTalk Server Accelerator for RosettaNet.

Partner Interface Processes and the RosettaNet Implementation Framework

RosettaNet defines electronic business guidelines for the IT Supply Chain as a series of specifications of business processes between partners in the distribution channel, known as *Partner Interface Processes* or *PIPs*. *RosettaNet Implementation Framework* (or *RNIF*) provides exchange protocols for quick and efficient implementation of PIPs. The Microsoft BizTalk Server Accelerator for RosettaNet supports a variety of PIP versions as well as RNIF 1.1. RosettaNet has recently published the RNIF 2.0 specification and it is expected that future versions of the Microsoft BizTalk Server Accelerator for RosettaNet will support this new specification.

PIPs and Clusters

The business processes or PIPs are categorized by groups. They are initially grouped into eight *Clusters* (starting from Cluster 0). A Cluster is a group of core business processes that represents the backbone of the trading network. Each Cluster is further divided into Segments or cross-enterprise processes that involve more than one type of trading partner. Each Segment, meanwhile, contains individual PIPs. The following table describes the eight Clusters, the Segments of each Cluster, and the individual PIPs within each Segment. The naming convention for PIPs is:

Cluster_Number + Segment_Number + PIP_Number

For example, PIP 0A1-Notification of Failure represents the first (there is only one in this particular case) PIP in Segment A of Cluster 0. Whereas the Cluster numbers and Segment numbers are continuous, with PIP numbers this is not always the case.

The BizTalk Server Accelerator for RosettaNet has built-in support for the eight most-used PIPs in three Clusters: RosettaNet Support, Product Information, and Order Management. However, as you will learn, the accelerator has been designed to facilitate easy addition of existing and up-and-coming PIPs through the use of a template approach. The following table lists the Segments and PIPs of these three clusters. You can get a complete list of RosettaNet Clusters, Segments, and PIPs from RosettaNet's Web site at http://www.rosettanet.org.

Cluster	Segment	PIPs
0: RosettaNet Support	0A: Administrative	0A1*: Notification of Failure
2: Product Information	2A: Preparation for Distribution	2A1*: Distribute New Product Information 2A2: Query Product Information 2A3: Query Marketing Information 2A4: Query Sales Promotion & Rebate Information 2A5: Query Technical Information 2A6: Query Product Lifecycle Information 2A7: Query Product Discontinuation Information 2A8: Distribute Product Stock Keeping Unit (SKU) 2A9: Query Technical Product Information 2A12: Distributed Product Master

Table 13-1 *Supported Segments and PIPs of these RosettaNet clusters* PIPs directly supported in BizTalk Server Accelerator for RosettaNet*

Cluster	Segment	PIPs
	2B: Product Change Notification	2B1: Change Basic Product Information 2B2: Change Marketing Information 2B3: Change Sales Promotion & Rebate Information 2B4: Change Product Technical Information 2B5: Change Product Lifecycle Information
	2C: Product Design Information	2C1: Distribute Engineering Change Status 2C2: Request Engineering Change 2C3: Distribute Engineering Change Response 2C4: Request Engineering Change Approval 2C5: Notify of Engineering Change Order 2C6: Notify of Engineering Change Implementation Plan
3: Order Management	3A: Quote and Order Entry	3A1: Request Quote 3A2*: Request Price and Availability 3A3: Request Shopping Cart Transfer 3A4: Request Purchase Order 3A5: Query Order Status 3A6: Distribute Order Status 3A7*: Notify of Purchase Order Management 3A8: Request Purchase Order Change 3A9: Request Purchase Order Cancellation 3A10: Notify of Quote Acknowledgement
	3B: Transportation and Distribution	3B1: Distribute Transportation Projection 3B2*: Notify of Advance Shipment 3B3: Distribute Shipment Status 3B4: Query Shipment Status 3B5: Request Shipment Change 3B6: Notify of Shipments Tendered
	3C: Returns and Finance	3C2: Request Financing Approval 3C3*: Notify of Invoice 3C4*: Notify of Invoice Reject 3C5: Notify of Billing Statement 3C6: Notify of Remittance Advice
	3D: Product Configuration	3D8: Distribute Work in Progress 3D9: Query Work in Process

Table 13-1 *Supported Segments and PIPs of these RosettaNet clusters* PIPs directly supported in BizTalk Server Accelerator for RosettaNet* (continued)

Introducing BizTalk Server Accelerator for RosettaNet

The BizTalk Server Accelerator for RosettaNet is a set of infrastructure, tools, and tutorials built on top of BizTalk Server 2000 as an add-on product to help you rapidly develop RosettaNet RNIF 1.1-compliant PIPs.

An Infrastructure for PIP Development

BizTalk Server Accelerator for RosettaNet provides a PIP-centric infrastructure for rapidly developing RNIF 1.1 solutions, including the following:

- **Roles** BizTalk Server Accelerator for RosettaNet uses the concepts of *Initiator Role* and *Responder Role* to describe the parties involved in transaction or notification processes. In a transaction process, an initiator (the requester) sends a request to a responder (the request handler) and the responder sends an acknowledgement back to the initiator. Later, after the responder finishes processing the request, it sends a response back to the initiator, and then the initiator sends another acknowledgement to the responder. In a notification model, an initiator (the notifier) sends a notification to a responder (the notification handler) and the responder sends back an acknowledgement message to the initiator. In a procurement scenario, the buyer plays the initiator role, sending a purchase order request to the supplier who acts as the responder. The supplier first sends an acknowledgement back to the buyer, indicating it has received the purchase order request. The supplier then processes the order and sends a response to the buyer. Upon receiving the response from the supplier, the buyer sends an acknowledgement message back to the supplier.
- **PIP Implementations** PIP implementations are pre-built, ready to use, XLANG schedules, directly mapped to the corresponding PIP specifications. Currently, there are eight PIP implementations available in BizTalk Server Accelerator for RosettaNet: 0A1, 2A1, 3A2, 3A4, 3A7, 3B2, and 3C4, located in individual PIP subfolders (for example, the PIP 3A4 Manage Purchase Order folder) under the <BizTalk Server Accelerator for RosettaNet Installation>\PIP SDK\PIP Implementations\Rnif 1.1 folder. Under each subfolder, there can be one or more pairs of requester/responder XLANG schedules.
- **PIP Patterns** Unlike PIP implementations, PIP patterns are extensible XLANG schedule templates that can be used as starting points for developing RNIF 1.1-compliant PIPs that are not part of the eight pre-built PIP implementations. There are two PIP patterns, Transaction and Notification,

located in the Transaction and Notification subfolder under the <BizTalk Server Accelerator for RosettaNet Installation>\PIP SDK\PIP Patterns folder. Again, each subfolder contains a pair of XLANG schedule templates (Initiator/Responder).

- **PIP Adapters** In BizTalk Server Accelerator for RosettaNet, PIP adapters are COM components that are used to facilitate the interaction of line-of-business (LOB) applications, BizTalk Messaging Services, and BizTalk Orchestration Services (for integration with their business partners). PIP adapters include *PIP Adapter SDK classes* (*CPIPAdapter*, *CPIPAdapterManager*, *CPIPAdapterSubmit*) which are glues that integrate BizTalk Messaging Services, BizTalk Orchestration Services, legacy systems and/or line-of-business (LOB) applications. Additionally, *PIP Adapter Auxiliary Classes* are used by the XLANG schedules to persist and retrieve string/integer data, interact with Registry, and perform other related tasks. Finally, *Application Adapters* are COM components that implement either the *StubInitiatorApplication* or the *StubResponderApplication* interface and provide a gateway between your LOB application and PIP implementation XLANG schedules.

A Rich Set of Tools

BizTalk Server Accelerator for RosettaNet provides a set of tools that help you to rapidly develop, administer, and test your RosettaNet PIP implementations. Every tool also ships with source code that can be used for developing and implementing BizTalk Server 2000 solutions.

The Messaging Configuration Wizard The Messaging Configuration Wizard is a code generation tool that you can use to generate necessary VBScript code to automatically create required BizTalk Server Messaging Objects (source and destination organizations, channels, messaging ports, document definitions, envelopes, and so on). These messaging objects are used in conjunction with corresponding PIP Implementation XLANG schedules and PIP SDK Adapters to provide a complete PIP implementation. You can think of it as creating the interactions in the RNIF layer.

Later in this chapter, you will learn how to use the Messaging Configuration Wizard to generate script code for setting up the BizTalk Server Messaging Services objects. When the time comes, we'll walk through the PIP Adapter Tutorial that ships with the BizTalk Server Accelerator for RosettaNet.

The PIP Administrator The PIP Administrator is a simple graphical user interface (GUI) that enables you to associate a specific RosettaNet PIP (such as 3A4, Purchase Order Request) with a corresponding PIP Implementation XLANG schedule. The physical file path location of the PIP Implementation XLANG schedules you specified are stored in a SQL Server database (BTSKInstances was created when you installed the BizTalk Server Accelerator for RosettaNet) so that they can be retrieved later during the run time by the PIP SDK adapter through appropriate lookup procedures.

Later in this chapter, you will learn how to use the PIP Administrator.

The PIP Schema Manager The PIP Schema Manager enables you to merge a RosettaNet Implementation Framework (RNIF) Document Type Definition schema into the *BizTalk Messaging RosettaNet Universal Message*. Later, you'll learn about the BizTalk Messaging RosettaNet Universal Message and how to use the PIP Schema Manager to merge PIP 1A1, Request Account Setup, into BizTalk Messaging RosettaNet Universal Message. The PIP Schema manager enables you to leverage new PIPs that utilize RNIF 1.1 when made available by RosettaNet rather than waiting for Microsoft to update the accelerator.

The PIP XLANG Schedule Tester The PIP XLANG Schedule Tester enables you to test your PIP XLANG schedule implementations by simulating either role (initiator or responder) in a RosettaNet transaction. When you test an initiator role, the PIP XLANG Schedule Tester plays the responder role, consuming request messages and submitting response messages. When you test a responder role, on the other hand, the PIP XLANG Schedule Tester simulates the initiator role, submitting request messages and handling response messages. The Tester application simulates message transfer over the Internet by using local message queues. Later in this chapter, you will learn how to use the PIP XLANG Schedule Tester to test the XLANG schedule, 3A2Request.skx, PIP 3A2 Request Price and Availability.

Developing PIP Implementations

To develop a PIP implementation using BizTalk Server Accelerator for RosettaNet, follow these steps:

1. Select an existing PIP implementation XLANG schedule or develop a new PIP implementation schedule from one of the PIP patterns (Transaction or Notification).
2. Develop an Application Adapter for either an LOB application, a legacy application, or a specific data source by implementing either the StubInitiatorApplication interface or the StubResponderApplication interface, depending on the role involved in the RosettaNet transaction. RosettaNet only manages the firewall-to-firewall interface. Once you have the document ready to give to the private process, you can utilize the adapter and BizTalk Server's EAI functionality to send to, or retrieve from, LOB applications.

3. Bind the PIP XLANG schedule to the Application Adapter you developed in Step 2.
4. Bind the PIP XLANG schedule to the BizTalk Server Messaging Service by replacing a Message Queuing port to the CPIPAdapterSubmit class.
5. Compile the PIP XLANG schedule and register it with the system through the PIP Administrator tool.
6. Run the PIP implementation, including the PIP XLANG schedules and related LOB applications.

The PIP Adapter Tutorial that ships with BizTalk Server Accelerator for RosettaNet contains PIP implementations for both initiator and responder roles of RosettaNet PIP 3A2, Query Price and Availability, as well as two simple applications that simulate LOB applications. We will walk you through the tutorial to demonstrate how to use the infrastructure and tools of BizTalk Server Accelerator for RosettaNet to implement RosettaNet PIP applications. Later, we'll also demonstrate how to use the PIP XLANG Schedule Tester to test a PIP implementation XLANG schedule, as well as teach you how to use the PIP Schema Manager to merge the PIP 1A1 DTD schema (Request Account Setup) into the BizTalk Messaging RosettaNet Universal Message.

Using the PIP Adapter Tutorial

In this section, you will use the PIP Adapter Tutorial that ships with BizTalk Server Accelerator for RosettaNet to get familiar with the process of implementing a RosettaNet PIP solution.

The Environment The PIP Adapter Tutorial is shipped as a Zip file named TutorialFiles.zip, located in \Program Files\Microsoft BizTalk Server Accelerator for RosettaNet\PIP SDK folder. Unzipping the Tutorial to C: drive (or any other hard drive) creates the following folders:

C:\Tutorial\Initiator\Application

C:\Tutorial\Initiator\Application Adapter

C:\Tutorial\Initiator\Bin

C:\Tutorial\Responder\Application

C:\Tutorial\Responder\Application Adapter

C:\Tutorial\Responder\Bin

The BizTalk Server Accelerator for RosettaNet online documentation has detailed descriptions about the application architecture of the Tutorial (under PIP Adapter Tutorial\Defining), the Roles, and Data Flow. The Tutorial is a simple implementation of RosettaNet PIP 3A2—the Price and Availability Query—including implementations for both initiator and responder. The Application folders contain LOB applications for both roles (initiator and responder), whereas Application Adapter folders contain application adapters. The Bin folder contains respective PIP Implementation XLANG schedules. You will work with the files in these folders to complete the set up of the Tutorial.

Application Adapters The BizTalk Server Accelerator for RosettaNet uses *Application Adapters* to provide the connection points for you to integrate BizTalk Messaging Services into your LOB, legacy applications, or third-party enterprise packages, such as ERP or CRM packages.

The PIP Implementation XLANG schedules as well as the PIP patterns in BizTalk Server Accelerator for RosettaNet contain stub COM components that are abstract COM interfaces (StubInitiatorApplication or StubResponderApplication) that serve as placeholders. You are responsible for creating concrete COM components that implement these interfaces. The Tutorial contains two application adapters, InitiatorAdapter and ResponderAdapter, both of which are VB ActiveX DLL projects, located in the appropriate Application Adapter folders. In either case, the VB project must have a reference set to Microsoft BizTalk Server Accelerator for RosettaNet PIP Application Interfaces 1.0 Type Library. This type library defines two COM interfaces, *IPIPInitiatorApplication* and *IPIPResponderApplication*. In your VB projects, you use the *Implements* keyword to make the stub code of the appropriate interface available.

The IPIPInitiatorApplication interface contains nine methods, while the IPIPResponderApplication interface has six methods, as detailed in the online documentation. In this tutorial, the InitiatorAdapter project contains a *CInitiator* class which implements the IPIPInitiatorApplication interface. For demonstration purposes, only the *HandleResponseMessage* method is implemented, which simply displays a message box with the flow ID (a GUID that represents a running XLANG schedule instance):

```
Private Sub IPIPInitiatorApplication_HandleResponseMessage( _
    p_strFlowID As String, _
    p_strRequestMessage As String, _
    p_strResponseMessage As String, _
    p_strErrDesc As String)

    MsgBox "Initiator Application Received Message: " _
           & p_strFlowID

End Sub
```

You still have to include the stubs for the rest of the methods in the IPIPInitiatorApplication interface, even though you won't implement them. This is a VB requirement.

Compile the InitiatorAdapter.vbp project since InitiatorAdapter.dll will automatically register it in the Registry. The IStubInitiatorApplication interface supports nine methods that can be called by the RosettaNet PIP XLANG schedules for the Initiator role (these are described in the Table 13-2). For detailed method signature and syntax, refer to the online documentation of the BizTalk Accelerator for RosettaNet.

Similarly, the ResponderAdapter Visual Basic project contains a single class module, *CResponder*, which implements the IPIPResponderApplication interface.

Method	Description
InitializeRequestMessage	Initializes a request message.
ValidateResponseMessage	Validates a response message. This is the primary method, as demonstrated in the Tutorial.
HandleResponseMessage	Handles a response message.
HandleError	Handles errors. This is an error trapper.
HandleRNException	Handles a RosettaNet exception.
HandleRNReceiptAcknowledgement	Handles a RosettaNet receipt acknowledgement.
HandleRNReceiptAcknowledgementException	Handles a RosettaNet receipt acknowledgement exception.
HandleUnexpectedResponse	Handles an unexpected response.
HandleUnexpectedSignal	Handles an unexpected signal.

Table 13-2 *The methods of the IStubInitiatorApplication interface*

In this case, you only implement one method, *StartRequestHandling*, and include the stubs for the rest of the methods:

```
Private Sub IPIPResponderApplication_StartRequestHandling( _
    p_strFlowID As String, _
    p_strRequestMessage As String, _
    p_strSkeletalResponseMessage As String, _
    p_strErrDesc As String)

    Dim FlowIDDataFile As String
    Dim XMLRequestMessageDataFile As String
    Dim XMLSkeletalResponseMessageDataFile As String

    MsgBox "Responder Application Received Message: " & _
           p_strFlowID

    FlowIDDataFile = "FlowID.xml"
    SaveDataToXML "<FlowID>" & p_strFlowID & "</FlowID>", _
                  FlowIDDataFile

    XMLRequestMessageDataFile = "RequestMessage.xml"
    SaveDataToXML p_strRequestMessage, _
                  XMLRequestMessageDataFile

    XMLSkeletalResponseMessageDataFile = "SkeletalResponseMessage.xml"
    SaveDataToXML p_strSkeletalResponseMessage, _
                  XMLSkeletalResponseMessageDataFile


End Sub
```

As you can see from the preceding code, the StartRequestHandling method displays another message box and writes three files to the hard disk, FlowID.xml (which contains the GUID for the initiator XLANG schedule instance), RequestMessage.xml (which contains the request message), and SkeletalResponseMessage.xml (which contains the skeletal response message).

The SaveDataToXML function loads the content of an XML document into a DOMDocument object and calls the Save method to persist the XML document to an external file on the hard disk:

```
Private Sub SaveDataToXML(Data As String, FileName As String)
    Dim DOM As New DOMDocument
    DOM.async = False
    DOM.loadXML Data
    DOM.save FilePath & FileName
    Set DOM = Nothing
End Sub
```

Unless you set the tutorial files in the D: drive, you need to modify the *FilePath* constant declaration to reflect the actual disk drive where you unzipped the Tutorial. For example:

```
Const FilePath = "C:\Tutorial\Responder\Bin\"
```

Compile ResponderAdapter.dll will automatically register the responder application adapter in the Registry.

The IStubResponderApplication interface supports six methods that can be called on by the RosettaNet PIP XLANG schedules for the Responder role, as described in the following table. For detailed method signatures and syntax, refer to the online documentation of the BizTalk Accelerator for RosettaNet.

Method	Description
StartRequestHandling	Starts request handling. This is the primary method as demonstrated in the Tutorial.
ValidateRequestMessage	Validates a request message.
HandleError	Handles an error.
HandleRNReceiptAcknowledgement	Handles a RosettaNet receipt acknowledgement.
HandleRNReceiptAcknowledgementException	Handles a RosettaNet receipt acknowledgement exception.
HandleUnexpectedSignal	Handles an unexpected signal.

Table 13-3 *Methods of the IStubResponderApplication interface*

PIP Implementation XLANG Schedules In this tutorial, you need to update two PIP XLANG schedules drawings, 3A2RequesterTutorial.skv and 3A2ResponderTutorial.skv, respectively. They are located in the appropriate Bin folders.

First, open the 3A2RequesterTutorial.skv XLANG schedule drawing. During the installation of BizTalk Server Accelerator for RosettaNet, a local private Messaging Queuing queue was created on the machine where the Accelerator is installed, .\private\RNMsgOut. By default, PIP implementation XLANG schedules (and the PIP patterns) send documents or acknowledgements to this private queue via a *SendRequestPort*. If you locate the SendRequestPort in the 3A2RequesterTutorial.skv XLANG drawing, you will find that the port is no longer connected to any actions. It is replaced by another port, *RNSendPort* which is bound to the COM component, CPIPAdapterSubmit, defined in the Microsoft BizTalk Server Accelerator for RosettaNet Submit Services type library. In this tutorial, this binding step was already done for you. In your own PIP implementations, however, you will be responsible for replacing the message queuing port.

You do, however, need to replace the stub placeholder with the application adapter you created earlier in this section. Locate the StubInitiatorApplication COM component, next to the *AppCalloutPort*, as shown in Figure 13-1.

Double-click the StubInitiatorApplication COM component to bring up the COM Component Binding Wizard. Navigate to the Class Information page, select InitiatorAdapter.CInitiator interface, as shown in Figure 13-2.

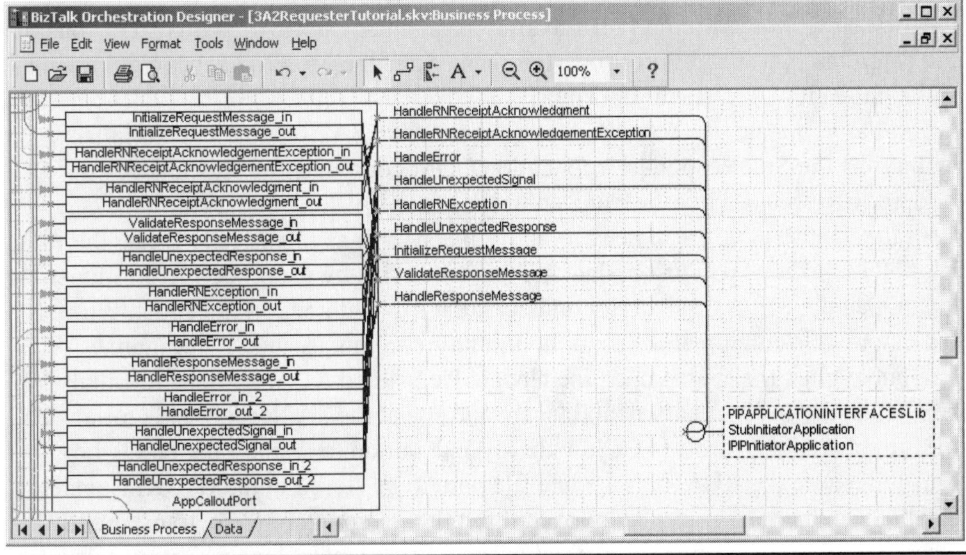

Figure 13-1 *Locating the StubInitiatorApplication COM component*

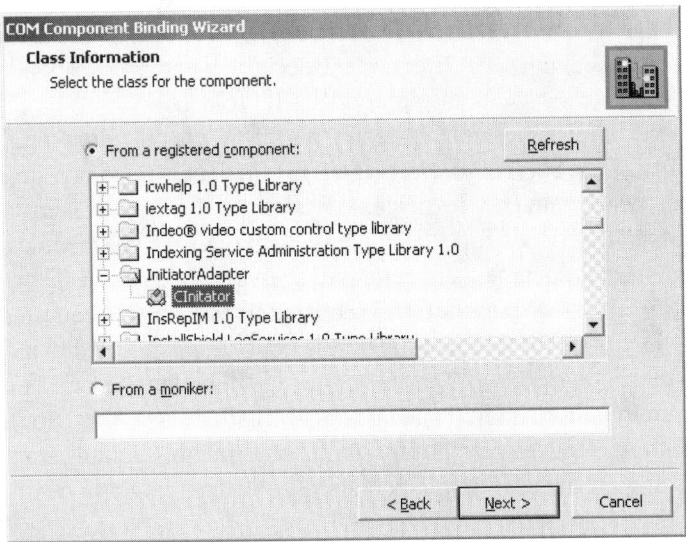

Figure 13-2 *Selecting the InitiatorAdapter.CInitiator interface*

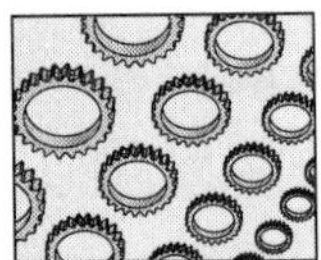

NOTE

There is a misspelling in the source code that ships with the tutorial. The CInitiator was misspelled as CInitator.

Click Next. In the Method Information page, click CheckAll and Next. Then click Finish on the Advanced Port Properties page. Save the XLANG schedule drawing and compile it to 3A2RequesterTutorial.skx.

Similarly, update the XLANG schedule drawing, 3A2ResponderTutorial.skv, by binding the StubResponderApplication COM component to Responder Adapter.CResponder interface and compiling it to 3A2ResponderTutorial.skx.

In the next step, you will need to notify the system as to where to locate the PIP XLANG schedules you just updated. You can do this by using the PIP Administrator tool. Open the PIP Administrator and click the row with 3a2 in the Global Process Indicator Code column and Yes in the Initiator column, as shown in Figure 13-3.

Double-click the row to open the Update Registered XLANG Schedule dialog box. Click the Browse button, and locate and select the 3A2RequesterTutorial.skx file, as shown in Figure 13-4. Click the Update button to dismiss the dialog box. This will cause the XLANG schedule file path to be stored in the BTSKInstances database so that later it can be invoked through the moniker syntax transparently when you call the appropriate method of the CPIPAdapterManager interface.

Similarly, you can update the XLANG schedule in the BTSKInstances database for 3A2ResponderTutorial.skx.

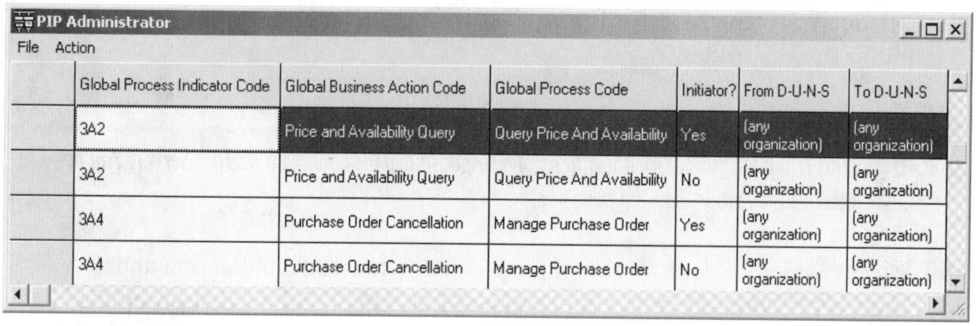

Figure 13-3 *Using the PIP Administrator*

BizTalk Messaging Objects Now that you have completed the appropriate PIP XLANG schedules, it is time to set up corresponding BizTalk Server Messaging Objects for the RNIF layer. You can use (and should use) the Messaging Configuration Wizard to complete this task. In this tutorial, you will need to create the BizTalk Server Messaging Services infrastructure for both the initiator and responder organizations. Therefore, you need to run the wizard two times. Follow the instructions documented in the PIP Adapter Tutorial\Creating Organizations, Ports and Channels section of the online documentation to create the BizTalk Server Messaging Services objects for both the initiator and responder roles.

Since the Tutorial uses the receiveRNO.asp file as the HTTP transport for some messaging ports, you need to copy this file from the \Program Files\Microsoft

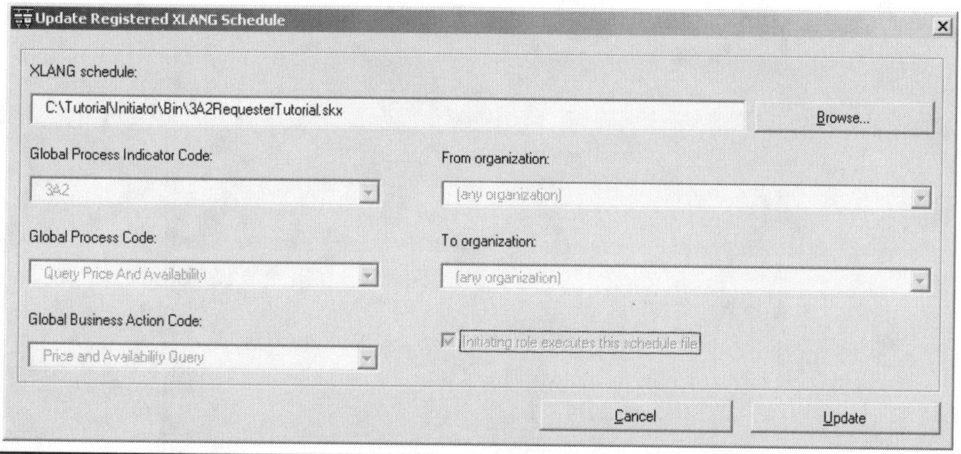

Figure 13-4 *Updating a registered XLANG schedule*

BizTalk Server Accelerator for RosettaNet\BTM Extensions\ASP folder to the \Inetpub\wwwroot folder.

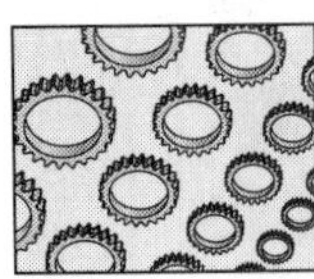

NOTE

This is similar but not identical to receiveresponse.asp included with BizTalk Server. You need to use this file rather than the base one.

LOB Applications For demonstration purposes, the InitiatorApplication and ResponseApplication are both simple Visual Basic applications that group the actions into steps. Figure 13-5 shows the GUI interface of the InitiatorApplication. As you can see, there are three numbered frame controls. Each contains at least one command button and sometimes several textboxes.

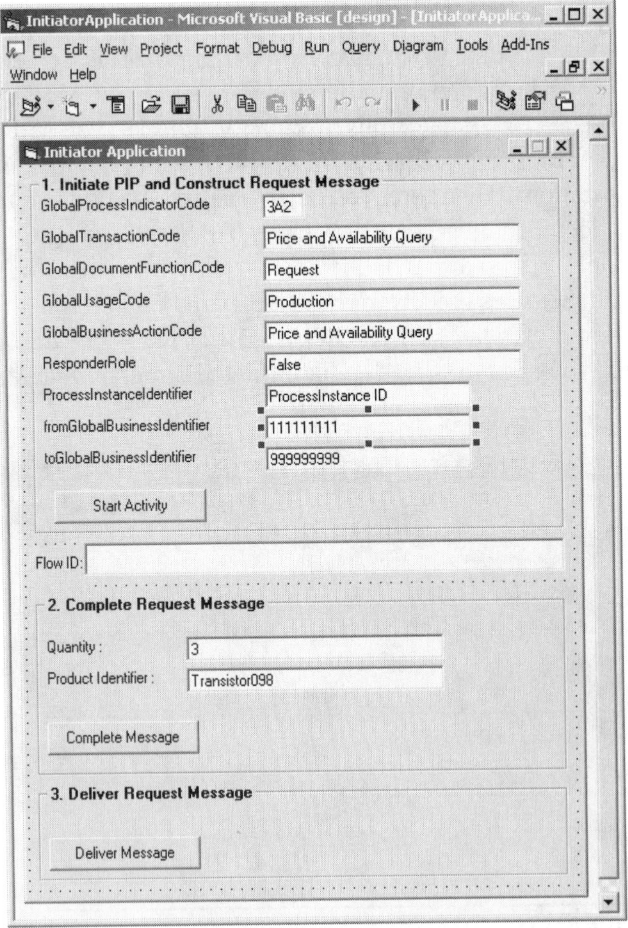

Figure 13-5 *The InitiatorApplication*

The Start Activity command control in Frame 1, Initiate PIP and Construct Request Message, calls the *StartActivity* method of the CPIPAdapterManager object, passes the values collected from the textboxes, and then displays the returned flow ID (the GUID of the running instance of the 3A2RequesterTutorial.skx XLANG schedule) in the textbox, txtFlowID:

```
Private Sub cmdStartActivity_Click()

    Set PIPAdapterManager = _
        CreateObject("PIPAdapterSDK.CPIPAdapterManager")

    strFlowID = _
    PIPAdapterManager.StartActivity( _
        txtGlobalProcessIndicatorCode.Text, _
        txtGlobalTransactionCode.Text, _
        txtGlobalDocumentFunctionCode.Text, _
        txtGlobalUsageCode.Text, _
        txtGlobalBusinessActionCode.Text, _
        txtResponderRole.Text, _
        txtProcessInstanceIdentifier.Text & Now(), _
        txtfromGlobalBusinessIdentifier.Text, _
        txttoGlobalBusinessIdentifier.Text, _
        strDocument)

    txtFlowID.Text = strFlowID

End Sub
```

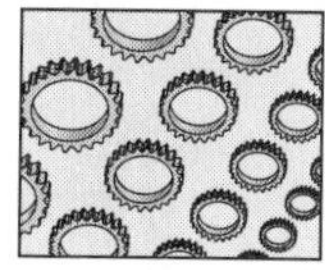

NOTE

By default, the text properties of the txtfromGlobalBusinessIdentifier and txttoGlobalBusinessIdentifier were set to "111111111" and "999999999," respectively. These are the DUNS numbers representing the source and destination organizations. If you followed the Tutorial instructions in the online documentation when you ran the Messaging Configuration Wizard, you should recall that you set the DUNS number of the source and destination organization to "SourceDUNS" and "DestinationDUNS," respectively. Therefore, you need to modify the Text properties of these two textboxes to reflect the DUNS numbers you set in the Messaging Configuration Wizard so they match.

The StartActivity method initiates a PIP XLANG schedule and constructs an XML message, using the following syntax:

Public Function StartActivity(_

ByVal p_strGlobalProcessIndicatorCode As String, _

```
ByVal p_strGlobalTransactionCode As String, _
ByVal p_strGlobalDocumentFunctionCode As String, _
ByVal p_strGlobalUsageCode As String, _
ByVal p_strGlobalBusinessActionCode As String, _
ByVal p_bIsResponderRole As Boolean, _
ByVal p_strProcessInstanceIdentifier As String, _
ByVal p_strfromGlobalBusinessIdentifier As String, _
ByVal p_strtoGlobalBusinessIdentifier As String, _
ByRef p_strMessage As Variant _
) As String
```

It returns a string that represents the flow ID (the GUID) of the running PIP XLANG schedule being initiated. All parameters are input parameters except for *p_strMessage*, which is an output parameter (indicated by the *ByRef* declaration). The following table describes the parameters of the StartActivity method:

Parameter	Description
p_strGlobalProcessIndicatorCode	A RossettaNet document element that indicates the global process indicator code. For example, 0A1, 2A1, 3A2, 3A4, and so on.
p_strGlobalTransactionCode	A RosettaNet document element that indicates the global transaction code. For example, "Price and Availability Query," "Request Purchase Order," and so on.
p_strGlobalDocumentFunctionCode	A RosettaNet document element that indicates the global document function code. It only accepts two possible values: Request or Response.

Table 13-4 *The parameters of the StartActivity method*

Parameter	Description
p_strGlobalUsageCode	A RosettaNet document element that indicates the global usage code, whether "Test" for testing environments or "Production" for production environments.
p_strGlobalBusinessActionCode	A RosettaNet document element that indicates the business action code. It uses a phrase that specifies a business action, such as "Price and Availability Query," "Request Purchase Order," and so on.
p_bIsResponderRole	A Boolean value that indicates whether the PIP is the responder role (True) or not (False).
p_strProcessInstanceIdentifier	The moniker for the PIP XLANG schedule.
p_strfromGlobalBusinessIdentifier	A RosettaNet document element that specifies the DUNS number of the source organization.
p_strtoGlobalBusinessIdentifier	A RosettaNet document element that specifies the DUNS number of the destination organization.
p_strMessage	The generated RosettaNet document.

Table 13-4 *The parameters of the StartActivity method* (continued)

The returned RosettaNet document of the StartActivity method call contains an empty ServiceContent node (<ServiceContent />). The Complete Message command button in Frame 2, Complete Request Message, completes the generated RosettaNet document by replacing the <ServiceContent /> empty element with the one in the C3A2PriceAndAvailabilityQuery.xml document (via the *replaceChild* method) and fills the *GlobalProductIdentifier* and *ProductQuantity* nodes with the contents of the appropriate textboxes.

```
Private Sub cmdCompleteMessage_Click()
    Dim XMLNODE As IXMLDOMNode

    XMLDOM.async = False

    XMLDOM.Load App.Path & _
        "\..\Bin\C3A2PriceAndAvailabilityQuery.xml"

    Set XMLNODE = XMLDOM.selectSingleNode( _
```

```
        "RosettaNetMessage/ServiceContent")
    XMLDOM.loadXML strDocument
    XMLDOM.documentElement.replaceChild XMLNODE, _
        XMLDOM.selectSingleNode("RosettaNetMessage/ServiceContent")

    XMLDOM.selectSingleNode(GPI).Text = _
        txtGlobalProductIdentifier.Text
    XMLDOM.selectSingleNode(PQ).Text = _
        txtQuantity.Text

    cmdDeliverMessage.Enabled = True

End Sub
```

The GPI and PQ in the preceding code listing are constants that are defined in the General Declaration section of the form. These represent the specific business information we want to complete in the RosettaNet document, the product identifier and the item quantity:

```
Const GPI = "RosettaNetMessage/ServiceContent/" _
        & "Pip3A2PriceAndAvailabilityQuery/" _
        & "ProductPriceAndAvailabilityQuery/" _
        & "ProductPriceAndAvailability/ProductLineItem/" _
        & "productUnit/ProductPackageDescription/" _
        & "ProductDescription/GlobalProductIdentifier"

Const PQ = "RosettaNetMessage/ServiceContent/" _
        & "Pip3A2PriceAndAvailabilityQuery/" _
        & "ProductPriceAndAvailabilityQuery/" _
        & "ProductPriceAndAvailability/ProductLineItem/" _
        & "ProductQuantity"
```

Finally, the Deliver Message command button in Frame 3, Deliver Request Message calls the *DeliverInitiationMessage* method of the PIPAdapterManager object, passing the flow ID, certificate, and the request message (prepared in Step 2):

```
Private Sub cmdDeliverMessage_Click()
    PIPAdapterManager.DeliverInitiationMessage strFlowID, _
        "NoCertificate", XMLDOM.xml
    Set PIPAdapterManager = Nothing
End Sub
```

The DeliverInitiationMessage method uses the following syntax:

```
Public Sub DeliverInitiationMessage( _
ByVal p_strFlowID As String, _
ByVal p_strSignatureCertificate, _
ByVal p_strMessage As String)
```

where *p_strFlowID* is the flow ID of the XLANG schedule to which the message will be delivered. *p_strSignatureCertificate* is the signature certificate associated with the initiation message (you are not using signature certificate in this tutorial, so you passed "NoCertificate" instead), and *p_strMessage* is the request message to be delivered.

The DeliveryInitiationMessage method call will deliver a request message to the running PIP XLANG schedule (3A2RequesterTutorial.skx in this case), which sends an unsigned message to BizTalk Server Messaging Services through the CPIPAdapterSubmit COM component (by calling the SendRNMessage method). The HTTP transport of the messaging port in turn submits the message again to BizTalk Server Messaging Services via the ReceiveRNO.asp ASP page, which transports the message to the responder PIP XLANG schedule (3A2ResponderTutorial.skx in this case) through the PIPAdapterSDK CPIPAdapterManager adapter (which implements the IPipelineComponent and IPipelineComponentAdmin interfaces).

Generally, you would implement all three of these calls in succession putting in data from your target application.

Now the data is on the responder side.

The Responder PIP XLANG schedule calls the StartRequestHandling method of the ResponderAdapter COM component, which displays a message box and persists three files to the \Tutorial\Responder\Bin folder as described earlier in this chapter. The Responder PIP XLANG schedule is then dehydrated, and thereafter waits for an acknowledgement message to arrive from the Initiator XLANG schedule. Recall that in Chapter 9 we explained that BizTalk Server Orchestration Services uses a dehydration/rehydration mechanism to preserve database and system resources for long-running processes. Keep in mind, it might take the responder a significant period of time to respond.

The ResponderApplication Visual Basic application (shown in Figure 13-6) has a simpler GUI interface than the InitiatorApplication.

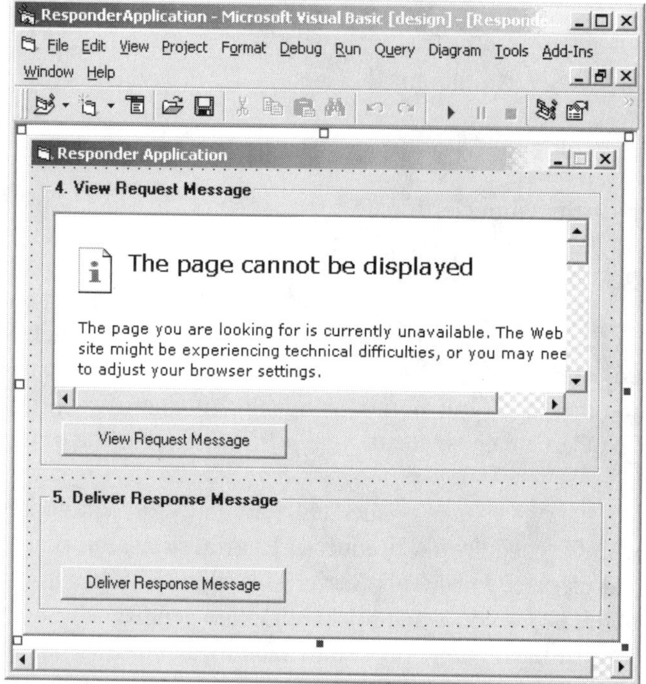

Figure 13-6 *The ResponderApplication*

As you can see, the ResponderApplication contains two steps. Step 4 (Frame 4), View Request Message contains a WebBrowser control and a command button, View Request Message. This step is purely for demonstration purposes only. It displays the RequestMessage.xml document persisted by the ResponderAdapter in the WebBrowser control.

```
Private Sub cmdViewRequestMessage_Click()
    wbXMLViewer.Navigate2 FilePath & "RequestMessage.xml"
End Sub
```

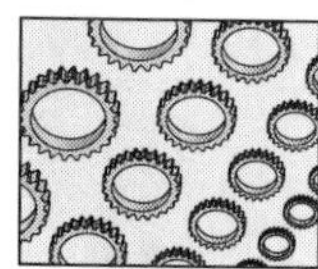

NOTE

As in the ResponderAdapter, you may need to change the value of the FilePath constant to reflect the actual path of the Tutorial, unless you unzipped it to the D: drive.

Step 5 (Frame 5), Deliver Response Message contains only a single command button, Deliver Response Message, which delivers a response message to the running instance of the Initiator PIP XLANG schedule. The command button calls a helper subroutine, *AssembleandDeliverResponseMessage*, to do the job:

```
Private Sub cmdDeliverResponse_Click()

    Dim FlowIDDataFile As String
    Dim XMLSkeletalResponseMessageDataFile As String

    FlowIDDataFile = "FlowID.xml"
    XMLSkeletalResponseMessageDataFile = "SkeletalResponseMessage.xml"

    AssembleandDeliverResponseMessage FlowIDDataFile, XMLSkeletalResponseMessageDataFile

End Sub
```

Here is the AssembleandDeliverResponseMessage subroutine:

```
Private Sub AssembleandDeliverResponseMessage( _
    FlowIDDataFile As String, _
    XMLSkeletalResponseMessageDataFile As String)

    Dim XMLDOM As New DOMDocument
    Dim XMLNODE As IXMLDOMNode
    Dim PIPAdapterManager As PIPAdapterSDK.CPIPAdapterManager
    Dim FlowID As String
    Dim SkeletalMessage As String
    Dim ServiceContent As String

    XMLDOM.async = False

    XMLDOM.loadXML RetrieveDataFromXML(FlowIDDataFile)
    FlowID = XMLDOM.documentElement.Text

    SkeletalMessage = RetrieveDataFromXML( _
        XMLSkeletalResponseMessageDataFile)

    XMLDOM.Load FilePath & "C3A2PriceAndAvailabilityResponse.xml"

    Set XMLNODE = XMLDOM.selectSingleNode( _
        "RosettaNetMessage/ServiceContent")

    XMLDOM.loadXML SkeletalMessage
    XMLDOM.documentElement.replaceChild XMLNODE, _
        XMLDOM.selectSingleNode("RosettaNetMessage/ServiceContent")
```

```
    Set PIPAdapterManager = CreateObject( _
        "PIPAdapterSDK.CPIPAdapterManager")
    Call PIPAdapterManager.DeliverResponseMessage( _
        FlowID, XMLDOM.xml)

    Set PIPAdapterManager = Nothing
    Set XMLDOM = Nothing

End Sub
```

The AssembleandDeliverResponseMessage subprocedure first loads the FlowID.xml and retrieves the Flow ID from the appropriate node. It then replaces the <ServiceContent /> node of the skeletal response message document with the one in the C3A2PriceAndAvailabilityResponse.xml. Finally, it calls the *DeliverResponseMessage* method of the CPIPAdapterManager COM component, which delivers the response message to the corresponding running instance of the 3A2RequesterTutorial.skx XLANG schedule, which is waiting for the response message. The flow in the 3A2RequesterTutorial.skx XLANG schedule then checks certificate information, and creates and sends an acknowledgement message to the ResponderTutorial.skx XLANG schedule through BizTalk Server Messaging Services (via the CPIPAdapterSubmit COM component). The RequesterTutorial.skx XLANG schedule then reloads, validates and handles the response message (corresponding to the acknowledgement message) that was created earlier in its process flow, cleans up, and ends.

The ResponderTutorial.skx XLANG schedule is then rehydrated and processes the arrived acknowledgement message (by calling the *HandleRNReceiptAcknowledgment* method of the IPIPResponderApplication interface (which contains no implementation in the ResponderAdapter), cleans up, and then ends.

The DeliverResponseMessage method uses the following syntax:

```
Public Sub DeliverResponseMessage( _

ByVal p_strFlowID As String, _

ByVal p_strMessage As String)
```

where *p_strFlowID* is the Flow ID of the running XLANG schedule to which you want to deliver the response message and *p_strMessage* is the response message.

Running the Tutorial To run the tutorial, start the InitiatorApplication.exe and the ResponderApplication.exe. To verify the process flows of the PIP Adapter Tutorial, it is recommended you also start an instance of the XLANG Event Monitor program (XLANGMon.exe) and arrange your screen so you can see all three applications at the same time.

Step 1: Click the Start Activity button on the InitiatorApplication.exe. You will see the sked moniker of a running instance of the 3A2RequesterTutorial.skx XLANG schedule displayed in the Flow ID text box. This can be verified by the appearance of a corresponding 3A2RequesterTutorial entry in the XLANG Event Monitor.

Step 2: Click the Complete Message button on the InitiatorApplication.exe to convert the skeletal request message to a complete request message.

Step 3: Click the Deliver Message button on the InitiatorApplication.exe to deliver the request message to the 3A2RequesterTutorial XLANG schedule. You will observe that the 3A2RequesterTutorial.skx XLANG schedule enters a loop (indicated by the __LoopModule entry). Another XLANG schedule instance, 3A2ResponderTutorial, appears in the XLANG Event Monitor. Next, a message box from the ResponderAdapter is displayed (as shown in Figure 13-7). Click OK to dismiss the message box and soon you'll see that the 3A2ResponderTutorial.skx XLANG schedule instance has become dehydrated.

Step 4: Click the View Request Message button on the ResponderApplication.exe. As we explained earlier in this chapter, this step is for demonstration purposes. It displays the contents of the request message in the WebBrowser control.

Step 5: Click the Deliver Response Message button on the ResponderApplication.exe. A message box from the InitiatorAdapter appears (as shown in Figure 13-8). Click OK to dismiss the message box. You will then notice that the dehydrated 3A2ResponderTutorial.skx XLANG schedule instance is rehydrated, and soon both 3A2RequesterTutorial.skx and 3A2ResponderTutorial.skx XLANG schedules are terminated.

Figure 13-7 *A message box from the ResponderAdapter*

Figure 13-8 *A message box from the InitiatorAdapter*

Testing a PIP Implementation

In this section, you will learn how to use the PIP XLANG Schedule Tester to test the 3A2Requester.skx PIP Implementation XLANG schedule located in the \Program Files\Microsoft BizTalk Server Accelerator for RosettaNet\PIP SDK\PIP Implementations\Rnif 1.1\PIP 3A2 Request Price and Availability\ folder. Before you can use the PIP XLANG Schedule Tester tool, you will need to use the PIP Administrator to update the file path for the 3A2 PIP (the Initiator role) so the system will know where to look for the correct XLANG schedules for 3A2 (the Initiator role). This process is similar to the way you configured the PIP Administrator for the 3A2RequesterTutorial.skx XLANG schedule, but this time, you will set the file path to \Program Files\Microsoft BizTalk Server Accelerator for RosettaNet\PIP SDK\PIP Implementations\Rnif 1.1\PIP 3A2 Request Price and Availability\3A2Requester.skx instead.

The 3A2Requester.skx XLANG schedule (and the corresponding XLANG schedule drawing, 3A2Requester.skv) is a "raw" PIP implementation which uses a private Message Queuing queue, .\private\RNMsgOut, to simulate the external trading partner. In this exercise, you will use the PIP XLANG Schedule Tester to load a request message and initiate the 3A2Requester.skx XLANG schedule. This polls the message from the private queue and loads a response message, sending it back to the running instance of the XLANG schedule (3A2Requester.skx). In this scenario, the PIP XLANG Schedule Tester plays a Responder role.

Setting Up Dialogs Start the PIP XLANG Scheduler Tester, then select Transaction Initiator from the Scenario Type drop-down box. Remove Send Signal Message from the Selected Dialogs list. Now your PIP XLANG Scheduler Tester should look like the one in Figure 13-9. Click Next.

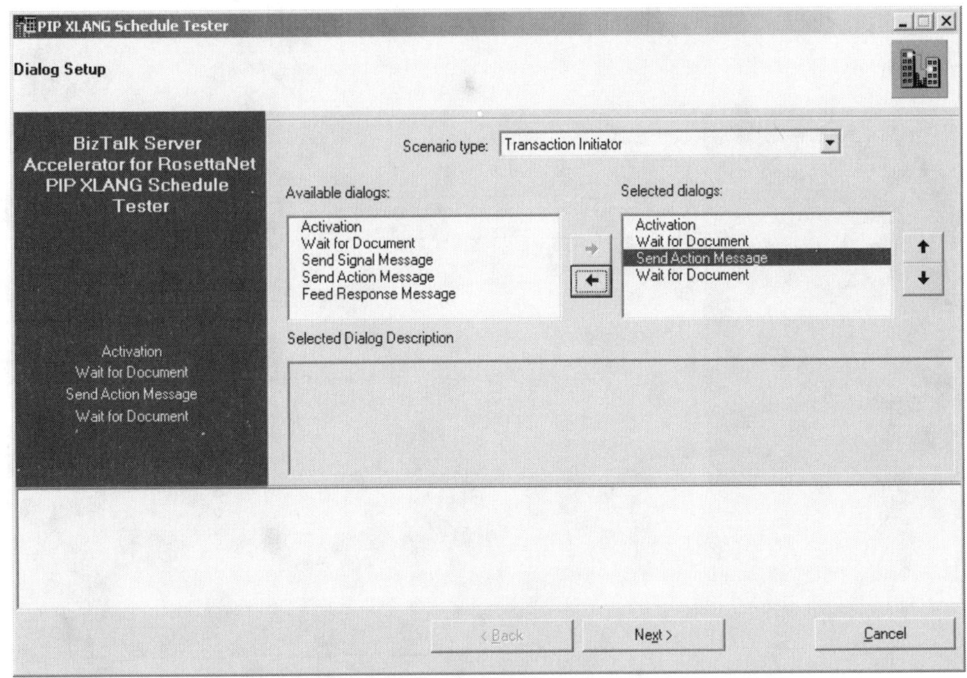

Figure 13-9 *The Dialog Setup page of the PIP XLANG Scheduler Tester*

Testing Dialogs In the Activation Dialog page, click the Browse button and select the RequestMessage.xml from the \Tutorial\Responder\Bin folder. You will use an existing request message generated in the previous section when you were running the PIP Adapter Tutorial. The content of the RequestMessage.xml document should appear in the middle of the PIP XLANG Schedule Tester page, as shown in Figure 13-10. Leave RNMsgOut in the Output Message Queue text box.

Click Next and you will see the Waiting for Document Dialog page. This will instantiate the 3A2Requester.skx XLANG schedule (indicated by the events listing on the lower panel of the PIP XLANG Schedule Tester page) which will send the RequestMessage.xml to the private queue, .\private\RNMsgOut. You can verify this by examining the private queue using the Computer Management MMC snap-in. Clicking the Poll Queue button will retrieve the message from the private queue and

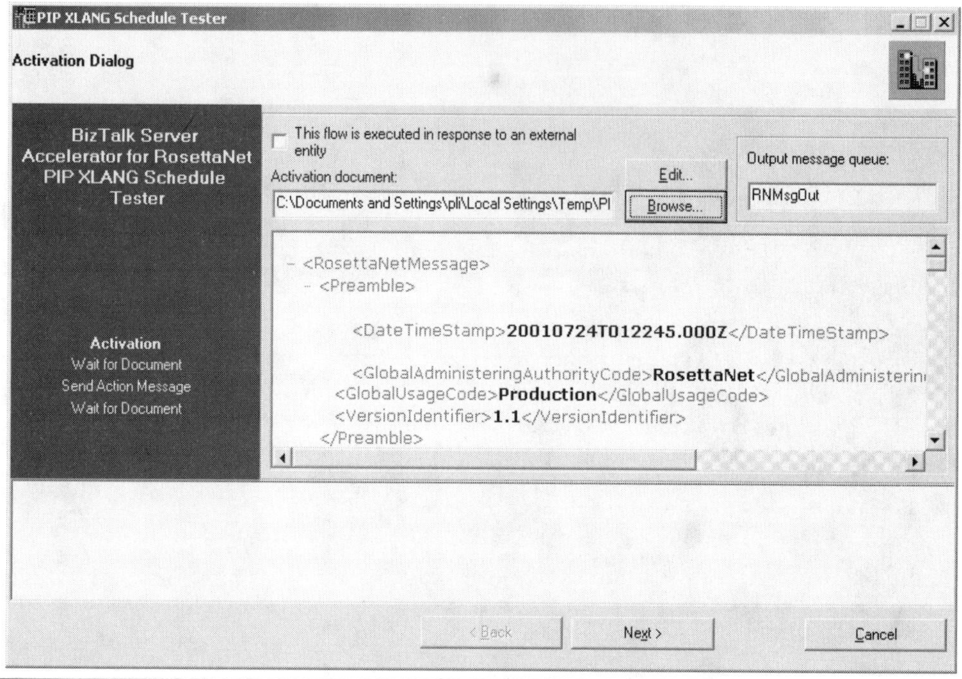

Figure 13-10 *The Activation Dialog page*

display it in the middle of the PIP XLANG Schedule Tester, as shown in Figure 13-11. Click Next.

In the Feed Response Message Dialog page, click the Browse button and select the SkeletalResponseMessage.xml document from the \Tutorial\Responder\Bin folder. The PIP XLANG Schedule Tester looks like the one in Figure 13-12 now.

Click Next and you will see the Wait For Document Dialog again. Clicking the Poll Queue button will display the SkeletalResponseMessage.xml in the middle of the PIP XLANG Schedule Tester. Click the Finish button and you are done with your test of the 3A2Request.skx XLANG schedule.

Using the PIP Schema Manager

In this section, you will learn how to message a RosettaNet Framework (RNF) 1.1 PIP DTD schema into the BizTalk Messaging RosettaNet Universal Message.

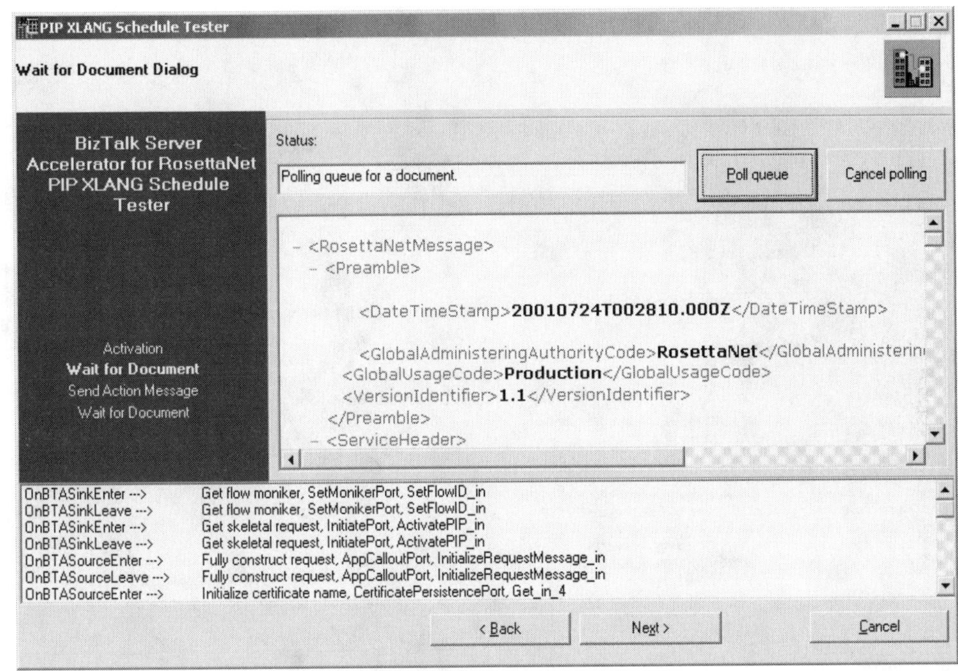

Figure 13-11 *The Wait For Document Dialog page*

BizTalk Messaging RosettaNet Universal Message BizTalk Server Accelerator defines a BizTalk Messaging RosettaNet Universal Message as a BizTalk Specification document designed to validate and map incoming and outgoing documents processed by BizTalk Server Messaging Services. This specification also serves as an intermediate representation for messages when they are processed by appropriate XLANG schedules. This specification document, RosettaNetMessage.xml is located in the \Program Files\Microsoft BizTalk Server Accelerator for RosettaNet\PIP SDK\SDK Repository\DocSpecs folder.

The BizTalk Messaging RosettaNet Universal Message contains a *RosettaNetMessage* root element and three child elements, *Preamble*, *ServiceHeader*, and *ServiceContent*. Figure 13-13 illustrates the partially expanded BizTalk Messaging RosettaNet Universal Message in BizTalk Editor

The Preamble element contains four child elements: DateTimeStamp, GlobalAdministeringAuthorityCode (currently RosettaNet only), GlobalUsageCode (Test or Production), and VersionIdentifier (currently 1.1).

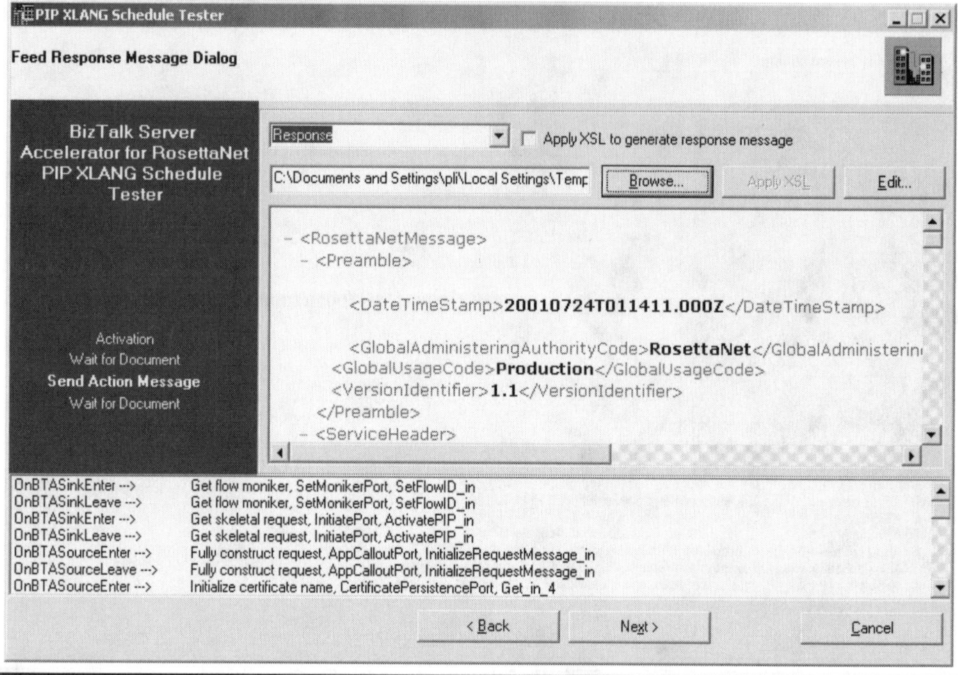

Figure 13-12 *The Feed Response Message Dialog page*

The ServiceHeader element contains business properties organized in a highly hierarchical manner.

The ServiceContent element contains schemas of all the existing PIP document types available in BizTalk Server Accelerator for RosettaNet or the PIP document types you imported using the PIP Schema Manager.

Merging a PIP DTD into the BizTalk Messaging RosettaNet Universal Message Merging a PIP DTD schema into the BizTalk Messaging RosettaNet Universal Message involves three steps. First, you import a PIP DTD into BizTalk Editor and save it as a BizTalk Specification. Secondly, you merge the saved PIP BizTalk Specification into the *Consolidated RosettaNet Message* specification, defined in the ConsolidatedMessage.xml document (also located in the \Program Files\Microsoft BizTalk Server Accelerator for RosettaNet\PIP SDK\SDK Repository\DocSpecs folder), using the PIP Schema Manager. Finally, you merge the Consolidated RosettaNet Message document into the BizTalk Messaging RosettaNet Universal Message, also using the PIP Schema Manager.

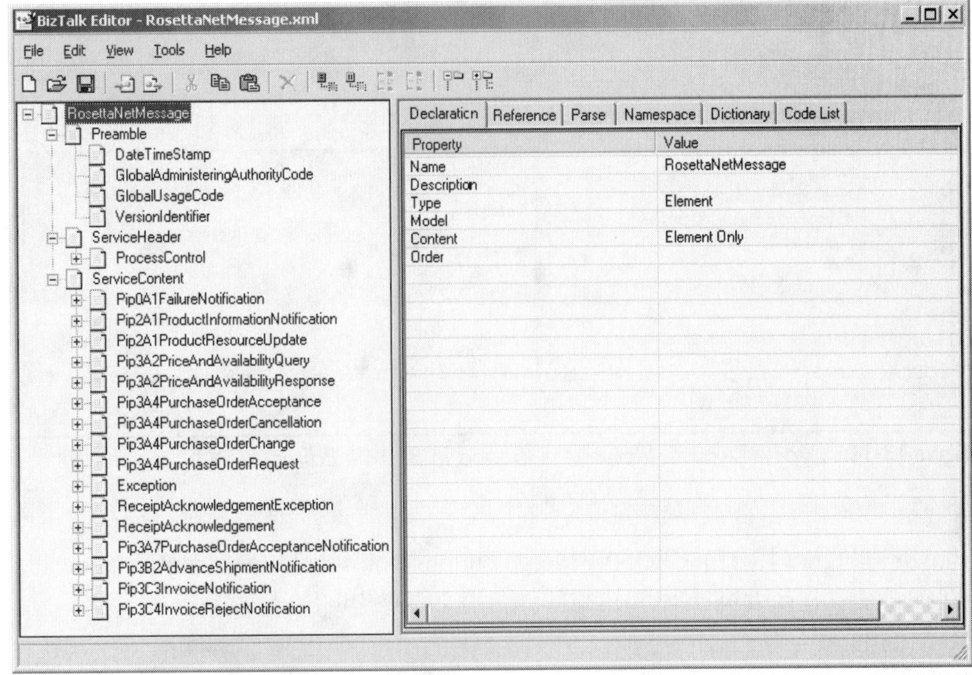

Figure 13-13 *The BizTalk Messaging RosettaNet Universal Message*

In this exercise, you will merge the DTD for RosettaNet PIP 1A1, Account Request, into the BizTalk Messaging RosettaNet Universal Message. You can download the DTD document (1A1_MS_B01_00A_AccountRequest.dtd) from the RosettaNet web site (http://www.rosettanet.org) in a zipped form (1A1_RequestAccountSetup.zip).

Step 1: Start BizTalk Editor and click Tools | Import… menu option. Select the Document Type Definition icon in the Select Import Module dialog box and click OK. Browse to 1A1_MS_B01_00A_AccountRequest.dtd and click OK. The Pip1A1AccountRequest is now loaded into BizTalk Editor, as shown in Figure 13-14. Save the BizTalk specification document as 1A1_MS_B01_00A_AccountRequest.xml.

Step 2: Start PIP Schema Manager. Click the first Browse button and select 1A1_MS_B01_00A_AccountRequest.xml that you created in Step 1. Click the second Browse button and select the ConsolidatedMessage.xml document. In the Output File textbox, specify a file path where you want the consolidated message to be saved and type **C_1A1_MS_B01_00A_AccountRequest.xml** as the filename (notice the C_ in the filename). Make sure the first OperationType, From Imported RosettaNet XML Schema To Consolidated RosettaNet Message, is selected (as

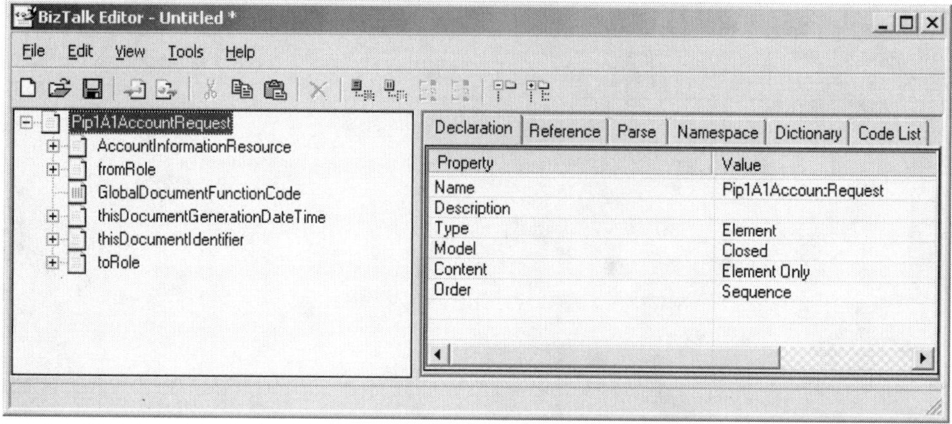

Figure 13-14 *Pip1A1AccountRequest is loaded in BizTalk Editor*

shown in Figure 13-15). Click the Merge button. You should see a confirmation message box that indicates the operation was successful.

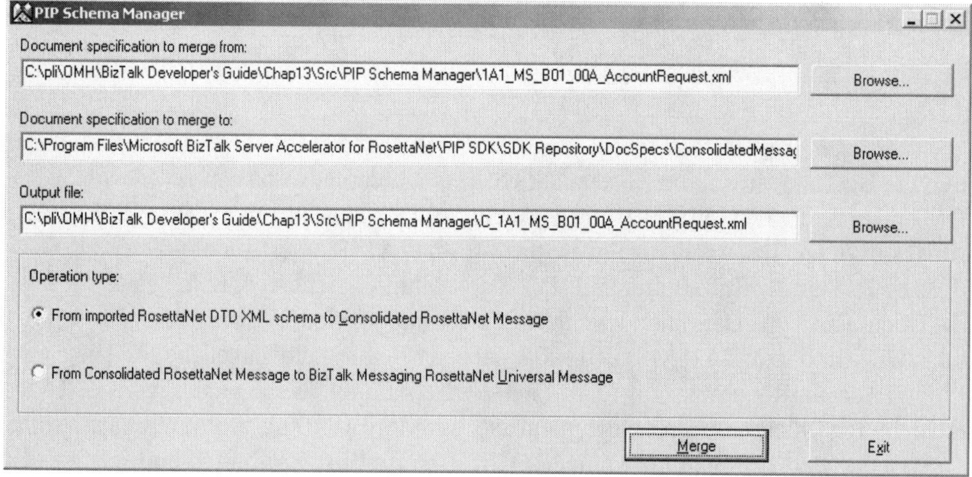

Figure 13-15 *Merging a PIP DTD schema into the Consolidated RosettaNet Message*

Step 3: In this step, you will use the PIP Schema Manager again to merge the Consolidated RosettaNet Message you created in Step 2 into the BizTalk Messaging RosettaNet Universal Message. Update the three textboxes so they look something like the ones in Figure 13-16. Make sure the second Operation Type, From Consolidated RosettaNet Message To BizTalk Messaging RosettaNet Universal Message, is selected (also shown in Figure 13-16). Click the Merge button to complete the operation. A confirmation message box should appear.

Open the PIP_1A1_MS_B01_00A_AccountRequest.xml document in BizTalk Editor and expand the ServiceContent node. You should see that a new node Pip1A1AccountRequest was imported, as shown in Figure 13-17.

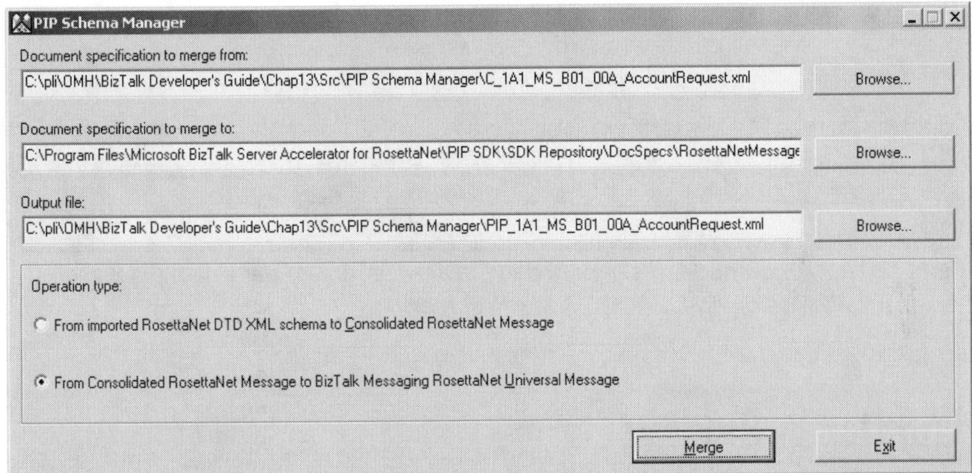

Figure 13-16 *Merging a Consolidated RosettaNet Message into the BizTalk Messaging RosettaNet Universal Message*

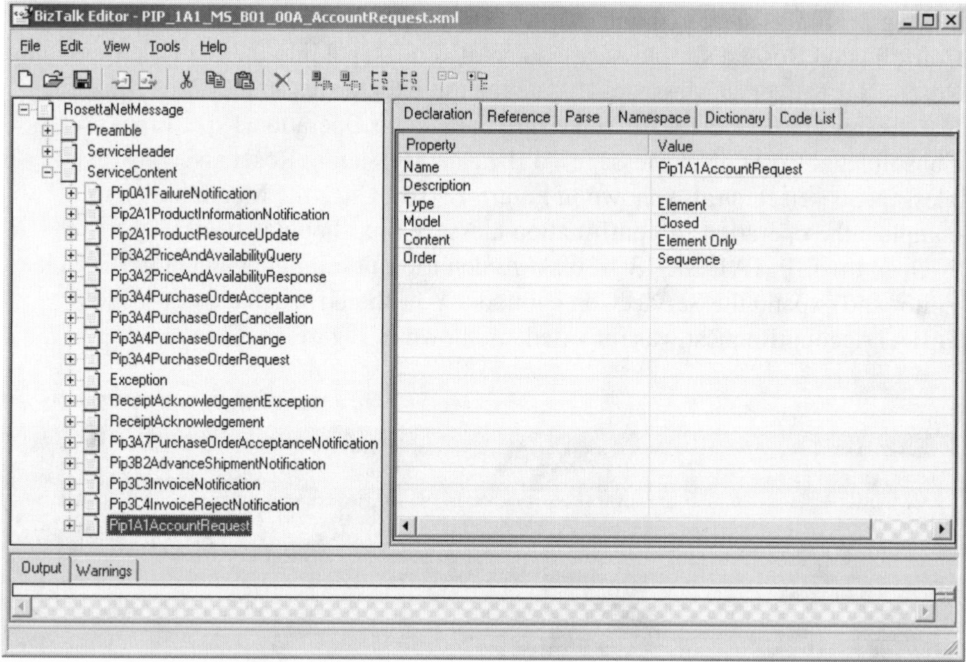

Figure 13-17 *A new node was imported to the ServiceContent element of the BizTalk Messaging RosettaNet Universal Message*

Chapter in Review

In this chapter, you learned how to use the BizTalk Server Accelerator for RosettaNet to rapidly develop RosettaNet PIP implementations that would otherwise prove a daunting task. The infrastructure, services, and a rich set of tools included in BizTalk Server Accelerator for RosettaNet were also discussed. After finishing this chapter, you should feel comfortable in using the BizTalk Server Accelerator for RosettaNet to develop RosettaNet solutions, either by using existing PIP implementation or by developing new PIP implementations that utilize appropriate PIP Partners.

CHAPTER

14

BizTalk Server Accelerator for HIPAA

IN THIS CHAPTER:

Introducing HIPAA

Introducing BizTalk Accelerator for HIPAA

Working with HIPAA-specific BizTalk Specifications

Using the Claim Processing Sample Application

Chapter in Review

In the last chapter, you learned how to use BizTalk Server Accelerator for RosettaNet to build B2B integration solutions for the IT and high-tech industry. In this chapter, you will learn about another BizTalk Server Accelerator—BizTalk Server Accelerator for HIPAA—and see how to use it to meet HIPAA compliance requirements for the health care industry.

You will first learn what HIPAA is and why it is so important for the health care industry. You will also discover what the various components are that make up BizTalk Server Accelerator for HIPAA, and how BizTalk Server and the HIPAA Accelerator can be used to help the health care industry meet HIPAA compliance standards. In addition, you will learn about the structure of HIPAA-specific BizTalk specifications and how to work with them. Finally, you will learn to use and extend the developer sample that ships with BizTalk Server Accelerator for HIPAA in order to build custom HIPAA-compliant BizTalk solutions.

Introducing HIPAA

In this section, you will learn what HIPAA is, what it covers, as well as who will be affected by it.

What Is HIPAA?

HIPAA stands for the *Health Insurance Portability and Accountability Act of 1996*. It is a set of standards that was agreed upon and set forth by both the U.S. Congress and the health care industry in 1996 for the electronic exchange of administrative and financial health care transactions to improve the efficiency and effectiveness of health care systems.

What Does HIPAA Cover?

HIPAA consists of a set of National Standards as well as a Standards Setting Process.

National Standards

HIPAA National Standards include Transaction and Code Set Standards (also known as *Transaction Sets*) for governing electronic health care transactions, Privacy Standards and Security Standards for addressing privacy and security concerns, Identifier Standards for uniquely identifying appropriate entities who are involved in electronic health care transactions by a National Provider Identifier, a National

Employer Identifier, and a National Health Plan Identifier. In addition, HIPAA Implementation Guides outline the proper format that should be followed.

At the core of HIPAA are the administrative and financial health care transaction sets, which include the following:

- Health claims and equivalent encounter information
- Enrollment and disenrollment in a health plan
- Eligibility for a health plan
- Health care payment and remittance advice
- Health plan premium payments
- Health claim status
- Referral certification and authorization
- Coordination of benefits

HIPAA defines the contents and document formats for the preceding transaction sets. Currently HIPAA has adopted ASC X12N EDI as the proper document format, as detailed in HIPAA Implementation Guides.

Standards Setting Process

The HIPAA Standards Setting Process includes the Private Sector Standards—Development and Federal Implementation Plan.

TIP

More information about HIPAA standards and FAQs are available from the Web site of the Office of the Assistant Secretary for Planning and Evaluation at http://www.aspe.hhs.gov/. HIPAA Implementation Guides can be purchased or downloaded for free (in PDF formats) from the Washington Publishing Company's Web site at: http://hipaa.wpc-edi.com/HIPAA_40.asp.

Who Is Affected by HIPAA?

The U.S. Department of Health and Human Services (HHS) published the Final Rule on Standards for Electronic Health Care Transactions on August 17, 2000. Federal law requires that by August 16, 2002, most organizations must adopt these standards (24 months after the Final Rule was published). Small health plans may make an exception for extending their current practices for another year (36 months after the publication of the Final Rule). Failure to adopt and comply to the Standards, however, can result in penalties of up to $25,000 and/or up to 10 years imprisonment.

Almost every entity in the health care industry will be affected by HIPAA, including providers (such as doctors, hospitals, and so on), payers (such as insurance companies), and clearinghouses (third parties that act on behalf of providers or payers).

Introducing BizTalk Accelerator for HIPAA

In this section, we will look at the challenges the health care industry is facing today when it comes to implementing HIPAA standards, and how BizTalk Server and BizTalk Server Accelerator for HIPAA help address them.

HIPAA Challenges

In order to comply with the HIPAA regulation in a timely manner, the health care industry is facing a number of challenges today, including the following:

- **Too many different document formats exist** Today, health care providers and health plans that process business transactions electronically must deal with many different formats. For example, for health care claims alone, more than 400 different formats exist today.
- **Disparate and dissimilar applications exist within organizations** Just as in any other industry, today, different systems and applications written in different languages and running on different platforms exist in health care organizations (providers, payers, clearinghouses, and the like), including line-of-business applications, legacy systems, and other proprietary, home-grown applications. Getting data from these applications and transforming them into HIPAA-required formats to submit them to trading partners is a very difficult task.
- **Speed to market** As the implementation deadline for HIPAA approaches, health care organizations face increasing pressures to get the HIPAA implementation in place in time.

The Rescue—BizTalk Server Accelerator for HIPAA

BizTalk Server Accelerator for HIPAA goes a long way in helping health care companies meet HIPAA compliance requirements. BizTalk Server Accelerator for HIPAA leverages the B2B and EAI platforms and Services of BizTalk Server and provides you with necessary components to rapidly build HIPAA-compliant BizTalk solutions. In this section, you will learn about the BizTalk Server Accelerator for HIPAA toolbox and understand how it can help health care organizations address the aforementioned HIPAA challenges.

What's in the Toolbox?

The installation process for BizTalk Server Adapter for HIPAA is very straightforward. You basically insert the CD into the CD-ROM and follow the onscreen instructions. After installing BizTalk Server for HIPAA, it will be accessible by selecting Start | Programs where you can find links to the online documentation and the planning guide (.chm files). BizTalk Server Accelerator for HIPAA is implemented very differently from the BizTalk Server Accelerator for RosettaNet. This is due to the differences in underlying standards upon which these two accelerators were built.

The RosettaNet Implementation Framework is a process-intensive framework in which business processes are defined as PIPs (Partner Interface Processes). As a result, the BizTalk Server Accelerator for RosettaNet leverages the Business Process Orchestration (BPO) feature of BizTalk Server Orchestration Services and provides a set of predefined, ready-to-use XLANG schedules called PIP implementations, as well as XLANG schedule templates that can be used as starting points when implementing custom solutions, referred to as PIP Partners. BizTalk Server Accelerator for RosettaNet also supplies a set of COM components, known as PIP Adapters (and the associated COM+ applications for holding them), that facilitate the BizTalk Orchestration and Messaging Services. In addition, BizTalk Server Accelerator for RosettaNet provides a set of tools for developing, debugging, testing, and deploying PIP implementation solutions. These components are collectively referred to as PIP SDK. Finally, it provides RosettaNet-specific parser/serializer components that help in processing RosettaNet documents, and a SQL Server database (BTSInstances) for storing appropriate metadata.

In contrast, HIPAA standards are document-centric—they define the formats and contents of the documents being electronically transacted among health care entities. To meet the unique requirements of HIPAA standards and address those HIPAA challenges the health care industry is facing today, BizTalk Server Accelerator is implemented as a set of components that leverage the power of BizTalk Server Messaging Services such as document validation, flexible mapping, Application Integration Components (AIC), and so on. As a result, the BizTalk Server Accelerator for HIPAA is much less complicated than the BizTalk Server Accelerator for RosettaNet. BizTalk Serve Accelerator for HIPAA is implemented as a set of “silent” server-side components (for example, they do not have a GUI interface and do not need to directly interact with the users). The BizTalk Server Accelerator for HIPAA provides the following components:

HIPAA *Transaction Set Schemas* BizTalk Server Accelerator for HIPAA provides all 12 HIPAA transaction set schemas in the form of BizTalk Specifications (a topic you learned about in Chapter 4). These schemas are jointly developed by Microsoft and the Washington Publishing Company, the publisher of the HIPAA Implementation Guides. The schemas are located in \Program Files\Microsoft BizTalk Server Accelerator for HIPAA\templates folder, as described in the following table.

Later in this chapter, you will see examples which use some of the BizTalk schemas, including 837Institutional_V1_wpc_multiple.xml, 835_V1_wpc_multiple.xml, and 837Dental_V1_wpc_multiple.xml.

HIPAA Transaction Set	BizTalk Schemas
270/271: Health Care Eligibility/Benefit Inquiry and Information Response	270_V1_wpc.xml 271_V1_wpc.xml
276/277: Health Care Claim Status Request and Response	276_V1_wpc.xml 277_V1_wpc.xml
278: Health Care Services Review—Request for Review and Response	278Request_V1_wpc.xml 278Response_V1_wpc.xml
820: Payroll Deducted and Other Group Premium Payment for Insurance Products	820_V1_wpc.xml
834: Benefit Enrollment and Maintenance	834_v1_wpc_multiple.xml 834_V1_wpc_single.xml
835: Health Care Claim Payment/Advice	835_V1_wpc_multiple.xml 835_V1_wpc_single.xml
837: Health Care Claim: Institutional	837Institutional_V1_wpc_multiple.xml 837Institutional_V1_wpc_single.xml
837: Health Care Claim: Dental	837Dental_V1_wpc_multiple.xml 837Dental_V1_wpc_single.xml
837: Health Care Claim: Professional	837Professional_V1_wpc_multiple.xml 837Professional_V1_wpc_single.xml

Table 14-1 *HIPPA Specifications for BizTalk*

A Custom BizTalk Map Document for Processing Receipts BizTalk Server Accelerator for HIPAA also includes a custom map, HipaaCanonicalReceiptTo4010-997.xml, which is also located in the \Program Files\Microsoft BizTalk Server Accelerator for HIPAA\templates folder. This map converts BizTalk canonical receipts to a X12 4010 977 receipt. Later in this chapter, you will see how to use this map to generate X12 EDI receipts.

HIPAA-specific X12 Parser Component BizTalk Server Accelerator for HIPAA provides a HIPAA-specific X12 parser component, CISHipaaParser.dll (ProgID: BizTalk.ParserHipaaX12.1), located in \Program Files\Microsft Biz Talk Server Accelerator for HIPAA folder. Figure 14-1 illustrates the HIPAA-specific X12 Parser in the Parser's tab of the BizTalk Server Group Properties dialog box. You can use the

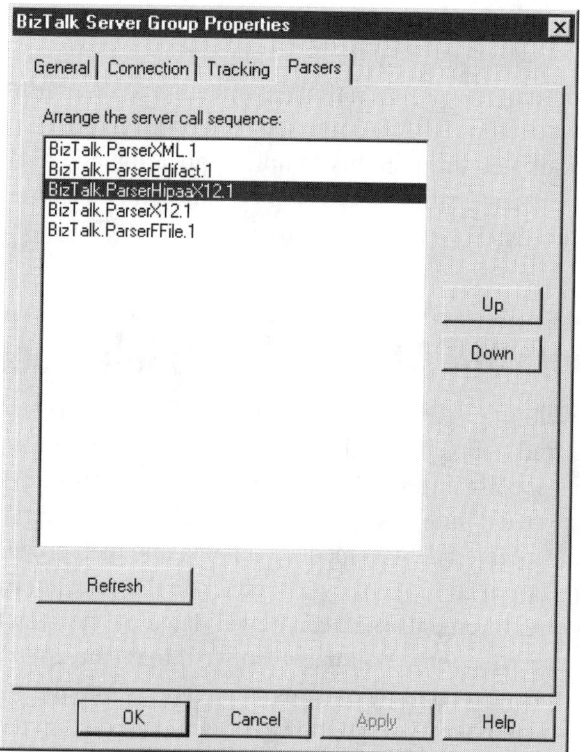

Figure 14-1 *HIPAA-specific X12 parser*

Up and Down arrow to rearrange the order of available parsers so that the most frequently used ones get executed before those less frequently used.

A HIPAA-specific Validation Component In addition, BizTalk Server Accelerator for HIPAA provides a custom validation component, HipaaValidateDoc.dll (ProgID: ValidateDoc.ValidateDocument.1), also located in the \Program Files\Microsoft BizTalk Server Accelerator for HIPAA folder. It is this validation component that makes it possible for you to validate HIPAA-specific X12 EDI document instances in BizTalk Editor. The use of the validation component is transparent to you, however. If you unregister this validation component (by running Regsvr32 with a /u switch, for example), you will not be able to validate HIPAA-specific X12 EDI document instances in BizTalk Editor.

Later in this chapter, you will learn how to use BizTalk Editor to validate HIPAA-specific X12 EDI document instances (with the help of the validation component, of course).

A Developer Sample Application Finally, BizTalk Server Accelerator for HIPAA ships with a Claim Processing developer sample application to demonstrate how to use the Accelerator to develop HIPAA-compliant solutions. In the last section of this chapter, we will walk you through this sample application and also show you how to extend this sample application to develop custom HIPAA solutions to fit your specific business needs.

Working with HIPAA-specific BizTalk Specifications

When you are developing HIPAA solutions using BizTalk Server Accelerator for HIPAA, you will find yourself spending a significant amount of time working with BizTalk document specifications, also known as schemas, that correspond to the transaction sets specified in the X12N HIPAA implementation guide. You may want to select an available HIPAA-specific schema and then create new applications or modify existing applications so they can generate the selected EDI transaction set that meets HIPAA requirements (i.e., can be validated by the selected HIPAA-specific BizTalk specification). You may also want to create appropriate maps that transform documents generated by existing applications into the standard HIPAA format. No matter which way you go, however, you will end up having to deal with one or more of the HIPAA-specific BizTalk specifications.

In this section, you will first learn about the structure of a HIPAA transmission. You will then learn how to validate existing document instances against an appropriate HIPAA-specific BizTalk schema using BizTalk Editor.

Document Structure

First of all, a HIPAA document instance is formatted according to the ANSI ASC X12 family of standards. Just as with any X12 document, a HIPPA X12 EDI document groups its data in a hierarchical manner. Figure 14-2 illustrates a fragment of a sample 837 Health Care Claim (Institutional) document with layers of header/trailer pairs. The outmost layer consists of an interchange control header (the ISA segment) and corresponding interchange control trailer (the IEA segment). This layer is sometimes referred to as an *interchange envelope*. The next highest layer is the functional group header and trailer pair, designated by the GS segment and GE segment, respectively. The next layer is the transaction set and begins with the ST segment and ends with the SE segment. Inside each interchange envelope you can have multiple functional groups (not shown in Figure 14-2), while the innermost layer, the transaction set, contains the business data. Inside each functional group you can have multiple detail transaction sets (again, not shown in Figure 14-2).

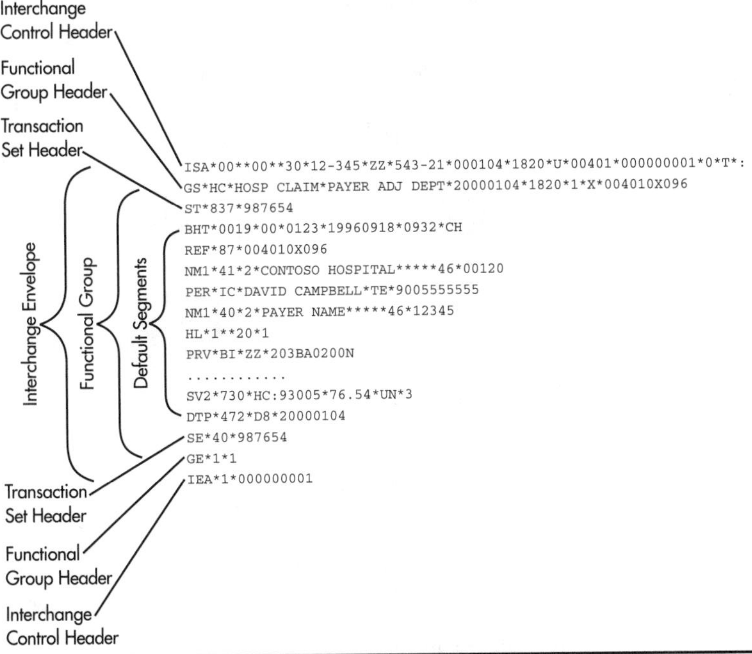

Figure 14-2 *The structure of a HIPAA transaction set document*

Another characteristic of the HIPAA document is that the structure is not flexible. You cannot arbitrarily add, remove, or modify any nodes (elements and/or fields in BizTalk specifications) in a HIPAA schema like you can in a regular X12 BizTalk schema.

Validating a HIPAA Document Instance

In this section, you will learn how to use the BizTalk Editor to validate a HIPAA document instance. You will use the sample file, 837I_ValidationInstance.txt, found in the SourceCode\Chap14 folder of the companion CD of this book. This file is created by removing all the "envelopes" (interchange control, functional group, and transaction set headers/trailers) from an original HIPAA 837 document, 937I.txt, located in the \Program Files\Microsoft BizTalk Server Accelerator for HIPAA\Samples\Claim Processing\TestData folder.

Now start BizTalk Editor and open the 837Institutional_V1_wpc_multiple.xml through the templates (select File | New | X12) specification from either the \templates folder of the BizTalk Server Accelerator for HIPAA installation or from the btshipaasamp WebDAV repository. From the Tools menu, select Validate Instance… Then browse to the 837I_ValidationInstance.txt document (you will need to specify All Files (*.*) as the Files Of Type in the Validate Document Instance dialog box to make the text files to appear). Select and click the Open button. Fill in necessary document delimiters as shown in Figure 14-3, and click OK. The XML representation of the 837I document instance should appear in the Output tab on the lower pane of the BizTalk Editor, as shown in Figure 14-4.

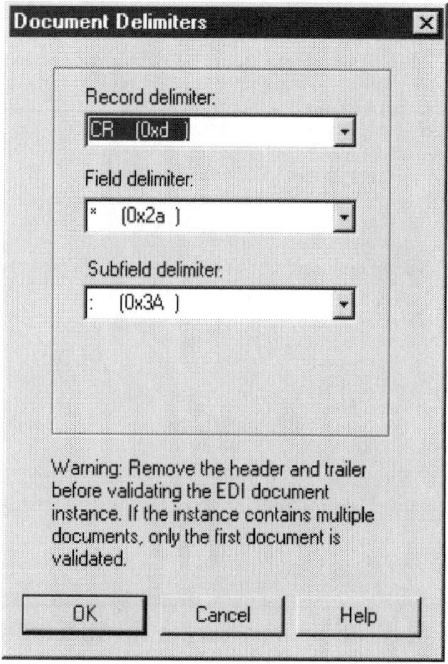

Figure 14-3 *Filling up document delimiters*

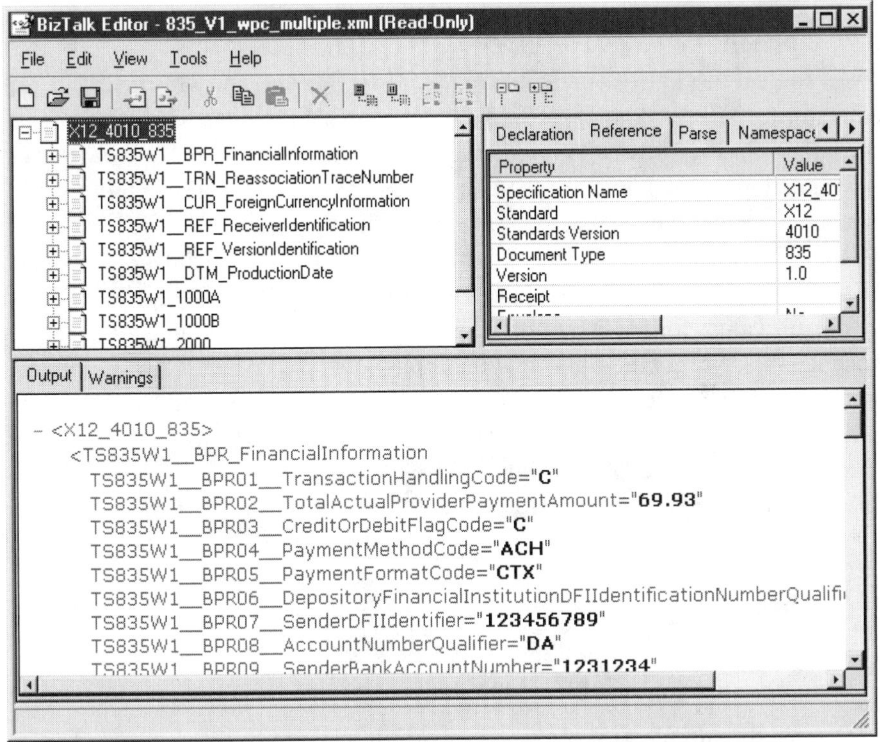

Figure 14-4 *The HIPAA document instance has been successfully validated*

Similarly, you can validate the 835_ValidationInstance.txt (located in the same folder as the 837I_ValidationInstance.txt) document instance against its document specification.

Using the Claim Processing Sample Application

The claims processing sample is designed to demonstrate how to build an application that tracks health care claims submitted by a provider (for example, a doctor's office, clinic, or hospital) and their corresponding payments, using the BizTalk Server Accelerator for HIPAA. We will first walk you through the sample application to see how it works, then show you how to extend the sample application to solve particular problems in some scenarios.

Install the Claims Processing Sample

You can find an Install.exe executable in the \Program Files\Microsoft BizTalk Server Accelerator for HIPAA\Samples\Claims Processing\setup folder. The source code for the Install.exe is also provided and is located in the sample folder. To set up the sample application, double-click Install.exe to launch the executable. Fill in appropriate information, such as database server name (clicking the Get Server List button will fill in the SQL Server drop-down box with a list of SQL Server names), username, and password for the receiving functions and the contact person's e-mail address and leave default values for the rest of the input boxes, as shown in Figure 14-5. Later you can change the configuration information through the Web pages. Click the Install button. If everything was fine, you will see a message box that confirms a successful installation. Otherwise, open the BtsHipaaSetup.log file that was created during the installation for the details of failures.

The installation executable performs the following tasks:

- Creates a COM+ application—BizTalk Accelerator for HIPAA—Claims Processing Sample—that hosts the COM components for the sample (AIC components and application-specific COM components).
- Writes application specific configuration data into the Windows Registry.
- Creates the sample SQL Server database, BTSHIPAA.
- Creates the sample Web site.
- Creates necessary BizTalk messaging objects (organizations, document definitions, channels, messaging ports, and so on).
- Create folders and receive functions for receiving claims and payments.
- Creates a scheduled task that kicks out an XLANG schedule (to check for possible payments that are overdue and then sends an e-mail notification if an address is found).

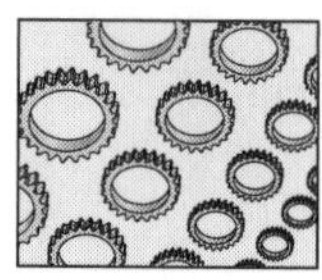

NOTE

By default, the claims processing sample application is configured for the Provider. You can also configure it for the Payer by selecting Payer as the Organization type during installation.

The sample application uses a SQL Server database, BTSHIPAA, to track claims and payments information for a fictitious provider, CONTOSO HOSPITAL. When a new HIPAA 837 claim document arrives, a receive function picks it up and submits it to the appropriate BizTalk channel to process it. An associated messaging port

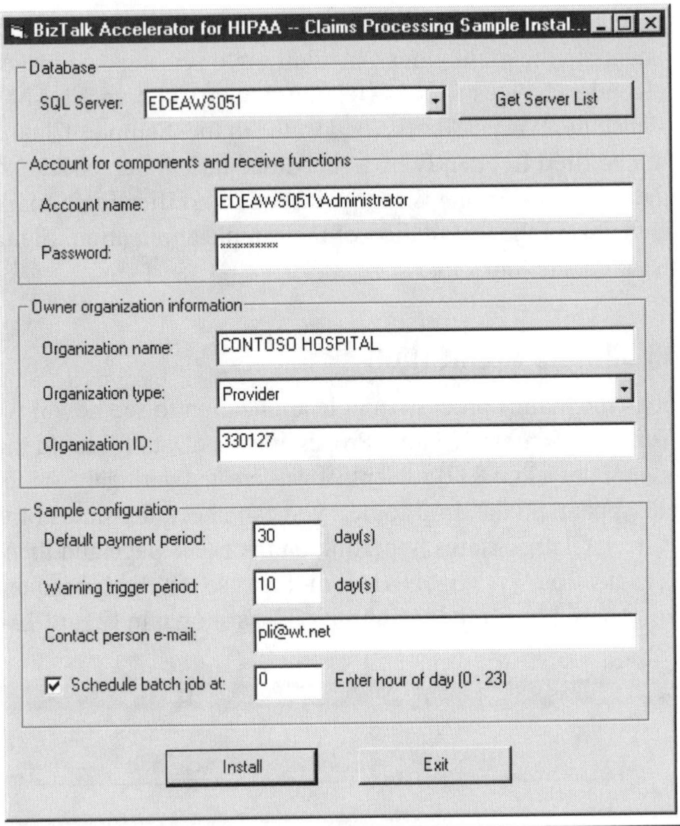

Figure 14-5 *Setting up the claims processing sample application*

invokes an appropriate AIC component which parses the information from the received document (in the intermediate BizTalk internal XML format) and stores the claim and the sub-items in the database and marks their status as "Submitted" (a value of 0 in the database).

When a HIPAA 835 payment document arrives, another receive function grabs it and sends it to BizTalk Server, where another AIC component is called which then parses the payment document and stores it in the database. The AIC component also correlates the payment document with a corresponding claim document and its sub-items and marks them as "Addressed" (a value of 1 in the database).

The Web site (http://localhost/btshippa) consists of many ASP pages which interact with the database through appropriate COM+ components (BTSHipaaSamp.dll, located in the \Samples\Claims Processing\BTHAIC folder) in the middle tier, allowing you to check the status information of a particular claim. It also permits you to modify the configuration stored in the Windows Registry (also through the COM+ components in the middle tier). In addition to serving ASP pages, the COM components provide services to the AIC components and an XLANG schedule. The XLANG schedule, ProcessAlerts.skx, located in the \Samples\Claims Processing\sked folder, will be fired frequently by a scheduled task which checks to see if there are any overdue payments. If one is found, it sends a notification e-mail to the address specified during the installation of the sample application. Figure 14-6 shows what the Web site looks like.

Running the Sample Application

Let's run through the claims process sample application to see how it works. Copy 837I.txt file from the \Samples\Claims Processing\TestData folder to the \Samples\Claims Processing\FilePickup\837I folder that was created during the sample installation. After the file disappears in the drop folder, you can check the status of the claim (clicking the Check Claims Status hyperlink on the home page and then clicking the name of the organization, PAYER NAME in this case, on the subsequent page) on the Web site—it should be marked "Submitted," as shown in Figure 14-7. You can

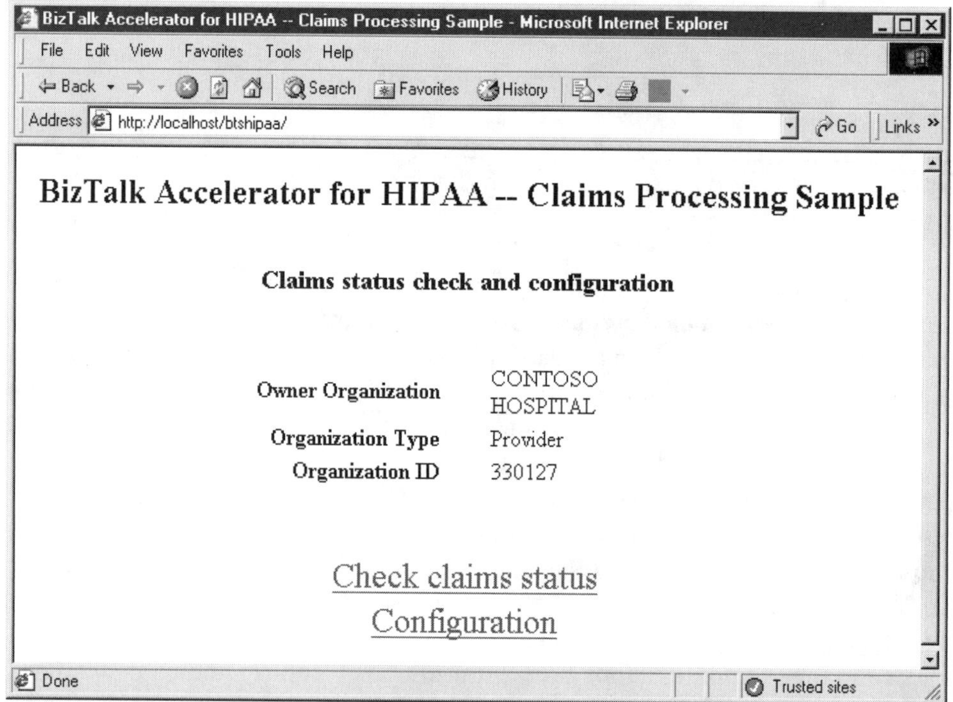

Figure 14-6 *The home page of the sample Web site*

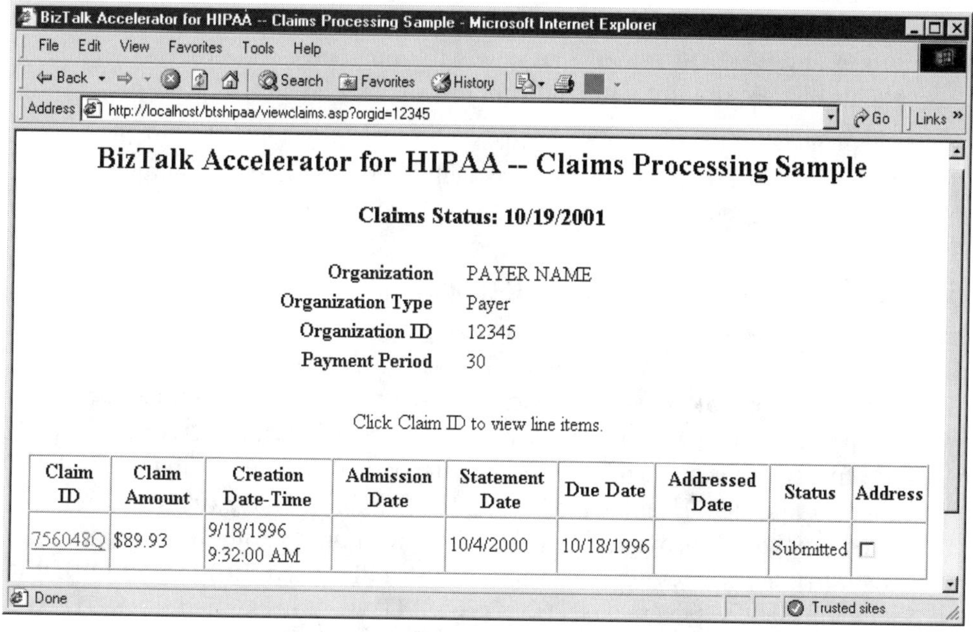

Figure 14-7 *Checking the claims status*

dig further to check the status of individual subitems by clicking the Claim ID hyperlink in Figure 14-7.

Now, copy 835.txt file from the \Samples\Claims Processing\TestData folder to the \Samples\Claims Processing\FilePickup\835 folder. After the file disappears in the drop folder, you can go back to the Web page to check the status of the original claim. You will find that the status is now marked as "Addressed" and most of the values in the grid have turned green. You can also check the status of the subitems, which should be marked as "Yes" in the Status column.

Processing Dental Claims

Now you will see how you can extend the sample application so that it can processes dental claims as well. Here is list of things you need to do:

- Select a new HIPAA-specific BizTalk specification for dental claims. You also need to create a sample document instance to test your solution. In addition, you can also create a corresponding 835 document instance for the payments.

- Create a new AIC component by adding a new class module in the sample Visual Basic project, BTHAIC.vbp, located in the \Samples\Claims Processing\BTHAIC folder. This new AIC component will process dental claims that are slightly different from the regular claims.
- Create necessary BizTalk Server messaging objects such as document definitions, messaging ports, and channels, as well as a receiving function to process the dental claim document.

Selecting HIPAA-specific BizTalk Specifications

The HIPAA transaction set you will be working with is 837-Health Care Claim: Dental, so you need to select 837Dental_V1_wpc_multiple.xml from the \Program Files\Microsoft BizTalk Server Accelerator for HIPAA\Templates folder.

To help you test your solution, you will also need some test data. You can find the 837D.txt file, which is created by modifying the data in Example 1, in the HIPAA Implementation Guide–Health Care Dental 837 (ASC X12N 837 (004010X097)), available for download from the WPC Web site mentioned earlier in this chapter. For demonstration purposes, we replaced the SUBMITTER and BILLING PROVIDER entries (and the address) with CONTOSO HOSPITAL. You can find file 837D.txt and 837D_ValidationInstance.txt (you'll use this file to validate the document against the schema) in the companion CD, located in \SourceCode\Chap14 folder. In addition, we also created a corresponding payment document, 835D.txt, so the dental claim can be addressed the same as any regular claim.

Creating a New AIC Component

In the regular claim processing scenario, the document is processed by the AIC component, or more accurately, the BTHAIC.Proc837I component. The source code in the Visual Basic class module, Proc837.cls, reveals how it works.

The class module implements the simple AIC interface, IBTSAppIntegration through the Implements statement in the general declaration area:

```
Implements IBTSAppIntegration
```

Then it declares a User Defined Type (UDT) for holding the structured data gathered from the document:

```
Private Type ClaimInfoType
    sAcctNum As String
    sProvID As String
    sProvName As String
```

```
    sClaimFreqCode As String
    sPayerID As String
    sPayerName As String
    vTotalClaimAmount As Variant
    dtCreationDateTime As Date
    dtStatementDate As Date
    dtAdmissionDate As Variant
    nLineItemNumCount As Integer
    arLineItems() As LineItemType
End Type
```

The *IBTSAppIntegration_ProcessMessage( )* function provides an entry point for the BizTalk Messaging Services to call during run time in order to pass the document from the channel (the outbound document). The implementation code of the function is pretty simple and looks like this:

```
Private Function IBTSAppIntegration_ProcessMessage( _
    ByVal bstrDocument As String) As String
    IBTSAppIntegration_ProcessMessage = ""

    On Error Resume Next
    Dim xmlClaimDoc As New MSXML2.DOMDocument
    xmlClaimDoc.loadXML bstrDocument
    ProcessClaim xmlClaimDoc
    If (Err.Number <> 0) Then
        m_oUtil.LogError "Unable to process claim.", _
        Err, m_sClaimDescription
    End If
    'The rest of code is omitted here for brevity.
    Set xmlClaimDoc = Nothing
End Function
```

The function first makes certain that the document being passed is a well-formed XML document. It does this by calling the Load method of the DOM object. It then calls the *ProcessClaim( )* subroutine to do the actual dirty work (the line is highlighted in the code listing), passing the document.

The ProcessClaim sub works like this: First it calls another subroutine *GetClaimInfo( )* which parses the documented being passed in and populates the ClaimInfoType UDT variable clm:

```
GetClaimInfo xmlClaimDoc, clm
```

It then checks to make sure the claim frequency code is 1, otherwise it quits:

```
If (clm.sClaimFreqCode <> "1") Then
    m_oUtil.LogMesg "Ignoring claim: Claim frequency code" _
        & " not equal to 1." & vbCr & m_sClaimDescription
    Exit Sub
End If
```

If everything has worked fine so far, the GetClaimInfo sub will call the appropriate SQL Server stored procedures through the BTSHipaaSamp.DbComp COM component, inserting data into the bth_claims and bth_ lineitems table, and optionally the bth_organizations table (if a new organization is presented in the document). All of these inserts are wrapped into a single ADO transaction.

The GetClaimInfo subroutine is the most document-specific piece. In this case, it contains specific code for parsing the 837I document: code that you need to adapt to process the dental claims. We will get into the details of this in just a moment.

To create the new AIC component, open the BTHAIC.vbp project and add a new class module, naming it Proc837D. Copy and paste the entire code from the Proc837I class module into the new class module and you are ready to start modifying.

Browse to the GetClaimInfo subroutine in the new class module and limit the scope of the code to pertain only to this procedure by clicking the Procedure View button, as shown in Figure 14-8.

Skip the local variable declarations and start modifying the first few blocks of code by replacing TS837Q3__XXX with TS837Q2__XXX. For example, replacing TS837Q3__BHT_BeginningOfHierarchicalTransaction with TS837Q2__BHT_BeginningOfHierarchicalTransaction. These are almost identical nodes found in both 837Institutional_V1_wpc_multiple.xml and 837Dental_V1_wpc_multiple.xml BizTalk schemas (we reformatted the following code segment a bit to improve its readability):

```
Set xde = xmlClaimDoc.selectSingleNode( _
    "//TS837Q2__BHT_BeginningOfHierarchicalTransaction")
sDate = xde.getAttribute( _
    "TS837Q2__BHT04__TransactionSetCreationDate")
sTime = xde.getAttribute( _
    "TS837Q2__BHT05__TransactionSetCreationTime")
clm.dtCreationDateTime = StringToDate(sDate, sTime)

Set xde = xmlClaimDoc.selectSingleNode( _
    "//TS837Q2_2010AA_NM1_BillingProviderName")
clm.sProvID = xde.getAttribute( _
    "TS837Q2_2010AA_NM109__BillingProviderIdentifier")
```

```
clm.sProvName = xde.getAttribute( _
    "TS837Q2_2010AA_NM103__BillingProviderLastOrOrganizationalName")

Set xde = xmlClaimDoc.selectSingleNode( _
    "//TS837Q2_1000B_NM1_ReceiverName")
clm.sPayerID = xde.getAttribute( _
    "TS837Q2_1000B_NM109__ReceiverPrimaryIdentifier")
clm.sPayerName = xde.getAttribute( _
    "TS837Q2_1000B_NM103__ReceiverName")

Set xdeClaimInfo = xmlClaimDoc.selectSingleNode("//TS837Q2_2300")

Set xde = xdeClaimInfo.selectSingleNode( _
    "./TS837Q2_2300_CLM_ClaimInformation")
clm.sAcctNum = xde.getAttribute( _
    "TS837Q2_2300_CLM01__PatientAccountNumber")
clm.vTotalClaimAmount = xde.getAttribute( _
    "TS837Q2_2300_CLM02__TotalClaimChargeAmount")
```

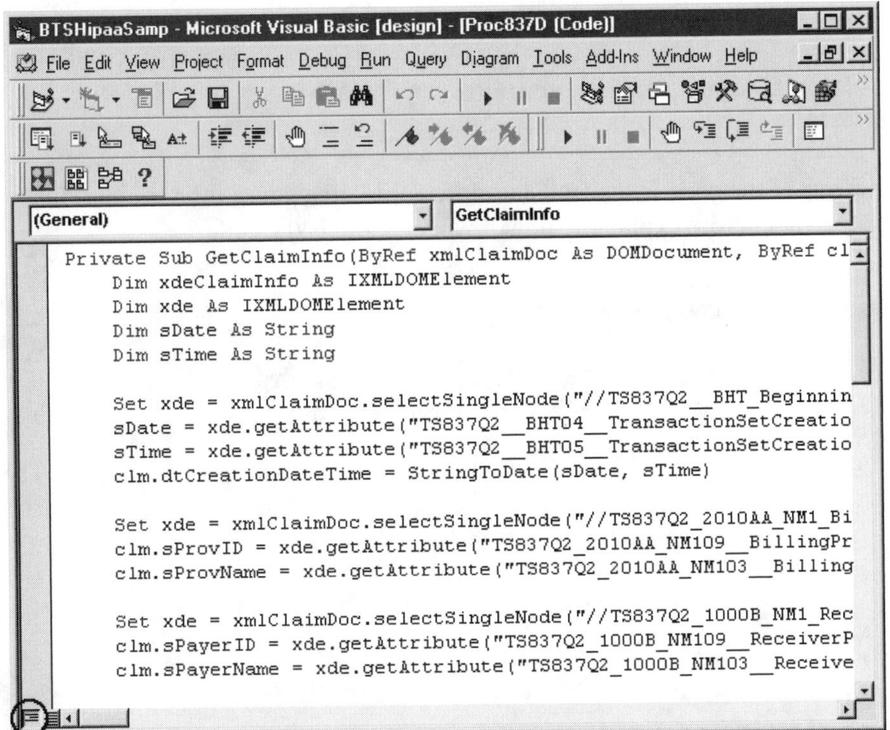

Figure 14-8 *The Procedure View button*

The next two blocks of code in the original class module deal with the TS837Q3_2300_CLM05_C023U1079 and TS837Q3_2300_DTP_StatementDates nodes of which none exists in our 837Dental_V1_wpc_multiple.xml schema. However, these are required fields in the database tables. For demonstration purposes, we hardcoded the claim frequency to 1 and the statement date to current date time, like this:

```
clm.sClaimFreqCode = 1
clm.dtStatementDate = Now()
```

The next block of the code is actually optional, because the node, TS837Q2_2300_DTP_DateAdmission, does not exist in the 837Dental_V1_wpc_multiple.xml schema, so that the *xde* variable will always be Nothing. In addition, the admission date is a nullable field in the database table. The code fragment looks like this:

```
Set xde = xmlClaimDoc.selectSingleNode( _
    "./TS837Q2_2300_DTP_DateAdmission")
If (xde Is Nothing) Then
    clm.dtAdmissionDate = Null
Else
    sDate = xde.getAttribute( _
        "TS837Q2_2300_DTP03__RelatedHospitalizationAdmissionDate")
    clm.dtAdmissionDate = StringToDate(sDate)
End If
```

The rest of the code in the GetClaimInfo subroutine gets a little trickier. Let's present it first before explaining how it works. Here is the code:

```
Dim xdnlLineItems As IXMLDOMNodeList
Dim li As IXMLDOMElement

Set xdnlLineItems = xdeClaimInfo.selectNodes("TS837Q2_2400")
clm.nLineItemNumCount = xdnlLineItems.length
If (clm.nLineItemNumCount > 0) Then
    ReDim clm.arLineItems(clm.nLineItemNumCount - 1)
    Dim i
    For i = 0 To clm.nLineItemNumCount - 1
        GetLineItemInfo xdnlLineItems(i), clm.arLineItems(i),
xdeClaimInfo
    Next i
End If
Set xde = Nothing
Set xdeClaimInfo = Nothing
```

Note the *GetLineItemInfo ( )* call in which we passed an extra parameter, *xdeClaimInfo*. This is because the structure of the 837Dental_V1_wpc_multiple.xml schema is different from the 837Institutional_V1_wpc_multiple.xml in terms of the nodes of interest. In the former case, some of the TS837Q2_2300_DTP_DateService node is located under the TS837Q2_2300 node, while the rest nodes are located under the TS837Q2_2400 node. In the latter case, everything is located under the TS837Q3_2400 node. The following is the modified GetLineItemInfo( ) subroutine. For comparison purposes, we left the original code in commented form instead of deleting it to help you understand the differences:

```
Private Sub GetLineItemInfo( _
    ByRef xdeLineItem, _
    ByRef li As LineItemType, _
    ByVal xdeClaimInfo As IXMLDOMElement)
    'Added a third input parameter.

    Dim xde As IXMLDOMElement
    Dim sDate As String

    'Set xde = xdeLineItem.selectSingleNode( _
        "./TS837Q3_2400_LX_ServiceLineNumber")
    Set xde = xdeLineItem.selectSingleNode( _
        "./TS837Q2_2400_LX_LineCounter")
    li.nLineItemNum = xde.getAttribute( _
        "TS837Q2_2400_LX01__AssignedNumber")

    'Set xde = xdeLineItem.selectSingleNode( _
        ".//TS837Q3_2400_SV202_C003U1880")
    Set xde = xdeLineItem.selectSingleNode( _
        ".//TS837Q2_2400_SV301_C003U1032")
    'li.sProcCode = xde.getAttribute( _
        "TS837Q3_2400_SV202_C00302U1882_ProcedureCode")
    li.sProcCode = xde.getAttribute( _
        "TS837Q2_2400_SV301_C00302U1034_ProcedureCode")

    'Set xde = xdeLineItem.selectSingleNode( _
        "./TS837Q3_2400_DTP_ServiceLineDate")
    Set xde = xdeClaimInfo.selectSingleNode( _
        "./TS837Q2_2300_DTP_DateService")
    'sDate = xde.getAttribute("TS837Q3_2400_DTP03__ServiceDate")
    sDate = xde.getAttribute("TS837Q2_2300_DTP03__ServiceDate")
    li.dtServiceDate = StringToDate(sDate)
End Sub
```

Now, save the new class module as Proc837D.cls and then recompile the BTHAIC.dll, making sure you set the Version Compatibility of the project to Binary Compatibility.

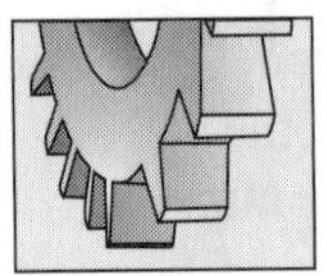

TIP

If you don't want to write the code by yourself, you can find the class module file (Proc837D.cls) on the companion CD, under \SourceCode\Chap14 folder and add it to the BTHAIC.vbp project, save the project, and then recompile.

Now you need to refresh the COM+ application—BizTalk Accelerator for HIPAA–Claims Processing Sample. You can do this by opening the Component Services MMC snap-in and expanding the Components node under that COM+ application. Delete BTHAIC.Proc835 and BTHAIC.Proc837I and reinstall all three components from the BTHAIC.dll.

Creating BizTalk Messaging Configuration Objects

Next, you need to create BizTalk messaging objects and a receive function to receive and process HIPAA dental claims.

Open BizTalk Messaging Manager and create a new document definition, BTSHIPAA_Samp_837D_Doc, and set the document specification to http://Localhost/BizTalkServerRepository/DocSpecs/btshipaasamp/837Dental_V1_wpc_multiple.xml WebDAV repository.

Now, create a new messaging port with the following properties:

- Name: BTSHIPAA_Samp_837D_Port
- Destination organization: BTSHIPAA_Samp_Payer_Org
- Primary transport: AIC - BTHAIC Proc837D

Then create a new channel from an organization with the following properties:

- Name: BTSHIPAA_Samp_837D_Chan
- Source organization: BTSHIPAA_Samp_Provider_Org
- Inbound and outbound document definition: BTSHIPAA_Samp_837D_Doc

Next, you need to create file receive functions in BizTalk Administration with the following properties:

- Name: BTSHIPAA_Samp_837D_RecvFunc

- File types to poll for: *.txt
- Polling location: C:\Program Files\Microsoft BizTalk Server Accelerator for HIPAA\Samples\Claims Processing\FilePickup\837D (you will need to create the 837D subfolder under \Samples\Claims Processing\FilePickup first).
- Channel name: BTSHIPAA_Samp_837D_Chan

Testing Your Solution

To test the dental claim processing solution, you simply copy the file 837D.txt to the \Samples\Claims Processing\FilePickup\837D folder and wait until it disappears. If you go back to the Provider's Web site and click the Check Claims Status hyperlink, you should find a new claim for INSURANCE COMPANY XYZ, as shown in Figure 14-9.

You can check the status of this new dental claim and its items. All of them should be marked as "Submitted" at this point.

Now copy the 835D.txt file to the \Samples\Claims Processing\FilePickup\835 folder and wait until the file disappears. If you check the status of the dental claim again, you should find that the status is now marked as "Addressed."

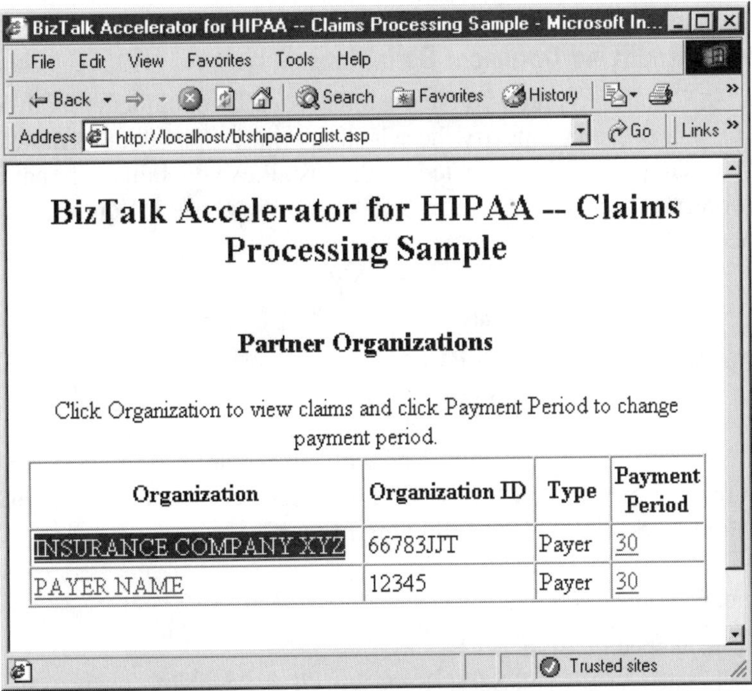

Figure 14-9 *A new dental claim is added to the system*

Outputting X12 EDI Documents and Processing Receipts

In the previous scenarios, we assumed that when we received the claim documents they were already in the HIPAA-specific X12 EDI format. The outbound documents are actually in the internal XML format (this is why the ProcessClaim subroutine works the way it does).

There is no HIPAA-specific serializer; it was rolled into BTS2K SP1 and is just the base X12 serializer (another post-Beta change). In this section, you will learn how to reconfigure BizTalk messaging objects in the sample claim application to output documents in the HIPAA X12 format. You will also learn how to generate an X12 977 receipt by transforming the BizTalk canonical receipt using the map provided in the BizTalk Server Accelerator for HIPAA.

To do this, you need to perform the following tasks:

- Create new document definitions and modify existing ones.
- Create two envelopes.
- Modify organizations, messaging ports, and recreate the channel.
- Create a pair of messaging ports and channels to deliver the receipts.

Creating and Modifying Document Definitions

Recall that in Chapters 3 and 6 you learned that for EDI documents (both X12 and EDIFACT), you needed to specify the selection criteria. The document definition BTSHIPAA_Samp_837I_Doc created by the Install.exe contains only partial selection criteria: functional_identifier and standards_version. You need to add two more selection criteria:

Name	Value
application_sender_code	HOSP CLAIM
application_receiver_code	PAYER ADJ DEPT

In addition, you need to create two new document definitions, one for the canonical receipt and another for the X12 977 receipt. The document definition for the canonical receipt has the following properties:

- Name: Canonical Receipt
- Document specification:
  http://LocalHost/BizTalkServerRepository/DocSpecs/Microsoft/Canonical Receipt.xml

- And the document definition for the X12 977 receipt has the following properties:
- Name: X12 977 Receipt
- Document specification: http://EDEALT031/BizTalkServerRepository/DocSpecs/Microsoft/997Schema.xml

The selection criteria is as follows:

Name	Value
functional_identifier	RC
standards_version	004010X977
application_sender_code	PAYER ADJ DEP
application_receiver_code	HOSP CLAIM

Creating Envelopes

To output documents in the EDI format, you need to use appropriate serializers. First, though, you need to create envelopes. In this exercise, you will create two, with the following properties:

Envelope Name	Format	Envelope Specification
HIPAA 837I Envelope	CUSTOM	http://EDEALT031/ BizTalkServerRepository / DocSpecs/BtsHipaaSamp / 837Institutional_V1_wpc_multiple.xml
977 Receipt Envelope	X12	N/A

Modifying Existing BizTalk Messaging Configuration Objects

Recall that in Chapter 6 you learned that when processing EDI documents, you cannot use the default organization qualifier, OrganizationName, due to length limitations. Therefore, you need to add two organization identifiers to the existing organization. For BTSHIPAA_Samp_Provider_Org organization, add an identifier with the following properties:

- Standard: ISO 6523: Organization Identification
- Qualifier: 30 (read-only)
- Value: 12-23456789

Also add an identifier for the BTSHIPAA_Samp_Payer_Org with the following properties:

- Standard: Mutually defined
- Qualifier: ZZ (read-only)
- Value: 9876543-21

Now you need to modify the messaging port and channel to specify the new organization qualifiers. In addition, you need to specify the envelope and associated properties for both the messaging port and the channel. The BizTalk Messaging Manager will prevent you from doing so, however. To work around this problem, you can first delete the channel, then recreate it later. So, go ahead and delete the channel BTSHIPAA_Samp_837I_Chan at this point.

Now switch to messaging port, BTSHIPAA_Samp_837I_Port, open it, and modify the following properties:

- Primary transport: file://C:\temp\HIPAA\837I%tracking_id%.txt
- Envelope information: HIPAA 837 Envelope
- Delimiters: Record - "<CR>", Field - "*", Subfield - ":"
- Interchange control number: 10001
- Organization Identifier: Mutually defined/98-7654321

Now you can recreate the channel BTSHIPAA_Samp_837I_Chan, with the following properties:

- Source organization: BTSHIPAA_Samp_Provider_Org
- Organization identifier: ISO 6523: Organization Identification/12-3456789
- Inbound and outbound document definition: BTSHIPAA_Samp_837I_Doc
- Group control number: 10001

Click the Advanced button in the Advanced Configuration page of the Channel Wizard and click the Envelope tab of the Override Messaging Port Defaults tab. Specify X12 serializer as the Serializer component, as shown in Figure 14-10.

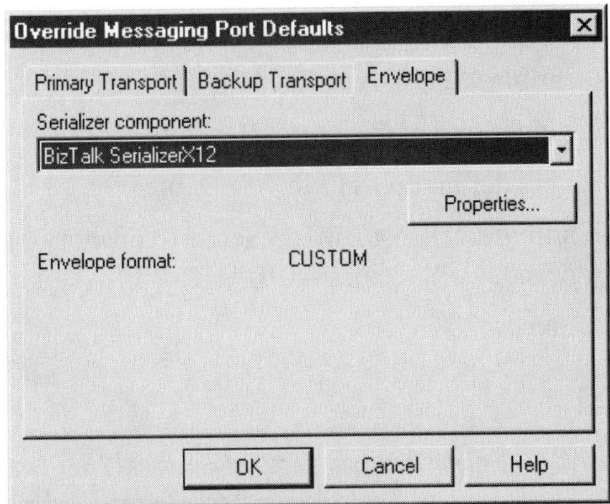

Figure 14-10 *Specifying the HIPAA-specific serializer*

Creating the Messaging Port and Channel for Delivering Receipts

Finally, you can create the messaging port and channel to deliver the X12 977 receipts. Create a new messaging port (to an organization) with the following properties:

- Name: BTSHIPAA_Samp_977_Port
- Destination organization: BTSHIPAA_Samp_Provider_Org
- Primary transport: file://C:\temp\HIPAA\977%tracking_id%.txt
- Envelope information: 977 Receipt Envelope
- Delimiters: >, *, ~
- Interchange control number: 20001
- Organization identifier: ISO 6523: Organization Identification/12-3456789

Then create a new channel (from an organization) with the following properties:

- Name: BTSHIPAA_Samp_977_Chan
- This is a receipt channel: Checked

- Source Organization: BTSHIPAA_Samp_Payer_Org
- Organization Identifier: Mutually defined/98-7654321
- Inbound document definition: Canonical Receipt
- Outbound document definition: X12 977 Receipt
- Map reference: http://LocalHost/BizTalkServerRepository/Maps/Microsoft/HipaaCanonicalReceiptTo4010-997.xml*
- Group control number: 2001

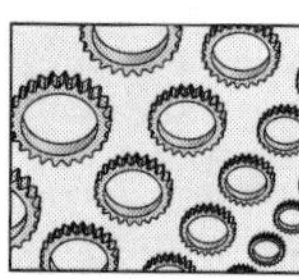

NOTE

A map is required to transform the canonical receipt into the X12 977 format. In this case, you cannot use the BizTalk Canonical Receipt document definition provided by BizTalk Server. If you use it, the outbound document definition will also be a BizTalk Canonical Receipt and therefore will become a read-only property. In addition, you need to copy the map to the BizTalk specification WebDAV repository prior to the creation of this channel.

As the last step, you need to specify the BTSHIPAA_Samp_837I_chan as the channel that generates the receipt by selecting the Generate receipt check box and specify BTSHIPAA_Samp_977_chan as the Receipt channel, as shown in Figure 14-11.

Test the Solution

To test the solution, you simply copy the 837I.txt file to the \Samples\Claims Processing\FilePickup\837I folder and wait until it disappears. You should then find two new documents in the C:\temp\HIPAA folder (or any folder you specified). One is the HIPAA 837 claim and the other is an X12 977 receipt.

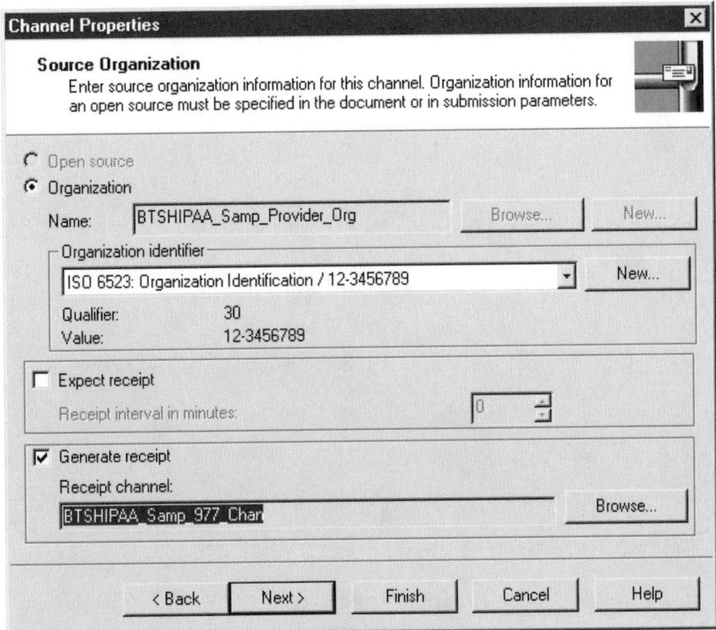

Figure 14-11 *Configuring the channel to generate the receipt and specifying the receipt channel*

Chapter in Review

In this chapter, you have learned about HIPAA and BizTalk Server Accelerator for HIPAA. By working with the exercises in this chapter to extend the claims processing sample application, you should now be familiar with the Accelerator, and on your way to creating great BizTalk HIPAA solutions.

PART VII

Bizet—BizTalk Server 2002

OBJECTIVES

- To master new and enhanced BizTalk Server 2002 features

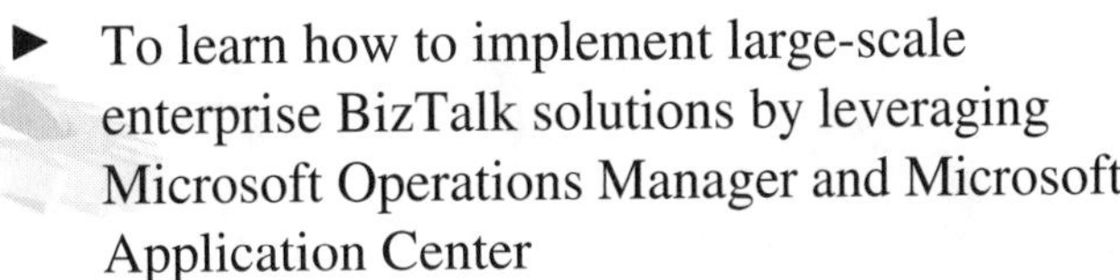

- To learn how to implement large-scale enterprise BizTalk solutions by leveraging Microsoft Operations Manager and Microsoft Application Center

CHAPTER 15

Introducing BizTalk Server 2002

IN THIS CHAPTER:

Introducing BizTalk Server 2002

The HTTP Receive Function

The BizTalk SEED Wizard – Enabling Trading Partners

Custom Counters

Improved BizTalk Editor and Mapper

New Orchestration Features

Chapter in Review

BizTalk Server 2000, codenamed Bizet, ships with Enterprise Edition only. It is an incremental release post BizTalk Server 2000, which provides commonly requested key functionality specifically in the areas of the development, monitoring, and deployment of large-scale BizTalk Server implementations in enterprises. This chapter will focus on the new features found in BizTalk Server 2002, and some development practices. The next chapter will conclude Part VII (and thus the entire book) with a discussion on monitoring and deploying large-scale BizTalk solutions by leveraging Microsoft Operations Manager (MOM) and Microsoft Application Center (another Microsoft .NET enterprise server).

Introducing BizTalk Server 2002

BizTalk Server 2002 is not an overhaul of BizTalk Server 2000. Rather, it is an incremental release that preserves and enhances the existing services and features available in BizTalk Server 2000 and leverages the enterprise management capabilities (such as monitoring and deployment) offered by Microsoft Operations Manager and Microsoft Application Center. BizTalk Server 2002 shares the same architecture with BizTalk Server 2000, including the four SQL Server databases (messaging, tracking, shared queue, and XLANG databases).

In this chapter, we will discuss the enhancements of BizTalk Server 2002 over BizTalk Server 2000, including the new HTTP receive function, the SEED Wizard tool, the Custom Counter component, and the new functionalities of BizTalk Editor and Mapper.

Installing BizTalk Server 2002

Before going further, let's take a moment to discuss the installation of BizTalk Server 2002. BizTalk Server 2002 will be shipped separately with Microsoft Operations Manager (MOM) and Microsoft Application Center. The use of MOM and/or Application Center is optional.

Installing BizTalk Server Only

The system requirements and installation procedures of BizTalk Server 2002 itself are very straightforward and are extremely similar to those of BizTalk Server 2000, as you learned in Chapter 2. As a result, we won't bore you by covering the steps in detail. Rather, we will only point out a few exceptions that you should pay attention to.

BizTalk Server 2002 requires Windows 2000 Server with Service Pack 2. In addition, the Orchestration Designer of BizTalk Server 2002 requires Microsoft Visio 2002, which is shipped with BizTalk Server 2002 and is also available as part of the Microsoft Office XP suite. As with the rest of the products in the Office XP suite, the first time you open Visio 2002 (or BizTalk Orchestration Designer) you will see the Microsoft Visio Professional 2002 Activation Wizard, and you will have to have the product activated to prevent the Activation Wizard from being displaying in the future. Activating the product is easy—just follow the Wizard's instructions.

BizTalk Server 2002 now uses the more secure Windows authentication rather than the legacy SQL authentication to talk to its databases. To do this, open SQL Server Enterprise Manager and expand the SQL Server group. Right-click the SQL Server for which you want to change the authentication mode and select Properties to bring up the SQL Server Properties dialog box. Click the Security tab and change the Authentication from SQL Server and Windows to Windows only, as shown in Figure 15-1. Click OK.

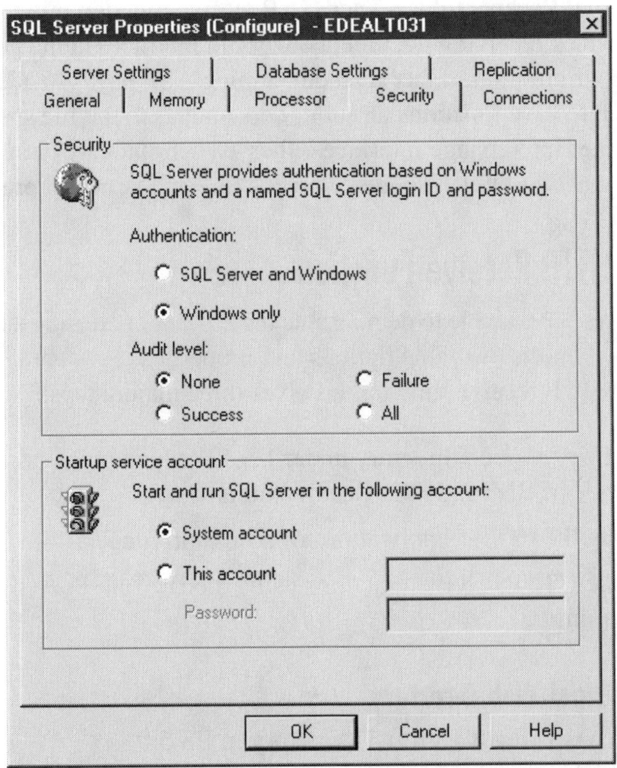

Figure 15-1 *Specifying the SQL Server authentication mode*

Installing MOM and Application Center

BizTalk Server 2002 leverages Microsoft's standard products for deployment, clustering/load-balancing through Application Center, and monitoring through Microsoft Operations Manager (MOM). These products are not bundled with BizTalk Server 2002, so you will need to purchase them separately. We will discuss Application Center and MOM and demonstrate how to leverage them to implement enterprise BizTalk Server 2002 solutions in the next chapter.

The HTTP Receive Function

While BizTalk Server 2000 supported HTTP transport through ASP pages that were independently managed, BizTalk Server 2002 introduced a third type of receive function—the HTTP receive function. An HTTP receive function is implemented as an ISAPI (short for Internet Server Application Programming Interface) extension in a COM DLL BizTalkHTTPReceive.dll which is located under the <BizTalk Server Installation>\HTTP Receive folder. The HTTP receive function provides an out-of-box solution that enables receiving documents over the Internet via the HTTP protocol with minimal configuration, rather than developing ASP pages to additional COM DLLs. An HTTP receive function can submit documents to the file system or through a COM call of the IInterchange interface either asynchronously or synchronously (through Submit and SubmitSync, respectively, as you learned in previous chapters).

Creating an HTTP Receive Function

Let's walk through an example to demonstrate the process of creating an HTTP receive function and explain the available options and properties.

Creating an HTTP receive function involves three major steps:

1. Creating a virtual Web directory under IIS 5.0 which points to a file folder where a copy of BizTalkHTTPReceive.dll is located.
2. Configuring the COM+ application for access privileges.
3. Creating the HTTP receive functions using the BizTalk Server Administrator MMC snap-in.

Creating the Virtual Web Directory

Follow these steps to create a Virtual Directory in IIS 5.0:

1. Create a folder in the root directory of the C drive named C:\ReceivePO.

2. Create a FileDrop subfolder under C:\ReceivePO.
3. Copy the BizTalkHTTPReceive.dll file from the HTTP Receive folder to the C:\ReceivePO folder you just created.
4. Open the Computer Management MMC snap-in and expand Services and Applications | Internet Information Services.
5. Right-click Default Web Site and select New | Virtual Directory. Name the Virtual Directory Alias as ReceivePO and point it to the C:\ReceivePO folder.
6. Make sure that the Execute (such as ISAPI applications or CGI) option is selected in the Access Permissions page of the Virtual Directory Creation Wizard.
7. When finished creating the Virtual Directory, right-click it and select Properties.
8. On the Virtual Directory tab of the ReceivePO Properties dialog box, change the Application Protection option from Medium (Pooled) to High (Isolated), as shown in Figure 15-2. Click OK to dismiss the ReceivePO Properties dialog box.

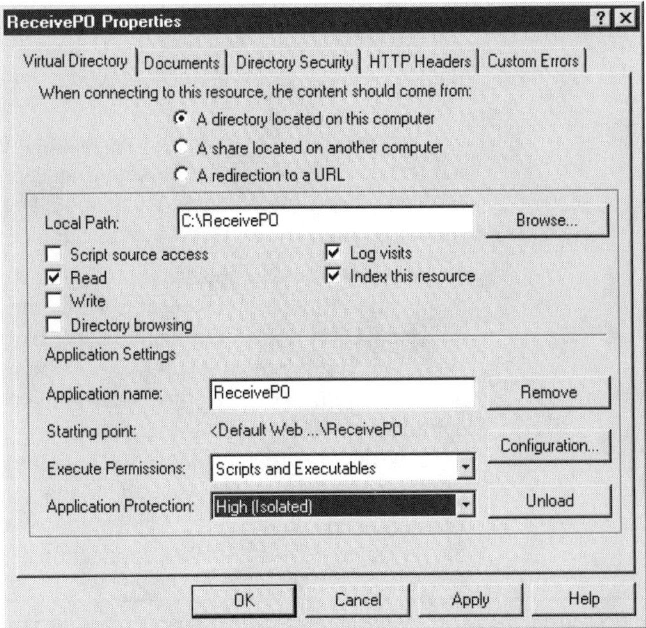

Figure 15-2 *Specifying the application protection level of the virtual directory*

Configuring the COM+ Application

Depending on the Application Protection level you set for the Virtual directory, you need to configure this COM+ application or the World Wide Web Publishing Services to set access privileges accordingly. The following table describes how to configure appropriate access privileges based on the Application Protection level.

For simplicity purposes, in this example, assume you logged on to the server using the administrator account, so you can set the Identity to Interactive user, as shown in Figure 15-3.

Application Protection Level	Do This...
Low (IIS Process)	1. Open Component Services MMC snap-in and click Services (Local) node. 2. Right-click World Wide Web Publishing Service in the right pane and select Properties. 3. Click the Log On tab and set the log on account to a user account that has access to BizTalk Message Management database and BizTalk Server Interchange Application and BizTalk Server Internal Utility COM+ applications.
Medium (Pooled)	1. Open Component Services MMC snap-in, right-click the IIS Out-of-Process Pooled Applications, and select Properties. 2. Click the Identity tab and set the account to the user that has access to the BizTalk Message Management database, BizTalk Server Interchange Application, and BizTalk Server Internal Utility COM+ applications.
High (Isolated)	1. When you create a Virtual Directory in IIS with the Application Protection level set to High, the system will create a COM+ application with a name like {IIS-{Default Web Site/Root/ReceivePO}. Open Component Services MMC snap-in, right-click this system-created COM+ application and select Properties. 2. Click the Identity tab and set the account to the user that has access to the BizTalk Message Management database, BizTalk Server Interchange Application, and BizTalk Server Internal Utility COM+ applications.

Table 15-1 *Configuring access privileges based on the Application Protection level*

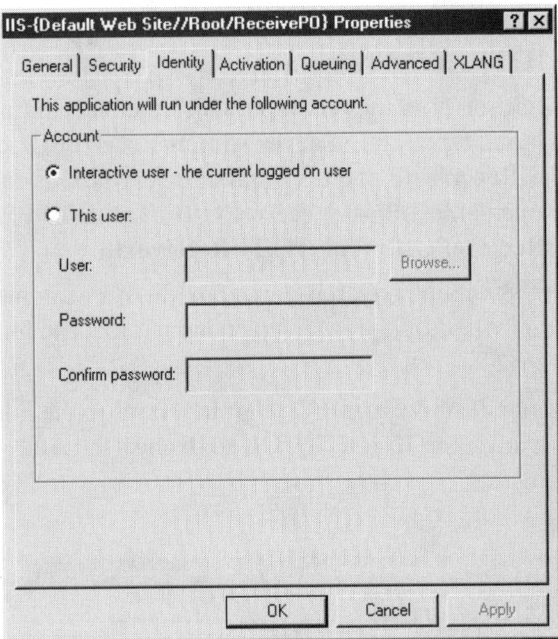

Figure 15-3 *Setting the Identity property for the COM+ application*

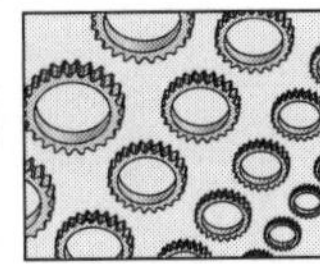

NOTE

Setting the Identity property of a COM+ application to Interactive user–the current logged on user will allow whoever logs on to the server access to the specified COM+ application. This is very convenient for development and debugging purposes. The down side of using Interactive user is that someone has to log on to the server. If you deploy the COM+ application into a production machine, it is highly recommended that you set to This user and associate it with a specific user account. In this way, it is not necessary to have someone log on to the server in order to access the COM+ application.

Creating and Configuring the HTTP Receive Function

Follow these steps to create and configure the HTTP Receive Function:

1. Open the BizTalk Server Administration MMC snap-in and expand Microsoft BizTalk Server 2002 | BizTalk Server Group (or the name of your custom BizTalk server group) to expose and highlight the Receive Functions node.
2. Select Action | New | HTTP Receive Function from the menu bar. This brings up the Add An HTTP Receive Function dialog box.

3. In the Add An HTTP Receive Function dialog box, enter **ReceivePO** as the Name of the HTTP receive function.
4. Select a BizTalk server in the server on which the receive function will run the drop-down list and type **/<BTSServerName>/ReceivePO/. BizTalkHTTPReceive.dll** in the Virtual directory box. For the local BizTalk server, you can enter **localhost/ReceivePO/BizTalkHTTPReceive.dll** or simply type **/ReceivePO/BizTalkHTTPReceive.dll**.
5. Select File in the Submit To: drop-down box. In this example, the HTTP receive function will drop the received document to a file folder you'll specify in the next step.
6. Enter **C:\ReceivePO\FileDrop\PO_%guid%.xml** in the File Path And Name: box, as shown in Figure 15-4. Click OK to dismiss the Add An HTTP Receive Function dialog box.

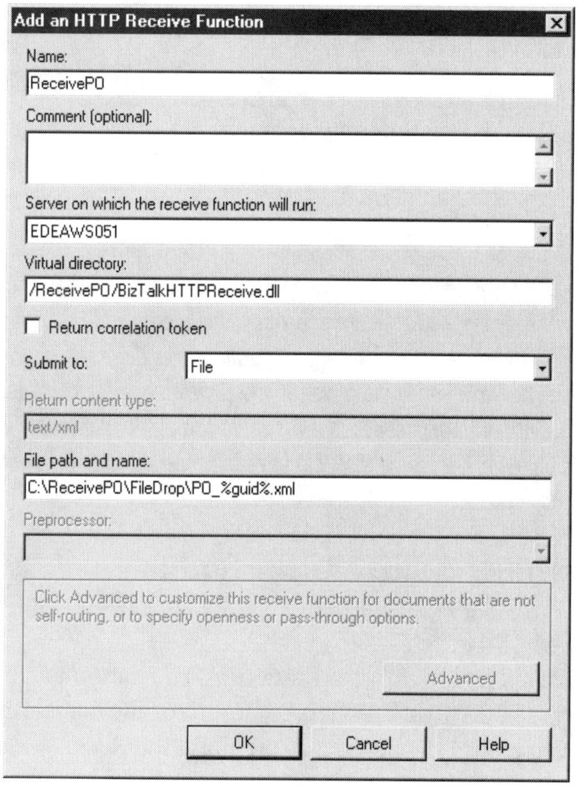

Figure 15-4 *Creating an HTTP receive function*

Submitting Documents to the HTTP Receive Function

After appropriately setting up the HTTP receive function, you can submit documents from a client machine through HTTP protocol. The following code listing illustrates how to submit the POReq.xml document to the HTTP receive function you created, using the *IXMLHTTPRequest* interface of the MSXML 3.0 parser. The inline comments explain how it works.

```
Dim doc, xmlHttp

on error resume next
' Create a DOM object and load POReq.xml.
set doc = CreateObject("MSXML2.DOMDocument")
doc.async = false
doc.load "POReq.xml"

if doc.parseerror <> 0 then
   wscript.echo "Error loading po document."
   wscript.quit
end if

' Create an XMLHTTP instance.
set xmlHttp = CreateObject("MSXML2.XMLHTTP")

' Change the machine of the following line to name of
' the BizTalk/Web Server you want to access.
' Post the POReq.xml document to the HTTP receive function
call xmlHttp.open ("POST", _
"http://EDEAWS051/ReceivePO/BizTalkHTTPReceive.dll", _
False)

xmlHttp.send doc.xml

if err = 0 then
    if xmlhttp.status = 202 then
        wscript.echo "PO was successfully submitted."
    else
        wscript.echo "PO submitting failed - " _
                     & xmlhttp.statusText
    end if
else
    wscript.echo "PO submitting failed - " _
              & err.description
```

```
end if

set doc = nothing
set xmlHttp = nothing
```

After successfully submitting the document to the HTTP receive function, you should find a document in the C:\ReceivePO\FileDrop folder with a name like PO_{059F2056-0BFD-4EF8-9B1A-BBDCE02C0AEB}.xml.

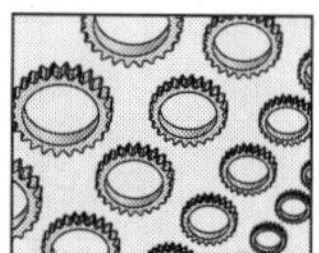

NOTE

The source code, SubmitPO.vbs, and the POReq.xml document (both can be found on the accompanying CD) must be placed in the save folder.

Minor Details

To make the example simple, we deliberately avoided the explanations for some details, such as the syntaxes of some options. Now it is time to discuss them.

Take a look at Figure 15-4 again. Notice the syntax for the Virtual directory. In this case, it was /ReceivePO/BizTalkHTTPReceive.dll. There are a couple of points we want to make here. First, don't prefix http:// in the URL. You can specify the server name if the Virtual directory is located on a remote server. Second, you can create multiple HTTP receive functions and have them all point to the same Virtual directory. To do this, you will need to specify a query string in the Virtual Directory text box as well as the corresponding submitting code. For example, suppose you want to create two HTTP receive functions, one for Buyer A and another for Buyer B. You can specify the Virtual directories as /ReceivePO/BizTalkHTTPReceive.dll?Buyer%20A and /ReceivePO/BizTalkHTTPReceive.dll?Buyer%20B, respectively. Notice the **%20** used in the query string. It is one of the URL encode methods for specifying URLs. %20 stands for a space.

Another thing to notice is the Return correlation token check box in Figure 15-4. Depending on how you set up the Submit To: option, the correlation token can contain either the submission GUID (for synchronous or asynchronous submission) or a filename (if you specified Submit To: as **File**, as in this example). An example of a correlation token follows:

```
<BizTalkHttpReceive>
  <CorrelationToken TokenType= SUBMIT>
C:\ReceivePO\FileDrop\PO_{059F2056-0BFD-4EF8-9B1A-BBDCE02C0AEB}.xml
<CorrelationToken>
</BizTalkHttpReceive>
```

In case asynchronous submission is specified for the Submit To:, the correlation token allows the processing of the document on the receiving side to appear to have a synchronous behavior.

You might also notice in Figure 15-4 that we used a *%guid%* in the filename (File Path And Name:). It is one of the three variables you can use in the filename. Other available variables include *%server%* and *%datetime%*. (Recall that in Chapter 3 you learned about the six symbols that can be used to specify the filename for the File Transport Protocol).

As mentioned before, in addition to File, you can also specify BizTalk–Asynchronously or BizTalk–Synchronously for the Submit To: box. If you specified BizTalk–Synchronously, you can also specify the Return content type, which is the HTTP response context type. The default is text/xml. In either case (synchronously or asynchronously), you can also specify a Preprocessor when appropriate and the Advanced button will become enabled which allows you to specify the Openness, envelope, channel, document definition and so on, just as you do when you create a File or MSMQ receive function.

Programmatically Creating HTTP Receive Functions

Just like File or MSMQ receive functions, you can also programmatically create an HTTP receive function through WMI APIs, as you learned in Chapter 7. The following code segment illustrates how to specify the properties specific to the HTTP receive functions. For detailed instruction about WMI and receive function programming, see Chapter 7 of this book.

```
If Not oReceiveFunctionInstance Is Nothing Then
    With oReceiveFunctionInstance
       .Name = "ReceivePO"
       .ProtocolType = 3
       .GroupName = "BizTalk Server Group"
       .PollingLocation = "/ReceivePO/BizTalkHTTPReceive.dll"
       .OpennessFlag = 1
       .IsPassThrough = False
       .DisableReceiveFunction = False
       .TransportURL = "C:\ReceivePO\FileDrop\PO_%guid%.xml"
       .HttpTransportType = 1
       .HttpReturnCorrelationToken = False
       .ProcessingServer=gHostName
       .Put_ (2) 'wbemChangeFlagCreateOnly
    End With
End If
```

The BizTalk SEED Wizard – Enabling Trading Partners

In a typical B2B integration scenario, setting up your trading partners is a very challenging and laborious task. For a large organization that has tens of thousands suppliers and wants to automate procurement withthem, the challenge will be multiplied. Fortunately, BizTalk Server 2002 has just introduced a new tool, BizTalk SEED Wizard, which enables you and your trading partner to quickly and easily set up, test, and deploy the necessary configuration and infrastructure for B2B integration, provided that the trading partner also uses BizTalk Server to receive and/or submit the document from/to your site.

The Roles and Responsibilities

The process of setting up your trading partner using BizTalk SEED Wizard involves both your organization and your trading partner. In this relationship, the party (your organization in this case) who initiates the process is referred as an *initiator* while the trading partners who participate in the process are referred to as *recipients*. Figure 15-5 illustrates the overall process of creating and deploying a SEED package, the roles involved, and their responsibilities.

As you can see in Figure 15-5, the initiator starts the process by creating a SEED package (Step 1) and makes it available for the recipients (Step 2). The information in the SEED package created by the initiator includes the organization name of the initiator, testing and production URLs for recipients to submit documents, and the specification and instance data of the sample document. When a recipient gets the SEED package, it configures the SEED package (Step 3), tests it locally and remotely (Step 4 and 5) and finally deploys the configuration (Step 6).

Creating and Configuring a Sample SEED Package

To demonstrate how to use BizTalk SEED Wizard to enable a trading partner, let's walk through an example (we'll explain the details of each step later). In this example, we will show you how to use BizTalk SEED Wizard to create, configure, test, and deploy a SEED package that involves the exchange of an invoice document.

Whereas I've used two computers in building this sample, for learning purposes it will be perfectly fine if you only have one computer available to you—you will be able to practice the example on a single machine.

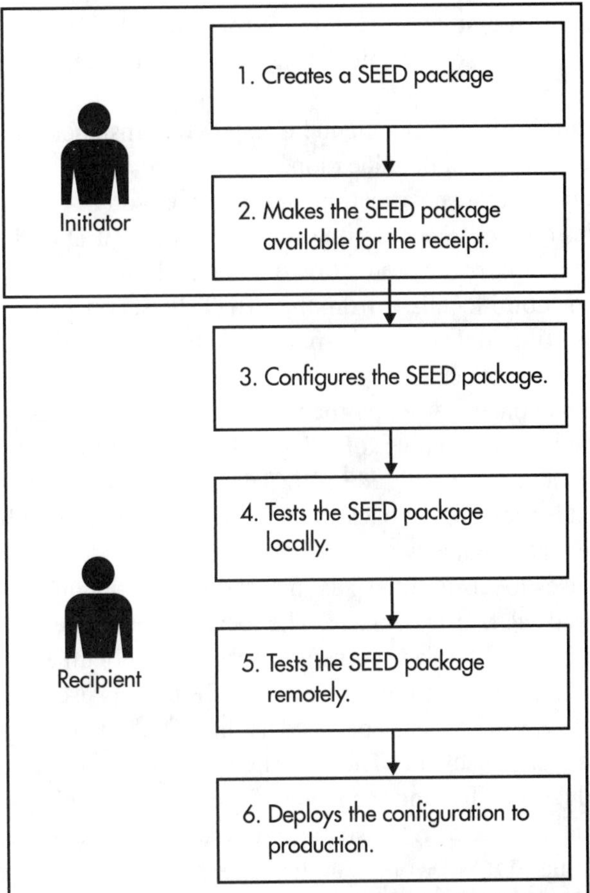

Figure 15-5 *Enabling trading partners using the BizTalk SEED Wizard*

The Initiator - Preparing the Document Specification and Instance

Before the initiator can start creating a SEED package, it needs to make the document specification and test instance availability. For demonstration purposes, we will use the CommonInvoice.xml BizTalk specification that ships with BizTalk Server.

On the machine that emulates the initiator role, start BizTalk Editor and retrieve the CommonInvoice.xml specification from the BizTalk WebDAV repository (under the Microsoft folder).

In BizTalk Editor, select Tools menu | Create XML Instance and save the instance as Invoice_Instance.xml to a disk location.

In addition to document specification and instance, you also need to create two Virtual directories on the IIS server, one for testing the SEED package, named SEEDTesting, and another for production, named SEEDProduction. Copy slingback.asp and submitlocal.asp from the <BizTalk Server Installation>\SEED\ folder to the respective folders that are pointed to by the two Virtual directories you just created.

The slingback.asp page is used by the recipients for remote testing of inbound documents. When the recipient uses BizTalk SEED Wizard to test the configuration remotely, the document is submitted to BizTalk Server synchronously through slingback.asp and is then copied back to the recipient and verified by BizTalk SEED Wizard to ensure that it matches the one it sent.

The recipient uses localsubmit.asp as the production URL after it successfully tested and deployed the SEED package. The localsubmit.asp retrieves the channel name from the submitted XML document to submit the document to BizTalk Server.

There is a third ASP page: trigger.asp. This ASP page is used for testing outbound documents remotely. This page is specified as the URL for remote test when the initiator creates a SEED package. The document submitted to the trigger.asp page contains the production URL and the name of the channel used by the recipient to process the document. The trigger.asp page submits the document to BizTalk Server with an open destination. We won't use the trigger.asp page in this example.

TIP

The source code of all three forementioned ASP pages can be found in the <BizTalk Server Installation>\SEED\ folder. You may want to modify them to fit your needs.

The Initiator – Packing the SEED

To create a SEED package using BizTalk SEED Wizard, use the following procedure:

1. While still on the same machine, start BizTalk SEED Wizard and select Create SEED Package, as shown in Figure 15-6. Click Next.
2. Type a name for the initiator organization in the Package Creating Process–Organization Information page of the BizTalk SEED Wizard. In this example, enter SEED Test Organization and click Next (the SEED Test Organization was created automatically when you installed BizTalk Server 2002).

Figure 15-6 *Creating a SEED package*

3. In the Package Creation Process–Document Specifications page of BizTalk SEED Wizard, click the Add button to bring up the Configure Document dialog box.
4. Specify the CommonInvoice.xml BizTalk Specification from the Microsoft BizTalk WebDAV repository as the Specification and the Invoice_Instance.xml document you created earlier as the Test Instance.
5. Specify the Inbound To Initiator option. In this example, you are emulating a scenario in which trading partners submit invoices to your organization.
6. In URL for remote test, enter: **http://MachineName/SEEDTesting/slingback.asp**.
7. In Production URL, enter: **http://MachineName/SEEDProduction/localsubmit.asp**. The Configure Document dialog box should now look like the one in Figure 15-7. Click OK to return to the BizTalk SEED Wizard's main page. The CommonInvoice.xml should now appear in the Documents list with the Inbound To Initiator button selected. Click Next.
8. Enter the path and filename for the SEED package. In this example, name the file Invoice_SEED.xml and click Finish.

The SEED package you just created is an XML document that contains the name of your organization (SEED Test Organization in this case), the URLs for testing

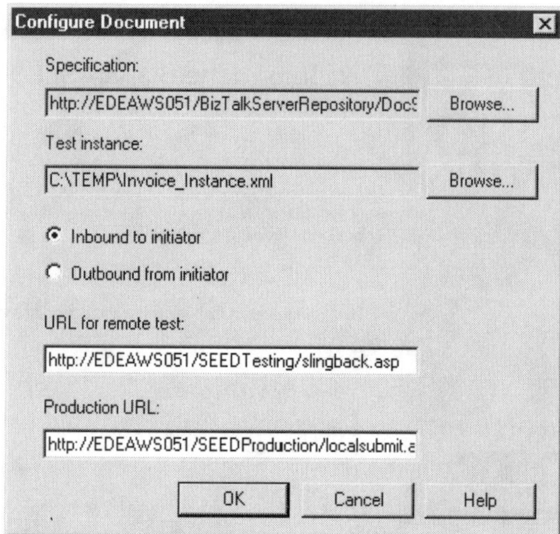

Figure 15-7 *Specifying document configuration information*

and production, an embedded BizTalk specification (CommonInvoice.xml), and an embedded XML document instance (Invoice_Instance.xml). It is now ready to be handed over to the recipient.

The Recipient – Configuring, Testing, and Deploying the SEED

On another machine that emulates your trading partner (or the same machine if you can't find a second one with BizTalk Server installed) use the following procedures to configure, test the SEED package, and deploy the configuration in the recipient's organization:

1. Start BizTalk SEED Wizard. Select Install SEED package (the second option in Figure 15-6). Click Next.
2. In the Package Installation Process–Package Selection page of BizTalk SEED Wizard, select the Invoice_SEED.xml package you created (or rather that the initiator created). The package information will be displayed in BizTalk SEED Wizard, as shown in Figure 15-8. Click Next.
3. On the next page, Package Installation Process–Test Information, leave the Time out and Interval for the defaults. Click Next.
4. On the Package Installation Process–Document Deployment page, select CommonInvoice.xml document and click the Configure button. The Inbound Document (to Initiator) Configuration dialog box appears. Fill up the information as indicated in Figure 15-9 (assuming the folders where created beforehand) and

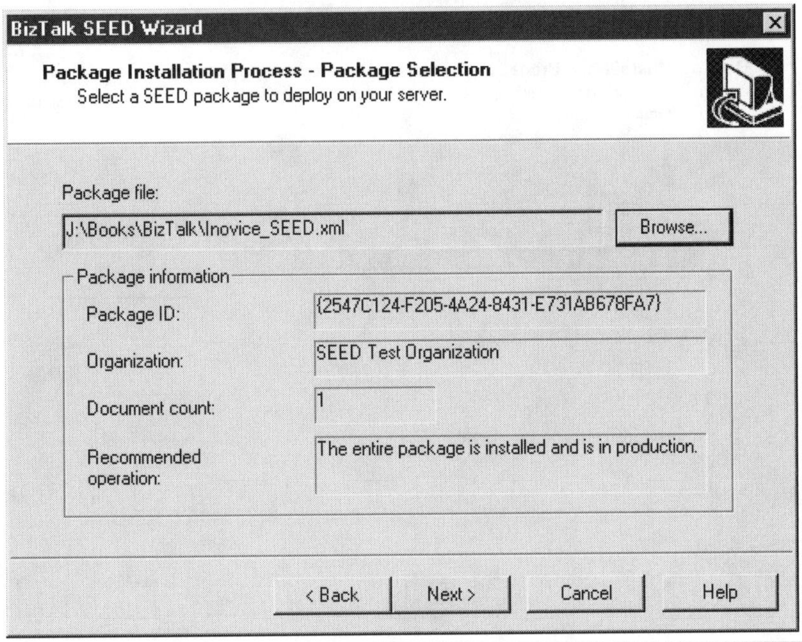

Figure 15-8 *Selecting a SEED package*

click OK to return to the main page of BizTalk SEED Wizard (see Figure 15-10). Now that you've completed the configuration of the document. You are ready to test the configuration and deploy it. The appropriate command buttons will be enabled when you move to the specific point later in the process.

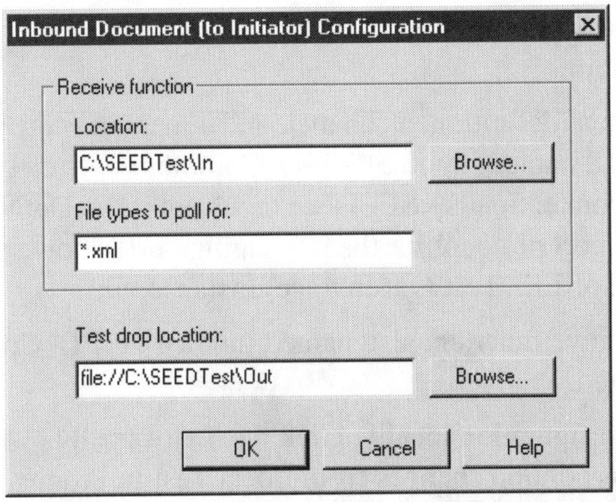

Figure 15-9 *Specifying inbound document configuration information*

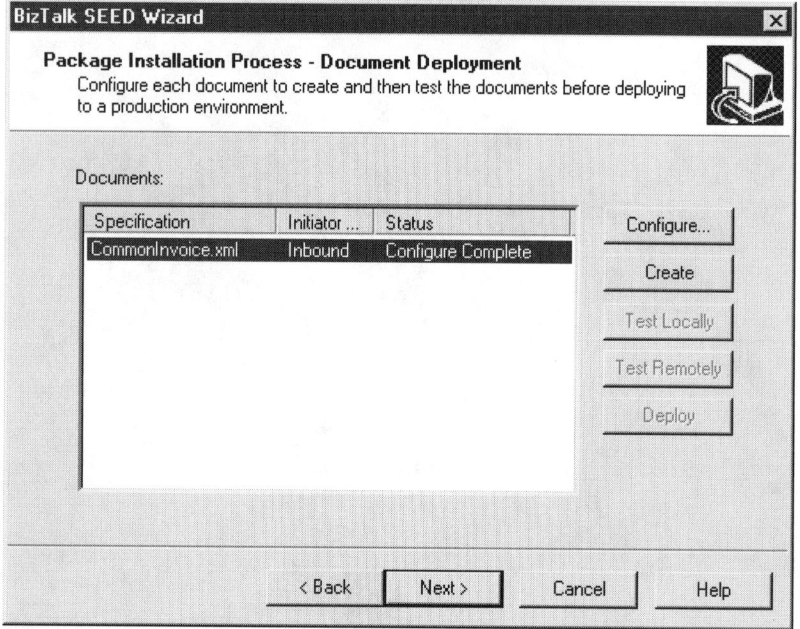

Figure 15-10 *Configuration of the document is complete*

5. Before testing the configuration, click the Create button. When the status column indicates "Create Passed," the Test Locally button will be enabled. At this point, several things have happened behind the scenes which established an infrastructure for you to test (locally and remotely) and deploy the configuration:
   - A new WebDAV folder was created under BizTalkServerRepository \DocSpecs\, named PEPs, which contains the CommonInvoice.xml specification.
   - A document definition, a channel, and a message port were created, all named Invoice_SEED_CommonInvoice. The naming convention is <SEEDPackageName_DocDefName>. The transport protocol for the messaging port is now specified as file://C:\SEEDTest\Out\Invoice_Instance.xml.
   - A file receive function, also named Invoice_SEED_CommonInvoice was created.
6. To test the configuration locally, click the Test Locally button. You will notice that the Status column changes from Local Test In Progress to Local Test Passed (hopefully) and the Test Remotely button should be enabled by now.

In addition, the transport protocol for the messaging port will be changed from File to HTTP and point to the remote testing site as the initiator specified when the SEED package was created. In this case, it is http://RemoteServerURL/SEEDTesting/slingback.asp.

7. The process of testing the configuration remotely is very similar to Step 6—you simply click the Test Remotely button and wait until the Status changes from Remote Test In Progress to Remote Test Passed.
8. The last step is simple, as well. Click the Deploy button (it should be enabled if the remote test was passed). If the Status indicates "Deploy Passed," the transport protocol for the messaging port will be changed again to http://EDEAWS051/SEEDProduction/localsubmit.asp. This is the production site as specified by the initiator.
9. To save the completed SEED package, click Next and Finish.

To actually start trading, the initiator needs to create an ASP page to accept orders.

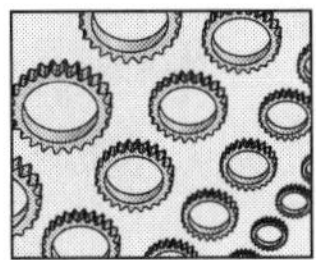

NOTE

When using BizTalk SEED Wizard to set up your trading partners, you should be aware of its constraints and limitations. For example, the recipients must also use BizTalk Server 2002 (whereas you can also use BizTalk Server 2000 to be a participant in SEED testing and deployment, the BizTalk SEED Wizard tool itself only ships with BizTalk Server 2002). Additionally, the BizTalk messaging infrastructure (channels, messaging ports, receive functions, and so on) that was set up by BizTalk SEED Wizard is used only for testing and is not meant for production purposes.

Custom Counters

Custom counters are a new feature of BizTalk Server 2002. Custom counters refer to two specific custom-built WMI classes that are created based on custom queries you defined against the BizTalk tracking database (InterchangeDTA). The query criteria for custom counters include the names or qualifiers of source and destination organizations of the documents, the name of the document definition, and the time range over which to accumulate the custom counter value.

You can use custom counters to acquire the number of documents in the tracking database that match your queries and to build custom applications to track specific documents. Additionally, custom counters can also be consumed by user-defined rules in Microsoft Operations Manager (MOM). MOM will be covered in the next chapter. In this chapter, you will learn how to create custom counters using the WMI API.

The WMI Classes

Custom counters are instances of two specific BizTalk WMI classes, *MSBTS_CustomCounterSetting* and *MSBTS_CustomCounter*. Figure 15-11 illustrates the interfaces of these two classes and their relationship. The MSBTS_CustomCounterSetting class enables you to create and validate custom counters, whereas the MSBTS_CustomCounter enables you to acquire information about the custom counter, such as how many matching documents are found, the name of the BizTalk Server group, and the name of the custom counter. For each instance of MSBTS_CustomCounterSetting class, a dynamic instance of MSBTS_CustomCounter class is automatically created. MSBTS_CustomCounterSetting and MSBTS_CustomCounter classes are derived from their respective Common Information Model (CIM) classes, *CIM_Setting* and *CIM_LogicElement*.

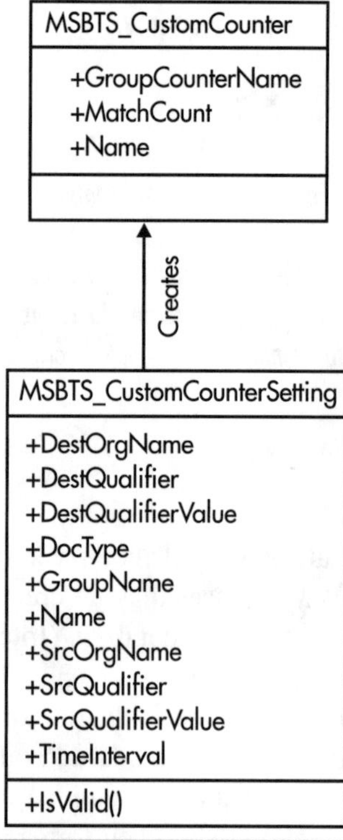

Figure 15-11 *The custom counter WMI classes*

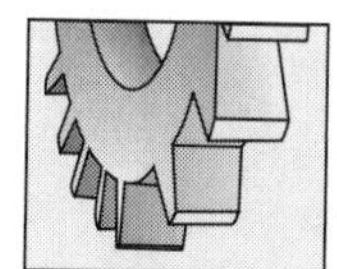

TIP

Windows Management Instrumentation (WMI) is Microsoft's implementation of Common Information Model (CIM). For more information about CIM, visit MSDN and search for "Common Information Model."

The MSBTS_CustomCounterSetting Class

You can use the MSBTS_CustomCounterSetting class to create, delete, and validate custom counters. The MSBTS_CustomCounterSetting class has the following properties that enable you to specify the query criteria for creating the custom counters:

Property	Explanation
Name	The name of the custom counter. You can use the Name property of the MSBTS_CustomCounterSettings to retrieve the MSBTS_CustomCounter instance.
SrcOrgName	The name of the source organization for the channel. For example, "Northwind."
SrcQualifier	The qualifier of the source organization for the channel. For example, "OrganizationName."
SrcQualifierValue	The value of the source organization qualifier for the channel. For example, "Northwind."
DestOrgName	The name of the destination organization for the messaging port. For example, "Supplier A."
DestQualifier	The qualifier of the destination organization for the messaging port. For example, "OrganizationName."
DestQualifierValue	The value of the destination organization qualifier for the messaging port. For example, "Supplier A."
DocType	The name of the inbound and/or the outbound document definition.
TimeInterval	Interval of time, in seconds, over which to accumulate the custom counter query value.

Table 15-2 *Criteria for creating custom counters*

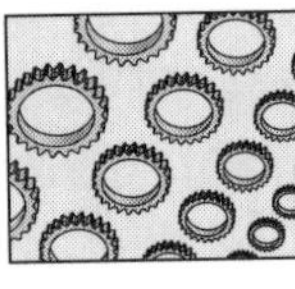

NOTE

You can use either the name of the source and destination organizations or their qualifier-value pairs. You cannot use both the names and the qualifier-value pairs at the same time, however. Using qualifier-value pairs enables you to fine-tune your query for documents that are processed by the channels and/or messaging ports associated with specified organization qualifiers. For example, using "Northwind" as the Name property will return all documents whose source organization for the channels or destination organization for the message ports are "Northwind," including those that use the default qualifier name (for example, OrganizationName) and those that use the custom qualifier name (for example, a D-U-N-S value). Using qualifier-value pairs and specifying as OrganizationName-Northwind will return only those documents whose channels or messaging ports are configured using OrganizationName as the qualifier, excluding the documents whose channels or messaging ports use other qualifiers, such as a D-U-N-S value.

The MSBTS_CustomCounterSetting class contains only one method, *IsValid*, that validates the custom counter creation parameters:

```
IsValid (ByRef bIsValidSrcOrg As Boolean, _
  ByRef bIsValidSrcId As Boolean, _
  ByRef bIsValidDestOrg As Boolean, _
  ByRef bIsValidDestId As Boolean, _
  ByRef bIsValidGroup As Boolean)
```

As you can see, all of the five parameters are declared as ByRef. Therefore they are all output parameters. A returned TRUE value indicates the specified object represented by the parameter is valid. A FALSE indicates an invalid object.

The MSBTS_CustomCounter Class

The MSBTS_CustomCounter class contains three properties and no method:

Property	Explanation
Name	The name of the custom counter. It has the same value as the Name property of the MSBTS_CustomCounterSetting object.
MatchCount	The number of the matching document found.
GroupCounterName	The names of BizTalk Server group and the custom counter, in the form of BizTalkServerGroupName/ CustomCounterName.

Creating Custom Counters

Because custom counters are instances of WMI classes, the process of creating a custom counter is very similar to the process of creating other BizTalk Server WMI classes, as you learned in Chapter 7.

To refresh your memory, here are the six steps of creating BizTalk Server WMI classes that we listed in Chapter 7:

1. Creating an instance of the SWbemLocator object.
2. Calling the ConnectServer method of the SWbemLocator object to the BizTalk server and returning a SWbemServices object.
3. Calling the Get method of the SWbemServices object to create an SWbemObject object.
4. Calling the SpawnInstance_ method of the SWbemObject object to create a new instance of the class.
5. Setting up properties for the class instance.
6. Calling the Put_ method and passing parameter 2 (wbemChangeFlagCreateOnly) to create the new class and saving it to the BizTalk Messaging Management database.

The following VBScript code segment illustrates how to create a custom counter, using BizTalk WMI API. We omitted the error handling code for clarity.

```
Const wbemChangeFlagCreateOnly = 2
Const CUSTCOUNTER_SETTING_NAMESPACE = "MSBTS_CustomCounterSetting"

Dim oLocator
Dim oServices
Dim oCustomCounterFactory
Dim oCustomCounterSetting
Dim oCustomCounter

Set oLocator = CreateObject("WbemScripting.SWbemLocator")
Set oServices = oLocator.ConnectServer(, "root/MicrosoftBizTalkServer")

Set oServices = GetObject( _

"Winmgmts:{impersonationlevel=impersonate}!root/MicrosoftBizTalkServer")
```

```
Set oCustomCounterFactory = oServices.Get(CUSTCOUNTER_SETTING_NAMESPACE)
Set oCustomCounterSetting = oCustomCounterFactory.SpawnInstance_

With oCustomCounterSetting
    .Name = "Custom Counter using Organizations"
    .SrcOrgName = "SrcOrg for Custom Counter"
    .DestOrgName = "DestOrg for Custom Counter"
    .DocType = "POReq"
    .TimeInterval = 300
    .GroupName = "BizTalk Server Group"
End With

oCustomCounterSetting.Put_(wbemChangeFlagCreateOnly)

oCustomCounterSetting.IsValid bSrcOrg, bSrcOrgId, bDestOrg, _
     bDestOrgID, bGroup

WScript.Echo "ValidityCheck: " & vbCrLf & _
      "SrcOrg " & CStr(bSrcOrg) & vbCrLf & _
      "SrcId " & CStr(bSrcOrgId) & vbCrLf & _
      "DestOrg " & CStr(bDestOrg) & vbCrLf & _
      "DestId " & CStr(bDestOrgId) & vbCrLf & _
      "Group " & CStr(bGroup)

Set oCustomCounter = oServices.Get( _
    "MSBTS_CustomCounter.Name=""" & oCustomCounterSetting.Name & """")

WScript.Echo "Counter Information: " & objCustomCounter.Name & vbCrLf & _
           "Matching Documents: " & objCustomCounter.MatchCount
```

Here's how it works:

First, after declaring constants and variables, you created an instance of the SWbemLocator object and called the ConnectServer method of the SWbemLocator object to the BizTalk server and returned an SWbemServices object (Step 1 and 2).

```
Set oLocator = CreateObject("WbemScripting.SWbemLocator")
Set oServices = oLocator.ConnectServer(,
"root/MicrosoftBizTalkServer")
```

Optionally, you can set up securities such as the authentication level, using the moniker syntax:

```
Set oServices = GetObject( _
    "Winmgmts:{impersonationlevel=impersonate}!root/MicrosoftBizTalkServer")
```

You can also use the alternative syntax to set up security levels like this:

```
OServices.Security_.ImpersonationLevel = wbemImpersonationLevelImpersonate
```

Next, you call the Get method of the SWbemServices object to create a SWbemObject object and then the SpawnInstance_ method of the SWbemObject object to create a new instance of the class (Steps 3 and 4):

```
Set oCustomCounterFactory = oServices.Get(CUSTCOUNTER_SETTING_NAMESPACE)
Set oCustomCounterSetting = oCustomCounterFactory.SpawnInstance_
```

At this point, you can set the properties for the class instance (Step 5):

```
With oCustomCounterSetting
    .Name = "Custom Counter using Organizations"
    .SrcOrgName = "SrcOrg for Custom Counter"
    .DestOrgName = "DestOrg for Custom Counter"
    .DocType = "POReq"
    .TimeInterval = 300
    .GroupName = "BizTalk Server Group"
End With
```

Then you can create the new class and save it to the BizTalk Messaging Management database (Step 6):

```
oCustomCounterSetting.Put_(wbemChangeFlagCreateOnly)
```

Now you can call the IsValid method and report the results to validate the custom counter:

```
oCustomCounterSetting.IsValid bSrcOrg, bSrcOrgId, bDestOrg, _
    bDestOrgID, bGroup
```

```
WScript.Echo "ValidityCheck: " & vbCrLf & _
      "SrcOrg " & CStr(bSrcOrg) & vbCrLf & _
      "SrcId " & CStr(bSrcOrgId) & vbCrLf & _
      "DestOrg " & CStr(bDestOrg) & vbCrLf & _
      "DestId " & CStr(bDestOrgId) & vbCrLf & _
      "Group " & CStr(bGroup)
```

Up to this point, you've created an instance of the MSBTS_CustomCounterSetting class, set up the query properties and validated the custom counter. Now it is time to retrieve the instance of the MSBTS_CustomCounter class and discover how many match documents are found. You use the Name properties of the oCustomCounterSetting object to retrieve the oCustomCounter object and the MatchCount property to report the number of matched documents:

```
Set oCustomCounter = oServices.Get( _
    "MSBTS_CustomCounter.Name=""" & oCustomCounterSetting.Name & """")

WScript.Echo "Counter Information: " & objCustomCounter.Name & vbCrLf & _
             "Matching Documents: " & objCustomCounter.MatchCount
```

Improved BizTalk Editor and Mapper

BizTalk Server 2002 has introduced a few improvements to BizTalk Editor and BizTalk Mapper tools.

New BizTalk Editor Features

The new features in BizTalk Editor include:

- The ability to create a native Instance for flat file and EDI documents, in addition to creating XML instances. This feature is available through the Tools menu option and will only be enabled when the specification that is loaded into BizTalk Editor is either a flat file (delimited or positioned) or an EDI file (X12 or EDIFACT).
- The ability to export XSD (XML Schema Definition) schemas in addition to XDR schemas. Figure 15-12 illustrates these new enhancements in BizTalk Editor. This feature is also available through the Tools menu option. This feature enables you to create schema in BizTalk Server for use with Visual Studio.NET. In BizTalk Server 2002, the engine is still based on XDR. Microsoft has committed to XSD support in a future version.

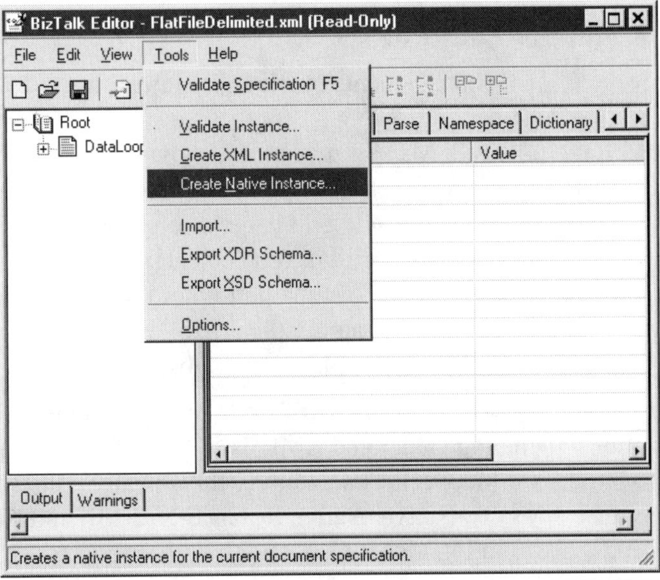

Figure 15-12 *New BizTalk Editor Features*

► A new tab has been added to the BizTalk Editor Options dialog box (also available through the Tools menu option), called Document Delimiters, which enables you to specify Record, Field, and Subfield delimiters for EDI documents, as shown in Figure 15-13.

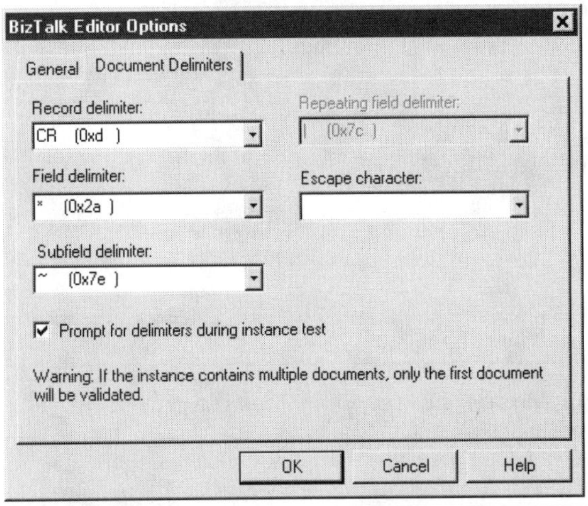

Figure 15-13 *The Document Delimiters tab is added to BizTalk Editor Options tab*

New BizTalk Mapper Features

There are some significant enhancements in BizTalk Mapper in the following areas:

- **Enhanced IDE** BizTalk Mapper now enables you to create multiple grid pages. This can be extremely helpful if you have used a lot of functoids in the map document. You can add a new grid page, delete (through the Edit menu option), and rename an existing grid page. You can navigate to a specific grid page by clicking the respective tap at the bottom of the page grid. If you have more than three grid pages, you can use the arrow keys to navigate between grid pages, as shown in Figure 15-14.
- **New Test Map options** The new BizTalk Mapper has added a number of testing options, including Generated XML To XML (the one supported in BizTalk Server 2000 Mapper), Generated XML To Native, Instance XML To XML, Instance XML To Native, Native Instance To XML and Native Instance To Native, as shown in Figure 15-15.

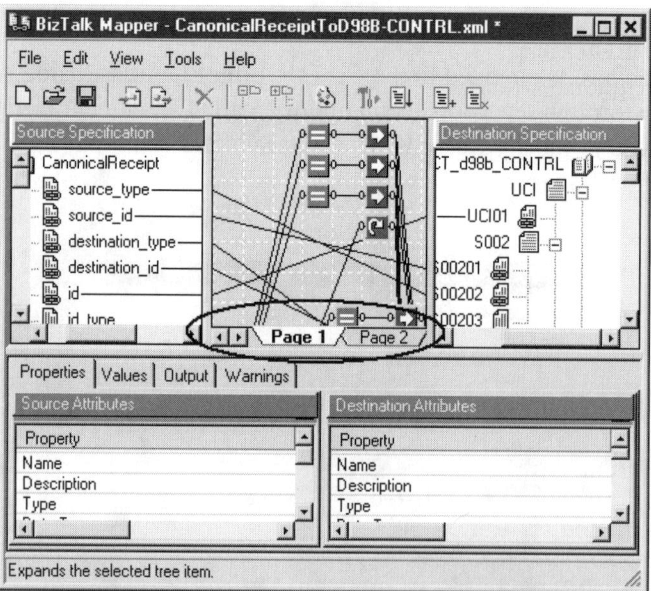

Figure 15-14 *BizTalk Mapper now supports multiple grid pages*

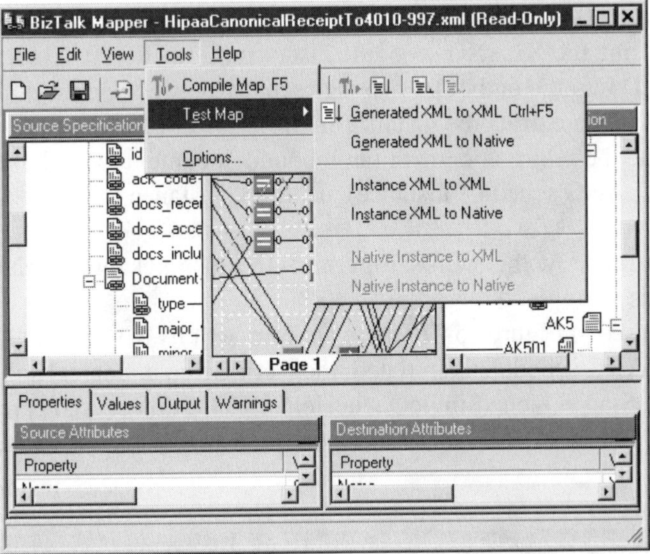

Figure 15-15 *New Test Map options*

- **Options dialog box** The new BizTalk Mapper has enhanced its BizTalk Mapper Options dialog box by adding two new tabs. The Document Delimiter tab is similar to the one in BizTalk Editor and is used for mapping EDI documents. The XSLT output tab enables you to specify whether to omit the XML declaration.
- **JScript support in functoids** The new BizTalk Mapper now allows you to use both JScript and VBScript for writing custom functiods.

New Orchestration Features

BizTalk Server 2002 offers several new Orchestration features, including use of a single Message Queuing queue for XLANG schedule correlation and the capability to pool your XLANG schedules instances.

Correlating XLANG Schedule Instances

Recall that in Chapter 9 you learned that to correlate the exchange of messages to XLANG schedule instances, you have to use per instance (MSMQ) queues. Now,

BizTalk Server 2002 enables you to use a single queue for this purpose. This is achieved by using the XLANG schedule instance ID (a GUID). You can incorporate this instance ID into the outbound message sent to an MSMQ queue. An external application can then extract the instance ID from the document retrieved from the queue and send the return document (an inbound document from the perspective of the running XLANG schedule instance), using the instance ID as the Label property of the message.

To demonstrate how this works, Figure 15-16 illustrates the XLANG schedule drawing of this example.

As you can see in Figure 15-16, there are four actions in this XLANG schedule. When the XLANG schedule is initiated, the Get POReq action calls the GetDoc method of the SingleQueue.SingleQueueHelper COM object, and is passed a PO document. The Send POReq action then sends the PO document into a private

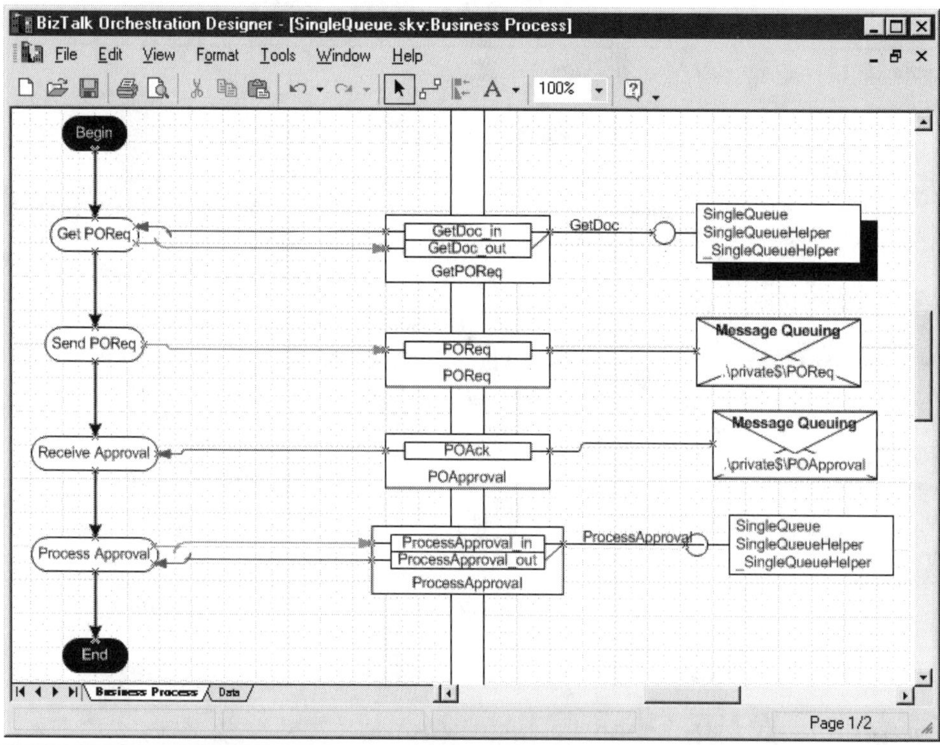

Figure 15-16 *Using a single queue for XLANG schedule instance correlation*

queue, POReq. In the Message Type Information page of the XML Communication Wizard, we specified Use Instance Id As Message Label and in the system field, Instance_Id_ appeared in the Message Type box, as shown in Figure 15-17. When an outbound message to an MSMQ queue is specified this way, a new constant is inserted into the Data page which you can incorporate into the outbound message like that shown in Figure 15-18.

The next action, Receive Approval, waits for a PO acknowledgement document from another MSMQ queue called POApproval that indicates whether the PO request is approved or not. You also need to specify the POAck message as Use Instance Id As Message Label so that when an acknowledge message arrives, its Label property will be automatically checked to see if it matches the Instance Id of the running XLANG schedule. If it does, the message will be retrieved from the queue and the XLANG schedule flows to the final action, Process Approval, which calls the ProcessApproval method of the COM object SingleQueue.SingleQueueHelper to display the contents of the acknowledgement document.

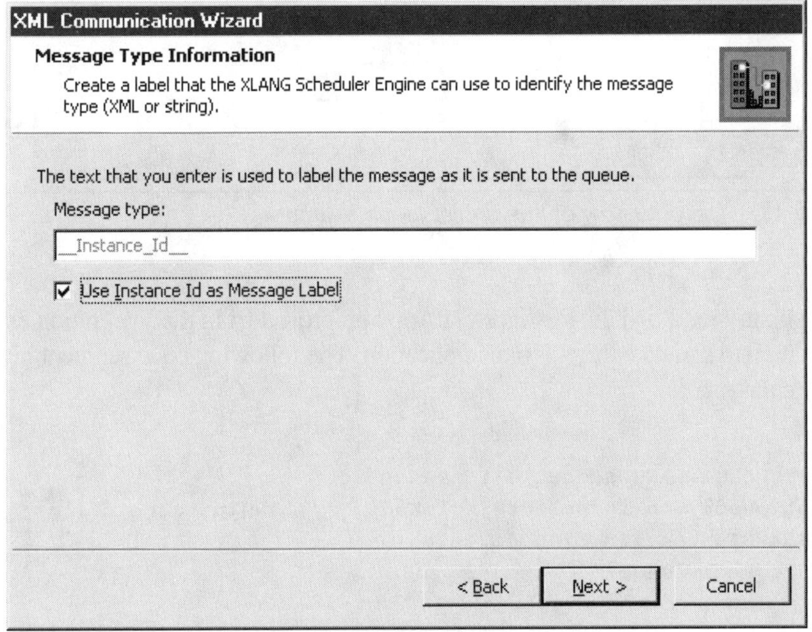

Figure 15-17 *Specifing Instance Id as the message label*

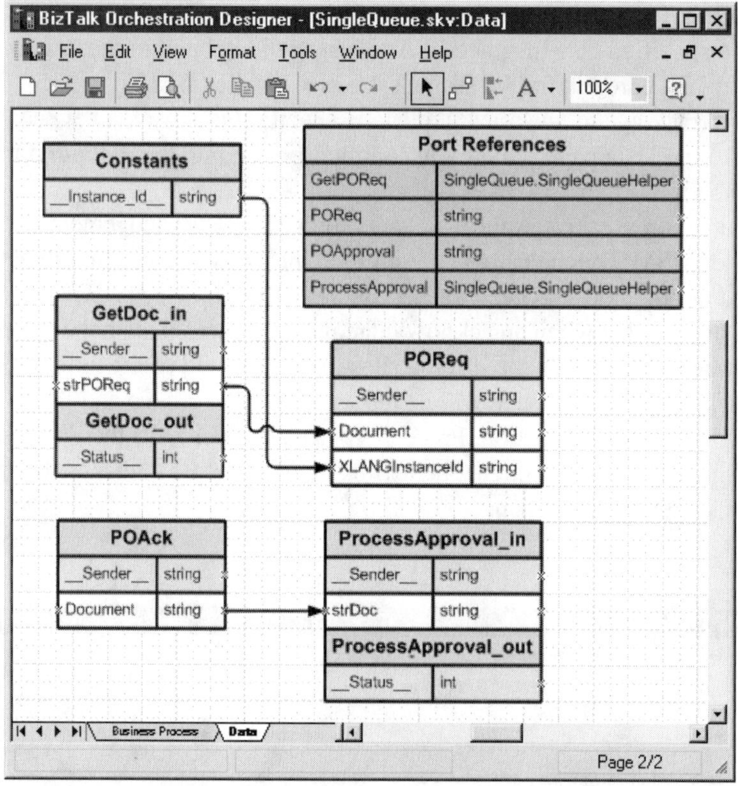

Figure 15-18 *The data flow of the SingleQueue example*

We slightly modified the POApprovalApp.vbp project from the Integration example in Chapter 9 to simulate the external application. The following code segment highlights the key changes:

```
'......
'Get the XLANG schedule instance id
Set oNode = oXML.selectSingleNode("//XLANGInstanceId")
sXLANGInstanceId = oNode.Text
'Set ReplyQueue
```

```
    sQPath = ".\PRIVATE$\POApproval"
    'Create the Acknowledgement document
    Set oAckDoc = CreateObject("MSXML2.DOMDocument")
    oAckDoc.async = False
    oAckDoc.loadXML "<POAck>" & vbCrLf _
& "  <Approval>" & sApprovalFlag & "</Approval>" & vbCrLf _
& "  <InstanceId>" & sXLANGInstanceId & "</InstanceId>" & vbCrLf _
& "</POAck>"
    oAckDoc.documentElement.setAttribute "OrderID", sOrderID
    oDestQInfo.PathName = sQPath
    Set oDestQ = oDestQInfo.Open(MQ_SEND_ACCESS, MQ_DENY_NONE)
    If oDestQ.IsOpen Then
       oMsg.Body = oAckDoc.xml
       oMsg.Label = sXLANGInstanceId
       oMsg.Send oDestQ, MQ_SINGLE_MESSAGE
    End If
```

The code extracts the Instance Id of the XLANG schedule instance, embeds the Instance Id into the acknowledgement document, and assigns the Instance Id as the Label property of the message to the MSMQ queue, POApproval, which is being watched by the running XLANG schedule instance.

To see this example in action, follow these steps:

1. Run the setup.cmd file to set up the environment.
2. Launch XLANG Event Monitor (XLANGMon.exe).
3. Launch POApprovalApp.exe for incoming PO requests.
4. Run the SingleQueue.vbs script file twice to initiate two XLANG schedule instances. At this point, you should see two running SingleQueue XLANG schedule instances in XLANG Event Monitor, identified by their corresponding Instance Ids.
5. Switch to POApprovalApp and click Approval or Deny. You will soon see a message box, displayed by a running instance of XLANG schedule. The Instance Id in the message box should match the Instance Id of the first XLANG schedule instance in XLANG Event Monitor.

Pooling XLANG Schedule Instances

Another new Orchestration feature in BizTalk Server 2002 is the ability to leverage COM+ object pooling services to pool XLANG schedule instances. The capability to pool XLANG schedule instances allows you to better utilize the machine resources and improve scalability. This feature is implemented by a BizTalk Server 2002-specific COM+ application, XLANG Schedule Pool, which contains 25 COM components, SimpleSkedPool.SimplePoolN.1 (where N represents the number of the pooling component, ranging from 1 to 25).

To enable the pooling of an XLANG schedule, you need to do two things:

- Enable object pooling for the particular COM component, SimpleSkedPool.SimplePoolN.1.
- Specify in the XLANG schedule drawing that you want to use pooling (throttling).

Enabling COM+ Components for Object Pooling

To enable object pooling of the COM+ component, open the Component Services MMC snap-in, expand My Computers | COM+ applications | XLANG Schedule Pool | Components. Right-click the particular COM component which enables you to pool objects (SimpleSkedPool.SimplePool1.1, for example) and select Properties. Click the Activation tab and specify the minimum and maximum pool size as well as the creation time out values, as shown in Figure 15-19.

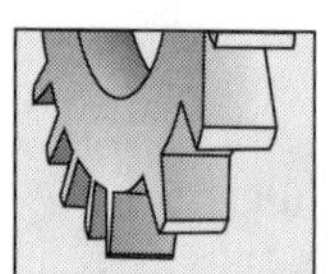

TIP

You need to clear the Disable Changes check box in the XLANG Schedule Pool COM+ application before you can enable object pooling for the COM components. To do this, right-click the XLANG Schedule Pool COM+ application in Component Services and select Properties. Click the Advanced tab and clear the Disable Changes check box.

Specifying the XLANG Schedule Drawing for Instance Pooling

To specify the XLANG Schedule for instance pooling, right-click the Begin shape in the XLANG schedule drawing and, select Properties. Click the Pool drop-down list and select one of the 25 pools available, as shown in Figure 15-20. The pool you specify in the XLANG schedule drawing should match the COM+ component whose object pooling has been enabled.

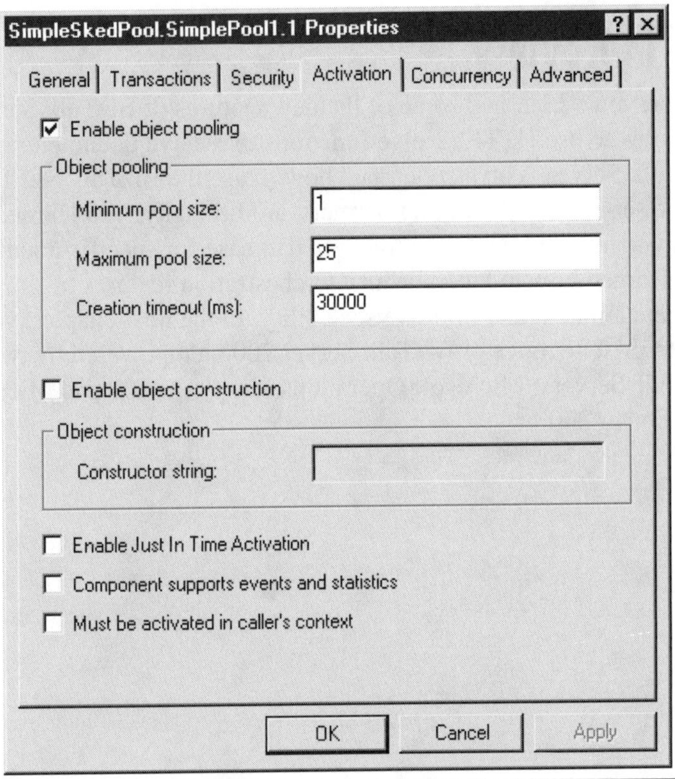

Figure 15-19 *Enabling object pooling for COM+ components*

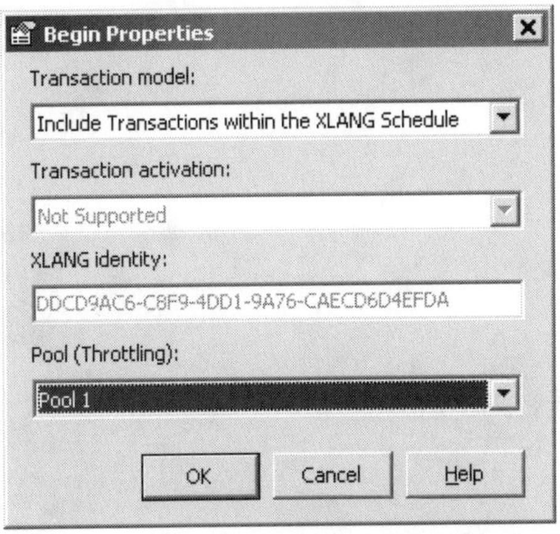

Figure 15-20 *Specifying the pool for the XLANG schedule*

Chapter in Review

In this chapter, you've learned some of the new features of BizTalk Server 2002—specifically, how to use HTTP receive functions to receive documents and submit them to BizTalk Server. You also learned how to use the BizTalk SEED Wizard to streamline the set-up of your trading partners. Additionally, you learned how to create custom counters to query the tracking database for specific documents. Finally, you learned how to leverage new Orchestration features to simplify your application development and improve scalability. In the next chapter, you will learn about the enterprise features of BizTalk Server 2002, empowered by two other Microsoft .NET Servers: Microsoft Operations Manager 2000 and Microsoft Application Center 2000.

CHAPTER

16

Managing with Application Center and MOM

IN THIS CHAPTER:

Microsoft Application Center 2000

Microsoft Operations Manager 2000

Chapter in Review

BizTalk Server 2002 only ships one edition: the Enterprise Edition. Its enterprise functionality relies heavily on two other Microsoft.NET servers: Microsoft Application Center 2000 and Microsoft Operations Manager 2000 (MOM). Microsoft Application Center provides all the services and features you need for creating, deploying, and managing Web- and component-based applications. MOM provides operation-oriented monitoring and managing functionality. Together, Microsoft Application Center and MOM provide you with a powerful foundation for administrating your BizTalk solutions in an enterprise environment. Whereas neither of the .NET servers ships with BizTalk Server 2002, the integrated modules (such as management packs) in BizTalk Server 2002 have greatly streamlined the integration of both .NET servers.

In this chapter, you will learn some basics about Application Center and MOM, from the perspective of BizTalk Server, and also learn how to utilize them with the appropriate modules in BizTalk Server 2002 to manage your enterprise BizTalk solutions.

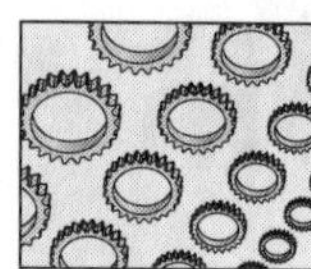

NOTE

You can use either Application Center or MOM with BizTalk Server 2002, and, as you will learn later, each of these .NET servers provides unique values in managing your enterprise BizTalk applications. When using them together, you can fully unleash the complementary services and features that come with both products.

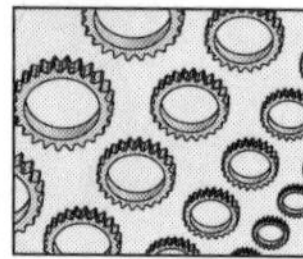

NOTE

Strictly speaking, you can also use Application Center and/or MOM with BizTalk Server 2000. However, the lack of integrated modules (such as BizTalk Application Center Applications and Management Packs) and other features in BizTalk Server 2000 make the use of these two products with BizTalk Server very difficult, if not impossible.

Microsoft Application Center 2000

Microsoft Application Center 2000 is a tool that helps you create, deploy, and manage Web- and component-based applications in an enterprise environment that greatly improves manageability, scalability, and reliability. In this section, you will learn how to install Application Center with BizTalk Server 2002. Afterward, we'll discuss Application Center architecture, learn about the rich set enterprise features of Application Center, and, finally, learn how to use Application Center to manage BizTalk Server 2002 applications.

Installing Microsoft Application Center 2000

Microsoft Application Center 2000 must be installed **prior** to the installation of BizTalk Server 2002. After installing Application Center and BizTalk Server 2002, you must also install the Service Pack 1 Beta for Application Center 2000, which can be found on the BizTalk Server 2002 CD-ROM.

Installing Application Center

Insert the Microsoft Application Center CD-ROM and click Install Microsoft Application Center 2000. The Microsoft Application Center 2000 Setup Box appears, showing three steps, as shown in Figure 16-1. If your computer already has Windows 2000 Service Pack 1 or Service Pack 2 installed, you can skip Step 1 and begin with Step 2 which installs the Microsoft Windows 2000 Post-Service Pack 1 fixes.

During the installation of Microsoft Windows 2000 Post-Service Pack 1 fixes, you should see a DOS prompt window that indicates the progress of SP2 hotfixes. At the end of this process, you will be prompted to reboot your computer to complete the installation of the hotfixes.

After you have all the necessary prerequisites installed, you can proceed to Step 3 by clicking Step 3: Install Microsoft Application Center 2000 and following the instructions displayed in the Setup Wizard. (If the Microsoft Application Center 2000 Setup Box does not appear, click on Install Microsoft Application Center 2000 on the main setup window to bring it up). If you want to install Monitoring Samples, you must select Custom Setup instead of Typical Setup.

After you have completed installing Application Center 2000, you can go ahead and install BizTalk Server 2002.

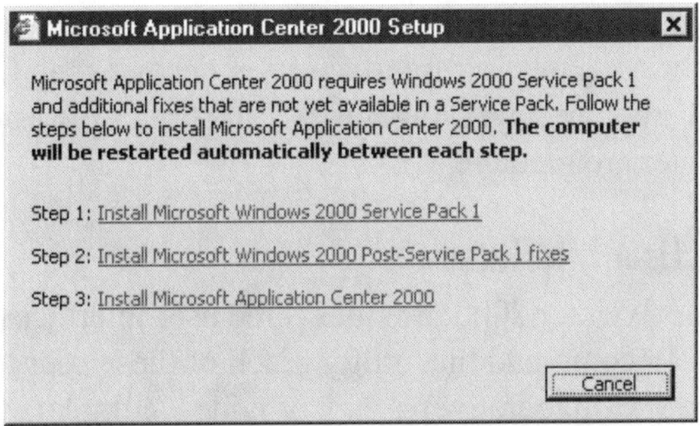

Figure 16-1 *Microsoft Application Center Setup*

Installing Service Pack 1 Beta for Application Center 2000

You must also install the Service Pack 1 Beta for Application Center 2000 in order to use Application Center with BizTalk Server 2002. The file, AC2000_SP1.exe, can be found in the \ACPatch folder of the BizTalk Server 2002 CD.

Application Center Overview

In this section, we'll introduce you to the Application Center architecture, discussing each of the architectural layers in order to give you an overview of Microsoft Application Center 2000.

Application Center Architecture

There are three major layers in Application Center architecture:

- The first layer is the User Interface which consists of an MMC snap-in, a Web interface, and a command line utility. Three additional MMC snap-ins, Health Monitor, Internet Information Service, and Component Services, are conveniently included in a consolidated MMC console. You can also add other snap-ins (for example, the Certificate snap-in) to the MMC console for easier administration.
- The second layer is the Feature Set, which includes Cluster Services, Load Balancing, Synchronization and Deployment, Monitoring, Programming Support, and so on. We'll discuss these shortly.
- The third layer is the Operating System, which consists of system-level services such as MMC, IIS, COM+, Network Load Balancing (NLB), Windows Management Instrumentation (WMI), and others.

In addition, the run-time version of SQL Server, the SQL Server version 2000 desktop engine, is also included for Application Center Event and Performance Logging and Monitoring. The User Interface layer accesses the Operating System layer through the Feature Set layer. Figure 16-2 illustrates the three major layers of the Application Center architecture.

Application Center User Interfaces

Microsoft Application Center 2000 provides three user interfaces, an MMC snap-in, a Web interface, and a command line utility. Each of these user interfaces provides unique functionalities. Collaboratively, they provide a complete tool set for performing comprehensive administration tasks in the Application Center.

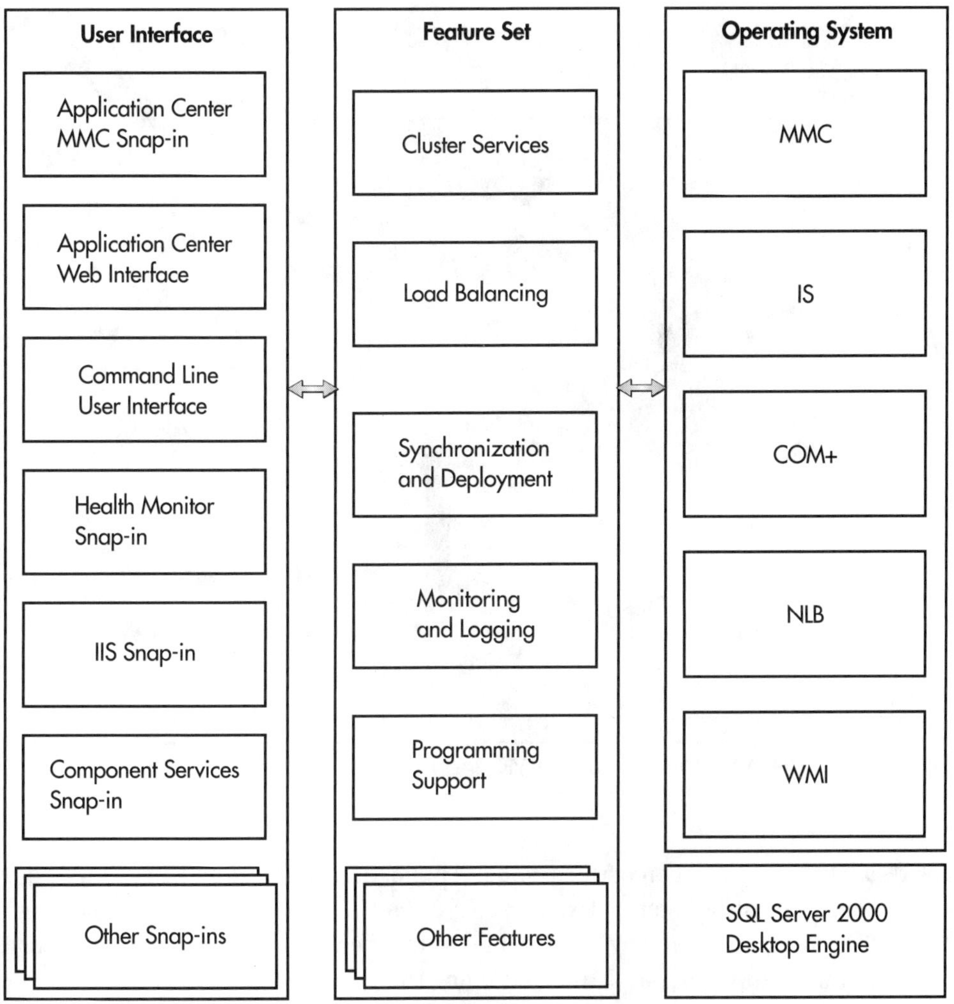

Figure 16-2 *Microsoft Application Center 2000 architecture*

The MMC Snap-In The Application Center MMC snap-in provides full access to most features in Application Center except for monitoring and limited cluster administration. The consistent MMC console interface enables system administrators to easily navigate and perform appropriate administration tasks. Three other MMC snap-ins, IIS, Health Monitor, and Component Services, are also included in the same MMC console for centralized administration, as shown in Figure 16-3. The Application Center MMC snap-in can be accessed by choosing Start | Programs | Administrative Tools | Application Center.

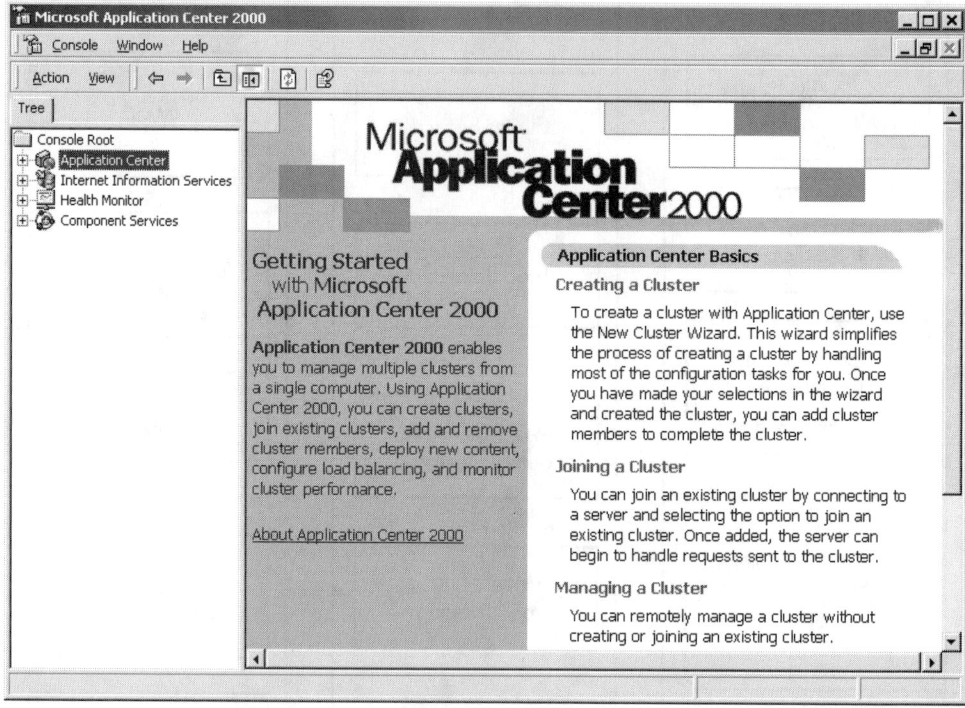

Figure 16-3 *The Application Center MMC snap-in*

The Web Interface You can perform some Application Center administration through its Web interface using Internet Explorer (5.5 or later), by entering the machine name (or the IP address) followed by the default port number 4242 of the Application Center 2000 Administration Site, as shown in Figure 16-4.

Through its Web interface, you can perform some of the administration tasks for Application Center 2000, including editing cluster IP addresses, adding/removing performance counters, viewing events, and monitoring (editing, enabling, and disabling), eather locally or remotely (with appropriate access privileges, of course).

The *Command Line Utility* The command line utility of Application Center also allows you to administer and manage the Application Center through the command line by executing appropriate commands directly or from within a script or batch file. The command line utility, AC.EXE, is located in the \Program Files\Microsoft Application Center folder and its path is set during the installation of Application Center so it can be executed from any directory. For a complete listing of available Application Center commands, refer to the Microsoft Application Center 2000 Resource Kit,

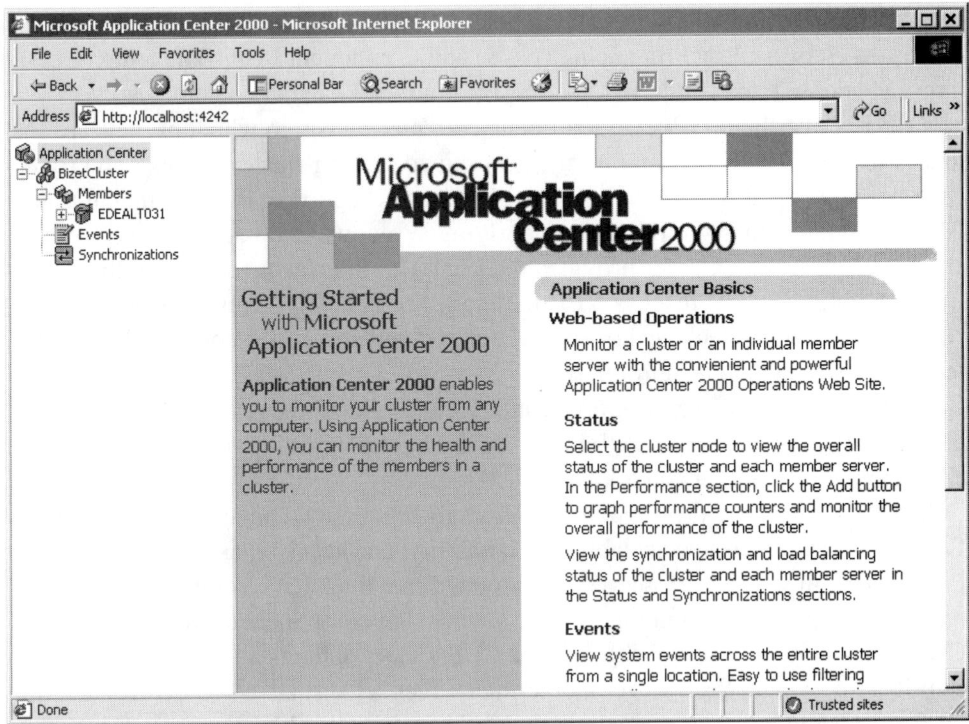

Figure 16-4 *The Web interface of Application Center*

available in Microsoft Reader format from the Application Center product Web site, http://www.microsoft.com/ApplicationCenter.

Important Application Center Features

Microsoft Application Center 2000 provides a rich set of features that enable you to manage your Web and component applications within and across enterprises, including cluster services, load balancing, deployment, monitoring, and so on.

Cluster Services A *cluster* is a group of servers managed by Application Center. Application Center Cluster Services supercedes the cluster services of Windows 2000 Advanced Server and enables you to easily create a cluster, add members to the cluster, or bring them offline through a wizard interface. Application Center Cluster Services provide a foundation on which other important services and features are based, such as load balancing, synchronization and deployment, centralized monitoring, high availability, and so on.

Load Balancing Application Center supports two types of load-balancing services: integrated Network Load Balancing (NLB) and Component Load Balancing (CLB). You can choose to use either NLB or CLB, or no load balancing at all.

NLB is a distributed IP-level load-balancing mechanism in which packets are sent to a virtual IP (VIP). NLB monitors the workload of each cluster member and routes each packet to an appropriate cluster member according to the load-balancing rules. NLB is actually carried out by the underlying Windows 2000 Advanced Server, whereas Application Center provides the user with interfaces to work with NLB. In this book, we won't discuss NLB in detail. For detailed information about how NLB works, read the technical overview at http://www.microsoft.com/windows2000/techinfo/howitworks/cluster/nlb.asp.

CLB is a feature of Application Center. It enables the invocation of COM+ components to be load-balanced. Later in this chapter, you'll learn how CLB works and how BizTalk Server can leverage CLB.

In a typical large-scale Windows DNA architecture, you can use both NLB and CLB to achieve improved scalability, availability, and security, as illustrated in Figure 16-5, in which Web servers are grouped into the NLB cluster (sometimes referred to as a *Web farm* in this context), where the component servers that host COM+ applications are grouped into the CLB cluster. Clients access the NLB cluster as if it were a single Web server (sometimes called a "Virtual Web Server") and the NLB transparently routes the call to an appropriate physical Web server. The Web server invokes appropriate COM+ component in the CLB cluster, which in turn accesses backend resources such as legacy systems and databases. You may notice that there are two firewalls in this architecture. The CLB cluster or the Web farm sits in between these two firewalls (an area that is known as the Demilitarized Zone, or DMZ).

Deployment and Synchronization By using the replication feature of Application Center 2000, you can easily deploy the applications that include contents (HTML, XML, ASP pages, and so on); components (COM+ applications) and configurations (IIS configuration, Network settings, COM+ configuration, Registry settings, Server certificates, and others) of your applications, including *BizTalk Artifacts*; a collection of BizTalk messaging objects (channels, messaging ports, schemas, document definitions, envelopes, and so forth); XLANG schedules; and other BizTalk resources (such as Message Queues, digital certificates, receive functions, COM+ applications, and so on) across the cluster, either automatically or on demand. In addition, you can replicate the content within a cluster or to another cluster. You will learn how to leverage the replication feature of Application Center to simplify the deployment of BizTalk Server applications later in this chapter.

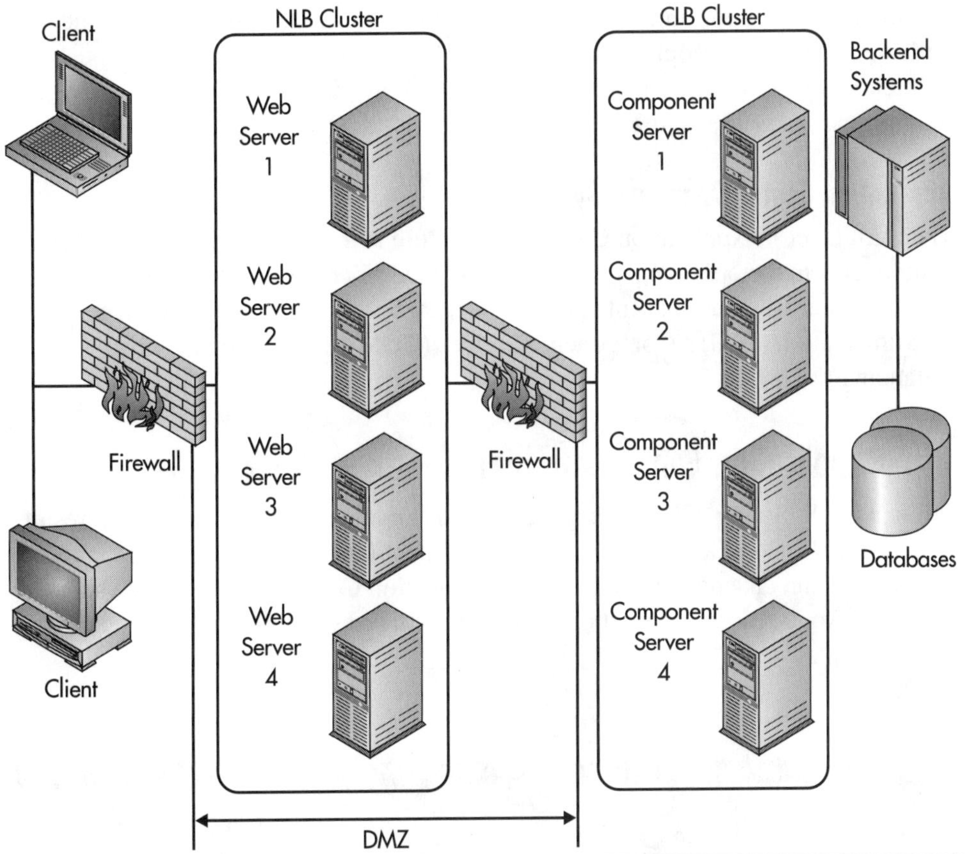

Figure 16-5 *Using both NLB and CLB in a Windows DNA application*

In addition, Application Center provides an automatic synchronization mechanism that can synchronize such resources as File System Paths, Registry Keys, Web Sites and Virtual Directories, COM+ Applications, and Data Sources.

CAUTION

Unlike the rest of the Application Center resources previously mentioned, BizTalk resources (the messaging objects) are not automatically synchronized. Post deployment changes and updates have to be manually synchronized (or re-deployed) across the cluster.

Monitoring Application Center provides sophisticated single machine monitoring capabilities, including performance monitoring via appropriate performance counters as well as health monitoring via the Health Monitor. Figure 16-6 illustrates the built-in performance monitor of Application Center 2000. Later in this chapter, you will learn how to use the Health Monitor (also shown in Figure 16-6) and WMI to monitor the Suspended Queue.

Application Center Operation System

The third layer in Application Center architecture is the Operation System. Major components in the operating system layer include Microsoft Management Console (MMC), Microsoft Internet Information Service 5.0 (IIS), Windows Management Instrumentation (WMI), Component Services (COM+), and Network Load Balancing (NLB).

Using Application Center with BizTalk Server 2002

From BizTalk Server 2002's perspective, you can leverage three major features of Application Center 2000: Deployment, Component Load Balancing, and Monitoring. Before you can take advantage of these Application Center features, make sure you have Application Center 2000 with SP1 Beta installed, as mentioned earlier in this chapter.

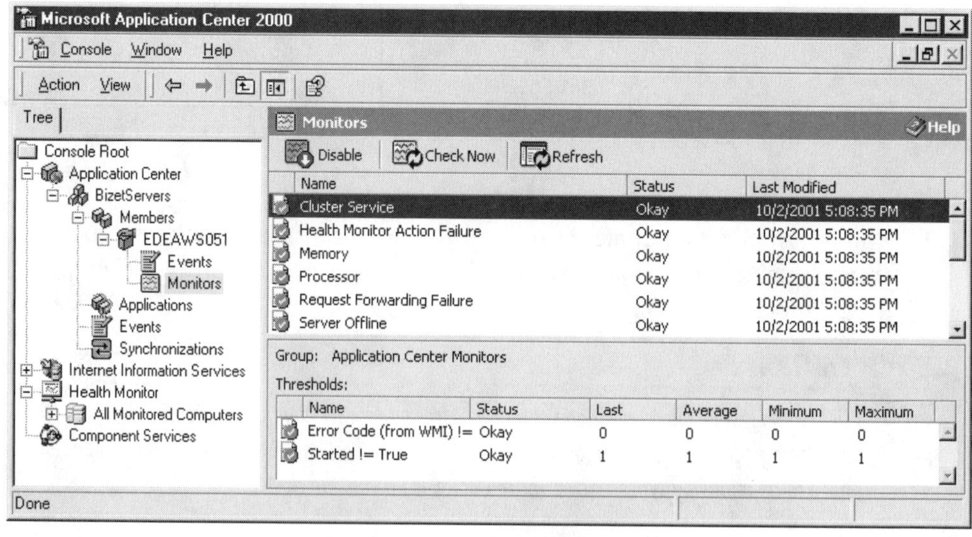

Figure 16-6 *Monitoring application performances and system health in Application Center*

Deploying BizTalk Applications

Deploying a BizTalk Application involves four major steps:

1. Creating a cluster.
2. Adding members to the cluster.
3. Creating the BizTalk application.
4. Deploying the BizTalk application.

Creating a Cluster To create a Web cluster, right-click the Application Center node in the tree view of the left pane and select Connect. In the Connect To Server dialog box, type in the server name (you can click the Browse button to select a server from the network), and select Manage Cluster For The Specified Server (as shown in Figure 16-7). Check the Connect As box, enter the appropriate credentials, and click OK.

In the New Server dialog box that appears, select Create A New Cluster, as shown in Figure 16-8, and click OK. The Welcome page of the New Cluster Wizard will appear. Click Next, then click Next again on the Analyzing Server Configuration page when the searching is completed.

On the Cluster Name and Description page, specify the name of the cluster and, optionally, a description as shown in Figure 16-9, and click Next.

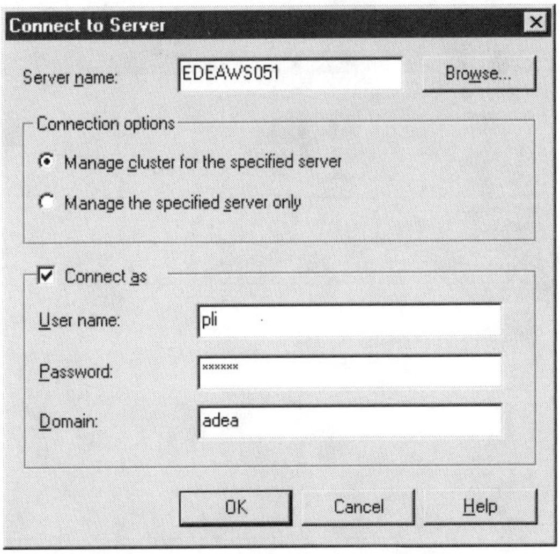

Figure 16-7 *The Connect To Server dialog box*

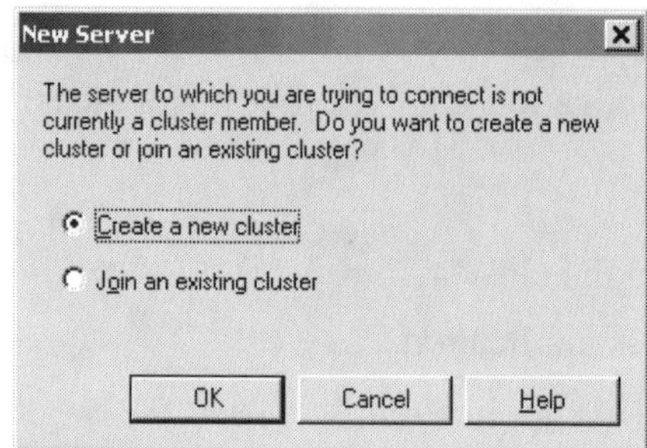

Figure 16-8 *The New Server dialog box*

On the Cluster Type page, choose the COM+ application cluster (other available options are General/Web cluster and COM+ routing cluster), and click Next. On the Load Balancing page, you can specify whether you want to use the cluster for load balancing or as a stager. In this scenario, you select the former, Other Load Balancing, and click Next. On the Monitoring Notifications page, you can optionally specify an e-mail address (and an e-mail server) to which alerts and notifications should be sent. Click Next, and then Finish.

Adding a Member to the Cluster After the cluster has been created, you are ready to add members (servers) to the cluster. To add a member to the cluster, right-click the

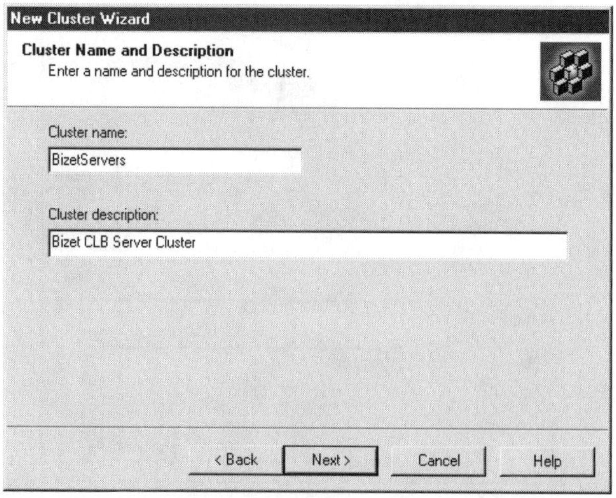

Figure 16-9 *Specifying the name and description of the cluster*

Application Center node, and select Connect. In the Connect To Server dialog box, enter the Server name and select Manage Cluster For The Specified Server. Select the Connect As check box and fill in the User name, Password, and Domain information as shown in Figure 16-10, then click Next.

The Welcome page of the Add Cluster Member Wizard appears. Click Next. In the Controller Name page of the Add Cluster Member Wizard, enter the name of the controller (the first server in the cluster) and fill in the necessary login information, then click Next. Click Next on the Analyzing Server Configuration page. Specify if you want to Automatically Synchronize This Cluster Member (highly recommended) on the Cluster Members Option page and click Next. Then click Finish.

The first member added to the cluster, as shown in Figure 16-11, is referred to as the *cluster controller*. You can add more members to the cluster in the same manner.

Creating a BizTalk Application Center Application In the context of Application Center 2000, an application is a collection of contents (HTML, XML, ASP pages, and so on), components (COM+ applications), and configurations (IIS configuration, Network settings, COM+ configuration, Registry settings, Server certificates, and so forth). When a cluster is created, four applications are created automatically: Default Web Site (Site #1), Administration Web Site (Site #2), AllSites, and Application

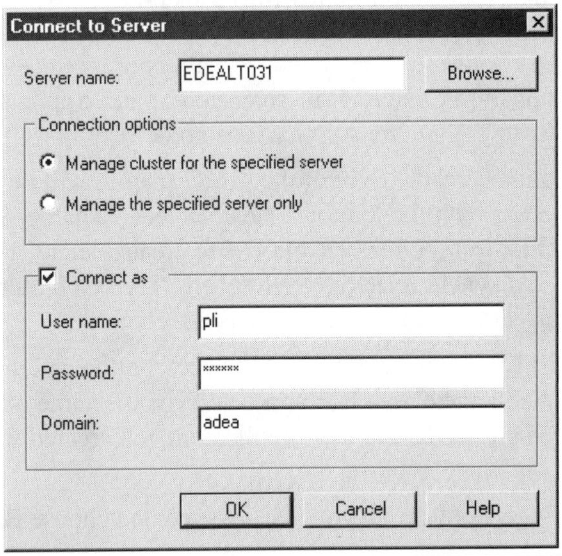

Figure 16-10 *Adding a server to the cluster*

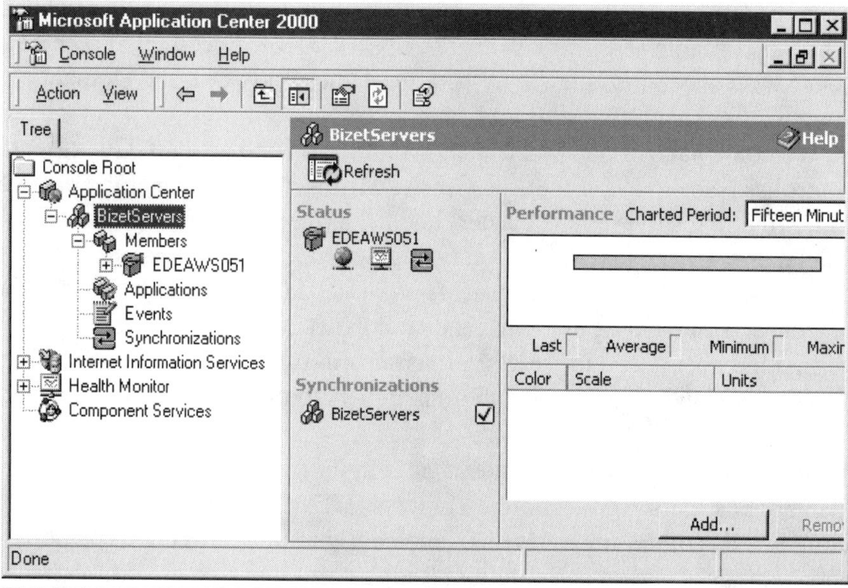

Figure 16-11 *The first member—the cluster controller (EDEAWS051)—has been added to the cluster*

Center Administrative. You can create other types of applications including BizTalk applications using the Application Center MMC snap-in.

Here's how to create a BizTalk Application:

1. Open the Application Center MMC snap-in. Expand Application Center and then the cluster to expose the Applications node.
2. Click Applications and the right of the MMC snap-in will be refreshed, which displays a tool bar with five buttons: New, Delete, Rename, Synchronize, and Refresh. The first four buttons enable you to create, delete, and rename your applications, and synchronize the deployment. The last button allows you to refresh the current page in the MMC snap-in.
3. To create a BizTalk Application, click the New button and the Create A New Application Web Page dialog box appears. Type the name of the BizTalk application and click OK. The new application you created will show up in the right pane of the MMC snap-in.
4. Highlight the new application you just selected and choose BizTalk as the Resource Type.

5. Click the Add button next to the Resource Type to bring up the Add Resource Web page dialog box, which lists the available BizTalk Resources, including BizTalkCustomCounter, BizTalkPortGroups (a port group is a distribution list in BizTalk Messaging Manager), BizTalkPorts, and BizTalkReceiveFunctions. You can click the Add button in the dialog box to add one resource at a time.

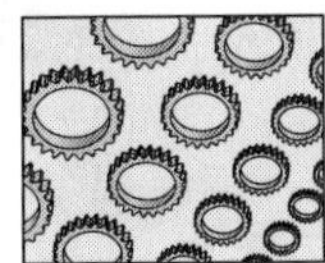

NOTE

Notice that here you have only four BizTalk resources, rather than the entire BizTalk artifacts. The reason for this is that BizTalk artifacts are a new concept that aren't currently visible in BizTalk Messaging Manager. This arrangement gives you a more granular control over deploying selected artifacts.

Figure 16-12 illustrates a BizTalk Application, *Bizet Application*, with all four available BizTalk resources.

To add an XLANG schedule to your BizTalk application, select File System Path from the Resource Type and follow the procedures as previously outlined. Other types of resources you can add to your BizTalk application include Registry Keys, Web Sites and Virtual Directories, COM+ Applications, and Data Source Names (DSNs).

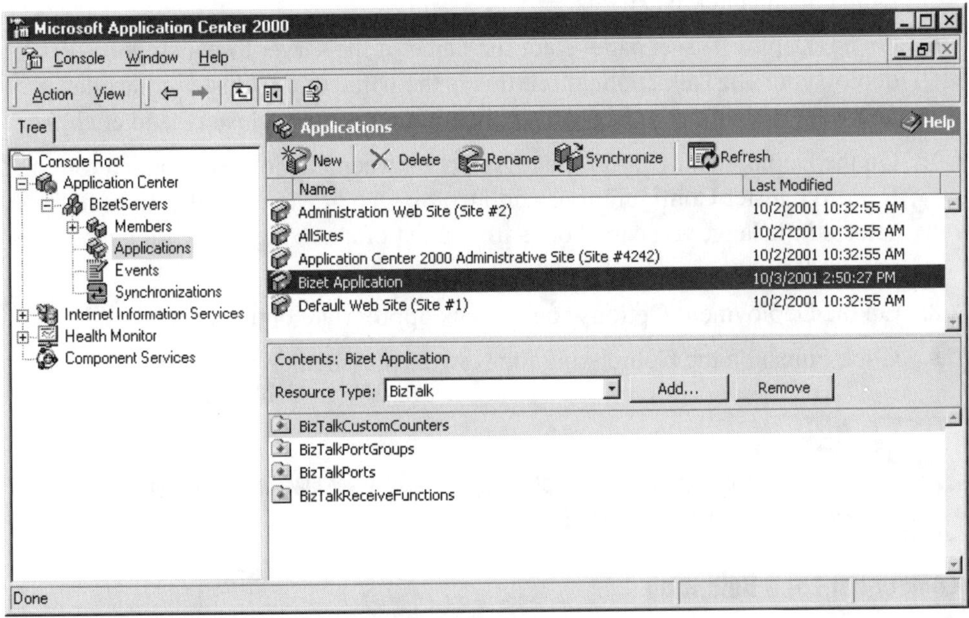

Figure 16-12 *Creating a BizTalk application*

Deploying the BizTalk Application You can use the Deployment Wizard of Application Center 2000 to deploy your BizTalk applications synchronously (intra-cluster) and asynchronously (across clusters). Although in most scenarios you will find yourself deploying BizTalk applications asynchronously (from development cluster to staging cluster to production cluster), the synchronous deployment can also be useful; for example, you enhanced some aspects of your BizTalk applications on one server in the development cluster and want to deploy them to all the other machines within the cluster. To deploy a BizTalk Application to a target server, follow these steps:

1. Open Application Center MMC snap-in, expand Application Center and then the cluster to expose the Applications node.
2. Right-click Applications and select New Deployment.
3. Click Next on the Welcome To New Deployment Wizard page.
4. On the Deployment Target Options page, give a meaningful name to your deployment (the default name is a timestamp) and select between Deploy Content Inside The Current Cluster and Deploy Content Outside The Current Cluster. Click Next.
5. On the Deployment Target Authentication page, fill in User name, Password, Domain, and click Next.
6. On the Deploy Target page, enter the name of the server to which you want to deploy your BizTalk application (this is the name of the cluster controller if you want to deploy the BizTalk application on another cluster), and click Add.
7. On the Deployment Options page, select between Deploy All Applications and Related Cluster Configurations and Deploy One or More Applications. (If you selected the later, you can choose from a list of available applications the ones you want to deploy.) Click Next.
8. On the Deployment Options page, check appropriate options and click Next.
9. Click Finish on the Completing the New Deployment Wizard page.

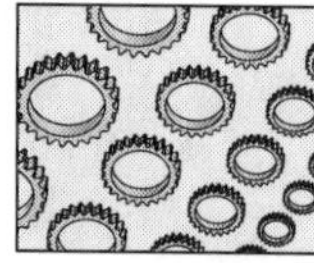

NOTE

To deploy an Application Center application, you need at least two members in the cluster, or you must have another cluster available.

Component Load Balancing

Component Load Balancing (CLB) is an Application Center 2000 feature which enables the invocation of the COM+ component to be load balanced. By using CLB, you can have multiple servers to process client requests (improve scalability), avoid single point of failure (improved availability), and utilize the role-based COM+ security. In this section, we will explain how CLB works (at a high level) and how to use CLB in BizTalk Server 2002.

How CLB Works CLB uses a routing mechanism to dynamically redirect the invocation requests from the client among the COM+ servers in the CLB cluster. There are at least two clusters involved in this scenario, a front-end cluster, which could be either a NLB cluster (the Web farm as you saw earlier in this chapter) or a COM+ routing cluster, and a CLB cluster, as shown in Figure 16-13.

When the application on one of the servers in the front-end cluster (a CLB cluster or a COM+ routing cluster) tries to create an instance of a COM+ component through

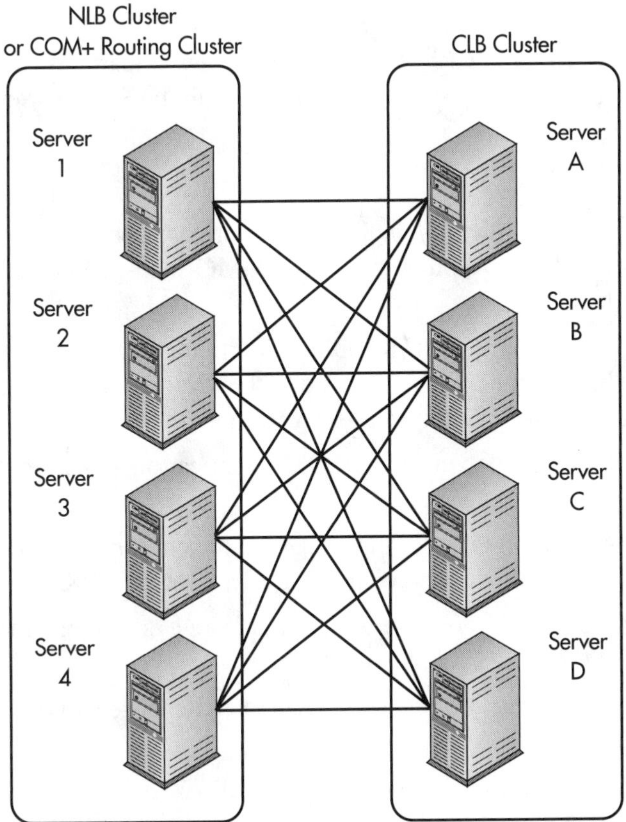

Figure 16-13 *Two clusters are involved in CLB*

some mechanism (for example, a CreateObject() VBScript call-in ASP page), instead of creating the component on the local machine, the CLB invokes a remote instance of the requested COM+ component on the *least busy* server (the one that has the least workload at the moment the invocation is requested) in the CLB cluster. CLB determines the workload of individual servers in the CLB cluster based on two things, a *Routing List* and a *Response Time Table*, both of which reside in the memory **on every member** in the front-end cluster. The Routing List is a list of available servers in the CLB cluster. It is created at the setup time and automatically updated throughout the front-end cluster. In addition to the Routing List, for every 200 milliseconds, the CLB also polls the CLB cluster to get a list response time of each server and creates a Response Time Table, which is a list of available servers sorted by the response time in ascending order. The CLB uses a round-robin mechanism to invoke the COM+ component on an appropriate server in the CLB cluster, according to the Response Time Table.

Using CLB in BizTalk Server 2002 In this section, you will learn how to use CLB to load balance an AIC component that is included in the BizTalk Server 2002 SDK sample.

Follow these steps:

1. Create a COM+ application in the Component Services MMC snap-in (available inside the Application Center MMC-snap-in) and name it "AIC CLB Example."
2. Install a new component, BTSAppInt.dll, into the COM+ application you just created. The component can be found in the \Program Files\Microsoft BizTalk Server\SDK\Messaging Samples\BTSAppIntegration\VB folder.
3. Right-click the component in the COM+ application and select Properties to bring up its properties page.
4. Click the Activation tab and select the Component Supports Dynamic Load Balancing check box, as shown in Figure 16-14. Click OK.
5. In the Application Center MMC snap-in, create a new application and name it "AICCLBApplication."
6. Select the new application you just created and choose COM+ Applications as the Resource Type.
7. Click the Add button and select the AIC CLB Example COM+ application you created in Component Services. The application should look like the one in Figure 16-15.

8. Deploy the AICCLBApplication to the target cluster as described earlier in this chapter.
9. Finally, build an initial routing list. To do this, right-click the cluster in the Application Center MMC snap-in and select Properties. Click the Component Services tab and the Add button to add the cluster members in the Component Servers list, as shown in Figure 16-16.

CLB for BizTalk.Interchange.1 By using Application Center, you can load-balance the BizTalk.Interchange.1 component. CLB for this component enables an HTTP transport to dynamically and transparently invoke the component from one of the servers in the cluster instead of a single server and call the Submit method. This will improve the scalability and avoid single point-of-failure.

To enable CLB for the BizTalk.Interchange.1 component, open the Component Services MMC snap-in and expand My Computer, COM+ Applications, BizTalk Server Interchange Application and Components. Right-click BizTalk.Interchange.1 and select Properties. Click the Activation tab and select the Component Supports Dynamic Load Balancing check box. Click OK.

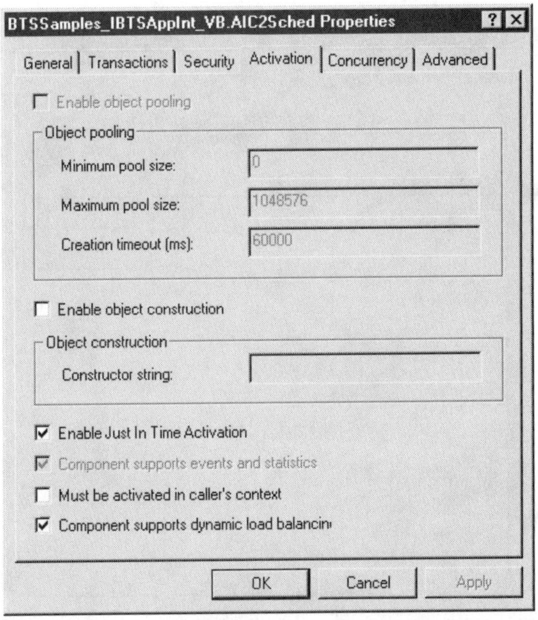

Figure 16-14 *Marking the COM+ component as supporting CLB*

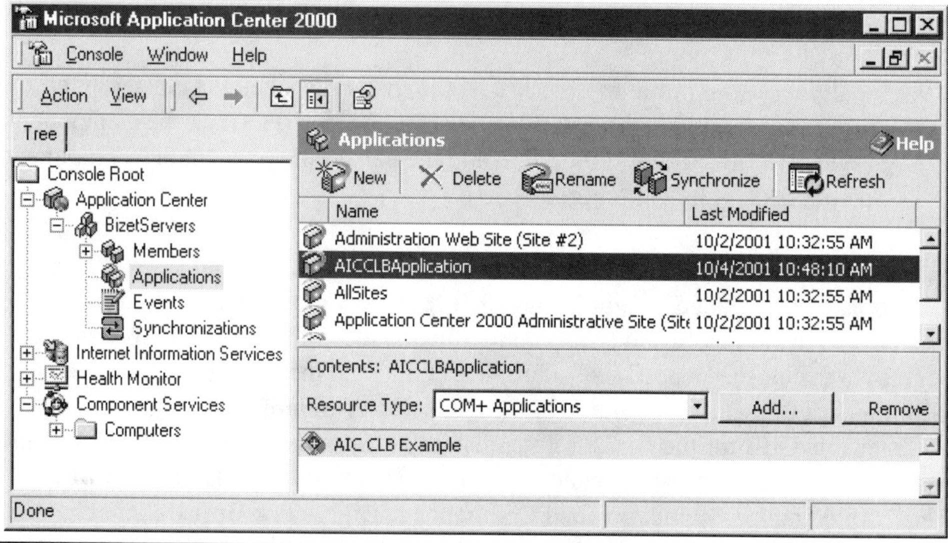

Figure 16-15 *Creating an Application Center application that supports CLB*

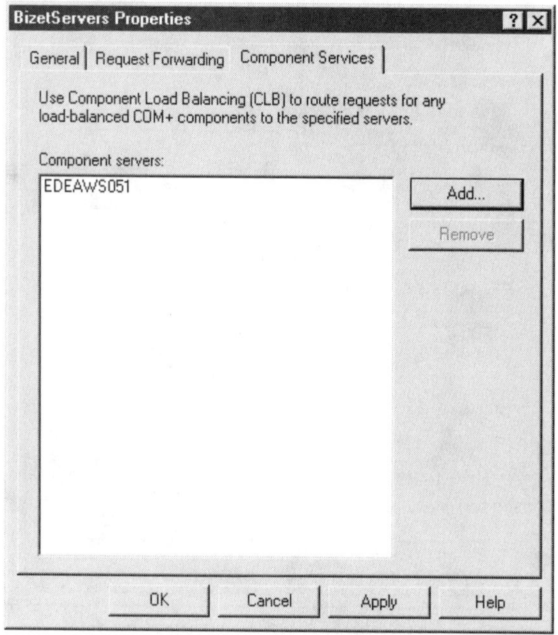

Figure 16-16 *Building a CLB routing list*

TIP

Before you change the configuration of the BizTalk.Interchange.1 component, you need to clear the Disable Changes check box on the Advanced tag of the Properties page of its hosting COM+ application—BizTalk Server Integration Application.

Using Health Monitor with BizTalk Server

As you will see in the next section, MOM provides enterprise quality monitoring for Bizet. For single-machine monitoring in smaller installations where you wish to define all the events of interest manually, you can also leverage Health Monitor in AC. Usually you would use one or the other, but not both… In this section, you will learn how to use the Health Monitor to monitor the WMI events raised by the Suspended Queue. The purpose is to give you some hands-on experience in using the Health Monitor with BizTalk Server 2002. For more information about Health Monitor, read Chapter 7 of the Application Center 2000 Resource Kit.

To monitor WMI events using Health Monitor, you need to create a pair of Health Monitor objects: a *data group* and a *data collector*. You use the data group to group related data points into a category and the data collect to receive and store WMI data (events). A data group can contain one or more data collectors. In addition to data groups and data collectors, you can also create custom *actions* in Health Monitor to define what you want to do about the events that have been collected by the data collectors.

To set up the Health Monitor to monitor Suspended Queue events, follow these steps:

1. In the Application Center MMC snap-in, choose Health Monitor | All Monitored Computers to expose the computers you want to monitor.
2. Right-click the computer whose Suspended Queue you want to monitor and select New | Data Group.
3. Give a name to the data group, such as WMI Events, and click OK.
4. Right-click the data group you just created and select New | Data Collector | WMI Event Query.
5. On the Details tab of the WMI Event Query Properties dialog box, click the Browse button next to the Namespace box and select ROOT\MicrosoftBizTalkServer from the list.
6. Click the Browse button next to the Class box and select MicrosoftBizTalkServer_ScheduledQueue from the list. As you work along, you will notice that a WMI query is automatically built for you and is displayed in the lower part of the WMI Event Query Properties dialog box.

7. At this point, the Properties list box should be populated by a list of available properties from which you can choose the one you want to monitor. In this example, select the QID check box.
8. Click the Message tab. Here you can customize the messages for both scenarios. In this example, you will use the default messages.
9. Click the Actions tab. Here you can specify what actions you would like to take when the event happens. Click the New Action Association button (the first button in the upper-right corner) to bring up the Execute Action Properties dialog box. Select Email Administrator from the Action To Execute list box. Click OK to dismiss the dialog box and then Click OK to close the Properties page.

Now that you have set up the Suspended Queue monitor and you are ready to test it out. You can use the Suspended Queue Monitoring SDK sample to test the monitor. This sample is designed to work with MOM (the topic of the second half of this chapter), but it will work just fine for our purposes here. Run the SuspendedQueueConfig.vbs VBScript in the \Program Files\Microsoft BizTalk Server\SDK\Messaging Samples\Suspended Queue Monitoring folder to set up necessary BizTalk messaging objects and receive functions. Follow the instructions in the Readme.txt file to run this sample. At the end of the process, you should have a document that ends up in the Suspended Queue and the administrator will receive an e-mail that looks like this:

```
Health Monitor Alert on EDEAWS051 at 9/24/2001 10:10:40 PM
BTS Suspended Queue Monitor : Critical condition
```

Now that you've learned enough about Microsoft Application Manager 2000 for managing and deploying enterprise BizTalk solutions, in the second half of this chapter, you will learn how to utilize Microsoft Operations Manager (MOM) to monitor your BizTalk applications.

Microsoft Operations Manager 2000

Microsoft Operations Manager 2000 (MOM) is a Microsoft product designed for Windows operations management. In this half of the chapter, we will introduce the Microsoft Windows management infrastructure and the roles and relationships of MOM and other complementary products. We will then discuss key MOM features. Finally, we will see how to leverage MOM to manage your BizTalk solutions. Before we delve into the discussion, let's first have MOM installed.

Installing MOM

In real-world scenarios, it's best to install different MOM components across the managed Windows Servers to achieve the greatest scalability. For demonstration and learning purposes, it will be just fine to have all the components installed on one machine. Here, we will choose the second option based on the consideration that most readers of this book probably don't have the luxury of having two or more computers running Windows 2000 Server. For instructions on how to install MOM on multiple machines, refer to the Microsoft Operations Manager 2000 Installation Guide, available in Microsoft Word format from the MOM product Web site, http://www.microsoft.com/mom.

There are two parts to MOM installation, the prerequisites and MOM. When you insert the Microsoft Operations Manager 2000 CD into the CD-ROM drive, the Autorun program will launch the main setup page, as shown in Figure 16-17.

Clicking Verify Prerequisites will bring up the Setup Prerequisites Wizard, as shown in Figure 16-18. As you can see in the figure, there are a total of 11 prerequisites. Some of them are disabled because they are already installed on the target computer. For example, Figure 16-18 indicates that there are three prerequisites missing from my computer before I install MOM: Access 2000 Run-time, Microsoft Office Graph Component, and MSDTC Logfile Size. The right pane displays the installation instructions for the selected item on the left. Depending on the configuration of the target computer, the available items may vary.

Select individual required prerequisites and click the blue hyperlink in the lower part of the Wizard screen to have them installed one by one.

The MSDTC Logfile Size item allows you to launch the Component Services MMC snap-in from the Setup Prerequisites Wizard so that you can configure the size of the MSDTC (Microsoft Districted Transaction Coordinator) log file. To do this, expend Component Services and then Computers. Right-click My Computer and select Properties. Click the MSDTC tab, the default log file size should be 4 MB (in the Capacity box).

Before you can reset the size of the log file, you need to stop MSDTC Windows service first. Click the Stop button to stop the MSDTC service (this will stop all he dependent Windows services, such as MSMQ). After the MSDTC service is stopped, change the Capacity to 512 MB and click OK. Click OK on the DTC Console Message box to confirm that you want to reset the existing MSDTC log file. You can restart the MSDTC Windows service by right-clicking My Computer in the Component Services MMC snap-in and selecting Start MS DTC.

After all the prerequisites are installed, click the Reboot button to reboot your computer.

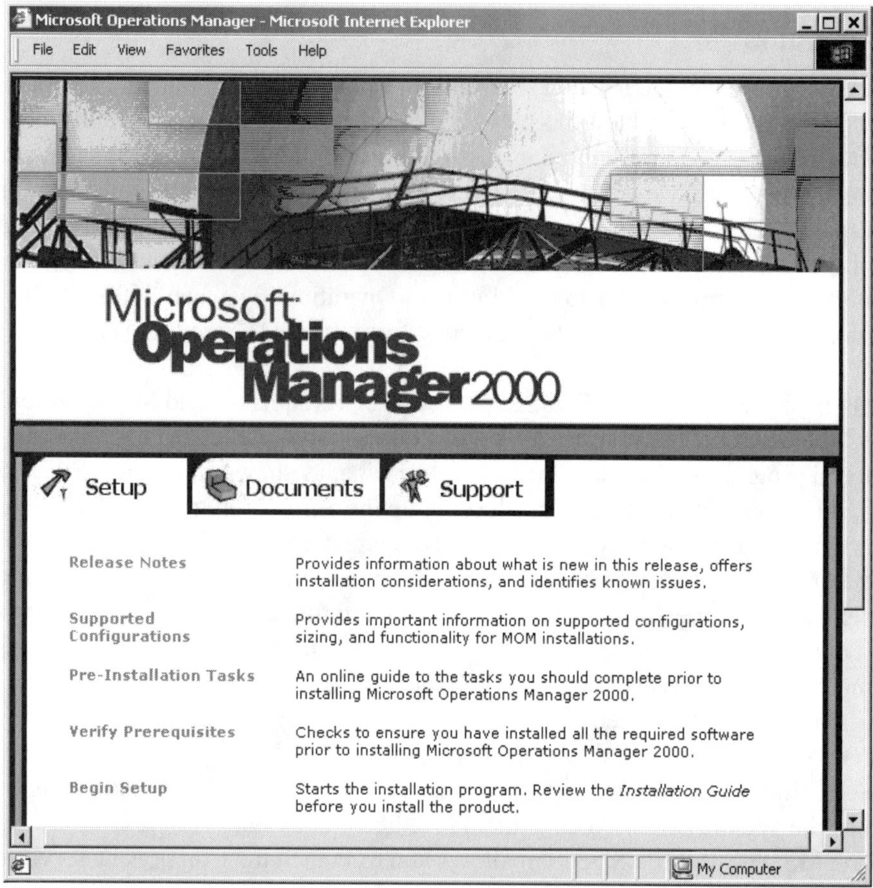

Figure 16-17 *Installing MOM*

MOM and Microsoft Systems Management Server

System management presents complex, multifaceted challenges, involving change and configuration management (provisioning), and operations management (real-time, dynamic monitoring). To resolve the issues associated with Windows system management, Microsoft provides comprehensive tools and technologies, including Microsoft Systems Management Server (SMS), MOM, and the Application Center you learned about in the first half of this chapter. Each product is designed to address a specific area of the system management and together they provide a complementary system management service in the Windows environment.

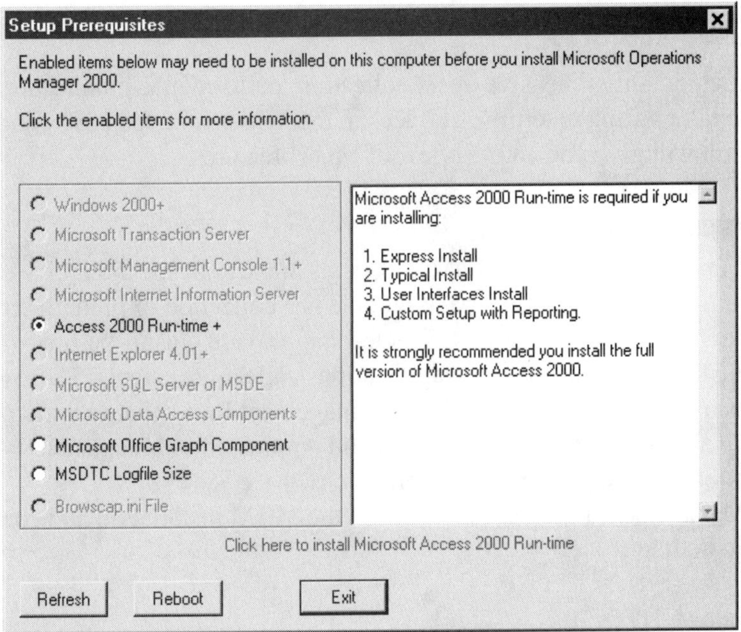

Figure 16-18 *Installing prerequisites*

Microsoft Systems Management Server 2.0 (SMS) is designed for change and configuration management related to the provisioning and configuration of enterprise systems throughout the life cycle of the hardware and software involved. SMS extends powerful Windows 2000 management features by adding detailed inventory, advanced software distribution and metering and remote diagnostics. Due to the scope of this chapter, we won't discuss SMS here. For more information, visit the SMS product Web site at http://www.microsoft.com/smsmgmt/default.asp.

Whereas SMS manages change and configurations of the enterprise systems, MOM takes care of the operations management. Operations management involves such tasks as monitoring a system's operational states, collecting system and application events, sending alerts and notifications based on collected events, and reporting system performance in regards to trends analysis and capacity planning.

SMS and MOM provide reciprocal and complementary services and form the Windows management infrastructure—operations management provides advance warning of the need for change and configuration management. In addition, as you learned in the first half of this chapter, Application Center 2000 embraces the functionalities of both worlds and provides a cluster-based centralized management platform for Windows and Web-based enterprise applications.

MOM 2000 Features

MOM provides comprehensive event collection, performance monitoring and alerting, and reporting enterprise services in the Windows 2000 environment. This section will give you an overview of MOM features.

Management Packs

The most important feature of MOM 2000 is its *Management Packs* (or *Management Pack Modules*). A management pack module is a collection of predefined rules, as well as Microsoft Knowledge Base articles that provide out-of-the-box solutions for monitoring and managing specific applications and environments. There are two categories of Management Packs: Base Management Packs that provide monitoring services to all critical Windows services, and Application Management Packs that help monitor specific systems and applications.

Base Management Packs are included in the MOM installation and contain the following modules:

- Windows 2000
- Active Directory Service
- File Replication Service (FRS)
- Windows Internet Name Service (WINS)
- Domain Name Service
- Internet Information Service
- Dynamic Host Configuration Protocol (DHCP)
- Routing and Remote Access
- Microsoft Transaction Service (MTS)
- Microsoft Message Queuing (MSMQ)
- Microsoft Distributed Transaction Coordinator (MSDTC)
- System Management Server 2.0
- Microsoft Operations Manager 2000
- Microsoft Terminal Server
- Microsoft Windows NT 4.0 operating systems log

Application Management Packs are separately developed by specific Microsoft application product teams or by third party vendors whose product can be monitored by MOM. The following is a list of some Application Management Packs available today:

- Exchange Server 5.5
- Exchange Server 2000
- Site Server 3.0
- SNA Server 4.0
- SQL Server 7.0
- SQL Server 2000
- Proxy Server 2.0

In addition, BizTalk Server 2002 ships with a MOM Management Pack that is located in the \MOM folder of the installation CD.

Application Management Packs can be imported, updated, and exported.

Centralized Management of Distributed Events

MOM enables you to collect a wide variety of system and application events in a distributed Windows environment and aggregate these events into a central event repository. You can consolidate and manage these distributed events either through the Microsoft Management Operations Manager MMC snap-in or through the Microsoft Operations Manager Web Console.

To access the MMC snap-in, select Start | Programs | Microsoft Operations Manager | MMC Interface.

To access the Web Console, open a Web browser such as IE 5 and enter the URL **http://*MachineName*/onepointoperations** (for example, http://localhost/onepointoperations). Answer the four questions on the Welcome To Microsoft Operations Manager Web Console page (or leave the default answers) and click Start Web Console at the bottom of the page to open the MOM Web Console.

Rule-based Monitoring and Intelligent Alerting

MOM allows you to create event monitoring and processing rules so that the captured events can either be used to trigger associated alerts and/or actions (e-mail or page notifications, commands, batch files, and so on) or aggregate with other events into a more significant event. Rules enable MOM to intelligently react to known events and trigger corresponding administrative alerts and actions. Rules can also be linked to resources such as Microsoft Knowledge Base articles, custom resolution documents, and others, so that when a particular event occurs, you can be instantly armed with related knowledge and information for solving the problem at hand.

Performance Monitoring

In MOM, you can monitor key performance thresholds through appropriate performance counters. Local and aggregated thresholds can be set to trigger appropriate alerts and/or actions in response to any changes in system or application performance.

Reporting

MOM has a built-in reporting tool, a custom Access reporting application (which requires the installation of Access 2000 Runtime Engine). The MOM reporting tool provides a rich set of out-of-the-box reports ranging from performance monitoring and trends analysis to capacity planning. To access the MOM reporting tool, click Start | Programs | Microsoft Operations Manager | Reporting.

Scalable Architecture

MOM uses a scalable architecture that enables you to manage tens of thousands of servers and handle hundreds of millions of events per day, with full redundancy and load balancing. Figure 16-19 illustrates the architecture of MOM.

As shown in Figure 16-19, the *Consolidator*, which has an associated *Agent Manager* component (not shown in Figure 16-19) for installing, uninstalling, and configuring intelligent *agents* (an agent is a service that runs on every monitored computer), interacts with the MOM database through the *Data Access Server* (*DAS*). DAS serves as a broker between the consolidator and the database and translates the requests from the consolidator into specific database operations. Intelligent agents are at the forefront in collecting and analyzing information and executing commands sent by MOM (through the consolidator). These agents are installed on each managed node along with local rules. The distributed architecture is what makes MOM extremely scalable—local rule storage and event processing reduces traffic and workload on the MOM Control Server, helping avoid bottlenecks, and guaranteeing higher performance from MOM.

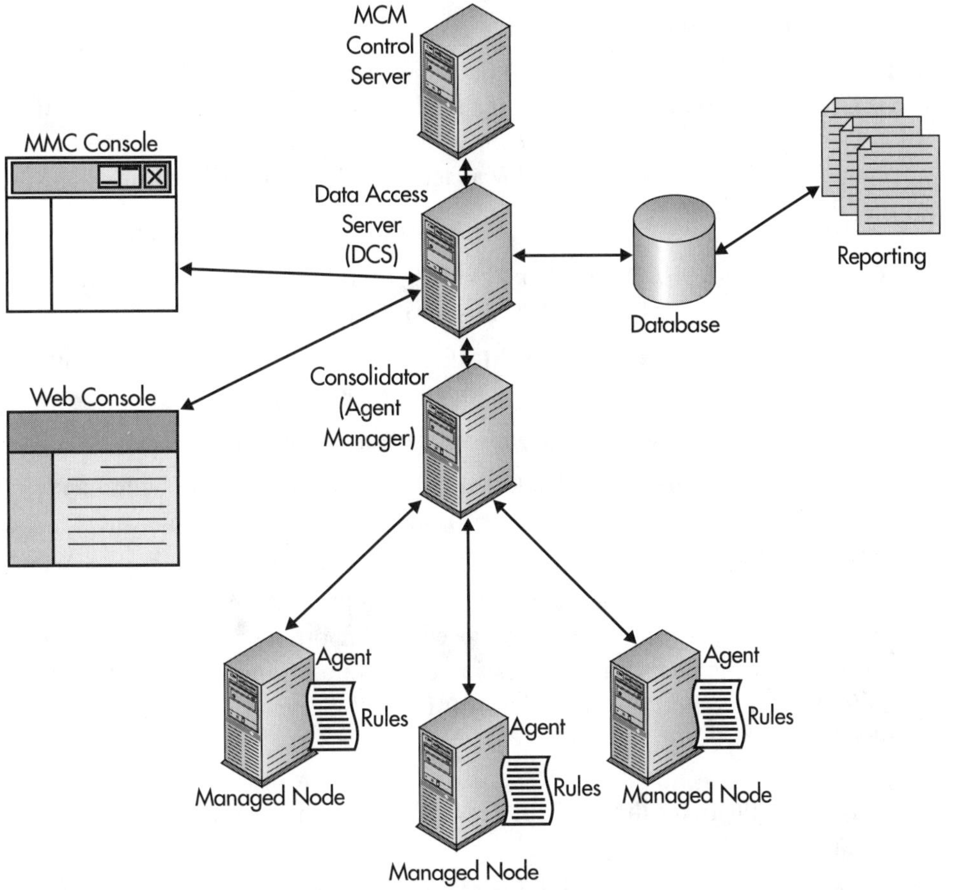

MCM Control Server
MMC Console
Data Access Server (DCS)
Database
Reporting
Web Console
Consolidator (Agent Manager)
Agent
Rules
Managed Node
Agent
Rules
Managed Node
Agent
Rules
Managed Node

Figure 16-19 *The scalable architecture of Microsoft Operations Manager*

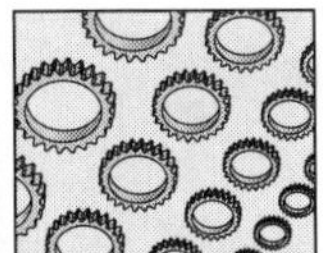

NOTE

Although Figure 16-19 illustrates the physical distributed architecture of a MOM installation, it is perfectly fine to install all the components on a single machine for learning purposes.

Using the BizTalk Server 2002 Management Pack

BizTalk Server 2002 provides a specific management pack module for Microsoft Operations Manager, the BizTalk Server 2002 Management Pack, which streamlines the monitoring of your enterprise BizTalk application through MOM.

Importing the Management Pack

The BizTalk Server 2002 Management Pack can be found in the \MOM folder of the BizTalk Server 2002 CD. You can install the BizTalk Server 2002 Management Pack either through the MMC console or by using the command line utility.

To import the BizTalk Server 2002 Management Pack into MOM using the MMC console, follow these steps:

1. Open the MOM MMC console by clicking Start | Programs | Microsoft Operations Manager | MOM Administrator Console.
2. In the tree view on the left of the MMC console, expand Operations Manager (Default) and then Rules to expose Processing Rule Groups.
3. Right-click Processing Rule Groups and select Import Management Pack.
4. On the Import Management Pack dialog box, click the Browse button and select BizTalk2002.akm from the BizTalk Server 2002 CD, under the \MOM folder.
5. Click the Import button at the bottom of the Import Management Pack dialog box. After a few seconds, you should see the Imported Processing Rule Groups dialog box which lists three processing rule groups: Samples, BizTalk Server 2002 Enterprise Edition, and Microsoft BizTalk Server. Click OK to dismiss the dialog box.

Figure 16-20 illustrates the BizTalk Server 2002 Management Pack in the MOM MMC console.

Alternatively, you can use the command line utility, ManagementModuleUtil.exe, located in the \Program Files\Microsoft Operations Manager\one point folder. For syntax details and instructions on the command line utility, see Knowledge Base article Q299594.

You can use the BizTalk Server 2002 Management Pack to manage Windows NT Event Rules, performance Counters, Partially Configured Rules, and User-Configured Rules.

Monitoring BizTalk Servers

The BizTalk Server 2002 Management Pack provides *processing rules* and performance counters that can be used to monitor BizTalk Server-related events and generate alerts and responses. A processing rule defines appropriate actions and responses for a specific event collected by MOM agents. Processing rules are grouped into specific categories, known as processing rule groups (PRGs). A PRG can have

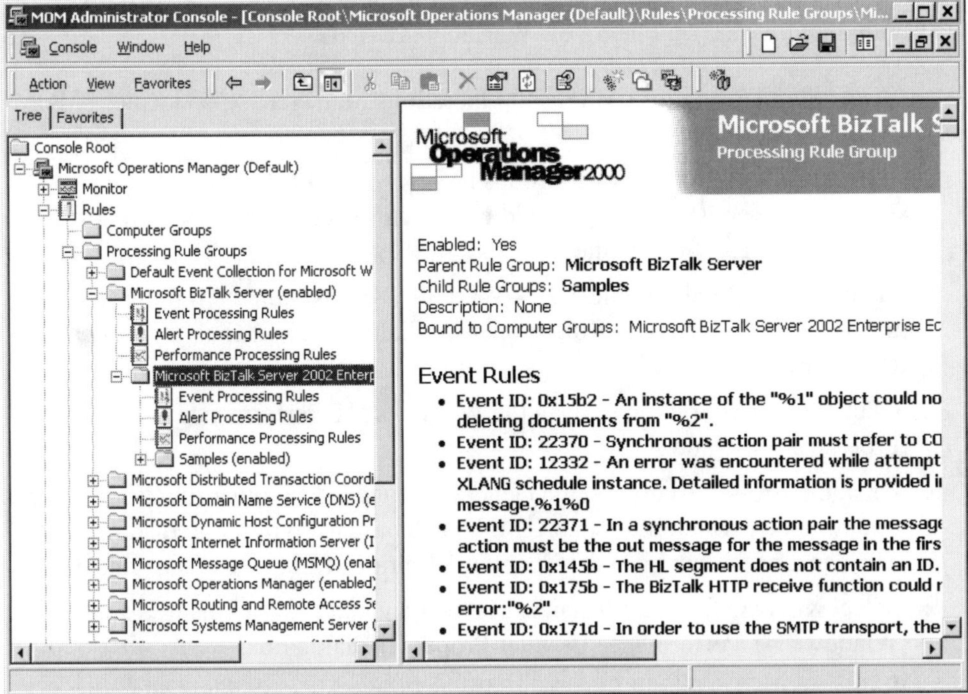

Figure 16-20 *The BizTalk Server 2002 Management Pack*

sub-PRGs, and you can access PRGs and process rules in the MOM Administrator Console.

BizTalk Server Processing Rules In the BizTalk Server 2002 Management Pack, the top-level PRG is Microsoft BizTalk Server, which is directly under the Processing Rule Groups. Underneath this PRG, there is a sub-PRG: Microsoft BizTalk Server 2002 Enterprise Edition.

There are three types of processing rules: event processing rules, alert processing rules, and performance processing rules. The BizTalk Server 2002 Management Pack provides hundreds of event processing rules and performance processing rules. All of the event processing rules in the BizTalk Server 2002 Management Pack are fully configured. Some of the performance processing rules in the BizTalk Server 2002 Management Pack are fully configured, whereas others are partially configured.

Partially configured rules are disabled by default in the MOM Administrator console. To enable a partially configured processing rule, you first need to complete its configuration. The following steps demonstrate how to enable the partially configured rule, Database File Size – Warning: XLANG.

1. Select Start | Programs | Microsoft Operations Manager Expand Rules | MOM Administrator Console.
2. Expand Rules | Process Rule Groups | Microsoft BizTalk Server | Microsoft BizTalk Server 2002 Enterprise Edition, then select Performance Processing Rules in the tree view on the left.
3. Double-click Database File Size – Warning: XLANG on the right pane to open the Threshold Processing Rule Properties dialog box and click the Data Provider tab.
4. Click the Modify button to open the Windows NT Performance Counter Properties dialog box.
5. Click the Browse Button on the General tab and select either the local server or remote server which hosts the XLANG database to be monitored and click OK. The name of the server in the Counter definitions from box will be updated.
6. Select XLANG from the Instance List box and click OK to dismiss the Windows NT Performance Counter Properties dialog box.
7. Return to the Threshold Processing Rules Properties dialog box and click the General tab.
8. Select the Enable check box and click OK.

In addition to these out-of-the-box processing rules in the BizTalk Server 2002 Management Pack, you can also define user-configured rules in MOM for monitoring those events, alerts, or custom counters for specific purposes. For instructions about how to create and manage processing rules, refer to the Microsoft Operations Manager User Guide, available in PDF format from the MOM product Web site at http://www.microsoft.com/mom.

BizTalk Server Views In MOM, you can create *views* to report performance counters and other vital information. BizTalk Server 2002 Management Pack offers dozens of views for BizTalk Messaging Services and Orchestration Services (XLANG). These views in the MOM Administrator can be accessed under Monitor | Public Views | Microsoft BizTalk Server | Microsoft BizTalk Server 2002 Enterprise Edition.

Using the Suspended Queue Alert Examples The BizTalk Server 2002 Management Pack provides processing rule samples for monitoring events, alerts, and performances. In addition, the SDK of BizTalk Server 2002 ships with some samples that you can use in conjunction with these processing rules for monitoring your BizTalk applications using MOM. In this section, we will walk you through the Event Processing Rules example, Sample: Suspended Queue Alert. In this example, you will learn how to use the sample processing rule to monitor the BizTalk Server Suspended Queue to generate alerts when the number of documents in the Suspended Queue reaches certain thresholds. In addition, you will also learn how to create a response that automatically sends an e-mail to appropriate administrators should the alert occur.

Before you get started, you need to enable the example processing rule by following these steps:

1. In MOM Administrator, expand Rules | Processing Rule Groups | BizTalk Server BizTalk Server 2002 Enterprise Edition | Samples.
2. Click Event Processing Rules in the tree view on the left and double-click Sample: Suspended Queue Alert in the right pane.
3. Select the Enabled check box and click OK.
4. Right-click the Rules in MOM Administrator and select Commit Configuration Change to force the agent to be updated.

Now you can set up the SDK sample, Suspended Queue Monitoring, located under \Program Files\Microsoft BizTalk Server\SDK\Messaging Samples\Suspended Queue Monitoring. Refer to the Readme.txt documentation for instructions about how to set up this sample application.

Run the sample as instructed in the Readme.txt. This will cause the submitted document (InvalidPO.xml) to end up in the Suspended Queue.

Switch back to the MOM Administrator and expand Monitor | All Open Alerts. You will see a BizTalk Error listed in the right pane.

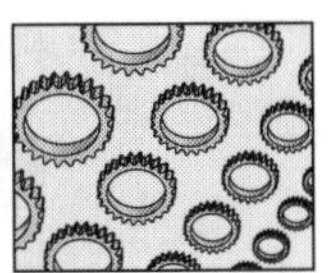

NOTE

The alerts in the MOM Administrator refresh every 14 minutes. As a result, you may not be able to see the Suspended Queue alert immediately after it was generated.

Next, let's demonstrate how to create a response in the sample processing rule so that an e-mail message will be sent to the appropriate notification group should a Suspended Queue alert occur. You can do this by following these steps:

1. Open the Event Processing Rule Properties dialog box for Sample: Suspended Queue Alert as described earlier in this section and click the Responses tab.
2. Click the Add button and select Send A Notification To A Notification Group.
3. In the Notification Group drop-down box on the Send A Notification To A Notification Group dialog box that pops up, click the New button.
4. On the Notification Group Properties dialog box, enter Bizet Administrators in the Name box.
5. Click the New Operator button and enter Bizet Operator in the Name box of the Operator Properties Wizard, then click Next.
6. On the E-mail page of the Operator Properties dialog box, enter the e-mail address where you want the alert to be sent, and click Next.
7. On the Page page of the Operator Properties dialog box, clear the Page The Operator check box, and click Next.
8. On the Command page of the Operator Properties dialog box, clear the Notify This Operator By External Command and click Finish to dismiss the Operator Properties dialog box.
9. Click Finish to dismiss the Notification Group Properties dialog box.
10. Click OK to dismiss the Send A Notification To A Notification Group dialog box.
11. Click OK to dismiss the Event Processing Rule Properties dialog box.

Now if you run the Suspended Queue Monitoring SDK sample again, in addition to the generated alert, those e-mail addressees in the Bizet Administrators notification group will get an alert e-mail message.

Chapter in Review

In this chapter, you have learned about the key features of Microsoft Application Center 2000 and Microsoft Operations Manager 2000 and how to use them to manage your BizTalk Server 2002 applications. In particular, you've learned how to leverage Application Center 2000 to build highly scalable, available, and reliable BizTalk Server 2002 solutions (cluster and load-balancing services), to deploy BizTalk Artifacts, and to monitor WMI events. Additionally, you've learned about the operations management features of MOM and the BizTalk Server 2002 Management Pack.

PART VIII

Appendixes

OBJECTIVES

- Master basic XML technologies
- Learn how to use XML Transformation
- Build XML applications
- Create Windows scripts components

APPENDIX

A

XML Fundamentals

IN THIS CHAPTER:

Writing Well-Formed XML Documents

Using Namespaces

Validating XML Documents

Appendix in Review

XML is the backbone of BizTalk technologies. The BizTalk Framework, meanwhile, is an XML-based specification. So is the SOAP protocol on which the BizTalk Framework is based. Additionally, BizTalk Server 2000 internally uses XML exclusively. For example, in BizTalk Server Messaging Services, business documents are either directly submitted to BizTalk Server as XML documents or converted to XML either with the default parsers (for well-known formats such as EDI, and flat text files) or via custom parsers (using the IBizTalkParserComponent interface for complex non-XML formats). Moreover, BizTalk Server document specifications and mapping specifications are XML Data Reduced (XDR) schemas (mapping specifications also have XSL stylesheets embedded in them). Furthermore, the BizTalk Orchestration Designer persists XLANG schedules as XML documents.

XML is a simple, elegant, yet powerful technology, and, along with its supporting languages such as XSLT and XPath, it has brought rapid changes to the Internet, EAI, and B2B integration arenas. The importance of XML has lead to the adoption of its technology in many other products besides BizTalk. As a matter of fact, the entire product line of Microsoft .NET enterprise servers has embraced XML. Even the Microsoft .NET platform itself, which uses Web Services technologies heavily, now includes strong support for XML. The same holds true for other programming tools, database products, and platforms such as Java and Oracle.

As a result, mastering XML has become so important to software developers that no one can afford to ignore it, no matter which programming language he or she uses, and no matter which platform. If you haven't mastered XML yet, it is time to do so. To help you get underway, Appendixes A, B, and C of this book is dedicated to XML and its related technologies. We will cover the basics of the XML language in this appendix. XSLT transformation will be addressed in Appendix B, and Appendix C will explain how to build XML applications.

Writing Well-Formed XML Documents

Like HTML, XML (or e**X**tensible **M**arkup **L**anguage) also originated from SGML (or **S**tandard **G**eneralized **M**arkup **L**anguage).

SGML is an international standard (ISO 8899) designed to create interchangeable, structured documents. It can be used for defining device-independent, system-independent methods of representing texts in electronic form. Although it has been around for more than a decade, the implementation costs of SGML, not to mention its complexity, has limited its use to government agencies, big business industries, the military, and academic research projects of various sizes.

HTML is a simplified version of SGML, used in the presentation of web pages. It employs a predefined, and therefore not extensible, set of *tags* (markup texts) to describe how the text within specific tags should be presented. For example, the following HTML segment tells a web browser that the phrase **Learn XML Now** should be displayed as bold text:

```
<B>Learn XML Now</B>
```

It achieves this by using a pair of HTML markup tags, <B></B>, which tell the web browser that anything within this specific set of tags should be in bold font. By using this simple markup mechanism, HTML has become the foundation of all web pages used worldwide.

Whereas HTML provides an excellent method for instructing web browsers how the segments of a document should be displayed, it has no way of telling the application that processes the document what is the content of the document, or its segments. In other words, HTML has no mechanism for describing the document data. This is where XML comes in, as a complement to HTML in the realm of web browser scenarios. XML was designed as a simplified version of SGML to help describe structured data. Take the phrase we used earlier as an example. The corresponding XML segment of that phrase may look like this:

```
<Title>Learn XML Now</Title>
```

This tells the document processor that the phrase is a title of a book or an article. It uses a pair of user-defined tags, <Title></Title> to describe the contents of the texts surrounded by the tags. The reach of XML data has been extended from inside the web browser to specific data transfer applications that facilitate B2B transfer between companies.

The Structure and Constructs of an XML Document

A document that is as simple as this one isn't particularly useful. Let's look at a more complete XML document to get a better idea of how an XML document is constructed:

```
<?xml version="1.0"?>
<?xml-stylesheet type="text/xsl" href="Books.xsl"?>
<!DOCTYPE Books SYSTEM "Books.DTD">
```

```
<!--Sample XML document-->
<Books>
  <Book ISBN="0-7897-2458-8">
    <Title>Visual Basic and COM+ Programming By Example</Title>
    <Publisher>QUE</Publisher>
    <Authors>
      <Author>Peishu Li</Author>
    </Authors>
    <Price>34.99</Price>
  </Book>
  <Book ISBN="0-07-213338-4">
    <Title>BizTalk Server 2000 Developer's Guide</Title>
    <Publisher>Osborne/McGraw-Hill</Publisher>
    <Authors>
      <Author>Peishu Li</Author>
    </Authors>
    <Price>59.99</Price>
  </Book>
</Books>
```

The preceding example is an XML document which describes two computer books. As you can see, a complete XML document can be roughly divided into two sections: a *Prologue* section that contains document metadata, and a *Document Body* section which can contain one or more sets of document data.

The Prologue

The first four lines of text in the previous sample XML document is the prologue of the document:

```
<?xml version="1.0"?>
<?xml-stylesheet type="text/xsl" href="Books.xsl"?>
<!DOCTYPE Books SYSTEM "Books.DTD">
<!--Sample XML document-->
```

In this example, the prologue contains an XML declaration, a Process Instruction (or PI), a DOCTYPE declaration, and a comment. Let's explain each of these sections of the prologue individually:

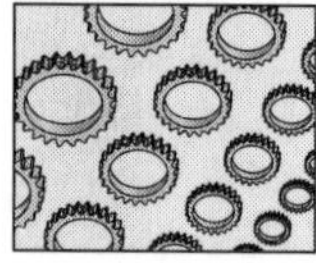

NOTE

The prologue of an XML document is not mandatory.

XML Declaration The first line of text in the sample XML document is an *XML declaration*:

```
<?xml version="1.0"?>
<?xml-stylesheet type="text/xsl" href="Books.xsl"?>
<!DOCTYPE Books SYSTEM "Books.DTD">
<!--Sample XML document-->
```

The XML declaration is optional. When included, however, it must appear as the very first line of the document. The version number is mandatory and must be placed in single or double quotes. It tells the XML processor what version of XML specification the XML document is compliant with. The current version is 1.0, and being such, this is the only valid entry for the XML version. The XML declaration starts with a "<?xml" and ends with a "?>".

Optionally, you can also include an encoding declaration like this:

```
<?xml version="1.0" encoding ="UTF-16"?>
```

The encoding declaration must immediately follow the version number and include a value that indicates which existing character encoding rule is being used in the XML document. The W3C XML recommendation requires that all XML parsers must be able to automatically recognize UTF-8 or UTF-16 Unicode encoding. If you choose to use other encodings for your XML document, however, you need to explicitly include an encoding declaration to notify the XML parser. The following example uses the ISO-8859-1 Latin 1 encoding method:

```
<?xml version="1.0" encoding ="ISO-8859-1"?>
```

In addition, you can also include an optional *standalone*:

```
<?xml version="1.0" standalone ="Yes"?>
```

The standalone declaration can have two possible values, "Yes" or "No." A value of "Yes" indicates that the XML document has an externally declared Document Type Definition (DTD) document that defines its structure. If the standalone declaration is omitted, a value of "No" is assumed. In this case, the XML document either has an *in-line DTD* embedded in the document or has no DTD at all.

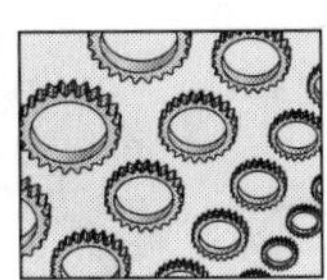

NOTE

We will discuss Document Type Definition (DTD) later in this appendix.

You can include both encoding and standalone declarations simultaneously or just use one of them. When you do this, the standalone declaration must appear last in the XML declaration:

```
<?xml version="1.0" encoding ="UTF-16" standalone ="Yes"?>
```

Process Instruction (PI) The second line of our sample XML document is a *Process Instruction* (PI):

```
<?xml version="1.0"?>
<?xml-stylesheet type="text/xsl" href="Books.xsl"?>
<!DOCTYPE Books SYSTEM "Books.DTD">
<!--Sample XML document-->
```

As its name implies, PI provides a means of passing application-specific information to a target application (e.g., XML processors). A PI must start with "<?" followed by a *target* that identifies the target application, which is then followed by a white space and the specific process instructions. The PI must end with "?>", like this:

<?Name_of_Target_Application Process_Instruction?>

In our example, the target identified, by "xml-stylesheet", signals the processor (in this case, the Internet Explorer 5.0 or above web browser) that an XML stylesheet, Books.xsl, is attached at the XML document's sample location.

PIs are optional and can appear anywhere in the XML documents (although here we used it in the prologue of the example). PIs don't have to follow the syntax and "well-formedness" rules of XML, as long as they are declared syntactically as outlined here.

DOCTYPE Declaration The third line of text in the prologue section of our sample XML document is a *DOCTYPE declaration*:

```
<?xml version="1.0"?>
<?xml-stylesheet type="text/xsl" href="Books.xsl"?>
<!DOCTYPE Books SYSTEM "Books.DTD">
<!--Sample XML document-->
```

If you use a Document Type Definition (DTD) to validate your XML document, you will need a DOCTYPE declaration. As you will learn later in this appendix, a

DTD is one of the mechanisms that defines the valid structure and constraints for the XML document.

Depending on which identifier you use, SYSTEM or PUBLIC, a DOCTYPE declaration could be in one of two forms:

<!DOCTYPE Root_Element SYSTEM “URI_Reference”>

or:

<!DOCTYPE Root_Element PUBLIC “Public_Identifier” “URI_Reference”>

The *URI_Reference* in the preceding DOCTYPE declarations is a *Universal Resource Identifier* (or *URI*) and must be placed inside quotes. A URI uniquely identifies a specific web resource. It could be a URL (Unique Resource Locator) such as “http://www.myorganization.com/mydocdef.dtd” or a relative path such as “Books.DTD” in our example.

When a SYSTEM identifier is used, you only need to provide a URI reference to identify the location of the DTD file. If the PUBLIC identifier is used, you also need to supply a public identifier in addition to the URI reference. A public identifier is usually a well-known resource, such as a standard body, and can usually be recognized by XML processors. A public identifier is defined in the following form:

Standard_Flag//Owner_Organization//Doc_Name//Language_Code

An example of a DOCTYPE declaration that uses the PUBLIC identifier looks like this:

```
<!DOCTYPE Books PUBLIC "-//BookStandardOrg//Book Documents//ENG"
"Books.DTD">
```

When a PUBLIC identifier is used, the XML processor will try to recognize the public identifier and load the appropriate built-in DTD document. If this process fails, the XML processor will locate the DTD document identified by the URI reference that follows the public identifier in the DOCTYPE declaration.

In addition to using external files, the DTD can also be embedded inside an XML document, as shown in the following example:

```
<?xml version="1.0" encoding="UTF-8"?>
<!DOCTYPE Sample [<!ELEMENT Sample (#PCDATA)>]>
<Sample>Sample Text</Sample>
```

The Root_Element in the DOCTYPE declaration is the highest level element of an XML document. We will explain elements shortly in this appendix.

Comments As in HTML, XML provides for document comments. Comments start with “<!—” and end with “-->“, as shown in our example:

```
<?xml version="1.0"?>
<?xml-stylesheet type="text/xsl" href="Books.xsl"?>
<!DOCTYPE Books SYSTEM "Books.DTD">
<!--Sample XML document-->
```

Although typically you may add comments to the prologue section of an XML document, a comment can actually appear anywhere in the document. Comments placed in the prologue usually describe the overview information that applies to the entire document. In-line comments are more suitable for describing a specific piece of the document, such as the processing logic in an XSL file, as you will see in Appendix B.

Document Body

In our Books XML example, everything beyond the fourth line of text (the comment line) is the document body. Whereas the prologue section may be optional, an XML document must have a document body. This body must have one or more *elements*, and may contain *attributes*, as well as a *CDATA section*. The following lists the document body section of our Books XML example, which consists of elements, attributes, and texts:

```
<Books>
  <Book ISBN="0-7897-2458-8">
    <Title>Visual Basic and COM+ Programming By Example</Title>
    <Publisher>QUE</Publisher>
    <Authors>
      <Author>Peishu Li</Author>
    </Authors>
    <Price>34.99</Price>
  </Book>
  <Book ISBN="0-07-213338-4">
    <Title>BizTalk Server 2000 Developer's Guide</Title>
    <Publisher>Osborne/McGraw-Hill</Publisher>
    <Authors>
      <Author>Peishu Li</Author>
    </Authors>
```

```
    <Price>59.99</Price>
  </Book>
</Books>
```

Elements Elements in XML provide a mechanism for identifying named sections of a document. The Books XML example contains six elements: Books, Book, Title, Publisher, Authors, Author, and Price.

An element consists of markup tags that identify the name, start, and end of the element. The markup tag that identifies the start of an element is called a *start tag* and is expressed as <Element_Name>. Similarly, the markup tag that signifies the end of an element is called an *end tag*, in the form of </Element_Name>. Therefore, a Title element can be expressed as:

```
<Title>BizTalk Server 2000 Developer's Guide</Title>
```

Here the name of this element is "Title". The Title element consists of a start tag, <Title> and an end tag, </Title>.

An element can contain attributes, texts, CDATA sections and other elements (called *child elements*). The hierarchical relationships between elements in an XML document can be represented as a tree structure. Figure A-1 illustrates the tree structure of the Books sample XML document.

The relationships illustrated in Figure A-1 can also be referred to using a family tree metaphor. For example, the Books element contains Book child elements. The Book element in turn contains Title, Publisher, Authors, and Price child elements.

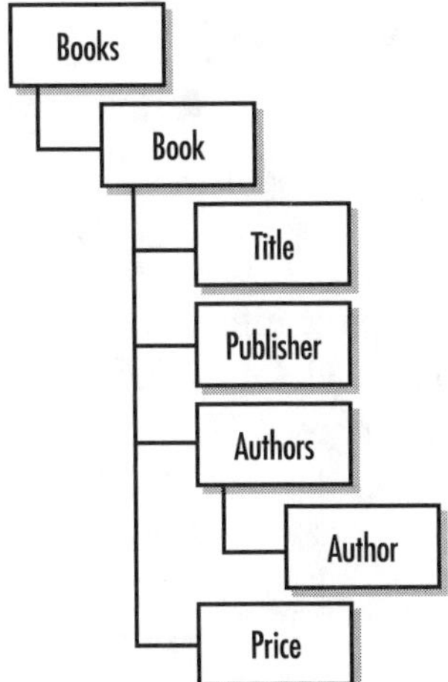

Figure A-1 *The relationships between elements in the Books XML sample*

The Books element is the parent element of the Book element, which in turn is the parent element of the Title, Publisher, Authors, and Price elements. The Authors element also contains child element(s)—for instance, the Author element(s). The highest level element, Books, is called a *root element*. As you will see later in this appendix, a well-formed XML document must have one, and only one, root element.

An element can be empty, without any child elements and/or *texts* (we will explain texts later in this appendix). An empty element can be represented in either of the following two syntaxes:

<Element_Name></Element_Name> or <Element_Name/>

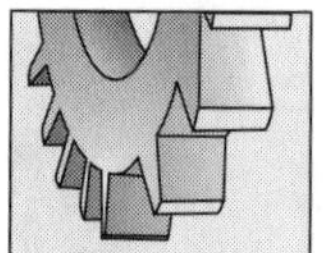

TIP

Microsoft Internet Explorer 5 or above contains a built-in XML parser (MSXML) which allows you to display an XML document directly inside the web browser (with the help of a default XSL stylesheet as we will explain in Appendix B). When an empty element is encountered, it is always displayed in IE 5 in the form </Element_Name>, even though the original file uses the <Element_Name></Element_Name> format. To update your MSXML, navigate to http://msdn.microsoft.com/xml and get the latest version, currently MSXML 3.0.

Attributes An element can also optionally contain attributes. An attribute is a name-value pair embedded in the start tag of the element as:

<Element_Name Attribute1_Name = "Value1" Attribute_Name2= "Value2"...>

For example, the Book element has an ISBN attribute:

```
<Book ISBN="0-07-213338-4">
  <!--Other elements have been omitted for brevity-->
</Book>
```

In addition to providing descriptive information about the element, attributes can also be used as an alternative to child elements. For example, we can use child elements to describe the dimensions of a box:

```
<Box>
  <Length>10</Length>
  <Width>8</Width>
  <Height>5</Height>
</Box>
```

Alternatively, we can also use attributes instead of child elements to describe the dimensions of the box:

```
<Box Length="10" Width="8" Height="5"/>
```

No one approach is better than the other. Choosing which to use is mostly a matter of design trade-off. Although the attribute approach tends to use less spaces due to the absence of some extra markup tags, the element approach, on the other hand, offers more flexibility and extensibility to the XML document. For example, you can add child elements to an existing element, but you cannot do the same to an attribute. The XML representation of an ADO recordset uses both attributes and elements rather than just elements. The XML version of query results in SQL Server 2000 can use both element only and element/attribute combinations, depending on user choice–although the default is to use both elements and attributes.

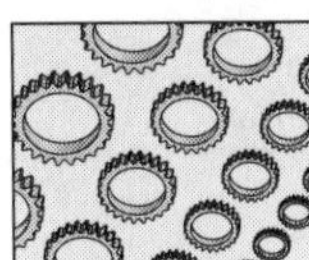

NOTE

An element that contains only attributes, and no textual information, is also considered an empty element.

Texts An element can optionally contain textual information called *text*. A text is surrounded by a *start tag* and an *end tag*. For example, the phrase "BizTalk Server 2000 Developer's Guide" inside the Title element is a text.

```
<Title>BizTalk Server 2000 Developer's Guide</Title>
```

Text usually appears at the leaf-level of an XML document tree, but elements that contain text can also have child elements.

CDATA Sections CDATA sections provide a mechanism for sheltering the document contents from XML parser validation. They can be used to escape text containing characters that would otherwise be recognized as markup symbols (for example, "<", ">", "&", etc.). It notifies XML parsers that anything included inside a 7CDATA section should not be parsed. The CDATA section is constructed using the following syntax:

```
<![CDATA[Contents_of_The_CDATA_Section]]>
```

For example, we can add two Contents elements to the Books XML document to describe the contents of the books. The first Contents element contains a CDATA section which uses ">", a preserved character in XML:

```
<Books>
  <Book ISBN="0-7897-2458-8">
```

```
    <Title>Visual Basic and COM+ Programming By Example</Title>
    <Contents><![CDATA[A book about programming COM+ services for
Visual Basic developers with > 1 year's experience in VB programming.
]]></Contents>
    <Publisher>QUE</Publisher>
    <Authors>
      <Author>Peishu Li</Author>
    </Authors>
    <Price>34.99</Price>
  </Book>
  <Book ISBN="0-07-213338-4">
    <Title>BizTalk Server 2000 Developer's Guide</Title>
    <Contents>An advance guide to BizTalk Server 2000</Contents>
    <Publisher>Osborne/McGraw-Hill</Publisher>
    <Authors>
      <Author>Peishu Li</Author>
    </Authors>
    <Price>49.99</Price>
  </Book>
</Books>
```

Others

So far, you have seen the majority of XML syntax constructs. In the following few sections, we will discuss how XML handles several special cases of character and entity references, white spaces, and language identification.

Character and Entity References Character and entity references provide a special way of representing characters so you don't have to directly type in the character from the keyboards.

A *character reference* refers to a specific character in the ISO/IED 10646 character set. An *entity reference* refers to the content of a named entity. To represent a character by its decimal code reference, use this syntax:

&#Decimal_Code;

The syntax for hexadecimal references is (notice the extra "x" after "&#"):

&#xHexadecimal_Code;

For example, the decimal code in the ISO/IED 10646 character set for letter "A" (capital letter) is 65, whereas its corresponding hexadecimal code is 41. Therefore, we can represent letter "A" in two ways: A or A as shown in the following example:

```
<char_ref_test>
  <dec>&#65;</dec>
  <hex>&#x41;</hex>
</char_ref_test>
```

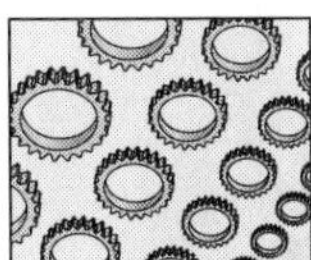

NOTE

In case you don't need to escape the character like in the previous example, you can always use the non-encoded expression as <normal>A</normal>.

When an XML parser encounters this XML document, it will interpret the text contents for both the dec element and the hex element as a capital letter "A". Figure A-2 illustrates how IE 5 displays the preceding XML document (IE 5 has a built-in XML parser—MSXML).

Character reference is useful in several special situations when you cannot directly enter the characters:

1. Characters that are used as part of the markups ("<", ">", "&", etc. This provides a more flexible alternative to the CDATA section approach. You can use entity references in a more granular manner than the CDATA section.)
2. Characters that are not available from the input device such as the keyboard of your computer (e.g., French characters on an English keyboard)
3. Characters that cannot be transported reliably through an operating system limited to one-byte characters

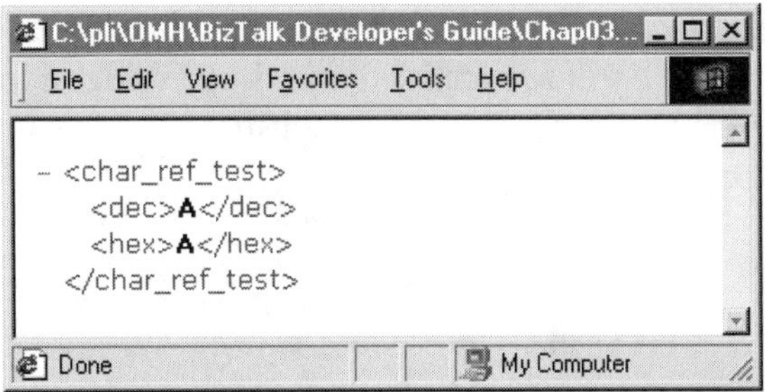

Figure A-2 *Both = and A are interpreted as capital letter "A" in IE 5*

XML provides five built-in entities that reference markup characters, as summarized in the following table:

Character	Entity Reference	Description
<	<	less than
>	≷	greater than
&	&	ampersand
‘	'	apostrophe or single quote
“	"	double quote

For example, a mathematical expression “X>Y” can be expressed as “X≷Y”. Similarly, a name “O’Reilly” becomes “O'Reilly”.

White Spaces White spaces refer to special characters such as spaces, tabs, and blank lines. Whereas the use of proper white spaces to indent the document greatly enhances its readability, white spaces are not always desirable in a delivered version of the document.

XML provides an *xml:space* attribute to tell XML processors how white spaces should be handled. The syntax of using the xml:space attribute is:

<Element_Name xml:space = “default”>

or

<Element_Name xml:space = “preserve”>

Setting the xml:space attribute to “default” will allow an XML processor to apply its default white space handling behavior, whereas a “preserve” value of the xml:space attribute tells the XML processor to preserve all the white spaces within the scope. The scope of the xml:space attributes applies to all descendants of the element where the attributes are used unless overridden by one of its child elements. Let’s use the Books example to demonstrate how the scope rule works for the xml:space attribute.

```
<Books>
  <Book ISBN="0-7897-2458-8" xml:space="preserve">
    <Title>Visual Basic and COM+ Programming By Example</Title>
    <Publisher>QUE</Publisher>
    <Authors xml:space="default">
      <Author>Peishu Li</Author>
```

```
    </Authors>
    <Price>34.99</Price>
  </Book>
  <Book ISBN="0-07-213338-4" xml:space="preserve">
    <Title>BizTalk Server 2000 Developer's Guide</Title>
    <Publisher>Osborne/McGraw-Hill</Publisher>
    <Authors>
      <Author xml:space="default">Peishu Li</Author>
    </Authors>
    <Price>49.99</Price>
  </Book>
</Books>
```

For this XML document, the XML processor will preserve all the white spaces for every Book element and its child elements except for the Authors elements and its child element, Author, which will be handled by the default white space handling behavior of the XML processor (either preserving the white spaces or ignoring them).

If the xml:space attribute is not used, it will be treated as if the xml:space="default" were used.

CAUTION

Not every XML processor supports the xml:space attribute. Check the documentation of the specific XML processor you want to use regarding the white space handling behaviors. Whereas MSXML parser supports the xml:space attributes, by default this attribute will be ignored unless the preserveWhiteSpace property of the DOMDocument object is set to true. You will learn about the DOM object models in Appendix C.

White spaces in attributes are usually normalized by most XML processors, i.e., tabs, carriage returns, and spaces are treated as single spaces. For example, the attribute in the following segment of an XML document is treated as "This is an excellent book!"

```
<Book Comments="This
is
an
excellent
book!"/>
```

In addition, white spaces must not be used before the XML declaration:

```
<?XML version="1.0"?>
```

Otherwise, the XML processor will report an error.

For end-of-line handling, XML treats the character sequence of carriage-return (#xD) and line-feed (#xA) as a single line-feed character (#xA). Any carriage-return character (#xD) that is not followed by a line-feed character (#xA) is also treated as a single line-feed character (#xA).

Language Identification XML provides an *xml:lang* attribute for you to specify the language in which the content is written. The values of the xml:lang attribute are language identifiers as defined by IETF RFC 1766 (available from **http://www.ietf.org/rfc./rfc1766.txt**). For example, the following segment of an XML document specifies that British English is used in the contents of a poem:

```
<Poem xml:lang="en-GB">
  <Title>My favourite colour</Title>
  <!-- the content of a British poem -->
</Poem>
```

Well-Formedness Rules

As of this section, we have introduced all the basic constructs of the XML syntax. XML is much less tolerant than HTML. To be qualified as a well-formed XML document, there are additional rules it must follow.

The Root Element

A well-formed XML document must have a single root element. For example, the following XML document is not well-formed because it has two root elements (two student elements):

```
<Student ID="800301">
  <Name>Joe Smith</Name>
  <Grade>3.5</Grade>
</Student>
<Student ID="800302">
  <Name>Mary Campbell</Name>
  <Grade>4.0</Grade>
</Student>
```

The built-in XML parser makes IE 5 a handy debugging tool that can help you construct XML documents. If you try to display the previous XML document in IE 5+, you will get an error, as shown in Figure A-3.

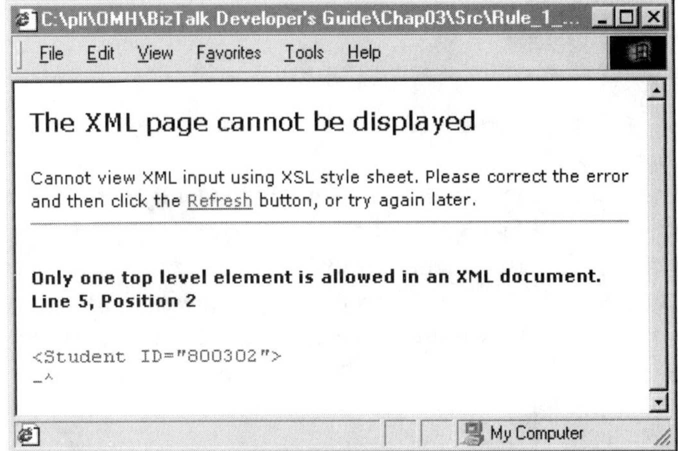

Figure A-3 *No root element error reported in IE 5*

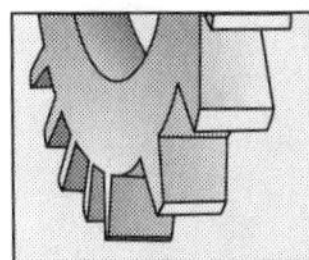

TIP

As you may already know from this book, you can use BizTalk Editor to create a specification (a BizTalk-specific XML document). In non-BizTalk scenarios, you can use the tools suggested in this Appendix.

The following XML document is well-formed:

```
<Students>
  <Student ID="800301">
    <Name>Joe Smith</Name>
    <Grade>3.5</Grade>
  </Student>
  <Student ID="800302">
    <Name>Mary Campbell</Name>
    <Grade>4.0</Grade>
  </Student>
</Students>
```

So is this one:

```
<Student ID="800301">
  <Name>Joe Smith</Name>
  <Grade>3.5</Grade>
</Student>
```

and so they display fine in IE5+.

End Tags Are Not Optional

In HTML, the following syntax is legal:

```
<P>Once upon a time, there was a mouse named Stuart Little.
```

It will start a new paragraph, and the browser will render it even if there is no corresponding </P> to close the paragraph.

In a well-formed XML document, however, a start tag must have a corresponding end tag, except in regards to empty elements. The following XML document is not considered well-formed, and will therefore generate an error, because the end tag </Paragraph> is missing:

```
<Paragraph>Once upon a time, there was a mouse named Stuart Little.
```

When displayed in IE5, the nature of the error will be appropriately reported, as shown in Figure A-4.

To fix the problem, add the missing end tag, </Paragraph>:

```
<Paragraph>Once upon a time, there was a mouse named Stuart Little.
</Paragraph>
```

Case Sensitivity

In HTML, markup tags are not case sensitive. For example, the following syntax is legal in HTML:

```
<B>BizTalk Server 2000 Developer's Guide</b>
```

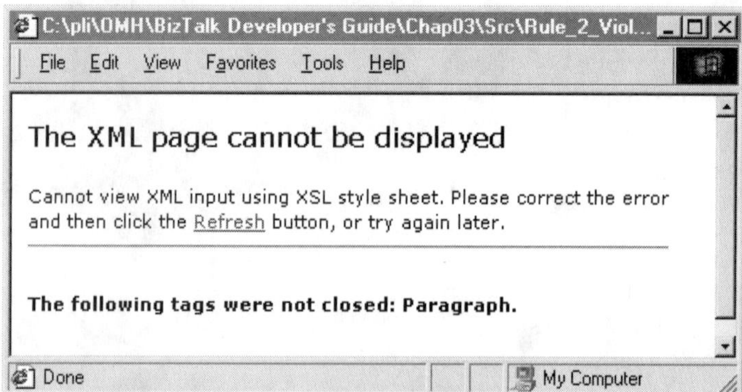

Figure A-4 *The end tag missing error reported in IE 5*

The web browser will render the text "BizTalk Server 2000 Developer's Guide" in a bold font.

In contrast, XML markup tags ARE case sensitive. <Strong> and <strong> are considered two different elements, and so is <STRONG>. If you save the preceding content into a file with an .xml extension and display it in IE 5, you will get an error as shown in Figure A-5.

You must complete each start tag with the case sensitive end tag. That is, you can use either <Strong></Strong> or <strong></strong> together , but not <Strong></strong> nor <strong></Strong>.

No Element Overlapping

In HTML, the following syntax is allowed:

```
<Strong><Em>BizTalk Server 2000 Developer's Guide</Strong></Em>
```

It will be formatted in a Web Browser as a Bold and Italic font. Note the strong element is interwoven with the Em element.

In XML, however, every tag (element) should be neatly nested. Overlapped elements like the previous one will cause an error to XML processors as shown in Figure A-6.

The correct syntax in XML is:

```
<Strong><Em>BizTalk Server 2000 Developer's Guide</Em></Strong>
```

where the Em element is completely nested inside the Strong element.

Figure A-5 *Case sensitivity error reported in IE 5*

Figure A-6 *Element overlapping error reported in IE 5*

Attribute Values Must Be Quoted

Placing the values of attributes in quotes is optional in HTML, as evidenced in the following example in which the attributes are not quoted:

```
<INPUT Type=Submit Value=Submit>
```

The preceding syntax will cause problems in XML. First, the value of attributes Type and Value are not quoted. Second, the INPUT element does not require an end tag </INPUT>. To be acceptable in XML, the previous syntax should be changed to the following (notice the shorthand syntax for empty element is used here):

```
<INPUT Type="Submit" Value="Submit"/>
```

Using Namespaces

Unlike HTML in which you have to use a set of predefined markup tags, XML provides a great flexibility and extensibility which allows you to define your own elements and attributes. XML was intended to be understandable for both humans and computer programs. The arbitrarily defined vocabularies (elements and attributes) in XML, however, can sometimes cause problems, especially for computer applications that are used to process XML documents.

Why Use Namespaces

Let's look at the following example describing a book order:

```
<Order>
  <ID>1001</ID>
  <Customer>
    <ID>30081</ID>
  </Customer>
  <Items>
    <Product>
      <ID>58390</ID>
      <Name>Computer Book</Name>
      <UnitPrice>59.99</UnitPrice>
    </Product>
    <Quantity>1</Quantity>
    <Price>59.55</Price>
  </Items>
</Order>
```

As you might have noticed, the ID element has been repeatedly used under three different contexts. The first ID uniquely identifies the order. The second ID identifies the customer. The third ID is a product identifier. This is not an issue for a human reader who can tell these IDs apart based on their contexts, our business knowledge about an order, or even our common sense. A computer program, however, does not have this kind of knowledge or common sense. There must be some way in which we can resolve this naming conflict. The solution to resolving naming conflicts in XML comes from using *namespaces*.

How to Declare Namespaces

A namespace defines a unique qualification for an element or an attribute, providing a context for computer programs to distinguish the elements that have the same names. Namespaces are declared by using the *xmlns* attribute, as in the following syntax:

<Element_Name **xmlns:**NameSpace_Prefix = "NameSpace_URI">

In the preceding order sample XML document, you can define three namespaces, one for orders, another for customers, and a third for products:

```
<Order xmlns:ord="http://www.xmlexampleorg.com/orders"
       xmlns:cust="http://www.xmlexampleorg.com/customers"
       xmlns:prd="http://www.xmlexampleorg.com/products">
```

After properly declaring the namespaces, you can use the prefix to qualify the elements and/or attributes in your XML documents:

```
<ord:Order xmlns:ord="http://www.xmlexampleorg.com/orders"
       xmlns:cust="http://www.xmlexampleorg.com/customers"
       xmlns:prd="http://www.xmlexampleorg.com/products">
  <ord:ID>1001</ord:ID>
  <cust:Customer>
    <cust:ID>30081</cust:ID>
  </cust:Customer>
  <ord:Items>
    <prd:Product>
      <prd:ID>58390</prd:ID>
<prd:Name>Computer Book</prd:Name>
      <prd:UnitPrice>59.99</prd:UnitPrice>
    </prd:Product>
    <ord:Quantity>1</prd:Quantity>
    <ord:Price>59.55</ord:Price>
  </ord:Items>
</ord:Order>
```

Now when the XML parser reads this document, it will understand which ID means what.

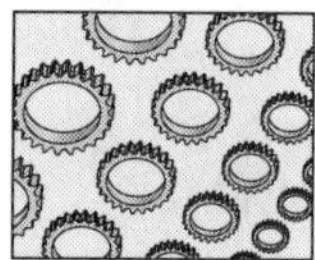

NOTE

A prefix is only a placeholder. You can use any name for the prefix as long as it conforms with the well-formedness constraints.

A namespace declared in this way is called *explicit declaration*. You can also use *default declaration* for namespaces. For example, another way to declare the orders namespace looks like this:

```
<Order xmlns="http://www.xmlexampleorg.com/orders">
```

Here the prefix "ord" has been left out. By using the default namespace, our orders XML document then becomes:

```
<Order xmlns="http://www.xmlexampleorg.com/orders"
       xmlns:cust="http://www.xmlexampleorg.com/customers"
       xmlns:prd="http://www.xmlexampleorg.com/products">
  <ID>1001</ID>
  <cust:Customer>
    <cust:ID>30081</cust:ID>
  </cust:Customer>
  <Items>
    <prd:Product>
      <prd:ID>58390</prd:ID>
      <prd:Name>Computer Book</prd:Name>
      <prd:UnitPrice>59.99</prd:UnitPrice>
    </prd:Product>
    <Quantity>1</Quantity>
    <Price>59.55</Price>
  </Items>
</Order>
```

For those elements (or attributes) without a namespace prefix, the default namespace (the order namespace) is implied.

The scope rule of namespace is similar to the rule for the xml:whitespace attribute. The first element where the namespace is declared determines the namespace of its child elements and/or attributes, unless overridden by one of its child elements that have their own namespace declaration. Let's look at the simplified version of our order XML document:

```
<Order xmlns="http://www.xmlexampleorg.com/orders"
       xmlns:cust="http://www.xmlexampleorg.com/customers"
       xmlns:prd="http://www.xmlexampleorg.com/products">
  <ID>1001</ID>
  <cust:Customer>
    <ID>30081</ID>
  </cust:Customer>
  <Items>
    <prd:Product>
      <ID>58390</ID>
    </prd:Product>
  </Items>
</Order>
```

The first ID element uses the default namespace for orders. The second ID implies use of the customers namespace, although the prefix "cust" is not explicitly used. Similarly, the third ID implies the products namespace (prd).

Validating XML Documents

We have discussed basic XML syntaxes, vocabularies, well-formedness constraints, and how to use namespaces to prevent possible naming conflicts. Using the knowledge you have learned so far in this appendix, you can build a perfectly well-formed XML document. This may be good for many situations, but there may be other instances where you want more control of the XML document's structure. For example, you may want to control what elements and attributes are allowed in an XML document and in which sequence they appear, how frequently a particular element or attribute should appear, what relationships are defined between different elements, and so on. In other words, you want to *validate* the XML document.

There are two mechanisms with which you can validate XML documents. They are Document Type Definition (DTD) and XML Schema. A valid XML document is one that follows the constraints defined by a DTD or an XML Schema. An XML document that conforms to the constraints of a DTD or XML schema is a valid XML document. DTD is a part of the SGML specification, an ISO standard, used for validations, but it does have some limitations, which you will see shortly in this appendix. XML Schema is now a W3C draft that will soon become a recommendation. XML Data Reduced (XDR) Schema is a functional subset of the XML Schema that Microsoft created to give their customers much of the advantages of XML Schema before W3C ratified an appropriate standard. For example, SQL Server 2000, Commerce Server 2000, ADO 2.5 and above, and BizTalk Server 2000 all use XDR Schema in their XML features.

DTD and XDR Schema will be the topics for the rest of this appendix. Let's discuss DTD first.

Document Type Definition (DTD)

You have seen a DOCTYPE declaration used to link a DTD to the Books XML sample document earlier in this appendix. Now it's time to go under the hood to see what the DTD document itself looks like. The following is a Books XML document, modified by adding a DOCTYPE declaration:

```
<!DOCTYPE Books SYSTEM "Books.DTD">
<Books>
  <Book ISBN="0-7897-2458-8">
```

```
    <Title>Visual Basic and COM+ Programming By Example</Title>
    <Publisher>QUE</Publisher>
    <Authors>
      <Author>Peishu Li</Author>
    </Authors>
    <Price>34.99</Price>
  </Book>
  <Book ISBN="0-07-213338-4">
    <Title>BizTalk Server 2000 Developer's Guide</Title>
    <Publisher>Osborne/McGraw-Hill</Publisher>
    <Authors>
      <Author>Peishu Li</Author>
    </Authors>
    <Price>49.99</Price>
  </Book>
</Books>
```

The following is the content of Books.DTD used to validate the Books XML document:

```
<!--Books.DTD-->
<!ELEMENT Books (Book+)>
<!ELEMENT Book (Title,Publisher,Authors,Price)>
<!ATTLIST Book ISBN  CDATA #REQUIRED>
<!ELEMENT Title (#PCDATA)>
<!ELEMENT Publisher (#PCDATA)>
<!ELEMENT Authors (Author+)>
<!ELEMENT Author (#PCDATA)>
<!ELEMENT Price (#PCDATA)>
```

As you can see, the entire DTD document consists of a number of ELEMENT and ATTLIST declarations that define elements and attributes as well as their content model.

Elements

Elements are declared in DTD as:

<!ELEMENT Element_Name Content_Model or Element_List>

There are three possible values for Content_Model, EMPTY, ANY, and #PCDATA, as summarized in the following table:

Content Model	Explanation
EMPTY	An element declared as EMPTY does not contain any child elements or texts. However, an empty element can have attributes. *Examples:* <!ELEMENT Customer EMPTY> <Customer /> or <Customer ID="123"/>
ANY	An element declared as ANY can contain any combination of child elements and texts. However, the element can just contain text only. Note: This content model is rarely used and is typically replaced by the Element_List declaration which provides more flexibility.
#PCDATA	#PCDATA stands for parsed character data. This content model is used to declare elements that contain only text. Examples: <!ELEMENT Title #PCDATA> <Title>BizTalk Server 2000 Developer's Guide</Title>

The Element_List is used to specify the relationship between elements separated by commas and enclosed in parentheses. The following additional characters are used to specify a particular pattern.

Character	Explanation
+	One or more elements can appear under the parent element
*	Zero or more elements can appear under the parent element
?	Zero or one element can appear under the parent element
|	Either one of the elements on each side of the "|" can appear
,	Used to separate different elements and determine the sequence of the elements

The following element declaration defines the Order element as having exactly one ID element, one or more Customer elements, and zero or more Items elements. These elements must appear in the sequence as defined:

```
<!ELEMENT Order (ID, Customer+, Items*)
```

The Items element in turn can have exactly one Product element, one Quantity element and one Price element, appearing in that order:

```
<ELEMENT Items (Product, Quantity, Price)
```

The Product element can have exactly one ID element, zero or one Name element, and exactly one UnitPrice element:

```
<ELEMENT Product (ID, Name*,UnitPrice)
```

The following example defines an Address element that has exactly one StreetAddress1 element, optionally one StreetAddress2 element, exactly one City element, either one State element or one Province element but not both, optionally either one ZipCode element or one PostalCode element but not both, and exactly one Country element:

```
<!ELEMENT Address
(StreetAddress1,StreetAddress2?,City,(State|Province),(ZipCode|Postal
Code)*,Country)
```

Attributes

The other important construct of an XML document is the attributes. For that, DTD provides an ATTLIST declaration, in the following syntax (The Attribute_Type and the Default_Value are optional):

<ATTLIST Element_Name Attribute_Name Attribute_Type Default_Value>

You can use one of the possible attribute types in the following table:

Attribute Type	Explanation
CDATA	Character data
ID	Used to uniquely identify an attribute
IDREF	Provides a reference to an element with an ID attribute
IDREFS	A number of IDREF separated by spaces. Provides a many to one relationship to ID
NMTOKEN	A name token
NMTOKENS	A number of NMTOKENS separated by spaces
ENTITY	Identifies an external entity
ENTITIES	A number of ENTITY separated by spaces

The following table summarizes the possible default values of an attribute:

Default Value	Explanation
#REQUIRED	Mandatory attribute
#IMPLIED	Optional attribute
#FIXED	A default value for the attribute must be supplied

Let's look at some examples. Here is the declaration for the ISBN attribute of the Book elements as shown in the Books.DTD document earlier in this section:

```
<!ATTLIST Book ISBN  CDATA #REQUIRED>
```

This simple example specifies that the ISBN attribute of the Book element is a character data and its appearance in the Books element is mandatory.

The following example demonstrates the use of the #FIXED with a value of "32" to permanently set the value for the FreezingPoint attribute of the Temperature element:

```
<!ATTLIST Temperature FreezingPoint #FIXED "32">
```

The following attribute declaration specifies the Country attribute of the Address element with a default value "USA":

```
<!ATTLIST Address CDATA Country "USA">
```

An optional attribute can be declared using #IMPLIED:

```
<!ATTLIST Address CDATA Country #IMPLIED>
```

The following example provides an enumeration of two possible values for the Gender attribute of the Student element, male or female, and default to female:

```
<!ATTLIST Student Gender CDATA #REQUIRED (male|female) "female">
```

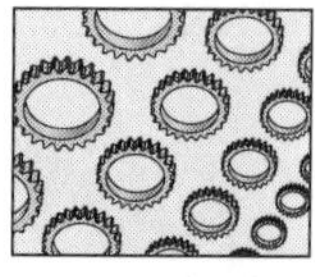

NOTE

Unlike elements, the order of attributes in an element is not important.

Entities

Entities in DTD are reusable units of contents. Earlier in this appendix we discussed five built-in entities used in entity reference. In this section, we will explore how entities can be used in DTD.

Entities in DTD are declared as:

<!ENTITY Entity_Name Entity_Content>

In the XML document, you refer to the entity as &Entity_Name;.

The following example demonstrates how to reuse the Shipper entity declared in DTD in an Order XML documentation:

```
<?xml version="1.0"?>
<!DOCTYPE Order [
<!--Elements and attributes declarations -->
<!ENTITY Shipper
'<Info>
   <Name>Lone Star Express</Name>
   <Type>Local Shipping Company</Type>
</Info>'
]
<Order>
  <!--Order details-->
  &Shipper;
</Order>
```

The entity can also be defined in an external file. For example, the Shipper entity might be defined in a ShipperEntity.txt file. To refer to an externally defined entity, you use the SYSTEM keyword:

<!ENTITY Entity_Name SYSTEM "Entity_Source">

For example, when you use an external entity file, the preceding XML document will look like this:

```
<?xml version="1.0"?>
<!DOCTYPE Order [
<!--Elements and attributes declarations -->
<!ENTITY Shipper SYSTEM "ShipperEntity.txt"
]
<Order>
  <!--Order details-->
  &Shipper;
</Order>
```

Notations

Notations provide a way to refer to non-textural data such as GIF and JPEG image files in XML documents. To declare a Notation, use the following syntax:

> <!NOTATION Notation_Name SYSTEM "External_AppName" or "Notation_Type">

The following examples demonstrate how to declare notations.

```
<!NOTATION jpg SYSTEM "LView.exe">
<!NOTATION gif SYSTEM "image/gif">
```

You can use the notation in the following manner:

```
<!ATTLIST Graphic FileType NOTATION (jpg|gif)>

<Graphic FileType="gif">
```

The Whole Picture

Now it's time to put the whole thing together. Let's go back to the DTD for our Books.xml. Here it is again:

```
<!ELEMENT Books (Book+)>
<!ELEMENT Book (Title,Publisher,Authors,Price)>
<!ATTLIST Book ISBN  CDATA #REQUIRED>
<!ELEMENT Title (#PCDATA)>
<!ELEMENT Publisher (#PCDATA)>
<!ELEMENT Authors (Author+)>
<!ELEMENT Author (#PCDATA)>
<!ELEMENT Price (#PCDATA)>
```

This time, it should look very straightforward to you. The first line defines the root element, Books. It says that the Books document consists of one or more Book elements. The next line defines the layout of the Book element. It contains a Title element, followed by a Publisher element, then an Authors element, and finally a Price element. The line after this defines a mandatory ISBN attribute for the Book element. The lines that follow define the Title, Publisher, Authors, Author, and Price elements. The Authors element contains one or more Author child elements, while the rest of the elements are texts (#PCDATA).

To refer to the DTD in the XML document, you can use the DOCTYPE declaration:

```
<!DOCTYPE Books SYSTEM "Books.DTD">
<Books>
<!--Document contents-->
</Books>
```

Alternatively, you can embed the DTD inside the XML document itself (in-line DTD):

```
<!DOCTYPE Books [
<!ELEMENT Books (Book+)>
<!ELEMENT Book (Title,Publisher,Authors,Price)>
<!ATTLIST Book ISBN  CDATA #REQUIRED>
<!ELEMENT Title (#PCDATA)>
<!ELEMENT Publisher (#PCDATA)>
<!ELEMENT Authors (Author+)>
<!ELEMENT Author (#PCDATA)>
<!ELEMENT Price (#PCDATA)>
]>
<Books>
<!--Document contents-->
</Books>
```

Limitations of DTD

Although DTD provides a great way of defining the structure constraints for an XML document, it has a number of limitations:

1. As DTD originated from the SGML specification, DTD itself does not use the XML syntax. This means there is a second syntax to learn: SGML syntax. It also means you cannot use regular XML APIs such as the Document Object Model (DOM) to access and manipulate the document structure defined in DTD (the metadata).
2. DTD does not support data types. All it has is character data, with no notion of integers, dates, reals, and other data types.
3. DTD uses a closed content model. You must follow exactly the sequence of elements defined in the DTD without deviation.

To overcome these limitations of DTD, Microsoft has proposed a better solution for defining the metadata of an XML document—XML Data, which was submitted to the W3C. The W3C also took submissions from other parties, such as DCD, SOX, and DDML, to create the XML Schema draft. Microsoft chose to give its customers the benefits of XML Schema before going through the long standardization process. The XML Data Reduced (XDR) Schema specification was created, this being a subset of XML Data and a functional subset of XML Schema. Microsoft has been implementing XDR support across all of their products and technologies, such as Microsoft .NET Servers (including BizTalk Server 2000) and ADO 2.5 or above. XDR Schema is the topic of the next section.

XML Data Reduced (XDR) Schema

Before we discuss the details of XDR Schemas, let's first look at a simple XDR Schema example. The following is an XDR equivalent of the Books.DTD you saw earlier when we discussed DTDs:

```
<?xml version = "1.0"?>
<Schema name="BooksSchema"
    xmlns="urn:schemas-microsoft-com:xml-data"
    xmlns:dt="urn:schemas-microsoft-com:xml-datatypes">
  <ElementType name="Books" content="eltOnly">
    <element type="Book" minOccurs="1" maxOccurs="*"/>
  </ElementType>
  <ElementType name ="Book" content="eltOnly" order="seq" >
    <attribute type ="ISBN" dt:type="string" required="yes"/>
    <element type ="Title" dt:type="string" minOccurs="1"
maxOccurs="1"/>
    <element type = "Publisher" dt:type="string" minOccurs="1"
maxOccurs="1"/>
    <element type = "Authors" dt:type="string" minOccurs="1"
maxOccurs="1"/>
    <element type = "Price" dt:type="float"  minOccurs="1"
maxOccurs="1"/>
  </ElementType>
  <AttributeType name="ISBN"/>
  <ElementType name = "Title" content="textOnly" />
  <ElementType name = "Publisher" content="textOnly" />
  <ElementType name = "Authors" content="eltOnly" >
    <element type = "Author" minOccurs="1" maxOccurs="*"/>
  </ElementType>
```

```
  <ElementType name = "Author" content="textOnly" />
  <ElementType name = "Price" content="textOnly" />
</Schema>
```

As you can see, an XDR Schema is itself a well-formed XML document. That is, the document consists of elements and attributes.

There are four major elements: *ElementType*, *AttributesType*, *element*, and *attribute*. They are used to define the core components of an XML document–elements and attributes. There are also other types of elements in XDR, like those used for declaring a schema document and setting namespaces (the *Schema* element), specifying the data types of elements and attributes (the *datatype* element), organizing and grouping contents of elements (the *group* element), and adding annotations to describe elements and attributes (the *description* element). By using these elements and their attributes, XDR Schema provides a better alternative to DTD for validating XML documentations. The advantages of XDR Schema are not restricted to its use of XML syntax. It also supports data types, and an open content model.

In the next few sections we are going to discuss all the elements used in XDR Schema and show you how to use them and their attributes to define the structure (the schema) of an XML document. We will also show you equivalent DTD declarations whenever appropriate to give you an opportunity to see how a particular structure is defined in both technologies.

Defining Elements

XDR Schema uses the ElementType element to define elements in a similar manner to the ELEMENT declaration in DTD. Here is the syntax for the ElementType element (we appropriately formatted the syntax to improve readability):

```
<ElementType
   name = “Name”
   content = “Element”
   model = “Openness”
   order = “Order_of_Child_Elements”
   dt:type = “Data_Type” >
   <!— optionally a list of child elements and/or attributes—>
</ElementType>
```

As you can see, the ElementType element can have five attributes, as described in the following:

The *name* attribute. This attribute determines the name of an element to be used in an XML document. The name attribute is required. You must specify a name for an element.

The *content* attribute. This attribute determines the type of element, i.e., whether an element should be empty or contain text, elements, or both. There are four possible values of the content attribute, as described in the following table:

Attribute Value	Description
Empty	This is an empty element.
EltOnly	The element can only contain child elements. It cannot contain any text.
TextOnly	The element can only contain text. It cannot contain child elements.
Mixed	The element can contain both child elements and text. This is the default value of the content attribute. When the content value is set to "mixed," the *minOccurs* and *maxOccurs* attributes (we will describe these two attributes shortly) of its child elements will be ignored by the XML processor that validates the XML document against the schema.

The *model* attribute. There are two possible values for the model attribute, "open" or "closed." The default value is "open." A closed element model is similar to the DTD element model in which an element can only contain child elements or attributes that are explicitly declared in the schema. An open element model, however, allows you to add additional elements and/or attributes that have not been explicitly declared in the schema. These additional elements and/or attributes can come from the same namespace or from a different namespace. This type of open element content model allows you to validate only part of an XML document and thus provide extensibility and flexibility to the schema.

The *order* attribute. This attribute determines the allowed ordering behavior for the element's child elements. There are three possible values for the order attribute:

Attribute Value	Description
One	Only one of a set of child elements is allowed. If you specify the order attribute to "one," you must also specify the model attribute of the ElementType element as "closed."
Seq	The child elements must appear in the sequence specified.
Many	Child elements can appear (or not appear) in any order. If you specify the order attribute as "many," the maxOccurs attributes of its child elements will be ignored by the XML processor.

The *type* attribute (dt:type). This attribute specifies the data type for the element. The prefix dt stands for the appropriate datatype namespace, as we will describe shortly.

When you declare an element that has child elements and/or attributes, you need to further specify which child elements and/or attributes this element has by using two additional elements—the *element* element and the *attribute* element.

The element that refers to an appropriate ElementType is also called *element* and has the following syntax:

```
<element
   type = “Type”
   minOccurs = “0_or_1}”
   maxOccurs = “1_or_*”
>
```

The attribute elements thus take the following form:

```
<attribute
   type = “Type”
   default = “Default”
   Required = “yes_or_no”
>
```

Both element and attribute elements use a *type* attribute to specify the element or the attribute defined elsewhere in the schema document. The rest of the attributes for the *element* and *attribute* elements are pretty self-explanatory.

The declarations for the Title, Publisher, Author, and Price element are straightforward. All of them contain only texts and not child elements:

```
<ElementType name = "Title" content="textOnly" />
<ElementType name = "Publisher" content="textOnly" />
<ElementType name = "Author" content="textOnly" />
<ElementType name = "Price" content="textOnly" />
```

These declarations are equivalent to the following DTD ELEMENT declaration:

```
<!ELEMENT Title (#PCDATA)>
<!ELEMENT Publisher (#PCDATA)>
<!ELEMENT Author (#PCDATA)>
<!ELEMENT Price (#PCDATA)>
```

The declarations for the Authors and Books elements are a bit complex. Both of them contain child elements. The Authors element contains one or more Author elements, so it appears as:

```
<ElementType name = "Authors" content="eltOnly" >
  <element type = "Author" minOccurs="1" maxOccurs="*"/>
</ElementType>
```

Notice the use of the *element* element. We specify the *type* attribute as "Author", which is an element we declared elsewhere in the schema (using the ElementType element). The *minOccurs* and *maxOccurs* attributes determine that the Author element should appear one or more times under the Authors element.

This DTD version of the Authors element is declared as:

```
<!ELEMENT Authors (Author+)>
```

The declaration of the Books element (the root element) is very similar to the Authors element:

```
<ElementType name="Books" content="eltOnly">
  <element type="Book" minOccurs="1" maxOccurs="*"/>
</ElementType>
```

And here is the DTD equivalent:

```
<!ELEMENT Books (Book+)>
```

The declaration of the Book element is a bit more interesting:

```
<ElementType name ="Book" content="eltOnly" order="seq" >
  <attribute type ="ISBN" dt:type="string" required="yes"/>
  <element type ="Title" dt:type="string" minOccurs="1"
maxOccurs="1"/>
  <element type = "Publisher" dt:type="string" minOccurs="1"
maxOccurs="1"/>
  <element type = "Authors" dt:type="string" minOccurs="1"
maxOccurs="1"/>
  <element type = "Price" dt:type="float" minOccurs="1"
maxOccurs="1"/>
</ElementType>
```

First, we used the order attribute of the ElementType element and specified its value as "seq". This means that the child elements of the Book element must appear in the sequence as they are specified in the schema. That is, the Title element must be followed by the Publisher element, then the Authors element, and finally the Price element.

Second, the dt:type attributes are used to specify the data types of these child elements: string data type for Title, Publisher, and Author elements; float data type for the Price element.

Third, we used two attributes, minOccurs and maxOccurs, and set both to "1" to specify that these elements must appear once and only once under the Book element.

Finally, we used the *attribute* element to specify that the Book element must have an ISBN attribute (this is indicated by the type attribute of the attribute element). The data type is specified as string. The required attribute is set to "yes" to signify that this ISBN attribute for the Book element is mandatory. The ISBN attribute is declared elsewhere in the schema using the AttributeType element as you will see shortly in the next section.

The DTD version of the Books element declaration has a much neater form:

```
<!ELEMENT Book (Title,Publisher,Authors,Price)>
```

Defining Attributes

To define an attribute for an element in XDR Schema, you use the AttributeType element in the following syntax:

```
<AttributeType
   name = "Name"
   default = "Default"
   dt:type = "Data_Type"
   dt:values = "Enumerate_Values"
   required = "yes_or_no" >
</AttributeType>
```

Most of the attributes of the AttributeType element are straightforward and similar to the element identifiers. The *values* (dt:value, where dt is the prefix of the datatype namespace you will see in the next section) attribute may need a little bit of explanation. The values attribute provides a means of specifying an enumeration of possible values for the attribute, each separated by white spaces. For instance, the following example allows the *format* attribute of the Book element to have three possible values, Paperback, Hardcover, and Multimedia, with a default of Paperback:

```
<AttributeType name = "Format" dt:type = "string"
      dt:value = "Paperback Hardcover Multimedia"
      default = "Paperback" required = "no" />
```

The DTD equivalent looks like this:

```
<!ATTLIST Book Format CDATA (Paperback|Hardcover!Multimedia)
"Paperback" #IMPLIED>
```

The declaration of the ISBN attribute is simple:

```
<AttributeType name = "ISBN" dt:type = "string" required = "yes"/>
```

Its DTD declaration is:

```
<!ATTLIST Book ISBN CDATA #REQUIRED>
```

Now you can reference these attributes in the declaration of the Book element like this:

```
<ElementType name = "Book" content = "eltOnly" order = "seq" >
  <attribute type = "ISBN" dt:type = "string" required = "yes"/>
  <attribute type = "Format" dt:type = "string" required = "no"/>
  <!--other element references-->
</ElementType>
```

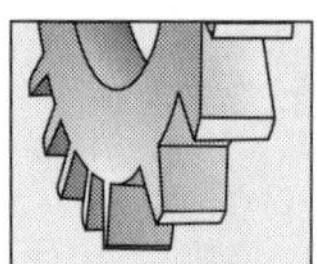

TIP

The ways of associating attributes with elements is different between XDR Schema and DTD. In XDR Schema, you reference the attribute inside the declaration of the element (in the ElementType), using the attribute *element as shown in the previous example. In DTD, on the other hand, you specify the name of the element inside the declaration attribute (in the ATTLIST).*

The Schema Information

The *Schema* element in XDR Schema allows you to specify the name of the schema document and appropriate namespaces:

```
<Schema name="BooksSchema"
    xmlns="urn:schemas-microsoft-com:xml-data"
    xmlns:dt="urn:schemas-microsoft-com:xml-datatypes">
```

When an external schema document is used, the *name* attribute is optional. If you use in-line schema as we will discuss shortly, you must specify the name.

The preceding example uses two standard namespaces, xml-data and xml-datatypes, both from the same Universal Resource Name (URN)— schemas-microsoft-com. The first namespace is the default namespace for the schema documents. The second namespace defines the available data types for the element and attributes of the schema.

In addition to these standard namespace declarations, you can also add custom namespaces and use an appropriate prefix to fully qualify the additional elements and attributes defined in your namespace. Of course, you must specify the model attribute of the ElementType element to "open."

Grouping

XDR Schema has a *group* element which is used under the ElementType element and allows you to specify constraints on a subset of child elements. The group element takes the following syntax:

<group order = "Order "minOccurs = "0_or_1" maxOccurs = "1_or_*">

The use of the *order* attribute of the group element is similar to the order attribute for the ElementType element:

<table>
<tr><th>Attribute Value</th><th>Description</th></tr>
<tr><td>One</td><td>Only one instance of each child element is allowed. This is similar to the "|" operator in DTD.</td></tr>
<tr><td>seq</td><td>The child elements must appear in the exact sequence as specified.</td></tr>
<tr><td>many</td><td>Child elements in the group can appear (or not appear) in any order.</td></tr>
</table>

The minOccurs and maxOccurs attributes are the same as for the *element* element we discussed before. Both of them have the default value of "1".

The following example uses a group element and sets its order attribute to "one", restricting the salary element to either an annual_salary child element or an hourly_pay element, but not both. The minOccurs and maxOccurs attributes are left out so there is only one occurrence of either case.

```
<ElementType name = "salary">
  <group order = "one">
    <element type = "annual_salary" />
    <element type = "hourly_rate" />
```

```
  </group>
</ElementType>
```

The DTD equivalent for the salary element declaration is:

```
<ELEMENT salary (annual|hourly)>
```

As a result, the following two instances of XML segments are both valid:

```
<salary>
 <annual_salary>50000</annual_salary>
</salary>
```

or:

```
<salary>
 <hourly_rate>25</hourly_rate>
</salary>
```

When used in conjunction with the ElementType element, the group element provides a flexible means of describing the content model of the child elements. In the following example, we specified the order attributes at both the element level and the group level:

```
<ElementType name = "address" order = "one">
  <element type = "street" />
  <element type = "city" />
  <group order = "seq">
    <element type = "state" />
    <element type = "zip" />
  </group>
  <group order = "seq">
    <element type = "province" />
    <element type = "postal" />
  </group>
  <element type = "country" />
</ElementType>
```

Both of the following address instances will be valid for the previous given schema:

```
<address>
  <street>123 XML Road</street>
  <city>XML Town</city>
```

```
  <state>XML State</state>
  <zip>12345</zip>
  <country>USA</country>
</address>
```

or:

```
<address>
  <street>123 XML Road</street>
  <city>XML Town</city>
  <province>XML Province</province>
  <postal>X1M2L3</postal>
  <country>Canada</country>
</address>
```

The DTD representation for the previous schema is:

```
<!ELEMENT address
(street,city,((state,zip)|(province,postal)),country>
```

Data Types

The *datatype* element of XDR Schema provides an alternative for the dt:type attribute of the ElementType and AttributeType elements. The following two schema segments are equivalent:

```
<ElementType name = "Title" dt:type = "string" content = "textOnly" />
```

or:

```
<ElementType name = "Title" content = "textOnly">
  <datatype dt:type = "string">
</ElementType>
```

TIP

Appendix A of this book lists all the data types supported in XDR Schema.

Annotation

XDR Schema provides a *description* element which allows you to add comments and annotations to any XDR Schema elements mentioned in previous sections. Because the description element is a standard XML tag, you can access its content more efficiently than the comments. The following example demonstrates how to use the description element to annotate the Books element:

```
<ElementType name = "Books">
  <description>
    This is the root element of the Books XML document.
  </description>
  <!--Other XML elements and attributes-->
</ElementType>
```

Referencing XDR Schema

Like with DTD, you can use an XDR Schema both externally or internally (in-line schema). To reference an XDR Schema that is externally defined, you use the namespace declaration, as demonstrated in the following example:

```
<Books xmlns = "x-schema:BooksSchema.xml">
  <Book ISBN = "0-7897-2458-8">
    <!--other elements-->
  </Book>
  <!--more book elements-->
</Books>
```

When you use the in-line schema, you use the following syntax:

<Root_Element xmlns:data="x-schema:#Schema_Name">

The Schema_Name following the "#" sign is the name attribute of the Schema element of your XDR Schema document. The following XML example uses an in-line schema in the Books XML document:

```
<Books xmlns:data = "x-schema:#BooksSchema">
  <Schema name = "BooksSchema"
    xmlns="urn:schemas-microsoft-com:xml-data"
    xmlns:dt="urn:schemas-microsoft-com:xml-datatypes">
    <!--The rest of the schema declaration-->
  </Schema>
  <Book ISBN = "0-7897-2458-8">
    <!--other elements-->
  </Book>
  <!--more book elements-->
</Books>
```

Introducing the XML Validator

We have demonstrated how to use both DTD and XDR Schema to define the structures of the XML document. In this section, we will introduce a very useful free XML validation tool that you can use to test your XML document instance against either a DTD or an XDR Schema to see if it is valid.

The tool is called XML Validator and can be downloaded from the MSDN download site at: **http://msdn.microsoft.com/downloads/samples/internet/xml/xml_validator/**.

Figure A-7 is a screen shot of the XML Validator.

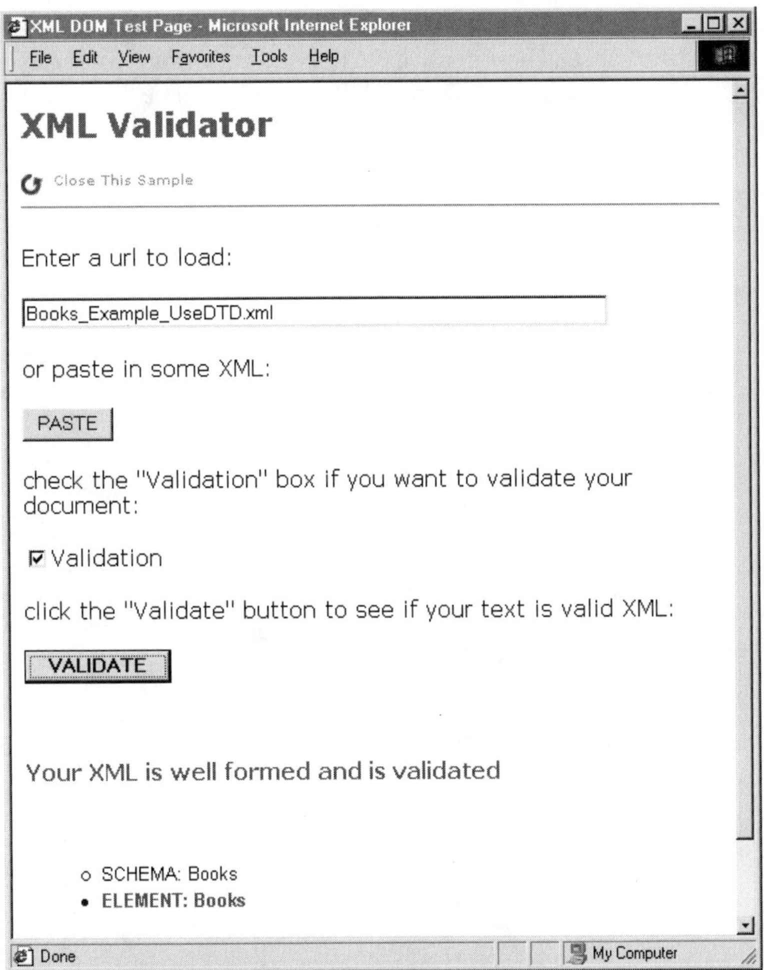

Figure A-7 *Usingt XML Validator to validate XML documents against DTDs or Schemas*

The XML Validator is an HTML-based tool with validating logics written in embedded Java Scripts (or VBScripts) to provide detailed information about the document being validated. The download package contains a readme.txt file that explains how to use the XML Validator.

Appendix in Review

The knowledge you gained from this appendix about XML builds a foundation for you to understand the technologies used in this book. We have covered the basics of XML documents, including elements, attributes, and other constructs. We also explained what the namespaces are and how to use them to avoid vocabulary conflictions. Finally, we showed you how to use both DTD and XDR schema to define the structure of XML documents and provide validations to them.

APPENDIX B

XSL Transformation (XSLT)

IN THIS APPENDIX:

- Introducing XSLT
- XPath Expressions
- XSLT Elements
- Appendix In Review

In the last appendix, you learned the fundamentals of authoring a well-formed, valid XML document. XML provides an elegant solution for describing structured data and makes it possible for separating the data from its presentation. XML enables developers to define custom vocabularies to address their specific business needs, using standard XML syntaxes.

This flexibility, however, sometimes comes with a price. For example, two organizations are likely to use different XML vocabularies (elements, attributes, and schemas) to describe the same business data, say purchase order. In order for these companies to electronically exchange the business documents (the purchase order), they need to transform the document from one XML format to another XML format. This is exactly what *XSLT* does.

XSLT, short for *XML Stylesheet Language Transformation*, is an XML application that transforms the XML structure to other document formats, including XML, HTML, text files, etc. In this appendix, you will learn the semantics of the XSLT language and see how to use it in examples.

Introducing XSLT

XSLT originated from its ancestor, XML Stylesheet Language (XSL), a language designed to help render the presentation of XML data in display devices such as Adobe PDF reader and Web browsers. XSL gets its name from the Cascading Stylesheet (CSS), a block of formatting descriptions that provides augmented control over presentation and layout of HTML. CSS is suitable for describing the HTML formatting behavior of simply structured HTML and XML documents. CSS determines how HTML tags are displayed, whereas XSLT determines how XML data is laid out. CSS does not provide a display structure that deviates from the structure of the source data, nor does it provide a means to transform the source XML document into another format. XSL was proposed to address the issues and limitations of CSS.

XSL consists of two components, a transforming language which becomes XSLT and an XML vocabulary that specifies the formatting semantics, *XSL Formatting Objects* (XSL FO). XSL FO is an XML application that addresses how to display complex formatting such as a PDF file. Unfortunately, discussion of XSL FO is beyond the scope of this appendix. Readers who are interested in knowing more about XSL FO can read J. David Eisenberg's article, "Using XSL Formatting Objects" on xml.com's Web site at: **http://www.xml.com/lpt/a/2001/01/17/xsl-fo/index.html**.

In this appendix, we will discuss XSLT only. For simplicity, XSL and XSLT are sometimes used interchangeably in technical literatures. You should bear in mind, however, that, strictly speaking, XSLT is a subset of XSL. In this appendix, however, we will stick to XSLT.

The Books Example

Before we get into the details of XSLT, let's first look at an example. The following is a Books XML document, similar to the one you saw in Appendix A, but this time it contains data for two programming books about XSLT.

```
<?xml-stylesheet type="text/xsl" href="books.xsl"?>
<Books>
  <Book ISBN="047146031">
    <Title>XSLT:Professional Developer's Guide</Title>
    <Publisher>John Wiley &amp; Sons</Publisher>
    <Authors>
      <Author>Peter Stark</Author>
      <Author>Johan Hjelm</Author>
    </Authors>
    <Price>49.99</Price>
  </Book>
  <Book ISBN="1861003129">
    <Title>XSLT Programmer's Reference</Title>
    <Publisher>Wrox Press Inc.</Publisher>
    <Authors>
      <Author>Michael Kay</Author>
    </Authors>
    <Price>34.99</Price>
  </Book>
</Books>
```

Let's assume that we want to display the contents of the preceding XML document in HTML, as shown in Figure B-1.

How can you do this? You might have noticed that the first line of the Books XML document looks like this:

```
<?xml-stylesheet type="text/xsl" href="books.xsl"?>
```

As you may recall, this line is a processing instruction (PI), like those described in Appendix A. It tells the XML parser (IE 5 Web browser in this case) that there is an

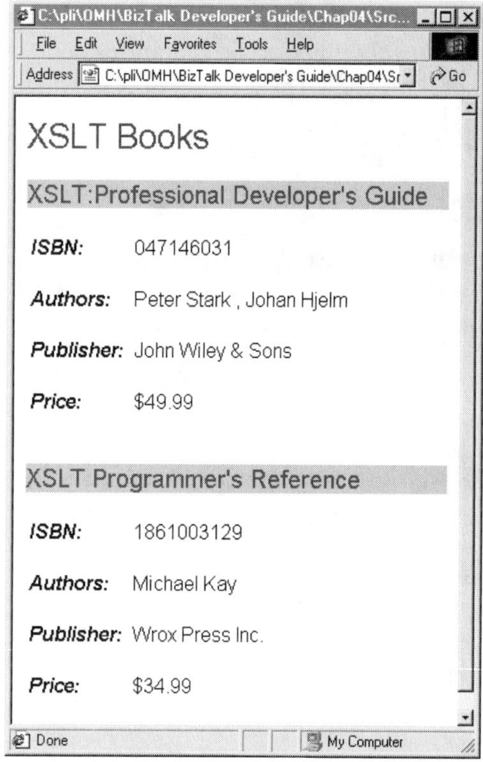

Figure B-1 *The HTML presentations of the Books XML document in IE's*

XSL stylesheet associated with it—the books.xsl that defines the output for the Books XML document, as you saw in Figure B-1. Here is the XSL stylesheet:

```
<xsl:stylesheet
    xmlns:xsl="http://www.w3.org/1999/XSL/Transform" version="1.0">
  <xsl:output method="html"/>
  <xsl:template match="/">
    <HTML>
      <BODY>
      <style type="text/css">
        <xsl:comment>
          H1 {font: 20pt "Arial"; color: blue}
          H2 {font: 15pt "Arial"; color: maroon;
              background-color: lightgrey}
          H3 {font: 12pt "Arial"}
        </xsl:comment>
```

```
      </style>
      <H1>XSLT Books</H1>
      <xsl:for-each select="Books/Book">
        <H2><xsl:value-of select="Title"/></H2>
        <TABLE border="0">
          <TR>
            <TD><H3><I><B>ISBN: </B></I></H3></TD>
            <TD><H3><xsl:value-of select="@ISBN"/></H3></TD>
          </TR>
          <TR>
            <TD><H3><I><B>Authors: </B></I></H3></TD>
            <TD>
              <H3>
                <xsl:for-each select="Authors/Author">
                  <xsl:choose>
                    <xsl:when test="position()!=1">
                      , <xsl:value-of select="text()"/>
                    </xsl:when>
                    <xsl:otherwise>
                      <xsl:value-of select="text()"/>
                    </xsl:otherwise>
                  </xsl:choose>
                </xsl:for-each>
              </H3>
            </TD>
          </TR>
          <TR>
            <TD><H3><I><B>Publisher: </B></I></H3></TD>
            <TD><H3><xsl:value-of select="Publisher"/></H3></TD>
          </TR>
          <TR>
            <TD><H3><I><B>Price: </B></I></H3></TD>
            <TD><H3>$<xsl:value-of select="Price"/></H3></TD>
          </TR>
        </TABLE>
      </xsl:for-each>
      </BODY>
    </HTML>
  </xsl:template>
</xsl:stylesheet>
```

As you can see, this simple XSL stylesheet is a well-formed XML document. In addition to the standard HTML elements (tags), the rest of the document contains a lot of XML elements under the namespace of xsl that is defined at the beginning of the XSL stylesheet document. These elements are called *XSLT elements*. A typical XSLT element takes the following form:

<xsl:Element_Name Attribute_Name = "Value"/>

In the XSLT world, the elements under the xsl namespace are the XSLT instructions or commands. These elements determine what kind of operation should be performed. The value of the attribute for an XSL element is a query expression called *XPath expression*. The XPath (XML Path Languages) expressions are used to identify the part of the source XML document upon which the operations should be performed.

For example, in the XSLT statement

```
<xsl:value-of select="Title"/>
```

the xsl:value-of element has a select attribute whose value is Title. This tells the XSLT processor to output the content of the Title element of the source XML document. In this case, Title is an XPath expression that identifies the Title element.

The entire XSLT language is built on these simple yet powerful semantics: an XSL element which defines the operations, and an optional attribute that uses an XPath expression to specify the address of the subset in the source XML document. We will start our discussion with the XPath query expression. Then we will discuss the XSLT elements. Finally, we will show you how to use these basic XSLT techniques to solve real world problems.

Useful Tools

In order for you to be able to follow the examples in this appendix, it will be helpful to install a few tools that are freely available from MSDN downloads:

Microsoft XML Parser (MSXML) 3.0

The first thing you need is the last version of Microsoft XML Parser (MSXML)—3.0. If you installed BizTalk Server 2000, MSXML parser will be automatically installed. Otherwise you can download it from the Microsoft download web site at: **http://download.microsoft.com/download/xml/Install/3.0/WIN98Me/EN-US/msxml3.exe**

I also recommend that you download the accompanying Software Development Kit—MSXSL SDK 3.0 from this URL: **http://download.microsoft.com/download/xml/SDK/3.0/WIN98Me/EN-US/xmlsdk.exe**. The SDK is an excellent XML resource that covers XML, XSLT, XDR Schemas, and Microsoft SAX2.0 parser, etc., with plenty of examples and tutorials to help you work with Microsoft XML technologies.

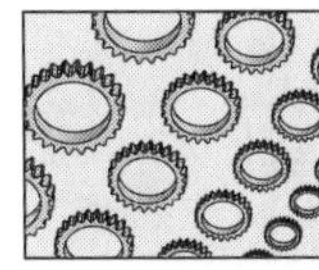

NOTE

*The XSLT processor that comes with IE 5 uses the old version of the XSLT specification with a namespace of **http://www.w3.org/TR/WD-xsl**. To update the XSLT processor to use the most recent XSLT specification (namespace: **http://www.w3.org/1999/XSL/Transform**), you should install the MSXML 3.0 parser in replace mode. To do this, you need to download the **xmlinst.exe** utility from **http://msdn.microsoft.com/msdn-files/027/001/469/XmlInst.exe**. For detailed information and instructions, refer to the MSXML SDK documentation.*

IE Tools for Viewing XSLT Output

IE 5 can display the desired HTML presentation defined by the XSLT stylesheet as illustrated in Figure B-1. It does not, however, allow you to view the intermediate XSLT output that generates the HTML presentation you saw in the web browser. You can download the IE 5 tools from **http://msdn.microsoft.com/msdn-files/027/000/543/iexmltls.exe**. Follow the instruction in the Readme.txt file of the download to install the tools. After the tools have been installed, you should be able to view the XSLT output by right-clicking on the IE web browser and selecting View XSL Output from the context-sensitive menu option. Figure B-2 illustrates the XSLT output view of our Books XML/XSL example.

In addition to viewing XSLT output, these tools also enable you to validate your XML document against a DTD or Schema from within the IE web browser.

Command Line XSLT Utility

The IE tools you downloaded in the preceding section work fine for viewing the XSLT output in the IE browser. Most of the time, however, you also need to have a persistent file for the XSLT output so you can pass it to other applications or exchange it with your business trading partners. This output file may or may not be an HTML document (in most cases, it is not), as it may not be appropriate for display in IE. In Appendix C, you will learn how to perform an XSLT transformation programmatically using Microsoft XML parser. For now, you can use a command line XSLT utility to help you generate the XSTL output files. This utility can be downloaded from: **http://msdn.microsoft.com/msdn-files/027/001/485/XSLTCommandLine.exe**.

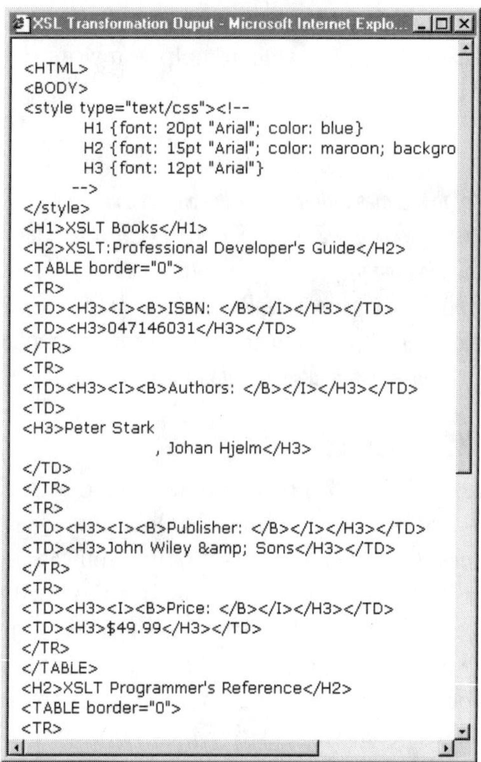


```
<HTML>
<BODY>
<style type="text/css"><!--
        H1 {font: 20pt "Arial"; color: blue}
        H2 {font: 15pt "Arial"; color: maroon; backgro
        H3 {font: 12pt "Arial"}
      -->
</style>
<H1>XSLT Books</H1>
<H2>XSLT:Professional Developer's Guide</H2>
<TABLE border="0">
<TR>
<TD><H3><I><B>ISBN: </B></I></H3></TD>
<TD><H3>047146031</H3></TD>
</TR>
<TR>
<TD><H3><I><B>Authors: </B></I></H3></TD>
<TD>
<H3>Peter Stark
                , Johan Hjelm</H3>
</TD>
</TR>
<TR>
<TD><H3><I><B>Publisher: </B></I></H3></TD>
<TD><H3>John Wiley &amp; Sons</H3></TD>
</TR>
<TR>
<TD><H3><I><B>Price: </B></I></H3></TD>
<TD><H3>$49.99</H3></TD>
</TR>
</TABLE>
<H2>XSLT Programmer's Reference</H2>
<TABLE border="0">
<TR>
```

Figure B-2 *View of the XSLT output from the IE tools*

The syntax for using this command line utility is:

MSXSL XML_Doc XSL_Doc -o Output_Doc

For example, the command for converting the books.xml document into books.htm using the books.xsl stylesheet would be:

```
msxsl books.xml books.xsl -o books.htm
```

where *-o* is one of the available options supported by msxsl.exe. For information about all the options, you can read the msxsl.doc Word document that comes with the download, or simply type **msxsl** at the DOS prompt and press ENTER.

XPath Expressions

XPath treats an XML as a tree of *nodes*. A node in the XML tree can be an element (element node), an attribute (attribute node), or a text (text node). There is also a special type of node called the root node. At any given time, the node the XSLT processor is using is called the *context node*.

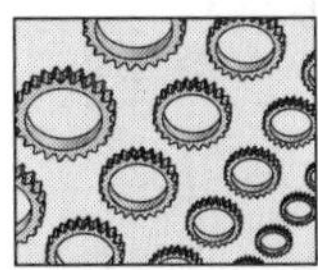

NOTE

A root node is not the same as the root element of the document. Rather, it is the parent of the root element.

An XPath expression is used to address or identify the parts in an XML document. It defines a query criterion that filters out a subset of the XML document, called a *node-set*. An XPath expression can be defined by either *location path* or an *XPath function*. For example, the "Books/Book" in our Books.xsl, our earlier XSL stylesheet, is a location path, whereas the "position()!=1" uses an XPath function, or rather the position() function (which will be explained later). In the following subsections, we will discuss location paths as well as XPath functions.

Location Paths and Location Steps

A location path selects a node-set (a set of nodes) specified by the path expression, defining a path relative to the context node. For example, assuming the XSLT processor is processing the first root node (the context node) of the Books XML example you saw earlier in this appendix, the following location path will return the second author of the book *XSLT: Professional Developer's Guide*—Johan Hjelm:

```
child::Books/child::Book[1]//child::Authors/child::Author[2]
```

As you can see, a location path consists of one or more *location steps*, separated by slashes (/). The preceding location path contains four location steps—child::Books, child::Book[1], child::Authors[1], and child::Author[2]. A location step consists of three parts: an *axis*, a node test, and optionally, one or more *predicates*. An axis specifies the relationship relative to the context node, defining a searching direction. A node test specifies a node type and *expanded-name* of the nodes returned by the location step. The optional predicates further refine the nodes returned by the location step. The axis and the node test are separated by a double colon (::). Predicates are placed inside square brackets. For example, in the location step child::Author[2], child is the axis, Author is the node test, and 2 is the predicate.

Now let's discuss axes, node tests, and predicates in more detail.

Axes

An axis determines the query directions. The child axis in the previous example is just one of the available axes for XPath location steps. The following table summarizes all the available axes:

Axis	Explanation
child	Returns the children of the context node. child is the default axis. When there is no axis specified in a location step, the child axis is assumed. For example, the location path child::Authors/child::Author is equivalent to Authors/Author
self	Returns the context node
descendant	Returns the descendants of the context node
descendant-or-self	Returns the descendants of the context node, including the context node itself
attribute	Returns the attribute of the context node
parent	Returns the parent of the context node
following	Returns all the nodes in the document that appear later then the context node
following-sibling	Returns the nodes that follow the context node and are at the same depth level in the document tree as the context node
preceding	Returns all the nodes in the document that appear earlier than the context node
preceding-or-self	Returns all the nodes that precede the context node and are at the same depth level in the document tree as the context node
ancestor	Returns all the ancestors of the context node, starting with its immediate parent
ancestor-or-self	Returns all the ancestors of the context node, starting with the context node itself
namespace	Returns the namespace nodes of the context node

Node Tests

A node test can by specified by an *expanded-name* which is a namespace prefix followed by a colon and then the qualified name (or QName). For example, myns:Book is an expanded name, where myns is a namespace prefix and Book is a

QName (the Book element in this case). For default namespace, the prefix can be omitted. The QName can be the name of an element or the name of an attribute.

In addition to expanded-names, you can also use the node test functions as described in the following table:

Node Test	Explanation
Node()	Will be true for a node of any type, including element, attributes, text, etc.
Text()	Will be true for a text node.
Comment()	Will be true for a comment node.
Processing-instruction()	Will be true for a PI node.

Predicates

A predicate provides additional filtering criterion (with respect to an axis) to further specify a subset of nodes specified by the axis and node test.

A predicate can be a number that indicates the location of the node in the node-set. For example, Author[2] selects the second Author element in a node-set that contains a collection of Author elements.

In addition, a predicate can also be a node-set function, as you will learn later in this appendix. For example, Author[position()=2] is equivalent to Author[2]. Here we use a node-set function, position(), to specify the second Author element.

Abbreviations

You may wonder why you did not see the :: and similar syntaxes we just described in the Books.xsl example. This is because we used an abbreviated syntax as specified by the W3C XPath specification. These abbreviated axes notations provide a convenient means for concisely describing some common cases. The following table lists some commonly used abbreviations and their corresponding axes:

Abbreviation	Axis
.	self::
//	descendant::
@	attribute::
..	parent::

For example, //Author (equivalent to descendant::Author) will return all the Author nodes at any depth in the document, starting from the child node of the context node. @ISBN (equivalent to attribute::ISBN) will return the ISBN attribute nodes of the context node.

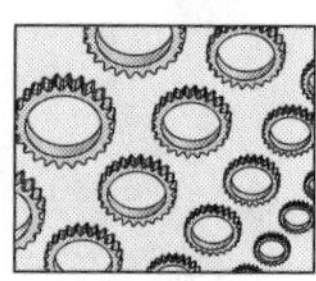

NOTE

You can mix the abbreviated syntax with the former syntax. For example, child::Books/child::Book[1]//Authors/Author[2]. Here, the first part of the XPath expression (before "//") is in the former syntax, whereas the second part is in the abbreviated syntax.

Special Characters and Operators

XPath uses several special characters and operators in the node tests as described in the following table:

<table>
<tr><th>Operator</th><th>Description</th><th>Example</th></tr>
<tr><td>*</td><td>Wildcard</td><td>Authors/* returns all the child nodes of the Authors element. Book/@* will return all the attributes of the Book element.</td></tr>
<tr><td>( )</td><td>Group operator. You can use group operators to override the default Precedence orders.</td><td>See the example for the set operator that follows.</td></tr>
<tr><td>|</td><td>Set operator</td><td>Book/(Title|Price) will return both the Title and Price element of a particular Book element.</td></tr>
<tr><td>[ ]</td><td>Filter operator</td><td>Author[2] returns the second Author element.</td></tr>
<tr><td>and</td><td>Logical AND</td><td>Book[Title and Price] will return the Book elements that contain both Title and Price elements.</td></tr>
<tr><td>or</td><td>Logical OR</td><td>Book[@ISBN or @Publisher] will return the Book elements that contain either the ISBN or Publisher attribute.</td></tr>
<tr><td>not()</td><td>Logical NOT</td><td>Book[not(@ISBN= "1861003129")] returns Book elements whose ISBN attribute values are not 1861003129.</td></tr>
<tr><td>=</td><td>Equal to</td><td>Book[@ISBN= "1861003129"] returns Book elements whose ISBN attribute value is 1861003129.</td></tr>
<tr><td>!=</td><td>Not equal to</td><td>Book[@ISBN!= "1861003129"] returns Book elements whose ISBN attribute values are not 1861003129.</td></tr>
<tr><td><</td><td>Less than</td><td>Book[number(Price)<40] will return Book elements whose price is less than 40 dollars. Note that we used a number() function here which will be explained shortly in this appendix.</td></tr>
</table>

Operator	Description	Example
<=	Less than or equal to	Book[number(Price)<=40] returns Book elements whose price is less than or equal to 40.
>	Greater than	Book[number(Price)>40] returns Book elements whose price is greater than 40 dollars.
>=	Greater than or equal to	Book[number(Price)>=40] returns Book elements whose price is greater than or equal to 40 dollars.

XPath Functions

By now you have seen a couple of XPath functions from our discussions on location paths, such as the position() function and the number() function. XPath uses several sets of functions to help evaluate expressions, including Node-Set functions, Number functions, String functions, XSLT functions, and Boolean functions.

Number Functions

XPath Number functions evaluate the argument expressions and return numbers or strings that can be used with comparison operators in filter patterns, as described in the following table:

Number Function	Description	Example
number()	Converts the expression into a number	Book[number(Price)>40] returns Book elements whose price is greater than 40 dollars. Here the number() function converts the text of the Price element into a number and than compares it with the number 40.
sum()	Converts the expressions of each individual node into numbers and then sums them up	sum(//Price) will convert the text of all the Price elements that are descendants of the context node into numbers and then sums them up.
round()	Rounds number to the closest integer	round(1.5) will return 2 whereas round(-1.9) will return -2.
ceiling()	Rounds to the smallest integer that is not less than the number being evaluated	ceiling(1.5) will return 2 whereas ceiling (-1.9) will return -1.
floor()	Rounds to the largest integer that is not greater than the number being evaluated	floor(1.5) will return 1 whereas floor(-1.9) will return -2.

String Functions

XPath provides a set of String functions that allow you to evaluate, format, and manipulate string expressions. These String functions are similar to those used in other procedural languages such as Visual Basic and Transact-SQL. The following table describes these String functions:

String Function	Description	Example
string()	Converts an object into a string	string(0 div 0) returns "NaN" (stands for Not a Number); string(1 div 0) returns "Infinity"; string(-1 div 0) returns "-Infinity"; string(20 div 5) returns literal string "4". The *div* operator used in the previous example performs floating-point division.
string-length()	Calculates the number of characters in a string	string-length("Transform") returns 9.
start-with()	Tests if the first string expression starts with the second string expression	start-with("Transform", "Trans") returns True, whereas start-with("Transform", "form") returns False.
contains()	Tests if the first string expression contains the second string expression	Both contains("Transform", "Transform") and contains("Transform", "form") return True, whereas contains("Trans", "Transform") returns False.
substring()	Returns a substring of the first string expression as specified by the second expression (a number that specifies the starting position) and optionally the third expression (a number that specifies how many characters should be returned)	substring("Transform", 1, 5) returns "Trans", whereas substring("Transform", 6) returns "form".
substring-before()	Returns the left side of the first expression before the occurrence of the second expression	substring-before("Dallas, Texas", ",") returns "Dallas".
substring-after()	Returns the right side of the first expression after the occurrence of the second expression	substring-after("Dallas, Texas", ",") returns "Texas".

String Function	Description	Example
concat()	Concatenates string expressions to form a new string	concat(“Dallas” “,” “Texas”) returns “Dallas, Texas”.
translate()	Replaces all occurrences of the second string expression in the first string expression with a third expression by the characters at the corresponding positions	translate(“Dallas TX”, “ “, “,”) returns “Dallas, Texas”.
normalize-space()	Strips out leading and trailing white spaces of the string expression. The normalize-space() function does not remove the inner white spaces within the string expression; use the translate() function for that purpose.	normalize-space(“ a b c “) returns “a b c”.

Node-Set Functions

Node-Set functions perform node-set related operations, such as returning a node set according to an expression, or providing information about a specific node, as described in the following table:

Node-Set Function	Description	Example
position()	Returns a number that represents the position of the context node in the node set	Expression “positions()<>1” excludes the first node.
last()	Returns a number that is equivalent to the number of nodes in the returned node set	Expression “//Book[last()]” returns the last Book element.
count()	Returns a number that represents the number of nodes in the returned node set	count(“//Book[number(Price)>40]”) returns the number of books whose prices are greater than 40 dollars.
id()	Returns a set of elements identified by the unique ID. If the expression is a node set, then a union of node sets is returned. Otherwise, a white space delimited string will be returned.	id(“ISBN”) returns elements with a unique ID ISBN attribute, whereas id(“ISBN”)/Title returns elements that have a unique ISBN attribute and a Title child element.

Node-Set Function	Description	Example
key()	Returns a set of elements specified by the <xsl:key> element with the same name	We will demonstrate how to use the key() function with the <xsl:key> element in the next section of this appendix.
name()	Returns the expanded name of the context node	name() returns the name of the context node (element or attribute).
local-name()	Returns the local portion of the expanded name of the context node	If the context node is "z:row", then local-name() will return "row".
namespace-uri()	Returns the namespace URI of the node set	namespace-uri() returns the default namespace URI of the XML document.
document()	Imports a node set from an external XML document into the XML document that is currently processed. The document() function provides a means for merging documents or segments of documents into a new document.	document("Books.xml"/Books/Book[@ISBN]) will retrieve the Book elements with an ISBN attribute from an external XML document Books.xml into the current document.

Boolean Functions

The following table describes the Boolean functions of the XPath language:

Boolean Function	Description	Example
boolean()	Evaluates the expression to a Boolean. Non-zero numbers (positive or negative) will return true. zero or NaN will return false. Null node-set or empty string will return false.	boolean(1=2) returns false.
not()	Reverses the evaluation of a Boolean expression	not(1=2) returns true.
lang()	Returns true if the language code in the expression matches the xml:lang attribute of the current node	Given the Books element as <Books xml:lang="en">, lang("en") returns true, whereas lang("de") returns false.

Boolean Function	Description	Example
true()	Returns true. This function is rarely used.	true() returns true.
false()	Returns false. This function is rarely used.	false() returns false.

XSLT Functions

XPath supports a set of functions that return information regarding the nodes in a node set. The following table describes these functions:

XSLT Function	Description	Example
current()	Returns the context node	current() functions the same way as the self::node() or ".".
function-available()	Returns a Boolean that indicates whether the function specified by the expression is a valid XPath function	function-available("number()") returns true whereas function-available("my-function") returns false.
element-available()	Returns a Boolean that indicates whether the element specified by the expression is a valid XSLT element	element-available("xsl:template") returns true whereas element-available("xsl:my-eleme nt") returns false.
system-property	Returns the system property information including xsl:version, xsl:vendor, and xsl:vendor-url properties	system-property("xsl:version") returns 1 for XSLT processors that implement the current version of XSLT specification.
unparsed-entity-uri()	Returns the path to the unparsed entities in a DTD. Empty string is returned when the entity specified does not exist.	If the entity is declared as <!ENTITY photo SYSTEM "my_photo.jpg" NDATA JPEG>]> in the DTD, then unparsed-entity-uri('photo') returns the path of the image file my_photo.jpg.
generate-id()	Generates a unique ID string that identifies the node in a node set that appears first in the document	generate-id("Book") returns an ID for the first Book element.
format-number()	Formats a number (the first argument) as defined by the pattern (the second argument)	format-number(10000, "#,###") returns 10,000.

XSLT Elements

Whereas XPath expressions provide a means to address the specific part of an XML document for the XSLT processor, XSLT elements provide specific processing instructions for the XSLT processor. Some XSLT elements use XPath expressions, some do not. When an XPath expression is used in an XSLT element, it is specified as the value of an attribute, such as *select*, *match*, *test*, etc.

In this section, we will briefly discuss various XSLT elements and how XSLT uses these elements to provide powerful processing functionalities, focusing on the important attributes. We will group our discussion of XSLT elements according to the specific functionality these elements support.

Declaring the Stylesheet

An XSLT stylesheet itself is a well-formed XML document. When you start writing an XSLT stylesheet, the first thing you need to do is declare the stylesheet using the *xsl:stylesheet* element.

xsl:stylesheet

As in the Books.xsl example you saw earlier in this appendix, everything in an XSLT stylesheet must be included inside the xsl:stylesheet element like this:

```
<xsl:stylesheet
    xmlns:xsl="http://www.w3.org/1999/XSL/Transform" version="1.0">
  <!-- the content of the XSLT stylesheet-->
</xsl:stylesheet>
```

The preceding example demonstrates a typical XSLT stylesheet declaration. It declares the xsl namespace and specifies the version number with which the XSLT processor complies to.

xsl:transform

The *xsl:transform* element is a synonym for the xsl:stylesheet. You can replace the xsl:stylesheet element with xsl:transform. The xsl:transform element is not typically used as the xsl:stylesheet element, though.

Determining the Output Type

XSLT supports transformation of XML documents to three different formats: XML, HTML, and text file. This is done by using the *xsl:output* element.

xsl:output

The formats of the output file are specified using the *method* attribute of the xsl:output element, as you saw in the Books.xsl example:

```
<xsl:output method="html"/>
```

Here we assign the value "html" to the method attribute to tell the XSLT processor that we want to transform the XML file to an HTML file.

In addition to "html," there are two other values you can set to the method attribute of the xsl:output element: "xml" and "text," for outputting XML and text files, respectively.

Using the xsl:output element is optional. When used, this element must immediately follow the stylesheet declaration (xsl:stylesheet or xsl:transform).

Dealing with Templates

The core of an XSLT stylesheet lies on the templates. A template in the XSLT stylesheet is a reusable block that defines the desirable output within a certain context. XSLT uses three elements to work with templates: *xsl:template*, *xsl:apply-templates*, and *xsl:call-template*. In addition, XSLT also offers several built-in templates.

xsl:template

The xsl:template element defines a template. For example, the Books.xsl uses only one template, defined as:

```
<xsl:template match="/">
  <!--the rest of the template definition-->
</xsl:template>
```

Here we used an XPath expression "/" to tell the XSLT processor to match the root element of the XML document (the Books element, in this case). This template will be called by the XSLT processor to output an HTML document.

You can also specify a name attribute for the template so that later the template can be called by its name:

```
<xsl:template name="tplTitle" match = "Title">
  <!--the rest of the template definition-->
</xsl:template>
```

The xsl:template element can have an optional *mode* attribute, provided that the match attribute is also used. This will allow the same element to be processed multiple times, each time producing a different result.

xsl:apply-templates

The xsl:apply-templates element allows the XSLT processor to apply appropriate templates. It uses a *select* attribute to find a match template that is defined elsewhere in the stylesheet:

```
<xsl:apply-templates select="Title"/>
```

It will apply the template that has a match attribute "Title".

If the select attribute is not supplied, the XSLT processor will try to match the node that is next to the context node. Thus, the following statement provides a recursive processing functionality that allows the XSLT process to continue processing remaining nodes:

```
<xsl:apply-templates/>
```

The following example uses the xsl:apply-templates element inside a template definition to allow the XSLT processor to continue processing after executing the current template:

```
<xsl:template match="Title">

  <B><xsl:apply-templates/></B>

</xsl:template>
```

xsl:call-template

The xsl:call-template element invokes a template through its name attribute. For example, the following XSLT statement calls the tmpTitle template we defined a little while ago:

```
<xsl:call-template name="tplTitle"/>
```

Unlike the xsl:apply-templates element, xsl:call-template does not change the current node or the current node-list. Therefore, the xsl:call-template is suitable for non-recursive scenarios.

xsl:call-template also allows passing in parameters, making calling an XSLT template more like a procedure call. We will show you how to do this when we discuss parameters later in this appendix.

Built-in Templates

XSLT provides a few built-in templates, including the following:

```
<xsl:template match="/|*"><xsl:apply-templates/></xsl:template>
```

This built-in template directs the XSLT processor to process all the nodes, starting from the root nodes.

```
<xsl:template match="text()"><xsl:value-of
select="."/></xsl:template>
```

This built-in template instructs the XSLT processor to output the text of the context node.

```
<xsl:template match="processing-instruction()|comment()"/>
```

This built-in template directs the XSLT processor to do nothing about instructions and comments.

When an XSLT stylesheet has no custom templates defined, the XSLT processor will apply these built-in templates which strip all markups from the source document and output only the texts. For example, if you apply the following template against our Books.xml example, you get the result shown in Figure B-3:

```
<xsl:stylesheet
  xmlns:xsl="http://www.w3.org/1999/XSL/Transform"
  version="1.0">
<xsl:output method="text"/>
</xsl:stylesheet>
```

These powerful built-in templates can sometimes produce undesired results, however. You can define custom template using the xsl:template element to suppress these built-in templates. For example, if you don't want to output any price information, you can define an empty template for the Price element like this:

```
<xsl:template match="Price"/>
```

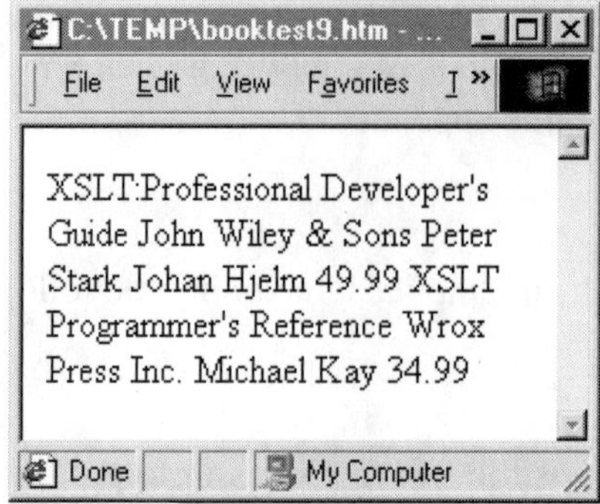

Figure B-3 *The output of built-in XSLT templates*

If you modify the simple stylesheet to (notice that we added two templates here):

```
 <xsl:stylesheet
  xmlns:xsl="http://www.w3.org/1999/XSL/Transform"
  version="1.0">
<xsl:output method="text"/>
<xsl:template match="/">
  <xsl:apply-templates/>
</xsl:template>
<xsl:template match="Price">
</xsl:template>
</xsl:stylesheet>
```

you will get the result shown in Figure B-4 where the prices are stripped out.

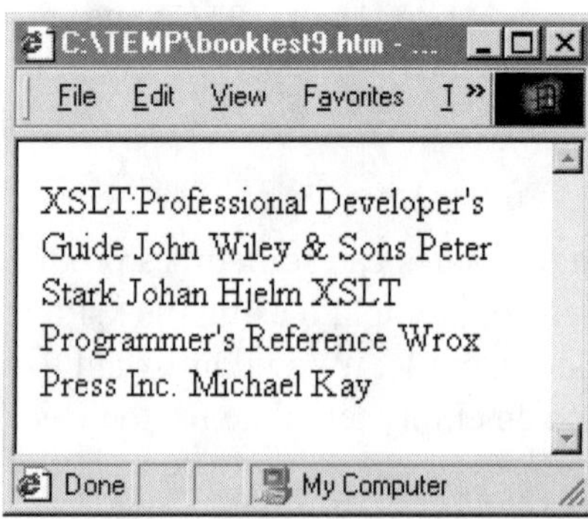

Figure B-4 *Using custom templates to override built-in templates*

In this stylesheet, the first template matches the root node and uses the xsl:apply-templates without supplying a matching criterion. This will cause the XSLT processor to recursively process all the nodes from the root node and generate a result as shown in Figure B-3. By using an empty custom template with a matching criterion, "Price", you override the built-in templates and cause the XSLT processor not to output texts of Price nodes, as illustrated in Figure B-4.

Dealing with Node Contents

XSLT provides several elements that allow you to insert and copy node contents. These elements include *xsl:value-of*, *xsl:copy*, *xsl:copy-of*. XSLT also offers an *xsl:decimal-format* element that, when used in conjunction with the format-number() XPath function, enables you to control the desired formatting of numbers.

xsl:value-of

The xsl:value-of element is one of the most used elements. It inserts the value of the context node into the output document. The xsl:value-of element uses a select attribute that defines an XPath expression to select the specific node. For example, the following:

```
<xsl:value-of select="Title"/>
```

inserts the text of the Title element into the output document. To insert the value of the ISBN attribute into the output document, do this:

```
<xsl:value-of select="@ISBN"/>
```

xsl:copy and xsl:copy-of

The xsl:copy element copies the context node into the output document whereas the xsl:copy-of element inserts subtrees and result-tree fragments into the target document.

Node created in the output document using the xsl:copy element has the same name, namespace, and type as the context node. Child nodes and attributes are not copied automatically; you need to explicitly call the apply-templates with a matching criterion "*|@*" to select both child nodes and attributes, as illustrated here:

```
<xsl:copy>
  <xsl:apply-templates match="*|@*"
</xsl:copy>
```

If you replace the highlighted line in the abbreviated Books.xsl stylesheet:

```
<xsl:stylesheet
    xmlns:xsl="http://www.w3.org/1999/XSL/Transform" version="1.0">
  <xsl:output method="html"/>
  <xsl:template match="/">
    <HTML>
      <BODY>
      <!--embedded CCS-->
      <H1>XSLT Books</H1>
      <xsl:for-each select="Books/Book">
        <H2><xsl:value-of select="Title"/></H2>
        <TABLE border="0">
          <TR>
            <!--Partial Table contents-->
          </TR>
          <TR>
            <TD><H3><I><B>Publisher: </B></I></H3></TD>
            <TD><H3><xsl:value-of select="Publisher"/></H3></TD>
          </TR>
          <TR>
            <!--Partial Table contents-->
          </TR>
        </TABLE>
      </xsl:for-each>
      </BODY>
    </HTML>
  </xsl:template>
</xsl:stylesheet>
```

with this:

```
<TD><H3>
  <xsl:copy>
    <xsl:apply-templates select="Publisher"/>
  </xsl:copy>
</H3></TD>
```

you will get the same output as shown in Figure B-1 earlier in this appendix.

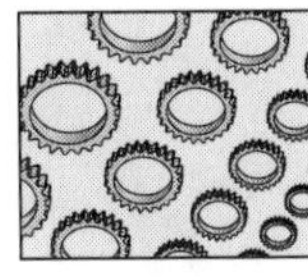

NOTE

As illustrated in the previous example, when the output of the XSLT stylesheet is an HTML document, the HTML tags must also be well-formed. For example, you should use <BR/> or <P/> instead of <BR>, or <P>. You should always place the value inside the quotes (for instance, use width = "1" instead of width = 1), and never use overlapping tags (use <B><I>My Book</I></B> instead of <B><I>My Book</B></I>).

Unlike the xsl:copy element, xsl:copy-of copies the entire content of the context node, including its attributes, child nodes, texts, etc., into the output document in the same order as the original document. If the context node is a simple element node, the xsl:copy will convert its content to a string and then insert it into the output document. Thus, the following segment:

```
<TD><H3>xsl:copy-of select="Publisher"</H3></TD>
```

is equivalent to the highlighted line in the abbreviated Books.xsl stylesheet.

xsl:decimal-format

The xsl:decimal-format element provides a means to alter the default behavior of the format-number() XSLT function. For example, the following segment:

```
<xsl:value-of select="format-number(100000.00, '###,###.00')"/>
```

will result in 100,000.00, representing the number ten thousand in U.S. convention.

You can use the xsl:decimal-format element to define a European convention named "en" and then call the format-number() XSLT function with a third argument to specify that the format with the name "eu" will be used, as illustrated in the following simple XSLT stylesheet:

```
<xsl:stylesheet xmlns:xsl="http://www.w3.org/1999/XSL/Transform"
version="1.0">
<xsl:output method="text"/>
<xsl:decimal-format name="eu" decimal-separator=","
grouping-separator="."/>
<xsl:template match="/">
<xsl:value-of select="format-number(100000.00, '###.###,00', 'eu')"/>
</xsl:template>
</xsl:stylesheet>
```

This will result in 100.000,00 (the comma and period are reversed).

Decisions and Loops

Like a procedure language, XSLT provides conditional processing capabilities. For example, the *xsl:if* element mimics a simple IF statement in most programming languages. Whereas other elements such as *xsl:choose*, *xsl:when*, and *xsl:otherwise* provide a similar functionality to the *if...else* constructs in other programming languages.

In addition, XSLT offers an *xsl:for-each* element that allows you to loop through the node-set selected.

xsl:if

The xsl:if element uses a *test* attribute to set the condition for the test. For example, the following segment uses the xsl:if element to determine if a comma should be added to the output, depending on whether context node is the last node in the node-set:

```
<xsl:if test="position()!=last()">
  , <xsl:value-of select="."/>
</xsl:if>
```

This can be useful when you need to create a comma-delimited list.

xsl:choose, xsl:when, and xsl:otherwise

When used together, these three XSLT elements provide a flexible conditional processing language construct, similar to the *case* or *switch...*construct in most programming languages. The syntax of using these three elements is:

```
<xsl:choose>
 <xsl:when test="condition_1">
  statement_1
 </xsl:when>
 <xsl:when test="condition_2">
  statement_2
 </xsl:when>

 ...........
 <xsl:otherwise>
  statement_n
```

</xsl:otherwise>
<xsl:choose>

The following segment is taken from our Books.xsl example:

```
<xsl:choose>
  <xsl:when test="position()!=1">
    , <xsl:value-of select="text()"/>
  </xsl:when>
  <xsl:otherwise>
    <xsl:value-of select="text()"/>
  </xsl:otherwise>
</xsl:choose>
```

This segment uses the conditional processing technique of XSLT to output a comma-separated list of author names.

xsl:for-each

The xsl:for-each element is one of the most frequently used. Its use is pretty straightforward, using a select attribute to select the node-set. In the Books.xsl example, nested xsl:for-each were used, as illustrated in the following segment :

```
<xsl:for-each select="Books/Book">
  <!--other XSLT instructions-->
  <xsl:for-each select="Authors/Author">
    <!--XSLT instructions for processing Author nodes-->
  </xsl:for-each>
</xsl:for-each>
```

Sorting

XSLT allows you to specify specific sorting orders with the *xsl:sort* element.

xsl:sort

The xsl:sort element requires use of a select attribute to define a sort key for the node. The xsl:sort element can be used as child elements of an xsl:apply-templates element or an xsl:for-each element. For example:

```
<xsl:apply-templates select="Books">
  <xsl:sort select="Price"/>
</xsl:apply-templates>
```

sorts the books according to their price.

The xsl:sort element can have an optional *order* attribute and an optional *data-type* attribute.

The value of the order attribute could be either ascending or descending. If the order attribute is not specified, then the default will be ascending, as in the previous example.

The value for the data-type attribute can be one of three: text, number, or a qualified name (QName). The data-type attribute with text specifies the sort should be in alphabetical order, whereas a number as the data-type attribute determines the sorting should be based on the numerical order. If a QName is specified as the value of the data-type attribute, the results of the evaluation of the QName will be converted into a string, which identifies the data type for determining the sorting order. The default value for the data-type attribute is text.

Variables, Parameter, Keys, and Decimals

In XSLT, you can declare and use variables, parameters, identify and access nodes in complex documents by keys. You achieve these tasks by using appropriate XSLT elements, including *xsl:variable*, *xsl:param*, *xsl:with-param*, and *xsl:key*.

xsl:variable

The xsl:variable element defines a variable and binds it with a value. As you may have already realized, in this context, the *variable* here may be more appropriately called a *constant*. As a matter of a fact, its behavior is closer to the constants declaration in other programming languages (i.e., its value will never change after it is defined).

To declare an xsl:variable element, use this syntax:

<xsl:variable name="var_name" select="XPath_expression"/>

When you refer to the variable later in the stylesheet, you add a dollar sign ($) prefix, like this: $var_name. The optional select attribute assigns a default value to the variable.

For example:

```
<xsl:variable name="discount" select="20"/>
<!--other XSLT instructions-->
<B>The cover price:$<xsl:value-of select="Price"></B><br>
<B><I>Our price:$<xsl:value-of select="Price">*&discount</I></B>
```

Alternatively, you can declare the discount variable like this:

```
<xsl:variable name="discount">20</xsl:variable>
```

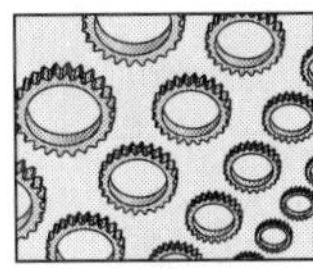

NOTE

If you use the select attribute, the content of the xsl:variable element must be empty.

xsl:param and xsl:with-param

The xsl:param element can do the same thing as the xsl:variable element does, in exactly the same way, as we just demonstrated in the previous example.

In addition, you can use the xsl:param element and the xsl:with-param element, along with the template elements (xsl:template, apply-templates, and xsl:call-template) to simulate functions and subroutines in an XSLT stylesheet as in a programming language.

We will skip introducing the syntax for the xsl:param because it is exactly the same as the xsl:variable element. The syntax of the xsl:with-param is also similar and looks like this:

<xsl:with-param name="param_name" select="XPath_expression">

The xsl:with-param has a required name attribute and an optional select attribute. The select attribute defines a query criterion that is used to match against the context node.

The following segment demonstrates how to use the xsl:with-param elements to perform a simple addition function:

```
<!--call the 'add' template-->
<xsl:call-template name="add">
<xsl:with-param name="var_1" select="4"/>
<xsl:with-param name="var_2" select="5"/>
</xsl:call-template>
<!--declare a template named 'add'-->
<xsl:template name="add">
<xsl:param name="var_1"/>
<xsl:param name="var_2"/>
<xsl:value-of select="$var_1*$var_2"/>
</xsl:template>
```

The template *add* defines two parameters, var_1 and var_2, and outputs (returns) the sum of the values of these two parameters, using the xsl:value-of element. This is very similar to a function definition in a programming language. The xsl:call-template calls the add template and passes two parameters via xsl:with-param and returns the sum of the values of these two parameters from the template.

xsl:key

The xsl:key defines a key to be used with the XPath key() function that provides an alternative means for accessing elements in an XML document. The syntax for the xsl:key element is:

<xsl:key name="key_name" match="pattern" use="expression"/>

A group of keys is similar to an index in a relational database. The values of the keys form a directory of elements in the XML document, and are generated by the *use* expression which provides an efficient access to the elements. The key() function has two arguments, called a key-value pair.

The xsl:key element is a top-level element, meaning it must be declared on the top of the XSLT stylesheet, directly under the xsl:stylesheet declaration. The following example uses the xsl:key element and the key() function and returns the title with the ISBN of 047146031 (XSLT:Professional Developer's Guide):

```
<xsl:stylesheet
    xmlns:xsl="http://www.w3.org/1999/XSL/Transform" version="1.0">
<xsl:key name="isbn" match="Book" use="@ISBN"/>
  <xsl:output method="html"/>
  <xsl:template match="/">
    <HTML>
      <BODY>
        <xsl:for-each select="key('isbn', '047146031')">
         <H3>
         <xsl:value-of select="Title"/>
         </H3>
      </xsl:for-each>
      </BODY>
    </HTML>
  </xsl:template>
</xsl:stylesheet>
```

Outputting XML Constructs

There are two ways in which you can insert XML constructs (elements, attributes, and so on) into the output document. You can use literal strings with custom XML tags (rather than the XSLT namespaces) to create elements and attributes. Alternatively, you can use the following XSLT elements to output XML constructs: *xsl:element*, *xsl:attribute*, *xsl:attribute-set*, *xsl:comment*, *xsl:processing-instruction*, and *xsl:namespace-alias*.

xsl:element

The xsl:element element allows you to output an XML element and has the following basic syntax:

<xsl:element name="element_name">text_content</xsl:element>

The following simple XSLT stylesheet:

```
<xsl:stylesheet
  xmlns:xsl="http://www.w3.org/1999/XSL/Transform" version="1.0">
<xsl:output method="xml"/>
<xsl:template match="/">
  <xsl:element name="MyElement">
My Test Element
</xsl:element>
</xsl:stylesheet>
```

will output the MyElement element like this:

```
<MyElement>My Test Element</MyElement>
```

xsl:attribute and xsl:attribute-set

You can use xsl:attribute elements to define attributes and bind them to your elements in the output XML document. Here is the syntax for xsl:attribute:

<xsl:attribute name="attribute_name">

The following example will add two attributes to the MyElement element:

```
<xsl:stylesheet
  xmlns:xsl="http://www.w3.org/1999/XSL/Transform" version="1.0">
<xsl:output method="xml"/>
<xsl:template match="/">
  <xsl:element name="MyElement">
    <xsl:attribute name="attr_1">attr_1</xsl:attribute>
<xsl:attribute name="attr_2">attr_2</xsl:attribute>
```

```
      My Test Element
   </xsl:element>
</xsl:template>
</xsl:stylesheet>
```

and generates the output like this:

```
<MyElement attr_1="attr_1" attr_2="attr_2">
My Test Element
</MyElement>
```

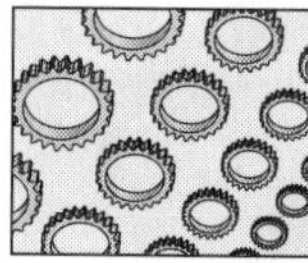

NOTE

Inside the <xsl:element>…</xsl:element> block, you must put the <xsl:attribute> elements before the text literals. Otherwise, the attribute will not be attached to the element.

Alternatively, you can use the xsl:attribute-set element to define a group of attributes and bind these attributes to the element. To define an attribute-set, use this syntax:

```
<xsl:attribute-set name="attribute_set_name">
  attribute_list
</xsl:attribute-set>
```

To bind an attribute-set to an element, you must use the literal tag name of the element instead of the xsl:element element, plus an xsl:use-attribute-sets attribute and set the name of the attribute-set as the value. The following example demonstrates the xsl:attribute-set technique:

```
<xsl:stylesheet xmlns:xsl="http://www.w3.org/1999/XSL/Transform"
version="1.0">
<xsl:output method="xml"/>
<xsl:template match="/">
  <MyElement xsl:use-attribute-sets="attrs">
     My Test Element
  </MyElement>
</xsl:template>
<xsl:attribute-set name="attrs">
<xsl:attribute name="attr_1">attr_1</xsl:attribute>
<xsl:attribute name="attr_2">attr_2</xsl:attribute>
</xsl:attribute-set>
</xsl:stylesheet>
```

This will generate output that exactly duplicates the preceding XSLT stylesheet.

xsl:comment

The xsl:comment element outputs a comments block and works like this:

<xsl:comment>Comment goes here</xsl:comment>

The Books.xsl example uses the xsl:comment to embed a CSS stylesheet inside the output HTML document:

```
<xsl:comment>
  H1 {font: 20pt "Arial"; color: blue}
  H2 {font: 15pt "Arial"; color: maroon;
  background-color: lightgrey}
  H3 {font: 12pt "Arial"}
</xsl:comment>
```

xsl:processing-instruction

The xsl:processing-instruction allows you to insert a PI in the output document and takes the following form:

<xsl:processing-instruction name="PI_name">
 PI_contents
</xsl:processing-instruction>

The following segment will generate the PI for an IE Web browser as shown in our Books.xml example:

```
<xsl:processing-instruction name="xml-stylesheet">
  <xsl:text>type="text/xsl" href="books.xsl"</xsl:text>
</xsl:processing-instruction>
```

It uses the xsl:text element to generate the PI as literal strings. Here is its output:

```
<?xml-stylesheet type="text/xsl" href="books.xsl"?>
```

xsl:namespace-alias

By default, XML will not allow you to use the different prefixes to refer to the same namespace within the same document. This can be a problem sometimes.

For example, your output document itself is an XSLT stylesheet. In this case, you will need a way to work out the namespace prefix limitation we just described.

Fortunately, XSLT provides an xsl:namespace-alias element which can create an alias prefix for the default prefix of a given namespace. Using this element, you can assign a temporary namespace to the alias prefix, apply the stylesheet, and then map the namespace to the default one.

The following example demonstrates how to use the xsl:namespace-alias element:

```
<xsl:stylesheet
  xmlns:xsl="http://www.w3.org/1999/XSL/Transform"
xmlns:alt="http://www.w3.org/1999/XSL/Transform-alternate"
  version="1.0">
<xsl:namespace-alias stylesheet-prefix="alt" result-prefix="xsl"/>
  <xsl:template match="/">
     <alt:stylesheet>
     <!--
        the contexts of the output stylesheet can use both
        prefixes: xsl: or alt:
     -->
     </alt:stylesheet>
  </xsl:template>
</xsl:stylesheet>
```

Dealing with White Spaces

You can use two XSLT elements to determine the default processing behavior of white spaces: *xsl:preserve-space* and *xsl:strip-space*. To generate outputs with desired white spaces, use the *xsl:text* element.

xsl:preserve-space and xsl:strip-space

The uses of xsl:preserve-space and xsl:strip-space are very straightforward. You use the former to preserve white spaces, and the latter to strip them. The syntaxes of these two elements are similar: both use an *element* attribute with a white space delimited list of element names to specify the scope of the declaration:

```
<xsl:preserve-space element=“el,t_1 elt_2 … elt_n”/>
```

and

```
<xsl:strip-space element=“elt_1 elt_2 … elt_n”/>
```

xsl:text

By default, all the white spaces defined in an XSLT stylesheet will be stripped out. You can use the xsl:text element to insert literal text including white spaces into the output document, as illustrated in the following segment example, which will generate three lines of text:

```
<xsl:text>Line One
Line Two
Line Three
</xsl:text>
```

Combining Stylesheets

You can import external stylesheets into the current stylesheet with three XSLT elements: *xsl:include, xsl:import*, and *xsl:apply-import*. These elements allow you to leverage existing XSLT styles to generate a new stylesheet and provide a modular solution.

xsl:include and xsl:import

The syntaxes of xsl:include and xsl:import are almost the same:

<xsl:include href="“external_stylesheet_url”/>

and

<xsl:import href="“external_stylesheet_url”/>

Both xsl:include and xsl:import use the *href* attribute to refer to the external stylesheet. There are some subtle differences between these two elements, as we will next explain.

To demonstrate the use of the xsl:include element, let’s rewrite the Books.xsl stylesheet this way:

```
<xsl:stylesheet
    xmlns:xsl="http://www.w3.org/1999/XSL/Transform" version="1.0">
<xsl:include href="include.xsl"/>
<xsl:output method="html"/>
<xsl:template match="/">
    <HTML>
      <BODY>
```

```
        <style type="text/css">
          <xsl:comment>
            H1 {font: 20pt "Arial"; color: blue}
            H2 {font: 15pt "Arial"; color: maroon; background-color:
lightgrey}
            H3 {font: 12pt "Arial"}
          </xsl:comment>
        </style>
        <H1>XSLT Books</H1>
        <xsl:for-each select="Books/Book">
          <H2><xsl:apply-templates select="Title"/></H2>
            <TABLE border="0">
            <TR>
              <TD><H3><I><B>ISBN: </B></I></H3></TD>
              <TD><H3><xsl:apply-templates select="@ISBN"/></H3></TD>
            </TR>
            <TR>
              <TD><H3><I><B>Authors: </B></I></H3></TD>
              <TD>
                <H3>
                  <xsl:for-each select="Authors/Author">
                    <xsl:choose>
                      <xsl:when test="position()!=1">
                        , <xsl:value-of select="text()"/>
                      </xsl:when>
                      <xsl:otherwise>
                        <xsl:value-of select="text()"/>
                      </xsl:otherwise>
                    </xsl:choose>
                  </xsl:for-each>
                </H3>
              </TD>
            </TR>
            <xsl:apply-templates select="Publisher"/>
            <xsl:apply-templates select="Price"/>
          </TABLE>
        </xsl:for-each>
        </BODY>
      </HTML>
  </xsl:template>
  <xsl:template match="Title">
    <xsl:value-of select="."/>
  </xsl:template>
```

```
<xsl:template match="@ISBN">
  <xsl:value-of select="."/>
</xsl:template>
<xsl:template match="Author">
  <xsl:value-of select="."/>
</xsl:template>
</xsl:stylesheet>
```

The example is a little long, but it still illustrates the point. As the first bolded line in the example indicates, we used the xsl:include element to include the external stylesheet, include.xsl, whose content looks like this:

```
<xsl:stylesheet
    xmlns:xsl="http://www.w3.org/1999/XSL/Transform" version="1.0">
<xsl:template match="Publisher">
  <TR>
    <TD><H3><I><B>Publisher: </B></I></H3></TD>
    <TD><H3><xsl:value-of select="."/></H3></TD>
  </TR>
</xsl:template>

<xsl:template match="Price">
  <TR>
    <TD><H3><I><B>Price: </B></I></H3></TD>
    <TD><H3>$<xsl:value-of select="."/></H3></TD>
  </TR>
</xsl:template>
</xsl:stylesheet>
```

It defines two templates, matched with Publisher and Price. When the two xsl:apply-templates are called (as we highlighted in the example code), the XSLT processor treats these templates as if they were defined inside the current stylesheet.

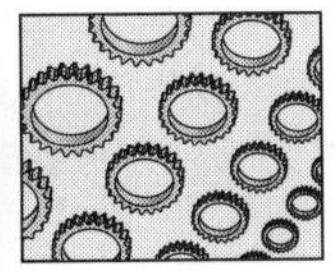

NOTE

The external template must be a complete XSLT stylesheet.

You can also use the xsl:import element in this way. For example, if you simply replace the xsl:include declaration with the following:

```
<xsl:import href="include.xsl"/>
```

It will give you the same results.

There are some subtle differences when you use xsl:import, however. When both the external stylesheet and the current stylesheet have templates by the same name, by default the template defined in the current stylesheet overrides the template defined in the external stylesheet (unless the xsl:apply-import is called, in which case the external template takes over the internal one). Let's modify our Books.xsl example again to demonstrate how it works.

```
<xsl:stylesheet
    xmlns:xsl="http://www.w3.org/1999/XSL/Transform" version="1.0">
<xsl:output method="html"/>
<xsl:import href="include.xsl"/>
<xsl:template match="/">
    <HTML>
      <BODY>
      <!--CSS Stylesheet goes here-->
      <H1>XSLT Books</H1>
      <xsl:for-each select="Books/Book">
        <H2><xsl:apply-templates select="Title"/></H2>
          <TABLE border="0">
          <!--other table rows omitted for brevity-->
          <xsl:apply-templates select="Publisher"/>
          <xsl:apply-templates select="Price"/>
        </TABLE>
      </xsl:for-each>
      </BODY>
    </HTML>
</xsl:template>
<!--other template omitted for brevity-->
<xsl:template match="Price">
<TR>
<TD><H3>Price: </H3></TD>
<TD><H3>$<xsl:value-of select="."/></H3></TD>
</TR>
</xsl:template>
</xsl:stylesheet>
```

Now, in the master stylesheet, there is also a Price template. It is almost the same as the Price template in the external stylesheet, include.xsl, except the <I><B></B></I> HTML font tags are left out. In this case, the Price template in the master stylesheet overrides the Price template defined in the external stylesheet. If you run this XSLT stylesheet against our Books.xml document, you will get the result shown in Figure B-5.

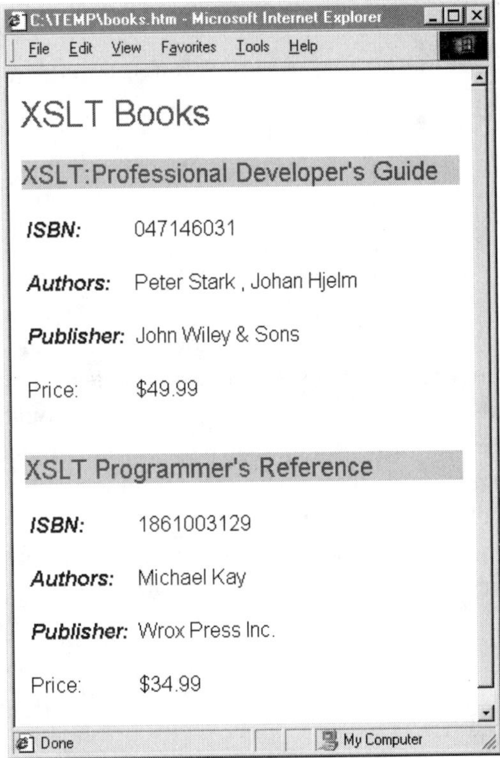

Figure B-5 *The effect of template rule overriding when using xsl:import*

As you can see in Figure B-5, the font of Price is now neither bold nor italic. This is what happens when the Price template in the master stylesheet takes control.

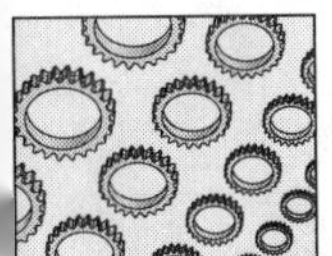

NOTE

Both xsl:include and xsl:import are top-level elements. They must be the direct children node of the xsl:stylesheet element.

Miscellaneous Elements

By now we have introduced almost all the XSLT elements. In this section, we are going to look at two additional elements: *xsl:number* and *xsl:message*. We will also introduce a MSXML 3.0 Parser specific element: *msxsl:script*.

xsl:number

The xsl:number element outputs a formatted number into the result tree. Its syntax looks like this:

```
<xsl:number level="single|multiple|any"
            count="pattern"
            from="patter"
            format="format_token"/>
```

The *level* attribute specifies at which level the format should be applied. The value of the *count* attribute (pattern) specifies what nodes should be counted at those levels. The value of the *from* attribute specifies where the counting starts. The value of the *format* attribute is a format token that specifies the number format. For example, "1" for numeric integer numbers, "01" with leading zero for two digits, "A" for alphabetic, "i" or "I" for Roman numbers, and so on.

The following example demonstrates how to use the xsl:number element to display authors for each book in our Books XML document:

```
<xsl:stylesheet xmlns:xsl="http://www.w3.org/1999/XSL/Transform"
version="1.0">
<xsl:output method="html"/>
<xsl:template match="/">
<HTML>
<BODY>
  <H2>XSLT Book Authors</H2>
  <xsl:for-each select="//Book">
  <H3><xsl:value-of select="Title"/></H3>
  <H4>Authors:</H4>
  <TABLE>
    <xsl:for-each select="Authors/Author">
    <TR>
      <TD>
        <xsl:number level="single" count="*" from="Books"
format="1"/>.
      </TD>
      <TD>
        <I><xsl:value-of select="text()"/></I>
      </TD>
    </TR>
    </xsl:for-each>
  </TABLE>
```

```
  </xsl:for-each>
</BODY>
</HTML>
</xsl:template>
<xsl:template match="text()"/>
</xsl:stylesheet>
```

This will generate the results shown in Figure B-6.

xsl:message

The xsl:message element sends a text message to the message buffer to display a message box. It has this syntax:

```
<xsl:message terminate="yes|no">
  Your message goes here
</xsl:message>
```

If you set the value of the terminate attribute to "yes," it will terminate the processing of the XSLT document and raise a trappable system-level error message. When used in conjunction with conditional processing elements, such as xsl:if,

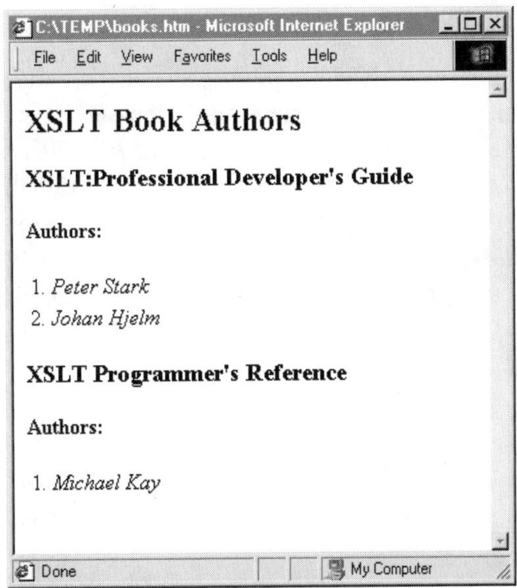

Figure B-6 *Using xml:number to display authors*

xsl:choose, and so on, the xsl:message provides a debugging mechanism that is similar to using the Print statements for debugging Transact SQL stored procedures.

msxsl:script

Finally, we introduce a Microsoft XSLT parser specific element—msxsl:script. This element extends the functionality of an XSLT stylesheet and allows you to create and use more powerful and flexible functions in Active scripting languages such as JScript or VBScript. The msxsl:script element is a top-level element and has the following syntax:

```
<msxsl:script
  language = "scripting_language"
  implements-prefix = "namespace_prefix">
  <![CDATA[functions_goes_here...]]>
</msxsl:script>
```

The *language* attribute specifies the scripting language to be used and can be either "JScript" or "VBScript." The *implements_prefix* attribute specifies a prefix for a user defined namespace.

Appendix in Review

In this appendix, we introduced XSLT, an XML dialect that enables you to transform a source XML document into other formats. We discussed XPath queries and XSLT elements and demonstrated how to use them, showing how flexible yet powerful they can be. The transformed document could be another XML document, an HTML document, or an EDI document. XSLT makes the important premise behind XML technology possible—separating the data from its presentation. BizTalk Server uses XSLT to map the documents between different trading partners. A BizTalk map contains an embedded XSLT stylesheet which performs the mapping between two different XML document schemas.

APPENDIX

C

Building XML Applications

IN THIS APPENDIX:

The Document Object Model (DOM)

The Simple API for XML (SAX)

Appendix in Review

XML is the backbone of the BizTalk technology. The BizTalk Framework 2.0 (as well as the SOAP protocol behind it) is an XML-based specification. In addition, BizTalk Server 2000 uses XML documents exclusively for its internal document interchanges.

In Appendix A and B, we have covered the XML basics, such as how to author a well-formed XML document and validate it using either a DTD or an XDR schema. In addition, we demonstrated how to create an XSLT document to transform an XML document into any desired document format.

Knowing the basic syntaxes and semantics of XML alone is not enough for building BizTalk solutions. As introduced in Chapter 2, BizTalk Server 2000 provides an open architecture that enables you to develop custom components to extend its functionalities. For example, you can build an Application Integration Component (AIC) to extend BizTalk Server Messaging Services. In addition, BizTalk Server uses XML internally as the intermediate format for both inbound and outbound documents of a messaging channel, no matter what their original formats are. As a result, we need an easy way to create, access, and manipulate the XML documents.

In this appendix, we will teach you how to create, access, and manipulate XML documents through two well-known XML *Application Programming Interfaces* (APIs), namely the *Document Object Model* (DOM) and the *Simple API for XML* (SAX). We will use the Microsoft MSXSL Parser 3.0 in the examples, because it supports both DOM and SAX APIs.

To facilitate our discussion, we will use the familiar Books.xml document (from Appendix A and B) with a few modifications—we added a "Subject" attribute and increased the number of books to four:

```
<?xml version="1.0"?>
<Books>
    <Book ISBN="047146031" Subject="XML">
    <Title>XSLT:Professional Developer's Guide</Title>
    <Publisher>John Wiley &amp; Sons</Publisher>
    <Authors>
      <Author>Peter Stark</Author>
      <Author>Johan Hjelm</Author>
    </Authors>
    <Price>49.99</Price>
  </Book>
  <Book ISBN="1861003129" Subject="XML">
    <Title>XSLT Programmer's Reference</Title>
    <Publisher>Wrox Press Inc.</Publisher>
    <Authors>
```

```
      <Author>Michael Kay</Author>
    </Authors>
    <Price>34.99</Price>
  </Book>
  <Book ISBN="0789724588" Subject="Visual  Basic">
    <Title>Visual Basic and COM+ Programming By Example</Title>
    <Publisher>QUE</Publisher>
    <Authors>
      <Author>Peishu Li</Author>
    </Authors>
    <Price>34.99</Price>
  </Book>
  <Book ISBN="0072133384" Subject="BizTalk">
    <Title>BizTalk Server 2000 Developer's Guide</Title>
    <Publisher>Osborne/McGraw-Hill</Publisher>
    <Authors>
      <Author>Peishu Li</Author>
    </Authors>
    <Price>59.99</Price>
  </Book>
</Books>
```

We will frequently refer back to this Books.xml document in the examples of this appendix.

The Document Object Model (DOM)

The Document Object Model (or DOM) uses a tree representation to describe structured, hierarchical data in an XML document. The tree structure sometimes is referred to as a *document tree* or *DOM tree*. Figure C-1 is a DOM tree of the Books.xml document.

DOM Objects

When the DOM parser, such as the MSXML DOM parser, reads an XML document, it creates a DOM tree in the memory and loads the contents of the entire XML document into the nodes of the tree. An application then accesses and manipulates the DOM tree through the DOM API. Figure C-2 illustrates this process:

In a DOM tree, each individual object is referred to as a *Node*. For example, in Figure C-1, there is a Document node (the document root), many element nodes

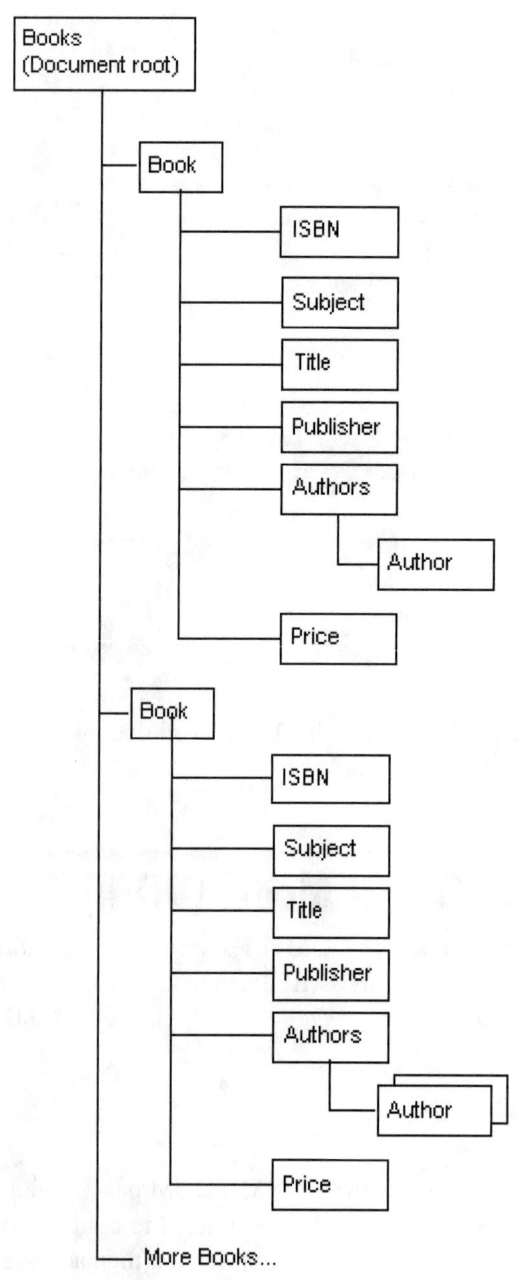

Figure C-1 *The tree structure of an XML document*

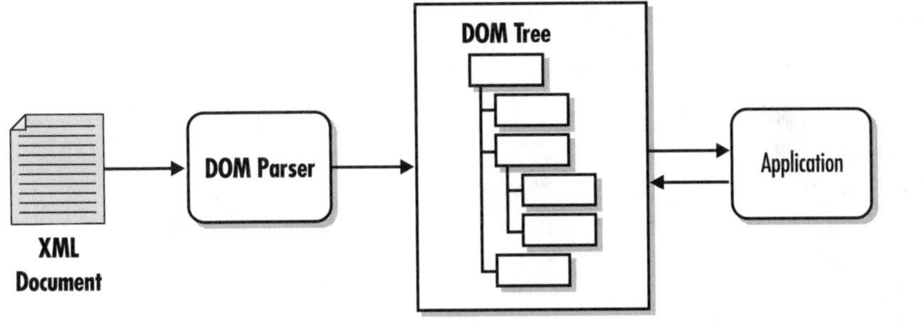

Figure C-2 *How a DOM parser processes an XML document*

(Books, Book, Title, Publisher, Authors, Author, Price, etc.) and attribute nodes (ISBN, Subject, etc.). There are also other types of nodes (not shown in Figure C-1) representing different parts of an XML document, such as namespace nodes, text nodes, PI nodes, comment nodes, CDATA nodes, and so on. DOM provides a set of objects or interfaces that map to the objects in a DOM tree. The following table describes the primary objects that are implemented in MSXML DOM parser:

DOM Object	Description
DOMDocument	Represents the XML document as a whole
IXMLDOMNodeList	Represents a node set, or collection of nodes
IXMLDOMNode	Represents a single node object in a node collection
IXMLDOMNamedNodeMap	Represents a collection of namespace attributes
IXMLDOMParseError	Returns detailed information of the last parse error

In this appendix, we will discuss these DOM objects through various examples. In addition, we will also introduce the IXMLHTTPRequest, as well as the ServerXMLHTTP and ServerXMLHTTPRequest objects. These objects are Microsoft's extension to the DOM object that support the HTTP protocol, and can be very handy when sending and receiving XML HTTP requests (a very useful feature for building applications that gets documents in and out of BizTalk Servers).

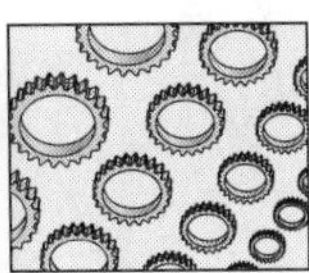

NOTE

For detailed information about MSXSL DOM objects, their properties and methods, please refer to the MSXML Parser SDK documentation.

DOMDocument

The *DOMDocument* object represents the content of an XML document. This object provides a main entrance to the XML document. You can also use it to load an XML document, to gather information about the XML document, to navigate through the DOM tree, and to create new nodes (elements, attributes, etc.).

The ProgID (Program ID) of the DOMDocument is **MSXML2.DOMDocument**. To create an instance of the DOMDocument object in Visual Basic, use one of the following methods:

```
'Assuming you have set a reference in your VB project to
'Microsoft XML, v3.0 (msxml3.dll).
Dim oXMLDoc As MSXML2.DOMDocument
Set oXMLDoc = New MSXML2.Document
```

Or:

```
Dim oXMLDoc As Object
Set oXMLDoc = CreateObject("MSXML2.DOMDocument")
```

The two methods are frequently referred to as *early-binding* and *late-binding* in Visual Basic documentation. The second example calls the *CreateObject* method to create an instance of the named object. This method is more flexible because it does not require you to reference a specific version of the XML parser type library, thus removing the version dependency, providing that the interface doesn't change. This is the way in which a scripting language such as VBScript and JScript creates an instance of object.

To load an XML document from an external file, you call its *Load* method of the DOMDocument. For example:

```
Dim oXMLDoc As Object
Set oXMLDoc = CreateObject("MSXML2.DOMDocument")
oXMLDoc.Load App.Path & "\Books.xml"
```

TIP

Here the App object in App.Path is a Visual Basic specific object, referring to the Visual Basic executable. The App.Path points to the path where the executable resides. In case the application is an ActiveX DLL, App.Path will be the path of the hosting application (the caller of the DLL).

To load an XML string, you call the *LoadXML* method instead:

```
oXMLDoc.LoadXML "<Books/>"
```

The *Save* method of the DOMDocument object allows you to save the content of the DOM tree in the memory to an external file:

```
oXMLDoc.Save App.Path & "\Books.xml"
```

The DOMDocument supports several *create* methods for generating a new node of a specific type. For example, to create an element, use the *createElement* methods, as illustrated in the following example:

First, declare related DOM objects:

```
Dim oXMLDoc As Object
Dim oNode As Object 'MSXML2.IXMLDOMElement
Dim oNode1 As Object 'MSXML2.IXMLDOMElement
Dim oNode2 As Object 'MSXML2.IXMLDOMElement
```

Then create a DOMDocument instance:

```
Set oXMLDoc = CreateObject("MSXML2.DOMDocument")
```

Now, create a Books element and append it to the document:

```
Set oNode = oXMLDoc.createElement("Books")
oXMLDoc.appendChild oNode
```

Next, create the Book child element for the root element:

```
Set oNode1 = oXMLDoc.createElement("Book")
oNode.appendChild oNode1
```

Now create the Title child element for Book element, and set its text context:

```
Set oNode2 = oXMLDoc.createElement("Title")
oNode2.Text = "XSLT:Professional Developer's Guide"
oNode1.appendChild oNode2
```

Finally, save the document:

```
oXMLDoc.Save App.Path & "\Books.xml"
```

As illustrated in the previous example, the createElement method returns an IXMLDOMElement object. You also need to call the *appendChild* method to append the element node you created from the appropriate parent node. Both the DOMDocument object and the IXMLDOMElement object support the appendChild method. This sample code will create a simple Books.xml document, as illustrated in Figure C-3.

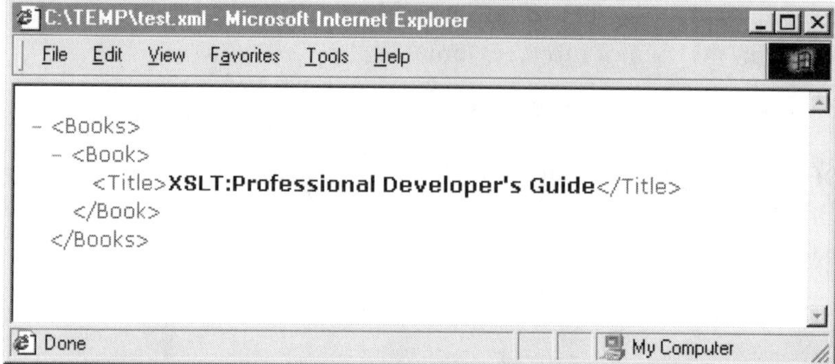

Figure C-3 *The simplified Books.xml document*

There is something missing from the preceding example, as you might have noticed. We need to add two attributes to the Title element, an ISBN and a Subject. To create an attribute, call the *setAttribute* method of the IXMLDOMElement object:

IXMLDOMElement.setAttribute "Attribute_Name", "Value"

To add the ISBN and Subject attributes to the Title element, insert the following two lines of code above oNode.appendChild oNode2:

```
oNode2.setAttribute "ISBN", "047146031"
oNode2.setAttribute "Subject", "XML"
```

The new code will generate a slightly enhanced version of the Books.xml document, as shown in Figure C-4.

In a similar manner, you can create the rest of the elements and attributes for the entire Books.xml document, as shown earlier in this appendix.

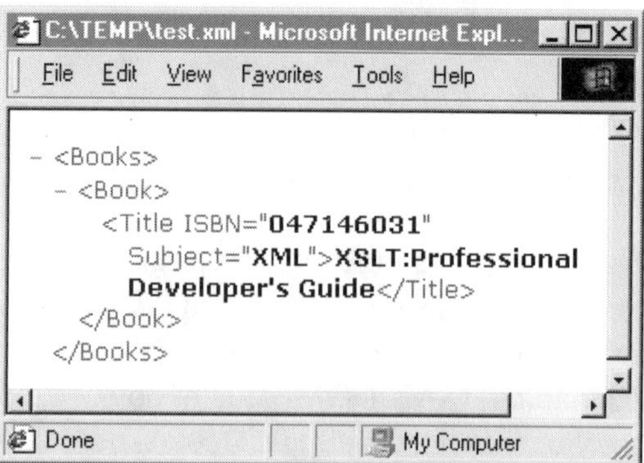

Figure C-4 *The enhanced Books.xml document*

The DOMDocument object supports several other *create** methods for constructing a new node. The following table lists the important ones:

Method	Description	Syntax
createComment	Creates a comment section, <!—…—>	oDOMDocument.createComment("Your_Comments")
createCDATASection	Creates a CDATA section: <![CDATA[…)]]>	oDOMDocument.createCDATASection("CDATA_Section")
createProcessingInstruction	Creates a PI. For example, <?xml-stylesheet type="text/xsl" href="Books.xsl"?>	oDOMDocument.createProcessingInstruction("Target","PI")

In addition, DOMDocument implemented in MSXML Parser 3.0 has a generic *createNode* method which has the following syntax:

Set oXMLDOMNode = oDOMDocument.createNode (Type, Name, NamespaceURL)

This method returns an IXMLDOMNode object, as we will discuss in the next section. Where the *Type* parameter refers to the type of node (or node type) you intend to create, as you will see in the next section. The *Name* parameter is the name of the node to be created. The *NamespaceURL* parameter specifies a namespace URL. When there is a prefix assigned to the namespace, the prefix will be used in the node to be created. Otherwise, it will be treated as the default namespace—there will be no prefix associated with the generated node.

CAUTION

The createNode method is MSXML Parser specific.

The DOMDocument supports a *getElementsByTagName* method that takes the element name as the input parameter and returns an IXMLDOMNodeList object as you will see in the next section. The following example calls the getElementsByTagName method of the DOMDocument object to return a node set and then loop through it to calculate the total prices of the books:

```
Dim oXMLDoc As New Msxml2.DOMDocument
Dim oNodeList As IXMLDOMNodeList
Dim i As Integer
Dim cTotal As Currency
oXMLDoc.async = False
```

```
oXMLDoc.Load App.Path & "books.xml"
Set oNodeList = oXMLDoc.getElementsByTagName("Price")
For i = 0 To (oNodeList.length - 1)
    cTotal = CCur((objNodeList.Item(i).text))
Next
Msgbox "The Total Cost of Books is $" & cTotal
```

You may notice that in the preceding code segment, there is a line that sets the *async* property of the DOMDocument object to False. The property is an MSXML parser specific property and is not supported by other XML parsers. Its default value is True. This means that by default, the MSXML parser will load an XML document asynchronously. This behavior could cause some problems, especially when the size of the XML file is large. For example, if you try to access the DOMDocument object and related objects before the document is completely loaded, a parser error will be returned. This is why most of the time we set the async property of the DOMDocument object to False to force the document to load synchronously.

If you do want to load the XML document asynchronously, MSXML parser provides a couple of events to let you check the loading status. The *ondataavailable* event fires when new data becomes available, so you can start parallel processing while the file is still loading. The *onreadystatuschange* event fires when the *readyState* property changes. You need to check the readyState property on both ondataavailable and onreadystatuschange events. There are four possible readyStates, as described in the following table:

readyState	Value	Description
LOADING	1	The document is being loaded but has not yet parsed.
LOADED	2	The document is being read and parsed, but the object model is not available yet.
INTERACTIVE	3	Part of the document is read and parsed. The object model is available for read-only.
COMPLETED	4	At this point, the document has been completely loaded and available for processing.

CAUTION

The async, readyState properties, and relevant events are MSXML parser specific.

In addition, you can also use DOMDocument to transform an XML document to the desired output format as defined by an XSLT stylesheet by calling its *transformNode* method or *transformNodeToObject* method. The following example transforms the Books.xml document to an HTML document Books.htm, using the Books.xsl XSLT stylesheet:

```
Dim oXML As Object 'Source XML document.
Dim oXSL As Object 'XSLT Stylesheet
Dim oFSO As Object 'FileSystemObject
Dim oFile As Object
Dim sOutput As String
Set oXML = CreateObject("MSXSL2.DOMDocument")
Set oXSL = CreateObject("MSXSL2.DOMDocument")
oXML.Load App.Path & "\Books.xml"
oXSL.Load App.Path & "\Books.xsl"
sOutput = oXML.transformNode(oXSL)
Set oFSO = CreateObject("Scripting.FileSystemObject")
Set oFile = oFSO.CreateTextFile(App.Path & "\Books.htm", True)
oFile.WriteLine sOutput
oFile.Close
```

The *transformNodeToObject* method works in a similar way. Instead of outputting the result to a string, this method creates an output object, such as a stream object, as illustrated in the following ASP code segment that sends the output of the transformation to the Response object so it will be directly displayed in the web browser:

```
<%
'code for instantiating and loading the objects
'omitted...
oXML.transformNodeToObject oXSL, Response
%>
```

The *XML* property of the DOMDocument object contains a read-only copy of the XML document the object represents.

IXMLDOMNode and IXMLDOMNodeList

The *IXMLDOMNode* represents a node of a specific type in the DOM tree. This is a generic object that can represent any type of node as indicated by its *nodeType* property. The following table describes the dozens of possible values for the nodeType property of the IXMLDOMNode object:

NodeType	Values	Description
NODE_ELEMENT	1	An element node
NODE_ATTRIBUTE	2	An attribute node
NODE_TEXT	3	A text node
NODE_CDATA_SECTION	4	A CDATA Section node
NODE_ENTITY_REFERENCE	5	Node representing the entity reference
NODE_ENTITY	6	An entity node
NODE_PROCESSING_INSTRUCTION	7	A PI node
NODE_COMMENT	8	A comment node
NODE_DOCUMENT	9	Node representing the XML document
NODE_DOCUMENT_TYPE	10	Represents the DTD indicated by the <!DOCTYPE> tag
NODE_DOCUMENT_FRAGMENT	11	Node representing a document fragment
NODE_NOTATION	12	A notation node

As we mentioned earlier, the IXMLDOMNode is a generic object. As such, some of its properties are only available for a specific nodeType. For example, the *nodeValue* property is only available for the nodes of type NODE_ ATTRIBUTE, NODE_TEXT, NODE_CDATA_SECTION, and NODE_COMMENT. For other node types, the nodeValue property is null. An attempt to access the nodeValue for these node types will generate an error.

The IXMLDOMNode object provides several properties and methods for working with its child nodes and siblings, such as the *firstChild*, *lastChild*, *nextSibling* properties, and *childNodes* property. The childNodes property returns a collection of child nodes represented by the *IXMLDOMNodeList* object.

The *appendChildNodes* and *hasChildNodes* returns a Boolean, indicating whether the existing node has any child nodes. The appendChild method will append a node of appropriate type to the existing node.

Additionally, there are two methods of the IXMLDOMNode object worth noticing—*selectNodes* and *selectSingleNode*. Both methods use an XPath expression as their input parameter. The selectNodes method returns the IXMLDOMNodeList containing all the qualified child nodes of the existing node. Whereas the selectSingleNode method will return the first matching child nodes.

TIPS

The selectNodes and selectSingleNode methods also apply to the DOMDocument object.

The IXMLDOMNodeList object represents a collection of nodes, where each node in the collection is of type IXMLDOMNode. When used together, these two objects provide a way for iterating through a list of nodes, similar to what is done to a database cursor.

You will see some examples that use the IXMLDOMNode and IXMLDOMNodeList objects later in this appendix.

IXMLDOMNamedNodeMap

The *IXMLDOMNamedNodeMap* provides a convenient way for iterating through a collection of namespaces and attributes. The attributes property of the DOMDocument and IXMLDOMNode objects will return IXMLDOMNamedNodeMap object.

The following code example illustrates the use of the IXMLDOMNamedNodeMap object:

```
Dim oXMLDoc As New MSXML2.DOMDocument
Dim oNode As IXMLDOMNode
Dim oNamedNodeMap As IXMLDOMNamedNodeMap
Dim i As Integer

oXMLDoc.async = False
oXMLDoc.Load App.Path & "\Books.xml"
Set oNode = oXMLDoc.selectSingleNode("//Book")
Set oNamedNodeMap = oNode.Attributes

For i = 0 To oNamedNodeMap.length - 1
    Debug.Print oNamedNodeMap.Item(i).baseName _
            & ": " & oNamedNodeMap.Item(i).Text
Next i
```

This will print the following contents to the Immediate Window of Visual Basic IDE:

ISBN: 047146031
Subject: XML

IXMLDOMParseError

A robust application must provide a way for reporting exceptions and handling errors. The DOM object model provides an *IXMLDOMParseError* object for you to detect and report any errors during the loading process of the XML document.

The IXMLDOMParseError can be retrieved by the *parseError* property of the DOMDocument object. It has the following read-only properties:

ParseError Property	Description
ErrorCode	A number that represents the error code. This is the default property.
Reason	The cause of the error.
Line	The line number that contains the error reported.
Linepos	The character position within the line where the error occurred.
Filepos	The character position within the file that contains the error.
SrcText	The full text of the line that contains the error.
url	The URL of the file that contains the error.

The following example illustrates the use of the IXMLDOMParseError object:

```
If oXMLDoc.parseError.errorCode <> 0 Then
    MsgBox "Parse Error: " & oXMLDoc.parseError.errorCode & vbCrLf & _
           "Reason: " & oXMLDoc.parseError.reason & _
           "Line: " & oXMLDoc.parseError.Line & vbCrLf & _
           "Position: " & oXMLDoc.parseError.linepos
    Exit Sub
End If
```

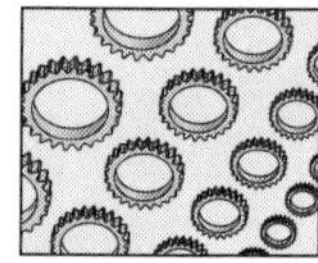

NOTE

The parse error is not a conventional error you can trap in a programming language like Visual Basic using its error trapping mechanism (which is the case with On Error statements in Visual Basic or VBScript). You must explicitly check the errorCode of the parseError property of the DOMDocument object, as we illustrated in the example. Additionally, whenever an error occurs while loading an XML document, the process will be terminated immediately. This means that if there is more than one error in the XML document, the parser will only detect the first error and stop the process.

By now, we have introduced you to all the MSXML DOM objects. A little later in this appendix, we will show you how to leverage the knowledge you've learned so far to build more advanced XML applications. In the meantime, let's introduce a couple of MSXML specific HTTP related objects.

XMLHTTP and ServerXMLHTTP

MSXML parser version 2.0 introduced an *XMLHTTP* object that enables you to send HTTP requests to a remote HTTP server. The XMLHTTP object implements the *IXMLHTTPRequest* interface. It provides a set of properties and methods for you to establish a connection to a remote HTTP server, set HTTP header information, send the request to the remote HTTP server, and process the server's response.

For example, to connect to the remote HTTP server, call the *Open* method of the XMLHTTP object:

```
Dim oXMLHTTP As Object
Set oXMLHTTP = CreateObject("MSXML2.XMLHTTP")
oXMLHTTP.Open "POST", _
            "http://MyWebServer/MyPage.asp"
```

The Open method takes two required parameters. The first required parameter is an HTTP method name such as POST, GET, PUT, PROPFIND, etc. The second required parameter is an absolute URL which points to the web page that your HTTP request is sent to. Optionally, you can also specify a Boolean parameter that determines whether the request is asynchronous or synchronous (the default is True, asynchronous), as well as specify a pair of parameters to be used as username and password in order to log on to a secure server.

After the connection to the remote HTTP server is established, set the HTTP header section by calling the *setRequestHeader* method of the XMLHTTP object:

```
oHTTP.setRequestHeader "Host", "YourWebServer"
oHTTP.setRequestHeader "Content-Type", "text/xml"
oHTTP.setRequestHeader "SOAPAction", sSOAPAction
```

The setRequestHeader method takes a pair of parameters, a header name and its value. The preceding example sets appropriate HTTP header information for an SOAP request.

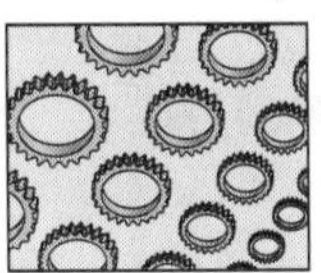

NOTE

For more information about SOAP (Simple Object Access Protocol), visit MSDN SOAP web site at: http://msdn.microsoft.com/soap/.

Now you are ready to send your HTTP request by calling the *send* method of the XMLHTTP object:

```
oXMLHTTP.send oXMLDoc 'oXMLDoc is an DOMDocument object
```

The send method has one parameter which is the request body. It could be an XML DOM document, as shown in the example, or a stream such as a string.

After you send the HTTP request, you can process the server response. Use one of the four properties of the XMLHTTP object: *responseBody*, *responseStream*, *responseText*, or *responseXML*, depending on the *Content-type* setting on your request. In our example, we used the responseXML to retrieve the content of the response:

```
set oHTTPResponse = oXMLHTTP.responseXML
'Now you can process the response via the
'oHTTPResponse object (an DOMDocument object)...
```

Whereas the XMLHTTP provides a great way for sending an HTTP request from a client to a remote server, this object is not optimized to be used as a server-side solution (where thread-safeness and multiple instancing are required) to send HTTP requests from one server to another server. For this reason, MSXML parser version 3.0 introduced another object—*ServerXMLHTTP*.

The ServerXMLHTTP object implements the *IServerXMLHTTPRequest* interface, which supports all of the properties and methods of the IXMLHTTPRequest interface plus a few newer methods such as *setOptions*, *setTimeouts*, and *waitForResponse*.

The ServerXMLHTTP object is designed to be used in server-side applications. It overcomes several shortcomings of the XMLHTTP object, such as dependency on WinInet for HTTP. It uses a "server-safe" subset of WinInet and offers enhanced reliability, security and multi-threading.

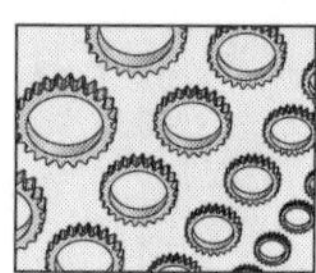

NOTE

If your HTTP or HTTPS servers are accessed via a proxy server, you need to use a WinHTTP proxy configuration utility, proxycfg.exe which can be downloaded from the following MSDN: ***http://msdn.microsoft.com/downloads/default.asp?URL-/code/sample.asp?url=/msdn-files/027/001/468/msdncompositedoc.xml****. For detailed instructions on the syntax of this proxy configuration utility, refer to the MSXML Parser SDK documentation.*

CAUTION

The ServerXMLHTTP only works on Windows NT 4.0 and Windows 2000 Servers. It won't work on Windows 9.x/ME systems.

Building XML Applications Using DOM

Using these primary DOM objects we introduced in the previous sections, you can build fairly complex and sophisticated XML applications. In this section, we will show you some examples to leverage the knowledge and techniques you have learned.

Navigating and Iterating an XML Document

This example shows the detailed information about Books in the Books.xml document. It does this by navigating and iterating the hierarchy of the DOM tree and displaying every piece of information it finds at a particular node level:

```
Private Sub cmdListBookDetails_Click()
    Dim oXML   As Object
    Dim oNodes As Object
    Dim oNode As Object
    Dim sBooksInfo As String

    On Error GoTo ErrorHandler
    Set oXML = CreateObject("MSXML2.DOMDocument")
    oXML.Load App.Path & "\books.xml"
    If oXML.parseerror.errorcode <> 0 Then
        MsgBox oXML.parseerror.reason
        Exit Sub
    End If
    sBooksInfo = "Programming Books"
    Set oNodes = oXML.selectNodes("Books")
    For Each oNode In oNodes
        If oNode.hasChildNodes Then
            sBooksInfo = sBooksInfo & ListNodes(oNode, 0)
        Else
            sBooksInfo = oNode.NodeName
        End If
    Next

    MsgBox sBooksInfo
    Exit Sub
ErrorHandler:
    MsgBox Err.Description
End Sub
```

Let's see how this works. After setting up the error trap by using the On Error statement, the function creates an instance of the DOMDocument object and loads the Books.xml document:

```
On Error GoTo ErrorHandler
Set oXML = CreateObject("MSXML2.DOMDocument")
oXML.Load App.Path & "\books.xml"
```

The next line then checks to see if there is any parse error while loading the document:

```
If oXML.parseerror.errorcode <> 0 Then
    MsgBox oXML.parseerror.reason
    Exit Sub
End If
```

If everything goes fine, it calls the selectNodes method with an XPath expression "Books" to return an IXMLNodeList object, oNodes. Because "Books" is the root node of the document, all the nodes in the document will be returned:

```
Set oNodes = oXML.selectNodes("Books")
```

Next, it loops through the oNodes list and either calls another function, *ListNodes*, to list the child nodes of each IXMLDOMNode object (oNode) or simply adds the node name to the list if there are no child nodes for a particular node:

```
For Each oNode In oNodes
    If oNode.hasChildNodes Then
        sBooksInfo = sBooksInfo & ListNodes(oNode, 0)
    Else
        sBooksInfo = oNode.NodeName
    End If
Next
```

ListNodes is a recursive function that does the actual work of navigating and iterating through the hierarchy of the DOM tree, retrieving detailed information for each node. Here is the ListNodes function:

```
Public Function ListNodes(ByVal oNode As Object, _
ByVal iIndent As Integer) As String

    Dim oItem As Object
    Dim oAttrs As Object
    Dim oNodesMap As Object
    Dim oNodes As Object
    Dim sListNodes As String

    On Error GoTo ErrorHandler
    iIndent = iIndent + 4
```

```
    'List the attributes if any for the particular node.
    Set oNodesMap = oNode.Attributes
    For Each oItem In oNodesMap
        sListNodes = sListNodes & vbCrLf & Space(iIndent) _
                   & oItem.NodeName & ": " & oItem.Text
    Next

    'List the texts of the element.
    Set oNodes = oNode.childNodes
    For Each oItem In oNodes
        If oItem.nodeType = NODE_TEXT Then
            sListNodes = sListNodes & ": " & oItem.Text
        Else
            sListNodes = sListNodes & vbCrLf & Space(iIndent) _
                       & oItem.NodeName
        End If
        If oItem.hasChildNodes Then
            sListNodes = sListNodes & ListNodes(oItem, iIndent)
        End If
    Next
    ListNodes = sListNodes
    Exit Function
ErrorHandler:
    ListNodes = Err.Description
End Function
```

Let's see how this works. The ListNodes function takes two input parameters, an IXMLDOMNode object and an integer, and returns a string that contains the detailed information it found about the nodes. The second input parameter helps to appropriately indent the list for better displaying:

```
Public Function ListNodes(ByVal oNode As Object, _
ByVal iIndent As Integer) As String
```

Each time the ListNodes function is called, it indents four more spaces:

```
iIndent = iIndent + 4
```

Then the function assigns the attributes property to an IXMLNamedNodeMap object, oNodesMap. If there is no attribute for a particular node, the oNodesMap will be null. Otherwise, it will be a collection of attributes:

```
Set oNodesMap = oNode.Attributes
```

In the later case, the function loops through the attributes collection using the *For Each …Next* construct and adds the attributes to the list:

```
For Each oItem In oNodesMap
    sListNodes = sListNodes & vbCrLf & Space(iIndent) _
                 & oItem.NodeName & ": " & oItem.Text
Next
```

Next, the function will call the childNodes method of the particular node. If the node has any child nodes, it will either list the name of the node for an element node or the text for a text node. If any of the child nodes themselves contain child nodes, the function will call itself to go one layer deeper in the hierarchy. In this recursive manner, all the information about the nodes will be listed:

```
Set oNodes = oNode.childNodes
For Each oItem In oNodes
    If oItem.nodeType = NODE_TEXT Then
        sListNodes = sListNodes & ": " & oItem.Text
    Else
        sListNodes = sListNodes & vbCrLf & Space(iIndent) _
                     & oItem.NodeName
    End If
    If oItem.hasChildNodes Then
        sListNodes = sListNodes & ListNodes(oItem, iIndent)
    End If
Next
ListNodes = sListNodes
```

The NODE_TEXT is a constant that is declared in the General Declaration section of the Visual Basic project:

```
Option Explicit
Const NODE_TEXT = 3
```

Figure C-5 shows the results.

Retrieving Specific Information about an XML Document

Navigating and iterating the DOM tree to get the information from all the nodes in the tree is great. But sometimes you may only be interested in certain information in an

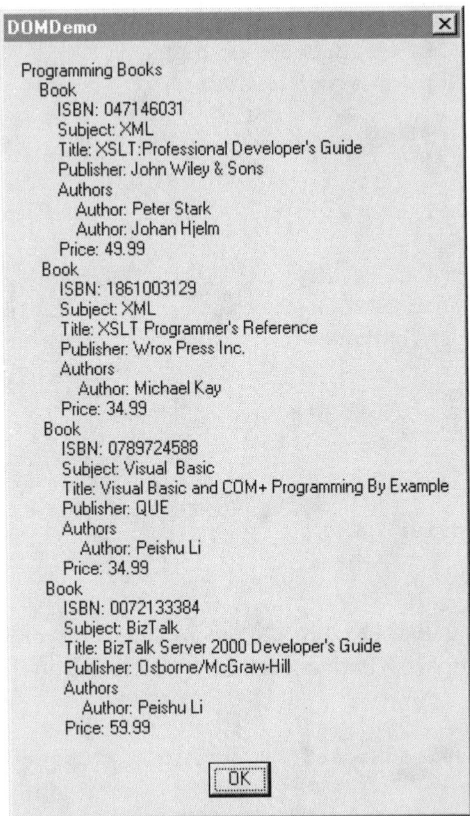

Figure C-5 *The detailed information about the books*

XML document. For example, you may want to get a list of XML titles from the Books.xml document. The following code demonstrates how to do this:

```
Private Sub cmdListXMLBooks_Click()
    Dim oXML As Object
    Dim oNodes As Object
    Dim oNode As Object
    Dim sBooksInfo As String

    On Error GoTo ErrorHandler
    Set oXML = CreateObject("MSXML2.DOMDocument")
```

```
    oXML.Load App.Path & "\books.xml"
    If oXML.parseerror.errorcode <> 0 Then
        MsgBox oXML.parseerror.reason
        Exit Sub
    End If

    sBooksInfo = "XML Books: " & vbCrLf & vbCrLf

    Set oNodes =
oXML.selectNodes("/Books/Book[@Subject='XML']/Title")
    For Each oNode In oNodes
        sBooksInfo = sBooksInfo & oNode.Text & vbCrLf & vbCrLf
    Next
    MsgBox sBooksInfo
    Exit Sub
ErrorHandler:
    MsgBox Err.Description
End Sub
```

In this example, we called the selectNodes method of the DOMDocument object and passed a more complex XPath expression, "/Books/Book[@Subject = 'XML']/Title":

```
Set oNodes = oXML.selectNodes("/Books/Book[@Subject='XML']/Title")
```

As we explained in Appendix B of this book, this XPath asks the XML parser to return a node set of Title element that is the child of the Book element whose Subject attribute equals "XML", and is also the child of the Books element.

The code next iterates through the node set and displays the contents:

```
For Each oNode In oNodes
    sBooksInfo = sBooksInfo & oNode.Text & vbCrLf & vbCrLf
Next
```

The result is shown in Figure C-6.

By using XPath expressions in conjunction with the DOM objects, you can also perform some calculations against the subset of nodes returned by the XPath

Figure C-6 *A list of XML books*

expression. For instance, you can calculate the total price for XML books, as we next illustrate:

```
Private Sub cmdGetXMLBookPrices_Click()
    Dim oXML As Object
    Dim oNodes As Object
    Dim oNode As Object
    Dim price As Currency

    On Error GoTo ErrorHandler
    Set oXML = CreateObject("MSXML2.DOMDocument.3.0")
    oXML.Load App.Path & "\books.xml"
    If oXML.parseerror.errorcode <> 0 Then
        MsgBox oXML.parseerror.reason
        Exit Sub
    End If

    Set oNodes =
oXML.selectNodes("/Books/Book[@Subject='XML']/Price")
    For Each oNode In oNodes
        price = price + CCur(oNode.Text)
    Next
    MsgBox "Total Price for XML Books = $" & price & "."
    Exit Sub
ErrorHandler:
    MsgBox Err.Description
End Sub
```

Figure C-7 shows the result.

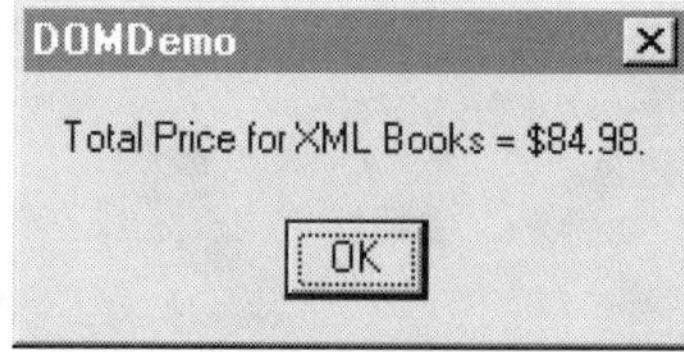

Figure C-7 *The total price for XML books*

Creating a COM Wrapper to DOM APIs

The previous examples demonstrated how to retrieve information from an XML document by using the DOM objects and XPath expressions. These techniques are important for building applications that process XML documents. For example, you may want to write an ASP page that receives and processes XML documents from BizTalk Servers. Or you may create a COM object for BizTalk Orchestration Services that takes an XML document as the input parameter of one of its functions.

In other scenarios, you may want to create an XML document based on the data you collected from an HTML form or from a database. To build an XML document using the raw DOM APIs, you have to use several DOM objects and maintain their relationships. This could be tedious and error prone. Instead, you can create a reusable COM component that wraps the raw DOM API calls into a single object to simplify the task. For demonstration purposes, we created a Visual Basic ActiveX DLL project, as shown in Figure C-8.

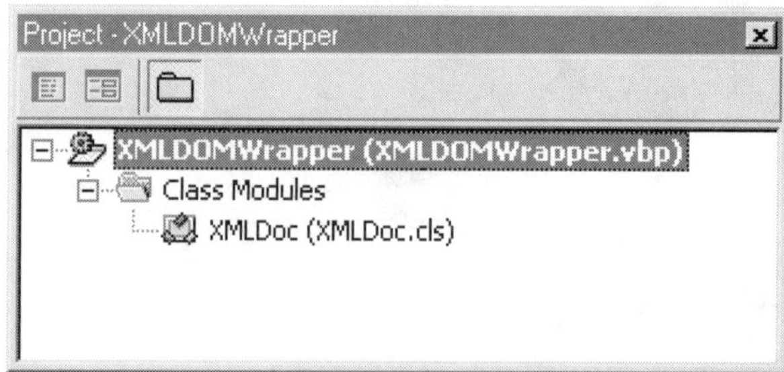

Figure C-8 *The XMLDOMWrapper Visual Basic ActiveX DLL project*

The XMLDOMWrapper project has a single class, XMLDoc, which supports the following properties and methods:

Property/Method	Description
CreateDoc	This method creates an internal DOMDocument object and sets its root element. This method must be called first before you call the rest of the methods of the Wrapper object, such as CreateElement, SetAttribute, etc.
CreateElement	This method creates an element for the internal DOMDocument object.
SetAttribute	This method sets an attribute for an element of the internal DOMDocument.
CreatePI	This method creates a processing instruction.
Save	This method saves the file to a URL you specify.
XML	This read-only property returns the XML document you build through the Wrapper object.
CurrentNode	This read-only property provides a bookmark of the current node.

The following is the implementation of the XMLDoc class:

```
'============================================================
' In the General Declaration section we declared two module
' level variables, the m_oXMLDoc holds the DOMDocument object
' internally and the m_oCurrentNode keeps track of the current
' node in the process so that the client application can
' bookmark it.
'============================================================
Option Explicit
Dim m_oXMLDoc As New MSXML2.DOMDocument
Dim m_oCurrentNode As MSXML2.IXMLDOMElement

'============================================================
' The CreateDoc() method
'============================================================
Public Sub CreateDoc(ByVal Root As Variant)
    On Error GoTo ErrorHandler
    Dim oRoot As MSXML2.IXMLDOMElement
    Set oRoot = m_oXMLDoc.CreateElement(Root)
    m_oXMLDoc.appendChild oRoot
```

```
    Set m_oCurrentNode = oRoot
    Exit Sub
ErrorHandler:
    Dim Number As Integer
    Dim Description As String
    Number = Err.Number
    Description = Err.Description
    Call RaiseError(Number, Description)
End Sub

'==============================================================
' The CreatePI() method
'==============================================================
Public Sub CreatePI(ByVal Target As Variant, _
                   ByVal Data As Variant)
    On Error GoTo ErrorHandler

    Dim oInstruction As MSXML2.IXMLDOMProcessingInstruction

    Set oInstruction = m_oXMLDoc.createProcessingInstruction(Target, Data)
    m_oXMLDoc.insertBefore oInstruction, m_oXMLDoc.documentElement
        Exit Sub
ErrorHandler:
    Dim Number As Integer
    Dim Description As String
    Number = Err.Number
    Description = Err.Description
    Call RaiseError(Number, Description)
End Sub

'==============================================================
' The CreateElement() method
'==============================================================
Public Function CreateElement(ByVal Parent As Variant, _
                         ByVal Name As Variant, _
                         ByVal Value As Variant) As Variant
    On Error GoTo ErrorHandler

    Dim oNode As MSXML2.IXMLDOMElement
    Set oNode = m_oXMLDoc.CreateElement(Name)
    If Len(Value) <> 0 Then
        oNode.Text = Value
```

```
    End If
    Parent.appendChild oNode
    Set m_oCurrentNode = oNode
    Set CreateElement = oNode
    Exit Function
ErrorHandler:
    Dim Number As Integer
    Dim Description As String
    Number = Err.Number
    Description = Err.Description
    Call RaiseError(Number, Description)
End Function

'==============================================================
' The SetAttribute() method
'==============================================================
Public Sub SetAttribute(ByVal Node As Variant, _
                        ByVal AttributeName As Variant, _
                        ByVal AttributeValue As Variant)
    On Error GoTo ErrorHandler
    Node.SetAttribute AttributeName, AttributeValue
    Exit Sub
ErrorHandler:
    Dim Number As Integer
    Dim Description As String
    Number = Err.Number
    Description = Err.Description
    Call RaiseError(Number, Description)
End Sub


'==============================================================
' The XML property (read-only)
'==============================================================
Public Property Get XML() As Variant
    On Error GoTo ErrorHandler
    XML = m_oXMLDoc.XML
    Exit Property
ErrorHandler:
    Dim Number As Integer
    Dim Description As String
    Number = Err.Number
```

```
    Description = Err.Description
    Call RaiseError(Number, Description)
End Property

'==============================================================
' The CurrentNode property (read-only)
'==============================================================
Public Property Get CurrentNode() As Variant
    On Error GoTo ErrorHandler
    Set CurrentNode = m_oCurrentNode
    Exit Property
ErrorHandler:
    Dim Number As Integer
    Dim Description As String
    Number = Err.Number
    Description = Err.Description
    Call RaiseError(Number, Description)
End Property

'==============================================================
' The Save() method
'==============================================================
Public Sub Save(ByVal Destination As Variant)
    On Error GoTo ErrorHandler
    m_oXMLDoc.Save Destination
    Exit Sub
ErrorHandler:
    Dim Number As Integer
    Dim Description As String
    Number = Err.Number
    Description = Err.Description
    Call RaiseError(Number, Description)
End Sub

'==============================================================
' The RaiseError() method (private)
'==============================================================
Private Sub RaiseError(ByVal Number As Integer, _
                       ByVal Description As String)
    Err.Raise Number, Description
End Sub
```

Compile the ActiveX DLL by choosing File, Make XMLDOMWrapper.dll… from the menu. The following is a sample client code that creates an XML document with one book, using the XMLDOMWrapper COM component:

```
Option Explicit

Private Sub Command1_Click()

    On Error GoTo ErrorHandler

    Dim oXML As Object 'XMLDOMWrapper.XMLDoc
    Dim oBookmarkNode As Object

    'Create an instance of the XMLDOMWrapper.
    Set oXML = CreateObject("XMLDOMWrapper.XMLDoc")

    'Create the document root.
    oXML.CreateDoc "Books"

    'Create a processing instruction - the XML declaration
    oXML.CreatePI "xml", "version=""1.0"""

    'Create the Book element.
    oXML.CreateElement oXML.CurrentNode, "Book", ""

    'Bookmark the Book node for later use.
    Set oBookmarkNode = oXML.CurrentNode

    'Add two attributes to the Book element.
    oXML.SetAttribute oBookmarkNode, "ISBN", "047146031"
    oXML.SetAttribute oBookmarkNode, "Subject", "XML"

    'Create the rest of the elements, node that the Author
    'element is the child of Authors, not the child of the
    'bookmark node which is the Book element.
    oXML.CreateElement oBookmarkNode, "Title", _
        "XSLT Programmer's Reference"
    oXML.CreateElement oBookmarkNode, "Publisher", _
        "Wrox Press Inc."
    oXML.CreateElement oBookmarkNode, "Authors", ""
```

```
    oXML.CreateElement oXML.CurrentNode, "Author", _
        "Michael Kay"
    oXML.CreateElement oBookmarkNode, "Price", "34.99"

    'Print the resulted XML document.
    Debug.Print oXML.XML
    Exit Sub
ErrorHandler:
    MsgBox Err.Description
End Sub
```

Here is the XML document it generates (we have added some white spaces to appropriately indent the document to increase its readability):

```
<?xml version="1.0"?>
<Books>
  <Book ISBN="047146031" Subject="XML">
    <Title>XSLT Programmer's Reference</Title>
    <Publisher>Wrox Press Inc.</Publisher>
    <Authors>
      <Author>Michael Kay</Author>
    </Authors>
    <Price>34.99</Price>
  </Book>
</Books>
```

As you can see, with the XMLDOMWrapper component, you can create an XML document with only a handful of calls. The Wrapper object encapsulates the complexity of the raw DOM APIs and makes the creation of an XML document much easier. You can enhance the Wrapper COM object by adding more methods and/or properties to suit your needs.

You may have noticed that all the public properties and methods take or return variant data types. This design will make the Wrapper COM object useful for scripting languages such as VBScript that don't support strong typing. The Wrapper COM object is thus "ASP-friendly."

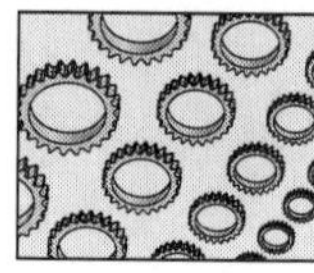

NOTE

The XMLDOMWrapper COM component has a dependency on the MSXML 3.0 Parser. To make it work, the MSXML 3.0 parser must have been installed on the machine. You can download MSXML 3.0 from ***http://msdn.microsoft.com/xml****.*

The Simple API for XML (SAX)

The Simple API for XML, or SAX API, was originally developed for Java language as a simple, fast, and low-level alternative to DOM API. MSXML 3.0 also implemented a SAX parser that supports SAX2 specification (a SAX2 parser). Unlike DOM API which parses an XML document and builds a DOM tree in the memory for applications to access and manipulate, SAX is an event-based API. Figure C-9 illustrates how SAX processes an XML document.

As shown in Figure C-9, the SAX parser reads the contents of an XML document and generates a series of events for the contents it encounters. An application implements appropriate event handlers and processes the events passed by the SAX parser. Events that a SAX parser generates include *StartDocument*, *EndDocument*, *StartElement*, *EndElement*, *Characters*, and so on. The way a SAX parser works is very much like a read-only, forward-only database cursor (sometimes referred as a *fire-hose cursor*). As it traverses the XML document, it reports everything it encounters in the document by firing an appropriate event and moving to the next part, until it reaches the end of the document. In other words, a SAX parser is a *push mode* XML parser.

Introducing MSXML SAX2 Parsers

The MSXML 3.0 (msxml3.dll) includes two SAX2 parsers, one for C++ and another for Visual Basic. The C++ SAX parser is implemented as a series of COM interfaces that maps to the Java SAX implementations. On top of the C++/COM SAX parser, MSXML 3.0 ships with a higher level COM wrapper for the Visual Basic programming language. The names of these C++/COM SAX interfaces are basically the same as those for Java SAX interfaces, except the prefix *ISAX* is added to the names. (Using I prefix is a COM naming convention for interfaces). The names for VB interfaces are similar; the *IVBSAX* prefix is used instead of ISAX.

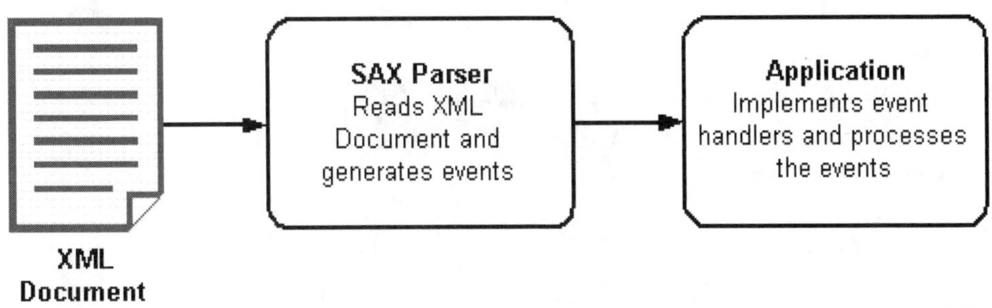

Figure C-9 *SAX is an event-based XML API*

For example, the *ContentHandler* interface in Java becomes ISAXContentHandler in C++, and IVBSAXContentHandler in Visual Basic. In this section, we will introduce the Visual Basic version of MSXML SAX2 parser.

The following table lists the primary interfaces of the MSXML SAX2 VB parser:

Interface	Description
IVBSAXXMLReader	Reads and parses the XML document and passes events to appropriate event handlers.
IVBSAXContentHandler	A primary handler that handles events such as StartDocument, EndDocument, StartElement, EndElement, Characters, etc. This is a primary event handler.
IVBSAXErrorHandler	Handles parsing errors. This interface has three events, error, fatalError and ignorableWarning. In the current version of MSXML SAX2, all the errors are considered fatal.
IVBSAXDTDHandler	Handles Document Type Definition-related events.
IVBSAXLexicalHandler	Handles DOCTYPE, comment, CDATA section, and entity-related events.
IVBSAXDeclHandler	Handles DTD-related events. An optional alternative to the IVBSAXDTD interface.
IVBSAXLocator	Reports the exact location (line, column) in the XML document when an event fires.
IVBSAXEntityResolver	Handles resolveEntity event. Not called in current MSXML SAX2 parser.
IVBSAXXMLFilter	Provides a filter that automatically passes events from upstream interfaces such as the IVBSAXXMLReader (or another IVBSAXXMLFilter interface) to a downstream interface such as IVBSAXEntityResolver, IVBSAXDTDHandler, IVBSAXContentHandler and IVBSAXErrorHandler (or another IVBSAXXMLFilter interface). This feature allows you to build a pipeline filtering solution.
IVBSAXAttributes	Allows a list of attributes to be accessed by indexes or QNames.

Parsing an XML Document Using MSXML SAX2 Parser

The steps for using MSXML SAX2 parser in Visual Basic to retrieve information from an XML document follows:

1. Set a reference to Microsoft XML, v3.0 (msxml3.dll) in the Visual Basic project.
2. Add a number of class modules. Each of them implements a specific type of SAX event handler, such as the IVBSAXContentHandler, IVBSAXErrorHandler, and so on.

3. Write code to appropriate event sinks. For those events to which you don't want to write code, you still need to implement an empty event (this is required by COM).
4. Inside your main code module, create an IVBSAXXMLReader object (the SAXXMLReader object) and associate appropriate event handlers with it (this process is sometimes referred to as Registering event handlers). Your main code module could reside in the same Visual Basic project as those class modules that implement appropriate event handlers, or it could reside in a client application if you wrap up the event handler classes into a COM object as will be illustrated in the example. A call to the *Parse* or *ParseURL* method of the SAXXMLReader object will trigger the appropriate events to be fired and captured by the associated event handlers.

Let's look at an example to demonstrate how to read information from an XML document using MSXML SAX2 parser. We decided to put all the class modules that implement appropriate SAX interfaces and event handlers into an ActiveX DLL project to provide some reusability. In addition, implementing specific interfaces involves an *early binding* process that is not supported in scripting languages such as VBScript and JScript. We can design the Wrapper component appropriately so it will be scripting language-friendly and usable in ASP and other scripting-heavy technologies.

Figure C-10 shows our VBSAX project.

The *CContentHandler* and *CErrorHandler* implement the IVBSAXContentHandler interface and the IVBSAXErrorHandler interface, respectively. Because they are simply event sinks and are not supposed to be accessible outside the component, we need to set the *Instancing* property of both classes to *2-PublicNotCreatable*. The *Wrapper* class, on the other hand, provides the entry point to the outside world whose

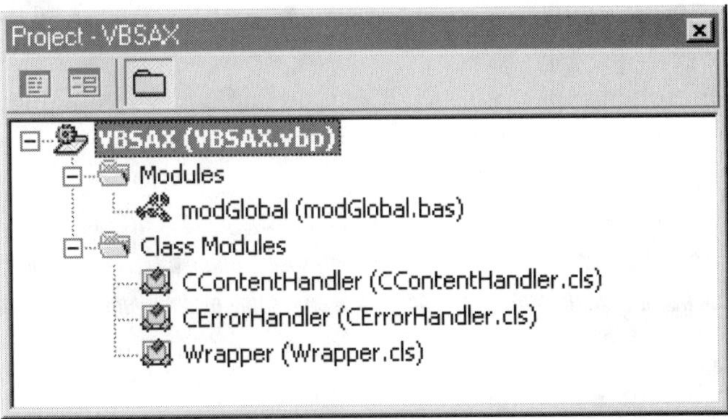

Figure C-10 *The VBSAX ActiveX DLL project*

instancing property should be set to *5-Multiuse*. The standard module modGlobal.bas holds to global variables that will be shared between different classes:

```
Option Explicit
Public g_sXML
Public g_sError
```

The code in the CErrorHandler class is very straightforward:

```
Option Explicit
Implements IVBSAXErrorHandler

Private Sub IVBSAXErrorHandler_fatalError(ByVal lctr As IVBSAXLocator, _
msg As String, ByVal errCode As Long)
    g_sError = g_sError & "*** error *** " & msg
End Sub

Private Sub IVBSAXErrorHandler_error(ByVal lctr As IVBSAXLocator, _
msg As String, ByVal errCode As Long)
    'Do nothing.
End Sub

Private Sub IVBSAXErrorHandler_ignorableWarning(ByVal oLocator _
As MSXML2.IVBSAXLocator, strErrorMessage As String, _
ByVal nErrorCode As Long)
    'Do nothing.
End Sub
```

Because the current MSXML SAX2 parser treats any error as fatal, we only actually implemented the *fatal* event, whereas we left the other two events empty. Notice the *Implements* VB keyword. The Implements statement makes the methods and properties, of the interface available to the Visual Basic classes that implement the interface.

For demonstration purposes, in the CContentHandler, we implemented four events and left the other events empty:

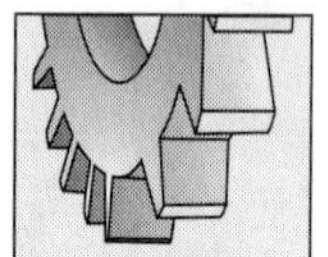

TIP

According to the COM (Component Object Model) specification, a class that implements a specific interface needs to declare all of the methods even if some of the methods don't really do anything.

```
Option Explicit
Implements IVBSAXContentHandler
```

```
Private Sub IVBSAXContentHandler_startElement(strNamespaceURI _
As String, strLocalName As String, strQName As String, _
ByVal attributes As MSXML2.IVBSAXAttributes)
    Dim i As Integer
    g_sXML = g_sXML & "<" & strLocalName
    For i = 0 To (attributes.length - 1)
        g_sXML = g_sXML & " " & attributes.getLocalName(i) _
        & "=""" & attributes.getValue(i) & """"
    Next
    g_sXML = g_sXML & ">"
End Sub

Private Sub IVBSAXContentHandler_endElement(strNamespaceURI _
As String, strLocalName As String, strQName As String)
    g_sXML = g_sXML & "</" & strLocalName & ">"
End Sub

Private Sub IVBSAXContentHandler_characters(text As String)
    text = Replace(text, vbLf, vbCrLf)
    g_sXML = g_sXML & text
End Sub

Private Sub IVBSAXContentHandler_processingInstruction(target _
As String, data As String)
    g_sXML = g_sXML & "<?" & target & " " & data & ">"
End Sub

Private Property Set IVBSAXContentHandler_documentLocator(ByVal _
RHS As MSXML2.IVBSAXLocator)
    'Do nothing.
End Property

Private Sub IVBSAXContentHandler_endDocument()
    'Do nothing.
End Sub

Private Sub IVBSAXContentHandler_endPrefixMapping(strPrefix _
As String)
    'Do nothing.
End Sub

Private Sub IVBSAXContentHandler_ignorableWhitespace(strChars _
```

```
As String)
    'Do nothing.
End Sub

Private Sub IVBSAXContentHandler_skippedEntity(strName _
As String)
    'Do nothing.
End Sub

Private Sub IVBSAXContentHandler_startDocument()
    'Do nothing.
End Sub

Private Sub IVBSAXContentHandler_startPrefixMapping(strPrefix _
As String, strURI As String)
    'Do nothing.
End Sub
```

The Wrapper class is a glue that ties an IVBXMLReader object and the two event handler classes together. Its *ParseURL* method directly wraps the ParseURL method of the IVBXMLReader:

```
Option Explicit

Friend Property Get XML() As String
    XML = g_sXML
End Property

Friend Property Let XML(ByVal sXML As String)
    g_sXML = sXML
End Property

Public Function ParseURL(ByVal sURL As String) As String
    Dim reader As New SAXXMLReader
    Dim contentHandler As New CContentHandler
    Dim ErrorHandler As New CErrorHandler

    g_sXML = ""
    g_sError = ""

    Set reader.contentHandler = contentHandler
    Set reader.ErrorHandler = ErrorHandler
```

```
    On Error GoTo ErrorHandler
    reader.ParseURL sURL
    ParseURL = XML
    Exit Function

ErrorHandler:
    If Len(g_sError) <> 0 Then
        ParseURL = g_sError
    Else
        ParseURL = Err.Description
    End If
End Function
```

Notice the use of the *Friend* keyword in the pair of Get/Let XML property procedures. It makes the XML property available only for read-write operations to the other two class modules, but not to the outside world.

Now let's compile the ActiveX DLL by selecting File, Make VBSAX.dll... from the menu. This will register the VBSAX.dll in Windows registry and make it available to other client applications. The following sample client code will print the content Books.xml document to Visual Basic's Immediate Window:

```
Dim oVBSAX As Object
Set oVBSAX = CreateObject("VBSAX.Wrapper")
Debug.Print oVBSAX.ParseURL(App.Path & "\Books.xml")
```

A call from the client on the *ParseURL* method of the VBSAX.Wrapper object will trigger the IVBXMLReader object to start parsing the XML document and firing appropriate events.

Filtering Specific Information with IVBSAXXMLFilter

The IVBSAXXMLFilter interface provides a means by which you can create a custom filter that sits between the SAXXMLReader object and the event to filter out specific information of interest in the XML document. You can also build a pipeline of filters where each filter in the pipeline performs a specific task, such as enforcing a business rule.

Let's use a simple example to give an idea of how the filter works. In this example, we are going to read the Books.xml document and calculate the total price for the XML books, as we did earlier in a DOM example. Figure C-11 shows the sample VB project that demonstrates how to use the IVBSAXXML filter.

The sample VB project has a form and three class modules. The CContentHandler and the CErrorHandler implement the IVBSAXContentHandler and the

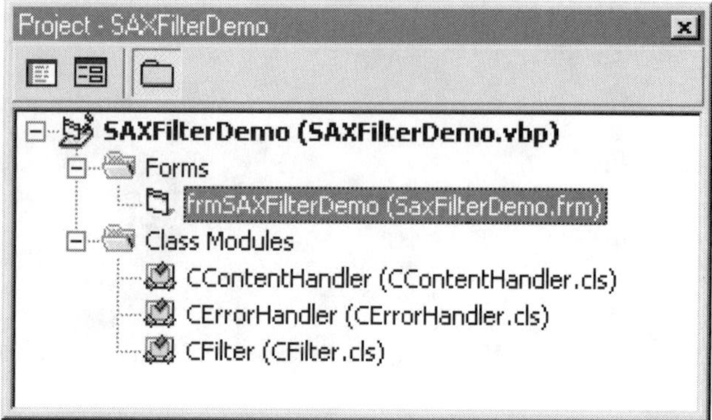

Figure C-11 *The SAXFilterDemo VB project*

IVBSAXErrorHandler interfaces, respectively. The CFilter implements the IVBSAXXMLFilter interface. The implementation of CErrorHandler is trivial; it simply displays a message on the fatal event. The implementation of the CContentHandler deserves some explanation, however. In its General Declaration section, we put the following code:

```
Option Explicit
Dim bXMLBook As Boolean
Dim bAddToTotal As Boolean
Dim iCount As Integer
Dim curTotal As Currency

Implements IVBSAXContentHandler
```

After the declaration of several module level variables, the Implements statement makes the events of the IVBSAXContentHandler available in the CContentHandler class. We only added code to the *startElement*, *characters*, and *endDocument* events, whereas we left the other events empty:

```
Private Sub IVBSAXContentHandler_startElement(strNamespaceURI As String, _
                                              strLocalName As String, _
                                              strQName As String, _
                                              ByVal oAttributes As
MSXML2.IVBSAXAttributes)
    Dim i As Integer
    If strLocalName = "Book" Then
        If oAttributes.getValueFromQName("Subject") = "XML" Then
```

```
            bXMLBook = True
         Else
            bXMLBook = False
         End If
    End If
    If bXMLBook = True And strLocalName = "Price" Then
        bAddToTotal = True
    Else
        bAddToTotal = False
    End If
End Sub

Private Sub IVBSAXContentHandler_characters(strChars As String)
    If bAddToTotal = True Then
        If Val(strChars) Then
            curTotal = curTotal + CCur(strChars)
        End If
        bAddToTotal = False
    End If
End Sub

Private Sub IVBSAXContentHandler_endDocument()
    MsgBox "Total price for XML books: $" & curTotal
End Sub
```

The startElement event checks the Subject attribute of the Book element and sets the bXMLBook flag to True if the value of the attributes is "XML." If a Price element is encountered, it will set the bAddToTotal flag to True. The characters event then checks if the bAddToTotal flag is true to decide if it should add the price to the total. The endDocument event displays the total price.

The following is the implementation of the CFilter class:

```
Option Explicit

Implements IVBSAXXMLFilter

Private Property Set IVBSAXXMLFilter_parent(ByVal RHS As
MSXML2.IVBSAXXMLReader)
    Dim contentHandler As New CContentHandler
    Dim errorHandler As New CErrorHandler
    Set RHS.contentHandler = contentHandler
    Set RHS.errorHandler = errorHandler
```

```
End Property

Private Property Get IVBSAXXMLFilter_parent() As
MSXML2.IVBSAXXMLReader
    'do nothing.
End Property
```

As you can see, the parent Set property procedure hooks appropriate event handlers to the upstream SAXXMLReader object. Here is the client code:

```
Private Sub Command2_Click()
    Dim reader As New SAXXMLReader
    Dim filter As IVBSAXXMLFilter
    'On Error Goto ErrorHandler
    Set filter = New CFilter
    Set filter.Parent = reader

    reader.parseURL App.Path & "\books.xml"
    Set filter = Nothing
    set reader = Nothing
    Exit Sub
ErrorHandler:
    Msgbox Err.Description
End Sub
```

Figure C-12 shows the results.

Using the MXXMLWriter Object

MSXML SAX2 parser provides a few interfaces to the original Java SAX2 specification. The IMXWriter interface is one of the MSXML SAX2 parser specific implementations. This interface implements the ISAXContentHandler, ISAXDTDHandler, ISAXErrorHandler, ISAXDeclHandler, and ISAXLexicalHandler

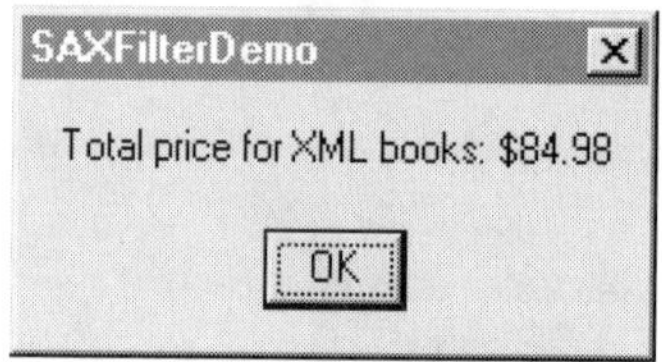

Figure C-12 *The total price for the XML books is returned by using the IVBSAXXMLFilter*

interfaces. The MXXMLWriter object implements the IMXWriter interface. As a result, when you use the MXXMLWriter object with the SAXXMLReader object, you can typecast the MXXMLWriter object to one of the event handlers it implements. The process of typecasting is also referred to as *registering*. After the MXXMLWriter object is typecast with the SAXXMLReader object, a call to the Parse or ParserURL method of the SAXXMLReader object will cause the content of the XML document to be written to the *output* property of the MXXMLWriter object. In case a parse error occurs, the error information will be outputted. The following example illustrates how to use the MXXMLWriter object with the SAXXMLReader object to read an XML file:

```
Private Sub Command1_Click()
    Dim oReader As Object 'MSXML2.SAXXMLReader
    Dim oWriter As Object 'MSXML2.MXXMLWriter

    On Error GoTo ErrorHandler

    'Create instances of the reader and the writer.
    Set oReader = CreateObject("MSXML2.SAXXMLReader")
    Set oWriter = CreateObject("MSXML2.MXXMLWriter")

    'Type cast the writer.
    Set oReader.ContentHandler = oWriter
    Set oReader.ErrorHandler = oWriter

    'Parse the XML document.
    oReader.ParseURL App.Path & "\Books.xml"

    'Display the output.
    Debug.Print oWriter.output

    'Clean up and exit.
    Set oReader = Nothing
    Set oWriter = Nothing
    Exit Sub
ErrorHandler:
    MsgBox Err.Description
End Sub
```

After you run the preceding code, the entire contents of the Books.xml document will be outputted to the VB Immediate window.

Additionally, you can use the MXXMLWriter object with an instance of the IVBSAXContentHandler object to manually create an XML document, as illustrated in the following example:

```
Private Sub Command1_Click()
    Dim oContentHdlr      As IVBSAXContentHandler
    Dim oXMLDcl           As IVBSAXDeclHandler
    Dim oAttr             As New SAXAttributes
    Dim oWriter           As New MXXMLWriter

    On Error Goto ErrorHandler
    'Cast type the writer.
    Set oContentHdlr = oWriter
    'Control the behavior of the XML output.
    oWriter.encoding = "UTF-8"
    oWriter.omitXMLDeclaration = True
    oWriter.indent = True

    'Create the XML document.
    With oContentHdlr
        .startDocument
        .processingInstruction "xml-stylesheet type=" & _
            Chr(34) & "text/xsl" & Chr(34) & " href=" & _
            Chr(34) & "books.xsl" & Chr(34), ""
        .startElement "", "", "Books", oAttr
        oAttr.addAttribute "", "", "ISBN", "", "047146031"
        .startElement "", "", "Book", oAttr
        oAttr.Clear 'Recycle the oAttr object.
        .startElement "", "", "Title", oAttr
        .characters "XSLT:Professional Developer's Guide"
        .endElement "", "", "Title"
        .startElement "", "", "Publisher", oAttr
        'Entities will be automatically escaped.
        .characters "John Wiley & Sons"
        .endElement "", "", "Publisher"
        .startElement "", "", "Authors", oAttr
        .startElement "", "", "Author", oAttr
        .characters "Peter Stark"
        .endElement "", "", "Author"
        .startElement "", "", "Author", oAttr
```

```
        .characters "Johan Hjelm"
        .endElement "", "", "Author"
        .endElement "", "", "Authors"
        .startElement "", "", "Price", oAttr
        .characters "49.99"
        .endElement "", "", "Price"
        .endElement "", "", "Book"
        oAttr.addAttribute "", "", "ISBN", "", "1861003129"
        .startElement "", "", "Book", oAttr
        oAttr.Clear
        .startElement "", "", "Title", oAttr
        .characters "XSLT Programmer's Reference"
        .endElement "", "", "Title"
        .startElement "", "", "Publisher", oAttr
        .characters "Wrox Press Inc."
        .endElement "", "", "Publisher"
        .startElement "", "", "Authors", oAttr
        .startElement "", "", "Author", oAttr
        .characters "Michael Kay"
        .endElement "", "", "Author"
        .endElement "", "", "Authors"
        .startElement "", "", "Price", oAttr
        .characters "34.99"
        .endElement "", "", "Price"
        .endElement "", "", "Book"
        .endElement "", "", "Books"
        .endDocument
    End With
    'Output the results.
    Debug.Print oWriter.output

    'Clean up the mess and quit.
    Set oContentHdlr = Nothing
    Set oXMLDcl = Nothing
    Set oAttr = Nothing
    Set oWriter = Nothing
    Exit Sub
ErrorHandler:
    Msgbox Err.Description
End Sub
```

When you use the IVBSAXContentHandler in this manner, you can directly call its methods (events) as shown in the example. This will cause the contents to be outputted to the typecast MXXMLWriter object.

CAUTION

When you use this technique to create an XML document, you should keep in mind that the MXXMLWriter object won't perform any syntax checking or validating. It is your responsibility to make the output XML document follow the rules of a well-formed XML document. For example, if you call a StartElement method without calling the corresponding EndElement method, you will end up with an element that has no end tag. Similarly, if you call the EndElement in the wrong place, you may get overlapped tags that violate the well-formedness rule of XML. It is strongly recommended you create a wrapper COM object to encapsulate the creating of elements and attributes, etc. into simpler methods and calls, and incorporate the XML rules inside the wrapper. Alternatively, you may consider using the DOM API to create the XML document as we demonstrated before.

Appendix in Review

In this appendix, we discussed two important XML APIs, DOM and SAX, and demonstrated how to use them to build real-world XML applications. The DOM API is a full-blown XML API that offers rich functionalities at the cost of memory resources, rendering it unsuitable for the processing of large XML documents. The SAX API provides a lightweight alternative to DOM but is not opted for handling random accessing, the transforming of documents, or write-intensive scenarios. These two APIs are quite compensative to each other. Which one to choose depends on what problem you are trying to solve. The knowledge and techniques you learned in this appendix will be of great value when building BizTalk and other XML-related solutions using MSXML parsers.

APPENDIX

D

Creating Windows Script Components

IN THIS CHAPTER:

Introducing Windows Script Components

Creating Windows Script Components

Appendix in Review

As you learned in Chapter 9, BizTalk Server 2000 Orchestration Services can use both COM components and Windows Script Components to provide synchronous communications. COM components are written in programming languages such as Visual Basic and Visual C++, whereas Windows Script Components are written in scripting languages such as VBScript and JavaScript. In this appendix, we will explain what Windows Script Components are, and teach you to how to create Windows Script Components that can be used in XLANG Schedules.

Introducing Windows Script Components

Windows Script Components, formerly known as *scriptlets*, is a technology that enables you to create reusable COM components in scripting languages such as VBScript and JavaScript. Strictly speaking, Windows Script Components are special XML documents that follow a specific schema (document structures, elements, and attributes) with embedded script code.

Windows Script Components provide an alternate way for creating COM components and have the following benefits:

- **Small and efficient** Windows script components are typically small XML files.
- **Easy to write** With the help of tools like the Windows Script Component Wizard, writing a Windows Script Component is as easy as writing a Visual Basic COM component. You can also select any scripting language with which you feel most comfortable, as long as the scripting language supports Microsoft scripting interfaces, including VBScript, JavaScript, and PERLScript.
- **Easy to maintain** .wsc files are XML documents (ASCII files). Modifying the implementations of a specific interface requires that the component be unregistered and reregistered, as long as you keep the interface intact. There is no recompilation involved. All you need to do is to save the .wsc file. In addition, as you will learn in this appendix, you can even invoke Windows Script Components using moniker syntax without registering the component in the system registry at all, thus the infamous "DLL Hell" problems usually associated with conventional COM components (ActiveX DLLs) will be avoided.
- **Easy to access the components' contents** Since Windows Script Components are XML documents, you can easily access the components' metadata or contents through standard XML APIs such as DOM or SAX parsers. For example, you can write an XSLT stylesheet that reads the contents of Windows Script

Components and generates Web Services Description Language (WSDL) files so your Windows Script Components will be available to the web clients through the SOAP protocol.

Windows Script Components Architecture

A Windows Script Component is an XML file with a .wsc extension. At minimum, a .wsc file must contain the following three pieces of information:

- Registry settings that help register and unregister the component in the system registry.
- Metadata that defines interfaces and their signatures.
- Embedded script code that implements defined interfaces.

After a Windows Script Component is registered (something we'll show you later in this appendix), its registry settings will look like that in Figure D-1.

As you can see from Figure D-1, the *InprocServer32* key of the Windows Script Components points to the path of the scrobj.dll, a system DLL known as the *script component runtime*. The *ScriptletURL* key contains the physical path to the .wsc file. When a client application tries to instantiate your Windows Script Component through its ProgID (for example, by calling the *CreateObject( )* method in Visual Basic or VBScript), it actually ends up creating an instance of the script component runtime instead. This runtime acts as the behind-the-scenes plumbing for your Windows Script Components by way of the appropriate *interface handlers*. An interface handler is an ActiveX DLL that provides a standard implementation of a specified interface. For example, the automation interface handler provides a standard OLE automation

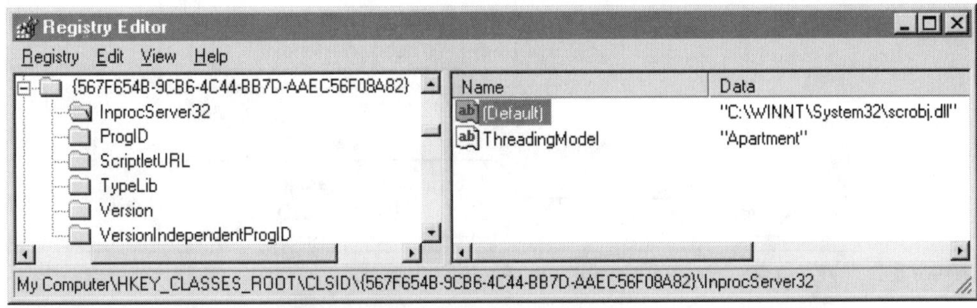

Figure D-1 *A Windows Script Component in the registry*

interface through which the properties and methods of your Windows Script Components can be exposed to the outside world. Whereas an ASP interface handler enables a Windows Script Component to get access to the various ASP object models such as Server, Application, Session, Request, and Response. Figure D-2 illustrates the architecture of Windows Script Components.

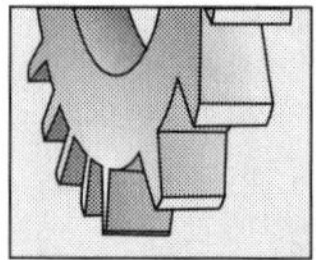

TIP

In the case of BizTalk Server Orchestration, the XLANG schedule is the client application of Windows Script Components.

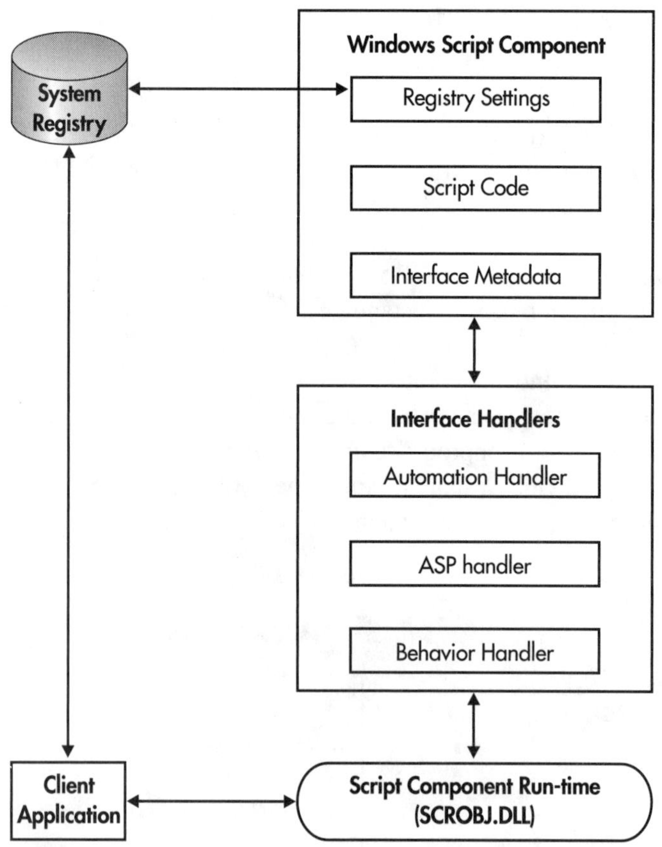

Figure D-2 *Windows Script Components Architecture*

Creating Windows Script Components

We mentioned earlier in this appendix that a Windows Script Component is an XML document that follows a specific schema with embedded script code. As a result, creating a Windows Script Component is really a matter of creating an XML document using those elements and attributes predefined in the Script Component Reference, which is available from the Microsoft Scripting Technology web site at http://msdn.microsoft.com/Scripting.

To help you quickly create Windows Script Components, Microsoft provides a Windows Script Component Wizard which can be downloaded from the aforementioned Microsoft Scripting Technology web site. The rest of this appendix will be devoted first to explaining the elements (and their attributes) defined in the Script Component Reference. Then later, when we teach you how to use the Windows Script Component Wizard to create Windows Script Components, you will have a better understanding of the Wizard's available options, and will know how to implement other functionalities not provided in the Wizard.

In this section, you will take a look under the hood of a Windows Script Component and see how it implements COM functionality using XML and scripts. Later in this appendix, when you learn to use the Windows Script Component Wizard, you will have a better understanding of what the options are and which ones to choose under which circumstances. If you're impatient to learn, you can jump to the "Using the Windows Script Component Wizard" section now and return to these pages when you're ready to get down to the nuts and bolts of Windows Script Components.

The Structure of a Windows Script Component

In this section, we look at what a Windows Script Component consists of.

A First Look - the Overall Structure

The following is the source code of the POReqUtil.wsc, a Windows Script Component you used in an XLANG schedule in Chapter 9.

```
<?xml version="1.0"?>
<component>

<?component error="true" debug="true"?>
```

```
<registration
description="POReq Utility Script Component"
progid="POReqUtil.POReqHelper"
version="1.00"
classid="{558FE2A0-4B07-11d5-BB83-0010A4BB0421}"
>

</registration>

<public>
<method name="CountItems">
<parameter name="sDoc"/>
</method>
<method name="Approval">
<parameter name="sDoc"/>
</method>
<method name="Denial">
<parameter name="sDoc"/>
</method>
</public>

<implements type="ASP" id="ASP"/>

<script language="VBScript">
<![CDATA[

function CountItems(ByVal sDoc)
  Dim oXML, iCountItems

  On Error Resume Next
  Set oXML = CreateObject("MSXML2.DOMDocument")
  oXML.async = False
  oXML.LoadXML sDoc
  iCountItems =  oXML.documentElement.selectNodes("//Item").length

  If Err = 0 Then
    CountItems = iCountItems
  Else
    CountItems = 0
    Err.Raise Err.Number
  End If
end function
```

```
Sub Approval(ByVal sDoc)
  Dim oXML
  Set oXML = CreateObject("MSXML2.DOMDocument")
  oXML.async = False
  oXML.LoadXML sDoc

  Msgbox "The following POReq document has been approved:" & _
         vbCRLF & vbCRLF & oXML.XML

end Sub

Sub Denial(ByVal sDoc)
  Dim oXML
  Set oXML = CreateObject("MSXML2.DOMDocument")
  oXML.async = False
  oXML.LoadXML sDoc

  Msgbox "The following POReq document has been denied:" & _
         vbCRLF & vbCRLF & oXML.XML

end Sub

]]>
</script>

</component>
```

As you can see, after the standard XML declaration, the entire component is enclosed in the <component> element. In this particular example, you only implemented one interface. If you want to implement multiple interfaces in a single Windows Script Component, you will need to wrap up individual <component> elements inside a <package> element like this:

```
<?xml version="1.0"?>

<package>

    <component id = "componentA">...</component>

    <component id = "componentB">...</component>

</package>
```

Each <component> element implements one interface. The <component> element has an ID attribute used to identify the component. This is similar to a single Visual Basic DLL project that contains multiple classes.

Underneath the <component> element you need to have three main sections, as illustrated in the following:

```
<component>

    <registration>...</registration>

    <public>...</public>

    <script>...</script>

</component>
```

A <registration> section provides information that helps register and unregister the Windows Script Component.

A <public> section defines the interface of your Windows Script Component.

Finally, the <script> section hosts the script code that implements the interface.

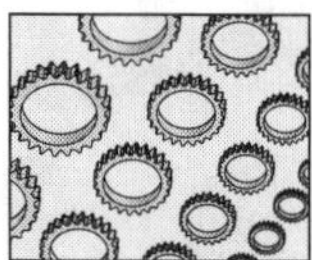

NOTE

XML elements are case-sensitive. It is recommended you use all lowercase for the elements in your Windows Script Components to avoid possible issues caused by the case-sensitivity of XML documents.

Being Registry Friendly

In order to make your Windows Script Components self-registering, a <registration> section is required. The <registration> element has four required attributes, one optional attribute and one optional subelement, as shown in the following:

```
<registration progid="progID"

                      classid="GUID"

                      description="description"

                      version="version"

                      [remotable=remoteFlag] >
```

```
   [<script>

      (optional registration and unregistration script)

   </script>]

</registration>
```

The value of the *progid* attribute specifies the Program ID of your Windows Script Component. For example, the Windows Script Component you used in Chapter 9 has a ProgID of "POReqUtil.wsc". This is the default ProgID generated by the Windows Script Component Wizard. This is fine if you only have one interface in the component. If your component implements multiple interfaces, however, you can use this convention to name the ProgID for your components:

"ScriptFileName.InterfaceName"

For example, "POReqUtil.POReqHelper".

The *classid* attribute specifies the CLSID of your component. For example, {558FE2A0-4B07-11d5-BB83-0010A4BB0421}.

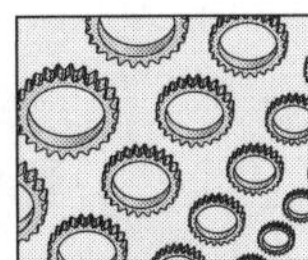

NOTE

As you will learn later in this appendix, when you use the Windows Script Component Wizard, the CLSID will be automatically generated for you. If you hand-code your Windows Script Component, or create your own tool to generate Windows Script Components, you will be responsible for providing the CLSID. You can either use the GUIDGen.exe utility that ships with Visual Studio 6.0 to manually generate the CLSID and copy to your Windows Script Component, or programmatically generate the CLSID by calling the appropriate system API.

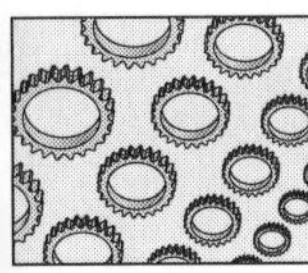

NOTE

Although both progid *and* classid *attributes are optional, you must specify at least one of them. When creating Windows Script Components to be used in XLANG schedules, you should always specify the progid. If possible, it is recommended you specify both.*

The *version* attribute allows you to specify the version of your components. For example, "1.00".

The optional *remotable* attribute is a flag that specifies whether your component supports DCOM (when the flag is "True"), so that a client application can invoke it from a remote machine.

Optionally, the <script> element provides a place where you can write script code that can be executed during the registration and unregistration of your Windows Script

Component. You must use two predefined functions, *register( )* and *unregister( )*, to host the code you want executed during registration and unregistration, respectively:

```
<script language="VBScript">
      Function register()
         'code inside this function will be executed
         'during the registration of the component.
      End Function
      Function unregister()
         'code inside this function will be executed
         'during the un-registration of the component.
      End Function
</script>
```

Defining Your Interface

You must include a <public> section to define your interface. An interface defines the attributes and behaviors of a component. In COM terminology, interfaces are defined by Properties (attributes), Methods (behaviors), and Events. Naturally enough, the <public> element can contain <property>, <method>, and <event> elements, as shown in the following:

```
<public>

    <property>...</property>

    <!—more properties—>

    <method>...</method>

    <!—more methods—>

    <event>...</event>

    <!—more events—>

</public>
```

Defining Properties To define a property for your component, use the <property> element, like this:

```
<property name="PropertyName">

   <get [internalName="getFunctionName"] />

   <put [internalName="putFunctionName"] />

</property>
```

The required *name* attribute of the property element specifies the name of a property. Unless the *internalName* attribute of a <get> or <put> element is used (as we will explain shortly), the value of the name attribute must match an appropriate global variable declared in the <script> section (which will be explained later in this chapter). Using the name attribute alone will define a property. This is similar to declaring a public variable in a Visual Basic class module to implement a property. A more robust way to implement a property in Visual Basic is to use property Get/Let (or Set) procedures. In a Windows Script Component, you can use the optional <get> and <put> elements to provide equivalents of VB property procedures. The <get> element enables you to define a Get property procedure, whereas the <put> element allows you to define a property Let or Set procedure (in VBScript, the data type is variant, so one <put> element is sufficient for both Let/Set procedures in Visual Basic).

The optional *internalName* attribute of the <get> or <put> element enables you to use alternate names to implement the property procedures. If you use the <get> or <put> element without using the internalName attribute, you must use the default names for the property procedures (i.e., get_PropertyName). You can implement a read-only property by using the <get> element without a corresponding <put> element. Similarly, you can implement a write-only property by providing a <put> element without a corresponding <get> element.

The following code segment defines a public-variable style property, PONumber:

```
<property name = "PONumber"/>
```

The following code segment defines a read-only property, PONumber. Because the internalName attribute is not used, you must name your Get property procedure *get_PONumber*.

```
<property name = "PONumber">
    <get>
</property>
```

The following code segment also defines a read-only property, PONumber. Here you can use *GetPONumber* as the name of the Get property procedure.

```
<property name = "PONumber">
    <get internameName = "GetPONumber">
</property>
```

Defining Methods In a Windows Script Component, methods are defined using the <method> element, in the following manner:

```
<method name="methodName"

               internalName="functionName"

               dispid=dispID>

   [<parameter name="parameterID1"

    <parameter name="parameterID2" … />]

</method>
```

The required *name* attribute specifies the name of the method. The use of the optional *internalName* attribute is similar to the internalName attribute of the <property> element. It enables you to specify an alternate name of a function or sub that implements the method. When this attribute is left out, you must use the value of the name attribute (methodName) as the name of the function or sub. The optional *dispid* attribute allows you to specify a COM dispatch ID so that the client can query your method through the *IDispatch* interface. Setting the value of the *dispid* attribute to "0" will define a default method for the component. The optional <parameter> element enables you to specify the parameters for your methods. The <parameter> element has a required *name* attribute for you to define the ID of the parameter. Since the scripting engine only supports variant data types, you don't need to specify the data type for the parameters. Neither do you need to specify the return types for your methods even if they are implemented as functions.

The *CountItems( )* method of our POReqUtil component is defined like this:

```
<method name="CountItems">
    <parameter name="sDoc"/>
</method>
```

Defining Events You can also define and implement events in Windows Script Components. Defining an event is straightforward, using the <event> element:

```
<event name =  "eventName"
          dispid = "dispatchID"/>
```

The *name* attribute specifies the name of the event and the *dispid* attribute, and is similar to the *dispid* attribute used in the <method> element, specifying the dispatch ID for the event. Here is an example that defines a POApproved event:

```
<event name = "POApproved" dispid = "1"/>
```

Implementing Your Interface

Now that you have provided information for your Windows Script Component to work with system registry and defined its interface, it is time to implement the interface to make your component functional. The entire implementation is done by wrapping your script code inside the CDATA section of the <script> element:

```
<script language = "ScriptingLanguage">

<![CDATA[

    <!— script code goes here—>

]]>

</script>
```

The <script> element has a required *language* attribute that specifies the scripting language to use. For example, the following code segment specifies that VBScript is used:

```
<script language = "VBScript">
```

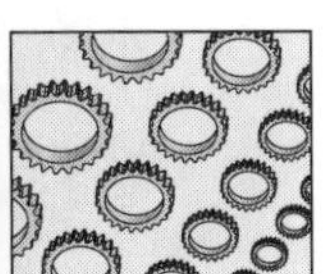

NOTE

Use the CDATA section if the XML declaration statement (<?XML version = "1.0"?>) is used. Refer to Appendix A of this book for information about CDATA section and XML.

Implementing Properties Depending on how a property is defined, the way you implement it varies. The following examples demonstrate how to implement the PONumber property you defined earlier in this appendix.

The following code segment implements the PONumber as a public variable-style property:

```
<property name = "PONumber"/>
...
<script language = "VBScript">
<![CDATA[
dim PONumber
]]>
</script>
```

The following code segment implements PONumber as a read-only property using the default name *get_PONumber*.

```
<property name = "PONumber">
    <get>
</property>
...
<script language = "VBScript">
<![CDATA[
function get_PONumber()
get_PONumber = ...
end Function
]]>
</script>
```

The following code segment also implements PONumber as a read-only property, but uses an alternate name for the function, *GetPONumber*:

```
<property name = "PONumber">
    <get internameName = "GetPONumber">
</property>
...
<script language = "VBScript">
<![CDATA[
function GetPONumber()
get_PONumber = ...
end Function
]]>
</script>
```

Implementing Methods Implementing methods in Windows Script Components is very similar to implementing methods in a programming language such as Visual Basic—using functions (and/or subs should VBScript be used).

Here is how the CountItems( ) method is implemented in the POReqUtil.wsc component:

```
function CountItems(ByVal sDoc)
  Dim oXML, iCountItems

  On Error Resume Next
  Set oXML = CreateObject("MSXML2.DOMDocument")
  oXML.async = False
  oXML.LoadXML sDoc
  iCountItems =  oXML.documentElement.selectNodes("//Item").length

  If Err = 0 Then
    CountItems = iCountItems
  Else
    CountItems = 0
    Err.Raise Err.Number
  End If
end function
```

Implementing Events To implement an event, you simply call the *fireEvent* method inside an appropriate function, passing the name of the event you defined. The following example demonstrates how to implement the POApproved event you defined earlier in this appendix, firing the event in the Approval( ) method (which is implemented as a sub):

```
<event name = "POApproved" dispid = "1"/>
...
<script language = "VBScript">
<![CDATA[
Sub Approval(ByVal sDoc)
  Dim oXML
  Set oXML = CreateObject("MSXML2.DOMDocument")
  oXML.async = False
  oXML.LoadXML sDoc
  fireEvent("POApproved")
  Msgbox "The following POReq document has been approved:" & _
         vbCRLF & vbCRLF & oXML.XML
```

```
end Sub
]]>
</script>
```

Other Things You Can Do in Windows Script Components

In addition to the required XML elements introduced previously to define and implement interfaces, you can also use a variety of techniques to build Windows Script Components. In this section, we will teach you how to use methods implemented in other script components of the same script file (the .wsc file), reference external COM objects to extend the functionality of your script component, implement interface handlers, use resources, and add comments.

Using Methods in Other Script Components of the Same Script File Windows Script Components infrastructure provides a *createComponent( )* function for you to make the methods implemented in other components in the same script file available to the current component, as illustrated in the following example:

```
<package>
    <component id = "POReq">
        <registration progid = "PO.POReq"/>
        <public>
            <method name = "Approval" />
        </public>
        <script language = "VBScript">
            <![CDATA[
              function Approval()
                  createComponent("Customer")
                  <!--other script code-->
              end function
            ]]>
         </script>
    </component>
    <component id = "Customer">
        <registration progid = "PO.Customer"/>
        <public>
            <method name = "GetShippingAddress" />
        </public>
        <script language = "VBScript">
            <![CDATA[
              function GetShippingAddress()
                  createComponent(Customer)
```

```
                <!--other script code-->
            end function
          ]]>
      </script>
   </component>
</package>
```

In the preceding code sample, the *GetShippingAddress( )* method is defined and implemented in the *Customer* component. Inside the *Approval( )* method of the *POReq* component (which is in the same script file), we called the createComponent( ) method and passed the ID of the Customer component. Now we can call the GetShippingAddress method from the instance of the POReq component in the client application in the following manner:

```
Dim oPOReq, oCustomer
Set oPOReq = CreateObject("PO.POReq")
Set oCustomer = oPOReq.Approval()
oCustomer.GetShippingAddress()
```

The preceding code segment is equivalent to:

```
Dim oCustomer
Set oCustomer = CreateObject("PO.Customer")
oCustomer.GetShippingAddress()
```

Referencing External COM Objects In addition to using the *CreateObject( )* method to reference external COM objects, as illustrated in the CountItems( ) method of the POReqUtil.wsc component, you can also use the <object> element. For example, the following statement,

```
Set oXML = CreateObject("MSXML2.DOMDocument")
```

in the CountItems( ) function can be replaced by the <object> element defined otherside the <script> element, which can then directly reference the object in the script code by its ID:

```
<object id = "oXML" progid = "MSXML2.DOMDocument"/>
<registration ... />
<public>
    <method name="CountItems">
        <parameter name="sDoc"/>
    </method>
```

```
</public>
<script language = "VBScript">
<![CD[
function CountItems()
  On Error Resume Next
  ' Now you don't need to call the CreateObject( ) method.
  ' Set oXML = CreateObject("MSXML2.DOMDocument")
  oXML.async = False
  oXML.LoadXML sDoc
  ' The rest of the function...
end function
]]>
</script>
```

Additionally, you can use the <reference> object to set a reference to the type library of a COM component. You can, afterwards, use the constants and enumerations defined in the type library, as illustrated in the following example, and then use the enumerated XML DOM constants in the script code:

```
<reference object = "MSXML2.DOMDocument.3.0" />
<registration ... />
<script>
<![CD[
function SomeXMLFunction(ByVal oNode)
  select case oNode.Type
    case NODE_ELEMENT
         ' ...
    case NODE_TEXT
         ' ...
    case NODE_ATTRIBUTE
         ' ...
  end select
  ' ...
end function
]]>
```

Implementing Interface Handlers Interface handlers provide the entry points for the script component runtime. By using the <implement> element, you can specify additional COM interface handlers for your script component. For example, to implement an ASP script component, you need to specify the *type* attribute of the <implement> element as "ASP" (just as with the Response object illustrated in the following):

```
<implement type = "ASP" />
```

Now you can use the ASP object models in your script code:

```
<script language = "VBScript">
<![CDATA[
function GetPONumber()
  ' ...
  Response.PONumber
  ' ...
end function
]]>
</script>
```

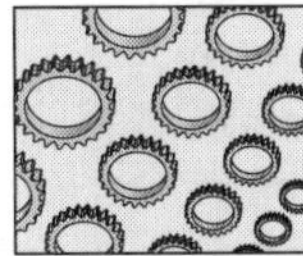

NOTE

The default interface handler of a Windows Script Component is "Automation".

Using Resources You can use the <resource> element and the *getResource( )* function to isolate strings or numbers that should not be hard-coded into the script component's scripts. Using this technique is similar to using the resource files (string tables, for example) in Visual Basic or Visual C++. They can be employed to simplify language localizations.

To use string or number resources in this manner, you first need to define the resource strings or numbers using the <resource> element. For example, to specify a greeting string, you specify the *id* attribute of the <resource> element and designate the contents of the greeting string as the text of the <resource> element, like this:

```
<resource id = "Greeting">
  Hello!
</resource>
```

Now, in your script code, instead of using hard-coded literal string like "Hello", you simply call the getResource function and pass on the ID of the <resource> element, as illustrated in the following:

```
<script language = "VBScript">
<![CDATA[
function SayHi()
  SayHi = getResource("Greeting")
end function
```

```
]]>
</script>
```

To return a French version of the greeting message, all you need to do is swap the contents of the <resource> element with an appropriate French word:

```
<resource id = "Greeting">
  Bonjour!
</resource>
```

Now, the SayHi method will return "Bonjour" instead of "Hello."

Debugging and Error Handling Windows Script Components provides a <?component?> processing instruction (PI) in which you can specify two flags (Boolean), *error* and *debug*.

Setting the error flag to "true" will cause the detailed error messages for syntax or run-time errors in the script component to be displayed; whereas the debug flag determines whether to enable debugging so you can use the script debugger to debug the script component.

If you don't explicitly specify these flags using the <?component?> PI, by default, the error flag is set to "true" and the debug flag is set to "false." You can overwrite the default behavior by using the following:

```
<?component error = "false" debug = "true"?>
```

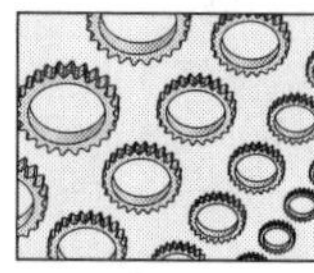

NOTE

When used, the <?component?> PI should be placed at the top of the script file but after the <?XML?> declaration. The error and debug flags are designed to be used for debugging purposes. You should turn them off when you deploy the script components in a production environment.

Documenting Your Script Component The <comment> element enables you to add some description about your script component. You can use the <comment> element anywhere in the XML document, but only after the <?XML?> declaration and any PIs. The <comment> element provides an alternate way to the <!— …—> comment block symbols which makes the retrieval of the comments a little easier.

The following example illustrates how to use the <comment> element to describe the CountItems( ) method:

```
<method name="CountItems">
    <comment>
    This method counts the total line items
```

```
    in the Purchase Order document.
    </comment>
    <parameter name="sDoc"/>
</method>
```

Using the Windows Script Component Wizard

Now that you have learned the nuts and bolts of Windows Script Components, you should be able to create a script component by generating an XML document using the standard elements and attributes discussed in previous sections. Hand coding a Windows Script Component, however, is tedious and error-prone. To help you rapidly develop Windows Script Components, Microsoft has created a Windows Script Component Wizard which is downloadable from the Microsoft Scripting Technology web site at http://msdn.microsoft.com/Scripting.

In this section, we will walk you through the process of creating the POReqUtil.wsc component (last seen in an XLANG schedule in Chapter 9), using the Windows Script Component Wizard.

Running the Windows Script Component Wizard

After having successfully downloaded and installed the Windows Script Component Wizard, you should be able to launch it by clicking Start | Program | Microsoft Windows Script and then selecting the Windows Script Component Wizard. In the first screen of the Windows Script Component Wizard, fill in the information about the script component, such as the name, ProgID, version number and so on (as shown in Figure D-3). Some of the information you input here will go to the <registration> element in the generated script component file.

Click Next. In the second screen of the Wizard, specify which language should be used, whether to use interface handler and which one to use, and whether you want to enable error and debug flags. In this example, you can keep the all the defaults, as shown in Figure D-4.

Click Next to go to the third screen where you can define the properties for your component. In this specific example, however, you don't use properties. So go ahead click the Next button to go to the fourth screen where you can define the methods for your script component. You will need to define three methods, CountItems, Approval, and Denial (as shown in Figure D-5).

Click Next and you will see the fifth screen where you can define events for your script component. In this example, you don't have events, so click the Next button to go to the last screen of the Wizard which displays a summary report about the script component you are going to create (shown in Figure D-6).

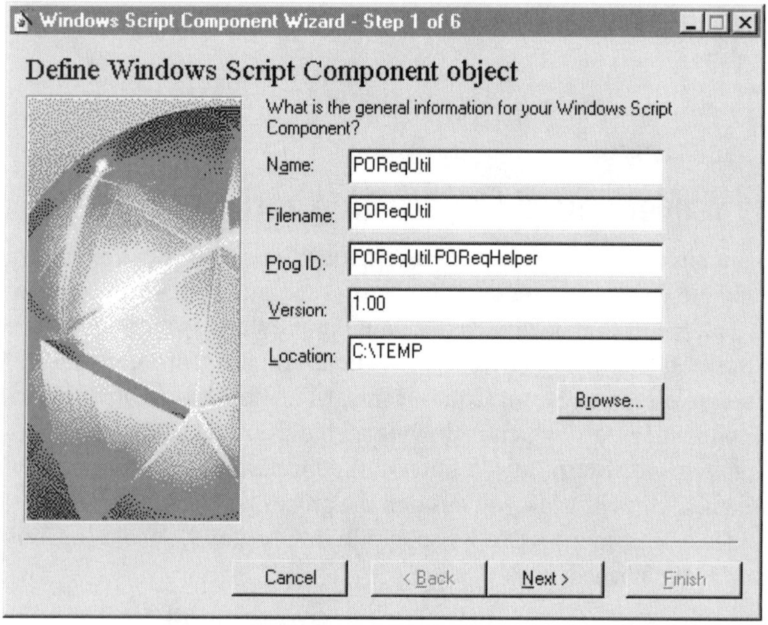

Figure D-3 *Defining the script component*

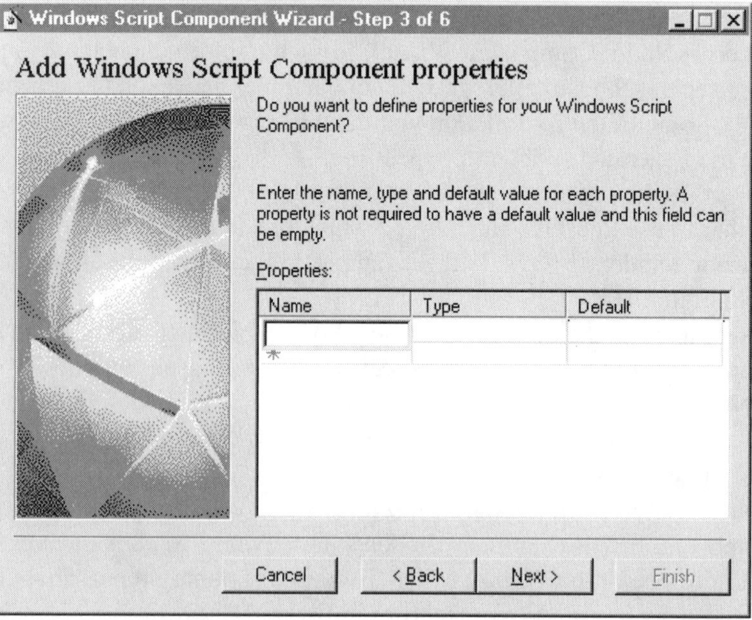

Figure D-4 *Specifying scripting language, interface handler, and error and debug flags*

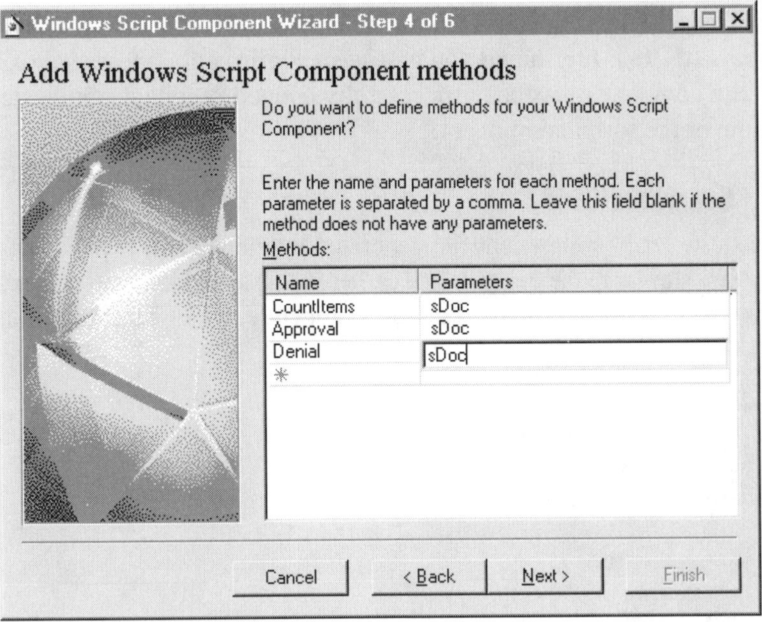

Figure D-5 *Defining methods for the script component*

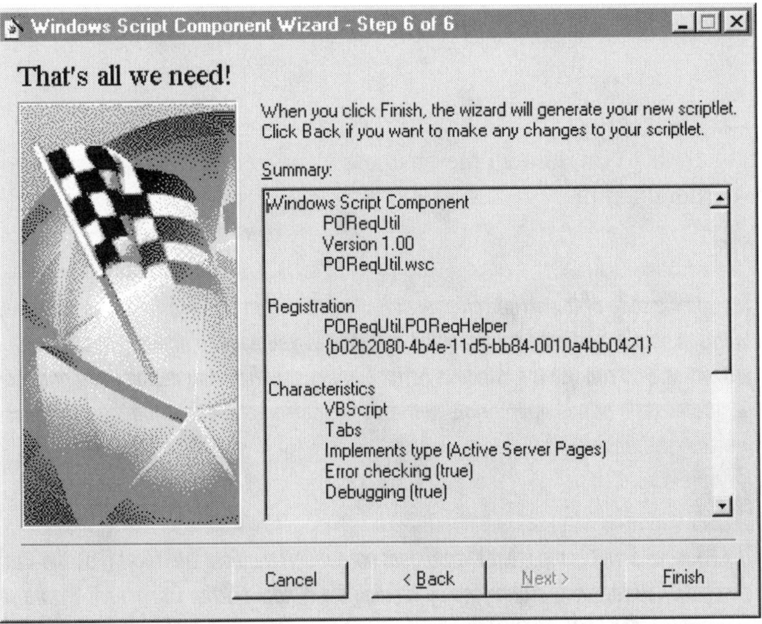

Figure D-6 *Checking the summary information about the script component*

You can drag the vertical scroll bar on the right of the screen to view the entire summary report. Click Finish and you will see a confirmation message box stating that the script component has been successfully created. It will also indicate the path and filename of the script component.

Modifying Generated Code

If you check the script component file generated by the wizard, POReqUtil.wsc, you will find it very similar to the one you saw earlier in this appendix, with one exception—the <script> section only contains skeleton script code, which resembles this:

```
<script language="VBScript">
<![CDATA[
function CountItems(sDoc)
CountItems = "Temporary Value"
end function

function Approval(sDoc)
Approval = "Temporary Value"
end function

function Denial(sDoc)
Denial = "Temporary Value"
end function
]]>
</script>
```

Your job here is to implement the business logic behind the skeleton code, as you saw in the earlier example.

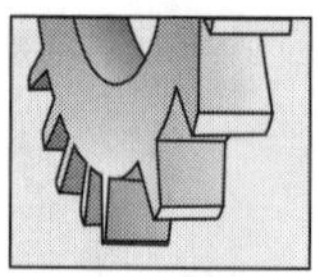

TIP

The sample code of this script component is available from this book's source code web download. In this example, you only implemented methods. If you need to implement both methods and properties, you can use the Windows Script Component Wizard to define them and then modify the generated code or add appropriate new code to implement them, using the guidelines explained in previous sections.

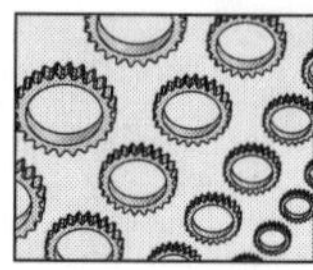

NOTE

The Windows Script Component Wizard does not support multiple interfaces (i.e., the <component> element). You can work around this by running the Windows Script Component Wizard several times, generating individual .wsc files each time. Then you can consolidate these separate .wsc files into a single .wsc file and wrap them into the <package> element, as described in previous sections.

Registering and Unregistering the Script Component

There are two ways in which you can register and unregister a script component.

1. You can register or unregister a script component by right-clicking the .wsc file in Windows Explorer and selecting Register or Unregister, respectively.
2. Or you can run the RegSvr32.exe utility as you would the ActiveX DLL components, using this syntax: regsvr32 [/u] scriptfile.wsc.

In addition, you can also generate a type library for the script component by right-clicking the script file in Windows Explorer and selecting Generate Type Library.

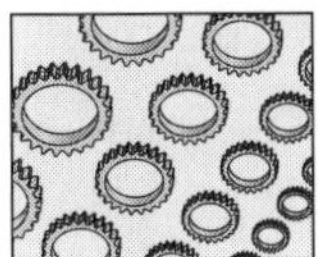

NOTE

*You can also use the GetObject() function with moniker syntax to avoid registering the script component at all. For example, to create an instance of the POReqUtil.POReqHelper script component without registering it, you call the GetObject() method and use the "**script**" moniker like this: Set oPOReqUtil = GetObject("script:C:\Orchestration\ApprovalPOReq\ApprovalReqUtil\POReqUtil.wsc")*

Appendix in Review

Windows Script Components provide an alternate way for writing COM components in scripting languages. They can be used in XLANG schedules of BizTalk Server 2000 Orchestration Services, in ASP pages, or anywhere you can use compiled COM DLLs. In this appendix, you have learned what Windows Script Components are and how to create them either by hand coding or by using the Windows Script Component Wizard.

Index

C

D

E

F

G

H

I

N

Q

R

S

U

V

W

INTERNATIONAL CONTACT INFORMATION

AUSTRALIA
McGraw-Hill Book Company Australia Pty. Ltd.
TEL +61-2-9417-9899
FAX +61-2-9417-5687
http://www.mcgraw-hill.com.au
books-it_sydney@mcgraw-hill.com

CANADA
McGraw-Hill Ryerson Ltd.
TEL +905-430-5000
FAX +905-430-5020
http://www.mcgrawhill.ca

GREECE, MIDDLE EAST, NORTHERN AFRICA
McGraw-Hill Hellas
TEL +30-1-656-0990-3-4
FAX +30-1-654-5525

MEXICO (Also serving Latin America)
McGraw-Hill Interamericana Editores S.A. de C.V.
TEL +525-117-1583
FAX +525-117-1589
http://www.mcgraw-hill.com.mx
fernando_castellanos@mcgraw-hill.com

SINGAPORE (Serving Asia)
McGraw-Hill Book Company
TEL +65-863-1580
FAX +65-862-3354
http://www.mcgraw-hill.com.sg
mghasia@mcgraw-hill.com

SOUTH AFRICA
McGraw-Hill South Africa
TEL +27-11-622-7512
FAX +27-11-622-9045
robyn_swanepoel@mcgraw-hill.com

UNITED KINGDOM & EUROPE (Excluding Southern Europe)
McGraw-Hill Education Europe
TEL +44-1-628-502500
FAX +44-1-628-770224
http://www.mcgraw-hill.co.uk
computing_neurope@mcgraw-hill.com

ALL OTHER INQUIRIES Contact:
Osborne/McGraw-Hill
TEL +1-510-549-6600
FAX +1-510-883-7600
http://www.osborne.com
omg_international@mcgraw-hill.com

LICENSE AGREEMENT